SOCIAL PROBLEMS
AND PUBLIC POLICY
Inequality and Justice

SOCIAL PROBLEMS
AND PUBLIC POLICY
Inequality and Justice

EDITED BY Lee Rainwater HARVARD UNIVERSITY

III⒯EIII ALDINE PUBLISHING COMPANY / *Chicago*

ABOUT THE EDITOR

Lee Rainwater, Professor of Sociology in the Department of Sociology and the John F. Kennedy School of Government at Harvard, received his M.A. and Ph. D. in sociology from the University of Chicago. He is Principal Investigator in the Research Program on Family Behavior and Social Policy, Joint Center for Urban Studies, Harvard and M.I.T. and is currently on the Board of Associate Editors of *Journal of Marriage and the Family,* and a member of the Advisory Board of the *Journal of Afro-American Studies.* Professor Rainwater's books include *The Moynihan Report and the Politics of Controversy* (senior author with William L. Yancey), *Behind Ghetto Walls: Black Families in a Federal Slum* (Aldine, 1970), and *What Money Buys: Inequality and the Social Meanings of Income* (In press).

309.173
R159a
1974
v.1

First published 1974 by
Aldine Publishing Company
529 South Wabash Avenue
Chicago, Illinois 60605

Library of Congress Catalog Card Number 72-97244
ISBN 202-30246-6 cloth; 202-30247-4 paper

PREFACE

THIS BOOK is designed as an introduction to social science perspectives on a broad range of social issues in American society. It is one of two companion volumes, dealing respectively with problems of inequality and justice and with problems of deviance and liberty; the volumes have been organized so that each can stand independently of the other.

Any one of the problems dealt with here is complex enough to merit the attention of a cadre of specialists. A book that seeks to survey contemporary social issues, therefore, cannot hope to provide an exhaustive or definitive analysis of each one. But there is a role for a survey that deals with the many different kinds of social problems of concern to American citizens and with the many different policy initiatives that are used to cope with these issues. From such a survey one can learn something about the common themes, predilections and quandaries that characterize this nation's response to its complexities, its patterns of inequality and injustice.

Given the tremendous variety of social problems of concern in our society, each selection in these volumes has to do several different kinds of duty. They have been chosen to cover as fully as possible the range of substantive problematic issues, the range of social science perspectives that can be brought to bear on issues of all kinds, and the range of social science methodologies used in studying modern society. Finally, the selections have been chosen to emphasize the contributions that can be made to understanding social problems by intensive and rigorous social science research.

Because these problems are of concern to so many in our society and because we all have available a good deal of information about many if not all of them, informal and impressionistic approaches often tell us a good deal about them. In this sense, every man is his own social scientist. Journalists and popular writers using this common sense approach to social problems may present in the mass media essays that are imaginative and incisive. As interpreters of social reality, they are formidable competitors to the social scientist, whose "ivory tower" and plodding approach often seems to yield less illumination than a good police reporter's work. Increasingly, however, the tools of social scientists are enabling them to produce information and analyses that contribute far more to our understanding than even the most insightful journalist can achieve. The selection in these volumes are designed to highlight the deeper and more fundamental understanding of social issues that can come from the rigorous analysis of government statistics, or from special sample surveys, or from in-depth ethnographic studies.

■ My editorial introductions to each selection appear in sans serif type (as here) and are set off from the text of the selections themselves by squares like those preceding and ending this paragraph. To assist the reader who wants to explore more fully the topics that are covered in this book, I have included suggestions for further reading at the end of each introduction. ■

The perspective on social problems that guided me in preparing this book was developed while working with a number of valued colleagues, in particular Irving Louis Horowitz and David J. Pittman during my years at Washington University, and Phillips Cutright, Herbert J. Gans, and Martin Rein during our time together at the Joint Center for Urban Studies of M.I.T. and Harvard. My wife, Carol Rainwater, has been an important contributor to this work, both in discussions over the years of most of the social issues covered here and more concretely through her assistance in selecting and assembling the articles included.

As on other occasions, I have benefited greatly from discussions with Aldine's publisher, Alexander J. Morin. Janet Braeunig of Aldine has responded magnificently to my not-so-orderly approach to editing this collection. And I thank Sally Nash for her competent handling of the complex process of manuscript preparation involved in preparing this book.

LEE RAINWATER

CONTENTS

Preface v

Introduction: The Study of Social Problems 1

I. MODERN PERSPECTIVES ON INEQUALITY AND SOCIAL PROBLEMS 15
  1. The New Egalitarianism, *Herbert J. Gans* 18
  2. Liberty and Equality, *Harold Laski* 26
  3. Social Inequality and Social Integration, *John H. Goldthorpe* 32
  4. On the Origin of Inequality Among Men, *Ralf Dahrendorf* 41
  5. The Dynamics of Distributive Systems, *Gerhard Lenski* 52
  6. Policy Analysis and Equality, *Martin Rein* 62

II. CLASS INEQUALITIES AND SOCIAL PROBLEMS 69
  7. Poverty in the United States, *Lee Rainwater* 70
  8. The American Distribution of Income: A Structural Problem,
    Lester C. Thurow and Robert Lucas 77
  9. The Welfare Crisis, *Martin Rein* 89
  10. The Guaranteed Income, *James Tobin* 103
  11. Education and Inequality 115
    11a. Inequalities in Higher Education, *W. Lee Hansen and
    Burton A. Weisbrod* 116
    11b. The Great Training Robbery, *Ivar Berg* 118
    11c. Schooling, IQ, and Income, *David K. Cohen* 124
  12. Working-class Family Life-styles and Social Alienation,
    Lee Rainwater 135
  13. Housing and Inequality 147
    13a. The Slum and Its Problems, *Lee Rainwater* 148
    13b. Improving Federal Housing Subsidies, *Bernard J. Frieden* 157
  14. Health and Inequality 168
    14a. Class and the Chance for Life, *Aaron Antonovsky* 170
    14b. The Lower Class: Health, Illness, and Medical Institutions,
    Lee Rainwater 179
  15. Who Needs Organized Family Planning Services?,
    Frederick S. Jaffe, Joy G. Dryfoos, and George Varky 188
  16. Taxes and Inequality, *Joseph A. Pechman* 201

III. INEQUALITIES OF STATUS 215

17. Black Unrest in the 1960s, *Thomas F. Pettigrew* 216
18. The 1960s: Decade of Progress for Blacks?,
    Reynolds Farley and Albert Hermalin 225
19. Attitudes Toward Racial Integration, *Andrew M. Greeley and
    Paul B. Sheatsley* 241
20. When the Melting Pot Doesn't Melt, *Nathan Glazer* 251
21. Sex Inequality 259
    21a. Sex Equality: The Beginnings of an Ideology, *Alice S. Rossi*..260
    21b. Women's Rights and the Drive for Day Care,
    *Charles L. Schultze, Edward R. Fried, Alice M. Rivlin,
    and Nancy H. Teeters* 268
22. Colonialism: The Case of the Mexican Americans,
    Joan W. Moore 280

IV. INEQUALITIES OF POWER 287

23. Equality of Voting, *Walter Dean Burnham* 288
24. Community Action and Neighborhood Control 299
    24a. Radical Decentralization, *Michael Lipsky* 300
    24b. Lower Class Life-styles and Community Action,
    Lee Rainwater 306
25. Power and Symbol in Administrative Regulation, *Murray Edelman*..313
26. The Vietnam War and Presidential Power, *Daniel Ellsberg* 322
27. American Military Policy and Advanced Weapons,
    James R. Kurth 336
28. The Politics of Culture in America, *Herbert J. Gans* 353

V. INTERNATIONAL STRATIFICATION AND INEQUALITIES 361

29. The Third World in International Stratification,
    Irving Louis Horowitz 362
30. World Population Crisis, *Kingsley Davis* 375
31. Inequality among Nations and International Redistribution,
    Ernst Michanek 389

VI. CONFLICTS OF EFFICIENCY, CHOICE, AND EQUALITY 393

32. Reason and National Goals, *Thomas Nagel* 394
33. Individual Adaptation and Collective Results, *Thomas C. Schelling*.403
34. Inequality, Affluence, and Environmental Problems,
    Barry Commoner 420
35. The City as Sandbox, *George Sternlieb* 431
36. Metropolitan Dispersal and Growth, *Commission on Population
    Growth and the American Future* 437

Index 450

SOCIAL PROBLEMS AND PUBLIC POLICY
Inequality and Justice

INTRODUCTION: THE STUDY OF SOCIAL PROBLEMS

"A social problem is a condition which is defined by a considerable number of persons as a deviation from some social norm which they cherish." This definition offered by Richard C. Fuller and Richard R. Myers some 30 years ago character-izes with considerable economy the kinds of issues sociologists typically study under the rubic of "social problems." As will quickly become apparent below, the "field" of social problems has a very different character from most of the sub-stantive areas of sociology, such as social stratification or interaction processes or the family.

In their efforts to define what social problems as traditionally studied have in common, Fuller and Myers noted that there is always a dual reference in the assertion that something is a social problem: (a) a reference to an objective condition, and (b) a reference to a subjective evaluation which defines that condi-tion as in some way undesirable, destructive, or immoral. They note further that the objective condition is verifiable, in the sense that impartial or trained observers can describe its nature and extent. But in order for a particular objective condition to be reasonably characterized as a social problem, it is necessary that members of the society see it as an undesirable departure from the ordinary course of things.

One could relax this latter condition somewhat and broaden the definition to include objective conditions that have or are believed to have consequences which, if understood, would be regarded as deviating from some social norm. These might be called "hidden social problems." I raise this issue not simply to make a pedantic point but to observe that one important consequence of living in a complex society like ours is that new undesirable consequences are constantly being discovered. Before these situations are fully communicated, the existence of the

This introduction is identical in both volumes of *Social Problems and Public Policy*, the first dealing with *Inequality and Justice* and the second with *Deviance and Liberty*. Nevertheless, I suggest that the reader of both volumes may wish to read the introduction again, to recapitulate the setting for the subsequent discussion.

problem may be known only to a few specialists; after they have been fully communicated, these situations are recognized as social problems by many people. Some aspects of environmental issues present particularly dramatic examples of this—for example, the dangers of nuclear fall-out.

The relationship of the social scientist to social problems is ambiguous; it has plagued research in this area from its inception and involves issues that are not really resolvable. Sometimes the social scientist is interested in studying the problem itself—for example, he may be interested in studying patterns of crime, understanding who commits crimes, and why and what their fate is. When he does this, he generally takes for granted the definition of crime as a social problem, although he may not fully share the social evaluations of crime that are prevalent at the time he does his work. On the other hand, and increasingly, social scientists have been interested not so much in studying the problem itself as in studying the processes by which society defines and takes action about problems. Here the social scientist focuses on the characterization of a given objective condition as a social problem. Indeed, as Howard S. Becker has noted, the social scientist may have to address the question of whether the objective condition which society defines as a problem really exists at all (as in the case of witchcraft, for example).

There are solid theoretical, policy, and ethical reasons for selecting either of these approaches to particular social issues, but they are really quite different, and this has frustrated all attempts to develop a closely reasoned "theory" of social problems. For our purposes here, we will certainly be better off if we start with the understanding that there is no "field" of sociology with theoretical coherence that can be called "social problems." We must look elsewhere for the vitality of this subject of study. Throughout the whole of sociology's growth from early in this century to the present, social problems consistently have attracted high interest among researchers, writers, teachers, and students. As we will see, the existence of the field has allowed many creative scholars to sharpen their analytic tools in the process of trying to understand particular problems. But trying to invest the study of social problems with theoretical precision has come to naught. We are left finally with the understanding that the subject is attractive because those who study society inevitably are also concerned with changing it, and naturally pay especial attention to its problematic aspects. Since social scientists are very much representative of their own society, they tend to bring to their work exactly the same range of subjective definitions about "problems" that others in the society have.

In short, practicing sociologists and students study social problems because they are concerned about them and they wish to use the tools of their discipline to illuminate them.

If the sociologist's interest in a particular problem is in its definitional aspect—that is, in how society comes to define a particular condition as a problem and how that definition is incorporated into ongoing social transactions—then he can achieve an adequate account within the bounds of the discipline itself. This approach is eminently sociological. If, however, one's interest is in the social problem itself, it is not possible to get very far by using only the tools of sociological analysis. Social problems are not simply *sociological* problems, but always involve other aspects of human behavior—economic, political, psychological, and historical. If we want to understand the problem itself rather than the process by which society defines it as a problem, then we must seek understanding from a broader perspective than that provided by the sociologist's expertise alone.

In these two volumes, the emphasis is primarily on the social problems themselves, although many of the selections deal with the social processes of problem definition because those processes in turn often create problems. We have not confined our selections to the work of sociologists; instead, selections from all the social sciences have been chosen in order to illustrate the broad range of social science theory and method that must be applied to gain the fullest understanding of social problems.

The range of social problems traditionally covered by sociology, however, has not been of equal concern to the other social sciences. It is in that sense that this field of study has seemed to "belong" to the discipline of sociology. Although in fact all such problems involve economic or political or psychological aspects, few of them have been subjected to study by specialists in those fields. In general, issues related to economic and political inequality, for example, have been heavily and creatively studied by the nonsociological disciplines. However, until recently there were many areas of deviant behavior and some areas of inequality that were almost exclusively the concern of sociologists and psychologists. It is only recently that we have begun to see interesting work on the economics of drugs or crime or the political aspects of abortion or "gay liberation." If a lively interest continues in research on these kinds of social problems from the perspective of different social sciences, we can look forward to an increasingly good understanding of them. In this way some of the disciplinary parochialism that has characterized much sociological work on social problems will be corrected.

FIVE SOCIOLOGICAL PERSPECTIVES ON SOCIAL PROBLEMS

Although sociology from its inception has been deeply involved in describing and analyzing social problems, the approach of sociologists to the subject has shifted markedly from time to time. Earl Rubington and Martin S. Weinberg have analyzed the development of five different sociological perspectives: (1) social pathology, (2) social disorganization, (3) value conflict, (4) deviant behavior, and (5) labelling.

Early sociologists, working in the period before World War I, tended to see social problems as manifestations of one or another departure from "normality" in society. They regarded society as an organism, and as with other organisms, it was possible to speak of its state of health and to point to particular conditions that were pathological. This view came easily at the time since it was consistent with deeply established assumptions about the importance of biological factors in social behavior, ranging from the role of inheritance in establishing mental superiority or inferiority to the role of climate in determining which nations prospered and which nations declined. The social pathologist tended to locate the causes of social problems in individuals who were defective in some way, who caused problems because they were feeble-minded or had criminal constitutions or some other weakness, or who gave in to immoral impulses or preyed on the weakness of others.

In more recent times, sociologists who find the *social pathology* perspective meaningful have spoken of society and its institutions as "sick." The causes of that sickness are generally located in the predatory character of particular classes or institutions within society. In this form, the social pathology perspective shades imperceptively into the two approaches that succeeded it in the development of sociology—social disorganization and value conflict. The emphasis on social pathology is perhaps best thought of as a primitive first approximation of a social scientific view of widely recognized problems in society. As the theoretical tools available to sociologists for analyzing social life have improved, this naive approach has been supplanted.

The second sociological perspective on social problems to gain ascendancy was that of *social disorganization*. After World War I, sociologists—particularly those associated with the University of Chicago—concentrated their attention on the dynamics of social life in the American city. They came to see the many social problems in the cities as the result of rapid social change, of the impact on social life and individuals of two major processes: urbanization from abroad and from rural areas within the United States, and the technological change attendant on advanced industrialization and the development of new products such as the automobile. The "Chicago School" sociologists who studied social pathologies such as crime, truancy, suicide, and tuberculosis made the surprising discovery that over a half a century of waves of immigration to the city, the same neighborhoods manifested continuing high rates of these problems although the immigrant groups that inhabited them changed from one generation to the next. They concluded that these environments somehow disorganized and disrupted the lives of their inhabitants. This social disorganization compounded the breakdown of rules and the inability of individuals to depend on a familiar set of expectations that could successfully guide their actions.

Just as the perspective of social pathology implicitly assumes an obverse condition of social normalcy, the perspective of social disorganization implicitly assumes the existence of social organization. Indeed, the latter perspective became of central importance for much of sociology between the two world wars because of a growing conviction on the part of sociologists that they were beginning to develop a scientific theory of how societies were put together. The central role of rules—of recipes for doing the work of society—in the theory of social organization sets up social disorganization as an everpresent companion. If the rules do not work, or if they are unclear or contradictory, then the group has a problem because it cannot carry forward its activity.

Much of the empirical research done during this period fit neatly into a framework emphasizing the central role of normlessness and cultural conflict. However, as time went on, more and more sociologists began to observe that many situations involving social problems did not fit under the rubric of social disorganization. In fact, much socially problematic behavior seemed highly organized and tightly integrated into the ongoing activity of society. Observations of this kind considerably strengthened a growing skepticism about the proposition that "bad things" in society or in individuals were producing the bad effects we call social problems.

This skeptical impulse eventually produced a third approach, usually called the *value conflict* perspective. It is this perspective on which we have drawn for our own general definition of social problems, accepting the position originally enunciated by Fuller and Myers (Rubington and Weinberg, 1971) who first brought into sharp focus the view that central to all such problems are "conflicts in the value scheme of the culture." In this view, problems occur not because things fall apart socially but because different groups in society have different interests, these interests conflict, and these conflicts precipitate conditions that at least some people regard as undesirable.

Fuller and Myers distinguish three kinds of social problems. First, there are *physical problems* which everyone regards as a threat to their welfare. Value conflict does not cause such problems (earthquakes, hurricanes, floods, droughts, etc.), but our way of adapting to them does involve conflicting interests, and disagreements arise concerning what should be done to cope with them.

A second kind of social problem they call the *ameliorative problem*. Here there is general consensus that an objective condition is undesirable, but people "are unable to agree on programs for the amelioration of the condition." Examples include crime, physical and mental disease, accidents, etc. These problems, unlike physical problems, are fully social in that both the objective condition and our responses to it are full of potentials for interest or value conflict.

A third kind of problem they call the *moral problem*. Here there is no agreement that the problematic condition itself is undesirable. Some groups in society believe it is a problem and others argue with equal vehemence that it is not, that it is in some way a "normal" social situation. Many of the conditions and processes we have included under the rubric of problems of inequality are of this type, in that there is not universal agreement that they are in fact problematic.

There is a kinship between this perspective and the social disorganization approach. For both, the central factor in social problems is that there is no homogeneity of social values. The notion that social problems were greatly heightened by the trends of urbanization and industrialization which was so obvious in earlier views is muted but nevertheless present here, as in the observation by Willard Waller that "social problems in the modern sense did not exist when every primary group cared for its own helpless and unfortunate. Social problems as we know them are a phenomenon of secondary group society in which the primary group is no longer willing or able to take care of its members."

More systematic attention to sociological theory as the starting place for sociological perspectives, in contrast to a conceptual apparatus inductively developed from empirical work, bore important fruits in the 1950's for the study of social problems. Ideas developed by Robert K. Merton as part of his more general interest in structural-functional theory were applied to a wide range of social problems, under the general rubric of "anomie" in a new theory of *deviant behavior*. A 1939 article by Merton on "Social Structure and Anomie" some fifteen years later had been applied in a fairly systematic way to studies of crime and delinquency and later even more broadly to other social problems ranging from drug use to poverty. Merton's theory was of considerable generality, seeking to account for all behavior that deviates from customary expectations. Instead of regarding social problems as manifestations of a lack of rules, he saw them as situations in which individuals learned the values of their society, but because they did not have access to approved ways of making those values effective for themselves, sought other ways of gaining culturally approved ends. Those "deviant" ways brought them into conflict with the dominant conceptions of conventional behavior. "Racketeering" is a particularly clearcut example. Poor but ambitious young men, lacking access to legitimate careers became gangsters, thus winning, by illegitimate means, the success denied them by thir impoverished backgrounds.

In this perspective, the norms of society are taken for granted; what is problematic is the individual's response in terms of those norms. If he has access to approved ways of achieving goals, he is unlikely to engage in deviant behavior; if he does not have access to achievement consistent with culturally approved models, he is likely to violate the rules and thus lay himself open to punitive responses on the part of society. Deviant behavior is seen as the product of strains built into society, stemming from a disjunction between what the culture offers as desirable and what the social structure actually makes available to all members.

This perspective encourages the student of social problems to pay close attention to the situation of individuals engaging in deviant behavior, to determine what kinds of stresses they are subjected to by their position in relation to the "opportunity structure" of society, and to point policy-makers toward altering that position in such a way that individuals can achieve their goals in more conventional ways. While a conflict between the "deviant" and the "normal" is recognized, that conflict is regarded as a secondary consequence of the fact that the deviants have not had an opportunity to become normals in the first place.

A strong reaction against this conception of the dynamics of deviance and social problems has informed the work of sociologists who have developed our final perspective—that of societal reaction or *labelling*. The labelling theorists want to attend not to the behavior of deviants so much as to the behavior of the normals who are engaged in labelling behavior *as* deviant. Their starting place is the process by which members of society select certain kinds of behavior that are labelled as rule violations out of the many kinds of behavior individuals present to those around them. Their criticism of the deviant behavior theorists is that their conception of rule violation is too mechanical. It assumes that the labelling process is automatic and highly predictable, given the details of the deviant's behavior. In fact, such writers as Lemert and Becker observed that exactly the same behavior may variously be ignored by society, mildly sanctioned, or subjected to the most intense and dramatic moral reaction (for example, the consumption of alcohol).

The process by which this reaction is established and the purpose of the process for society, the labelling theorists argue, is far more interesting than the evaluation of the deviant act itself. Further, they observe, the reaction of the deviant to his situation is not simply a matter of his choices as determined by the opportunity structure but is also adapted to the societal reaction. Thus, Lemert's concept of "secondary deviance" refers to those aspects of the behavior of the deviant that are generated by his effort to adopt to the fact that he is (or potentially may be) labelled by the larger society as deviant. For example, much of the behavior of the drug user is seen as adaptive to the illegal situation in which he finds himself rather than as a result of drug use as such. The "deviant subculture" that grows up when persons engaged in a given kind of deviant behavior spend considerable time with each other is as much a product of their cooperative endeavor to defend themselves against the responses of society as it is intrinsic to their initial deviant commitment.

In summary, the perception of social problems in these five perspectives has differed dramatically. For the social pathologist, the problem is the defective character of individuals in society (or in a later version, the defective character of social institutions). For the sociologist who focuses on social disorganization, the problem is the ineffectiveness of rules for organizing constructive social processes. For the value conflict theorist, the problem can be understood only as a result either of conflicts among groups in society or of conflicting interests held by a single individual. For the deviance theorist, the problem lies in the instigations to rule violation created by the unequal distribution of opportunities for self-realization in society. For the labelling theorist, the problem is very much in the eye of the beholder, and in the process by which society separates its members into the moral and the immoral, the conforming and the deviant.

The theorists who developed these different perspectives have tended to emphasize (and perhaps to exaggerate) their incompatibility. To some extent the differences are more a result of preferred subject matter than anything else. Many modern investigators have combined at least the last three perspectives—those of anomie theory, labelling theory, and value conflict—in ways that yield a much more richly detailed and subtle picture of socially problematic situations and behavior than any investigator working only within one tradition is likely to be able to do.

ANALYZING SOCIAL PROBLEMS

The analysis of particular social problems requires that the analyst learn something of how the problematic situation came to be defined as it is, and how the particular actions that make up the problem came to be established. In their analysis of "the natural history of a social problem," Fuller and Myers offer the view that all social problems go through three definable stages—one might say three logically necessary stages—for the complete development of an "institutionalized" problem. These stages are (1) awareness, (2) policy determination, and (3) reform. With respect to most problems of concern to society and to social scientists, these stages are not observable separately, since society has long ago reached the third ("reform") stage of concern with problems such as crime, economic dependency, political corruption, etc. However, since what the problem is and how it is to be dealt with changes in its details over time (the definition of "crime," for example), Fuller and Myers' admonition to be sensitive to the sequence of stages is still very useful.

In the beginning there must be the definers—those who offer in some vigorous and convincing way a definition of particular conditions as a social problem, as a situation that challenges important values and produces undesired consequences. Then there will generally follow discussion about what should be done about the newly-diagnosed problem. Once decisions are made about what should be done, there is a final stage of doing it. Fuller and Myers call this "reform," but we might adopt the more general term of "policy action." Since in the real world problems seldom go away, most social action on social problems has to do with changing slightly the definition of what is the problem or the prescription of what might be done about it or, even more commonly, changing slightly the procedures by which a policy is administered and executed within a general social prescription.

The social scientist who is interested in a given social problem needs to start with a concern about how and to whom that problem is salient. There are several different levels of salience that one can readily observe. In terms of increasing breadth of concern, these may be categorized as follows:

1. *Detached scholarly diagnosis.* It sometimes happens that scholars (not only social scientists but also biological and physical scientists, legal scholars, etc.) observe social situations they believe can be defined as problematic in the light of established values and norms. They may write or speak about their diagnoses, without engaging a wider audience than their own colleagues. Some of the earliest work that eventuated in a broader concern with automotive safety, for example, can be seen as having begun at this level.

2. *The voice in the wilderness.* Somewhat more public and at the same time more individual is the activity of persons who undertake to publicize and dramatize situations which they and perhaps only a small group of others see as a problem. The most dramatic example of this kind in recent times is that of Rachel Carson, whose book, *Silent Spring,* first announced to a wide audience the environmental threat posed by pesticides. History is full of examples of voices in the wilderness who were initally treated as crack-pots (and, of course, for many voices in the wilderness that evaluation never changes).

3. *Pressure-groups.* Here those involved in asserting the existence of a problem encompass a broader group than either specialized scholars or the friends of a voice in the wilderness. A group of individuals, for reasons that seem sufficient and compelling to them, vigorously assert the existence of a problem against what they see as the indifference or resistance of society. Sometimes such groups persist over long periods of time with no apparent effect on the way society deals with the problematic situation. Then for reasons that may be quite difficult to disentangle the circumscribed issue may find itself augmented in the following ways:

4. *Pervasive elite concern.* The most significant transition in the evolution of a social problem may take place when the issue comes to be defined as important by individuals who conceive of themselves as part of the elite, as "knowledgeable persons." Racism in America, for example, was more the province of pressure groups than otherwise until the early 1960's, when it became an issue which could not be ignored by any individual who wished to claim that he was knowledgeable, judicious, and constructive-minded about society.

5. At the broadest level, a social problem may evoke considerable *society-wide concern;* it may be considered important not just by the elite (or sometimes not even by the elite) but by the man in the street. Some of the most interest-

ing political situations in a democratic society occur where the elite misperceive the concerns of the man in the street, and his concerns come to represent a political embarrassment to the elite. A recent example is the case of crime as a social problem, which achieved apparently very high salience among the public before that fact was clearly perceived by most of the elite. This disjunction of perceptions provides an important avenue of opportunity for aspiring politicians to move into more powerful positions.

These different levels of saliency in terms of the variable of "awareness" can be used to analyze not only social problems as such but also issues of policy determination and execution. A given policy approach may be confined to a particular set of scholars or a voice in the wilderness or a particular pressure group, or it may be the conventional wisdom within the elite or the wider society. Similarly, particular approaches to policy execution may be localized in each of these different groups. The social scientist who wishes to understand the pattern of social action involved in a given problematic issue needs to examine the varieties of awareness, policy determination, and policy execution that exist among these different levels of society at any given time.

For each group that has some awareness of the problem, or for all groups taken together, one can raise the following kinds of questions, and answers to each of them are necessary if we are to have a full understanding of the problem.

What is the problem? That is, what is the objective condition to which those who define the problem direct our attention?

Who are the people whose behavior constitutes the problem, and what are their characteristics?

How broad is the domain of the problem? That is, is it highly circumscribed ("teenagers vandalizing high schools during the summer vacation"), is it extremely pervasive in its penetration of various aspects of social life ("moral breakdown and permissiveness in our society"), or is it in between?

How much policy thinking is there about the problem? Is it one which, whatever the level of awareness, is not being much attended to by those with the power to make policy, or is it regarded as already routinely handled and therefore not subject to policy reassessment, or is it very much on the agenda of those who initiate policy?

What is in fact being done? Is this a social problem for which policy is more symbolic than actual, is political rhetoric the principal form of policy, or is the problem subject to considerable bureaucratic institutionalization and ongoing activity?

Given the level of policy action, to what extent does policy in fact affect the problem, either in terms of decreasing or increasing its prevalence or altering its form through the mechanisms we have discussed above as "secondary deviance?"

The social scientist whose interest in a social problem is not substantive, in the sense that he does not wish to make an independent contribution to public policy on the issue, may address himself to these questions simply to contribute to basic knowledge about how societies in general or a particular society operates: defining and taking action to understand social problems is itself of the essence of the ongoing life of human societies. But as we have noted, social scientists have generally studied social problems in good part because they wish to contribute to their constructive resolution.

Sometimes the upshot of the social scientist's study has been to suggest that "the problem itself is the problem," that is, that there is no real damage done to society by the condition causing complaint and that society would be better off if it were simply redefined as not a problem. As we will see, the social scientists on the U.S. Commission on Pornography essentially came to that conclusion. Or the social scientist may take the problem as seriously, or more seriously, than society in general, and set about seeking to develop knowledge that will be useful in coping with it.

What kinds of contributions can social science make? Howard S. Becker has suggested five areas in which social scientists can contribute. First, he says, the social scientist can help by "sorting out the differing definitions of the problem." Because problems are defined in different ways by different groups in society (and have been defined in different ways at different times in the history of the same society), discussion often produces more confusion than necessary because participants operate on the incorrect assumption that theirs is the only way of stating the issue. The social scientist who spells out different definitions of the problem and shows how they are related or contradictory provides the raw material for reconciling those differences in ways that could lead to more useful policy consideration.

Second, the social scientist can assist by analyzing the assumptions made by interested parties about how the problematic situation is constituted and operates. Those who are participants in policy determination and execution processes all operate on the basis of implicit models about what goes on in the world. These assumptions may conflict, just as definitions of the problem may conflict, and they may or may not be accurate. They are generally not complete or accurate over the whole range of social action entailed in the problem. The social scientist therefore seeks to make explicit the implicit models held by different participants in the problem-defining and resolving process.

Then he is in a position to make a third contribution, the one that is most distinctively a product of his expertise: testing various assumptions about the problem against empirical reality. The social scientist brings to bear a set of methodological and theoretical tools to assess the facts of the matter. This is simply said, but the complexity of the social facts involved in even the most apparently simple social problem is formidable indeed. As many social scientists and philosophers of science have observed, facts are not neutral. Students and activists concerned with any problem acquire interests in their particular definitions of its nature, definitions which analysis often shows are more a product of the organizational requirements of those involved than of their detached assessment of the reality with which they deal.

The structure of putative facts that shores up conventional ways of dealing with problems is extremely complex, and a great deal of social science activity involves simply demonstrating the inaccuracy of pieces of this structure. This is a fairly dismal task; indeed in recent times it has seemed that sociology may replace economics as "the dismal science." Over and over again sociologists seem able to demonstrate that various institutions designed to do something about a problem do not work—job training programs don't cure poverty, prisons do not rehabilitate criminals, more money spent on schools doesn't increase learning, etc. In the long run, however, social scientists are committed to the belief that a necessary though not sufficient condition for dealing constructively with social problems is a more accurate model of the social processes involved in each of them.

Becker observes that an accurate model of social processes makes possible the social scientist's fourth contribution—that of "discovering strategic points of intervention in the social structures and processes that produce the problem." The sociologist's assessment of the various kinds of social transactions that add up to the problematic situation allows him to imagine interventions which might have the effect of ameliorating the problem or doing away with it entirely. If he understands the dynamics of the problem, he is in a better position to predict the consequences of policy innovations. Recently there has been considerable interest among social scientists in large-scale experiments to test innovations and in particular to test the effectiveness of small variations in them. The New Jersey negative income tax experiment that was completed in the early 1970's is the largest example of such experimentation to date. Here different amounts of guaranteed income and different tax rates on the earnings of persons who received benefits from the plan were tested against each other and against a control group of low-income families who received no benefits. The experiment's designers hoped that analyzing the results of this experiment will yield greater precision in dealing with some aspects of the poverty problem. Some social scientists, particularly economists and political scientists, have for some time been involved in an effort to design intervention strategies to deal with social problems. Sociologists have been less involved in such activity, but it seems likely that in the future they will be more concerned with this kind of innovation design and testing research.

Many social scientists evince considerable ambivalence about a fifth contribution they can make toward the solution of social problems. They can, Becker notes, "suggest alternative moral points of view from which the problem can be assessed." Sociologists have long struggled to dissociate themselves from social philosophy and to establish their detachment as scientists. Yet involvement with the pragmatic issues of social problems often pushes them imperceptibly toward that earlier role. The social scientist often discovers when he offers alternative policy recommendations for dealing with a problem that he runs up against moralistic objections to his proposed innovations. In this situation, he often shifts his attention from the facts as such to analyzing the relationship between particular moral prescriptions ("crime should be punished") and the broader moral and humanitarian values to which those prescriptions are related as means to ends. He may suggest that in terms of these more basic moral views, a different set of operational moral standards might prove more constructive. These different standards, in turn, may serve to legitimate policy innovations that have not been previously considered acceptable. Since moral standards often conflict, this kind of analytic work generally proves crucial to resolving the policy impasses that often characterize serious social problem issues.

THE ORGANIZATION OF THESE VOLUMES

I have organized my coverage of social problems issues under two main rubrics: problems of inequality and problems of deviance. Problems of inequality are defined in terms of the values having to do with justice, equal treatment, equal humanity, which are supposed to inform public policy in the United States. The issues subsumed under the rubric of deviance involve another established natural value, that of liberty, of individual choice, of the determination of one's own best interest, free from arbitrary interference by the state, and with the security to exercise it.

The focus of these volumes is firmly substantive rather than disciplinary. That is, we are interested in social problems as areas of application of the social sciences to important social issues. We take it that it is their interest in problems and policy that brings students to a course in social problems, and that an interest in application characterizes an increasing number of sociologists. In pursuing this focus, however, we have made extensive use of the work of sociologists whose interest in social problems is perhaps more for what their analysis can tell one about the basic dynamics of human society than for policy purposes. It is commonly true in the social as in the physical sciences that an interest in research important for the development of the discipline in fact turns out to provide knowledge that is crucial for understanding some quite practical matter.

Many students of social problems end up pursuing careers in the public professions. It is important that before they specialize in a particular area (housing, welfare, education, health, corrections, etc.), those who are going to pursue such careers understand something of the general nature of social problems and the many themes that tie them together, themes having to do both with the problematic behavior itself and with the common responses on the part of political and administrative institutions.

Already public service work directed to social problems is a major industry in America, and all indications are that it will become even larger in a generation's time. Yet one major conclusion from research on these activities over the last decades is that they have a great capacity for dehumanizing those they are designed to serve, and very little capacity for resolving the social issues that lead to their establishment. I hope the germs of better kinds of intervention can already be found in the knowledge of today's social scientists.

A most convenient compendium of articles representative of different perspectives on social problems can be found in Earl Rubington and Martin S. Weinberg (eds.), *The Study of Social Problems: Five Perspectives* (Oxford University Press, 1971). The editors' analysis of the history and interrelations of the perspectives discussed above is particularly useful for the student. The articles by Fuller and Myers referred to above are included in this compendium, as is the article by Willard Waller. The reader also will be interested in the editor's introduction in Howard S. Becker (ed.), *Social Problems: A Modern Approach* (John Wiley and Sons, 1966).

Another overview of the relationship between sociology and social problems analysis, representing a structural-functional approach, is Robert K. Merton's

"Social Problems and Sociological Theory," in Robert K. Merton and Robert A. Nisbet (eds.), *Contemporary Social Problems* (Harcourt, Brace, 1961). One of the most incisive analyses of the relationship between the personal, political, and professional ideologies of sociologists and their work on social problems is in C. Wright Mills, "The Professional Ideology of Social Pathologists" (*American Journal of Sociology*, September 1943). For a more recent analysis of some of these issues, see Irving Louis Horowitz, "The Sociology of Social Problems: A Study in the Americanization of Ideas," in his *Professing Sociology: Studies in the Life Cycle of Social Science* (Aldine, 1968). See also Alvin W. Gouldner, "Anti-Minotaur: The Myth of a Value-Free Sociology" (*Social Problems,* Volume 8, Number 3, Winter 1962, pp. 199 ff.), and the contributions by the editors in *Alvin W. Gouldner and S. M. Miller, Applied Sociology* (The Free Press, 1961).

I.

MODERN PERSPECTIVES
ON INEQUALITY
AND SOCIAL PROBLEMS

THE ABSENCE OF justice or equity in how the resources of society are distributed to individuals and groups has long been a fertile source of socially problematic situations. In order to understand the intimate connections between these social problems and a distribution of goods and services judged inequitable by the standards of a society, we need first to examine how sociologists have studied inequality—which they usually call in more technical terms, "social stratification."

In Part I, we consider several philosophical and scientific approaches to issues of social inequality. Sociologists make heavy use of a tripartite division of society developed by Max Weber: a political (or legal) order, a social order, and an economic order. Different groups within these segments of the stratification system he called "classes" (defined by their chances to enjoy the fruits of economic resources), status groups (defined by their standing along a continuum of social honor or prestige), and parties or political groups (defined in terms of their greater or lesser capacity to influence communal action). Some sociologists have used Weber's ideas as if he conceived of these three orders as independent of each other. Although he did argue that for analytic purposes it was important to distinguish among these hierarchies and to analyze each in systematic detail, he was very much aware of their interpenetrations, of their overlapping and the mutual and simultaneous causality that runs from one to another.

In this volume we have used the rubrics of class, status, and power to organize a group of selections dealing with inequality and social problems. In Part II we cover inequalities in market chances, that is, in the relationships of people to economic institutions broadly conceived. In Part III we examine status inequalities, principal among which in our society are inequalities of racial and ethnic group membership and inequality between the sexes. In Part IV we analyze inequalities in power, ranging from such clearly party-oriented activities as voting to inequalities in the power of a variety of institutions that are important in a complex society like ours.

Part V expands on some of these issues to the international level. In most discussions of inequality the focus is on a given nation, but we have become more and more aware in the past generation of the importance of inequalities among nations, particularly between the so-called "underdeveloped countries" and advanced industrial nations. "International stratification," to use Irving Horowitz's term, includes all three orders of inequality. Most dramatically, of course, nations differ in their economic resources and productivity, but as Horowitz notes in Selection 29, there are also severe status inequalities compounded of racism and ethnic rivalries as well as the sense of moral superiority so long characteristic of the Western world. Finally, there are great political inequalities among nations that manifest themselves in the division of the world into major and minor powers and nations with no power to speak of at all.

Inequality, and its attendant injustice, is not the only great problem of complex societies, and even when we add deviant behavior we have not exhausted the kinds of problems that may be recognized by human societies, although most of them can be subsumed under one rubric or the other. In addition, an important issue in all social groups has to do with the efficient allocation of resources in terms of the choices and goals their members make and pursue. There are many connections between issues of efficiency and choice and issues of inequality and justice. Therefore in Part VI we have included several selections that address questions of efficiency, choice, and the conservation of resources. Each of these selections in one way or another highlights the interrelationships between goals of equality and goals of efficiency, and illustrates some of the impacts that pervasive patterns of social inequality may have on efforts to maximize efficiency and the conservation of resources.

The selections in the following Parts have been chosen to illustrate different ways in which patterns of social inequality are related to particular social problems that concern people in American society today. (Although the selections refer to American society, in fact the issues they deal with are for the most part common to all industrial societies.) First, patterns of social inequality may be regarded as problems because they are believed to be unjust in and of themselves. For example, no greater reason for regarding racial discrimination as a social problem is needed than that it is unjust in terms of American values. But there are other relationships between inequality and social problems. Many of the selections suggest that particular problems are second-order consequences of the extreme degree of inequality in American society; sometimes these are consequences of inequalities in market resources, sometimes in power, sometimes in status. Here the consequences of being in an inferior position in one or all of these respects may produce behavior that is judged as problematic or immoral. Such is the argument developed by those who emphasize the deviant behavior perspective in approaching social problems. They see particular kinds of problems as arising from the lack of access of individuals with low resources to conventional opportunity structures.

Finally, there is a relationship between inequality and social problems that arises from the problematic side effects of the efforts by those with advantages to maintain their place in the system. The anxieties generated by the necessity to struggle for advantage in structures of class, power, or status, it is widely believed, generate problems through their effects on peoples' feelings of fraternity and community, and by the patterns of inefficiency they introduce in the use or destruction of resources.

1. THE NEW EGALITARIANISM

HERBERT J. GANS

Reprinted from Saturday Review, *May 6, 1972. Copyright 1972 by Saturday Review, Inc. Herbert J. Gans is Professor of Sociology at Columbia University and a Senior Research Associate at the Center for Policy Research in New York City. He has published two classic studies of American urban communities and has written extensively on urban policy, poverty, and the role of the mass media in American society.*

■ Analysts of society—no less than all of us as we go through our daily lives—are likely to become so involved with the special situations, qualities, and terminologies of particular social issues that they end up not seeing the forest for the trees. In this selection Herbert J. Gans discovers a forest by tying together several social movements of the 1960s and showing how they all share a renewed emphasis on the goals and values of equality. To be sure, each particular group and movement pursues greater equality for its own group, but as the "liberations" of the 1960s followed one on another, both activists and commentators became impressed by a common theme in their programs; as Gans shows, that common theme is equality. The equality movement can be dated from 1955 with the beginning of the Montgomery bus boycott designed to destroy Jim Crow seating in buses. With that incident began a decade of civil rights activities—the sit-in movements for equal public accommodation and the voting rights drives for equal political representation, which culminated in the Black power movement, and, with these movements of the Black revolution as models, the liberation movements for other minority groups, for women, and for homosexuals.

These challenges to the nation's accustomed ways of sorting, ranking, and categorizing people became ever more general and began to inform a new ethic of egalitarianism at a fairly abstract level, so that even ordinary individuals began to apply the principle of equal treatment in the context of ordinary social relationships—within factories, within families, between citizens and public servants. Gans concludes his exploration of the new egalitarianism by considering the question of how the United States can move toward a more egalitarian society in a way that will accord with its traditions and with the U.S. character.

The classic discussion of the ambivalence in American society between values of democracy, equality, and unequal achievement is found in Alexis de Tocqueville's *Democracy in America,* available in several paper and hardback editions. In *The First New Nation* (New York: Basic Books, 1963), Seymour Martin Lipset analyzes the conflict between equality and inequality that has characterized the United States from its founding to the present. A useful collection of articles dealing with civil rights and Black power movements is found in Gary T. Marx, *Racial Conflict, Tension, and Change in American Society* (Boston: Little, Brown, 1971). In *Levittowners* (New York: Pantheon, 1967) and *People and Plans* (New York: Basic Books, 1968), Gans presents an analysis of the urban-suburban poverty and racial crises that provide the social structural base for many of the movements that converge in the new egalitarianism. ■

I

ALTHOUGH THE FUNDAMENTAL IDEA of the Declaration of Independence is that "all men are created equal," Americans traditionally have been more interested in life, liberty, and the pursuit of happiness than in the pursuit of equality. In the last decade, however, their interests have begun to shift, and equality may be on its way to becoming as significant as liberty in the hierarchy of American goals.

The shift began approximately on the day in 1955 when Mrs. Rose Parks of Montgomery, Alabama, decided that she was no longer willing to sit in the rear of a bus. Much has been written about the ensuing political and social unrest, but few observers have emphasized that the revolts of the

18

Blacks, the young, and others have a common theme: the demand for greater equality by the less than equal. Blacks have agitated for racial equality through black power; students, in high schools as well as in colleges, have demanded more power on the campus; teen-agers have begun to claim the sexual freedom now available to young adults, and in less public ways they—and even younger children—have sought more equality within the family. And, of course, many women are now demanding equality with men, and homosexuals with heterosexuals.

Similar developments have been occurring in the economy and the polity. Wage workers have begun to demand guaranteed annual incomes and the other privileges that salaried workers enjoy. Public employees have struck for wage equity with workers in private industry. Assembly-line workers have sought better working conditions and more control over the operation of the line. Enlisted men have called for reductions in the power of officers.

In politics the 1960s saw the emergence of the drive for community control—attempts by urban residents to obtain more power over their neighborhoods. Subsequently, community control broadened into a movement to reduce the power of bureaucracies at all levels of government and of professionals over their clients; for example, of doctors over patients, teachers over parents, and planners over homeowners. Consumers have called for more control over what goods are to be produced and sold, environmentalists over how they are to be produced. Stockholders have demanded a greater role in the decisions taken by management.

Few of these demands have been explicitly phrased in terms of equality; most of those making the demands have spoken of autonomy and democracy. Many have actually asked for more liberty. Still, if all of these demands are put together they mean more income for some and higher costs for others, more power for some and less for others. If the demands were heeded, the eventual outcome would be greater overall equality.

No one can accurately predict whether or not these demands will be heeded, but egalitarian ideas are cropping up with increased frequency among politicians and in the media. Senator Fred Harris's populist presidential campaign, which called for some income redistribution, was short-lived, but Senator George McGovern has proposed a comprehensive tax reform program along the same lines, and Governor George Wallace occasionally injects egalitarian notions into his campaign speeches. Widely read journalists, such as Tom Wicker, Jack Newfield, and *New Republic's* TRB, have talked and written about the need for equality. In March [1972] an article entitled "Equality" appeared in *Fortune*; it sought, rather gingerly, to prepare the business community for a more egalitarian future.

II

The current interest in equality cannot be explained away as the plaints of discontented minorities and newly radicalized public figures. It stems from the fact that America's is, and always has been, a very unequal society. Take the distribution of income. The poorest fifth of the U.S. population receives only 4 percent of the nation's annual income, and the next poorest fifth only 11 percent, while the richest fifth gets about 45 percent, and the 5 percent at the top over 20 percent. Inequality of assets is even greater: 1 percent of the people control more than a third of the country's wealth. Although many Americans now own some stocks, 2 percent of all individual stockholders own about two-thirds of stocks held by individuals.

The same inequality exists in the business world. Of the almost 2 million corporations in America, .01 percent controls 55 percent of the total corporate assets; 1.1 percent controls 82 percent. At the other end of the spectrum, 94 percent of the corporations own only 9 percent of the total assets. Even the public economy is unequal, for the poor pay a larger share of their incomes for taxes than other groups; people earning less than $2,000 pay fully half of their incomes in direct and indirect taxes as compared with only 45 percent paid by those earning $50,000 or more. Moderate income groups are not much better off; people earning $8,000 – $10,000 a year pay only 4 percent less of their income than those making $25,000 – $50,000.

Of course, the poor get something back from the government through welfare and other subsidies, but then so do the affluent, especially through indirect subsidies in the guise of tax policies, such as the oil depletion allowance, crop supports, and tax exemptions granted to municipal bond purchasers. Philip Stern, author of *The Great Treasury Raid* and himself a multimillionaire, recently described these subsidies as "a welfare program that reverses the usual pattern and gives huge welfare payments to the super-rich but only pennies to the very poor." Stern estimated that the annual subsidies came to $720,000 per family for people with million-dollar incomes, $650 per family for the $10,000 – $15,000 middle-income group, and $16 per family for the under-$3,000 poor.

Political inequality is also rampant. For example, since about 13 percent of the population is poor in terms of the official poverty line, an egalitarian political system would require that almost 50 congressmen and 13 senators be representatives of the poor. This is not the case, however, even though big business, big labor, and even less numerous sectors of the population have their unofficial representatives in both houses of Congress. While Supreme Court action has finally brought about the one-man, one-vote principle in electing these representatives, the seniority system maintains the traditional pattern of inequality, and so a handful of congressmen and senators, many from rural districts, still hold much of the real power on Capitol Hill. Affluent individuals and well-organized interest groups in effect have more than one vote per man because they have far greater access to their elected representatives than does the ordinary citizen and because they can afford to hire lobbyists who watch out for their interests and even help to write legislation.

III

These patterns of inequality are not new; although America has sometimes been described as a nation of equals and as a classless society, these are simply myths. To be sure, America never had the well-defined classes or estates that existed in Europe, but from its beginning it has nevertheless been a nation of unequals. For example, in 1774, among the minority of Philadelphians affluent enough to pay taxes, 10 percent owned fully 89 percent of the taxable property. Over the last 200 years the degree of economic inequality has been reduced somewhat, but in the last 60 years—since reliable statistics on income distribution have become available—that distribution has changed little.

Although the ideal of a nation of equals has existed in American life from the beginning, it has, in fact, never been pursued very energetically in either the economy or the polity. Even the ideal that every boy could be president of the United States or chairman of the board of General Motors has rarely been achieved; most of our presidents have been rich, and studies of the origins of American businessmen show that in the 19th century, as now, the large majority have themselves been sons of businessmen.

Nevertheless, over the last 200 years most Americans seem to have put up quietly with the prevailing inequality. Today, however, the traditional patience with inequality has disappeared, and for three reasons.

First, many Americans are now beginning to realize that the frontier, by which I mean the opportunity to strike out on one's own and perhaps to strike it rich, is closing down. The literal frontier in the West was closed before the turn of the century, but until recently other frontiers were still thought to be open. Rural people hoped that they could become independent by saving up for a farm; factory workers by going into business, perhaps opening a gas station or small work-shop; and middle-class people by entering the independent professions.

Today these hopes have begun to disappear, for the family farm is economically obsolete, the small store cannot compete with the chain, and the independent professions now consist more and more of salaried employees. Of course, there are still exceptions, and every year a few well-publicized individuals strike it rich, but their small number only proves the rule. Most Americans now realize that they will spend their working lives as employees and that they can best improve their fortunes by making demands on their employers and, because the government's role in the economy is rapidly increasing, on their political representatives.

Second, as people have voiced more political demands, they have also become less patient with political inequality, particularly with their increasing powerlessness as bureaucracies and corporations continue to get bigger. Indeed, many of the demands for change that sprung up during the 1960s were fledgling attempts to fight powerlessness and to redress the political imbalance.

Third, the affluence of the post-World War II era has enabled many Americans to raise their incomes to a point where they are no longer preoccupied solely with making ends meet. As a result, new expectations have emerged, not only for a higher standard of living but also for improvements in the quality of life and for greater power to control one's destiny. And, more than ever before, people believe that the economy and the government should help them achieve their new expectations.

IV

What people demand is not necessarily what they will get, as the lingering recession of the last few years and the continuation of the war in Vietnam have persuasively demonstrated. Still, the demands associated with the equality revolution will not recede, and

if America is to have any chance of becoming a more stable society, it must also become a more egalitarian society.

Once upon a time inequality helped to America great. The country was built out of the energy of restless entrepreneurs, the labor supplied by the unequal, and the capital generated from both. Today, however, inequality is a major source of social instability and unrest and is even a cause of the rising rates of crime, delinquency, and social pathology—alcoholism, drug addiction, and mental illness, for example. The conventional wisdom maintains that crime and pathology are caused largely by poverty, but during the 1960s poverty declined while crime and pathology increased. In these same years, however, inequality did not decrease; by some estimates, it actually grew worse.

One conventional measure of inequality is the number of people who earn less than half of a country's median family income. In the United States between 1960 and 1970, when this median rose from $5,620 to $9,870, the number earning half the median dropped only 1 percent—from 20 to 19. One can also define inequality by measuring how far the poor are from the median income. In 1960 income at the poverty line, earned only by the richest of the poor, came to 50 percent of the median; by 1970 it came to only 40 percent. In other words, during the decade the poverty line rose far more slowly than the median income, and the inequality gap between the poor and the median earners actually widened by a full 20 percent.

This gap is not just economic, however; it also produces social and emotional consequences. Inequality gives rise to feelings of inferiority, which in turn generate inadequacy and self-hate or anger. Feelings of inadequacy and self-hate, more than poverty, account for the high rates of pathology; anger results in crime, delinquency, senseless violence—and, of course, in political protest as well. But inequality also has less dramatic consequences. For example, because they cannot afford to dress their children properly, some poor mothers refuse to send them to school; shabby clothes may protect a youngster from the elements—a flour sack made into a suit or dress will do that—but shabby clothes also mark the child as unequal, and mothers want to protect their children from this label even at the cost of depriving them of schooling.

The social and emotional consequences of inequality are also felt by moderate income people, especially the almost 40 percent of Americans who earn above the poverty line but below the median income. For example, many young factory workers now realize, as their fathers could not afford to realize, that they hold unpleasant jobs without much chance of advancement or escape, and that much blue-collar work is inferior to white-collar jobs, which are now the norm in the American economy. In fact, the pathology and the protest normally associated with the poor is beginning to develop among factory workers as well. Hard drugs are now showing up in blue-collar neighborhoods, and strikes over working conditions, such as the recent one at the General Motors plant in Lordstown, Ohio, are increasing in number and intensity.

Indeed, if the most serious inequalities in American life are not corrected, people who feel themselves to be most unequal are likely to find new ways of getting even with America. New kinds of school, factory, and office disturbances, ghetto unrest, and dropping out of the system can be expected, and more crime in middle-class urban neighborhoods and suburbs is likely, for crime has always been a way by which at least some poor people can obtain a primitive kind of income redistribution when society pays no heed to their inequality.

Inequality does not harm only the unequal; it hurts the entire society. The last 10 years have demonstrated the fragility of the American political fabric, but the social fabric is also weak. Old sources of stability have disappeared, as has much of the traditional American culture that once provided satisfactions even under inegalitarian conditions. The small towns and rural areas that gave people a sense of rootedness, which compensated them for their poverty, are being depleted by out-migration. In the cities the ethnic groups, which maintained the peasants' necessary resignation to European inequality and provided group cohesion and a close-knit family life as compensation, are now Americanized. (Although a revival of ethnic identity may be taking place currently, the old cultures are not being resuscitated, for the new ethnic identity is political and actually calls for more equality for ethnics.) Increasingly, Americans today are members of a single mainstream culture, partly urban, partly suburban, and distinguished primarily by differences in income and education. The mainstream culture pursues values long identified with the American way of life, mainly individual and familial comforts, security, and self-improvement; but it strives for ever higher levels of these, and with ever rising expectations that they will be achieved. As a result, mainstream culture rejects traditional rural, ethnic, and other values that call for modest expectations of comfort, security, and self-improvement and that thus accept the prevailing inequality.

The continued rise in expectations makes it likely that America will enter a period of greater economic and political conflict, for, when almost everyone has higher expectations there must inevitably be conflict over how these expectations are to be met and just whose expectations are to be met first and foremost.

America has always endured conflict, of course; after all, economic competition is itself a form of conflict. But conflict can tear society apart unless it can be resolved constructively. This is possible only if the participants in the conflict have, and feel they have, a chance to get what they want or, when this is not feasible, to get about as much as everyone else—if, in other words, the conflict ends in a compromise that meets everyone's needs as fairly as possible. But if the participants in the conflict are unequal, those with power and wealth will almost always get what they want, whether from government or from the economy.

Conflicts can best be compromised fairly if the society is more egalitarian, if differences of self-interest that result from sharp inequality of income and power can be reduced. The more egalitarian a society, the greater the similarity of interests among its citizens, and the greater the likelihood that disagreements between them can be settled through fair compromise. Also, only in a more egalitarian society is it possible to develop policies that are truly in the public interest, for only in such a society do enough citizens share enough interests so that these policies can be considered to be truly public ones.

V

Consequently, the time has come to start thinking about a more egalitarian America and to develop a model of equality that combines the traditional emphasis on the pursuit of liberty with the newly emerging need to reduce inequality. As Daniel Patrick Moynihan put it in the famous "Moynihan Report" of 1965, Equality of Opportunity must be transformed into Equality of Results. Equality of Opportunity simply enables people with more income and better education to win out over the less fortunate, even when the competition itself is equitable. Equality of Results means that people begin the competition more equal in these resources; therefore, the outcome is likely to be more equitable. Equality of Results does not mean absolute equality, however, either of income or of any other resource. It does mean sufficient reductions in present inequities to erase any insurmountable handicaps in the competition.

Models or methods for achieving equality have generally been *collectivist;* they call for replacing private institutions with public agencies that will take over the allocation of resources, typically through a nationalization of industry. This approach assumes that all resources belong equally to all people and that public ownership will bring about equality. When all the people own everything, however, they really do not own anything, enabling the officials who govern in the name of the people to make themselves more than equal politically and to restrict others' political liberties. This seems to be an almost inevitable outcome of collectivist policies, at least in poor countries, even though these policies have also reduced overall economic inequality.

An American equality model must be *individualist;* it must achieve enough equality to allow the pursuit of liberty to continue but not restrict equal access to liberty for others. An individualistic model of equality begins with these assumptions: that people are not ready to stop competing for material or nonmaterial gain or self-improvement; that they will not, for the sake of equality, become altruists who repress their ego-needs for the public good; and that they are not ready to surrender control over their own lives to a government, however democratic, that doles out liberty and equality through collective ownership of all resources. Consequently, an individualist model would aim for greater economic equality, not by nationalizing industry but by distributing stock ownership to larger numbers of people, as Louis Kelso, among others, has suggested.

Similarly, the model would not provide the same public or private goods and services to everyone; rather, it would attempt to equalize income and then let people decide to spend that income on goods and services of their own choosing. Nor would everyone have the same income. Instead, the model would enable people to maximize their earnings through their own efforts; it would create more equality through tax and subsidy policies, as in Sweden and Great Britain, for example. Greater equalization of incomes after taxes should not significantly reduce incentive, for even now rich people continue trying to make more money although most of the additional earnings goes to the tax collectors.

VI

The reconciling of equality and liberty is not simple, and only a great deal of public debate can determine how it ought to be done. It is not simply a matter of giving up a little liberty for a little equality. There are many kinds of equality—economic, social, political, and sexual, among others. Which kinds are most important, how much equality is needed, and which resources, powers, rights, and privileges need to be equalized and which need to be allocated on libertarian principles must be debated.

Nevertheless, some of the basic requirements of a more egalitarian society can be outlined. The American political-bureaucratic complex must be restructured so that it will attend to the demands of average citizens rather than of those best organized to apply maximal political pressure or the largest campaign contributions. The right combination of centralization and citizen control has to be found to make this complex both effective and democratic, responsive to majority rule as well as to the rights of minorities, at state and inferior levels as well as at the federal level. Some basic services, such as health, education, legal aid, and housing, should be available to everyone at a decent level of quality, so that, for example, the poor would not be confined to slums or public housing projects but could choose from the same kind of housing as everyone else. They would obtain rent subsidies to help pay for it.

The economy must also be democratized; corporations need to become more accountable to consumers and the general public, and they must be required to shoulder the social and other indirect costs of their activities. Stock ownership has to be dispersed, taxes must be made progressive, and subsidies should be used extensively for egalitarian purposes. Unemployment and underemployment have to be eliminated and the poverty line raised so that the gaps between those at the bottom, middle, and top are reduced and so that eventually no one will earn less than 75 percent of the median income: $7,500 by today's income figures. Whether a ceiling on top incomes is economically necessary remains to be seen, although it may well be socially desirable. Even now there is considerable uproar over millionaires who pay no taxes. Nevertheless, more income equality cannot be achieved solely by redistributing some of the great wealth of the superrich; redirecting the benefits of future economic growth to the now less than equal and imposing higher taxes on the corporations and the top fifth of the population would also be necessary. Still, greater income equality can be brought about without excessive soaking of the rich; S. M. Miller has estimated that if only 10 percent of the after-tax incomes of families earning more than $15,500 were shifted to those earning less than $4,000, the income of persons earning less than $4,000 would increase by more than half.

America is today sufficiently affluent to afford more income equality without great sacrifice by anyone. The Gross National Product is currently so high that if it were divided equally among all Americans, a family of 4 would receive $19,000. Part of the GNP must be used for investment, of course, but if what economists call Total Personal Income were divided up, a family of 4 would still receive $15,600, fully half as much again as the current median family income.

A more egalitarian America is thus economically feasible, but it would not be politically achievable without considerable political struggle. The more than equal would fight any inroads on their privileges, but even the less than equal might at first be unenthusiastic, fearful that promises would not be kept and that, as has so often happened in the past, high-sounding policy proposals would continue to result in legislation benefiting the wealthy and powerful. The less than equal would soon rally to genuinely egalitarian legislation, but the affluent would still have to be persuaded that money and privilege alone cannot buy happiness in a conflict-ridden society and that the current American malaise, from which they suffer as much as others, will disappear only with greater equality. Indeed, I am convinced that what Daniel Bell has called the postindustrial society cannot be held together unless private and public resources are shared sufficiently to give every American a fair chance in the pursuit of liberty. That is why equality is likely to become an increasingly insistent item on the agenda of American politics.

2. LIBERTY AND EQUALITY

HAROLD LASKI

Reprinted by permission of George Allen & Unwin Ltd. from Harold J. Laski, A Grammar of Politics, Yale University Press, 1925, second edition, 1930. Harold J. Laski, having received honors at the school of Modern History at Oxford in 1914, served as a lecturer in history and political science from 1914-1926 at McGill, Harvard, Yale, and Cambridge Universities and at the London School of Economics and Political Science. In 1926 he went to London University as Professor of Political Science. He was a well-known and influential member of the British Labor Party and served on its executive committee from 1936-1949. The author of a number of books and articles, he was a strong advocate of socialism and planned economy, and his influence has extended beyond his death in 1950.

■ Liberty and equality, Harold Laski notes, often have been taken as at least partly contradictory social goals. It has been argued that as society allows a wide range of personal liberty its exercise inevitably will produce inequalities among persons. Or, more commonly, the antiequality argument states that liberty suffers to the extent that equalitarian patterns are made part of our social institutions. In this selection Laski argues for the primacy of equality because no universal liberty is possible unless people have what he calls "a minimum basis of civilization." The argument put forward by the antiequalitarian conservatives who would exalt liberty over equality resolves inevitably into liberty for the few and both inequality and restriction for the rest. Though Laski's is the political rhetoric of several decades ago, it nevertheless accords quite well with modern social science orientations to issues of stratification and personal well-being. Laski's work provides a nice bridge between some of the highly abstruse treatments of equality in 19th century political philosophy and modern social science concepts.

John Rawls's recent book, *A Theory of Justice* (Cambridge, Mass.: Harvard University Press, 1971), has given us a powerful analysis of the ethical basis for equalitarian social norms, a subject philosophers have long neglected. All who seek to connect social science, public policy, and philosophical equalitarian perspectives should read this book. An earlier treatment in the tradition of Fabian concerns is R. H. Tawney's classic *Equality*, which is available in several editions. A convenient collection of legal and philosophical discussions of equality is found in William T. Blackstone, ed., *The Concept of Equality* (Minneapolis: Burgess Publishing Co., 1969). A less sanguine view of equality as a political goal is in Ralf Dahrendorf, "Liberty and Equality," in *Essays in the Theory of Society* (Stanford, Calif.: Stanford University Press, 1968). The classic modern discussion in favor of economic liberty and against equality is that of Milton Friedman in *Capitalism and Freedom* (Chicago: University of Chicago Press, 1962). ■

NO IDEA IN THE WHOLE REALM of political science is more difficult than the concept of equality. To minds so ardent for liberty as Tocqueville and Lord Acton, liberty and equality were antithetic things. It is a drastic conclusion. But it turns, in the case of both men, upon a misunderstanding of what equality implies. Equality does not mean identity of treatment. There can be no ultimate identity of treatment so long as men are different in want and capacity and need. The purpose of society would be frustrated at the outset if the nature of a mathematician met a response identical with that to the nature of a bricklayer. Equality does not even imply identity of reward for effort so long as the difference in reward does not enable me, by its magnitude, to invade the rights of others.

Equality, broadly, is a coherence of ideas each one of which needs special examination. Undoubtedly, it implies fundamentally a certain leveling process. It means that no man shall be so placed in society that he can overreach his neighbor to the extent which constitutes a denial of the latter's citizenship. It means that my realization of my best self must involve as its logical result the realization by others of their best selves. It means such an ordering of social forces as will balance a share in the toil of living with a share in its gain also. It means that my share in that gain must be adequate for the purposes of citizenship. It implies that even if my voice be weighed as less weighty than that of another, it must yet receive consideration in the decisions that are made. The meaning, ultimately, of equality surely lies in the fact that the very differences in the nature of men require mechanisms for the expression of their wills that give to each its due hearing. The power, in fact, of the ideal of equality lies in the historical evidence that so far in the record of the state the wills of men have been unequally answered. Their freedom, where it has been gained, has accordingly been built upon the unfreedom of others. Inequality, in a word, means the rule of limited numbers because it secures freedom only to those whose will is secure of respect. They will dominate the state and use its power for their own purposes. They will make the fulfillment of their private desires the criterion of public good.

Equality, therefore, means first of all the absence of special privilege. . . . In the penumbra of equality, [that phrase] means, in the political sphere, that my will, as a factor in the counting of heads, is equal to the will of any other. It means that I can move forward to any office in the state for which men are prepared to choose me. It means that I am not to find that there are persons in the state whose authority is qualitatively different from my own. Whatever rights inhere in another by virtue of his being a citizen must inhere, and to the same extent, in me also. There is no justification in such a view for the existence of an hereditary second chamber. For, obviously, in the second generation of such an assembly men exercise political authority not in virtue of their own qualities, but by reason of parental accident. So, also, no office that carries with it power

can ever be rightly regarded as an incorporeal hereditament, for that is to associate important functions with qualities other than fitness for their performance. The exclusion of any man, or body of men, from access to the avenues of authority is always, that is to say, a denial of their freedom.

Equality means, in the second place, that adequate opportunities are laid open to all. By adequate opportunities we cannot imply equal opportunities in a sense that implies identity of original chance. The native endowments of men are by no means equal. Children who are brought up in an atmosphere where things of the mind are accounted highly are bound to start the race of life with advantages no legislation can secure. Parental character will inevitably affect profoundly the quality of the children whom it touches. So long, therefore, as the family endures—and there seems little reason to anticipate or to desire its disappearance—the varying environments it will create make the notion of equal opportunities a fantastic one.

But that is not to say that the opportunities created may not be adequate. We can at least see first that all men are given such training as seems, in the light of experience, most likely to develop their faculties to the full. We can at least surround those circumstances with the physical media without which the training of the mind can hardly be successful. We can, where we discover talent, at least make it certain that it does not perish for want of encouragement. These conditions do not exist today. Children who come hungry to school cannot, on the average, profit by education in like degree to those who are well fed. The student who is trying to do his work in a room which serves for the various tasks of life cannot find that essential isolation without which the habit of thought can rarely be cultivated. The boy and girl who have to assume that at 14 they are bound to pass into the industrial world rarely acquire that frame of mind which searches with eagerness for the cultivation of intelligence. In the modern world, broadly speaking, opportunity is a matter of parental circumstance.

Boys of a certain social status may assume that they will pass from the secondary school to the university. Boys whose parents are, broadly, manual workers will in the vast majority of cases be inevitably destined to manual work also. There is no reason to decry either the value or the dignity of manual work; but there is every reason to examine the social adequacy of a system which does not at every point associate the best training available with those whose qualities most fit them to benefit by that training. We do not want—possibly we cannot afford—to prolong the period of education unduly. But no state has established conditions of reasonable adequacy until the period of education is sufficiently long, first, to ensure that the citizen knows how to use his mind, and second, that those of special capacity are given that further training which prevents the wastage of their talent. . . .

The provision of adequate opportunity is, therefore, one of the basic conditions of equality, and it is mainly founded upon the training we offer to citizens. For the power that ultimately counts in society is the power to utilize knowledge; and disparities of education result, above all, in disparities in the ability to use that power. I am not pleading for equality of function. I am pleading only for the obvious truth that without education a man is not so circumstanced that he knows how to make the best of himself and that therefore, for him, the purpose of society is, *ab initio,* frustrated. Once men are in that situation where they can know themselves; the use they make of their opportunities becomes subject to principles of which equality is only one.

But if we agree . . . that a democratic state regards its members as equally entitled to happiness, it follows that such differences as exist must not be differences inexplicable in terms of reason. Distinctions of wealth or status must be distinctions to which all men can attain, and they must be required by the common welfare. If a state permits the existence of a hereditary aristocracy it must be because it is capable of proof that a heredi-

tary aristocracy multiplies the chances of each man's realizing his best self. If we are to have an economic system in which the luxury of a few is paralleled by the misery of the many, it must be because the common welfare requires that luxury. In each case the proposition is open to historical disproof. A hereditary aristocracy is bound, sooner or later, to use its political power to general disadvantage, unless, like the peerage of France, it has ceased to be anything but a faded memory. A state divided into a small number of rich and a large number of poor will always develop a government manipulated by the rich to protect the amenities represented by their property. It therefore follows that the inequalities of any social system are justified only as it can be demonstrated that the levels of service they procure are obviously higher because of their existence. It is obvious that a general must have larger powers than a private because, thereby, the purpose of an army is more likely to be fulfilled. It is obvious that a statesman in office must be so remunerated that he is not oppressed by narrow material cares; and that might well involve placing him in a financial rank higher than a bootmaker or a shop assistant. In each case the measure of difference is conceived in social terms. It is set in a principle which is demonstrably rational. It is fitting the circumstances of function to the environment of which it has need.

Such a view admits, at least as a matter of theory, of fairly simple statement in institutional terms. The urgent claims of all must be met before we can meet the particular claims of some. The differences in the social or economic position of men can only be admitted after a minimum basis of civilization is attained by the community as a whole. That minimum basis must admit of my realizing the implications of personality. Above that level, the advantages of the situation I occupy must be advantages necessary to the performance of a social function. The advantages I enjoy must be the result of my own effort, because they are the return to me for my own services, and I am clearly not entitled to enjoy them as the result of someone else's services. One man is not entitled to a house of 20 rooms until all people are adequately housed; and 1 man, even in that environment, is not entitled to a house of 20 rooms because his father was a great advocate or a large industrialist. The things that are due to me are the rights I must enjoy in order to be a citizen, and the differential advantages which society adjudges inherent in the particular occupation I follow. . . .

If all this is true, equality is most largely a problem in proportions. There is an aspect in which the things without which life is meaningless must be accessible to all without distinction in degree or kind. All men must eat and drink and obtain shelter. But those needs are, in their turn, proportionate to what they do. My wants are my claims to find a harmony of impulses. I do not want the same harmony if I am a miner as I shall want if I am a surgeon. But the system which obtains must not satisfy the claims of the surgeon at the expense of the miner's claims. My urgent needs are not less urgent than the needs of any other person, and they are entitled to equal satisfaction. Once urgency is satisfied superfluity becomes a problem of so fixing the return to service that each man can perform his function with the maximum return to society as a whole.

In this aspect, the problem of proportions is largely an economic problem. It is a question of the methods we use to determine the claim of each citizen upon the social dividend, and of the environment which surrounds the application of those methods. There have been famous answers to this problem. We have been told that response should be made in terms of need, or in terms of contribution; it has been insisted that identity of response is alone adequate. Of these solutions that which would reward me by what I do for society is certainly the least satisfactory. For it is impossible in any genuine way to measure service. We cannot say what Newton or Lister, Shakespeare, or Robert Owen were

"worth" to their fellow citizens. We cannot measure the contribution of a banker against the contribution of a bricklayer. Often enough, as in the case of Galileo, for example, we may not be able to see how vast in truth the contribution is. Nor, it may be argued, is the communistic solution adequate. For, in the first place, there is no total identity of needs between men; nor is their effort so equal as to merit an identical return. The communistic principle is adequate up to the point where human urgencies are in question; it is not adequate after that point. And it is adequate only so far as its application wins the result of a deliberate effort on the part of those whose needs are satisfied to do work of civic quality. And since to do work of civic quality involves differentiation of function, it is, I think, clear that when the primary needs of all men are met, the differences they encounter must be differences their function requires; requirement involving always the context of social benefit.

But this, it will be argued, is to assume sufficiency. It implies that there is in fact enough to go round, whereas we know that the productivity of men does not suffice for their wants. What we ought rather to do is to allow the free play of capacity to win response to its need and let those prosper who show the power to triumph in the race. The answer involved in this attitude is far less simple than it seems. If the state exists for social good, "capacity" can only mean capacity to add to social good. It is not in the least certain that the exercise of talent in a society like our own does in fact result in social benefit. Capacity, in short, must run in the leading-strings of principle. It must be excited to the end our institutions have in view. And since that end is the achievement of happiness for each individual, it seems obvious that we must, if the margin be insufficient, suffer equally by its insufficiencies. We can never, therefore, as a matter of principle, justify the existence of differences until the point is reached when the primary claims of men win a full response. I have no right to cake if my neighbor, because of that right, is compelled to go without bread. Any social organization from which this basis is absent by denying equality denies all that gives meaning to the personality of men.

Equality, therefore, involves up to the margin of sufficiency identity of response to primary needs. And that is what is meant by justice. We are rendering to each man his own by giving him what enables him to be a man. We are, of course, therein protecting the weak and limiting the power of the strong. We so act because the common welfare includes the welfare of the weak as well as of the strong. Grant, as we may well grant, that this involves a payment by society to men and women who limp after its vanguard; the quality of the state depends on its regarding their lives as worth preserving. To act otherwise is to regard them not as persons but as instruments. It is to deny that their personality constitutes a claim. It is deliberately to weight institutions against a section of the community. If they are to harmonize their impulses in the effort after happiness, such bias is inadmissible. For it is utilizing their service not for their own well-being, but for the well-being of others. That is essentially the definition of slavery.

It is no answer to this view to urge that it bases social organization upon a principle hitherto inoperative in history. The decay of previous systems has been most largely based on the fact that it was inoperative. Men have seen institutions pass, or have cooperated to destroy institutions, precisely because they did not see in them the forces which sought response to what made them men. Nor are we seeking to compel all citizens to win from life an identical response. We seek identity only up to the level where the facts insist upon identity. We argue that some will not starve quietly if others have abundance. We urge that the conference of knowledge upon some while others are excluded from its benefits is, in fact, their exclusion from the purpose of the state. And no other principle, as a working system, will effect the results the state has in view. For immediately we admit

privilege within the area of equal need, it will use every weapon at its disposal to multiply its access to special benefits. The history of privileges is not a history of voluntary abdication in terms of social welfare; it is rather the history of a careful limitation of the idea of social welfare to those who enjoy the opportunity it offers. It is only, as a consequence, by making identity the basis of our institutions, and differences an answer to the necessities of social functions that we can make our society call into play the individuality of men.

Here it is immediately important to insist on certain conditions upon which alone that basis of identity may be maintained. A first essential is approximately equality of wealth. I do not mean by that the absence of varying rates of payment for effort. I mean only that the rate of payment shall not so differ that merely in virtue of those differences men can exert an unequal pressure upon the fabric of institutions.

That unequal pressure obviously exists today. There are men in every community whose power is built not upon what they are or do, but upon the possessions they embody. The influence they exercise is not a tribute to themselves but an offering to their wealth. They act by owning. They command the service of others to the performance of functions built upon a private will not necessarily relevant to the social welfare. They can direct the flow of production into channels notable only for their wastefulness. They can dominate the supply of news, and so influence to their own ends the working of political institutions. They can adjust the economic power of the community to purposes fatal to the welfare of those who have nothing but their labor to sell. The desire, for instance, of the great iron masters of France to dominate the heavy industries of Europe may well send the next generation to die on the battlefield. Where there are great inequalities of fortune, there is always inequality of treatment. It is only when no man merely by virtue of his possessions can influence the course of affairs that the equal interest of men in the results of the political process can secure validation. The surest way to that end is to prevent those disparities of wealth which permit the owners of fortune to manipulate unfairly the mechanisms of power.

Broadly, I am urging that great inequalities of wealth make impossible the attainment of freedom. It means the dictation of the physical and mental circumstances which surround the less fortunate. It means the control of the engines of government to their detriment. The influence of the great corporations upon the legislative system of the United States is only a supreme example of that control. Hardly less deleterious is the way in which it controls the intellectual environment it encounters. It is able to weight the educational system in its interest. It is able, by the rewards it offers, to affect the propertyless brainworker to its service. Since the judiciary will be largely selected from its paid advocates, legal decisions will largely reflect the lessons of its experience. Even the churches will preach a gospel which is permeated by their dependence upon the support of the wealthy.

Political equality, therefore, is never real unless it is accompanied by virtual economic equality; political power, otherwise, is bound to be the handmaid of economic power. The recognition of this dependence is in the main due to the explanation of historic evolution, and it is, indeed, almost as old as the birth of scientific politics. Aristotle pointed out the equation between democracy and the rule of the poor, between oligarchy and the rule of the rich. The struggle to remedy economic disparity is the key to Roman history; it is at the root of English agrarian discontent. It underlies the sermons of John Ball, the *Utopia* of More, the *Oceana* of Harrington. The early history of socialism is most largely the record of a perception that the concentration of property other than labor power in a few hands is fatal to the purpose of the state. It was that perception which Marx, in the *Communist Manifesto,* made the foundation of the most formidable political philosophy in the modern world. For though the materialistic interpretation of history is an overemphasis of one link in the chain of causation, it is the link most intimately related to the experience of ordinary men. It is overwhelmingly right in its insistence that either the state must dominate property, or property will dominate the state.

For, as Madison wrote, "the only durable source of faction is property." But it is obvious that to base the differences between men on a contest for economic wealth is to destroy the possibility of a well-ordered commonwealth. It is to excite all the qualities in men—envy, arrogance, hatred, vanity—which prevent the emergence of social unity. It is to emphasize a competition based on their separation, instead of a competition based upon their mutual interest. As soon as we postulate approximate equality of wealth, our methods of social organization enable us to respond to men's needs in terms of the substance of those needs. We are the more bound to this effort immediately we admit the logic of universal suffrage. For to confide to the mass of men the control of ultimate political power is broadly to admit that the agencies of the state must be utilized to respond to their needs. They involve, if they are to be satisfied, such a distribution of influence over authority as will balance fairly the incidence of its results among the members of society. It means, that is, that I must adjust my scale of wants to social welfare as that is organized in terms of a valuation which equally weights the primary needs of citizens; and that valuation remains ineffective if my power is a function not of my personality but of my property.

3. SOCIAL INEQUALITY AND SOCIAL INTEGRATION

JOHN H. GOLDTHORPE

Reprinted from Advancement of Science, *Vol. 26, No. 128, December 1969. This selection is the text of a paper given to Section N of the British Association for the Advancement of Science, Exeter Meeting, 1969. John H. Goldthorpe is a Fellow of Nuffield College, Oxford University. A leading British sociologist, he has written extensively on issues of social stratification. His best-known works deal with the impact of economic affluence on British workers and their families.*

■ Many social thinkers have identified social problems not so much as issues of social inequality but as issues of social integration; they have emphasized a lack of consensus in society. Since Durkheim's work sociologists have made heavy use of the concept of anomie, certainly one of the central, guiding paradigms of the sociological perspective. Drawing on the great wealth of empirical research in the area of industrial relations, Goldthorpe seeks to show that marked social inequality in modern societies must serve to undermine social integration, and that without sharply reducing inequality anomic patterns cannot be reduced in such societies. He seeks to show that "disorderly" industrial relations and the "wages jungle" are consequences of patterns of inequality that cannot be legitimated. The "unprincipled" nature of the unequal distribution of rewards serves as a constant destabilizing influence, encouraging each group of workers to "get theirs." Goldthorpe believes that in the analysis of particular applied problems it is incumbent on applied sociologists not to take existing patterns of inequality as given, because no solutions to social problems exist within the unequal system. Instead, applied sociologists should face up to the often unpleasant need to explain that conflict and lack of integration are routinely generated consequences of a highly unequal distribution of resources.

Readers interested in comparing the American patterns of inequality described in this book with comparable patterns in Britain are referred to W. G. Runciman, *Relative Deprivation and Social Justice: A Study of Attitudes Towards Inequality in Twentieth Century England* (Berkeley: University of California Press, 1966); John H. Goldthorpe, David Lockwood, Frank Beckhofer, and Jennifer Platt, *The Affluent Worker: Industrial Attitudes and Behavior,* 3 vols. (Cambridge University Press, 1968, 1969); and Peter Townsend, ed., *The Concept of Poverty* (New York: American Elvier Publishing Co., 1970). Classical empirical sociological studies of inequality and integration are Alfred W. Jones, *Life, Liberty and Property* (New York: Lippincott, 1941), and Robert E. Lane, *Political Ideology: Why the American Common Man Believes What He Does* (New York: Free Press, 1962). An analysis of the views of one group of Americans (Bostonians) on issues of equality and justice is found in Lee Rainwater, *What Money Buys* (New York: Basic Books, 1974). ■

I WISH TO MAKE three points about the general nature of social inequality before turning to the problem with which my paper will be centrally concerned: that is, the problem of the *implications* of inequality for social integration. The three points are the following.

1. Social inequality, in societies such as ours, is manifested in a very wide variety of ways—wider than is usually recognized in public discussion of the matter. For example, inequalities in economic resources tend, relatively speaking, to receive a fair amount of attention. The finding reported by Meade that 5 percent of the population own 75 percent of all personal wealth has figured quite frequently in recent political argument, as have data on the number of households whose members could be regarded as living in poverty—on incomes, say, below the "National Assistance" level. But far less is heard

of the further marked inequalities that are involved in the ways in which economic rewards are actually gained—most importantly, in the content of work tasks and roles. There is, however, by now ample evidence to show that wide differences exist between occupations and jobs in the extent to which they offer possibilities of *intrinsic* satisfaction to the individuals engaged in them or, on the other hand, are a source of psychological or social deprivation. To take an obvious contrast, the inequalities in reward between professional employment and factory work are clearly not confined to the differences in their income levels.

Again, one aspect of inequality in work which it *has* of late been somewhat fashionable to point to, and to decry, is that of the status differences which operate among different categories of employee in most industrial organizations; for instance, in such matters as methods of payment, "clocking-in" and lateness rules, toilet, canteen or car parking arrangements. But discussion of these questions has usually been carried on without any reference to the far more basic inequality represented by the steep gradient of *authority* within such organizations—which, in fact, status distinctions serve largely to symbolize.

The tendency here illustrated to conceive of inequality in a piecemeal manner, rather than as a multiform and pervasive phenomenon, results, I would argue, from a failure to appreciate in what, fundamentally, social inequality consists. This leads me to my second point.

2. Social inequality in all its manifestations can be thought of as involving differences in social power and advantage: power being defined as the capacity to mobilize resources (human and nonhuman) in order to bring about a desired state of affairs; and advantage as the possession of, or control over, whatever in society is valued and scarce. Power and advantage are thus closely related. Power can be used to secure advantage, while certain advantages constitute the resources that are used in the exercise of power.

Moreover, different forms of power and advantage tend in their very nature to be convertible: economic resources can be used to gain status or to establish authority; status can help to reinforce authority or to create economic opportunities; positions of authority usually confer status and command high economic rewards, and so on.

In this perspective, then, the way in which inequality structures virtually the whole of social life can be readily understood. Differences in social power and advantage, simply because they imply differences across the whole range of life-chances, always tend, other things being equal, to become generalized differences. Furthermore, it is important to add that this effect operates not only from one area of social life to another but also through time. Inequalities of condition at any one point in time create inequalities of opportunity for future achievement. For example, the intergenerational aspects of this phenomenon could be said to constitute the central problem thus far for the sociology of education. The results of research in this field provide impressive evidence of how, notably through the agency of the family, the stability of social strata tends to be maintained—despite the growing importance of education to career chances and the development of policies aimed at reducing nonacademic influences on educational attainment.

3. It has, therefore, to be recognized that structures of social inequality of both condition and opportunity—or, in other words, systems of social stratification—are inherently highly resistant to change. The members of higher strata have the motivation and in general the resources to hold on to their position and to transmit it to their children, while the members of lower strata are often caught up in vicious circles of deprivation. This is not, of course, to suggest that change in stratification systems cannot, or does not, occur; but rather that any significant reduction in the degree of inequality will require purposive, well-designed and politically forceful action to this end—that it is unlikely to come about simply as the unsought-for

consequence of technological advance, economic growth, or any such like secular trends. Such developments may well modify certain forms of inequality; but they appear just as likely to accentuate others.

Indeed, far from industrial societies having "built-in" processes which steadily diminish inequality—as some writers have claimed —what is striking, at least in the British case, is the frequently very limited effect of even the deliberate pursuit of equality through governmental action. For example, as already implied, the egalitarian aspects of educational policy over the last half-century or so have resulted in only a very slight lessening in class differentials in educational opportunity— despite the fact that over the same period an enormous expansion of educational facilities has occurred. In a similar way, major improvements in medical services and general standards of health have failed over a long period to produce any appreciable reduction in relative class differentials in infant mortality and in many kinds of morbidity. And finally in this respect it may be noted that inequalities in incomes, after being somewhat diminished in the war and immediate postwar period, subsequently stabilized and then from around 1950 appear, if anything, to have widened again.

In sum, one may say that social inequality, as observed in present-day Britain, takes the general form of a substantially self-maintaining structure of social groupings differentiated multi-fariously and often extremely in terms of the power and advantage that their members enjoy. What, then, are the consequences of this inequality for the integration of British society; that is to say, for the extent to which the actions of individuals and groups tend regularly to comply with recognized norms, and to be thus consistent with, rather than in conflict with or unrelated to, the expectations and actions of other individuals and groups?

This question, in certain of its aspects, has in fact been examined by a number of recent writers, who have adopted a similar initial approach. They have started from the observation that in Britain considerable and abiding inequality does not apparently give rise to deeply divisive conflicts in which the existing social structure, political institutions included, is frequently and fundamentally called into question. They have then gone on to infer from this, not unreasonably, that the resentment of inequality among the less favored sections of the population is neither particularly widespread nor particularly militant—and especially if comparisons are made with the situation in certain other societies. Thus, the somewhat more specific problem which emerges from this approach is the following: why is it that, given the prevailing degree of social inequality, there is no widely supported and radical opposition to the existing sociopolitical order, and that at all levels of the stratification hierarchy attitudes of acceptance, if not of approval, are those most commonly found? At this point, analyses tend to divide into two main types which one might conveniently label "social-psychological" and "culturalist." The first type is best displayed in the work of Runciman.

Briefly, Runciman's argument is that to account for the discrepancy between the objective degree of inequality in British society and the actual awareness and resentment of this inequality, we must consider the "reference groups" in terms of which individuals in the lower social strata assess their position. That is to say, we must consider the other groups in society—real or imagined—with which members of less favored groups habitually *compare* themselves in evaluating their rewards, opportunities, and social deserts generally, and in relation to which their expectations and aspirations are formed. If, for instance, the reference groups adopted by a certain membership group are located fairly closely in the stratification hierarchy to the membership group's own position, then the degree of felt inequality is likely to be quite slight, no matter what the overall range of factual inequality may be. A strong sense of grievance is only to be expected if reference groups are selected in a more "ambitious" way so that considerable inequality is perceived and is then, on the basis of the comparison made, regarded as illegitimate and unjust. In other words, the degree of *relative deprivation*—deprivation which is subjectively experienced and which may thus influence political behavior—is primarily determined *by the structure of reference groups* rather than by the structure of inequality itself as the sociologist might describe it.

Runciman's own research, using both historical and survey methods, indicates that among the British working class reference groups are, and generally have been, restricted in scope; and that while some variation in this respect can be traced over time and from one form of inequality to another, no consistent trend is evident toward wider ranging comparisons. Consequently, the disruptive potential that social inequality might be thought to hold remains in fact suppressed; social integration is furthered through perceptual and conceptual limitations.

Turning secondly to the "culturalist" type of analysis, it should be said that this has been chiefly elaborated by American social scientists interested in the question of the social bases of stable and effective democracy. In treating Britain as one of the relatively few countries whose polity might be thus described, these investigators have been led to examine—with differing degrees of directness —such issues as the following. Why among lower social strata in Britain is there not far more alienation from a political system which is elitist in itself and under which many other forms of inequality persist? Why is there no longer in Britain, if indeed there ever was, a powerful class-based social movement seeking radical structural changes of an egalitarian kind, and prepared if necessary to challenge existing political institutions in pursuit of its objectives?

In the explanations that are offered for the absence of these possible threats to stable democracy, major emphasis is laid on the nature of British "political culture"; that is, on the pattern or "mix" of attitudes which research has shown to exist in British society toward political institutions and political life

in general. Like other countries in which democracy flourishes, the argument runs, Britain has, in the course of her historical development, built up a political culture of a distinctive type. It is one characterized primarily by the *balance* that holds, even across lines of class and party, between participant, activist attitudes on the one hand and acquiescent, passive attitudes on the other; between emotional commitment to political principal and cool pragmatism; between consensus on matters of procedure and conflict over particular issues.

Through their socialization into this culture from childhood onward, it is held that the majority of citizens come to feel a sense of unfanatical, but generally unquestioning, allegiance to the established political order, and one that is unlikely to be seriously disturbed by any grievances they may have over the distribution of social power and advantage. Such grievances do not lead to alienation from the political system since there is wide acceptance of the "democratic myth"— the myth that the individual can influence political decisions and outcomes—and the system itself is not therefore seen as exploitive. Moreover, attitudes toward the political elite tend to be ones of trust, if not of deference, and the exercise of government authority is generally accepted as legitimate. For example, in one study survey data are presented to show that manual workers who believe that there are inordinately powerful groups in British society (such as "big business") are as much prepared to allow government a wide sphere of authority as are workers who do not share in this belief. In other words, grievances arising out of inequality do not tend to become so highly politicized that established political institutions and processes are themselves challenged. Political awareness is in any case at only a moderate level, and politics is only rarely a central life interest. Consequently, the availability of the ordinary citizen for involvement in "unstabilizing" mass movements is low; the political culture effectively inhibits the radical political action which marked social inequality might otherwise be expected to generate.

Clearly, social-psychological and culturalist points of view on the issue in question are not incompatible: they could, rather, be represented as complementary and mutually supportive on the following lines. Because the reference groups of lower strata have remained generally restricted, political issues stemming from social inequality have tended to be relatively "mild" and capable of being resolved or accommodated by existing political arrangements. This has, therefore, helped a basically "allegiant" political culture to form. Reciprocally, the development of such a culture has been inimical to the spread of ideological thinking—as, say, on the matter of social justice—which could lead both to a heightened awareness of inequality and deprivation and to greater recognition of their political dimensions. In short, social psychological processes of the kind examined by Runciman could be seen as a necessary condition of the political culture of British democracy, while this culture in turn, once established, favors the persistence of these processes.

Despite the various criticisms with which they have met, the analyses I have reviewed do, in my opinion, go some important part of the way to explaining why the consequences of inequality in Britain are not socially divisive in an extreme degree. But what has to be kept in mind, and what I wish here to emphasize, is that for the most part these analyses treat the problem of inequality and integration only from one particular angle. As I earlier noted, the focus of interest is on the possible *political* implications of inequality; and what is in effect illumined is chiefly the question of why among the British working class there is found no significant support for political ideas and movements of a revolutionary cast, nor even the widespread *incivisme* which characterizes sections of, say, the French or Italian working class. However, there are other major aspects of the problem which may be distinguished, and ones which have

been curiously neglected. In particular, I would advance the view—as the central thesis of this paper—that the most far-reaching implications of inequality for the integration of British society occur not in the political sphere but rather in that of economic life; and that they are manifested not in a situation of fundamental class struggle but rather in a situation of anomie; that is, in a situation in which, to stay close to the original Durkheimian notion, there is a lack of *moral* regulation over the wants and goals that individuals hold. . . .

My two central arguments [are] the following: first, that social inequality in Britain appears to pose no direct threat to the stability of the political order—because this is, as it were, "insulated" from the potentially disruptive consequences of inequality by a combination of social-psychological and cultural influences; but second, that the existence of inequality, of an extreme, unyielding, and largely illegitimate kind, does militate seriously against any stable normative regulation in the economic sphere—because it militates against the possibility of effective value consensus on the distribution of economic, and other, resources and rewards.

Of these two arguments, it is, I imagine, the latter that will be the more likely to provoke dissent, and chiefly perhaps among social scientists with "applied" interests in the field of industrial and economic policy; for it obviously suggests that much of their present endeavor will meet with relatively little success. However, as a way both of rounding off this argument and leading on to my own, concluding, observations on policy issues, I would like to draw attention to one further point—somewhat obvious but often neglected—with implications that may be still more unwelcome to those colleagues in question. This is the point that, in spite of frequent attempts, it has not proved possible to give a satisfactory explanation of the persisting degree and form of inequality, in Britain or in any advanced society, by reference primarily to "external" constraints, and without reference to the purposive exercise of their power and advantage by more privileged groups and strata. In other words, it has not proved possible to explain social inequality otherwise than as a structure with important self-maintaining properties.

For example, attempts to relate social inequality or particular aspects of it—say, in incomes—to differences in the so-called "natural" attributes of individuals have repeatedly failed; and chiefly because social variation is regularly found to be of a different order of magnitude from natural variation. In advanced societies the dispersion of even earned income has a proportionate range of as wide as 50 or perhaps 100 to 1: no conceivably relevant natural attribute has been shown to vary to such an extent. Again, it is by now evident enough that established structures of inequality yield little to explanation in terms simply of the operation of "impersonal" market forces—in terms, that is, of the interaction of supply and demand in regard to different types of labor service. Labor economists themselves, as much as educational sociologists, have demonstrated the considerable restrictions that occur on the "supply" side, as a result of various forms of inequality of opportunity. Consequently, the existence of the essentially "non-competing groups" which social strata form distorts the labor market into a highly imperfect condition; and the "imperfections" themselves lie outside the scope of pure economic analysis. Finally, one should note, attempts by sociologists to revamp classical economics in the guise of "functional" theories of social stratification have scarcely been convincing. Even if one leaves aside the basic problems of how to determine the functional exigencies of a social system or the relative functional importance of positions and roles within it, a logical limitation of such theories must still be stressed: that is, they are adequate only to explaining why *some degree* of social inequality should occur—not why the actual pattern of inequality is as it is.

In short, then, one may assert that attempts to account for observable social inequality in terms simply of constraints, whether stemming from genetics, economics, or "societal" imperatives, are at best of very limited value. Through their very inadequacies, such attempts point to the degree to which the phenomenon of social stratification must be seen as an autonomous one: as a phenomenon which has to be explained largely as the outcome of social action and interaction in the form of competition and conflict, the basis for which being always the inequality in power and advantage previously existing.

This being so, there are, I think, two implications of note. First, since prevailing patterns of inequality cannot be represented as the direct consequence of ineluctable exigencies, it is hard to see how they can be "scientifically" legitimated as *necessary* features, either of the human condition in general or of the functioning of a particular type of society. In itself, of course, this fact is unlikely to be of much significance for the attitudes toward social inequality which are actually held among the population at large: it seems probable that inequality is indeed quite widely accepted as deriving either from "natural" differences or from (what sociologists would call) "functional imperatives." But this situation then points to the second implication which I see as important. Namely, that when concerned with problems arising out of competition and conflict, such as those found in economic life, applied social scientists must seriously ask themselves whether they do not have an obligation to state, clearly and insistently, that the context of inequality in which these problems typically exist is neither unalterable nor indisputably desirable, and need not, therefore, be taken as a "given." In other words, they must consider whether they are not obliged to emphasize what they know about the nature of social inequality, including its self-perpetuating but "man-made" characteristics, and thus try to redress a situation in which, as Runciman has put it, "From the moment almost of birth, attitudes to the social structure are conditioned by pressures in which the ideal of social justice plays little if any part."

If applied social scientists do act in this way, they may well, of course, make their task of piecemeal social reconstruction even more difficult than I have already suggested; that is, by increasing awareness and resentment of inequality, especially among disadvantaged groups and strata, and thus reducing further the likelihood of their willing cooperation. But if, on the other hand, our social and economic engineers keep silent on the matter of inequality—if they attempt rather to build on the fact that the full extent of inequality is often unrealized and its sources misunderstood—then they are, willy-nilly, applying their knowledge and expertise in a partial way. And on this account, whatever their intentions may be, they lay themselves open to the charge of acting as "the servants of power."

I am, then, arguing not only that attempts at reconstituting normative order in economic life have small chances of success under existing conditions of inequality, but further that these chances will be still smaller if social scientists acknowledge an obligation to propagate the findings of examinations of this inequality and to relate these findings to the issues in which they seek to intervene. For it can scarcely be denied that such knowledge is likely to be corrosive of those beliefs and attitudes which, it seems, contain grievances arising out of inequality to a level that is "manageable" at all.

This, I recognize, may be thought a very negative position to adopt, and in certain respects it obviously is. However, I should like to observe that there is one conclusion with constructive possibilities to which my analysis does lead on directly; that is, that if the problem of anomie in economic life is to be attacked effectively, then the problem of social inequality must be attacked simultaneously. It can, I think, be argued, as a matter of sociology rather than ideology, that in a society that is both industrial and democratic relatively stable normative order in economic life can *only* be created through norms being underpinned by some minimum degree of value consensus—as opposed to

merely customary limitations on wants and goals. And such consensus in turn cannot be achieved without the distribution of economic resources and rewards, and indeed the entire structure of power and advantage, becoming in some sense "principled"—becoming, that is, more capable of being given consistent rational and moral justification. In other words, the advantage of social justice has to be seen not as some lofty and rather impractical ideal, the further pursuit of which must wait upon the attainment of such basic objectives as "getting the economy right," but rather as an important *precondition* of mitigating current economic difficulties. Such a lesson had to be learned once in the 19th and earlier 20th centuries, when governments were forced to recognize, as one historian has remarked, that social welfare policies were not "mere sweeteners of the hard rigors of a system of individualist compulsions," but represented rather "social provisions against waste of life and resources and against social inefficiency—not concessions." Governments now apparently need to learn that in a society with a highly complex division of labor, in which the possibilities of malintegration are correspondingly great, social inequality which is extreme and without legitimation will continually frustrate the orderly and efficient conduct of industrial and economic affairs generally: or, as Durkheim more succinctly put it, that "all external inequality compromises organic solidarity."

This is not the place to spell out in detail how the normative reconstruction of economic life and the reduction of social inequality might proceed together. But certain general possibilities are evident enough. For example, several writers have already observed that attempts to regularize industrial relations at enterprise level, so as to facilitate grievance procedures and checks on wage movements, inevitably raise afresh issues of industrial democracy: issues of the right of employees to participate in management and economic decision-making going beyond the scope of collective bargaining. And at least one economist has been prepared to recognize that effective answers to the key "micro" problems of incomes policy may well entail "changes in concepts of managerial structure, authority and control." Again, as regards incomes policy in "macro" terms, Professor Wootton more than a decade ago argued the need for such a policy to be *expressly related* to egalitarian objectives, in order to counteract the self-reinforcing character of social inequality and to give the structure of earnings a clearer moral basis; otherwise, the support of large sections of the population could neither be asked for nor expected. Professor Wootton in fact points to the genuinely radical conception of an incomes policy addressed not simply to problems of inflation, but, more basically to those of social integration and the furtherance of democracy. Such a policy, rather than being devised as an essentially economic instrument, would be framed as part of an overall social policy, with economic considerations being admissible only as and when their imperative nature could be actually demonstrated.

In adumbrating such possibilities, there are two things I should make quite clear. First, I do not for a moment underestimate the difficulties that would be involved in realizing them—not least as a result of the direct opposition which could be safely predicted from those whose power and advantage would be diminished. Second, I am not attempting here to argue for the desirability of developments of the kind in question in any absolute sense—though such a case might no doubt be made. What I am trying to establish is that these possibilities exist, and that unless and until something on these lines is accomplished, then the present anomic character of economic life will remain. I recognize that from a number of value positions the goal of greater equality may be given only low priority, or that inequality may even be regarded as a good in itself. Moreover, I do not believe that the sociologist *qua* sociologist is able to impugn such positions directly. But what *can* be argued sociologically is that those who are prepared to accept social inequality more or less as it presently exists must *also* be prepared to accept "disorderly" industrial relations, the "wages jungle" and general economic "free-for-all" more or less as *they* now exist—or, as the one remaining possibility, to support attempts at entirely authoritarian solutions to these problems. This last course of action, however, would be perhaps the most effective way of breaking down the insulation of the British political system from issues and grievances stemming from inequality—the insulation which the national political culture has hitherto provided. In other words, it would carry the very real threat of extending economic into political instability.

Finally, to turn from possibilities to probabilities, one has, I think, to accept that for the foreseeable future by far the most likely outcome is the continuance of the present state of affairs; that is, of a situation of persisting, marked inequality and also of chronic industrial unrest and of general economic infighting between interest groups under the rules mainly of "catch-as-catch-can." Such a forecast is indicated by the fact that the egalitarian restructuring of our society, which could be achieved only as a work of political will, expertise and force, does not now appear to be even on the agenda of any major political party. For those who find this situation an unacceptable one, the main hope, at this stage at least, must lie in attempts at analysis and persuasion; in attempts, that is, to demonstrate, as cogently and as widely as possible, just what the concomitants of existing social inequality are, and how they block the aspirations found in many groups and strata—and not only among the less privileged—for a society in which resources are more rationally and cooperatively used. The highest degree of optimism that egalitarians can permit themselves—the belief that the *need* for greatest equality will eventually prevail—is aptly expressed in one further passage which I take from Durkheim, from near the end of *The Division of Labour.*

The task of the most advanced societies is then, one could say, a work of justice. . . . Just as the ideal of less developed societies was to create or maintain as intense a common life as possible, in which the individual was absorbed, so our ideal is to invest our social relationships with ever greater equity in order to ensure the free development of all socially useful potentialities. When one thinks, though, that for centuries men have been content with a much less perfect justice, one begins to ask if these aspirations might not perhaps be due to fits of gratuitous impatience; if they do not represent a deviation from the normal state of affairs, rather than an anticipation of the normal state of the future; in short, whether the way of curing the disorder they make manifest is through

satisfying them or rejecting them. What we have already established . . . enables us to answer this question precisely. There are no needs more firmly grounded than these impulsions, for they are a necessary consequence of the changes that have occurred in the structure of societies. . . . In the same way as earlier peoples needed, above all, a common faith to live by, we ourselves need justice; and we can be sure that this need will become increasingly exigent if, as seems in every way likely, the conditions that govern social evolution remain unchanged.

4. ON THE ORIGIN OF INEQUALITY AMONG MEN

RALF DAHRENDORF

Excerpted from Essays in the Theory of Society *with permission of the publishers, Stanford University Press. Copyright* © *1968 by the Board of Trustees of the Leland Stanford Jr. University. Ralf Dahrendorf is a leading member of the FDP, the small German political party in the classical liberal mode, which shares power with the Social Democratic Party. He has been a member of the German Parliament. Before embarking on a career in public life, he was Professor of Sociology at the University of Constanz. His major sociological interests have been in social stratification and the place of social conflict as a central explanatory principle in political and sociological theory.*

■ Men at all times have puzzled over their differences in rank, honor, and privileges. They have sought to explain these differences and have thereby produced a variety of interesting stories about how men come to live the lives they do. The puzzlement about how the existence of social ranks is to be understood has played a major role in philosophy and, Ralf Dahrendorf suggests, is perhaps the central issue of the relatively new science called sociology. The same issue has played an important role in other social sciences: in some branches of psychology that seek to explain social rank by individual differences in specific capacities and general intelligence; in economics, where issues of the distribution of resources were a principal concern until a preoccupation with the dynamics of economic growth superseded them; in political science, which Harold D. Lasswell once defined as the study of "who gets what, when, and how"; and in anthropology, which has cataloged and theorized about the tremendous variety of social hierarchies found in the different cultures of the world.

Dahrendorf traces the origin of social inequality—not in the historical sense but in the sense of its basic sources in any society—to the idea that societies are communities of persons who operate under rules that some members realize more fully in their behavior than others. Variable conformity to norms, then, becomes both the source of an ineradicable level of inequality in a society and the central dynamic of change in society, since those members who are disadvantaged by the norms are thereby motivated either to change their opportunities relative to the norms or to change the norms themselves.

Social problems are regularly produced as a result of these stratification processes. A social problem can be recognized when the inequalities produced by the application of norms and sanctions are judged by someone in some sense to be unfair or to have consequences that are destructive. Similarly, a fertile source of problems is the conflict provoked by the efforts of those whom the reigning values disadvantage. Sometimes the problems are defined in terms set by those who uphold the established norms—for example, "race riots"— and sometimes by those who would change the established system so that it includes presently disadvantaged groups—for example, norms about the appropriate age for citizenship.

Dahrendorf's theoretical explorations in social stratification are developed in detail in other papers in *Essays in the Theory of Society* and an earlier book, *Class and Conflict in Industrial Society* (Stanford, Calif.: Stanford University Press, 1959). He has applied his theoretical expertise to a study of modern German society, *Society and Democracy in Germany* (New York: Anchor Books, 1969).

The various contributors to the debate over the social sources of inequality are well represented in Reinhold Bendix and S. M. Lipset, eds., *Class, Status and Power* (New York: Free Press, 1966). Other reviews of the issues covered here can be found in T. B. Bottomore, *Classes in Modern Society* (New York: Random House, Vintage Books, 1969), and *Elites and Society* (New York: Pelican Books, 1966). A wide range of articles that describe social stratification in the United States is in Jack L. Roach, Llewellyn Gross, and Orville Gursslin,

Social Stratification in the United States (Englewood Cliffs, N.J.: Prentice-Hall, 1969).

The greatest amount of empirical sociological research on stratification has been directed toward understanding occupations. Two of the most important works in this tradition are Albert J. Reiss, Jr., *Occupations and Social Status* (New York: Free Press, 1961), and Peter M. Blau and Otis Dudley Duncan, *The American Occupational Structure* (New York: Wiley, 1967). A perspective that concentrates on potentials for conflict and social change is C. Wright Mills, *White Collar* (New York: Oxford University Press, 1951). The meshing of honor and privilege at the top of the social order are dealt with in the American context in E. Digby Baltzel, *Philadelphia Gentlemen: The Making of a National Upper Class* (New York: Free Press, 1958), and in W. Lloyd Warner, *Yankee City*, 1 vol. ed., (New Haven, Conn.: Yale University Press, 1963). ■

WHY IS THERE INEQUALITY among men? Where do its causes lie? Can it be reduced, or even abolished altogether? Or do we have to accept it as a necessary element in the structure of human society?

I shall try to show that historically these were the first questions asked by sociology. By surveying the various attempts to answer them a whole history of sociological thought might be written, and I shall at least give some indication of how this may be so. So far, however, as the problem of inequality itself is concerned, this history has achieved little more than to give it a different name: what was called in the 18th century the origin of inequality and in the 19th the formation of classes, we describe today as the theory of social stratification—all this even though the original problem has not changed and no satisfactory solution to it has been found. In this essay I shall attempt a new explanation of the old problem, one that in my opinion will take us a few steps beyond the present state of our thinking.

The younger a branch of scholarship is, the more concerned are its historians to pursue its origins back at least as far as Greek antiquity. Historians of sociology are no exception to this rule. But if one regards the problem of inequality as a key to the history of sociology, it can be clearly shown not only that Plato and Aristotle were definitely not sociologists, but also why they were not. It is always awkward to ascribe to an academic discipline a precise date of birth, but this discussion may help us to date the beginnings of sociology with reasonable plausibility.

In 1792, a gentleman by the name of Meiners, described as a "Royal British Councillor and *rite* teacher of worldly wisdom in Gottingen," wrote some reflections on "the causes of the inequality of estates among the most prominent European peoples." His results were not especially original.

In all times inequality of natures has unfailingly produced inequality of rights. . . . If the negligent, the lazy, the untrained, and the ignorant were to enjoy equal rights with those who display the corresponding virtues, this would be as unnatural and unjust as if the child had rights equal to those of the adult, the weak and cowardly woman rights equal to those of the strong and courageous man, the villain the same security and respect as the meritorious citizen.

Meiners's reflections are a version, highly characteristic of his time, of an ideology that to the present day, and with only minor refinements, is invoked by all societies that are worried about their survival to reassure themselves of the justice of their injustices. By repeating in a simplified form the errors of Aristotle, such societies assert a pre-established harmony of things natural and social, and above all a congruence of natural differences between men and social differences between their positions. It was Aristotle, after all, who said:

It is thus clear that there are *by nature* free men and slaves, and that servitude is agreeable and just for the latter. . . . Equally, the relation of the male to the female is *by nature* such that one is superior and the other inferior, one dominates and the other is dominated. . . . With the barbarians, of course, the female and the dominated have the same rank. This is because they do not possess a naturally dominating element. . . . This is why the poets say, "It is just that Greeks rule over barbarians," because the barbarian and the slave are *by nature* the same.

Now this is just the attitude that makes impossible a sociological treatment of the problem—i.e., an explanation of inequality in terms of specifically social factors expressed in propositions capable of being empirically tested.

So far, I have talked about social inequality as if it were clear what is meant by this notion. Obviously, this is a somewhat optimistic assumption. The lathe operator and the pipe fitter, the general and the sergeant, the artistically gifted child and the mechanically gifted child, the talented and the untalented, are all pairs of unequals. Yet these inequalities are evidently themselves rather unequal, and have to be distinguished from one another in at least two respects. First, we must distinguish between inequalities of natural capability and those of social position; second, we must distinguish between inequalities that do not involve any evaluative rank order and those that do. If we combine these two approaches, four types of inequality emerge, all of which we shall have to discuss. In relation to the individual there are (1) *natural differences of kind* in features, character, and interests, and (2) *natural differences of rank* in intelligence, talent, and strength (leaving open the question of whether such differences do in fact exist). Correspondingly, in relation to society (and in the language of contemporary sociology) there are (3) *social differentiation* of positions essentially equal in rank, and (4) *social stratification* based on reputation and wealth and expressed in a rank order of social status.

Our interest here is primarily in inequalities of the stratification type. On the question of what these are, or, more technically speaking, how they can be measured, no consensus has so far been reached, nor has a suggestion been offered that would make a consensus possible. I am accordingly making an arbitrary decision here when I distinguish the distributive area of stratification—the explicandum of our theoretical discussion—from nondistributive inequalities such as those of power. According to this distinction, wealth and prestige belong to the area of stratification, even if they are assembled to a considerable extent by one person; property and charisma, by contrast, are nondistributive. How wealth and prestige relate to each other, and especially whether they are mutually convertible and can therefore be reduced to one concept, one single "currency" of social stratification, is an important technical question that I cannot go into here.

Aristotle was concerned as we are here to examine the origin of the fourth type of inequality, social stratification. However, by trying to explain social stratification—as so many authors of antiquity, the Christian middle ages, and modern times did after him—in terms of assumed natural differences of rank between men, he missed precisely that type of analysis which we should today describe as sociology. In consequence, his analysis subjects a potentially sociological problem to assumptions that transcend the realm of social fact and defy the rest of historical experience. That this attitude helped to delay the birth of sociology by more than 20 centuries is perhaps no great loss, considering the political consequences of so unhistorical an explanation. I believe that Rousseau was right, for all his polemical tone, when he argued that it did not make sense

to investigate whether there might not be an essential connection between the two inequalities [the natural and the social]. For it would mean that we must ask whether rulers are necessarily worth more than the ruled, and whether strength of body and mind, wisdom, and virtue are always found in the same individuals, and found, moreover, in direct relation to their power or wealth; a question that slaves who think they are being overheard by their masters may find it useful to discuss, but that has no meaning for reasonable and free men in search of the truth.

This is Rousseau's argument in his prize essay of 1754 on "The Origin of Inequality among Men and Whether It Is Legitimated by Natural Law." Unlike his earlier essay of 1750 on "The Moral Consequences of Progress in the Arts and Sciences," this essay was not awarded the prize of the Dijon Academy. I do not know why the judges preferred the essay of "a certain Abbé Talbert" (as one editor of Rousseau's work describes him); but conceivably they began to feel uneasy about the radical implications of their own question. For the new meaning given by Rousseau and his contemporaries to the question of the origin of inequality involved a revolution in politics as well as intellectual history.

The pivotal point of the Aristotelian argument—if I may use this formula as an abbreviation for all treatments of the problem before the 18th century—was the assumption that men are by nature unequal in rank, and that there is therefore a natural rank order among men. This presupposition collapsed in the face of the assumption of natural law that the natural rank of all men is equal. Politically, this meant that together with all other hierarchies, the hierarchies of society also lost their claim to unquestioning respect. If men are equal by nature, then social inequalities cannot be established by nature or God; and if they are not so established, then they are subject to change, and the privileged of today may be the outcasts of tomorrow; it may then even be possible to abolish all inequalities. A straight road leads from such reflections to the Declaration of the Rights of Man and Citizen of 1789: "Men are born and remain free and equal in rights. Social differences, therefore, can only be based on general utility."

In terms of intellectual history, the same process meant that the question of the origin of inequality was now phrased in a new and different—i.e., sociological—manner. If men are by nature equal in rank, where do social inequalities come from? If all men are born free and equal in rights, how can we explain that some are rich and others poor, some respected and others ignored, some powerful and others in servitude? Once the question was posed in these terms, only a sociological answer was possible. With good reason, then, Werner Sombart and others have seen the beginnings of sociology in the works of those authors who first tried to give a sociological answer to this question—notably the French *philosophes,* the Scottish moral philosophers and political economists, and the thinkers of the German Enlightenment in the second half of the 18th century. . . .

Since Talcott Parsons first published his "Analytical Approach to the Theory of Social Stratification" in 1940, there has been an unceasing debate over the so-called "functional" theory of social stratification. Almost all major American sociologists have taken part in this debate, which—unknown though it still is on the Continent—represents one of the more significant contributions of American sociology toward our understanding of social structures.

The chief immediate effect of Parson's essay of 1940 was to acquaint American sociologists with the idea of a theory of social stratification. The largely conceptual paper published by Parson's disciple Kingsley Davis in 1942 was also mainly preparatory in character. The discussion proper did not begin until 1945, when Davis and Wilbert E. Moore published "Some Principles of Stratification." . . . Rousseau and his successors . . . had regarded inequality as a historical phenomenon. . . . Since there had once been a period of equality, the elimination of inequality was conceivable. Davis and Moore, by contrast, saw inequality as a functional necessity in all human societies—i.e., as indispensable for the maintenance of any social structure whatever—and hence as impossible to eliminate.

Their argument . . . runs as follows. There are in every society different social positions. These positions—e.g., occupations—are not equally pleasant, nor are they equally important or difficult. In order to guarantee the complete and frictionless allocation of all positions, certain rewards have to be associated with them—namely, the very rewards that constitute the criteria of social stratification. In all societies, the importance of different positions to the society and the market value of the required qualifications determine the unequal distribution of income, prestige, and power. Inequality is necessary because without it the differentiated (occupational) positions of societies cannot be adequately filled.

Several other writers, among them Marion J. Levy and Bernard Barber, have adopted this theory more or less without modification. But it has been subjected to severe criticism, and despite several thoughtful replies by the original authors, some of the criticisms seem to be gaining ground. The most persistent critic, Melvin M. Tumin, has presented two main arguments against Davis and Moore (in two essays published in 1953 and 1955). The first is that the notion of the "functional importance" of positions is extremely imprecise, and that it probably implies the very differentiation of value that it allegedly explains. The second is that two of the assumptions made by Davis and Moore—that of a harmonious congruence between stratification and the distribution of talent, and that of differential motivation by unequal incentives—are theoretically problematical and empirically uncertain.

This second argument was bolstered in 1955 by Richard Schwartz, whose analysis of two Israeli communities showed that it is in fact possible to fill positions adequately without an unequal distribution of social rewards. Buckley charged Davis and Moore in 1958 with confusing differentiation and stratification; unfortunately, however, his legitimate objection to the evaluative undertones of the notion of "functional importance" led in the end to an unpromising terminological dispute. Since then, criticism of the functional theory of stratification has taken two forms. Some critics have followed Dennis Wrong, who in 1959 took up Tumin's suggestion that Davis and Moore had underestimated the "dysfunctions" of social stratification—i.e., the disruptive consequences of social inequality; the conservative character of the functional theory has been emphasized even more clearly by Gerhard Lenski. Other critics have raised methodological objections, questioning the value of a discussion of sociological universals that ignores variations observed in the workings of real societies.

But the significance of the American debate on stratification is only partly to be found in its subject matter. In this respect, its main conclusion would seem to be that social inequality has many functions and dysfunctions (that is, many consequences for the structure of societies), but that there can be no satisfactory functional explanation of the origin of inequality. This is because every such explanation is bound either to have recourse to dubious assumptions about human nature or to commit the *petitio principii* error of explanation in terms of the object to be explained. Yet this discussion, like its historical predecessors, has at several points produced valuable propositions, some of them mere remarks made in passing. With the help of these propositions, let us now attempt to formulate a theory of social stratification that is theoretically satisfactory and, above all, empirically fruitful.

The very first contribution to the American debate on stratification, the essay by Parsons, contained an idea which, although untenable in Parsons's form, may still advance our understanding of the problem. Parsons tries to derive the necessity of a differentiated rank order from the existence of the concept of evaluation and its significance for social systems. The effort to formulate an ontological proof of stratification is more surprising than convincing—as Parsons himself seems to have felt, for in the revised version of his essay, published in 1953, he relates the existence of a concept of evaluation to the mere probability, not the necessity, of inequality. In fact, Parsons's thesis contains little more than the suggestion, formulated much more simply by Barber, that men tend to evaluate themselves and the things of their world differently. This suggestion in turn refers back to Schmoller's "psychological assumption" of a human tendency to produce evaluative rank orders, but it also refers—and here the relation between evaluation and stratification begins to be sociologically relevant—to Durkheim's famous proposition that "every society is a moral community." Durkheim rightly remarks that "the state of nature of the eighteenth-century philosophers is, if not immoral, at least amoral." The idea of the social contract is nothing but the idea of the institution of compulsory social norms backed by sanctions. It is at this point that the possibility arises of connecting the concept of human society with the problem of the origin of inequality—a possibility that is occasionally hinted at in the literature but that has so far gone unrealized.

Human society always means that people's behavior is being removed from the randomness of chance and regulated by established and inescapable expectations. The compulsory character of these expectations or norms is based on the operation of sanctions—i.e., of rewards or punishments for conformist or deviant behavior. If every society is in this sense a moral community, it follows that there must always be at least that inequality of rank which results from the necessity of sanctioning behavior according to whether it does or does not conform to established norms. Under whatever aspect given historical societies may introduce additional distinctions between their members, whatever symbols they may declare to be outward signs of inequality, and whatever may be the precise content of their social norms, the hard core of social inequality can always be found in the fact that men as the incumbents of social roles are subject, according to how their roles relate to the dominant expectational principles of society, to sanctions designed to enforce these principles.

Let me try to illustrate what I mean by some examples which, however difficult they may seem, are equally relevant. If the ladies of a neighborhood are expected to exchange secrets and scandals with their neighbors, this norm will lead at the very least to a distinction between those held in high regard (who really enjoy gossip, and offer tea and cakes as well), those with average prestige, and the outsiders (who, for whatever reasons, take no part in the gossiping). If, in a factory, high individual output is expected from the workers and rewarded by piecework rates, there will be some who take home a relatively high paycheck and others who take home a relatively low one. If the citizens (or better, perhaps, subjects) of a state are expected to defend its official ideology as frequently and convincingly as possible, this

will lead to a distinction between those who get ahead (becoming, say, civil servants or party secretaries); the mere followers, who lead a quiet but somewhat anxious existence; and those who pay with their liberty or even their lives for their deviant behavior.

One might think that individual, not social, inequalities are in fact established by the distinction between those who for essentially personal reasons (as we must initially assume, and have assumed in the examples) are either unprepared for or incapable of conformism and those who punctiliously fulfill every norm. For example, social stratification is always a rank order in terms of prestige and not esteem—i.e., a rank order of positions (worker, woman, resident of a certain area, etc.), which can be thought of independently of their individual incumbents. By contrast, attitudes toward norms as governed by sanctions seem to be attitudes of individuals. There might therefore seem to be a link missing between the sanctioning of individual behavior and the inequality of social positions. This missing link is, however, contained in the notion of social norm as we have used it so far.

It appears plausible to assume that the number of values capable of regulating human behavior is unlimited. Our imagination permits the construction of an infinite number of customs and laws. Norms—i.e., socially established values—are therefore always a selection from the universe of possible established values. At this point, however, we should remember that the selection of norms always involves discrimination not only against persons holding sociologically random moral convictions but also against social positions that may debar their incumbents from conformity with established values.

Thus if gossip among neighbors becomes a norm, the professional woman necessarily becomes an outsider who cannot compete in prestige with ordinary housewives. If piecework rates are in force in a factory, the older worker is at a disadvantage by comparison with the younger ones, the woman by comparison with men. If it becomes the duty of the citizen to defend the ideology of the state, those who went to school before the establishment of this state cannot compete with those born into it. Professional woman, old man, young man, and child of a given state are all social positions, which may be thought of independently of their individual human incumbents. Since every society discriminates in this sense against certain positions (and thereby all their incumbents, actual and potential), and since, moreover, every society uses sanctions to make such discrimination effective, social norms and sanctions are the basis not only of ephemeral individual rankings but also of lasting structures of social positions.

The origin of inequality is thus to be found in the existence in all human societies of norms of behavior to which sanctions are attached. What we normally call the law— i.e., the system of laws and penalties—does not in ordinary usage comprise the whole range of the sociological notions of norm and sanction. If, however, we take the law in its broadest sense as the epitome of all norms and sanctions, including those not codified, we may say that the law is both a necessary and a sufficient condition of social inequality. There is inequality because there is law; if there is law, there must also be inequality among men.

This is, of course, equally true in societies where equality before the law is recognized as a constitutional principle. If I may be allowed a somewhat flippant formulation, which is nevertheless seriously meant, my proposed explanation of inequality means in the case of our society that all men are equal *before* the law but they are no longer equal *after* it—i.e., after they have, as we put it, "come in contact with" the law. So long as norms do not exist, and insofar as they do not effectively act on people ("before the law"), there is no social stratification; once there are norms that impose inescapable requirements on people's behavior and once their actual behavior is measured in terms of these norms ("after the law"), a rank order of social status is bound to emerge.

Important though it is to emphasize that

by norms and sanctions we also mean laws and penalties in the sense of positive law, the introduction of the legal system as an illustrative *pars pro toto* can itself be very misleading. Ordinarily, it is only the idea of punishment that we associate with legal norms as the guarantee of their compulsory character. The force of legal sanctions produces the distinction between the lawbreaker and those who succeed in never coming into conflict with any legal rule. Conformism in this sense is at best rewarded with the absence of penalties. Certainly, this crude division between "conformists" and "deviants" constitutes an element of social inequality, and it should be possible in principle to use legal norms to demonstrate the relation between legal sanctions and social stratification. But an argument along these lines would limit both concepts—sanction and stratification—to a rather feeble residual meaning.

It is by no means necessary (although customary in ordinary language) to conceive of sanctions solely as penalties. For the present argument, at least, it is important to recognize positive sanctions (rewards) as both equal in kind and similar in function to negative sanctions (punishments). Only if we regard reward and punishment, incentive and threat, as related instruments for maintaining social norms do we begin to see that applying social norms to human behavior in the form of sanctions necessarily creates a system of inequality of rank, and that social stratification is therefore an immediate result of the control of social behavior by positive and negative sanctions. Apart from their immediate task of enforcing the normative patterns of social behavior, sanctions always create, almost as a by-product, a rank order of distributive status, whether this is measured in terms of prestige, or wealth, or both.

The presuppositions of this explanation are obvious. Using 18th-century concepts, one might describe them in terms of the social contract (*pacte d'association*) and the contract of government (*pacte de gouvernement*). The explanation sketched here presupposes (1) that every society is a moral community, and therefore recognizes norms that regulate the conduct of its members; (2) that these norms require sanctions to enforce them by rewarding conformity and penalizing deviance.

It may perhaps be argued that by relating social stratification to these presuppositions we have not solved our problem but relegated its solution to a different level. Indeed, it might seem necessary from both a philosophical and a sociological point of view to ask some further questions. Where do the norms that regulate social behavior come from? Under what conditions do these norms change in historical societies? Why must their compulsory character be enforced by sanctions? Is this in fact the case in all historical societies? I think, however, that whatever the answers to these questions may be, it has been helpful to reduce social stratification to the existence of social norms backed by sanctions, since this explanation shows the derivative nature of the problem of inequality. In addition, the derivation suggested here has the advantage of leading back to presuppositions (the existence of norms and the necessity of sanctions) that may be regarded as axiomatic, at least in the context of sociological theory, and therefore do not require further analysis for the time being.

To sum up, the origin of social inequality lies neither in human nature nor in a historically dubious conception of private property. It lies rather in certain features of all human societies, which are (or can be seen as) necessary to them. Although the differentiation of social positions—the division of labor, or more generally the multiplicity of roles—may be one such universal feature of all societies, it lacks the element of evaluation necessary to explain distinctions of rank. Evaluative differentiation, the ordering of social positions and their incumbent scales of prestige or income, is effected only by the sanctioning of social behavior in terms of normative expectations. Because there are norms and because sanctions are necessary to enforce conformity of human conduct, there has to be inequality of rank among men.

Social stratification is a very real element of our everyday lives, much more so than this highly abstract and indeed seemingly inconsequential discussion would suggest. It is necessary, then, to make clear the empirical relevance of these reflections, or at least to indicate what follows from this kind of analysis for our knowledge of society. Such a clarification is all the more necessary since the preceding discussion is informed, however remotely, by a view of sociology as an empirical science, a science in which observation can decide the truth or falsity of statements. What, then, do our considerations imply for sociological analysis?

First, let us consider its conceptual implications. Social stratification, as I have used the term, is above all a system of distributive status—i.e., a system of differential distribution of desired and scarce things. Honor and wealth, or, as we say today, prestige and income, may be the most general means of effecting such a differentiation of rank, but there is no reason to assume that it could not be effected by entirely different criteria. As far as legitimate power is concerned, however, it has only one aspect that can be seen as affecting social stratification, namely patronage, or the distribution of power as a reward for certain deeds or virtues. Thus to explain differences of rank in terms of the necessity of sanctions is not to explain the power structure of societies; it is rather to explain stratification in terms of the social structure of power and authority (using these terms to express Weber's distinction between *Macht* and *Herrschaft*). If the explanation of inequality offered here is correct, power and power structures logically precede the structures of social stratification.

It is hard to imagine a society whose system of norms and sanctions functions without an authority structure to sustain it. Time and again, anthropologists have told us of "tribes without rulers," and sociologists of societies that regulate themselves without power or authority. But in opposition to such fantasies, I incline with Weber to describe "every order that is not based on the personal, free agreement of all involved" (i.e., every order that does not rest on the voluntary consensus of all its members) as "imposed"—i.e., based on authority and subordination. Since a *volonté de tous* seems possible only in flights of fancy, we have to assume that a third fundamental category of sociological analysis belongs alongside the two concepts of norm and sanction: that of institutionalized power. Society *means* that norms regulate human conduct; this regulation is guaranteed by the incentive or threat of sanctions; the possibility of imposing sanctions is the abstract core of all power.

I am inclined to believe that all other categories of sociological analysis may be derived from the unequal but closely related trinity of norm, sanction, and power. At any rate, this is true of social stratification, which therefore belongs on a level of generality lower than power. To reveal the explosiveness of this analysis we need only turn it into an empirical proposition: the system of inequality that we call social stratification is only a secondary consequence of the social structure of power.

The establishment of norms in a society means that conformity is rewarded and deviance punished. The sanctioning of conformity and deviance in this sense means that the ruling groups of society have thrown their power behind the maintenance of norms. In the last analysis, established norms are nothing but ruling norms—i.e., norms defended by the sanctioning agencies of society and those who control them. This means that the person who will be most favorably placed in society is the person who best succeeds in adapting himself to the ruling norms; conversely, it means that the established or ruling values of a society may be studied in their purest form by looking at its upper class. Anyone whose place in the coordinate system of social positions and roles makes him unable to conform punctiliously to his society's expectations must not be surprised if the higher grades of prestige and

income remain closed to him and go to others who find it easier to conform. In this sense, every society honors the conformity that sustains it, i.e., sustains its ruling groups; but by the same token every society also produces within itself the resistance that brings it down.

Naturally, the basic equating of conformist or deviant behavior with high or low status is deflected and complicated in historical societies by many secondary factors. (In general, it must be emphasized that the explanation of inequality proposed here has no immediate extension to the history of inequality or the philosophy behind it.) Among other things, the ascriptive character of the criteria determining social status in a given epoch (such as nobility or property) may bring about a kind of stratification lag; that is, status structures may lag behind changes in norms and power relations, so that the upper class of a bygone epoch may retain its status position for a while under new conditions. Yet normally we do not have to wait long for such processes as the "*déclassement* of the nobility" or the "loss of function of property" which have occurred in several contemporary societies.

There are good reasons to think that our own society is tending toward a period of "meritocracy" as predicted by Michael Young—i.e., rule by the possessors of diplomas and other tickets of admission to the upper reaches of society issued by the educational system. If this is so, the hypothesis of stratification lag would suggest that in due course the members of the traditional upper strata (the nobility, the inheritors of wealth and property) will have to bestir themselves to obtain diplomas and academic titles in order to keep their position; for the ruling groups of every society have a tendency to try to adapt the existing system of social inequality to the established norms and values—i.e., their own. Nevertheless, despite this basic tendency we can never expect historical societies to exhibit full congruence between the scales of stratification and the structures of power.

The image of society that follows from this exceedingly general and abstract analysis is in two respects nonutopian and thereby antiutopian as well. On the one hand, it has none of the explicit or concealed romanticism of a revolutionary utopia à la Rousseau or Marx. If it is true that inequalities among men follow from the very concept of societies as moral communities, then there cannot be, in the world of our experience, a society of absolute equals. Of course, equality before the law, equal suffrage, equal chances of education, and other concrete equalities are not only possible but in many countries real. But the idea of a society in which all distinctions of rank between men are abolished transcends what is sociologically possible and has a place only in the sphere of poetic imagination. Wherever political programs promise societies without class or strata, a harmonious community of comrades who are all equals in rank, the reduction of all inequalities to functional differences, and the like, we have reason to be suspicious, if only because political promises are often merely a thin veil for the threat of terror and constraint. Wherever ruling groups or their ideologists try to tell us that in their society all men are equal, we can rely on George Orwell's suspicion that "some are more equal than others."

The approach put forward here is in yet another sense a path out of utopia. If we survey the explanations of inequality in recent American sociology—and this holds for Parsons and Barber as it does for Davis and Moore—we find that they betray a view of society from which there is no road leading to an understanding of the historical quality of social structures. In a less obvious sense this is also true, I think, of Rousseau and Marx; but it is more easily demonstrable by reference to recent sociological theory. The American functionalists tell us that we ought to look at societies as entities functioning without friction, and that inequality among men (since it happens to exist) abets this functioning. This point of view, however useful in other ways, may then lead to conclusions like the following by Barber: "Men

have a sense of justice fulfilled and of virtue rewarded when they feel that they are fairly ranked as superior and inferior by the value standards of their own moral community." Even Barber's subsequent treatment of the "dysfunctions" of stratification cannot wipe out the impression that the society he is thinking of does not need history anymore because everything has been settled in the best possible way already: everybody, wherever he stands, is content with his place in society, and a common value system unites all men in a big, happy family.

It seems to me that whereas an instrument of this kind may enable us to understand Plato's Republic, it does not describe any real society in history. Possibly social inequality has some importance for the integration of societies. But another consequence of its operation seems rather more interesting. If the analysis proposed here proves useful, inequality is closely related to the social constraint that grows out of sanctions and structures of power. This would mean that the system of stratification, like sanctions and structures of institutionalized power, always tends to its own abolition. The assumption that those who are less favorably placed in society will strive to impose a system of norms that promises them a better rank is certainly more plausible and fruitful than the assumption that the poor in reputation and wealth will love their society for its justice.

Since the "value system" of a society is universal only in the sense that it applies to everyone (it is in fact merely dominant), and since, therefore, the system of social stratification is only a measure of conformity in the behavior of social groups, inequality becomes the dynamic impulse that serves to keep social structures alive. Inequality always implies the gain of one group at the expense of others; thus every system of social stratification generates protest against its principles and bears the seeds of its own suppression. Since human society without inequality is not realistically possible and the complete abolition of inequality is therefore ruled out, the intrinsic explosiveness of every system of social stratification confirms the general view that there cannot be an ideal, perfectly just, and therefore nonhistorical human society.

This is the place to recall once again Kant's critical rejoinder to Rousseau, that inequality is a "rich source of much that is evil, but also of everything that is good." There is certainly reason to regret that children are ashamed of their parents, that people are anxious and poor, that they suffer and are made unhappy, and many other consequences of inequality. There are also many good reasons to strive against the historical and therefore, in an ultimate sense, arbitrary forces that erect insuperable barriers of caste or estate between men. The very existence of social inequality, however, is an impetus toward liberty because it guarantees a society's ongoing, dynamic, historical quality. The idea of a perfectly egalitarian society is not only unrealistic; it is terrible. Utopia is not the home of freedom, the forever imperfect scheme for an uncertain future; it is the home of total terror or absolute boredom.

5. THE DYNAMICS OF DISTRIBUTIVE SYSTEMS

GERHARD LENSKI

■ The forms of stratification in different societies have important effects on the way social issues arise and are dealt with. Lenski's theory of stratificaton systematically relates power, privilege, and prestige to the socio-technological stage of development of human societies. His synthesis of historical materials on stratification in different societies over the centuries provides a context for understanding the particular form stratification takes in modern industrial societies, a form that is nevertheless animated by the same basic human propensities to pursue power and privilege that have operated in all societies.

Lenski shares with Dahrendorf an understanding that the existence of stratification guarantees conflict between the have-nots and the haves as the have-nots seek to strike a better bargain for themselves. His emphasis on constitutionalism touches on the issues of social integration that Goldthorpe discusses, although Lenski seems considerably less sanguine about the possibilities for an equalitarian solution to the failure of integration that inequality engenders.

A classical early study that relates social stratification to levels of technological development is L. T. Hobhouse, G. C. Wheeler, and M. Ginsberg, *The Material Culture and Social Institutions of the Simpler Peoples* (London: Chapman and Hall, 1930). A more recent cross-cultural empirical study of some of these issues is found in Alvin W. Gouldner and Richard A. Peterson, *Notes on Technology and the Moral Order* (Indianapolis: Bobbs-Merrill, 1962). A theory about the role of the military in forming stratification systems that has considerably influenced Lenski is developed by Karl A. Wittfogel in *Oriental Despotism: A Comparative Study of Total Power* (New Haven, Conn.: Yale University Press,

1957). Lenski's book does not contain a full discussion of social stratification in the United States; for this the reader is referred to Joseph A. Kahl, *The American Class Culture* (New York: Holt, Rinehart & Winston, 1957 and revisions); and Richard P. Coleman and Bernice L. Neugarten, *Social Status in the City* (San Francisco: Jossey-Bass, 1961). For a text/reader that relies heavily on American materials see Jack L. Roach, Llewellyn Gross, and Orville R. Gursslin, eds., *Social Stratification in the United States* (Englewood Cliffs, N.J.: Prentice-Hall, 1969). ■

SOON AFTER PRESIDENT KENNEDY's election in the fall of 1960, Americans were again reminded of one of the curious features of their national life. When the President selected Robert S. McNamara for the post of Secretary of Defense, the press reported the substantial financial sacrifice the nominee would be forced to make. While still only a vice-president of the Ford Motor Company, McNamara received salary and other compensation in excess of $400,000 a year. With his promotion to the presidency of the company (just prior to his appointment as Secretary of Defense) he was certain to make substantially more. By contrast, as Secretary of Defense for the nation he received a salary of only $25,000, or roughly 5 percent of what he would have received as president of the Ford Motor Company.

Few Americans seem to have been greatly surprised by these facts, and fewer still were shocked or disturbed. Like the natives of Lewis Carroll's remarkable Wonderland, they saw nothing strange or incongruous in their surroundings.

Yet if one reflects on this matter, one cannot help being impressed by its curious quality. The same man with the same skills and talents moves to a post of far greater importance, and undoubtedly a more trying one, and finds his compensation reduced 95 percent. In his new position, where he bears much of the burden of the defense of the nation, he receives a salary no greater than that of thousands of minor executives in industry.

If this were but an isolated instance, we might regard it as an interesting oddity, a curious exception to the rule, and think no more about it. But such is not the case. Even a superficial examination of American life reveals innumerable instances in which the rewards men receive bear little or no relation to the value of the services they render or the sacrifices they make in their performance. Many substantial fortunes have been built in a few short years by speculation in stocks and real estate, often with borrowed funds, but the public record reveals no instance in which a great fortune was ever established by a lifetime of skilled and conscientious labor in the foundries, shops, or mills of this country. Entertainers who reach the top in their field receive several hundred thousand dollars a year. By contrast, the top pay for public school teachers, regardless of ability, is not greatly in excess of $10,000 a year [$15,000 by 1970]. Playboys like John Jacob Astor III live lives of ease and indolence, while the vast majority of those who do the work which makes this way of life possible struggle to make ends meet.

What is the explanation of this situation which, like Wonderland, grows curiouser and curiouser the more we examine it? What principles govern the distribution of rewards in our society and in others? What determines the magnitude of the rewards each man receives?

These questions have long been argued and debated. In modern times they have become the heart and core of a special field of study within sociology known as "social stratification." This label has been unfortunate for it encourages a seriously oversimplified view of modern social structure. Even worse, it fosters an excessive concern with questions of structure at the expense of more basic problems concerning the processes which generate these structures.

This field might better be identified as the study of the "distributive process." Virtually all the major theorists in the field, regardless of their thoretical and ideological biases, have sought to answer one basic question: *Who gets what and why?* This is the question which underlies all the discussions of classes and strata and their structural relationships, though in some recent empirical research it seems to have been almost forgotten. . . .

TWO LAWS OF DISTRIBUTION

. . . If those postulates [about the nature of man and society] are sound, one would predict that almost all the products of men's labors will be distributed on the basis of two seemingly contradictory principles, *need* and *power.*

In our discussion of the nature of man, it was postulated that where important decisions are involved, most human action is motivated either by self-interest or by partisan group interests. This suggests that power alone governs the distribution of rewards. This cannot be the case, however, since we also postulated that most of these essentially selfish interests can be satisfied only by the establishment of cooperative relations with others. Cooperation is absolutely essential both for survival and for the efficient attainment of most other goals. In other words, men's selfish interests compel them to remain members of society and to share in the division of labor.

If these two postulates are correct, then it follows that *men will share the product of their labors to the extent required to insure the survival and continued productivity of those others whose actions are necessary or beneficial to themselves.* This might well be called the first law of distribution, since the survival of mankind as a species depends on compliance with it.

This first law, however, does not cover the entire problem. It says nothing about how any *surplus*—i.e., goods and services over and above the minimum required to keep producers alive and productive—which men may be able to produce will be distributed. This leads to what may be called the second law of distribution. If we assume that in important decisions human action is motivated almost entirely by self-interest or partisan group interests, and if we assume that many of the things men most desire are in short supply, then, as noted before, this surplus will inevitably give rise to conflicts and struggles aimed at its control. If, following Weber, we define power as the probability of persons or groups carrying out their will even when opposed by others, then it follows that *power will determine the distribution of nearly all of the surplus possessed by a society.* The qualification "nearly all" takes account of the very limited influence of altruistic action which our earlier analysis of the nature of man leads us to expect.

This second law points the way to another very important relationship, that between our two chief variables, power and privilege. If privilege is defined as possession or control of a portion of the surplus produced by a society, then it follows that *privilege is largely a function of power, and to a very limited degree, a function of altruism.* This means that to explain most of the distribution of privilege in a society, we have but to determine the distribution of power.

To state the matter this way suggests that the task of explaining the distribution of privilege is simple. Unfortunately, this is not the case since there are many forms of power and they spring from many sources. Nevertheless, the establishment of this key relationship reduces the problem to more manageable proportions, since it concentrates attention on one key variable, power. Thus if we can establish the pattern of its distribution in a given society, we have largely established the pattern for the distribution of privilege, and if we can discover the causes of a given distribution of power we have also discovered the causes of the distribution of privilege linked with it.

To put the matter this way is to invite the question of how the third basic element in every distributive system, *prestige*, is related to power and privilege. It would be nice if one could say that prestige is a simple function of privilege, but unfortunately this does not seem to be the case. Without going into a complex analysis of the matter at this point, the best that can be said is that empirical evidence strongly suggests that *prestige is largely, though not solely, a function of power and privilege, at least in those societies where there is a substantial surplus.* If this is true, it follows that even though the subject of prestige is not often mentioned in this [article], its pattern of distribution and its causes can largely be deduced from discussion of the distribution of power and privilege and their causes in those societies where there is an appreciable surplus.

Graphically, the relationship between these three variables, as set forth in the propositions above, can be depicted in this way:

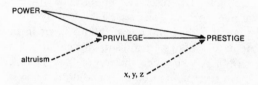

The solid lines indicate major sources of influence, the dashed lines secondary sources.

Power is the key variable in the triad from the casual and explanatory standpoint. Hence, it is with this variable that we shall be primarily concerned in the analysis which follows.

THE VARIABLE ASPECTS
OF DISTRIBUTIVE SYSTEMS

As the statement of the two laws indicates, the second law does not have any effect on the distributive process until the conditions specified in the first have been satisfied. Until the necessities of life have been made available to enough productive, mutually interdependent members of the group, there is no surplus to be fought over and distributed on the basis of power. Thus, as a first hypothesis we would be led to predict that *in the sim-*

plest societies, or those which are technologically most primitive, the goods and services available will be distributed wholly, or largely, on the basis of need.

As the productivity of societies increases, the possibility of producing a surplus steadily increases, though it should be noted that the existence of a surplus is not a function of technological advance alone. Even though we cannot say that the surplus available to a society increases proportionately with advances in the level of technology, such advances increase the probability that there will be a surplus and also that there will be a sizable surplus. Hence, as a second hypothesis we are led to predict that *with technological advance, an increasing proportion of the goods and services available to a society will be distributed on the basis of power.*

In view of the dualistic basis of the distributive process, and the variations to which this must necessarily give rise, it would be unwise to attempt to develop a single general theory of distribution or stratification to cover all societies. Rather, we will gain far more if we follow the example of the economists in their analyses of the behavior of markets. As they discovered years ago, it is impossible to create a single general theory of market behavior except of the most limited nature. In order to deal effectively with most of the more complex aspects of market behavior, it is necessary to take account of the existence of different kinds of markets. This has led to the distinction between theories of perfect and imperfect competition. The latter can be further subdivided into theories of oligopoly, monopoly, monopsony, and so forth. In other words, on closer inspection the theory of market behavior turns out to consist of a small number of general principles which constitute the general theory of markets, and a whole series of more limited principles applicable only under specific conditions.

The same approach is required in stratification theory, if our analysis up to this point is sound. If the first two laws of distribution and the two hypotheses based on them are valid, then *the nature of distributive systems will vary greatly, depending on the degree of* technological advance in the societies involved. The variations should be every bit as great as those which differentiate markets where perfect competition prevails from those where imperfect competition holds sway. . . .

While the foregoing is reason enough to base our special theories on societal types defined in technological terms, there is one other great advantage derived from this approach. Past research has made it clear that technology is never an isolated variable in sociocultural systems. On the contrary, it tends to be linked fairly closely with a whole series of other variables which evidently stand in a dependent relationship to it. This is especially true of many social organizational variables which are linked with distributive systems and tend to define their limits of possible variation—e.g., nature and extent of division of labor, maximum community size, etc. Hence, *by classifying societies on the basis of technology, we are, in effect, simultaneously controlling, wholly or in part, many other relevant variables.* . . .

To say that many other characteristics of human societies vary with technology is not to say that all do. Clearly some do not, and others do so only to a limited degree. Wilbert Moore has suggested that supernatural beliefs and aesthetic forms are not so closely correlated with technology as most forms of social organization. The same may also be true of certain basic aspects of family life. However, while these exceptions deserve recognition and careful consideration, they do not vitiate the basic principle involved.

It should also be noted that classifying societies on the basis of the nature of their technology does not imply that all those in a single category have *identical* distributive systems any more than that all oligopolistic markets function the same way. Obviously there are variations within each societal type just as within each type of market, and an effort will be made to identify and account for the more important of them. However, these may be thought of as *second-order variations,* which are best dealt with after the first-order variations have been established and the internal uniformities associated with them clearly delineated.

. . . If the size of a society's surplus affects the nature of its distributive system, and if the size of the surplus depends to some degree on the nature of the physical environment, then we should predict that *differences in the physical environment will lead to secondary differences in distributive systems*. More specifically, the richer the environment, the larger the surplus and the greater the importance of power in the distributive process.

There are also reasons for predicting that the influence of environmental differences will be greater in primitive societies than in those which are technologically more advanced. To begin with, technological advance makes possible the geographical expansion of societies, and the larger the territory occupied by a society, the less the probability that the total environment will be extremely favorable or unfavorable and the greater the probability that it will include a mixture of favorable and unfavorable land. Hence, environmental variation should be less among the larger, technologically advanced societies than among the smaller, more primitive. In addition, technological advance frequently means the development of alternative solutions to the various problems of production. Technologically advanced societies, therefore, should be less hampered by environmental limitations than primitive societies are, and thus *environmental variation should have less effect on the level of productivity in advanced societies than in primitive*.

Another important source of secondary variation has been identified by Stanislaw Andrzejewski in his important but neglected book, *Military Organization and Society*. As he has shown, both deductive logic and empirical data indicate that *the degree of inequality in societies of a given level of technological development tends to vary inversely with what he calls "the military participation ratio"*—that is, *the proportion of the adult male population utilized in military operations*. Where most adult males are utilized for such purposes, the degree of inequality tends to be less than in those in which military needs are supplied by a small force of military specialists. Thus, this factor can also be used to explain some of the secondary variations which are found among societies of the same technological type.

A third source of secondary variations which can be anticipated is the technological variation which exists even among societies classified in the same category. No two societies are identical from the technological standpoint, and their classification into technological types is based on similarities (or identity) with respect to certain fundamental characteristics and ignores secondary differences. If primary differences in technology cause major differences in distributive systems, *one would expect these secondary differences in technology to generate lesser differences in distributive systems*. Thus, one would expect considerable differences between a society in the first stages of industrialization and one which is highly industrialized, just as one would expect differences between a hunting and gathering society with no alternative mode of food production and one which has some rudimentary forms of horticulture to supplement its diet. . . .

FORCE AND ITS TRANSFORMATION

Of the two principles which govern the distributive process, need and power, the first is relatively simple and poses few problems of great importance or difficulty. Unhappily, the same cannot be said of the second. Of all the concepts used by sociologists, few are the source of more confusion and misunderstanding than power. Hence it is necessary to spell out in some detail the nature of this concept and how it functions in the distributive process.

As a starting point, it may be well to return briefly to one of the postulates introduced [earlier]. There it was assumed that survival is the chief goal of the great majority of men. If this is so, then it follows that *the ability to take life is the most effective form of power*. In other words, more men will respond more readily to the threat of the use of *force* than to any other. In effect, it constitutes the final court of appeals in human affairs; there is no appeal from force in a given situation except the exercise of superior force. Hence force stands in the same relationship to other forms of power as trumps to the other suits in the game of bridge, and those who can exercise the greatest force are like those who control trumps.

This fact has been recognized by countless observers of the human scene in every age. As Pascal put it, "Not being able to make that which is just strong, man has made that which is strong just." Cicero made the same point when he said, "Laws are dumb in the midst of arms," and Hobbes asserted that "Covenants without the sword are but words, and of no strength to secure a man at all."

This principle is also recognized by the leaders of nations, the practical men of affairs. Every sovereign state restricts, and where possible prohibits, the independent exercise of force by its subjects. States may be tolerant of many things, but never of the growth of independent military organizations within their territories. The reason is obvious: any government which cannot suppress each and every forceful challenge to its authority is overthrown. Force is the foundation of sovereignty.

On this point there is no dispute between conservatives and radicals. Their arguments are concerned only with the ends served by the state's use of force. Conservatives insist that might is employed only as the handmaiden of right, to restrain and rebuke those who put self-interest above the common good, while radicals maintain that the state employs might to suppress right, in defense of selfish interests.

If force is the foundation of political sovereignty, it is also the foundation of the distributive system in every society where there is a surplus to be divided. Where coercive power is weak, challenges inevitably occur, and the system is eventually destroyed and replaced by another based more firmly on force. Men struggling over control of the surplus of a society will not accept defeat so long as there is a higher court of appeals to

which they may take their case with some likelihood of success and profit to themselves.

The principle involved here is essentially the same as the principle of escalation with which modern military men are so concerned. Small wars based on small weapons inevitably grow into more deadly wars utilizing more deadly weapons if, by advancing the level of conflict, one of the parties anticipates turning defeat into victory. Similarly, in the case of conflicts within societies, the parties involved are always motivated to take the issue to the final court of appeals so long as there is the likelihood of benefiting by it. While men will not resort to armed revolution for trivial gains, when control over the entire surplus of a society is involved, the prospect is more enticing. The attractiveness varies directly with the weakness of the current regime.

Nevertheless, as Edmund Burke, the famed English conservative, recognized, "The use of force alone is but temporary. It may subdue for a moment; but it does not remove the necessity of subduing again: and a nation is not governed, which is perpetually to be conquered." Though force is the most effective instrument for seizing power in a society, and though it always remains the foundation of any system of inequality, it is not the most effective instrument for retaining and exploiting a position of power and deriving the maximum benefits from it. Therefore, regardless of the objectives of a new regime, once organized opposition has been destroyed it is to its advantage to make increasing use of other techniques and instruments of control, and to allow force to recede into the background to be used only when other techniques fail.

If the new elite has materialistic goals and is concerned solely with self-aggrandizement, it soon discovers that the rule of might is both inefficient and costly. So long as it relies on force, much of the profit is consumed by the costs of coercion. If the population obeys only out of fear of physical violence, a large portion of the time, energy, and wealth of the elite are invariably consumed in the effort to keep it under control and separate the producers from the product of their labors. Even worse, honor, which normally ranks high in the scale of human values, is denied to those who rule by force alone.

If materialistic elites have strong motives for shifting from the rule of might to the rule of right, ideologically motivated elites have even stronger. If the visions and ideals which led them to undertake the terrible risks and hardships of revolution are ever to be fulfilled, the voluntary cooperation of the population is essential, and this cannot be obtained by force. Force is, at best, the means to an end. That end, the establishment of a new social order, can never be fully attained until most members of society freely accept it as their own. The purpose of the revolution is to destroy the old elite and their institutions, which prevent the fulfillment of this dream. Once they are destroyed, an ideological elite strives to rule by persuasion. Thus *those who seize power by force find it advantageous to legitimize their rule once effective organized opposition is eliminated.* Force can no longer continue to play the role it did. It can no longer function as the private resource of a special segment of the population. Rather it must be transformed into a public resource used in the defense of law and order.

This may seem to be the equivalent of saying that those who have at great risk to themselves displaced the old elite must now give up all they have won. Actually, however, this is not at all necessary since, with a limited exercise of intelligence, force can be transformed into authority, and might into right.

There are various means by which this transformation can be effected. To begin with, by virtue of its coercive power, a new elite is in a good position to rewrite the law of the land as it sees fit. This affords them a unique opportunity, since by its very nature law is identified with justice and the rule of right. Since legal statutes are stated in general and impersonal terms, they appear to support abstract principles of justice rather than the special interests of particular men or classes of men. The fact that laws exist prior to the events to which they are applied suggests an objective impartiality which also contributes

to their acceptance. Yet laws can always be written in such a way that they favor some particular segment of society. Anatole France saw this clearly when he wrote, "The law in its majestic equality forbids the rich as well as the poor to sleep under bridges, to get in the street, and to steal bread." . . . In short, laws may be written in such a way that they protect the interests of the elite while being couched in very general, universalistic terms.

Often a new elite finds that it does not even need to change the laws to accomplish its ends. Typically the old laws were written to serve the interests of the holders of certain key offices, and once these offices have been seized, the new elite can use them as resources to build their fortunes or attain other goals.

Institutions which shape public opinion serve as a second instrument for legitimizing the position of new elites. Through the use of a combination of inducements and threats, educational and religious institutions, together with the mass media and other molders of public opinion, can usually be transformed into instruments of propaganda for the new regime. A determined and intelligent elite working through them can usually surround itself with an aura of legitimacy within a few months or years.

The concept of "propaganda," or the manipulation of consensus, is an integral element in the synthetic theory of stratification. A recognition of this phenomenon and the special role it plays in the distributive process enables us to avoid the impasse which has driven Dahrendorf and others to despair of ever reconciling the conservative and radical traditions. Consensus and coercion are more closely related than those who preach the Janus-headed character of society would have us believe. *Coercive power can often be used to create a new consensus.*

There is probably no better example of this than the Soviet Union. Here a small minority seized control of the machinery of state in 1917 and used the coercive powers of the state to transform the educational system of the nation and the mass media into one gigantic instrument of propaganda. Within a single generation the vast majority of

Russians were converted to a sincere and genuine support of most of the basic elements of the Communist Party's program.

In the short run, propaganda may be used to support a great variety of programs and policies adopted by an elite. In the long run, however, its basic aim is the dissemination of an ideology which provides a moral justification for the regime's exercise of power. Gaetano Mosca put it this way:

Ruling classes do not justify their power exclusively by *de facto* processes of it, but try to find a moral and legal basis for it, representing it as the logical and necessary consequences of doctrines and beliefs that are generally recognized and accepted.

Most of the theories of political sovereignty debated by philosophers have been intellectualized versions of some popular ideology. This can be seen in the now discredited belief in the divine right of kings. In our own day, the belief in popular sovereignty serves the same justifying function. A basic element in our current American ideology is the thesis expressed by Lincoln that ours is a "government of the people, by the people, for the people." Another basic element is incorporated in Francis Scott Key's oft-sung phrase, "the land of the free." It is difficult to exaggerate the contribution of these beliefs to the political stability of our present political system and of the distributive system based on it.

Finally, the transformation of the rule of might into the rule of right is greatly facilitated by the pressures of daily life, which severely limit the political activities of the vast majority of mankind. Though the majority may become politically active in a significant way for a brief time in a revolutionary era, the necessity of securing a livelihood quickly drives most from the political arena. For better or worse, few men have the financial resources which enable them to set aside their usual economic activities for long. As a result, the affairs of state in any civilized society, and in many that are not, are directed by a small minority. The majority are largely apolitical. Even in popular democracies the vast majority do no more than cast a ballot at infrequent intervals. The formulation of public policy and the various other tasks required by the system are left in the hands of a tiny minority. This greatly facilitates the task of a new regime as it seeks to make the transition from the rule of might to the rule of right. . . .

When a political cycle survives for an appreciable period of time, the nature of the middle classes and their relation to the political elite gradually changes. In eras of constitutional rule there is a tendency for these classes to arrogate to themselves certain of the powers and privileges of the elite. This is not difficult since it is their normal function to act on behalf of the elite. Powers delegated often become powers lost; once lost they are not easily recovered. Thus it appears that *the greater the degree of constitutionalism in a society, the less the middle classes function merely as agents of the elite and the greater their personal independence, autonomy, and security.* This is an important development; . . . however, it should not be allowed to obscure the more basic relation between the middle classes and the elite which continues even in an era of constitutionalism.

Up to this point we have viewed the struggles for power and privilege chiefly from the standpoint of the elite, noting how, by various means, they bring the surplus of society under their control. This is only half the story, however, since in sociology, as in physics, *actions produce reactions.* Thus the exercise of power and privilege by elites invariably produces reactions by other members of society. These are no less important than the actions which produce them; hence they will be our primary concern for the remainder of the chapter. . . .

Of all the many reactions to the exercise of power and privilege in societies, the one most valued by the elites themselves is that of *competition among nonelites for positions in their employ.* In order to attract the best qualified men to these important middle stratum positions, elites make them more desirable than other nonelite positions. In the case of certain key positions, the inducements are substantial. A vigorous competition naturally develops for these positions, and members of the elite are only too happy to encourage it since they are the chief beneficiaries. Whatever expenses they incur can easily be recouped many times over when these positions are filled by capable, zealous, and loyal men.

Every system of power and privilege also sets in motion a deadly *struggle for survival among the offspring of the common people*, except in those societies which are able to control reproduction or in which there is a temporary shortage of population such as may be created by major plagues, famines, or other disasters. Unhappily, mankind has always been able to produce more offspring than society can maintain, especially when the economic surplus is skimmed off by a privileged elite. Usually there has not been land enough for every farmer's son to farm, nor farmers enough for every farmer's daughter to marry. Hence some of the common people of almost every generation have been reduced to the status of beggars, criminals, and prostitutes. Such persons have usually had short lives, since at this level the competition for survival is intense. From the standpoint of the elite, the struggles which developed among the common people have been a matter of little concern, since human fecundity always insured an ample supply of qualified producers. In fact, these struggles probably served the interests of the elite by diverting attention from their own exploitative role, thus affording them a considerable measure of security against popular protest and revolution.

A third reaction to the exercise of power and privilege is one which usually annoys elites but represents no serious threat to their security or status. This is the response of *petty thievery* by those in subordinate positions. Wherever household servants are employed, petty thievery is almost taken for granted. In many societies it is common practice for craftsmen to keep part of the materials with which they work for their own private use, and peasants often hide a portion of their harvest from tax collectors or from landlords with whom they have sharecropping arrangements. Such practices are irritating to elites, but because the losses are small and involve many isolated incidents, it is usually not worth their

while to do much about them. Occasionally, when some flagrant violation is detected, the offender may be punished severely in the hope of intimidating others, but this procedure rarely stops the practice.

A fourth type of reaction to the exercise of power and privilege manifests itself in the *efforts of members of the middle classes to gain control over powers, privileges, and resources traditionally reserved to the elite*. Most elites, when they come to power, limit control over key resources to their own number. For example, in many societies the ownership of land has been the privilege of a noble elite. Similarly, the franchise was limited at first to the wealthy.

This situation causes great insecurity for members of the middle classes, since their position of modest power and privilege is so largely dependent on the continuing goodwill of their superiors. If they lose favor, they have no resources to fall back on. Hence, there is a natural desire to gain control of some resources which would free them from this dependence. Not only does this hold the promise of greater security for the future, it also insures greater power and privilege in the present.

Certain members of the middle classes have not only the motives, but also the means to implement them. This is especially true of officials serving an elite which is anxious to withdraw from the tiresome tasks of managing its own affairs to cultivate the art of leisure. As with petty thievery, such action is so subtle in character that an elite is often oblivious to its existence until it is too late to do anything about it.

This particular pattern of reaction to the exercise of power and privilege is especially important because it plays such an important role in the development of constitutional government. Those who respond this way are men of cunning rather than men of force, to use Pareto's terms. Because of this, they find a complex system of law well suited to their purposes, and they strive by every means at their disposal to increase the law's importance and power.

A fifth type of reaction to power and privilege manifests itself in *crimes of violence directed against members of the elite and their agents.* More often it is against the latter since, as the working arm of the elite, they come into more frequent contact with the lower classes, who are the chief offenders. These crimes are always taken very seriously. The severity of the punishments undoubtedly reflects a recognition of the existence of widespread, latent hostility toward the holders of power and the realization that anything less than prompt and severe punishment may encourage more widespread violence. Furthermore, when crimes of this sort occur, the interests of the elite and the middle classes coincide and all the holders of power line up on the same side, thus making for a very unequal contest.

Up to this point, the reactions with which we have been concerned have all involved the uncoordinated actions of individuals. Sometimes, however, the exercise of power and privilege in a society leads to *collective* reactions by large numbers of the common people. For the moment we shall be concerned only with the nonviolent cases.

This type of action is possible only under two conditions. Either there must be a constitutional regime in power which recognizes the right of the common people to organize in defense of their own interests, or the ruling elite must be hard pressed by foreign foes and badly in need of the military service of the common people. A good example of the latter may be seen in the early successes of the Roman plebeians in their struggles with the patricians in the fifth century B.C. It is probably no coincidence that this type of reaction has become so much more common in the last century in the Western world. Ever since the French Revolution drastically changed the techniques of warfare by introducing conscription and the mass army, elites have been much more dependent on the common people. This may well have been one of the major reasons for the extension of the franchise in the last century and for the growing acceptance by elites of labor unions, workingmen's political parties, and all the other organizations designed to promote and protect the interests of the common people. . . .

The net effect of these many and varied reactions to the exercise of power and privilege by political elites is the strengthening of the tendency toward constitutional government. Constitutional government is, in essence, government which is based more on consent than on force. To obtain this consent, some concessions are required.

In effect, constitutional government rests on the foundation of an exchange which serves the interests both of the elite and of the other segments of the population. The elite forswear the use of violence except under more or less specified conditions, hence introducing an element of predictability and order into the life situation of the others. In exchange they receive the consent of others to their rule, which includes the tacit support of their use of force when it is in keeping with the dictates of the law. In a sense, there is something approximating a social contract, but since it is between unequals, it differs from the idealized versions described by earlier writers.

Thus the views of both conservatives and radicals contain an element of truth. Government does indeed rest on the foundation of consent, as the conservatives have maintained, but it also rests on the foundation of force, as the radicals have asserted. In short, both positions are true, but neither is the whole truth.

6. POLICY ANALYSIS AND EQUALITY

MARTIN REIN

Reprinted from "Social Policy Analysis as the Interpretation of Belief," Journal of the American Institute of Planners, September 1971, pp. 297-301, 305-7, 309. Martin Rein is Professor of Urban Studies and Planning at the Massachusetts Institute of Technology. He has written extensively on the analysis of social policy in the areas of poverty, welfare, and community action.

■ As many sociologists have pointed out, social scientists identify and analyze social problems because implicitly or explicitly they are concerned with changing society in directions that seem constructive and useful to them, or that accord with their own interests (which often seems to amount to the same thing). Some—but fewer over time—take the position that their interest in analyzing society does not imply a desire to change it. More often, however, social scientists have an explicit concern with social policy, although their concerns are not always immediately involved in their work.

Thus, many sociologists are concerned with policy analysis, and Martin Rein seeks to show in this article the ways in which values, operating principles, preferred strategies of change, and empirical data interact in the process of analyzing and acting on social policy as it is carried out in the variety of governmental and nongovernmental agencies that are "doing something" about social problems. His article reflects a growing awareness among those engaged in public policy that their earlier reliance on highly technical models of what they do has not, in fact, protected them from the need to make hard choices about the goals and values to which their activity is directed. For Rein this means that the social policy analyst needs to face the role of ideology in his work. He believes that at the most profound level social policy is informed by one's values about equality and inequality and that greater self-conciousness about equalitarian issues can lead to better policy.

These issues have been discussed with great cogency by C. Wright Mills, "The Professional Ideology of Social Pathologists," in *Power, Politics and People* (New York: Oxford University Press, 1963); by Howard S. Becker, "Whose Side are We On?" in *Social Problems: A Modern Approach* (New York: Wiley, 1966);

and by Alvin W. Gouldner, "The Sociologist as a Partisan: Sociology and the Welfare State," *American Sociologist*, May 1968.

For analyses of the relationship between beliefs and policy, see Martin Rein, *Social Policy: Issues of Choice and Change* (New York: Random House, 1970); Martin Rein and Peter Marris, *Dilemmas of Social Reform*, rev. ed., (Chicago: Aldine, 1973); and Daniel P. Moynihan, *Maximum Feasible Misunderstanding* (New York: Free Press, 1970). An excellent case study of the role of social beliefs and practices in relation to a particular policy is Richard Titmuss, *The Gift Relationship: From Human Blood to Social Policy* (London: Allyn and Unwin, 1971). See also Nathan Glazer, "The Limits of Social Policy," *Commentary*, September 1971, and S. M. Miller, "The Limits of Social Policy," *New Society*, August 1971. ■

SOCIAL POLICY IS, ABOVE all, concerned with *choice among competing values*, and questions of what is morally or culturally desirable can never be excluded from the discussion. Indeed, I regard the primary subject matter of policy as egalitarianism—a concern with the problems involved in the more equitable distribution of social goods. . . .

My starting point is that it is not only sterile to pursue techniques of analysis divorced from issues of purpose, but it is also misleading because techniques arise to serve purposes and therefore imply value assumptions. But, if it is no good simply pursuing techniques, neither is it good just to debate issues of social values. Such a debate can easily drift into an abstract argument about social ideals. The outcomes of such an analysis must be unconvincing, for the analyst isn't, and doesn't claim to be, a moral authority—so he has no particular role in this debate. The worthwhile course is one which relates the actual working of social policy to questions of value. And this, it seems to me, has two aspects. The first is analogous to jurisprudence in the teaching of a law— the analysis of the principles underlying different conceptions of policy. These principles are not the same as the fundamental value choices which direct the goals of policy, but rather they are *operating principles.* They represent an attempt to integrate various social ideals with a practicable rule of application. Such, for instance, are principles of universal coverage, or selection by need, or citizen participation, or the principles for allocation of educational, housing, and welfare subsidies, or the institutional forms for distributing benefits. Still, however ingenious are these rules for transforming purpose to program, by themselves they are insufficient. We must also look at *implementation outcomes*—how purposes and results relate to each other, what dilemmas and consequences arise from trying to implement a conception of social justice.

Therefore, the study of social policy involves the interaction between values, operating principles, and outcomes. If any of these is lost sight of the analysis tends to be nonproductive. Simply comparing values and outcomes (as radical idealists often do) leads to a diffuse revolutionary frustration—since there is no examination of strategy. Simply comparing values and principles of policy is to surrender to doctrine and to the debate of abstract images of good practice because they are presumed to be consistent with our ideals. Simply comparing principles and outcomes alienates idealists who do not accept that the argument can be conducted only within the framework of present legislative possibilities—and it easily becomes parochial for it indicts the system without specifying which components must be altered to achieve greater harmony between ideals and practice. The debate about values is detached ideology, while the debate about principles of implementation succumbs to doctrinaire insulation. To review outcomes without attention to purposes offers no criteria for assessing the desirability of the results. Finally, when the

match between purpose, principles, and outcomes is found to be weak, the analyst must suggest politically acceptable changes either in ideals or in policy or both. Proposals for change will be influenced by judgments about what is politically feasible, since analysis is inspired by the desire to be useful in helping to implement social ideals.

THE PURPOSES OF POLICY

That belief systems and values play a special role in defining research questions is now widely accepted in social science. But . . . we have been content to assert that values are important and to substitute this assertion for an analysis of either the nature of the value complexes which inform research questions or the consequences of holding one or another belief system. . . .

Here in brief are the salient features of a belief system concerning social policy and the "welfare state." Central in the system is the view held about *equality,* where at least two extreme positions can be identified. The liberal tradition holds that equality helps civilize society and, by promoting fraternal bonds and decreasing the structural sources of discontent, also assures its stability. The conservative tradition regards equality that is produced by public policy as a constraint on personal freedom and a threat to economic growth because it weakens those economic incentives that are needed to encourage work, risk-taking, and the assumption of managerial responsibility or undesirable jobs. While the conservative position rejects egalitarianism, it embraces that form of humanitarianism which seems to assure a minimum protection for all citizens; that is, the elimination of subsistence poverty is held as an ideal. The instruments of intervention to reduce poverty or inequality are as sacrosanct as the ideals they service, for the ideology of means is as formidable as the ideology of ends. Some view the market and economic growth as the most efficient means to improve well-being, and when these fail, cash transfers are preferable because they also preserve personal liberty. Others, while recognizing the beneficial effects of growth, seem more preoccupied with its cost. Market imperfections are troublesome, and while cash transfers are still accepted, social services seem the more critical elements in the strategy of redistribution. Proponents of both belief systems acknowledge that the more broadly social policy is defined the less redistributive is its effect. Some think situational and environmental forces reinforce policy, thus inhibiting life chances, while others regard the political system as sufficiently open so that individual initiative can overcome these constraints, using policy as an ally in its mission.

EFFICIENCY, CHOICE, EQUALITY

While competing systems of belief affect the purposes that social policy addresses, the ordering of priorities within a belief system presents equally demanding conflicts. One of the central concerns in social policy is establishing priorities, or reconciling the goals of economic efficiency, freedom of choice, and equality when they conflict. Here then is a fertile field in which the preferences of the analyst intrude, whether subtly or overtly.

The commonly accepted practical strategy for resolving conflicts between efficiency, choice, and equality usually translates into a preference for cash transfers as contrasted with benefits in kind. The argument runs as follows: concerns about choice and equality should be expressed in general legislation for taxation of income and wealth and by direct cash transfers, which allow the recipient to spend his additional income as he pleases. Efficiency is best achieved by action designed to make the market operate more competitively. Tobin explains the economists' preference for general egalitarianism as follows:

While concerned laymen who observe people with shabby housing or too little to eat instinctively want to provide them with decent housing and adequate food, economists instinctively want to provide them with more cash income. Then they can buy the housing and food if they want to, and if they choose not

to, the presumption is that they have a better use for the money. To those who complain about the unequal distribution of shelter or food, our first response . . . is that they should look at the distribution of wealth and income. If the social critics approve that distribution, they they should accept its implications, including the unequal distribution of specific commodities.

Of course, not all economists are willing to accept the heroic assumptions that taxation and cash transfers are neutral with respect to allocative efficiency, or more controversially, that inefficiencies in the distribution of subsidized commodities present a very large problem, even when the subsidies are substantial. In addition to these criticisms, Aaron and von Furstenberg have tried to show that the argument in support of cash transfers is built on an inappropriate model, where the rationale for *social* action is based on a *one*-person model in which it is assumed that "the donor cares only how the recipient perceives his own welfare." The more the presumed preferences of the donors of public largess are taken into account, the more the rationale for public policy leads to a willingness to restrict the consumer's freedom of choice. . . .

But even acknowledging the extensive use that governments do make of in-kind programs (such as distribution of free food commodities; food stamps which reduce the cost of food items; medicare for the aged and then medicaid for other groups in need; public housing; and, in recent years, a series of differentiated earmarked housing subsidies—such as rent supplements), we need not assume that the only underlying motive for such action is to control the behavior of the poor by restricting their consumption. Tobin argues that interest in specific egalitarianism can arise because "the social conscience is more offended by severe inequality in nutrition and basic shelter, or in access to medical care or legal assistance, than by inequality in automobiles, books, clothes, furniture, boats, etc. Can we somehow remove the necessities of life and health from the prizes that serve as incentives for economic activity . . . ?"

Thus, equitable distribution of specific resources may often be justified not on the grounds of expanding personal freedoms, but rather on the premise of containing them to reduce the discomforts of the well-to-do or to conform to the ideals of the donors. Socialist theoreticians have also generated similar arguments. For example, Crosland explains: "the first argument for greater equality is that it will increase social contentment and diminish social resentment." To what extent does greater equality produce political stability and discourage social deviations? Some analysts, like Glazer, have tried to show that though the relative economic position of Negroes has improved and thus inequalities have been narrowed, neither stability nor conformity has followed. "As the Negro's situation improves, his political attitudes are becoming more extreme." Donnison has noted, as if in direct response to Glazer's observations, the "societies that grow more equal may prove to be not more, but much less, fraternal. . . . Liberals who lose their nerve at this discovery are apt to turn against equality, and liberty too." If equality does not necessarily promote conformity and stability, and if these are valued, then more direct, coercive programs may be regarded as necessary. The exercise of administrative discretion in the allocation of those social services which are needed and wanted by the poor facilitates their use as a method to promote conformity to standards of "acceptable" behavior.

The ideological positions that policy analysts take with respect to this ancient issue of choice and equality also provide them with the framework for proposing new programs and the criteria for evaluating established ones. Without ideology, Joan Robinson has pointed out, we never would have thought of the important questions to pose. But ideology also provides criteria of judgment which lead to selective inclusion of data in order to argue a coherent position. . . .

A critique of the inefficiencies of the market may be inspired by a commitment to the more equitable distribution of selected commodities, especially those which seem essential for life or future earnings potential. Thus, Arrow's analysis of the role of uncertainty in the medical market provides a rationale for selective egalitarianism. But a desire to make markets more efficient can also be a subtle argument for increased inequalities. . . .

The value perspectives we have reviewed cluster together and serve as core ideas for both conservative and liberal interpretations of social policy. . . . Research in social policy inspired by politically conservative groups . . . has emphasized the importance of freedom of choice, of the market as a mechanism of intervention, and of the importance of income as it contributes to extending the quality of life. In a democratic society these strategies, when combined, appear to restrict the redistribution of resources and, thus, preserve inequalities. Liberal and more radical groups have tended to distrust the market as a mechanism of distribution and to emphasize the redistribution of noneconomic and economic resources by social policy outside the market, thereby promoting equality as a social aim. However, conservative thought has influenced the liberal-radical position. Increasingly, attention is being given to the problems and issues of choice, freedom, and the role of the market.

In this context, it is interesting to note that the criticisms of the political right and the political left in the United States are in agreement that one of the major defects of America's welfare state is that it has created a bureaucracy that has robbed clients of their rights and freedoms. The left is especially critical of the emerging new forms of the welfare state, for it views them as a new system of social control which seeks conformity as the price of security. As the liberal and the radical have come to accept the conservative emphasis on freedom of choice, some have increasingly turned to the role of the market as a mechanism for expanding freedoms, and to a scheme to promote local control through the decentralization of service systems.

But the link between ideology and policy is not that simple and tidy. For example, local community control has been the hallmark of political conservatives, while the liberals favored increasing centralization of public services on the assumption that equity was more likely to be achieved by centralized administration. But as issues of freedom, dignity, control, and choice emerged as priorities in welfare policy, liberal doctrine has been challenged. The net effect has been a fusing of the positions of the political right and left, leaving many analysts feeling that ideology is no longer an important factor either in politics or in the analysis of policy issues. As these traditional lines are redefined, many value priorities have been subjected to vigorous reassessment. Policy analysis is no longer ideologically based on an integrated belief system about efficiency, choice, and equality and how they relate to each other. Nevertheless, analysts continue to assign priorities to these competing aims, and these priorities do serve as a loose basis for the analysis and interpretation of specific policy issues. . . .

POLITICAL FEASIBILITY

Analysis of policy issues is also shaped by the analyst's search for solutions that are politically feasible. The commitment to feasibility is based on a desire to influence the development of policies. Since political considerations play a prominent, if not the dominant, part in shaping policy, the analyst will shape his analysis so that it takes account of these political factors. In making this statement I do not wish to suggest a crass sellout of beliefs or a gross distortion of evidence in order to produce politically usable reports and recommendations. Nevertheless, in subtle but important ways the wish to be relevant influences policy analysis. The most obvious way that this takes place is by failure to press the analysis to those root causes that at present are politically unresponsive to change. Thus, "welfare colonialism" or white racism as causes of poverty and social unrest are unacceptable interpretations in one era, while they may be ideas in good currency in another. . . .

I am not challenging the relationship between policy and politics, but rather examining different approaches to it. The first approach attempts to document how politics affects policy choice. One practical purpose of such inquiries is to present a spectrum of policy options that might be relevant under different political environments. In practice, this often results in a criticism of new policies because it is based on an inaccurate assessment of political possibilities. The second approach uses research as a political strategy to win acceptance for changes or to protect vulnerable programs when they are under attack. . . .

The conception of political feasibility is often closely associated with the idea of incremental change. The theory of disjointed incrementalism holds that, in the end, muddling and compromise are the only rational approaches to the management of conflicting multiple and ambiguous goals. . . . The dilemma of democracy is how to redistribute resources to politically weak and inarticulate groups in the interests of justice, without producing political and social instability, violence, and revolution. Every policy analyst must come to terms with the philosophy of incrementalism. His assessment of the ability of specific policies to cope with the problems for which they are designed will rest upon whether he repudiates, embraces, or compromises with the doctrine of incrementalism.

There are some alternative radical, but not revolutionary, approaches to providing changes on behalf of marginal and disadvantaged groups. One approach rests on the belief that concessions can be won by strategies of disruption. Cloward and Piven have recently argued that improvement for the poor is best created by exploiting the natural rage of those who are aggrieved, who spontaneously seek redress by a politics of dissension rather than consensus. Organizers who try to channel these efforts into more formal organizational structures for barter by bargaining undermine their viability, because the poor lack the sophistication to convert process to gain.

. . . Yet even these more radical approaches to change accept that a gradual and evolutionary process, contained by professionalism and cooperation, is at work. But the distrust of incrementalism encourages at least an openness to competing views of what is politically feasible.

CONCLUSIONS

This article has identified the terrain of policy not by its subject matter but by its procedures of analysis. I have tried to demonstrate how values inform analysis in every aspect of the procedure. What implications follow from this interpretation of policy analysis? The close relationship between values and modes of analysis does not invalidate policy analysis, but it does imply that there will never be one "true analysis." Every analysis must be judged good or bad within the framework of its value assumptions. The study of policy can be most insightful when it examinies afresh the critical assumption on which action proceeds. One such assumption is the context within which the analysis is framed, including definitions of and choices between constraints and options, which are typically governed by belief or opportunity or both.

This also suggests, at least implicitly, what might be the stance of those who undertake policy analysis. Their most demanding task is identification of their own values, along with an understanding of how these values blatantly and subtly bias analysis. "The excessive involvement in one's own value preferences may inhibit accurate observation . . . [the analyst] will do his job better if he is personally capable of a measure of temporary suspension of passions in the process of achieving his highly valued goals." I believe that this temporary detachment can be encouraged by the recognition that many of the values we most strongly cherish may at least partially conflict. The task is to apply this general principle to the particular case. But, in the end, detachment is not a substitute for action. We must make choices, and these are finally based on brute preference. To search for some olympian platform supposedly detached from values is illusory.

Even if the analyst is successful in discovering his values, he soon faces an ethical problem in how to act on his prejudices. An explicit statement of values may weaken the political case for reform. The concealment of values, by tactical ambiguity or denial—which takes the form of a retreat into an impartial, dispassionate, value-free scientific stand—threatens moral integrity. . . .

II.

CLASS INEQUALITIES
AND SOCIAL PROBLEMS

AS WE HAVE seen in the introduction to Part I, Max Weber defined "class" situations as involving people who have in common a given set of life chances by virtue of their economic situation—their possession of goods and opportunities for income. He referred to "the typical chance for a supply of goods, external living conditions, and personal life experiences, insofar as this chance is determined by the amount and kind of power or lack of such to dispose of goods or skills for the sake of income in a given economic order." Following this definition, we include in this Part selections dealing with problems that in one way or another have to do with class—with access to goods and services and the ability to offer labor for income in the marketplace.

Several of the selections deal with the U.S. income distribution and with policies designed to alter that distribution or at least to ameliorate its most extreme effects. This reflects the fact that in American society the life chances of individuals are affected primarily by their chances to acquire income.

A popular policy seeking to moderate income inequalities involves the educational system, in an effort to raise "human capital" by providing greater educational opportunity. Therefore we have included several selections dealing with the relationship between social inequality and education. Finally, we consider the consumption side, spending income rather than getting it, as another aspect of the stratification of life chances. We look at housing and health as two strategic kinds of consumption affecting the life chances of individuals and families, and we look at taxes as they affect the ability to consume given one's place in the income distribution.

7. POVERTY IN THE UNITED STATES

LEE RAINWATER

Reprinted from Toward A National Urban Policy *edited by Daniel P. Moynihan.* © *1970 by Basic Books, Inc., Publishers, New York. Lee Rainwater is Professor of Sociology at Harvard University.*

■ Poverty under one name or another has been a constant object of charitable and welfare activity in the United States during the industrial and postindustrial eras. This selection and the one that follows by Lester Thurow consider problems of the low-income group from the perspective of their inequality of income relative to others rather than in terms of the low absolute level of their subsistence. Until quite recently, however, minimum subsistence has dominated most public discussion of poverty. It has been assumed that the people who at any given time are considered poor are poor because they live below some minimum standard of living; if this is the case, and if economic growth proceeds far enough, no one will have to live below that standard of living and we will no longer have the problem of poverty.

However, it is possible to demonstrate by historical research that the minimum standard of living representing the poverty line in each previous decade had been exceeded by all but a tiny portion of the population within one generation's time. Yet at no time over the past 100 years has the problem of poverty not been of concern to policymakers. Sometimes it has been in the forefront of public and political attention, as in the second half of the 1960s; at other times it has been more the province of specialists and a few dedicated polemicists; but always a "war on poverty" has had its advocates and expert strategists.

This selection seeks to show some of the sociological and social-psychological conditions of inequality that constantly generate the group at the bottom of the social hierarchy who are considered to be poor.

Readers interested in how poverty has been defined in the past should consult Oscar Ornati, *Poverty Amid Affluence* (New York: Twentieth Century Fund, 1966). An interesting contemporary analysis of poverty at the beginning of the 20th century is Robert Hunter, *Poverty: Social Consciousness in the Progressive Era* (New York: Harper & Row, 1965). Robert Lampman, *Ends and Means of Reducing Income Poverty* (Chicago: Markham, 1971), contains a useful statistical analysis of the changing composition of the population that lived on less than poverty-line incomes between 1947 and 1967. Issues related to the effects of definitions of how we think about poverty and make policy to deal with it are covered in several important articles in Peter Townsend, ed., *The Concept of Poverty* (New York: American Elsevier, 1970). ■

FROM THE PERSPECTIVE of the material standard of the world at large, American poverty is a curious phenomenon indeed. Americans call a family of husband, wife, and two children poor if it receives about $4,500 a year or less in income, but that is an amount that many families in Western Europe would consider quite adequate, and an amount that many families in less industrialized countries would consider quite luxurious. A family considered poor in the United States, were it to transport its material possessions and household to many other countries in the world, would discover itself in terms of material affluence suddenly to be no longer poor, but well above average in economic standing. If a comparison is made on the historical rather than geographical basis, the same kind of seeming paradox obtains. Forty years ago well over half of American families received what today is considered a poverty income. Yet at that time few of the families involved would in fact have considered themselves poor, and poverty as a national problem was not at all such a central focus of public concern and policy as it is today.

Over the past seven or eight years the poverty problem has been of rising interest and common concern to American scholars and intellectuals, and from that interest and concern there has gradually grown an ever greater commitment on the part of policy makers and political figures to the goal of somehow eliminating what we call poverty. The War on Poverty, conceived by President Kennedy and launched by President Johnson, was the political outcome of researches conducted by American scholars over a generation's time on a complex of problems revolving around the fact that there continues to exist in American society a small but significant proportion of families who are socially and economically disadvantaged.

The concern with poverty apparent in the work of these scholars, and in the work of applied professionals such as social workers, has generally been manifest as a concern with those families who live below certain levels considered to be minimally adequate for subsistence. The poverty standards that have grown up in connection with the calculation of social welfare budgets and the like have been based on the assumption that there is a certain amount of income that is necessary simply to subsist. Indeed, these budgets have often been in large part determined by the cost of food for a family. (Since it is known that families at low income levels spend about one-third of their income on food, the subsistence level has been calculated simply as three times the amount of money that is necessary to provide a minimally adequate diet for a family of given size.) Yet we now know that these "subsistence income levels" have tended to rise faster than has the cost of living, so that what would be considered a subsistence level income today is far above the subsistence level income of 20 or 40 years ago even when price increases are taken into account.

All of this suggests that what is called poverty in the United States is a relative matter—relative to time and place and how well off the rest of the populaton is—and not a question of some absolute level of subsistence that is unchanging over time. Once this point of view is adopted the dimensions of the poverty problem are quite different.

While, in terms of an absolute standard, poverty has diminished dramatically in the United States, in terms of any reasonable relative definition of poverty there has been little if any change. For example, taking today's poverty line, over the past 15 years the proportion of families who would be considered poor has been cut in half.

But this kind of economic definition of poverty has never really been central to the things that concern Americans, intellectuals and men in the street alike, about social and economic disadvantage. In fact it has been the social problems which seem to accompany poverty that have perplexed and frustrated the nation. One could well argue that it really matters very little if some people continue to earn a great deal less than the average family income so long as they are doing slightly better each year economically, and so long as in fact most of them have the opportunity to acquire reasonable amounts of food, have a roof over their heads, and clothes to keep them warm. The concern with the problem of poverty is motivated by the many specific social problems which seem somehow related to the fact that there exists in the society a group of people removed from the accustomed affluence of average American life. Some of these problems have to do with the fact that a significant minority of men and women, boys and girls, are not able to establish themselves within the institutions that keep the society going economically—these are the problems of adolescents leaving school before they have graduated from high school (which in the United States is increasingly regarded as the minimum adequate education), of children from these families tending not to achieve adequately in school and once they have entered the labor market tending to have rather high rates of unemployment and irregular employment.

The poor are, in short, marginal to the major training and productive institutions of the society. Another kind of problem has to do not so much with the productive sectors of the society but rather with the fact that the same substantial minority of the population seems to be disproportionately involved in various kinds of deviance from the standards presumably held for all members of the society—here we become concerned with the problems of crimes of violence and of property, with problems of juvenile delinquency, illegitimacy, physical and mental disease, divorce and separation, and of mothers who have young children but no husbands and are unable to support their families adequately. Most recently all of these problems have reached a new level of expression in the widespread rioting and mass violence that affected most of the major American cities during the 1960s.

The social scientists who have been most concerned with these social problems have not been economists but, rather, sociologists, anthropologists, and psychologists. They have tended to define these problems as those of social class rather than simply as problems of income, and from their perspectives the problem of poverty appears as the problem of the existence of a lower-class group in the society. The specific social problems enumerated above—crime, illegitimacy, poor school achievement, and so forth—have been seen by these behavioral scientists as arising from the generalized situation of the lower class, each such problem being only one particular expression of a more general malaise that comes from living at the bottom of the social hierarchy. After several decades of intensive research and theoretical exploration of this complex of problems it is now possible to begin to see some of the ways in which the behavioral scientists' emphasis on social and cultural processes interact with the economists' concerns with income and income distribution.

The behavioral scientists have learned that most of the problems of those who live at the lower class level, and the problems that lower class people in turn make for the rest of the society, can be understood if conceptualized as a result of the lower class person's efforts to adapt to and cope with the relative deprivation of being so far removed from the average American standard. The people who are called poor and near-poor live a life

somewhat separated from that of the stable working and middle class members of the society. The latter have generally been doing very well indeed in terms of material affluence; in many ways they have found their lives more and more gratifying as the country has progressed economically, even as the sense of alienation of the relatively most deprived has increased.

The lower class is defined by two tough facts of life as it is experienced from day to day and from birth to death. These are the facts of deprivation and of exclusion: the lower class is deprived because it is excluded from the ordinary run of average American working and middle class life, and it is excluded because it is deprived of the resources necessary to function in the institutions of the mainstream of American life (which is, after all, working, not middle, class). The most basic deprivation is, of course, the lack of an adequate family income, but from this deprivation flows the sense so characteristic of lower class groups of not having the price of admission to participation in the many different kinds of rewards that ordinary society offers, most of which cost money, but also a good many others (education, for example) that do not.

But deprivation and exclusion are only the beginning of the troubles of the lower class, and sometimes in day-to-day life they do not really loom largest as barriers to a sense of reasonable satisfaction and security about who and where one is. The economic system and the system of social segregation operate to concentrate lower class people into particular communities. In those communities, by virtue of their own troubles and by virtue of the indifference and exploitative attitudes of the rest of the society, there grows up a system of institutionalized pathology (to use Kenneth B. Clark's phrase in *Dark Ghetto*) which characterizes ghettos and slum neighborhoods. It is this world, more than the objective facts of deprivation and exclusion per se, that impinges most directly on the lower class child as he grows up and on the lower class adult as he lives from day to day.

Let me illustrate this point about the direct, immediately experienced relevance of institutionalized pathology with an example. From my own research and from a careful analysis of studies during the Depression and after, I feel reasonably certain that the proportion of lower class marriages which break up do so primarily because the husband is not able to be a stable wage earner. That is, they break up because of "deprivation," and the exclusion from ordinary life that follows from it. However, in a study in which we asked a representative sample of women in a public housing project why their marriages broke up, we discovered that the women themselves did not give low income or their husbands' inability to find work as the most frequent reasons for their marriages breaking up. Instead, some 50 percent of them said that their marriages broke up because their husbands were unfaithful, played around in the streets, or drank too much, and another 27 percent indicated that their marriages broke up because the husbands *would not* work or give them enough money. In other words, from the wives' point of view, the breakup of the marriages was the fault of the husband, and not an unwilled result of living in highly depriving circumstances.

Perhaps this is just another way of saying that lower class people, the same as the rest of us, are not capable of being detached and impersonal about the events of their daily lives. But this is a very important fact, because when such incidents are multiplied thousands of times in the interactions of husbands and wives, parents and their children, friends and neighbors, and when this kind of individual faultfinding comes to dominate the contacts that lower class people have with the functionaries on whom they depend in social agencies, educational institutions, housing authorities, and the like, an institutionalized system exists in which lower class people are constantly subjected to "moral damage" in their interactions with others. By their very peers, and even more by their "superiors," they are deprived of a right which even the most uncivilized and primitive people that anthropologists have studied routinely accord their members—that is, the right to consider oneself and to be considered by others a worthwhile and valid representative of the human race.

To me this is the central damaging fact of lower class existence. The potential for an attack on one's moral worth is ever-present for lower class people. Depending on their particular situations they learn to expect such attacks from other family members, from their peers, from their neighbors, and most predictably from the caretakers with whom they have contact.

But lower class people have responded to this reality of their lives with all of the resourcefulness and imaginativeness that human beings can bring to bear in dealing with their difficulties. Their ways of coping with these dangers (as well as more obvious physical dangers and socioeconomic frustrations that come from their deprived and excluded existence) work in the sense that they are effective in maintaining daily lives that are for the most part tolerable, though seldom highly gratifying. At the same time these ways of coping with the dangers with which their world presents them also have a negative feedback into the system of social relations of the group in that they sometimes precipitate further problems for the individual and set problems of adaptation for others in the group and for outsiders. When social scientists speak of the tangle of pathology of ghetto and slum worlds they refer to these negative feedback effects of the adaptive mechanisms of lower class people, although they are also aware that the same mechanisms may well be the only ones that are meaningfully available to the individual who grows up in a lower class world.

It is in the light of this very abbreviated assessment of the social and cultural situation of the lower class that we can assess most effectively the appropriateness of the public policy response to the problems of American poverty. In general, American poverty policy has been oriented to a minimum subsistence idea of what constitutes poverty. The main goals of War on Poverty programs have been to provide services which alleviate some of the problems that result from poverty—as in the provision of special health, legal, housing, family life, and education programs—and to develop other programs that will train the poor to behave in ways that would allow them to attain jobs which pay about the minimum subsistence level of income. In other words, the War on Poverty has sought a two-pronged attack which on the one hand changes the poor person into a more conventional person in terms of style of life and work-oriented habits, and at the same time makes opportunities available to him so that he can translate his new social and technical skills into a stable job.

The results of these programs, however, have so far been discouraging. Some supporters of the War on Poverty programs argue that this lack of success is simply a result of the token financing of the program—after all, they argue, how can one expect to eradicate poverty with an annual expenditure by the Office of Economic Opportunity of less than $100 per poor person. Among social scientists, however, there is increasing skepticism that the services and opportunity programs could achieve significant impact on the poverty problem even with vastly increased budgets.

This skepticism comes from the recognition of the two cardinal facts about American poverty outlined earlier: first, that American poverty is a phenomenon of relative deprivation and not living below some absolute minimum subsistence level, and second, that the behavior of poor people which often seems to interfere with their taking advantage of services and opportunities represents an inevitable adaptation to their situation of relative deprivation, an adaptation that will not easily be given up unless there is some very basic change in the situation to which they must adapt. Therefore, these social scientists argue that the goal of any seriously intended War on Poverty must be that of reducing income inequality by insuring a minimum income floor such that no American family has a standard of living significantly below that of the average family. The first stage of such a program would

be directed at those who receive less than half of the median family income; their incomes would be increased to half the median. This program would affect about 20 percent of American families. But it seems likely that many of the social problems associated with poverty would not be more than moderately reduced and that the second stage of an income equalization program would have to take as its goal the increasing of family incomes in the lower 40 percent of the population so that a minimum family income floor of around $5,000 would be established.

These are formidable goals indeed, and once they have been formulated the question immediately arises whether it is possible, either economically or politically, to achieve such goals.

The United States' socioeconomic system is in many ways a highly stable one; so stable, in fact, that it can tolerate without serious dislocation even an ongoing low-level revolt of the disadvantaged in its cities. (For example, there was hardly a ripple on Wall Street as riots swept Newark and Detroit and numerous smaller cities.) This American socioeconomic system can and does insure an increasing affluence for the nation as a whole, an affluence that is brought home to working and middle class families each year as a slightly higher standard of living. But this same system also operates in such a way that a large portion of the population is doomed to live removed from the rest, and it seems by now quite clear that there are no self-corrective mechanisms in the system that will, in fact, gradually reduce the size of the population that lives in "the other America." In addition to the purely economic forces which preserve a highly unequal income distribution, racial prejudice and discrimination, both historically and currently operative, continue to reinforce inequality and frustrate most government efforts to alleviate the problem through legal measures, job training, improved educational programs for the so-called culturally disadvantaged, and so forth. Obviously, it will take a major change in the way the nation conducts its affairs and allocates it resources to alter the socioeconomic hierarchy in such a way that the problems associated with poverty and racial exploitation no longer exist. The curious thing about this change is that, were it made, it would probably result in even higher levels of affluence and social stability than now exist, but the nation nevertheless pulls back from the price that would have to be paid to bring about these conditions.

The economists and sociologists who have been concerned with this problem have suggested that the following kinds of measures will be necessary to begin to reduce income inequality. First of all, the nation's economy will have to be operated in such a way that there is tight full employment. That is, the 4 percent unemployment rate that the United States now considers acceptable must be sharply reduced to something in the 2 percent range. In addition, because a great many of the poor are immediately capable of functioning only at the unskilled and semiskilled levels, there will have to be specific government financing designed to create work for persons who have those kinds of skills. In fact, there is a great deal of such work that needs to be done, particularly in the public sector of the economy—in hospitals, in schools, in various local municipal services. During the Great Depression of the 1930s such programs were put into effect to solve the very high unemployment of that time, but they were regarded as temporary expedients. Now the problem is to build in government-stimulated demand for work in the public sector that will provide stable and secure jobs—year in, year out—not on a temporary basis.

Along with the provision of jobs, it would, of course, be necessary to see to it that wages paid for these jobs were such as to provide incomes that approximate the average American standard. This means that minimum wages in both the public and private sectors would have to be pegged to at least three-quarters of the wage necessary to earn the median family income, and that unemployment compensation payments would have to be similarly high. Such high minimum wages and unemployment compensation could be economically feasible only in the context of very tight full employment.

Finally, because a significant minority of the poor are not able to work—because they are mothers of many children or because they are disabled—it is apparent that there would have to be some guaranteed minimum income provisions applicable to families in which there is no wage earner or in which the wage earner cannot earn sufficient income. Recently, many such guaranteed income programs have been suggested, the most popular being the negative income tax and the family allowance. As these programs are examined and tested for their costs and other significant features, it is very likely that a guaranteed income plan will emerge which provides a reasonable income floor without at the same time significantly reducing the incentive of able-bodied persons to work.

A price will, of course, have to be paid for such programs. The low productivity of a good many poor workers will have to be subsidized for a number of years, perhaps for a generation. However, this price can be easily exaggerated, since the introduction of a large group of even unskilled workers would have the effect of increasing the Gross National Product both directly and in terms of the demand generated for goods and services by the now more affluent former poor. In any case, from the point of view of sociologists, whose assessment of research on the lower class emphasizes the necessity of changing lower class situations before lower class adaptations can occur, it seems that whatever the price, only in this way can the problem of poverty be eventually resolved. If it is resolved by this kind of income strategy, then one can expect at the very least that the next generation of the poor will have acquired through their schooling and through normal job training programs sufficient skills to earn their own way in society so that the cost would be, in the main, a onetime cost.

Along these lines, then, it seems that the intellectual problems of understanding poverty and of developing social policies that would resolve the problem over the long term are gradually approaching solution. But the solution of the intellectual problem, of course, in no way guarantees that the poverty problem will be solved in the real social, economic, and political world. For too long the nation's creative political efforts have been absorbed in trying to come to terms with the United States as policeman of the world, particularly in Southeast Asia, a problem beside which the problem of American poverty tends to pale as a contemporary challenge. It is unlikely that the challenge of income inequality will be seriously addressed by the nation so long as the policeman involvement continues at its present level.

In the long run, however, the destructiveness of American poverty (and its twin, racial prejudice and exploitation of the black and other minority groups) will eventually place it high on the national agenda, not only on humanitarian grounds but also because without a solution to these problems it seems likely that the American city as we know it today will itself be destroyed.

8. THE AMERICAN DISTRIBUTION OF INCOME: A STRUCTURAL PROBLEM

LESTER C. THUROW and ROBERT LUCAS

Reprinted from Proceedings of the Joint Economic Committee of the Congress of the United States *(Washington, D.C.: Government Printing Office, March 17, 1962). Robert Lucas is in the Department of Economics at U.C.L.A. Lester Thurow is Professor of Economics and Management at the Sloan School of Management, Massachusetts Institute of Technology. He has written extensively on the economics of poverty and racial discrimination, on income distribution in the United States, and on the U.S. tax system.*

■ The distribution of income and wealth in capitalist countries has been a subject of intermittent concern to social scientists. At some times the topic has generated interest not only among scientists but also among politicians and ordinary citizens. At other times the issue has not excited much interest at all, being somehow regarded as settled or, to the extent that it remained problematic, self-correcting. From the 1930s into the 1960s a general presumption seems to have been that various social, political, and economic forces were increasing equality in the distribution of income and wealth. To be sure, no one believed that millionaires had ceased to represent a distinctive social type or that there were no more poor people. However, there was a sense that economic growth, unionization, the income tax, greater educational opportunity, and a decline in artificial barriers to achievement together added up to a long-term trend that would narrow the gap between the haves and the have-nots in the United States as well as in most West European countries. By the late 1960s, however, it had become evident that no clear-cut trend toward equalization was apparent.

In the United States it seems that the distribution of income has not shifted markedly since before the Great Depression of the 1930s. Perhaps there was some slight equalizing during the Depression and World War II, but even this seems to have been a one-time shift and not part of a trend toward equality. Thurow starts his examination of income inequality from the central fact that U.S. society seems to generate and regenerate, year in and year out, essentially the same distribution of income among persons and families. If one

believes, as many social policy analysts do, that maldistribution of income is a central factor in causing a wide range of social problems, then it becomes important to analyze the structural bases for that maldistribution. This Thurow does, taking up one by one the characteristics of the economy that produce the particular pattern of income inequalities we find in this country.

The most important sociological analysis of the relationship between occupation, education, and income is found in the work of Otis Dudley Duncan and his students, beginning with Peter M. Blau and Otis D. Duncan, *The American Occupational Structure* (New York: Wiley, 1967). An excellent integration of a broad range of sociological and economic studies dealing with income inequality is found in Christopher Jencks et al., *Inequality: A Reappraisal of the Effects of Family and Schooling in America* (New York: Basic Books, 1972). Thurow has dealt with the interaction between low income and racial discrimination in *Poverty and Discrimination* (Washington, D.C.: Brookings Institution, 1969). A review of economic theory about the distribution of income is found in Martin Bronfenbrenner, *Income Distribution Theory* (Chicago: Aldine, 1971). The first thoroughgoing empirical study of the distribution of income and economic welfare is that of James N. Morgan, Martin H. David, Wilbur J. Cohen, and Harvey E. Brazer, *Income and Welfare in the United States* (New York: McGraw-Hill, 1962). A useful presentation of census and other data on income distribution and its correlates is in Herman P. Miller, *Rich Man, Poor Man*, rev. ed. (New York: Thomas Crowell, 1971). ■

77

THE ROLE OF MONEY INCOMES

ALL OF THE AXIOMS used to praise market economies (capitalistic or socialistic) depend on a fundamental condition. If a market economy starts with an optimum distribution of income, then a market economy will efficiently and equitably produce and distribute goods and services. Other conditions are necessary to insure that market economies really work, but the whole structure of justifications for market economies depends on this initial condition. If the condition is not met, the most perfectly functioning market economy will be inefficient and unjust. It is simply starting out with the wrong distribution of economic voting power.

One of the main functions of government is to establish the right distribution of economic voting power. Not only must it establish such a distribution initially, it must continually reestablish such a distribution. Market economies will efficiently and equitably produce and distribute goods and services if they start with the optimum initial distribution of economic voting power, but market economies will not automatically regenerate such a distribution. Using tax and transfer policies, governments must be continually modifying market distributions of income.

But what is the right, optimum, or desired distribution of income? Fundamentally, the answer cannot be found in economic analyses. It is a moral problem that revolves around our collective judgments as to the proper degree of equality or inequality. Some individuals may want a society with complete equality in private purchasing power; others may want a large degree of inequality. In essence the fights over progressive versus regressive tax structures, level of welfare, and social security benefits are all disputes over the optimum distribution of money incomes. Living in one society, however, we must all agree on some common degree of equality. . . .

Although foreign examples and experiences do not provide conclusive proof of how the American population would react to different distributions of income, they provide informa-

tion on the response patterns of other human beings. Interestingly, the pretax distributions of income in Sweden, the United Kingdom, and West Germany are not noticeably different from that in the United States. All four countries seem to have approximately an 8 to 1 ratio between the average income of the richest quintile of the population and the poorest quintile of the population. Surprisingly, the country with by far the most rapid rate of growth has the most equal distribution of pretax income. In Japan the average income of the richest quintile is less than five times as large as that of the poorest quintile. In at least one culture, the world's highest rate of economic growth and a relatively equal distribution of market incomes seems compatible.

Analysis should, however, focus on post- rather than pretax incomes. Substantial equalization may come about in the process of taxation or in the process of distributing public goods and services. In the United States the pre- and posttax distributions of income are not noticeably different. When all of our taxes (local, state, and federal) are added together, progressive taxes seem to be canceled by regressive taxes, leaving a proportional tax system. As a result, taxes reduce everyone's income by the same percentage and leave relative incomes unchanged. Either pre- or post-tax, the richest quintile has approximately eight times as much income as the poorest quintile. In contrast, in Sweden substantial equalization in living standards comes about through the distribution of public goods and services. Although U.S. public expenditures are also redistributive, they are nowhere nearly so redistributive as those in Sweden. In the United Kingdom a much more progressive income tax leads to a more equal distribution of posttax income. . . .

There are two methods for redistributing income and wealth. In the first approach the federal government simply uses its tax rates and transfer payment system (negative taxes) to transform any market distribution of income into its desired distribution of income. If the marketplace does not generate enough equality, a progressive tax system is adopted to create equality. If the marketplace generates too much equality, a regressive tax system is adopted to create inequality. In the second approach the federal government adopts policies to alter the market distribution of income itself. Policies to improve the education of low (or potential low) income individuals are an example of such an approach. By reducing educational differentials the country seeks to reduce income differentials. . . .

Although this paper focuses on money incomes, the authors are well aware that money incomes are not the only determinants of welfare or the quality of life. Public services, friends, security, clear air, and a host of other factors influence welfare and the quality of life. At the same time, however, money incomes remain a principal component of the quality of life. Not surprising, most professions to the contrary seem to come from those with above-average incomes.

THE AMERICAN DISTRIBUTION OF INCOME AND WEALTH

FAMILY INCOMES

In the 22 years from 1947 to 1969 the median American family income has risen from $4,972 to $9,433 (in 1969 dollars). . . . The income distribution has been basically stable in the postwar period, but there have been noticeable changes. Whether they are significant depends on the view of the beholder (see Table 8.1). The average income of the richest 20 percent of all families has fallen

from 8.6 to 7.3 times that of the poorest 20 percent of all families. The average income of the richest 5 percent of all families has fallen from 36.6 to 21.6 times that of the poorest 5 percent of all families.

Relative incomes are only one measure of dispersion, however. Constant and even falling relative differences are compatible with increasing absolute differences in a world with rising incomes. In 1947 the average income of the richest 20 percent of all families was $10,565 higher than that of the poorest 20 percent of all families; in 1969 it was $19,071 higher (in 1969 dollars). The real gap between the poorest and richest 5 percent of all families rose from $17,057 to $27,605 (in 1969 dollars) despite the sharply declining differences in relative incomes.

Analysis of the family income distribution indicates that all income classes seem to be sharing in the fruits of economic growth. Incomes seem to be growing at about the same rate in most income classes. Measured in relative terms some equalization of the distribution of income is occurring; measured in absolute terms some further dispersion of income is occurring.

Within the distribution of family earnings, wives are playing an increasingly important role. The probability of having a working wife rises as a husband's earnings rise until his earnings reach the average level for husbands. As his earnings continue to rise, her probability of working declines (see Table 8.2). Measured in relative terms, working wives make the distribution of income more equal. The relative differences in female earn-

TABLE 8.1

PERCENTAGE SHARE OF AGGREGATE BEFORE-TAX INCOME GOING TO FAMILIES

	1947	1950	1956	1960	1965	1969
Lowest fifth	5.0	4.5	5.0	4.9	5.3	5.6
Second Fifth	11.8	12.0	12.4	12.0	12.1	12.3
Middle Fifth	17.0	17.4	17.8	17.6	17.7	17.6
Fourth fifth	23.1	23.5	23.7	23.6	23.7	23.4
Highest fifth	43.0	42.6	41.2	42.0	41.3	41.0
Top 5 percent	17.2	17.0	16.3	16.8	15.8	14.7
Bottom 5 percent	0.47	—	—	—	—	0.68

ings across male earnings classes are simply not so great as those in male earnings (see Table 8.2). The maximum average contribution for a wife is only 2.4 times as large

TABLE 8.2
HUSBAND-WIFE EARNINGS (1969)

Husband's Earnings ($1,000)	Probability of Working Wife	Median Earnings of Wife*
$0 - 1	34.9%	$ 879
1 - 2	36.0%	720
2 - 3	46.0%	1,087
3 - 4	45.7%	1,052
4 - 5	48.5%	1,214
5 - 6	46.3%	1,321
6 - 7	49.2%	1,524
7 - 8	47.2%	1,489
8 - 10	44.9%	2,075
10 - 15	37.6%	1,205
15 - 25	30.7%	903
25 & up	19.2%	570

*Includes husband-wife families with and without working wives.

as that of the wives in the lowest income class. In addition, husbands with high earnings have wives with lower average earnings than those of the poorest husbands.

Working wives make the absolute gap between poor and middle income families larger but reduce the income gap between middle and high income families. The largest contribution to family earnings ($2,075 per year) is made by wives of husbands earning $8,000 to $10,000 per year, while wives with husbands at the bottom of the earnings distribution earn $879, and wives with husbands at the top of the earnings distribution earn $570.

Postwar increases in female participation rates have resulted in some relative equalization of the distribution of income. They have reduced the absolute income gaps between middle and upper income families, but they also have increased the absolute income gaps between poor and middle income families. Given the existing distribution of female participation rates by their husbands earning class, the areas with the greatest potential for further increases are at the top and the bottom of the income distribution. If improve-

ments in job opportunities were to entice these wives into the labor force, poor family incomes would rise relative to middle class family incomes, but rich family incomes would also rise relative to middle class family incomes.

If income opportunities were opened so that women had the same potential earning capabilities as males, the impact would depend on the extent of selective mating. To the extent that males with high potential earning capabilities marry females with high potential earning capabilities and males with low potential earning capabilities marry females with low potential earning capabilities, equal income opportunities for women would make the family income distribution more dispersed. Since actual mating habits are not apt to match males with higher earning capabilities with females with low earning capabilities, increasing female income opportunities will probably make the actual distribution of family incomes more dispersed. This would occur unless high income males choose to select wives who are willing to stay at home.

MINORITY GROUPS

Minority groups are participating in the same general growth in incomes as the White majority. While average White family incomes were growing from $5,194 to $9,794, the average family incomes of Blacks and other races were growing from $2,660 to $6,191 (from 51 percent to 63 percent of White incomes; see Table 8.3).

TABLE 8.3
RATIO OF BLACK AND OTHER RACES TO WHITE MEDIAN INCOMES

1947	51%	1963	53%
1949	51%	1965	55%
1952	57%	1966	60%
1954	55%	1967	62%
1958	51%	1968	63%
1960	55%	1969	63%

Based on econometric analyses of the relationships between Black incomes and the business cycle, Black incomes might have been expected to rise to about 57 percent of White incomes in 1969 but not to 63 percent. The difference is an indication of some movement toward more income equality for minority groups. Once again, however, relative improvements are compatible with absolute deteriorations. From 1947 to 1969 the absolute difference between Black and White family incomes rose from $2,534 to $3,603 (in 1969 dollars).

In terms of income distributions, the distribution of income among Blacks and other races is slightly more unequal than the distribution of income among Whites (see Table 8.4). While the richest 20 percent of all

TABLE 8.4

PERCENTAGE SHARES OF
AGGREGATE INCOMES IN 1969

	White	Black and Other Races
Lowest Fifth	6.0	4.7
Second Fifth	12.6	10.8
Middle Fifth	17.6	16.9
Fourth Fifth	23.4	24.4
Highest Fifth	40.4	43.1
Top 5 Percent	14.8	14.7

Black families have 43.1 percent of all Black family income, the richest 20 percent of White families has 40.4 percent of all White family income.

The major source of income gains for minority groups has been geographic mobility. Blacks have increasingly moved out of the South, where their relative incomes are low, to the North and West, where their relative incomes are higher. In 1970, Blacks earned 57 percent of White incomes in the South, 71 percent in the Northeast, 73 percent in the North Central region, and 77 percent in the West. Based on the geographic movements that have actually taken place among Blacks between 1950 and 1970, Black incomes should have risen by about 12 percentage points relative to White incomes. In fact, they have risen by about 10 percentage points. Thus geographic movement more than accounts for the observed increase in Black incomes. Up to 1969 antidiscrimination programs seemed to be having little impact on average Black

incomes. Although geographic movement can be a powerful source of relative income gains, it is inherently limited. If all Black families were to move out of the South, Black incomes would still only be about 75 percent of White incomes.

Improvements in female incomes and job opportunities will also tend to lead to a widening gap between Black and White family incomes. In 1969, 53 percent of all Black wives were working in the paid labor force, while only 38 percent of all White wives were doing so. At high incomes the difference is even more extreme. Of all Black families with incomes over $15,000, 73 percent had a wife in the paid labor force, while only 48 percent of all White families with incomes over $15,000 per year had a wife in the paid labor force. As a consequence, better income opportunities for existing female workers would tend to equalize Black and White incomes, but better income and job opportunities that succeeded in attracting more female workers into the labor force would tend to increase the dispersion between Black and White incomes. There are simply more White wives remaining to be attracted into the labor force.

In addition to Blacks, Spanish-speaking Americans and American Indians are the principal groups with below-average incomes. The average income for Spanish-speaking Americans is $5,641 (in 1969), or $350 less than that of Blacks. American Indians make even less (probably around $3,000 per family). Although ethnic Americans often consider themselves to be subject to discrimination, all of the major ethnic groups have average incomes above those of native Americans (see Table 8.5). In 1969 the range was from $11,554 for Russian-American families to $8,127 for Irish-Americans. In contrast, other Americans (natives) had average incomes of only $7,671.

FEMALE INCOMES

Almost no changes have occurred in the relative earnings of males and females since 1939. In 1939 year-around full-time female

TABLE 8.5

MEDIAN FAMILY INCOMES

Origin		Origin	
English	$8,324	Polish	$ 8,849
German	$8,607	Russian	$11,554
Irish	$8,127	Spanish	$ 5,641
Italian	$8,808	Other	$ 7,671

workers earned 58 percent of male earnings; in 1969 they earned 59 percent. Once again constant relative differences imply increasing absolute differences. In 1939 the real income gap was $1,570 (in 1969 dollars) between year-around full-time male and female workers; in 1969 it was $3,526.

The overall consistency masks quite dramatic changes for Black females. Between 1939 and 1969 year-around full-time White female earnings fell from 61 percent to 58 percent of their male counterparts, while the earnings of year-around full-time Black female earnings rose from 51 percent to 69 percent of their Black male counterparts. Since year-around full-time Black male earnings were rising from 45 percent to 69 percent of their White male counterparts (most of this increase occurred during World War II), year-around full-time Black female workers earnings rose from just 38 percent to 82 percent of their White counterparts.

Family incomes, however, did not equalize at the same rate. White women were moving into the year-around full-time labor force much faster than were Black women. Rising White female participation rates managed to offset much of the income gains of Black workers. . . .

WEALTH

Distributions of wealth are available less frequently than those of income, but occasional measurements have been made. In 1962 the Federal Reserve Board conducted a survey of the ownership of all private assets. At that time, the wealthiest 20 percent of the population owned over 75 percent of all private assets, while the poorest 25 percent of all families had no net worth (their debts equaled their assets) (see Table 8.6). The wealthiest 8 percent of the population owned 60 percent of all private assets; the wealthiest 1 percent owned over 26 percent of all private assets.

TABLE 8.6

FAMILY DISTRIBUTION OF NET WORTH IN 1962

Net Worth Class ($1,000)	Cumulative Distribution of Families	Cumulative Distribution of Total Net Worth
Negative	8.1	—0.2
$0 - 1	25.4	0.0
1 - 5	42.7	2.1
5 - 10	56.9	6.6
10 - 25	81.3	23.8
25 - 50	92.5	40.9
50 - 100	97.6	55.9
100 - 200	98.6	61.3
200 - 500	99.5	74.2
500 & over	100.0	100.0

As these data indicate, the distribution of wealth is much more unequal than the distribution of income. While the richest 20 percent of all families have 41 percent of total income, they own 75 percent of all assets. While the poorest quintile has 5.6 percent of total income, they have no net worth. Wealth is also closely associated with income. Those with high net worths have high incomes (see Table 8.7).

ECONOMIC MOBILITY

What is the probability of individuals moving from one income distribution point to another over the course of a year, a lifetime or a generation? What is the conditional probability of a son's income given his father's income? With perfect intergenerational mobility, knowing a father's income provides no information about his son's income. With no intergenerational mobility, knowing a father's income provides all of the information necessary to predict a son's income. Economic mobility of this type is important since society's value judgments about the equity or inequity of a particular income distribution may depend on the degree of economic mobility (annual, lifetime, or in-

TABLE 8.7

1962 DISTRIBUTION OF INCOME AND WEALTH*

Income ($1,000) \ Net Worth ($1,000)	All Families	Negative	$0-1	1-5	5-10	10-25	25-50	50-100	100-200	200-500	500-1,000	1,000 & up
0-3	100%	12	31	16	15	17	7	1				
3-5	100%	15	22	22	12	17	8	3				
5-7.5	100%	7	14	21	17	28	8	4	1			
7.5-10	100%	3	5	19	16	37	14	5	2			
10-15	100%	1	3	9	13	34	24	11	4	1		
15-25	100%			2	8	18	30	26	7	7	1	
25-50	100%				1	2	7	20	31	30	5	3
50-100	100%						1	3	13	37	27	20
1,000 & up	100%								1	4	61	35

*Blanks indicate less than 0.5 percent

tergenerational) within it. A high degree of economic mobility may make us more willing to tolerate inequalities at any point in time. If incomes were given out on a lottery basis, any annual income distribution, no matter how unequal, could be consistent with a completely equal lifetime income. Although it is not extensive, there is some data on economic mobility.

Studies of poverty families indicate that about 70 percent of the families that were in poverty last year are in poverty this year. Of the remaining 30 percent, 11 percent were dissolved from death and other causes, and 19 percent escaped from poverty. Of the 19 percent who escaped, 8 percent were still within $1,000 of the poverty line, 4 percent were within $2,000 of the poverty line, and 7 percent were more than $2,000 away from the poverty line. Families who escape from poverty in any one year also have a significant probability of falling back into poverty in succeeding years. As a consequence, poverty data would seem to indicate a low degree of economic mobility among the poverty population. Such evidence, however, does not prove a low degree of economic mobility for other parts of the income distribution.

Data on the use of income-averaging provisions of the federal income tax laws indicate that only 0.7 percent of all returns found it profitable to average their incomes over a 5-year period in 1968. To be eligible for income averaging, 1968 income needed to exceed the average of the 4 previous years by 33.3 percent and by a minimum amount of $3,000 or more. Such data would indicate that economic mobility in high income ranges is rather low. Few individuals have large fluctuations in their annual incomes. As a result, distributions of income would probably not be noticeably different if they were collected on a lifetime rather than an annual basis.

Intergenerational economic mobility is even less well charted. Sociologists rather than economists have studied intergenerational mobility. They have focused on occupational mobility rather than economic mobility partly because of their interests and partly because

of a lack of data on intergenerational economic mobility. Given the wide ranges of incomes within occupations, the lack or presence of occupational mobility indicates little about economic mobility. Intergenerational occupational mobility is not high, but this conclusion does not necessarily lead to the same conclusion for economic mobility.

FUTURE TRENDS

In the absence of governmental policies to the contrary, future trends in the distribution of income are apt to mirror the trends of the postwar period. These trends seem firmly established in the American economy. Without government actions to alter them, they can be expected to continue.

As a result, the distribution of family income probably will remain reasonably constant when measured in relative terms but will continue to disperse when measured in absolute dollars. The largest unknown factor in such a prediction revolves around the impact of women's liberation. If the current movement toward women's liberation were to open up new job opportunities for women and succeed in attracting more women into the labor force, the distribution of family income might become more dispersed on either measure. More working wives would raise family incomes at all levels, but the family incomes of the rich would grow more rapidly than those of the less-well-off. Wives of high income males have the greatest potential for entering the labor force since they currently have the lowest labor force participation rates.

The rise in minority incomes relative to the majority will depend heavily on geographic movements from the South to the North and West. To the extent that this trend continues, Black incomes will rise relative to White incomes. To the extent that it slows down, Black incomes will cease rising relative to Whites. In this area the major unknown factor is the future impact of equal opportunity programs and antidiscrimination laws. As yet these programs do not seem to be having a noticeable impact on relative incomes, but they may start to do so in the future. Although the changes are not visible in national averages, small groups, like young northern Black male college graduates, may be advancing as a result of these programs.

Given the long-run consistency in male-female wage differentials there is no reason to believe that these differentials will change as the result of economic forces. If they are to change, it will be the result of political or sociological forces. As yet no changes are visible.

Given postwar changes in the distribution of income and the likelihood that the same types of changes will occur in the immediate future, the body politic must explicitly decide whether it wants changes in the distribution of income. Without such decisions and programs to bring the desired changes about, the distribution of income will not be noticeably different from the present. . . .

ALTERING THE STRUCTURE OF MARKET INCOMES

Historically both governmental policies and economic analysis have concentrated on supply-side efforts to alter the distribution of earnings. Programs were designed to educate or train individuals so that they had the skills and personal characteristics necessary to fill higher income jobs. Underlying such programs was a particular view of how labor markets work. According to this theory the supply of low income workers would be reduced in the process of such education and training programs. As a result, wages for low income workers would rise. Conversely, the supply of high income workers would be enlarged, and their wages would be reduced. Thus education and training would have a three-pronged effect on the distribution of income. (1) Some individuals would be raised from low income jobs to high income jobs; (2) wages for low income jobs would rise; and (3) wages for high income jobs would fall. The result—a more equal distribution of market earnings. . . .

But differences in personal characteristics do not explain all or even most of the observed differences in wages and salaries. Only 30 percent of the observed income differences between Black and White males can be attributed to differences in personal characteristics. The remaining 70 percent is explained in terms of demand-side phenomena (wage and job discrimination, full employment, etc.). Between women and men, demand-side elements are even more important. After standardizing for all of the personal characteristics that are demanded in the labor market, women earn only 50 percent of what men earn. The remaining 50 percentage points are explained by differences in the demand for women and men. As a consequence, no program for altering personal characteristics can hope to equalize income of Black and Whites or male and females. Efforts must be directly focused on relative wages and job characteristics.

If historical experience is to be used as any guide to the factors that are necessary to cause an increase in the quality of the income distribution, it is necessary to go back to the Great Depression and World War II. In both instances the distribution of income seems to have become noticeably more equal. From 1929 to 1941 the share of total income going to the bottom 40 percent of the population rose from 12.5 percent to 13.6 percent, while the share of income going to the top 5 percent fell from 30 percent to 24 percent, and the share of income going to the top 20 percent fell from 54.4 percent to 48.8 percent. From 1941 to 1947 the share going to the bottom 40 percent rose to 16 percent, while the share going to the top 5 percent fell to 20.9 percent, and the share going to the top 20 percent fell to 46 percent. In both cases alterations in the demand side, rather than the supply side, of the market seem to have provided the mechanism for equalizing incomes.

In the Great Depression an economic collapse was the mechanism for changes. Individual fortunes were lost, firms collapsed, and a wage structure emerged that was noticeably more equal than that before the collapse. While interesting, the deliberate collapsing of an economy in order to equalize the distribution of income is not a policy that commends itself. World War II is more interesting from this vantage point.

As a result of an overwhelming social and political consensus that the economic burdens of the war should be relatively equally shared, the federal government undertook two major actions. First, it instituted a very progressive income tax (more progressive than the current federal income tax) that converted a regressive tax system into a mildly progressive tax system. Second, it used a combination of wage controls and labor controls to equalize market wages. This was accompanied by a conscious policy of restructuring jobs to reduce skill requirements and to make use of the existing skills of the labor force. To some extent, old skill differences were simply cloaked with a new set of relative wages, and to some extent skill differentials were actually collapsed. When put together the two factors led to an equalization of market incomes that was not dissipated after the war ended.

To some extent, the wage policies of World War II were a deliberate attempt to change the sociology of what constitutes "fair" wage differentials. To some extent, the sociological judgments changed as a result of the war (war burdens were to be equally shared), and this was reflected in wage patterns. As a consequence of the widespread consensus that wage differentials should be reduced, it was possible to make a deliberate attempt to reduce wage differentials. While it may be difficult to alter sociological judgments on the definition of "fairness," such changes are an important ingredient in any attempt to alter the structure of wages. Since wage negotiators always look at relative wages as well as absolute wages, it is very difficult to change relative wages unless the participants believe that relative wages should, as a matter of "fairness," be changed.

Efforts to restructure skill differentials in the production process are also an essential ingredient of any plan to alter the structure of incomes. . . . Research and development expenditures [should be directed] toward alter-

ing the mix of labor skills required. At the moment almost all of our research and development expenditures are devoted toward discovering new products. Some of these expenditures might be directed toward discovering new (and perhaps cheaper) techniques of producing old products. Skill differentials could be deliberately collapsed as a matter of public policy.

Perhaps it is impossible to generate a consensus on the desired degree of equality without a major war, but there are certainly actions that can be taken to reduce barriers to shifts in the relative distribution of income. The first is to minimize fears of job competition by insuring a full or overly full employment economy that *never* suffers from business cycles and recession. If existing employees fear that every new employee is a potential competitor for their jobs, they will simply refuse to provide the informal on-the-job learning that is necessary for an effective transfer of skills. Second, in a world of labor *shortages* every employer has an incentive to go beyond his existing labor force—to recruit and upgrade workers that he would not otherwise recruit or upgrade. . . . Labor shortages will not automatically generate the desired distribution of income, but labor shortages are a necessary ingredient in any policy to do so. Even in wartime, labor shortages, as much as desired to equalize wartime burdens, explain the observed restructuring of the labor force.

In addition to an economy with substantial and persistent labor shortages, it is necessary to think of how the government can directly compress wage differentials without resort to the elaborate wartime structure of wage and labor controls. The answer must be found in public employment opportunities. Instead of adjusting its wage scales to the private economy, the public sets its wages at the desired level and places pressure on the private economy to adjust to the public wage structure. . . . At the lower end of the wage structure, the federal government would abandon the minimum wage law and replace it with a guaranteed job at some minimum wage. Thus the government might guarantee to employ everyone who wants work at $2 per hour. This would force the private economy to pay a minimum wage of $2 per hour, but it would also eliminate the adverse unemployment effects that spring from higher minimum wages. To compress the private wage structure, the federal government would set its wage scales in the appropriate manner and subsidize state and local governments to set their wage scales in the appropriate manner.

To encourage changes in the relative wage structure of the private economy, manpower expenditures should also shift from their present focus on personal background characteristics to a focus on the real objectives—a restructuring of incomes. If the objective is to alter the distribution of wages and salaries, expenditures should be directed toward this purpose. The easiest method for doing this is to establish a system of payments that rewards employers for altering their relative distribution of wages and salaries.

For example, a system of bonuses could be constructed where employers would be paid depending on the degree to which they raised the wages of their low income workers relative to the national average. If there were a desire not to have any worker earning less than 50 percent of the national average, and the average wage of $4 per hour was rising at 6 percent per year, employers would receive bonuses for raising the wages of employees earning less than $2 per hour faster than 6 percent per year. Since the bonus would not be large enough to cover the full cost of raising wages, employers would be left with the problem of the precise method of increasing the productivity of low wage workers. For some workers this might involve more training, for some workers this might involve a restructuring of jobs within a firm, and for some workers new employers might find it easiest to make use of their talents. In any case, the government would let the private economy determine the best technique for altering relative wages. It would merely stand ready to pay a bonus for any alterations that actually occurred.

Such a system has the advantage that the government pays only for the output it wants. If relative incomes change, it pays. If relative incomes do not change, it does not pay. It is not involved with paying for different inputs, such as training, that may or may not cause the desired results. The program is either successful or it has a zero cost. If it has a zero cost or a low cost (indicating little change) the initial bonus level is too small and must be increased to bring about the desired results. (This may very well happen, since only experimentation with different bonuses could determine the right bonus level.)

Any rapid improvement will also require some kind of quota system to place pressure on major organizations to bring their wage and salary structures into line with the desired national structure of incomes. To be effective, any quota should focus on the ultimate objective—a change in the distribution of income. Firms could be allowed to set their own time path of compliance as long as there was a final time deadline on complete compliance, but they would be fined for any deviation from their own path. For example, firms might be required to bring their wage and salary distribution into conformity with national objectives over a 10-year period, but allowed to set their own path subject to some minimum rate of progress (say 5 percent per year) toward the ultimate goal. The goal would be expressed in terms of the firm's income distribution. Thus if the aim were to aid minorities, the firm would be required to pay an appropriate fraction of the income in each quintile of its income distribution to minorities. . . .

An adequate package of government programs to alter the structure of incomes would include the following: (1) research and development expenditures directed toward finding techniques of production that used new skill mixes; (2) efforts to alter sociological judgments about "fair" wage differentials; (3) fiscal and monetary policies designed to create labor shortages; (4) public wage scales deliberately set to force the private sector of the economy to adjust to them; (5) a system of direct bribes to encourage compression of the private wage structure and to help pay for it; and (6) a set of flexible quotas. With such a package of public policies, the relative structure of earnings undoubtedly could be compressed.

While these programs would compress the wage structure, they would also have some adverse side effects. A program to compress the structure of incomes would probably make the inflation problem worse. Some of the new production techniques might be more expensive than the old, groups would fight to preserve historic wage differentials, labor shortages would lead to wage increases as firms bid against one another for labor, and a compression of the wage structure probably would come about by raising low wages rather than lowering high wages. Viewed in the context of income compression, inflation is not necessarily a negative factor. While inflation certainly creates horizontal inequities (two individuals with equal incomes before inflation may have unequal incomes after inflation), these do not seem to differ noticeably across different income classes. Horizontal inequities seem to be just as great among the rich as among the poor. Vertically, the combination of full employment and inflation is an equalizing agent. The poor catch up with the rich and the middle class. During periods of full employment and inflation, expanding job opportunities benefit the poor relatively more than the rich, and wage differentials tend to be compressed. While there are certainly poor people who are hurt by inflation, the poor, as a group, are helped by inflation. . . .

Most of the current government instruments for reducing inflation, such as creating recessions, limiting interest rates for small savers, and resisting cost-of-living escalators only serve to make the poor worse off. . . . The poor are asked to pay the price necessary to stop inflation for the rest of society. . . . Most policies to cause income equalization would create more inflation and the current set of policies for suppressing inflation create more income inequality.

[A] second income distribution goal is to alter the shape of minority income distributions so that they resemble that of the majority. To the extent that a poverty program is successful, the distributions will be equalized at the bottom (no one will be below the minimum allowable income) but they will not be equalized at the top. While training programs have a role to play, the basic problem is once again on the demand side of the market.

There are millions of Blacks, Spanish-speaking Americans, other minorities, and women who have all of the necessary qualifications to be promoted into better jobs than those they now hold. Yet they are not promoted. The problem is not solely one of increasing the supply of potentially qualified people but also of increasing the demand for minority laborers. . . .

CONCLUSIONS

If a restructuring of incomes is desired, it can be brought about. Substantial efforts, however, must be directed toward altering the demand for labor as opposed to altering the personal characteristics of individuals looking for work. Without such efforts on the demand side of the market most programs for altering personal characteristics will have little payoff. Such has been the case in the past and will be the case in the future.

It must be realized, however, that the current structure of market incomes is deeply embedded in the American economy. There are no easy solutions. Any set of programs that actually altered the structure of incomes would require enormous political pressure on its behalf. From the point of view of economics, tax-transfer policies are by far the easiest to implement; yet these are probably the most difficult to implement from a political viewpoint. Unfortunately, there simply are no governmental policies that will just slightly affect the economy yet cause large changes in the market distribution of earnings.

9. THE WELFARE CRISIS

MARTIN REIN

■ Although not planned as such, the principal American device for dealing with income inequality has become "welfare," or more particularly the program of Aid to Families with Dependent Children. As many writers have observed, this program was somewhat an afterthought to the Social Security Act of 1935. The notion was that as social insurance provisions of the act and general economic health provided the basic support that families needed, the AFDC program would wither away, becoming each year a smaller and smaller proportion of the total welfare bill. Charity in the form of public assistance was to be replaced by social insurance covering old age, unemployment, workmen's injury and illness, etc. In fact, it has been the other way around. From slightly more than half a million recipients in 1936, the AFDC caseload has risen to an estimate for 1973 of over 12.5 million persons and an estimated $7.8 billion in payments.

So the "residual" program has become a prime subject of policy analysis and public debate. Martin Rein's article reviews the development of the AFDC program, the various efforts to "reform" it, and the variety of psychological, sociological, and economic explanations that social scientists and others have advanced, particularly during the past decade, to explain the welfare problem. These explanations are more than academic exercises, since the diagnosis of welfare they embody becomes an important element in decisions about policy to deal more effectively with the problem of maintaining family incomes.

A useful review of the current status of the welfare program and income support programs generally can be found in the annual Brookings Institution's reviews of the federal budget; an example is Charles A. Schultze et al., *Setting National Priorities: The 1973 Budget* (Washington, D.C.: Brookings Institution, 1972). Administrative and political aspects of the welfare crisis are analyzed in Gilbert Steiner, *The State of Welfare* (Washington, D.C.: Brookings Institution, 1971). The Piven-Cloward theory to which

Rein refers in his article can be found in Frances F. Piven and Richard A. Cloward, *Regulating the Poor: The Functions of Public Welfare* (New York: Pantheon Books, 1971). A useful analysis of the variations in AFDC programs and the relationship among income maintenance, migration, and labor force participation can be found in the President's Commission on Income Maintenance Programs, *Technical Studies* (Washington, D.C.: Government Printing Office, 1969). An empirical analysis of the choices and tradeoffs between welfare and employment is found in Elizabeth F. Durbin, *Welfare, Income and Employment* (New York: Praeger, 1969). ■

THE AID TO DEPENDENT Children program was established under the Social Security Act of 1935. Since its inception it has undergone a major transformation in clientele, benefits, and size. The act established two major approaches to relieving economic want: contributory social insurance, in which entitlement to benefits was based on an earned right in that it related to past contributions; and public assistance, which was distributed only after a demonstrated test of need. Social insurance was initially extended only to the old and unemployed—the old through a nationally administered old-age insurance system, the unemployed through a federal system largely controlled by the states. Over the years insurance was extended to cover widows, dependent children, disabled, medical care expenses, and the maintenance of income during periods of illness (a program adopted in only four states). Public assistance was conceived of as a transitional program until the social insurance program matured in adequacy of benefits and extensiveness of coverage. In implementing federal aid to public assistance Congress included the categories of need already aided in some of the states, most specifically the aged, the blind, and dependent children. In establishing the grant maximum for which states could receive federal reimbursement no provision was made for mothers of dependent children. The House Ways and Means Committee set the figure as provided under the Veterans' Pension Act for children of servicemen killed in action, overlooking altogether that the widows of these servicemen received in addition a pension, while the mothers of the newly created ADC program would not. In its origins public assistance was conceived of as a transitional program whose benefits were limited to a narrow category of persons presumed to be out of the labor force. The Social Security Act assumed an orderly world divided between those who paid contributions and those who received gratuities; it was confident that in time the first program would displace the second.

This tidy conception of social security proved utterly inadequate. Public assistance was gradually extended to other groups, almost paralleling the development of social insurance. Thus in time the disabled, the medically indigent, parents of children who cared for dependent children, and those male adult family heads who had exhausted their unemployment insurance were entitled to benefits. (As coverage was extended the program changed its name from Aid to Dependent Children (ADC) to Aid to Families with Dependent Children (AFDC).) Today the largest category of assistance is the program for the medically indigent, known as medicaid, in which approximately 10 million persons receive aid at a total cost of over $5 billion. As public assistance was gradually extended to new categories of need, it became converted into a mass program. The proposed Family Assistance Plan would further extend coverage to those employed full time. While coverage under the program has broadened, the original philosophy, which held that public assistance should retain its transitional and residual character, has not been abandoned. Thus public policy is committed to reducing the number of persons who receive public assistance.

THE CHANGING CHARACTER OF AFDC

The clientele of the AFDC program has changed in at least three important respects. First, the causes of a child's dependency have altered dramatically. Nationally, fathers of 7 of every 10 children receiving ADC in 1940 were either dead or incapacitated; in only 3 cases out of 10 was the father absent from the home. In 1971 the father was absent from the home in 76 percent of the cases; in 14.1 percent he was dead or incapacitated. Of all families receiving AFDC in 1971, 28 percent were families in which the father was not married to the mother; 5 percent were families that the father had deserted. Separation with or without a court decree and divorce counted for an additional 30 percent. The changing composition of the AFDC program reflects in part the changes in the composition of poverty. Between 1960 and 1968 the percentage of poverty-level families headed by females had increased from 24 to 35 percent. There has also been a shift in the racial composition of the AFDC caseload since 1948 when 31 percent of recipients were non-White. However, during the decade of the great expansion in rolls the proportion of non-White AFDC recipients has remained unchanged. In 1961 and in 1971, 8 percent of the caseload was non-White.

In addition to changes in the family structure and the racial composition of the program, perhaps the most dramatic change is that welfare mothers are increasingly regarded as capable of being employed. The concept of employability is elusive. A recent national survey of 35 countries, undertaken by the Department of Health, Education and Welfare, defined employment ability with respect to the characteristics of the AFDC mother. Mothers who had completed 12 years of education or who had a record of previous employment in skilled blue-collar or white-collar jobs were defined as having high employability. Based on this definition, the survey found that potential employables among women receiving AFDC had risen from 25.3

percent in 1961 to 44.5 percent in 1968. Moreover, 80 percent of those so classified as high employables also expressed a desire to work if they could find a steady job.

Not only are more AFDC mothers regarded as employable but also, in 1971, 28 percent were in the labor force or in training while they received AFDC. Of these, 9 percent were in full-time employment, 6 percent were in part-time employment, 5.7 percent were looking for work, and 6.8 percent were enrolled or awaiting enrollment in training programs. Parents with older children and more education were also more likely to work.

SOURCES AND LEVELS OF INCOME

In addition to welfare the AFDC mother receives income from a variety of sources, such as social security, child support, and her own earnings. Between 1961 and 1967 income from all other sources increased from 19 to 35 percent. While welfare payments clearly remain the primary source of family income, they are by no means the exclusive source. For a growing proportion of families welfare serves as a supplement to the full-time earnings.

Not only have the sources of income become more varied but the average monthly cash payment also has increased substantially. Between 1963 and 1971 the average weekly AFDC payment increased by 67 percent, while the average spendable earnings of all private employees increased by only 42 percent.

These national averages mask the substantial rise in cash payments that has taken place in some selected states. If high benefit and low benefit states are divided, we find that in the high benefit states benefits have increased more rapidly than average earnings and prices. When the values of food stamps and medical benefits also are taken into account, the increase is, of course, even more significant. As the value of benefits has increased and the sources of income for the AFDC recipient have become more varied

in the absence of national standards, the traditional regional inequities have grown, and inequities between the fully employed poor and the AFDC recipient also have become more visible. The growth of this inequity is a compelling rationale for the creation of a federal program to supplement the wages of the working poor.

THE RISE OF WELFARE IN THE UNITED STATES

The normative problem is whether to contain the precipitous rise in the public assistance program known as Aid to Families with Dependent Children (AFDC). Between 1954 and 1967 the AFDC caseload grew at an annual rate of about 7 percent; then between 1967 and 1971 the rate of growth accelerated to about 18 percent per annum. During this time AFDC grew from a third of the total public assistance program to well over two-thirds, and as the numbers in the program have increased at an accelerated rate, the incidence of family dependency also has grown dramatically. In 1955, 3 percent of all families had received aid; in 1969 the proportions jumped to 6 percent of the child population.

HEW INTERPRETS THE RISING ROLLS

In its budgetary justification of the welfare program before the House Committee on Appropriations, the Department of Health, Education and Welfare offered the following interpretation of the reason for the absolute and relative rise of the AFDC program. For clarity I have elaborated the details somewhat.

1. The increase in broken families and the child population. Between 1940 and 1968 the illegitimacy rate more than tripled from 7 to 24 illegitimate births per 1,000 women aged 15 to 44, and the proportion of all births that were illegitimate rose from 1 to 25 to 1 to 10. Overall, one out of every four

women ever married was not living with a husband.

2. Increased awareness of the availability of public assistance, in part related to the efforts of community action, welfare rights, and civil rights groups.

3. The indirect case-finding effects of the medicaid program, which in some states, such as New York, were advertised in order to ensure that those entitled received benefits. Routine inquiries for the medicaid program also may have resulted in the discovery of applicants who were also eligible for assistance payments.

4. Changes in eligibility requirements authorized by federal law. In 1969, for example, 28 states had adopted a legislative ammendment that permits earnings of up to $50 per child or $150 per family to be disregarded in determining eligibility. Another provision adopted in 43 states permits children to receive assistance after 18 if attending school. Children and parents who were dependent because of the unemployment of the employable parent were included in a new program developed in 1961. A foster care component also was added. These various extensions of coverage added over 800,000 persons to the AFDC rolls by 1970. In addition, the Supreme Court struck down the more important provisions that prevented many persons from receiving AFDC. In 1968 the court declared unconstitutional the man-in-the-house rule that held that a man living in an AFDC home was responsible for the children's support; the decision precluded cutting off aid because the mother cohabited with a man not obligated by law to support the children. In 1969 the court invalidated the residency requirements for public assistance.

5. The continuing difficulties of unskilled and untrained persons in obtaining employment and earnings adequate to sustain their families. Race compounds the problem, since non--White unemployment rates, particularly among young people, are two to three times those of Whites. HEW predicted that in the future rates would continue to rise, because when all of these factors are taken into account only a third of all poor children are receiving AFDC benefits.

In its explanation to Congress HEW focused on the variety and complexity of the forces that were increasing AFDC caseloads —a laundry list of items. However, this had a focus. In particular they called attention to demographic and economic influences, to increased access, to changes in laws and regulations, and to court interpretations of both.

The argument implicit in the HEW presentation is that the rise in welfare is due to inconsistency in government policy in that Congress and the courts are acting to expand the program, while at the same time Congress is making somewhat weaker efforts to contain its growth. Also, the program is a victim of broad social and economic changes in the society. These forces have created a rise in the number of single-parent families.

Neglected in this interpretation is the argument about a change in local administrative practice toward greater leniency in qualifying applicants. Nationally the proportions of applications accepted declined from 66 percent in 1948 to 54 percent in 1953, showing only a modest change over the decade. However, by 1970 the percent of applications received and approved increased sharply to 81 percent. In a study of 11 major cities presented in a special report to the House Ways and Means Committee evidence showed that staff hiring procedures significantly affected the size of the caseload. There was a strong positive association between the proportion of the cities' poor population in receipt of AFDC and the rate of casework turnover, the relative youth of caseworkers, and an inverse correlation with caseworkers' professional orientation. It is the professional caseworkers, considering the needs of both the applicant and the agency, who serve as effective rationers of welfare benefits. The program not only was easier to get into but also increasingly more attractive. (For evidence see the discussion later in this chapter.)

In short, what HEW left out of its seemingly comprehensive list was the view that welfare had become a system that was much easier to get into and also more desirable in its own right, since the value of benefits increased more rapidly than prices and wages. How can we account for these omissions? Are they best understood in technical, political, or moral terms?

To the extent that the analysis made use of social scientific tools of inquiry we might say that it encountered conceptual difficulties; its model of explanation was underspecified. That is to say, it omitted important variables in its explanation. The selection of explanatory variables is related to a theory about what caused the rise, and the theory is faulty because it is incomplete. Alternatively, the theory may be inadequate, but no measures of the phenomena are available, and so these important variables are omitted for practical reasons.

It might as well be argued that the difficulty was political rather than conceptual or technical in that those who wrote the report were eager to protect the bureaucracy that employed them, and the list of explanations developed suggests that such a motive is plausible. Of course, to use the term *motive* may be misleading because it implies that a conscious process is at play. The authors may, however, be unaware that their interpretation was inspired by any motive other than understanding the events they tried to explain. All attempts to infer intent from behavior encounter this difficulty, but this doesn't inhibit the curious observer from conjecture.

Finally, the omissions may be related to a matter of taste or style. Some people are attracted to institutional rather than personal explanations, others to national rather than local explanators. Taste is in turn related to values, belief, and ideology, for without them one does not know how to select from an infinite number of possible alternatives. But is all this beside the point because the empirical validation of a theory is independent of the values that inspired it? Impartial evidence can in principle refute the validity of passionately held views. But can they? While a good deal of social reality is knowable through social scientific techniques, not everything is. We need therefore to distinguish between what is unknown and unknowable. This distinction may be useful to keep in mind, however. Even that which in principle is knowable may for practical reasons remain unknown, at least in the short run.

First, it is very difficult to gather empirical evidence about the most interesting policy questions. For example, while in principle it is possible to document the extent of welfare abuse, its relationship to administrative laxity, and the rising case rolls, in practice such a study might so intrude into the legally protected right to privacy that we may judge that given these constraints a definitive answer may be unknowable. In a different political context a more adequate answer may be forthcoming; but now, in this new environment, their scientific neutrality will be suspect.

Second, it is very difficult in practice to establish casual relationships. Is the rise in single-parent families "caused" by the availability of AFDC benefits or is the program better understood as a response to change in population at risk, caused by other factors. Interpretations about the underlying processes depend on a theory about the line of causality. It is extremely difcult to disentangle cause and effect. In principle it should be possible, through such techniques as regression analysis by the use of a comprehensive model, to explain and quantify the relative importance of each explanation in accounting for the welfare rise. But the weighing of explanatory factors is bedeviled with its own technical problems. For example: results will vary depending on the order in which the variables are introduced into the analysis; variables are often highly related to one another so that it is not possible to state which factors are most important (that is the problem of colinearity); and many regression equations account for only a small proportion of the variations in the dependent variable. Thus technically dispassionate studies either produce indifferent results or themselves lead to technical controversies. These may be settled in time with better data, for they are intrinsically knowable, but in the short run they contribute little to resolving the immediate policy debate.

I want to isolate three major competing interpretations of the rise in welfare and comment on their policy implications. I have selected these three views not for their scientific respectability but for their political relevance to the debate about how or whether the rise in the rolls should be halted. Each theory identifies a primary dimension, and each marshals selected evidence to support its view. It is the outlook—i.e., the line of explanation—that shapes the policy analysis and provides a graceful continuity between the facts cited and the course of action recommended.

THE WEAKENING OF TRADITIONAL FAMILY TIES

Some years ago Daniel P. Moynihan observed that the AFDC rates were rising while unemployment rates were declining. Before 1962 the increase in AFDC closely paralleled increases in unemployment levels as economic factors contributed to family disorganization. As in Sweden, the processes that linked the aggregate level of unemployment with changes in the number of welfare cases were not well understood. One interpretation held that men who were unable to secure jobs and had exhausted their unemployment insurance left their families, confident that their economic position would not suffer further as a result of their departure because the family would secure new sources of entitlement to income from welfare. Indeed, since these AFDC benefits were not available if the husband remained at home, maintaining family solidarity threatened economic viability. However, family pathology and especially the increased disorganization of the Black family in the middle and late 1960s came to displace economic factors as primary causal agents in the rise as unemployment declined but AFDC rolls advanced unrelentingly. The proportion of families who were abandoned and, to a lesser extent, the increase in unmarried mothers bearing illegitimate children were good indexes of family pathology.

Why should family disorganization increase during periods of economic growth and declining rates of unemployment? The availability of welfare is assumed to play an important contributing role in this problem as the response itself acts to generate and intensify the problem of disorganization. But by what specific processes does welfare serve as a causal agent to family disorganization? It is generally conceded that a full understanding of that process is lacking. Several interpretations have emerged, though, each supported by some fragmentary evidence.

First is the view that there is a direct link between welfare entitlement and family structure. Thus the AFDC breadwinner(s), acting like economic man, tries to alter the family structure to maximize its economic position. Because the absence of the father is a precondition for the receipt of benefits, families reconstitute themselves in order to become eligible for these benefits. But in New York City where the absence of the father is no longer a requirement for the receipt of benefits, families still continue to break up. In 1961 there were 12,000 deserted families on welfare in New York City; by 1968, with a stagnant population and a vigorous economy, the number of desertions rose 6-fold to 80,000 families. Moreover, illegitimacy during the same period doubled from 20,000 to 46,000 families. To explain why families continue to break up when no readily apparent external force is propelling them in this direction, a more psychological interpretation is offered. Welfare grants go to the mother, and the father comes to play only a marginal economic role within the family since he is robbed of his function as a breadwinner. Bereft of his central role, the father abandons his family. This line of reasoning draws on research studies undertaken during the great American Depression, when the role crisis experienced by male breadwinners during a period of very high unemployment was explored in some depth.

Those who distrust social psychological interpretations seek to revive an economic analysis of the increase of family abandonment. They argue that breakup of families is only a pretense to enable the family to enjoy both welfare benefits and earnings from employment. Moreover, little anxiety and guilt is associated with this type of fraud when it is interpreted as a form of repatriation for injustices done to the Black community. This interpretation is, of course, supported by a widely shared folk culture that profoundly believes that welfare and fraud are linked more intimately than welfare and distress.

Finally, there are those who believe that welfare expands the range of choices available to low income wives, for it provides an income source other than earnings. This alternative to earnings is even more attractive when it is administered with dignity, and the benefit levels do not diverge sharply from the prevailing community wage structure. Welfare maintains economic viability without threatening personal identity and freedom. This expands the choices a woman enjoys. She may choose to stay with a man who earns very little and remain on welfare, or she may continue on welfare and seek new social ties that might be more personally satisfying. Given such a choice, on balance more women choose to leave their husbands. Thus, according to this interpretation, rather than the man's abandoning the woman in an effort to restore his dignity when he is robbed of an economic role in the family unit, it is the woman who forsakes the man as her freedom of choice expands.

POLICY IMPLICATIONS

Those who focus on family disorganization as a primary causal factor in the rise of AFDC call attention to the ancient conflict between adequacy and social integration. Long ago the Charity Organization Society believed that a beneficent and compassionate society that administered the dole loosely and without systematic method encouraged people to exploit the welfare system. Uncoordinated charities enabled families to receive benefits from several sources, thus making welfare competitive to work. As more and more individuals exploited the inadequacies of the administration of welfare (then called the Poor Law), the economic viability of the society was threatened as people chose the dole over work. Modern proponents of this view have a very similar line of argument, though they no longer attribute the rise to uncoordinated charities so much as to either administrative laxity or, more generously, a liberal philosophy of entitlement combined with adequate benefit levels. But they also argue that with 15 percent of the population of New York City in receipt of benefits the economic stability of the city is threatened by the increase in welfare roles. The rise in AFDC exposes this difficult dilemma. Nathan Glazer summarizes with clarity and force this point of view.

The dilemma of income maintenance is that, on the one hand, it permits the poor to live better and with greater dignity. But on the other, it also permits them to live with less incentive to work, and with less incentive to form those close units of self-support—family in the first case, but also larger units—that have in the past formed the fabric of society. . . . But the history of our efforts to expend policies of income support suggest that inevitably, as we do the first, we also contribute to the second.

Clearly, given the cruel choice that must be made, Glazer favors strengthening the traditional constraints on which a civil society must rest. Hence he is drawn to the position that the incentives to work must be strengthened. In the conflict between dignity and incentive, while no clear and unequivical choice can ever be made, dignity must always be preserved at the cost of incentive, or the integrity of the whole system will be threatened.

WELFARE AND THE
MALDISTRIBUTION OF INCOME

This position holds that the rise in the AFDC benefit levels and the lagging of wage levels for certain groups have been major contributing factors in the rise in AFDC. In some high benefit states, benefit levels on AFDC have exceeded the poverty line. Between 1963 and 1971 the average AFDC payment rose by 67 percent, while the average spendable earnings of all private employees increased by only 42 percent. This contrasts with the earlier pattern. In 1962 average AFDC payments and spendable average weekly earnings of all private employees rose by about two-thirds. One explanation of the willingness of states to spend more money on benefit levels is cited by Irene Lurie, who explains that the 1965 change in the formula for federal matching of state benefit costs gave states 25 percent more funds. Substantial increases in the value of food stamps and medicare benefits for AFDC clients also helped make the program even more attractive.

Nationally, benefit levels on AFDC were rising more rapidly than price and wage levels, thus increasing the real benefits of AFDC and making them competitive with earning levels. Earnings of minority groups and unskilled groups in particular have failed to keep pace with this rise in benefit levels, and these are the groups most likely to seek out welfare. Bernstein estimates that the family income of Blacks in New York City rose by 7.6 percent between 1959 and 1968, whereas White income rose by 15.6 percent. Drawing on such data, Gordon tried to relate the distribution of income in New York City to the rise in welfare benefits. He estimated that the number of eligibles doubled between 1964 and 1968 and increased by yet another 22 percent between January and November 1968. But despite this tripling of caseloads the proportion of eligibles accepted for AFDC has actually declined, standing at only about half of the pool of eligibles. Thus even a liberal administration failed to make an impact on the problem of the underutilization of welfare.

The rise in welfare then is accounted for not so much by changes in administrative practices as by the increase in the pool of eligible persons brought about by higher benefit levels. In August 1968 AFDC benefit levels were increased by an average of 7 percent, an amount equal to about $250 per year for a family of 4 persons. So close is the wage and benefit system that even this modest increase produced stunning results.

"The slight dollar increase immediately causes an increase of 300,000 in the number of eligibles . . . and after the August increase, close to half of the city's minority population lived in families that were eligible to receive welfare payments."

Similar conclusions were reached from a study of supplementary benefits in Britain. Atkinson argued that despite the vigorous efforts to recruit, through a national take-up campaign, those who are eligible for supplementary benefits, the rise in numbers of persons who receive benefits is better accounted for by changes in the numbers of persons eligible rather than by increased effectiveness in reaching the eligible who failed to utilize the benefits to which they were entitled. In short, then, the population on welfare rises when benefits increase, because the pool of potentially eligible persons is thereby expanded. In periods when benefits rise more rapidly than wages and prices, or when the wage levels of minority and low income groups fail to keep pace with increasing benefit levels, this increase can be very substantial.

POLICY INTERPRETATION

This interpretation calls attention to the importance of integrating social and economic policies. This rather general and vague conclusion does not, of course, suggest a specific direction that a policy must take, but it points to a dilemma somewhat different from that Glazer identified.

If benefit levels increase at the same rate that average wages increase, and if low wages increase at a rate slower than that of average wages, then welfare benefits and low wages will continue to overlap. It follows that each increase in benefit levels will substantially broaden the size of the population eligible for welfare. Should welfare recipients and those outside the productive community be permitted to share fully in the life of that community as consumers? An affirmative answer conflicts with more traditional views that employment through the pursuit of a trade or profession is the only wholly acceptable means of acquiring an income, and that those who do not, or cannot, maintain themselves in this way should at all times be subject to some economic incentive to do so. According to this latter view, benefit levels should in principle lag behind wage levels. But if we believe that the poor should participate as consumers in the society, then benefit levels and wage levels should bear a closer relationship to each other, even if the net effect of such a policy is to increase the number of persons who receive welfare payments. At the same time, the real wages and income of minority groups and low wage groups should be narrowed relative to the average earning, either by increasing their productive capacities through training or by redistributing resources independent of the economic contribution they make. When these approaches are combined, the lower end of the income distribution scale is narrowed.

WELFARE AND CIVIL DISORDER

Frances Fox Piven and Richard Cloward recently developed an elaborate thesis that tries to link together the increase in welfare and the increase in civil disorder. They argue that relief expands to cope with disorder and contracts when stability is restored. A market system is characteristically plagued by periods of depression or stages of modernization, and the net effect of both of these processes is to displace large numbers of individuals from employment. Dependency in the United States in recent years is to a substantial degree a reflection of what Tobin called the final and painful phase of the liquidation of the 19th-century agricultural system in the South. When less work is available the daily routine and discipline of employment no longer serve to regulate the behavior of the heads of households. As the work role is weakened other integrative roles such as those that derive from meeting family obligations are also weakened. The net effect of these processes is that the allegiances that tie the

worker to society become less effective. When stability is threatened, civil disorder erupts. How does society cope with these disorders? Relief expands to cope with them. In part, welfare serves as a device for quieting the discontent of those whose way of life is threatened by economic change. But it also serves as a mode of control similar to that routinized work performs. Even economically useless work is socially useful in this sense. As a result, work behavior is a condition in getting welfare.

But welfare did not rise during the 1950s when planter and tenant relationships were disrupted and the economic displacement of the Black was most in evidence. There was a time lag. Blacks migrated to cities and, together with the White move to the suburbs, helped alter the character of American cities. At about the same time structural changes in the labor market created job scarcity in the low wage sector; as a result, Black unemployment levels rose. To maintain a subsistence level everyone in the family had to work, a process that disrupted the family and contributed to its disorganization. New solutions were sought. At first it was hoped that the needs of the displaced could be accommodated by the reform of other systems of intervention. Programs such as delinquency prevention, community mental health, community action, and model cities developed as ways to cool the ghetto out.

All these programs had in common an effort to direct resources at the neighborhood level, bypassing state government and on occasion city government as well. These federal programs were inspired by a concern for votes and to quell disorder. But as limits of these programs emerged and discontent with them grew, there were increased efforts to turn in a new direction in order to improve the rising militant demands of Blacks. The logical response was to provide plentiful jobs at adequate wage levels, but an open employment policy challenged the entrenched interest groups in both labor and management. After 1964 the rising volatility of the Black community, which took the form of long, hot summers, and the rising importance of the Black vote in large cities made it increasingly imperative that some effective public response would be forthcoming. This task was left to public welfare, and once again welfare was called on to perform its historic tranquilizing role when even civil disorder rose and seemed to threaten the stability of society. At about the same time that welfare administration became more responsive to the economic needs of Blacks, those who worked in the manpower and community action programs came to realize that they could not reach their primary objective through these programs, and so they began to organize the poor to take advantage of the benefits they were entitled to. They helped create the Welfare Rights Organization, which aided those on welfare to secure a wide range of services and benefits. These forces combined to swell the welfare roles.

As in the other interpretations, we find a strong story line that includes two views about the rise in welfare. On the one hand welfare recipients were subject to technological changes and economic fluctuations; on the other hand they were influenced by national and urban managers who by responding to threats to their position altered benefit levels, influenced the exercise of professional discretion, and shaped the rules of eligibility. Elites eased the granting of relief as a way of quieting turbulence in the city. Since welfare also served as a mechanism of control, emphasis was placed on getting the welfare mother to work, and work rules became required as a condition for getting relief. Welfare thus served as a means for routinizing, integrating and controlling the behavior of those whose ties to society had been weakened. In this sense welfare became a substitute for the role of the family and the role of employment as mechanisms of social integration. But when stability is restored welfare no longer needs to serve this purpose. As the elites become less concerned with unrest and inequalities, the rolls begin to drop and the anomaly of dependency marching hand in hand with prosperity passes away.

POLICY IMPLICATIONS

I have perhaps taken some liberties with the Piven and Cloward interpretation of the forces behind the welfare rise, but I tried as well to be faithful to the main argument. The thesis is provocative and suggestive. It anticipates a decline in welfare rolls at a time when public concern is riveted on their rise. Hence liberals are eager to prevent an erosion of the gains that were won in the preceding era. Central to this argument is that local welfare administrators responded to the civil disorder by becoming more liberal in the standards of eligibility used, the adequacy of welfare benefits, and the frequency with which currently active cases were reviewed and closed. These changes allowed a larger proportion of persons who applied to be accepted; their average length of stay on welfare increased; and the proportion of cases closed for reasons of noncompliance declined. In time as it became known that the welfare system was "easy to get into" the number of applications also increased. A more responsive administration reached out to those entitled to benefits and thus reduced the problem of underutilization. (This is an interpretation somewhat different from that developed by Gordon, who argued that despite administrative liberality, takeup rate among the eligible population did not increase.)

As we enter a period of stability, when the turbulence of the cities cools and elites feel they can control unrest, we can anticipate new policies aimed at tightening administration. Welfare rolls then will begin to contract. The liberal will try to find ways to consolidate the gains won during the liberal era. To determine how this might be done will require much ingenuity. Perhaps administration can be made to slow down the rate of accommodation to the changed political climate. Of course, conservatives will be eager to exploit it and to accelerate the introduction of a more restrictive administration. The common themes in this analysis concern the administrative responsiveness of the guardians of the welfare bureaucracy to external pressure exercised by both elites and welfare clients.

CURRENT STRATEGIES TO REDUCE WELFARE ROLES

Three main strategies have been used to limit welfare: eligibility as deterrence, social service as rehabilitation and opportunity, and training and income incentives as preparation for work. Eligibility restriction and social services have been the traditional ways in which welfare rolls were contained. The idea that a positive income strategy could provide an economic incentive to enter or return to work is relatively new. All of these strategies proved abortive in stemming the rise in the welfare caseloads during the late 1960s. Policy for the 1970s seems committed to making the administrative solution work by relying on more stringent eligibility review, lower benefit levels, and work requirements. Each strategy is reviewed.

ELIGIBILITY RESTRICTIONS

Perhaps the earliest explicit strategy for containing assistance through eligibility restrictions was embodied in the principles of the New Poor Law of 1834 and was known as the doctrine of less eligibility. This doctrine asserted that as a matter of principle the situation of a person in receipt of relief "shall not be made really or apparently eligible as the situation of the independent laborers of the class." At one time this doctrine was harshly interpreted. It meant loss of personal freedom when aid was given only to those who accepted the workhouse test, loss of the franchise when recipients were denied the right to vote, and finally loss of personal dignity when benefits were meager in amount and harshly administered. Over time the principles of 1834 have been substantially liberalized, and the ideals of the right to live have been affirmed. Nevertheless, a modern version of less eligibility persists. It finds expression not only with respect to the level of benefits but also in the way people are treated in local welfare departments and in their own homes.

The reliance on eligibility restrictions to limit the numbers in receipt of welfare appears to follow a cyclical pattern. During the prosperous period from World War II to 1950 welfare rolls increased sharply from 871,802 to 2,235,477. The percentage of non-Whites also increased from 21 percent in 1942 to 31 percent in 1948. "The response of many states to political pressures, financial strain and public indignation was to impose more stringent eligibility requirements and, in a few instances, to reduce the size of the grant. There was a proliferation of eligibility requirements." And the allegations of fraud and mismanagement created natural pressure for the review of eligibility procedures.

While eligibility rules were clearly used to deny aid, it was not until the 1960s that employability rules in Newburgh, New York, and suitable home rules in Louisiana emerged as a public debate. National attention was riveted on these issues. The federal administrators challenged the principle of less eligibility. They announced that Louisiana would not qualify for federal funds if they denied ADC to a child on the grounds of an unsuitable home as long as the child remained in the home. Parental fitness and suitable home rules were discouraged by federal government policy because they seemed to contribute to the practice of racial discrimination and because they encouraged intrastate variation in eligibility requirements and thus conflicted with the principle of uniformity of state practice. The Supreme Court decision reaffirmed and extended all federal action. The court declared that states could not deny welfare benefits to mothers because an able-bodied man lived in the house. They rejected the man-in-the-house rule. Residency requirements as a condition for the receipt of benefits were also declared unconstitutional by the Supreme Court on the ground that they denied equal protection under the law. Decreased reliance was placed on eligibility restrictiveness as a strategy for reducing caseloads, in contrast to the 1935 congressional action that affirmed the principle that states could consider "moral" qualifications as a condition for granting aid.

But if there is a cyclical reliance on eligibility restriction as a means of constraining the numbers of recipients, then we can antici- pate a return to this strategy in the future. There is clear evidence that Congress has moved in this direction. In November 1970 the Senate Finance Committee voted without a quorum to restore to states the right to impose one-year residency requirements and to enact man-in-the-house rules. The use of eligibility requirements as a condition for the receipt of aid was established in the 1967 amendments to the Social Security Act and reaffirmed in the Family Assistance Plan. The Talmadge amendments of 1972 require that all employable AFDC recipients be referred to state employment agencies for work. Some states have also required re- cipients to pick up their checks at the em- ployment service.

Rules of eligibility are a device for making receipt of public assistance more difficult or easier to secure. Philosophically a humane society rejects eligibility restrictiveness as its primary strategy for decreasing caseload rolls. Instead, other approaches are sought.

SERVICES AS A STRATEGY FOR REDUCING THE CASELOAD

The idea that casework and other social services could play a major role in the preven- tion and rehabilitation of economic depend- ency is the critical assumption on which a service strategy is based. This assumption has ancient roots in the history of the Poor Law. It is based on the commonsense assumption that the resourceful use of personal influence can change character and thereby rescue individuals from dependency.

Not long after the Social Security Act of 1935 was passed, there began a sustained attempt to intrude services within the public assistance program. Most of the early efforts proved abortive. However, in 1956 during the Eisenhower administration an important shift of purpose was introduced. The original purpose of the public assistance program in the Social Security Act was limited to helping states by providing financial aid. This aim was broadened to include three other purposes —promoting self-care and self-support and

strengthening family life. With the social se- curity amendments of 1962 the servcie strate- gy was attempted on a large scale.

What specifically was to be done to reduce dependence? Essentially the strategy rested on four specific approaches. (1) Caseworkers need to have more time to deal with their clients; therefore, smaller caseloads com- bined with more professional supervision was crucial. A worker should carry no more than 60 cases, and no supervisor should have more than 5 workers. Time to help was a precondition for the rendering of more ef- fective services. (2) Caseloads should be classified with respect to client problems and, where possible, appraised on likelihood that a client could be helped with his problem. The legislation required states to conduct a social survey and plan for services for all families with children. (3) *Direct* services should be rendered by the caseworker in the form of counseling, guidance, or referral for other services. This is the basic caseworker method. (4) Direct service was to be reinforced by *enabling* services, which called for consulta- tion on legal, social, educational, medical, and other problems and by *complimentary* services, such as homemaker and day care. Because social services were defined as all activities initiated on behalf of the reduction of clients' problems, demonstration projects and community planning as well as direct, enabling, and complimentary services also were included as relevant aspects of this strategy.

Five years after implementation of the serv- ice amendments the singlemost accurate con- clusion to be reached was that there was no possible way of discerning what services were rendered and how effective they were. By 1967 it was estimated that the annual costs of these services in AFDC had reached $228 million. Welfare workers had also sub- stantially increased from about 41,000 in 1960 to 141,000 in 1967. A federal statisti- cal report on social services could list the areas in which services were rendered (health care, family functioning, protection of chil- dren, self-support and others) and the propor- tion of cases classified as having received services in these areas. However, "the meaning of the terms is nowhere specified and the activities they are supposed to reflect are by no means clear, but . . . probably reflect the case workers' checking off of what are essentially subject areas. There is, of course, no way to explore whether anything was accomplished."

While it is not possible to say what, if anything, happened or how effective were these events or nonevents, this does not mean that nothing was learned. Experience from administrative reviews by federal officials showed that an elaborate process of case classification, which was in principle so essential to the proper diagnosis of need, to the intelligent referrals, to an efficient allocation of personnel, and to responsible accounting of effort, was self-defeating. In short, the effort to create a system of accountability produced a sea of paperwork that threatened to deluge the entire operation and in the end may have perversely reduced the time and energy that workers could exert in the rendering of services. All this made the argument for the simplification of eligibility procedures seem very compelling.

WORK, TRAINING AND ECONOMIC INCENTIVES

The presumption that AFDC recipients were unemployable and outside the work force became untenable in 1961 when the federal government extended coverage to families headed by an unemployed male parent (AFDC-UP). The need for the new law was clear, since the original Social Security Act denied assistance to families headed by an able-bodied male. The presence of employable parents on relief prompted Congress in 1962 to amend the Social Security Act to subsidize employment programs for relief recipients; until 1962 all AFDC recipients were presumed to be outside the work force, and public assistance funds could not be used to provide work. States were encouraged to adopt Community Work and Training (CW&T) programs designed to offer work relief rather than cash payments, and hopefully also to help AFDC-UP recipients

achieve economic independence. By their nature such work-relief projects serve many aims. They can embody the principle of less eligibility, for by setting conditions on the receipt of the cash grant they may deter requests for aid. They can be viewed as "social services," providing work discipline and nourishing work habits; and they can provide a base for training in the acquisition of new skills as a form of on-the-job training.

By 1967 the House Ways and Means Committee was profoundly concerned about the rising AFDC rolls, which it found had at that time doubled in the last decade. The Committee sought "a new direction for AFDC legislation." Its main element was the Work Incentive Program, whose provisions made work training mandatory for individuals. The Work Incentive provisions sought to strengthen training, redefine the nature of rehabilitative and supportive services, and place much greater emphasis on economic incentives. Moreover, the WIN program consolidated its target population by aiming only at public assistance recipients. But the results are discouraging. Of the 200,000 persons who left the program through September 1971, only 22 percent had completed training and remained employed during the 3- to 6-month follow-up period. Median hourly earnings for females who graduated WIN were below $2 per hour. As a result WIN earnings were seldom sufficient to enable a graduate of the program to leave welfare altogether. WIN encouraged combining work and welfare.

There is general agreement that only a minority of welfare recipients ever will be able to get off relief through employment. Only 40,000 left welfare after completing training. For a 4-person, female-headed family, hourly earnings of $2.25 or more on a full-time basis would be needed to remove recipients from AFDC rolls in 30 states. In only 9 states could the family head earn less than $2 per hour and become completely self-supporting. In New Jersey hourly earnings of $3.18 are required to remove a family of 4 from relief, and this amount was exceeded by only 2 other states. The anticipation that many will earn their way off relief is overly optimistic. Leonard Hausman, for example, has estimated that in the mid-sixties no more than one-third of AFDC mothers and two-thirds of AFDC-UP fathers could have earned as much as they received from welfare.

CONCLUSION

The strategy of training, service, and incentives devised during the decade of the 1960s to reduce the numbers on welfare has been vigorously dynamic. The concept of services has changed from professional consulting to concrete support (such as day care). There was also a shift in emphasis from make work to manpower training, and cash supplements to encourage participation in training and income disregards to encourage participation in work were increasingly important. But despite its flexibility the strategy was weak in implementation and flawed in conception.

It appears then, that a viable welfare reform to reduce the size of the welfare rolls must be integrated with economic policies that are directed at higher levels of employment and higher wage levels and a broader social policy that takes into account the pattern.

10. THE GUARANTEED INCOME

JAMES TOBIN

Reprinted from Agenda for the Nation, *(ed.) Kermit Gordon (Washington, D.C.: Brookings Institution, 1968). Copyright © 1968 by the Brookings Institution, Washington, D.C. James Tobin is Sterling Professor of Economics at Yale University. He was a member of the Council of Economic Advisors under President Kennedy. He has written extensively on international economic issues and has been influential in the discussion of the economics of poverty and race. He was president of the American Economic Association in 1971.*

■ As frustration over the welfare crisis in the 1960s grew both in Congress and within the executive branch of government, the idea of a guaranteed income attracted more and more attention. At first nothing could seem so "un-American" as to guarantee every individual a certain minimal level of living. Yet if one looks at the full implications of the kind of welfare state that has, in fact, developed in the United States and is accepted by almost all politicians regardless of party, it becomes clear that a great deal of guaranteeing of welfare is going on already. Indeed, one of the first advocates of a guaranteed income, the conservative economist Milton Friedman, sought to replace various antipoverty efforts with a single income grant phrased as a "negative income tax," as much to eliminate waste and lessen bureaucratic domination as for purely humanitarian reasons.

Rapid acceptance of the idea of a guaranteed income—from the initial responses among intellectuals in the early 1960s to Richard Nixon's proposal of a "Family Assistance Plan" in 1969—is testimony, among other things, to the effectiveness of a small group of economists and social policy experts. From bases of operation in the Office of Economic Opportunity and the Department of Health, Education and Welfare, they managed to work out specific negative income tax proposals and reasonably clear specifications of administrative mechanisms and costs. Without the advent of large-scale computer processing of socioeconomic data it would have been difficult to develop the specifics of these plans in order to demonstrate their feasibility.

Planning for a negative income tax as a replacement for welfare was also the occasion for fielding the largest controlled social experiment to date. Because many analysts were deeply concerned about the effects of a guaranteed annual income on incentives to work, an experiment organized and controlled by a group of economists and funded by the Office of Economic Opportunity was run in several cities to test the extent to which negative income tax payments might result in a family reducing its own employment level. Families were recruited for the experiment and randomly assigned to various negative income tax treatments or to a control group that received no payments. Early analysis of the results of this experiment suggests no adverse effects on incentives from income maintenance payments. These findings are very encouraging to the proposal's advocates.

President Nixon's original proposal for his Family Assistance Plan (FAP) would have established a guaranteed minimum of $1,600 for a family of four. FAP's advocates proposed that Congress should increase this minimum to $2,400 or more per year in the course of its passage. For a variety of political and technical reasons, however, the Family Assistance Plan still had not passed the Congress three years after its introduction. It is apparently quite difficult to integrate a new system of benefits into the existing patchwork of social welfare of various kinds—for housing, medical care, day care, and the like. By this time a new presidential campaign had rolled around, and the idea was sufficiently established—at least among liberals—for Senator George McGovern to propose a new form of guaranteed income (a credit income tax) at a higher benefit level and integrated into a reformed income tax system.

James Tobin's article here, along with his earlier writings, has proved among the most influential in establishing the idea of a guaranteed annual income as a desirable substitute for AFDC and other income maintenance programs. In this article Tobin reviews the rationale for income redistribution as an antipoverty strategy and then compares a negative income tax, a credit income tax, and children's and adults' allowances as alternative redistribution mechanisms. Tinkering with the distribution of income is a complex matter that requires considerable care and technical acumen if consequences are to be fully anticipated. Tobin suggests something of that complexity as he keeps our attention on the fundamental issues.

A convenient collection of articles dealing with guaranteed income proposals is found in ed., Theodore R. Marmor, *Poverty Policy* (Chicago: Aldine, 1971). Marmor's conceptual framework for comparing income maintenance alternatives is useful for those interested in understanding the significant ways in which income proposals vary. A fascinating insider's account of the development of the Nixon Family Assistance Plan is found in Daniel P. Moynihan, *The Politics of a Guaranteed Income: The Nixon Administration and the Family Assistance Plan* (New York, Random House, 1973). One of the earliest guaranteed income proposals not related to family or children's allowances is found in Lady Juliet Rhys Williams, *Something to Look Forward To* (London: McDonald & Co., 1943). Milton Friedman's negative income tax is presented in *Capitalism and Freedom* (Chicago: University of Chicago Press, 1962). The other principal proponent of a guaranteed income, particularly influential because he related the necessity for guaranteed income to automation and the cybernetic revolution, is Robert Theobald; see his *Free Men and Free Markets* (London: Clarkson and Tatton, 1953). The Negative income tax experiment and its analysis are described in Larry N. Orr, Robinson G. Hollister, and Myron J. Lefcowitz, *Income Maintenance: Interdisciplinary Approaches to Research* (Chicago: Markham, 1971). ∎

STRUCTURAL AND DISTRIBUTIVE STRATEGIES IN ANTI-POVERTY POLICY

PUBLIC POLICY CAN TAKE two basic approaches to the war on poverty. One is structural: to raise earning capacities, equipping the poor of this generation and the potential poor of the next with the means to earn above-poverty incomes through normal employment. The other is distributive: to make up income deficiencies by direct government grants in cash or in kind or by subsidized employment.

The structural approach has two facets, the market and the individual. Labor markets, as currently organized, prevent many individuals from exploiting fully the earning capacities they have. Racial discrimination in employment and housing, restrictions on entry into organized trades, minimum wage regulations, failures of communication between employers with vacancies and potential applicants—these and other labor market imperfections bar some workers from competing for jobs they could perform and shunt them into unemployment, underemployment, or low-paid work. Public policy could try to promote more effective competition in labor markets, though not without encountering strong opposition from workers and employers who are sheltered by the existing barriers.

With respect to the individual, structural policy seeks to build up what economists call his human capital—the health, education, skill, experience, and behavior on which the future market value of his labor depends. This general principle is so clearly in accord with American ideals of fair play and equality of opportunity that it receives wide assent. An improved distribution of human capital poses a competitive threat to those who benefit from scarcity, but it is a diffuse and remote one. The trouble is that we are not very expert in making social investments in human capital. Adult education, training, and retraining are difficult, slow, and costly processes.

The two approaches, structural and distributive, compete for the taxpayer's dollar. But they are in an important sense complementary, for the following reasons.

1. There are some deficiencies of earning power that structural policy and economic progress can never wholly remedy: large families, families without breadwinners, blindness and other physical disabilities, obsolete skills, old age, and so on. Programs to

maintain and supplement incomes are necessary to handle these cases.

2. The structural approach, even under the most favorable circumstances and with the most generous financing, is bound to take a long time. Labor markets and educational systems cannot be changed quickly. Furthermore, many of the necessary changes in these institutions will not bear fruit for a generation. Meanwhile people are poor.

3. It is tempting to dismiss the distributive approach as a palliative that deals only with symptoms, and to favor the structural approach as an attack on basic causes. But the metaphor is false. Poverty today leads to poverty tomorrow. Inequality of condition means inequality of opportunity. Poverty and inequality perpetuate themselves in children whose capacities and motivations to learn are impaired—perhaps by physical handicaps due to malnutrition or inadequate medical care before or after birth, perhaps by intellectually and culturally deprived homes and neighborhoods. Improvement in the conditions under which children are born and raised will increase, not diminish, their earning capacities as adults . . . .

REFORM OF PUBLIC ASSISTANCE

The serious failings of the present system of public assistance can be summarized as follows.

1. *Inadequate coverage.* The restrictive categories of eligibility exclude millions of poor people, especially among the working or employable poor. Even within the eligible categories, many people in need receive no assistance because of state residence requirements, overstrict local administration, or simple ignorance.

2. *Antifamily incentives.* Eligibility rules for AFDC penalize financially the formation and maintenance of intact families.

3. *Inadequacy of benefits.* In most states benefits are inadequate. Under AFDC the states determine their own standards of need and decide how fully to meet them. The needs of a mother and 3 children, as esti-

mated by the states, varied in January 1965 from $124 per month in Arkansas to $376 per month in Alaska. In most states actual benefit payments fall short of their own calculations of need. As a result, actual maximum payments to a mother with 3 children varied from $50 per month in Mississippi to $246 in New York. No state was paying benefits to families at the official poverty level.

4. *Incentives for uneconomic migration.* The wide differences in benefits, eligibility rules, and administrative practices encourage migration to the wealthier and more liberal states, compounding the problems of northern cities. AFDC cases have more than doubled in New York and California since 1961, and these two states alone account for more than half of the 1 million increase in the caseload since 1964.

5. *Disincentives to work and thrift.* Reduction of benefits on account of the recipient family's own earning and saving amounts to a heavy tax on work and thrift.

6. *Excessive surveillance.* Complex administrative determinations concerning the eligibility, need, and resources of every applicant and recipient must be continuously made. The overburdened caseworker is a combination detective, social worker, advocate, and judge. This surveillance is costly; administration takes about 10 percent of the costs of public assistance. At the same time, the system often increases and perpetuates the recipients' incapacity to manage their own affairs.

7. *Inequities.* The present system gives rise to serious inequities. Unlike income taxation, which is designed to narrow but not to reverse initial differences in income, the present system changes economic ranks in an arbitrary and haphazard manner. Eligible households are made better off than ineligible households with the same or higher initial income. Households in generous states are better off than similar households in low benefit states. Some taxpaying families are worse off than some households receiving aid.

This list of problems suggests the agenda of issues in reform of public assistance: How should benefits be related to household size and composition, and to the earnings and other resources of the recipient? How should assistance be financed? How should it be administered? Should there be a nationally uniform system? . . .

"COSTS" OF REDISTRIBUTIONS TO THE POOR

From the point of view of the nation as a whole, a pure internal income transfer is, as a first approximation, costless. That is, no productive resources are used; no labor or capital or land needs to be diverted from other purposes, public or private. In this sense, transfers are fundamentally different from other government expenditures, which divert productive resources into, say, fighting wars or building schools. Transfer programs may, of course, have secondary consequences for the size and composition of national output. Administrative costs are real enough, though fractional; taxes and benefits may affect the behavior of the individuals involved, by altering their incentives to work, for example; and the beneficiaries of transfers may use the funds differently from the taxpayers. But exhaustive government expenditures have these consequences, too, in addition to their primary claim on productive resources.

The costs that concern taxpayers are not the social costs but the additional taxes they will have to pay—or tax cuts they will have to forgo—in order to increase the incomes of the poor. There are many different ways in which this burden might be distributed among the nonpoor. In the discussion that follows it is assumed that the additional taxes are federal taxes on personal income. A measure of the cost of a public assistance program is then the additional income tax which must be collected from the nonpoor, taken as a group. This may be measured either in dollars of total additional revenue as of any given year, or in the equivalent increase in the effective average rate of tax on the personal income of the nonpoor.

But under many proposals, benefits would not be confined to the poor. Indeed, it would not be fair or sensible to aid households with initial incomes of $2,999 at the expense of households with initial incomes of $3,001. Therefore, the burden of the nonpoor as a group is a net figure, concealing some redistribution within the group from higher to lower income taxpayers. "Horizontal" redistributions may be involved as well, for example, between taxpayers with different numbers of dependents or different kinds of income. Some proposals draw a simple sharp line between beneficiaries and payers of additional tax, and in those cases it is possible to calculate the transfer between these two groups as well as the net transfer between poor and nonpoor. The redistribution from nonpoor to poor may be called the *primary redistribution* of a program of public assistance, and the transfers within the nonpoor group the *secondary redistribution*.

The poor received $16 billion in 1966 and needed $27 billion. The poverty "gap"—the aggregate deficit of the incomes of the poor below their poverty thresholds—was $11 billion in 1966, less than 2 percent of total personal income, 69 percent of the actual personal income of the poor. This was the gap remaining after the incomes of the poor had benefited from existing governmental transfers, including $4.5 billion of cash public assistance. It is an illusion, of course, to think that poverty could be eliminated by $11 billion additional expenditures. For if the government guaranteed everyone a poverty-line income, in the sense of making up any shortfalls, the poor would have no reason— and many nonpoor very little reason—to earn as much as they do now. The poor would not lose by working less, or gain by working more. This would be the 100 percent tax rate implicit in old-fashioned public assistance.

Suppose the government pays every household its poverty-line income and takes back not 100 percent but some fraction of the poor household's initial income. How much transfer to the poor would then have to be made? How much would this exceed current

TABLE 10.1

TRANSFER TO POOR REQUIRED IN 1966 TO ELIMINATE $11 BILLION POVERTY GAP,
AT SELECTED TAX RATES
(In billions of dollars)

Item in Calculation	Tax Rate			
	2/3	1/2	1/3	0
1. Total poverty-line income	27.1	27.1	27.1	27.1
2. Offsetting tax on initial income of poor (tax rate X $11.7 billion)	7.8	5.9	3.9	0
3. Required benefit payments (1−2)	19.3	21.2	23.2	27.1
4. Current public assistance	4.3	4.3	4.3	4.3
5. Additional transfer required to eliminate gap (3−4)	15.0	16.9	18.9	22.8

public assistance? Initial incomes of the poor, before public assistance, aggregated $11.7 billion in 1966. Assuming that this figure is unaffected by the tax rate, the calculation is the simple one given in Table 10.1. Making up the $11 billion gap requires $15 billion with a rate of two-thirds, $22.8 billion with no tax. The table makes clear a general point: the redistributive cost of guaranteeing any level of income is greater the lower the tax rate—at least before allowance is made for the unknown incentive effects of the rates themselves.

THE CREDIT INCOME TAX

The credit income tax, proposed by Earl Rolph and others, is a scheme for integrating public assistance with a vastly simplified and reformed system of income taxation. Radical as it is, the proposal deserves a serious hearing. It serves, moreover, as a convenient point of reference for considering less far-reaching reforms.

Suppose that every man, woman, and child in the country was entitled to receive $750 a year from the federal government, and obligated to pay the government one-third of his income (not including the $750). The $750 is a credit against the tax. It is also a guaranteed income, the final income an individual would receive if he had none of his own. Anyone else would end up with more final income, even though he would receive a smaller net amount from the government, or actually pay tax to the government. The system is summarized in Table 10.2.

TABLE 10.2

EFFECT OF THE CREDIT INCOME TAX AT SELECTED INITIAL INCOME LEVELS

Initial Income before Payment to or from Government	Gross Offsetting Tax (1/3 of 1)	Net Benefit (+) or Tax Paid (−) ($750 − 2)	Final Income after Payment to or from Government (1 + 3)
$	$ 0	$+ 750	$ 750
300	100	+ 650	950
600	200	+ 550	1,150
900	300	+ 450	1,350
2,100	700	+ 50	2,150
2,250*	750	0	2,250
3,000	1,000	− 250	2,750
9,000	3,000	−2,250	6,750
12,000	4,000	−3,250	8,750

*Break-even income.

Individuals with incomes of $2,250 would receive no net benefit and pay no net tax; $2,250 (more generally, the credit divided by the tax rate) can be termed the *break-even income*. If an individual has an initial income above $2,250, the government takes one-third of the excess. Symmetrically, if an individual's initial income is below $2,250, the government makes up one-third of the shortfall. The net benefits can be regarded as "negative income taxes."

Under the proposal, a family could pool its guarantee credits provided it also pooled its members' incomes. In the example of Table 10.3, the addition of another dependent would be worth $750 in reduced net taxes or added net benefits. Credits play a role in this scheme similar to that of personal exemptions in the present federal income tax. But there is one important difference. The guarantee or credit is of the same value, $750 in the example, whatever the income of the taxpayer. A personal exemption for a dependent is worth more to a high bracket than to a low bracket taxpayer. The prevailing $600 exemption is worth $420 to a taxpayer rich enough to be taxed at a marginal rate of 70 percent; $84 to a lowest bracket taxpayer; and nothing to a family too poor to pay income tax. To help large rich families but not large poor families is anomalous social policy.

Part of the logic of a negative income tax is that poor families should in equity be able to cash in their unused exemptions.

A simple proposal like the one illustrated in Table 10.3 is neutral with respect to the

grouping of individuals. A person is worth the same—$750 in the example—whether he is a dependent member of a large taxpaying unit or a separate one-person unit. His income is subject to the same tax—one-third in the example—in either case. No set of individuals can gain at the expense of the government either by splitting into several units or by combining into one.

The average per capita net benefit or tax depends in a simple manner on average per capita income:

$$Net\ revenue\ per\ capita =$$
$$(Tax\ rate \times initial\ income\ per\ capita) - tax\ credit,$$

or:

$$\frac{Net\ revenue\ per\ capita}{Initial\ income\ per\ capital} =$$
$$Tax\ rate - \frac{Tax\ credit}{Initial\ income\ per\ capita}$$

At the 1966 level of $3,000 personal income per capita, the average gross tax under the illustrative proposal would be $1,000, the average net tax $250. Thus the tax would yield the government 8.33 percent of personal income (33.33 percent − 25 percent) after all benefits or negative taxes were paid. (The federal income tax now yields about 10 percent of personal income, but little more than 9 percent after current public assistance transfers are paid.) Raising the guarantee from 25 to 30 percent of average income— that is, to the poverty line of $900 per capita —would require an increase of 5 points in the tax rate.

Real income per capita increases 2.5 percent per year. Assuming the guarantee is held constant in purchasing power, net revenue from a credit income tax will rise as a share of personal income 2.5 percent per year. Alternatively, this is the amount by which the flat tax rate can be reduced if no increase in revenue, relative to personal income, is needed. A hypothetical redistribution to the poor is calculated in Table 10.4.

The proposal also involves, of course, a large secondary redistribution among the nonpoor. A family of 4 would pay no tax unless its income exceeded $9,000. Benefits to nonpoor families below the break-even incomes might total $29 billion. The burden would

TABLE 10.3

EFFECT OF CREDIT INCOME TAX ON INITIAL INCOME OF $6,000, BY SELECTED SIZE OF FAMILY

Size of Family	Net Benefit (+) or Tax (−)	Final Income
1	$−1,250	$4,750
2	− 500	5,500
3	+ 250	6,250
4	+1,000	7,000

TABLE 10.4

HYPOTHETICAL REDISTRIBUTION FROM NONPOOR
TO POOR IN 1966, COMPARING EXISTING PUBLIC
ASSISTANCE WITH CREDIT OF $750 PER CAPITA AND TAX RATE OF ONE-THIRD

Characteristic	Poor	Nonpoor	Total
1. Number of persons (millions)	29.7	163.7	193.4
2. Percent of total population	15.3	84.7	100.0
3. Average income per capita			
a. Before taxes and public assistance	$ 395	3,471	$3,000
b. After taxes and public assistance*	$ 539	3,150	$2,750
4. Credit income tax			
a. Gross (1/3 3a)	$ 132	$1,157	$1,000
b. Net ($750 — 4a)	+$ 618	—$ 407	—$ 250
c. Final income (3a + 4b)	$1,013	$3,064	$2,750
5. Additional redistribution			
a. Per capita (4c — 3b)	+$ 474	—$ 86	0
b. Aggregate (billions)	+$ 14.1	—$ 14.1	0

* These entries assume actual public assistance totaling $4.3 billion and an income tax that raises from the nonpoor this amount and additional revenue of 8.33 percent of personal income.

fall mainly on higher income taxpayers, and among them mainly on taxpayers with income not now taxable. At present taxable income is only 46 percent of personal income. With this degree of slippage it would take a nominal tax rate of 70 percent to produce an effective tax rate of one-third. That is why the advocates of the credit income tax propose wholesale elimination of exclusions, deductions, and exemptions.

The uniform tax rate has great technical advantages, it eliminates all incentive to shift income, either in fact or in appearance, from one year to another or from one taxpaying unit to another. The structure is still progressive because of the tax credit or guarantee, which diminishes relative to income as income rises. As for progression in the rate structure itself, it is argued, the high rates applicable to high incomes are more apparent than real; the law is riddled with ways to escape these rates, particularly when the high incomes are derived from property. But marginal rates could be increased at high incomes.

CHILDREN'S ALLOWANCES AND ADULTS' ALLOWANCES

The credit income tax proposal can be modified in a number of different ways. The most important are the schedule of credits for households of varying size and composition and the structure of tax rates in relation to income.

A uniform per capita guarantee makes no allowance for economies of scale in family living or for differences in consumption requirements between adults and children. It favors large families, especially those with young children, as against single adults and small families. A high cash value for an additional child may be an undesirable incentive. For these reasons, it might be better to provide higher credits for adults, single or married, than for children, and also to reduce and eventually eliminate credit for an additional child as the size of family rises. An example is given in column 2 of Table 10.5. A schedule of this kind, however, introduces legal and economic problems that the flat per capital allowance avoids. A youth's claim on the government may depend on whether he is an "adult" or a "child," and the value of a child may depend on what household claims him as a member. Nevertheless, it seems perfectly feasible to set up and enforce some reasonable legal definitions.

An entirely different approach is to allow credits *only* for families with children. The

TABLE 10.5
ILLUSTRATIVE SCHEDULES RELATING CREDITS TO FAMILY SIZE

	Household's Credit or Guaranteed Income				
	(1)	(2)	(3)	(4)	(5)
			Half of personal exemptions and minimum standard deductions	Children's allowances	
Size of family	Constant per capita	Guarantees near poverty lines		modest	antipoverty
1	$ 750	$1,000	$ 450	$ 0	$ 0
2	1,500	2,000	800	0	0
3	2,250	2,600	1,150	200	1,800
4	3,000	3,200	1,500	400	2,400
5	3,750	3,600	1,850	600	3,000
6	4,500	4,000	2,200	800	3,600
7	5,250	4,200	2,550	1,000	4,200
8	6,000	4,400	2,900	1,200	4,800
9	6,750	4,400	3,250	1,400	5,400

Note: The table assumes that the first two members of a household are adults. If there is only one adult, entries in column 2 for households of two or more persons would be $400 less, and entries in columns 4 and 5 would be moved up one line.

United States is the only advanced country that does not pay children's allowances. In other countries allowances are paid for all children, without regard to parents' income, although in some cases the allowances are taxable. But they are in almost all cases too small to be the major form of assistance to families in serious poverty. The purposes of the allowances are, rather, to improve "horizontal" equity between small and large families of the same incomes, whether poor or rich, and in some countries to *raise* the birth rate.

A children's allowance plan in this spirit is illustrated in column 4 of Table 10.5. Paid to the parents of all children under 19, of whom there were 75 million in 1966, these allowances would cost $15 billion gross, or about $12 billion net if they were subject to regular income tax. Of the net benefits, nearly 80 percent would go to families above the poverty line. If the program were financed by a uniform increase in income tax rates, the end result would be a modest but dubious redistribution from childless taxpayers to large families, and very little redistribution from rich to poor.

If children's allowances are intended to be of significant help to destitute families, they must be much more generous, as in column 5 of Table 10.5. Moreover, since no help is

to be given to childless couples, the value of the first child would have to be very high indeed. To offer so large a financial incentive for women to start having children is risky social policy. With allowances on the scale of column 5, it is necessary to abandon the appealing idea of a universal payment subject to no test of need except the regular income tax. The net cost, of the order of $65 billion as of 1966, would exceed the yield of the federal income tax. Yet nothing would have been done for 18 million poor childless adults.

NEGATIVE INCOME TAX PROPOSALS

The credit income tax involves a large politically difficult secondary redistribution, which can be diminished in magnitude by abandoning the flat tax rate and by partially offsetting the credits or guarantees with a special high tax on low initial incomes. This is the technique of most negative income tax (NIT) proposals.

Consider, for example, the proposal made by Milton Friedman and others to pay each nontaxpayer half the difference between (1) the sum of his personal exemptions and standard deductions and (2) his initial income. The amounts that a household with no other income would receive are shown in Table 10.5, column 3. Benefits would decline by 50 percent of other income—that is, the income would be taxed at 50 percent. The breakeven levels would be twice the entries in column 3. At those incomes households would begin to pay regular income tax, just as they do now. The tax rate would fall from 50 percent to the first-bracket rate under the tax code (14 percent in the absence of the temporary surcharge enacted in 1968).

If the Friedman plan were superimposed on existing public assistance, about half the poverty gap, $5.5 billion as of 1966, would be made up—a bit less because the break-even levels fall short of the poverty lines. To finance the plan, regular income tax rates would have to be raised two points. If the plan replaced current public assistance, as Friedman suggests, its net cost would be only $2.5 billion or $3 billion as of 1966, but it would reduce the aggregate poverty gap only by the same amount.

Column 2 of Table 10.5 shows a more generous schedule of guarantees. This, too,

could be combined with a 50 percent offsetting tax on other income. Break-even incomes would range from $2,000 for a single adult to $8,800 for a family of 8. But the 50 percent tax rate would continue to apply at higher incomes until it produced the same tax liability as the regular income tax code. Above the "tax break-even" income the regular rates would apply. For illustration, the calculation of tax, negative or positive, for a couple with two children is given in Table 10.6. The tax break-even income is $7,920. For incomes above that point the normal tax calculation supersedes the special NIT calculation. The marginal tax rate falls abruptly from 50 percent to 17.1 percent, and then rises again with income.

The primary redistribution involved in this proposal is roughly the $17 billion required to close the poverty gap with a 50 percent tax, as calculated in Table 10.1. The secondary redistribution is difficult to estimate, but it is of the order of $5 billion. About half of 4-person families, for example, had incomes below $7,920 in 1966 and would have bene-

TABLE 10.6

COMPARISON OF EFFECTS OF EXISTING INCOME TAX AND
PROPOSED NEGATIVE INCOME TAX, FOR MARRIED COUPLE WITH TWO CHILDREN AT
SELECTED INCOME LEVELS

Initial Income	Net Benefit (+) or Tax (−)		Final Income		Marginal Tax Rate	
	NIT*	1966 tax law	NIT	1966 tax law†	NIT	1966 tax law
$ 0	$+3,200	$ 0	$3,200	$ 0		
1,000	+2,700	0	3,700	1,000	50 %	0 %
2,000	+2,200	0	4,200	2,000	50	0
3,000	+1,700	0	4,700	3,000	50	0
4,000	+1,200	− 140	5,200	3,860	50	14
5,000	+ 700	− 290	5,700	4,710	50	15
6,000	+ 200	− 450	6,200	5,500	50	16
6,400‡	0	− 511	6,400	5,889	50	15.3
7,000	− 300	− 603	6,700	6,397	50	15.3
7,920§	− 760	− 760	7,160	7,160	50	17.1
8,000	− 772	− 772	7,228	7,228	17.1	17.1
10,000	−1,114	−1,114	8,886	8,886	17.1	17.1

*$3,200 less 50 percent of initial income, or the tax under the 1966 tax law, whichever is algebraically larger.
†Figures shown assume standard deduction of $600 or 10 percent of initial income, whichever is larger. The 10 percent deduction when applicable makes the effective marginal tax rate 10 percent lower than the nominal rate for the bracket; that is why the marginal rate is 15.3 percent in the 17 percent bracket and 17.1 percent in the 19 percent bracket.
‡NIT break-even income.
§Tax break-even income.

fited from the plan. Beneficiaries other than current recipients of public assistance would have been subject to higher marginal tax rates, 50 percent compared with zero to 17 percent now. This change could have serious disincentive effects, just as the reduction in marginal rate of tax from 100 or 66.66 percent would improve incentives for public assistance clients.

A proposal of this type is, in effect, a credit income tax grafted onto the present income tax structure. The dip in the marginal tax rate creates some problems. Whenever marginal tax rates vary there is an inducement to shift income, both in appearance and in reality, to tax returns with lower marginal rates. This may mean the return for this year, last year, or some other person. In the present instance, there would be some incentive for concentrating income in time, in order to have it taxed at low marginal rates rather than at 50 percent. A more serious difficulty is the incentive for family-splitting: a father or potential stepfather with a good income may do better for himself and for a mother and her children by filing separately and paying regular income tax; if he joins the group, his income will be taxed at the 50 percent rate, depriving the mother and children of benefits they could otherwise claim. Although cases of this kind would be by no means as frequent or as serious as under AFDC, they point up the advantages of a uniform tax rate.

The two NIT examples both assumed a 50 percent tax rate. There is nothing sacred about 50 percent, or even about a constant rate. Lowering the tax rate in the more generous plan, while keeping the same schedule of credits, would increase the cost of both the primary and secondary redistributions. The Friedman proposal could be modified to change the tax rate to 25 percent while holding the break-even incomes constant. Then the guarantee levels shown in column 3 of Table 10.5 would be cut in half. So would the aggregate transfer: The government would be making up only a quarter of the deficit of each poor family. As an interim measure,

Robert Lampman has suggested guarantee levels at a quarter of the poverty line, zero tax on incomes up to half the poverty line, and 50 percent tax thereafter. His purpose is to concentrate aid on the working poor.

Taxable income as defined for the federal income tax is so poor a definition of need that to use it as the base for negative income tax payments would be a travesty of common sense and social justice. Society does not want to pay benefits to people with low taxable income but with ample resources—wealth, tax-exempt interest, capital gains, pensions, social security stipends, college fellowships, large itemized deductions, gift receipts, and so on. Consequently, negative income taxation requires a much more inclusive definition of income as the base for the offsetting tax.

Such a definition is feasible but admittedly involves a philosophical inconsistency. If taxable income as now defined is so obviously deficient as a test of need, why is it a good test of ability to pay? The illogic here is what leads Rolph and other advocates of the credit income tax to insist on a thorough reform, resulting in a single inclusive definition of income.

Americans, as noted above, are mortally afraid that some potential workers will choose idleness even at the expense of income. The total disqualification of households containing potential workers, as attempted in the present system of public assistance in most states, has proved disastrous. But does sufficient incentive to work remain after a tax of one-third or one-half is levied on earnings? Does the carrot need to be supplemented by a stick?

One possibility would be not to count potential workers in reckoning the guarantees to which the household unit is entitled, to presume that they have incomes at least sufficient to wipe out their credits. Thus if the credit for a potential worker were $1,000 and the offsetting tax rate were 50 percent, he would be presumed to be earning income at a rate of $2,000 a year even if his actual income were lower. This presumption would deprive his family of the $1,000 but not, as under AFDC, of the amounts to which it is entitled on account of its other members.

The presumption should be removed, and the potential worker's entitlement restored, in any month for which a federal manpower officer in his locality certified that, whether due to temporary personal disabilities or lack of suitable job or training opportunities, he could not earn income at the presumed rate. In this manner, a federal program of creating, financing and coordinating job and training opportunities could be meshed with a program of income supplementation.

CONCLUDING REMARKS

Poverty in the United States, as officially measured, has declined dramatically in this decade, thanks to the sustained expansion of the economy and the restoration of full employment. But the poverty that remains has become a greater threat to the social order. This is the decade of the Black's claim to full equality in all aspects of American life. Although the economic conditions of Blacks have markedly improved during the boom of the 1960s, they suffer much more than their share of poverty, unemployment, and urban squalor. The transformation of the American economy and population from rural to urban is still going on. Ultimately it will be the engine of great improvement in the lives of Black immigrants to cities and their children, as it has been for previous immigrants. But the transition is long, difficult, and dangerous.

The acute problem is the inability of many employable males to earn enough to support their children. The result is usually a family in poverty unrelieved by public assistance. With increasing frequency, however, the mother and children are left on their own, and "go to welfare." The basic solution in the long run is to build up earning capacities by education and work experience. Meanwhile, people are poor, and their children are raised under handicaps that may destine them to be poor, too.

The present system of public assistance has failed. Inadequate in coverage and in bene-

fits, perverse in its incentives, it fosters the very conditions it is supposed to relieve.

We urgently need a reformed and nationalized system of income assistance that does not exclude employable men and their families. In my opinion, this should be meshed with the federal income tax. The credit income tax seems the fairest and simplest solution. But it will take a long time to develop political consensus for so drastic a reform, and meanwhile something must be done. The merit of the negative income tax approach is that a workable and equitable system of aiding the poor can be introduced within the framework of present federal income taxation.

Which NIT proposal should it be?. . . Meanwhile, I would venture the opinion that the tax rate should not exceed 50 percent. I also find it hard to justify guarantee levels significantly below poverty lines except as a temporary and transitional feature of a new system.

Together these specifications imply a system like the one illustrated in Table 10.5, column 2, and in Table 10.6. This is a costly proposal, and if the budgetary resources could not be found at once, it could be gradually introduced as follows: Keep the suggested break-even incomes, which for most family sizes are roughly twice the poverty thresholds. Start by making up, say, only one-quarter of the amount by which a household's income falls short of this break-even level, and step up the rate gradually until it reaches 50 percent. During the transition the existing public assistance system would be gradually phased out. But states and localities that wished to augment the benefits available to the poor under the federal NIT system would be able to do so, perhaps even with some federal financial help.

The main obstacles to reform are ideological and fiscal. The widespread, if largely groundless, fear of freeloading can be met by making part, not all, of the assistance to families conditional on the willingness of employable members to present themselves for work or training, and by providing assistance in a way that rewards self-reliance. The budgetry cost is formidable, especially if we impose on ourselves the rule that taxes can never be increased. But the war on poverty is too crucial to be relegated to the status of a residual claimant for funds that peace in Asia and the normal growth of tax revenues may painlessly and gradually make available.

When asked to make sacrifices for the defense of their nation, the American people have always responded. Perhaps some day a national administration will muster the courage to ask the American people to tax themselves for social justice and domestic tranquillity. The time is short.

11. EDUCATION AND INEQUALITY

■ The next three selections deal with the relationship of education to class position. Most Americans believe that the more education you have, the better you do in life. Most Americans also believe that the more educated the population, the better we can solve all our problems. Education is thus the most popular solution both for the individual's desire for success and mobility and for society's need to solve its problems. Indeed, so powerful is its mystique that some observers believe education is America's state religion.

The issues of public policy connected with education are many and extremely complex. The most traditional issue concerns equality of educational opportunity. Americans have long felt that in order for each person to achieve the most in terms of his ability and motivation, educational opportunities should be readily available and, to the extent that society's affluence allows, free. Over time, more and more Americans have been able to complete more schooling, until now we have reached a point where the average young person is expected to finish at least a couple of years of college.

Free public education, then, is a principal mechanism by which our society endeavors to redistribute resources toward those who are less well off, and at the same time to produce benefits for the society as a whole by increasing the knowledgeability and skill, the human capital, of the nation. In their pathbreaking and highly controversial study of the subsidies embodied in the California higher education system, W. Lee Hansen and Burton Weisbrod challenge the notion that state-financed higher education in fact involves such a redistribution of resources from the better-off to the less-well-off classes in society.

Another aspect of the education issue involves what has sometimes been called "credentialism." The more society relies on formal education as its basic training device, the more do individuals find that educational credentials are essential if they are to have access to jobs and opportunities for promotion. As these credentials become more and more important, mere experience in the labor market is downgraded. An emphasis on educational credentials has been said to be justified in that as the economy has become more technical and complex, a more highly educated work force is necessary. Ivar Berg attacks this notion in his research on the relationship between education and job qualifications. His conclusion is apparent in the title of this article—"The Great Training Robbery." He believes that employers, sometimes to their own as well as to the workers' detriment, artificially inflate educational requirements for jobs because of prejudices that have no direct relationship to production or quality. In this he provides additional support for the points Lester Thurow makes on income distribution in Selection 8.

Finally, an even more abstract issue relates to the kind of society toward which we are moving as science and technology become more and more complex. It has been argued that we are in the process of become a "meritocracy"—a society in which each person's class position is determined by his ability to contribute to the well-being and stability of society, an ability that in turn is determined primarily by his innate intelligence as it is formed and directed by the educational system. In the late 1960s, there was a rebirth of interest in the impact of genetic factors on social position, perhaps because of frustration at the failure of various educational programs in the ghettos and among poor people generally. This antieducational backlash sought to point up the apparent failures of social reformers to change people through social intervention programs. It was argued that Black children and poor children continued to perform less well on intelligence and achievement tests and to earn less money later in life because their innate abilities were simply not so great as those of White and economically better-off children. David K. Cohen examines this issue with a care and detachment not often matched during this period by either the new social Darwinians or their critics. He points to findings in several careful and methodologically sophisticated studies which suggest that success—as measured by either occupational status or income—is not actually accounted for by such factors as IQ (the neo-Darwinians' candidate) or family socioeconomic background (the environmentalists' candidate). In the process he demonstrates that, for all our faith in it, education is a far-from-perfect avenue to success in life. Cohen concludes that the evidence shows—conventional wisdom notwithstanding—

that being stupid is not what is responsible for being poor in America (and by the same token, of course, being smart is not what is responsible for being well-off in America).

Perhaps the most important conclusion to be drawn from these three articles is that the time has come for a searching examination of exactly what role education does play in the workings of our system of determining one's chances in life. Given the results of these investigations, the conventional wisdom about the role of education can no longer be taken for granted. Once we know how education really does operate in our stratification system we can begin to ask questions about the gains and losses from our particular way of using education and about proper goals for education. It may well be that the result of such an examination would be to downgrade markedly the importance of education as the instrument of choice for fostering equality in American society.

The growing role of college education in American stratification is discussed in Christopher Jencks and David Riesman, *The Academic Revolution* (Garden City, N.Y.: Doubleday, 1969). Murray Milner, Jr., *The Illusion of Equality* (San Francisco: Jossey-Bass, 1972) analyzes the American belief that a more equal and just society can be built by expanding opportunities for education.

Much of the recent interest in the role of education in increasing opportunity has been stimulated by a concern with racially segregated schools, South and North. Sociologist James S. Coleman's *The Coleman Report* on equality of opportunity in the schools has proved a continuing stimulus to research on the role of education and on stratification generally. This study is critically assessed by several social scientists in Frederick Mosteller and Daniel P. Moynihan, eds., *On Equality of Educational Opportunity* (New York: Random House, 1972). ■

11a. INEQUALITIES IN HIGHER EDUCATION

W. LEE HANSEN and BURTON A. WEISBROD

Reprinted from W. Lee Hansen and Burton Weisbrod, "The Equality Fiction," The New Republic, Sept. 13, 1969, by permission of The New Republic, © 1969, Harrison-Blaine of New Jersey, Inc. W. Lee Hansen and Burton Weisbrod are Professors of Economics at the University of Wisconsin. Their study—reported in full in Benefits, Costs, and Finance of Higher Education *(Chicago: Markham, 1969)—was carried out for the Joint Committee on Higher Education of the California State Legislature. As higher education has consumed larger and larger proportions of state budgets, the question of what it's all for has received increasing attention. An influential critique of the Weisbrod-Hansen thesis will be found in Joseph A. Pechman, "A Review of Hansen and Weisbrod's 'The Distribution of Public Higher Education in California,' " Journal of Human Resources, Summer 1970.*

THE CLAIM THAT the American system of higher education contributes to equality of educational opportunity is largely fiction. This year [1969] well over $11 billion of tax funds spent on higher education will seriously violate the egalitarianism principle. Seemingly, public colleges and universities are open to all, but the truth falls far short of this. In practice, a perverse redistribution of higher education subsidies from low income to high income families takes place. Those with the most need for higher education are getting the least in terms of public benefits.

Studies of public higher education have recently been completed for the states of California, Florida, and Wisconsin. Because our study of California is the most comprehensive we shall focus on it. . . .

California possesses a vast and in many respects a model system of public higher education. Tuition is zero. College campuses abound, with at least a junior college in every sizable community. And it has the largest percentage of any state's high school graduates going on to college. Undergraduate students all receive large public subsidies, although the amounts differ greatly with the type of school attended. A student fortunate enough to attend the University of California in the mid-1960s received an average subsidy of about $5,000, but a California State College student only $3,000, and a junior college student about $1,000. Of course, some got even larger subsidies: a student completing 4 years at the university received a total subsidy of over $7,000. By "subsidy" we mean the difference between tuition—which in California is zero—and the sum of average instructional costs (professors' salaries, operating expenses, etc.) and the capital costs (the value of services provided by building, equipment, and land).

Many youngsters, however, received no subsidies at all, because they do not go to college (or, at least, not to a public college in their own state), and many others receive little because they are in college only briefly.

The highest subsidies go to students at the University of California (UC). But UC accepts only the upper eighth of all high school graduates, and these are largely children from well-to-do family backgrounds. Students from families with incomes above $25,000 are 4 times as likely to be eligible as are those from families with incomes below $4,000. Moreover, among eligible students, twice as large a percentage from high income families actually attend the UC as do those from low income families. The selectivity process restricts the availability of large subsidies to all but high income families. The end result is that California's three higher education systems—the University, the State Colleges (SC), and the Junior Colleges (JC) —educate three different general classes of students and, in turn, provide three different levels of subsidies. (The same is true for

many other states—including Florida, Wisconsin, Michigan, and Illinois, to name a few—that have a multiple-tiered higher education system.) The UC has the highest income students—their family incomes average more than $12,000—and provides the largest subsidies—$5,000 per student. Meanwhile, the JCs attract the lowest income students— with $8,800 average family income—and provide the lowest subsidies—about $1,000. The SC students are in between, with family incomes of $10,000 and subsidies of $3,800. Thus, the average subsidy received by students at the UC is 30 percent greater than that received by SC students, and is 400 percent greater than the JC subsidy—in spite of the fact that "need," as reflected by family income, runs in the opposite direction.

The upshot: even in California, with its extensive higher education system, over 40 percent of families with college-age children receive *no public subsidy at all,* while a most fortunate 10 percent receive subsidies over $5,000.

Consideration of the taxes people pay does not alter these striking redistributional effects. There is no satisfactory way to isolate the taxes that go for education, and so we can only compare *total* state and local taxes (for all public services) with the subsidies provided by public higher education. However, higher education consumes roughly 10 percent of state and local tax revenue in California, whose state-local tax system is essentially proportional to income over most of the income range.

The inescapable conclusion is that the structure and financing of public higher education in California heightens rather than narrows inequalities in economic opportunities. The situation is no different in other states. State tax systems are either proportional (to income) or regressive (i.e., high income taxpayers pay a smaller percentage of their income in taxes than low income persons).

Nationally, a larger percentage of low than of high income youngsters drop out of high school and so are not eligible to receive any higher education subsidies. Those low income students who are eligible to go to higher educational institutions most often wind up at institutions where the education subsidy is lowest. And they are more likely to drop out before graduation. For these and other well-known reasons, the cards are stacked against low income youngsters. Yet because tax revenues are used to support higher education, the anomalous result is lower income families not only do not receive significant amounts of public higher education subsidies but actually pay a larger fraction of their income in taxes to support higher education than do more affluent families. At a time when pressures are mounting to reduce disparities between privileged and disadvantaged, it is clear that something has gone awry. The mythology of equal educational opportunity for all is just that: mythology.

It is clear that the present structure and financing of public higher education needs to be reformed. One important possibility is to revamp the tax structure, making state and local taxes more progressive. This would increase taxes most for higher income families and wipe out some but not all of the redistributive effects. But it wouldn't discriminate between families with and without children in college, or between those in public and private colleges.

Another approach is to set tuition much closer to the full instructional and capital costs of college, and then to provide financial aid to students who cannot afford the full cost. This is essentially what private schools now do through their financial aid programs. Judging from the recent actions of state legislatures in raising tuition and fees, there is some sentiment for moving in this direction even at public colleges. Unless, however, every increase in tution for those who can afford it is accompanied by an increase of loan and scholarship funds for those who cannot afford it, the goal of greater equality of opportunity will continue to be only a distant vision. Unhappily, while tuition rates at public colleges are rising rapidly, student aid funds are lagging and federal student loan and scholarship funds are actually drying up.

More important than either of these reforms, public subsidies should be available to *all* young people, not just college students. Those for whom the best way to increase earning power is through apprenticeships, on-the-job training or night school deserve an equal chance in their struggle for productive and satisfying lives.

11b. THE GREAT TRAINING ROBBERY

IVAR BERG

Reprinted by permission of Transaction, Inc. from "Rich Man's Qualifications for Poor Man's Jobs," Transaction Vol. 6 (March 1969). Copyright © 1969 by Transaction, Inc. Ivar Berg is Professor of Sociology at Columbia University. His selection condenses some of the major points of his book, Education and Jobs: The Great Training Robbery *(New York: Praeger, 1970). Our commonsense assumptions that education makes for better job performance have been formalized as the economics of human capital. Two economists who have taken the lead in developing this line of thinking are Theodore W. Schultz and Gary Becker. Professor Schultz's seminal article on investment in human capital is reprinted along with other useful articles in Marc Blaug, ed.,* Economics of Education *(New York: Penguin Books, 1969). Professor Becker's view are developed in his* Human Capital *(New York: Columbia University Press, 1964).*

IT IS NOW A WELL-KNOWN FACT that America offers more and more jobs to skilled workers while the increase in unskilled jobs has slowed down. Newspaper articles regularly remind us that we have a shortage of computer programmers, and, at the same time, too many unskilled laborers. The conventional solution is to correct the shortcomings of the labor force by educating more of the unemployed. Apart from its practical difficulties, this solution begs the important question: Are academic credentials important for *doing* the job—or just for *getting* it?

My studies of manpower use indicate that although in recent years requirements for many jobs have been upgraded because of technological and other changes, in many cases education requirements have been raised arbitrarily. In short, *many employers demand too much education for the jobs they offer.*

Education has become the most popular solution to America's social and economic ills. Our faith in education as *the* cure for unemployment partly reflects our inclination as a society to diagnose problems in individualistic terms. Both current and classical economic theories merely reinforce these attitudes; both assume that the labor supply can be significantly changed by investments in education and health. Meanwhile private employers, on the other side of the law of supply and demand, are held to be merely reacting to the imperatives that generate the need for better educated manpower. . . .

Unfortunately, economists and public planners usually assume that the education that employers require for the jobs they offer is altogether beneficial to the firm. Higher education, it is thought, means better performance on the job. A close look at the data, however, shows that here reality does not usually correspond with theory.

In recent years, the number of higher level jobs has not increased as much as personnel directors lead us to believe. The big increase, rather, has been in middle level jobs—for high school graduates and college dropouts. This becomes clear when the percentages of jobs requiring the three different levels of education are compared with the percentages of the labor force that roughly match these categories. The comparison of census data with the U.S. Employment Service's descriptions of 4,000 different jobs also shows that (1) high education jobs have expanded somewhat faster for men than for women; (2) those jobs in the middle have expanded faster for women than for men; and (3) that highly educated people are employed in jobs that require *less* education than these people actually have.

The fact is that our highly educated people are competing with lesser educated people for the jobs in the middle. In Monroe County, N.Y. (which includes Buffalo), the National Industrial Conference Board has graphically demonstrated this fact. Educational requirements for most jobs, the board has reported, vary with the academic calendar. Thus, requirements rise as the end of the school year approaches and new graduates flood the market. Employers whose job openings fall in the middle category believe that by employing people with higher-than-necessary educations they are benefiting from the increasing educational achievements of the work force. Yet the data suggest that there is a "shortage" of high school graduates and of people with post high school educations short of college degrees while there is a "surplus" of college graduates, especially females.

The economic and sociological theories that pour out of university computers have given more and more support to the idea that we, as a society, have more options in dealing with the supply side of employment—with the characteristics of the work force—than with demand.

These studies try to relate education to higher salaries; they assume that the income a person earns is a valid measure of his job performance. The salaries of better educated people, however, may not be closely related to the work they do. Female college graduates are often employed as secretaries; many teachers and social workers earn less than plumbers and others who belong to effective unions. What these rate-of-return studies lack is productivity data isolated according to job and the specific person performing the job.

In any event, it is circular reasoning to relate wage and salary data to educational achievements. Education is often, after all, the most important criterion for a person's getting a job in the first place! The argument that salaries may be used to measure the value of education and to measure the "value added" to the firm by employees of different educational backgrounds may simply confirm what it sets out to prove. In jobs for which educational requirements have not been thoughtfully studied, the argument is not an argument at all, but a self-fulfilling prophecy.

Despite the many attempts to relate a person's achievements to the wages he receives, researchers usually find that the traits, aptitudes, and educational achievements of workers vary as greatly *within* job categories as they do *between* them. That is, people in job A differ as much from one another as they differ from people in job B. Only a small percentage of the labor force—those in the highest and those in the lowest job levels—are exceptions. And once workers become members of the labor force, personal virtues at even the lower job levels do not account for wage differences—intelligent, well-educated, low level workers don't necessarily earn more than others at the bottom of the ladder. Marcia Freedman's study of employment patterns for Columbia's Conservation of Human Resources project indicates that, although many rungs of the organizational ladder are linked to differences in pay, these rungs are not closely related to differences in the employees' skills and training.

Educational requirements continue to go up; yet most employers have made no effort to find out whether people with better educations make better workers than people with inferior educations. Using data collected from private firms, the military, the federal civil service, and public educational systems, and some collected from scratch, I have concentrated on this one basic question.

Business managers, supported by government leaders and academics interested in em-ployment problems, have well-developed ideas about the value of a worker's educational achievement. They assert that with each increment of education—especially those associated with a certificate, diploma, or degree—the worker's attitude is better, his trainability is greater, his capacity for adaptation is more developed, and his prospects for promotions are rosier. At the same time, those workers with more modest educations, and especially those who drop out of school, are held to be less intelligent, less adaptable, less self-disciplined, less personable, and less articulate.

The findings in my studies do not support these assertions.

A comparison of 4,000 insurance agents in a major company in the Greater New York area showed that an employee's productivity—measured by the dollar value of the policies he sold—did not vary in any systematic way with his years of formal education. In other words, those salesmen with less education brought as much money into the company as their better educated peers. When an employee's experience was taken into account, it was clear that those with *less* education and *more* experience sold the most policies. Thus, even an employer whose success in business depends on the social and psychological intangibles of a customer-client relationship may not benefit from having highly educated employees. Often factors such as the influence of colleagues and family obligations were more significant in explaining the productivity of agents.

In another insurance agency, the job performances of 200 young female clerks were gauged from the number of merit salary increases they had received. Researchers discovered that there were *no* differences in the performance records of these women that could easily be attributed to differences in their educational backgrounds. Once again, focusing on the educational achievements of job applicants actually diverted attention from characteristics that are really relevant to job performance.

At a major weekly news magazine, the

variation in educational achievement among over 100 employees was greater than among the insurance clerks. The magazine hired female college graduates as well as high school graduates, for clerical-secretarial positions. While the employers argued that the girls needed their college degrees to qualify for future editorial jobs, most editorial positions were *not* filled by former secretaries, whether college graduates or not, but by college graduates who directly entered into those positions. And although the personnel director was skeptical of supervisors' evaluations of the secretaries, the supervisors determined the salary increases, and as many selective merit-pay increases were awarded to the lesser educated secretaries as to the better educated secretaries.

Executives of a larger well-known chemical company in New York told me that the best technicians in their research laboratory were those with the highest educational achievement. Therefore, in screening job applicants, they gave greater weight to a person's educational background than to his other characteristics. Yet, statistical analysis of relevant data revealed that the rate of turnover in the firm was positively associated with the employees' educational achievement. And a close look at the "reasons for leaving" given by the departing technicians showed that they intended to continue their educations. Furthermore, lesser educated technicians earned higher performance evaluations than did their better educated peers. Understandably, the employer was shocked by these findings.

OVEREDUCATED ARE LESS PRODUCTIVE

The New York State Department of Labor's 1964 survey of employers suggests that technicians often possess educational achievements far beyond what employers themselves think is ideal for effective performance. Thousands of companies reported their minimal educational requirements to the Labor Department, along with their ideal requirements and the actual educations of the technicians they employed. In many industries and in respect to most types of technicians, the workers were better educated than they were required to be; in 10 out of 16 technical categories they were even better educated than their employers dared hope, exceeding the "ideal" requirements set down by the employers.

Upper and middle level employees are not the only ones who are overqualified for their jobs. Nor is the phenomenon to be observed only in metropolitan New York. In a study of eight Mississippi trouser plants, researchers found that the more education an employee had, the less productive she was. Several hundred female operators were paid by piece work, and their wages therefore were a valid test of workers' productivity. Furthermore this study showed that educational achievement was positively associated with turnover: The better educated employee was more likely to quit her job.

Education's negative relationship to jobs can be measured not only by the productivity and turnover of personnel, but also by worker satisfaction. It may be argued that dissatisfaction among workers leads to a desirable measure of labor mobility, but the funds a company spends to improve employee morale and make managerial personnel more sensitive to the needs of their subordinates strongly suggest that employers are aware of the harm caused by worker dissatisfaction. Roper Associates once took a representative sample of 3,000 blue-collar workers in 16 industries in all parts of the United States. Among workers in lower skilled jobs, dissatisfaction was found to increase as their educational achievements increased.

These studies of private firms suggest that many better educated workers are assigned to jobs requiring low skill and that among the results are high turnover rates, low productivity, and worker dissatisfaction. Nonetheless, the disadvantages of "overeducation" are best illustrated by employment practices of public school systems.

EDUCATED TEACHERS OPT OUT

Many school districts, to encourage their teachers to be highly educated, base teachers' salaries upon the number of credits they earn toward higher degrees. However, data from the National Opinion Research Center and the National Science Foundation's 1962 study of 4,000 teachers show that, like employees elsewhere, teachers become restless as their educational achievements rise. Elementary and secondary school teachers who have master's degrees are less likely to stay in their jobs than teachers with bachelor's degrees. And in a similar study done by Columbia Teachers College, it was evident that teachers with master's degrees were likely to have held jobs in more than one school system.

Thus, for school systems to tie pay increases to extra credits seems to be self-defeating. Teachers who earn extra credits apparently feel that their educational achievements reach a joint beyond which they are overtrained for their jobs, and they then want to get administrative jobs or leave education for better paying jobs in industry. The school districts are, in a sense, encouraging teachers not to teach. This practice impedes the upgrading of teacher qualifications in another way. Thanks to the extra-credit system, schools of education have a steady supply of students and therefore are under little pressure to furnish better and more relevant courses.

For the most part, though, employers in the public sector do not suffer from problems of unrealistic educational requirements. For a variety of reasons, they do not enjoy favored positions in the labor market and consequently have not been able to raise educational requirements nearly so fast as the private employer has. But for this reason alone, the experiences of government agencies are significant. How well do their employees with low education backgrounds perform their jobs?

The pressure on the armed forces to make do with "what they get" has forced them to study their experiences with personnel. Their investigations clearly show that a person's educational achievement is not a good clue to his performance. Indeed, general tests developed for technical, military classifications and aptitude tests designed to screen individual candidates for training programs have turned out to be far better indicators of a person's performance. . . .

These . . . data do not conclude that education is unimportant, or that formal learning experiences are irrelevant. Rather, it points out the folly of confusing a man's driver's license with his driving ability. Just as different communities have different safety standards, so schools and school systems employ different kinds of teachers and practices. It should surprise no one that a person's credentials, by themselves, predict his performance so poorly. . . .

Perhaps the military's most impressive data came from its experiments with "salvage" programs, in which illiterates and men who earn low scores on military classification tests are given remedial training. According to research reports, these efforts have been uniformly successful—as many graduates of these programs develop into useful servicemen as the average, normal members of groups with which they have been regularly compared. . . .

Wartime employment trends make the same point. During World War II, when demand for labor was high, both public and private employers adapted their recruiting and training to the labor supply. Productivity soared while a wide range of people mastered skills almost entirely without regard to their personal characteristics or previous circumstances. Labor's rapid adjustment on the job was also considered to be expensive. Labor costs, it was argued, had gone up during the war, and unit productivity figures were cited as evidence. These figures, however, may have been misleading. Since the majority of wartime laborers were employed in industries with "cost-plus" contracts—where the government agreed to reimburse the contractor for all costs, plus a certain percentage of profit—such arrangements may have reduced the employer's incentives to control costs.

The important lesson from the war period seems to be that people quickly adjust to work requirements once they are on the job. . . .

Few organizations in the United States have had to adapt to major technological changes as much as the Federal Aviation Agency has. Responsible among other things for the direction and control of all flights in the United States, it operates the control-tower facilities at all public airports. With the advent of jet-powered flights, the FAA had to handle very quickly the horrendous technical problems posed by faster aircraft and more flights. Since no civilian employer requires the services needed by the FAA in this area, the agency must train its own technicians and control tower people. The agency inventively confronted the challenge by hiring and training many new people and promoting those trained personnel it already had. Working with the background data on 507 men, . . . it would seem that, at this high level, education would surely prove its worth.

Yet in fact these men had received very little formal education, and almost no technical managerial training except for the rigorous on-the-job training given by the FAA itself. Of the 507 men in the sample, 211, or 42 percent, had no education or training beyond high school. An additional 48, or 10 percent, were high school graduates who had had executive training courses. Thus, more than half of the men had had no academic training beyond high school. . . .

The FAA's amazing safety record and the honors and awards given to the tower controllers are good indicators of the men's performance. The FAA's Executive Selection and Inventory System records 21 different kinds of honors or awards. Only one-third of the men have never received any award at all. Half of the 77 percent who have been honored have been honored more than once. And a relatively high percentage of those with no education beyond high school received four or more awards; those with a B.A. degree were least likely to receive these many honors. Other breakdowns of the data confirm that education is not a factor in the daily performance of one of the truly demanding decision-making jobs in America.

The findings reported in these pages raise serious questions about the usefulness of raising educational requirements for jobs. They suggest that the use of formal education as a sovereign screening device for jobs adequately performed by people of lower educational achievements may result in serious costs—high turnover, employee dissatisfactions, and poorer performance. Programs calculated to improve employees' educations probably aim at the wrong targets, while programs calculated to reward better educated people are likely to miss their targets. It would be more useful to aim at employers' policies and practices that block organizational mobility and seal off entry jobs. . . .

Unfortunately, attempts to change people through education have been supported by liberal-intellectuals who place great value upon education and look appreciatively upon the economic benefits accruing to better educated Americans. Indeed, one of the few elements of consensus in present-day American politics may well be the reduction of the gap between the conservative and liberal estimate of the worth of education.

Obviously, the myths perpetuated about society's need for highly educated citizens work to the disadvantage of less educated people, particularly non-Whites who are handicapped whatever the state of the economy. Information obtained by economist Dale Hiestand of Columbia does not increase one's confidence that educational programs designed to help disadvantaged people over 14 years old will prove dramatically beneficial. Hiestand's studies show that even though the best educated non-Whites tend to have more job mobility, they are more likely to enter occupations that are *vacated* by Whites than to compete with Whites for *new* jobs. Since the competition for middle education jobs is already very intense, it will be difficult to leapfrog Blacks into jobs not yet vacated by Whites, or into new jobs that Whites are likely to monopolize.

Now, nothing in the foregoing analysis should be construed as suggesting that education is a waste of time. Many jobs, as was stated at the outset, have changed, and the need for education undoubtedly grows quite aside from the monetary benefits individuals derive from their educations. But I think it is fundamentally subversive of education and of democratic values not to see that, in relation to jobs, education has its limits.

As the burden of evidence in this article suggests, the crucial employment issue is not the "quality of the work force." It is the overall level of employment and the demand for labor in a less than full employment economy.

11c. SCHOOLING, IQ, AND INCOME

DAVID K. COHEN

Reprinted from "Does IQ Matter?", Commentary, April 1972, by permission. Copyright © 1972 by the American Jewish Committee. David K. Cohen is Professor of Education and Director of the Center for Educational Policy Research at Harvard University. His article summarizes the results of several different studies carried out at the center, some of which are reported more fully in Christopher Jencks, Inequality: A Reappraisal of the Effect of Family and Schooling in America *(New York: Basic Books, 1972). Thomas I. Ribich,* Education and Poverty *(Washington, D.C.: Brookings Institution, 1968) also deals with these issues from a somewhat different perspective.*

THE LAST FOUR OR FIVE YEARS have not exactly been years of glory for American liberals. Some of the reasons for this—like the war or the President—are ephemeral. At least one other, however—the depressing performance of recent liberal social programs—probably is not. The poor record of the social legislation of the '60s has seriously shaken confidence in traditional liberal reform strategies, and since education has always occupied a favored role in those strategies, it has come in for a good share of the questioning. The apparent failure of programs like Headstart has raised doubts as to whether investment in education for the poor will promote equality.

Most commentators have responded to this development in a characteristically American fashion. The failure of earlier programs has been attributed to inadequate resources, indifferent professionals, or intractable bureaucracies. Reform can proceed, we are told, only when more money is spent, or when educational institutions are made more responsive, or when the professions are made more accountable. In response to apparent failure a whole new generation of optimistic proposals has sprung up.

A few critics of Great Society programs, however, have been less hopeful. Some ask whether education is in fact the mechanism by which the distribution of wealth, power, or status has been affected in America. If schooling has not promoted equality among Whites, after all, it would be a little silly to expect it to do so for Blacks. Others have asserted that the failure of educational programs owes more to the deficiencies of poor children than to the defects of their schools. If the sources of school failure among the poor are either habits of mind imposed by culture or intellectual barriers imposed by heredity, they argue, it hardly makes sense to spend money on school improvement programs that rest on contrary assumptions.

Each of these two major lines of thought raises serious questions about received liberal doctrine, because each suggests that institutions or individuals are not as malleable as we have hitherto assumed. But there has been greater fascination with the question of deficiencies in the poor than with the possible limits of schooling as an equalizing strategy. A few years ago, in an essay in the *Harvard Educational Review*, Arthur Jensen reviewed the evidence on group differences in intellectual ability and school achievement; everything showed large and consistent gaps among groups. On the average, children whose families were poor or Black did much less well on tests than children whose families were well-to-do, or White. Jensen also pulled together a considerable body of research which suggested that differences in intelligence among individuals seemed to be caused more by heredity than by environment. And finally he ventured the idea that heredity may explain intellectual differences among groups as well as it appears to account for differences among individuals. . . .

[Then] Richard J. Herrnstein, a Harvard psychologist, published an essay in the *Atlantic Monthly* which generated quite a stir. Herrnstein broadened, refined, and defended arguments laid down earlier. He maintained that what IQ tests measure is an important and stable human attribute. He marshaled evidence that IQ differences among individuals are mostly accounted for by genes, not by environment. And he pressed the idea that intelligence is an increasingly powerful influence on the allocation of status, wealth, and power in advanced industrial societies. Although Herrnstein did point out the difficulty of generalizing from individual to group differences, his essay questioned the traditional liberal idea that stupidity results from the inheritance of poverty, contending instead that poverty results from the inheritance of stupidity.

These arguments, of course, are nothing new. The heritability of IQ first became a major public fixation in reaction to the turn-of-the century deluge of poor European immigrants. It bubbled to the surface once again just after the *Brown* decision in 1954, when racial mixing in public schools seemed to loom on the horizon. And not surprisingly it reemerged when the disappointing results of recent school-improvement programs for the poor became known. As this little chronicle may suggest, recent attention to the subject is not wholly the product of scientific interest. While the heritability of IQ holds a constant fascination for psychologists and demographers, most of the time they are the only people who care enough about the matter even to mention it. Only when there are broader issues involving ethnic or racial minorities—in which the character of the culture, or the allocation of public resources, or the composition of society is at stake—does the relationship between genes and IQ reach the front page of anything other than arcane professional journals.

But while this may help us understand the recent interest in the IQ question as a social phenomenon, it doesn't say much about the arguments themselves. *Does* heredity account for most individual differences in IQ? Does it account for class and racial differences in IQ? Is IQ really a good measure of intelligence, or a good predictor of the things that make for success in America?

Of all these issues, the role of heredity in making for differences in individual IQ has been the most thoroughly probed. One way of approaching it has been to compare the intelligences of identical twins who have been raised in different environments. Since identical twins have the same genetic endowment in all respects, any difference in their IQs that are not due to errors in measurement would presumably be traceable to differences in environment. In general, studies show that only about 20 or 30 percent of the variation in the IQs of twins can be attributed to variations in their environment—the rest presumably due to heredity.

Another approach has been to compare the intelligence of unrelated children reared together. Since their genetic material can safely be assumed to have nothing in common, any relationship between their IQs would probably be the result of environmental similarity. Studies of this kind have yielded roughly the same results as the research on twins—namely, that only about 20 or 30 percent of the variation in IQ is attributable to environment.

This evidence is nothing to sneeze at, but it might easily be misinterpreted. For one thing, genes and environment may interact in ways which would lead to overestimates of genetic influence: a child with a low IQ will probably be treated accordingly, while a brighter child would get more stimulation. This could easily enhance the bright child's IQ while depressing the dull child's even further; in studies of the sort summarized here, such effects, which are really environmental, would all be marked down to heredity. The magnitude of effects like these has never been estimated, nor is it clear that it could be.

Another problem with the twin studies has to do with the distribution of environments. Identical twins reared apart are nearly as rare as hen's teeth, and constriction in the range of their environments might overstate the importance of heredity. However, while the environments studied do not fully cover the available extremes in the United States or Britain, the range was still pretty considerable. That is, in at least a few cases one twin was sent to Scarsdale to grow up, and the other to Hoboken.

But let us suppose that instead of going to Scarsdale one twin had been placed in some sort of superenriched environment, absolutely booming and buzzing with the varieties of stimulation that psychologists regard as brain food. We don't know very much about the effects of changing the intensity of environments or of reversing inequalities in their distribution. The few small experiments that have been conducted here and there around the country suggest that certain varieties of stimulation do produce considerable IQ gains in disadvantaged children. Some of them, in fact, have produced gains of roughly the same magnitude as the gap which on the average separates the IQ of Blacks and Whites. These programs have involved either highly structured pre-schools or home-visiting programs designed to improve effectiveness of parents as teachers. They generally last about nine months or a year. In one experiment now under way in Milwaukee, however, children from poor families have been exposed to far more intense stimulation than usual. Instead of being visited by a teacher once a week, or being placed in a highly structured preschool in the mornings, children and their families are absolutely bombarded with environmental stimuli. The initial results show quite phenomenal IQ gains—often on the order of 30 or 40 points. It is much too soon to tell whether the gains will last. Evidence from other experiments indicates that as the experience recedes into the past so does its effect diminish. Three or four years after most such experiments end, researchers find that the gains have by and large vanished. No one knows what would happen if the experiments were more intense, or if they lasted for nine years instead of nine months. And for the immediate future, at least, these questions will remain unanswered.

One important point about all these studies, then, is that they show the malleability of IQ. But another is that the results are still compatible with the general pattern of findings on the relative influence of heredity and environment on IQ. Thus, to say (by way of example) that genes seem to account for 80 per cent of the variation among the IQs of individuals is not necessarily to say that only 20 percent of anyone's IQ is malleable. No one knows whether there is a "ceiling" on environmental effects or not, or what it might be. . . .

It would be astonishing if people ever stopped arguing about the relative influence of heredity and environment on individual IQ differences. Hereditarians will always point to evidence which shows that (things being what they are) more of the variability in IQ is explained by heredity, and environmentalists will always be able to point to evidence which encourages the belief that if environments were radically altered, IQ's might be sharply changed. Since these phenomena are not mutually exclusive, and since experiments to test the limits of environmental effects are unlikely to be devised, the argument will probably continue for the next 30 years in much the same terms as it has for the last 30.

The question of chief interest, of course, is not that of individual but of group differences. The sources of such differences, however, are not nearly so well illuminated by research. That there is a substantial gap in test scores between the races seems clear. What people want to know is whether the gap is a result of differences in heredity or environment, but the answer is hard to get at. The same conditions which make for interest in the question—the existence of large differences in both measured ability and social achievement—make it very difficult to decide where cause ends and effect begins. It is hard to figure out whether poverty causes low IQ or low IQ causes poverty, because they tend to occur in the same persons. The very people who are continually suspected of being genetically underendowed with respect to IQ have also been socially underendowed with respect to environment. This means, for example, that the full range of environmental differences that characterized native WASPs in the 1920s did not characterize immigrant Italians, and as a result it would have been well-nigh impossible to find comparable samples of Italians and WASPs on whom to conduct research.

The same holds for Blacks and Whites today. One can investigate the relative influence of heredity and environment among Blacks, just as in the studies of White children summarized earlier. But such studies of Black children would only tell us how much of the IQ variation among Blacks themselves is due to heredity; they would not tell us how much of the gap in test scores *between* the races is due to heredity and how much to environment. We can imagine ways to get around this problem: study unrelated Black and White children who were raised in the same home; or study a population of Black and White adults who have had the same environments; or (as one wag has suggested) find several pairs of identical twins who have been reared apart and each pair of whom consists of one White and one Black twin. But simply listing the examples reveals the problem: securing Blacks and Whites with the same environments is only a little easier than securing Blacks and Whites with the same natural parents. The environmental dif-

ferences America has created between Blacks and Whites are profound and ancient, and they can be expected to endure for some time. Until such differences have become a thing of the past for at least some Blacks, it is hard to see how respectable research can be done on the sources of the racial IQ gap. It is likely, however, that by the time such social equality is attained, either the environmentalists will be proved right by the disappearance of the IQ gap, or the very fact of social equality will cause everyone to lose interest in the question. Who now cares whether Italians have lower or higher IQs than native White Americans?

Oddly enough, in most of the arguments about genes and IQ over the past 30 years much greater attention has been paid to the question of the relative importance of circumstances and heredity than to figuring out exactly what IQ means, or what it is good for. Most people with very high IQ's seem very smart, and most people with very low IQ's seem very stupid. But people in between —which is where almost everyone is—are full of surprises. The fact that the tests can distinguish extremes so evident in everyday life inclines one to believe they measure something important. The fact that things get unclear in the middle, however, should make one dubious as to the value of the measuring-stick for most of everyday life.

What do IQ tests measure? Some people naively believe they provide a summary index of a general human ability to cope, but this would appear unlikely: think of the psychologist next door who nearly became unhinged trying to put together a hi-fi kit, or of the university sociologists who lost their shirts running a consulting firm, or of the brilliant computer freak who is incapable of writing an intelligible English sentence.

There are psychologists who believe that IQ tests measure one dimension of some more general and unified underlying intelligence. Perhaps, but at the moment it is hard to know. Psychologists are not in agreement on the elements of this underlying intelligence, and available research shows that sometimes the elements in question are connected only weakly or not at all. In fact, IQ is about the only thing psychologists *have* learned to measure with much validity or consistency, and as a result good research on the relation between IQ and other aspects of intelligence or personality is not plentiful.

Finally, there are people who think that intelligence is simply the ability to perform well at whatever one's social situation seems to require. This is obviously true in some ways, but in extreme form the notion is not really useful at all. Does it make sense to . . . argue that a high school student who flunked out and then became a successful numbers runner is just as smart as the valedictorian of his high school who couldn't get a job after graduation? Intelligence may not be timeless and unitary, but pushed to the extreme the relativist view dissolves in horrible contortions.

No doubt this debate could go on forever —in fact it probably will—but most people would not wish to pursue it. They assume a social definition of intelligence; they care about not what it is as a psychological construct, but how it works as a phenomenon in society. Indeed, many of those who worry about the proper definition of IQ do so chiefly because they think it is becoming the central criterion for distributing the good things of life. People care about IQ because they regard it as the basis on which society's rewards and punishments are allocated; they believe that America is becoming a society in which status and power are now, and will increasingly be, a function of brains.

This view is so widely held that it has become a sort of secular catechism. It certainly is repeated often enough, and in many different connections. Radicals attack America for allocating rewards on the basis of technical talent rather than need or human value; liberals bemoan the fact that discrimination has kept members of minority groups from competing on their own merits; Jews fear the demise of merit standards in employment and education, and Blacks attack the standards themselves as racist. Conservatives used to attack merit standards too, on the ground that some things were more important than

intelligence, but the fact that this argument no longer has enough credibility to be used in defense of privilege—it is now employed only on behalf of the poor—suggests how widespread is the belief that meritocracy is upon us.

In the light of this concern, the fuss over IQ is indeed . . . important. . . . However muddy the tests or biased their results, they exist; in a meritocracy of the sort we are said to have, such tests would undoubtedly be a major criterion for the allocation of rewards. The basic question, then, is whether, and how much, IQ counts in America in terms of status and power.

Perhaps the best place to begin is in the schools. Schools, after all, are where IQ is supposed to have its greatest impact, because it is in schools that children get routed on the various educational tracks which are presumed to play a considerable role in their chances for wealth and status later on. Really bright children are supposed to be routed into college preparatory work, and really not-so-bright children into vocational courses. Those in between are assigned to "general," business, or similar curricula. Then everyone graduates and goes to work, or drops out, or goes to college, and moves on to his appointed niche.

This picture is far from being wholly false, but it is by no means as true as most educators make it out to be. Take, for example, what is probably the most critical decision made during a child's school career: the kind of high school program he will follow. In a perfectly meritocratic system based on IQ this decision would rest exclusively on test scores; in a perfect caste system it would rest exclusively on one's inherited status. In the United States things are much more confused. According to studies of curricula assignments of high school students, measured ability is only one among several influential factors; others include the social and economic status of a student's family, his own aspirations for a career, and the degree of encouragement his parents have offered to those aspirations. The most comprehensive studies suggest in fact that these latter three influences on placement in high school are only slightly less important than measured ability.

Of course, a good deal happens to children in school before they even reach the point where decisions are made about their high school curriculum. They are graded and grouped from the very beginning, and all of these classification procedures undoubtedly have some impact—if not on how children regard themselves at least on what the teachers think about them. But the assignment of children to ability groups, like the assignment to curricula, seems to be determined by all sorts of things in addition to IQ. And grades too seem to be influenced as much by the attitudes of the children, their behavior toward authority, and their general demeanor as by their test scores.

But the most important point is that all of these factors together—ability, aspirations, inherited status, etc.—account for less than half of the actual variation in the assignment of students to one high school track or another. A majority of the differences among students in this respect, in other words, are caused by something other than either status or brains. This is not as odd as it might seem. Some of the differences probably arise from mistakes is assignments—bright children who want to go to college but lose out because of a slip or who are incorrectly assigned because of a perverse teacher. Some of the differences probably are caused by variations in the attitudes and motivation of the family, which seem to have a considerable impact on schooling decisions quite independently of parents' status or children's ability; lots of poor parents push their children very hard, and lots of non-poor parents don't. And some of the differences probably are caused by variations in deportment or motivation, or the encouragement students get from teachers, or other factors that usually go unmeasured. In short, if we consider only measured intelligence or inherited status, we cannot explain most of the variation in placement of students in high school.

What is the relative importance of IQ and inherited status as far as getting into college

is concerned? Here, after all, is one of the great divides in American life. A college degree is regarded increasingly as the only sure way to gain access to the good things in this society, and certainly college entrance is the goal toward which so much of the work of the schools is supposed to be aimed. How great a role does IQ play here?

If we look only at the relative influence of tested ability and inherited social and economic status, the available evidence does not show that college entrance is chiefly determined by academic ability. In fact, the relative importance of these two influences seem to be roughly equal. Consider, for example, a high school senior whose family is in the lowest fifth of the population with respect to both social status and test scores. Not only is this young person less bright than at least 80 percent of all high school seniors, but his family is less affluent than at least 80 percent of American families. In the early 1960s, he had roughly 1 chance in 10 of entering college the year after high school graduation.

By way of contrast consider his friend down the street, similarly situated with respect to family circumstances, but in the top fifth of the ability distribution. His family is poorer than over 80 percent of the population, but he is smarter than over 80 percent of all high school seniors. He has roughly 6 chances in 10 of entering college the year after graduating high school.

A comparison of these two seniors reveals that among poor students, when family circumstances are roughly the same, more brains means a much better chance of going to college.

What about more advantaged students—do IQ and status operate in the same way? Consider two seniors who come from families in the upper fifth of the distribution of social advantages and economic status. If one of them fell in the bottom fifth of the ability distribution, he would have roughly 4 chances in 10 of going to college. If the other fell in the top fifth of the ability distribution, he would have 9 chances in 10 of going to college. This comparison reveals that brains are a help at the top of the social pyramid, just as at the bottom: rich boys and girls with high IQs go to college more often than rich boys and girls with low IQs.

But now a comparison of the first pair of students with the second pair reveals that getting rich (moving from the bottom to the top of the social pyramid), is nearly as big a help in increasing a student's chances of going to college as getting smart (moving from the bottom to the top of the IQ distribution). More precise analyses of the data on college-going confirm the impression gained from these examples: measured intelligence is of slightly greater influence on college attendance than inherited status. This is a great deal different from a world in which going to college is wholly determined by family position, but it is far from a world in which going to college is wholly determined by intellectual ability.

Once again, however, these comparisons do not reveal what must be the most important fact—namely, that ability and status combined explain somewhat less than half the actual variation in college attendance. As in the case of curriculum placement, we must turn to other factors—motivation, luck, discrimination, chance, and family encouragement or lack of it—to find likely explanations. Existing research provides support for the idea that these other factors do play a role (although it does not afford comprehensive estimates of their relative importance).

Thus, while academic ability or intelligence is important to educational success, other factors, measured and unmeasured, seem to have at least as much weight in determining who gets ahead in the world of American schools. But this in turn raises an absolute swarm of problems. If test scores are only moderately important, should steps be taken to increase their influence? Or would relying more heavily on test scores in order to lessen the influence of social inheritance leave less room for people to be selected on other criteria, such as motivation? If the influence of inherited status on selection ought to be reduced, how great should the reduction be?

In a perfect meritocracy, after all, the objective would be to remove the effect of any social advantages parents had achieved on the life-chances of their children—but what sort of society would that be? Would it be consistent with a society of nuclear families? Does anyone want a society in which every child has an equal chance to be a clamdigger or a cardiac surgeon, subject only to IQ differences? The idea seems bizarre, for it suggests a social ratrace which would make the Great American Status Scramble look like a party game for retired schoolmarms. And if a perfect meritocracy seems like a perfect neurotic nightmare, then just how much, or how little, of an educational advantage would we want families to be able to pass along to their children?

Anyone who thinks about these questions for more than ten seconds will realize that no easy answers are available. More equality in education would be a good thing, and it is sensible to suppose that this implies some effort to reduce the influence of social and economic inheritance on school success. But the questions reveal that we have no well-formed conception of how much the impact of families ought to be reduced, or how much of a role IQ ought to have in reducing it. Nor, indeed, is it clear that IQ should bear that burden at all. Distributing rewards in accordance with IQ scores, after all, is not the only known device for reducing social and economic differences, even in education.

Of course, one's view on these last issues will depend in part on the role one thinks intelligence actually plays in the allocation of adult status and power. If it turned out that IQ was crucial, it would be hard to maintain that it ought not to be the principal means for discriminating among school children. So before going any further with these questions about meritocracy in schools, it might be wise to find out just how important IQ is once people get out of them. I will deal with occupational status first, because that is what seems to fascinate most writers on the subject.

One way of looking at this question . . . is by pointing to the evidence on the average

IQs of people in different occupations. Thus, manual laborers turn out to have much lower IQs than professors of theology, and this is assumed to mean that IQ is an entry requirement for these occupations. But simply presenting the gross differences begs all the basic questions. First, the averages don't reveal the considerable dispersion of IQs within occupational groups, which reveals that there are lots of people in working-class jobs whose IQs are in the same range as those in higher status occupations, and vice versa. But more significantly, listing IQ differences among occupations only tells us that differences exist; it does not tell us how important IQ was in getting people into those occupations.

A satisfactory account would indeed require that we know the IQs of people in different occupations, but it would require other information as well. We would need to know, for example, how far people got in school and what social and economic advantages their parents had, because these might have a real impact on their own occupational status as adults to say nothing of their IQs. Armed with evidence of this sort —which is hard to come by because it covers almost the entire life cycle—we could compare the relative importance of IQ and other influences on the sorts of jobs adults wind up with. Now we do in fact have a good deal of research which shows that people who stay in school longer wind up on the average with higher status jobs, and that on the average people who begin life with more social and economic advantages wind up with more of them as adults. But when researchers try to assess the relative importance of education and social inheritance they begin to part company. Some argue that staying in school is a considerably more important influence on occupational attainment than inherited status; others find the opposite to be true. The former category of researchers also tend to think of America as a relatively open society, in which schooling serves as a vehicle of social mobility from one generation to another. Researchers in the second category tend to think of America as a relatively closed society, in which the schools mostly transmit the same status from parents to children. Since both judgments are manifestly true to some degree, and since the evidence is not entirely adequate to resolve the matter, the argument will continue for some time. But what is important for our purposes is not how much mobility there is, or to what extent schooling contributes to it; rather we want to know whether IQ has an effect on occupational status which is *independent* of these two influences.

The available evidence suggests that it does not. IQ seems to have little or no independent effect on the sorts of jobs people wind up with as adults, all other things being equal. IQ does help moderately and indirectly, because it has a moderate influence on how long people stay in school, and the length of their stay in school affects the sorts of jobs they get. But once the influence of schooling is taken into account, IQ appears to have no independent relation to occupational success. If a meritocracy is a society in which intelligent people do well regardless of their parents or their schooling, America is not such a society.

To make this concrete, consider several adults who differ in every aspect under discussion here—jobs, IQs, length of stay in school, and social and economic backgrounds. The differences in their inherited status and in the length of time they stayed in school account for a fair proportion (somewhat less than half) of the differences in the status of their jobs. Since those who have higher IQs will have stayed in school somewhat longer, IQ can be said to have a moderate effect on occupational status. But when people with equal amounts of schooling are considered, differences in their IQs turn out to account for none of the differences in the status of their jobs. Having a higher IQ is no help in getting a higher status job for people who have the same educational attainment and the same social and economic background. In addition, there is an abundance of studies showing that the grades of college students are not related either to their income or to their occupational status once they get out of college; similarly, research on what differentiates good from bad workers (within broad occupational categories) shows that workers who produce more or who are rated highly by their supervisors generally do not have higher test scores, although they do tend to have "better" attitudes, greater "motivation," better "deportment"—in effect, more of the attributes which also seem to make for success in school.

Thus, the process of selection to occupations in America does not appear to be more than mildly dependent on IQ. And here too, as in the case of high school placement and college entrance, recent research has shown that IQ, schooling and inherited status together account for less than half of the variation in the occupational attainment of American males. More than half of the differences in the job status of American men is explained neither by their IQ, nor by how long they went to school, nor by the social economic advantages (or burdens) they inherited. Some of these unexplained differences are undoubtedly due to errors in the ways sociologists measure things, but others are probably due to such imponderables as enterprise, motivation, the luck of the draw, and preferences unrelated either to brains or to economic background.

That, however, is not the end of the matter. Whatever the evidence may suggest about the modest influence IQ presently exerts on occupational selection, the popular mythology is that it is much greater now than it was 50 years ago. America, we are told, is a "knowledge society"; we are moving into a post-industrial age, in which talent will rule. Yet when we turn to historical evidence concerning the role of IQ in occupational selection, once again we find little support for such claims. If IQ were becoming a more important force in occupational selection we would expect the IQ averages of people in any occupation to have become more similar over time: the IQs of professional people should have grown more nearly equal as merit selection proceeded, and the same would be true of blue-collar workers. But the fragmentary evidence we have suggests this is not true:

the dispersion of IQs within occupational categories for native American whites seems to have remained pretty stable over the last four or five decades. Similarly, if IQ were becoming more important we might expect the intellectual level of intellectually demanding occupations to rise, and the level of undemanding jobs to fall. But no such development seems to have taken place. Finally, if IQ were becoming more important to adult success, we would imagine that the main instrument by which IQ makes itself felt in America—schooling—would have become more important to getting a job. But according to the historical evidence concerning the effect of schooling on occupational attainment over the past four or five decades, education seems to bear no more powerful relationship to the job one gets today than it did earlier in the century.

Now all of this evidence is partial, and subject to a variety of caveats. But the striking thing is that nowhere can we find any empirical support for the idea that brains are becoming increasingly more important to status in America. Of course, this by itself is not incompatible with the observation that "knowledge" is an increasingly central aspect of life. For one thing, measures of occupational status are based on opinion surveys in which random samples of the American people are asked about the relative prestige of occupations. Thus, the "importance" of intellectual work would appear to change only if people thought its prestige was changing. But in general public attitudes toward the relative prestige of various occupations have changed very little over time, so that, paradoxically, intellectual work may in fact be becoming more important even though this is not reflected in the measures used by sociologists. No one has ever actually set out to measure how much more important technological and scientific work is now than in 1920, and probably no one ever will.

But even if we assume that brains *are* becoming more important or powerful (a moot point in my view), other things are changing as well. Fifty years ago most Americans never finished high school, and only a tiny percentage went on to college. Now almost everyone finishes high school, and more than one third go on to some form of post-secondary education. This means that lots of ordinary people who would never have had the chance 50 years ago to be doctors or teachers or engineers, have the chance today. If brains are becoming more powerful at the same time as schooling becomes more universal (and thereby opens up opportunity through the power of certification), the two tendencies may cancel each other out. Of course I am speculating here, but observed evidence would tend to support this view, and to suggest also how complicated the relationship among intelligence, status, and power can be; some social forces may be acting to intensify the connection at the same time as others are weakening it. . . .

Another cause of the connection between schooling and adult success may be that schools are becoming the principal vehicle for "professionalizing" occupations. Especially in the marginal and semimarginal professions, adding educational requirements for certification and licensing is a way of enhancing the standing and respectability of a given line of work in the eyes of its practitioners and clients. It also is a way of persuading people that the occupation in question is up-to-date, modern, and in touch with the latest wisdom. And it often is a way (as with teachers, for example) of getting a bigger paycheck. But whatever the explanation, the additional educational requirements cannot be said to have much relation to job performance.

When schooling becomes necessary to later occupational standing for essentially nonintellectual reasons, various unhappy consequences can result. One such consequence is the subversion of the legitimate purposes of educational institutions, and the breeding of contempt for what they do; another is the creation of an occupational selection system in which the ability to remain glued to the seat of a chair for long periods of time becomes a prime recommendation for advancement. (The ability to sit still is useful for many purposes, but especially among chil-

dren it may not be related to the ingenuity, enterprise, and cleverness which any lively society would want to promote.) Under such a system of occupational selection, we are as likely to produce an unhealthy accumulation of boredom and discontent as we are to create a dangerous maldistribution of intellect.

Developments like these are the more distressing because of the greater uniformity they promise, both in what people do and in how they think about it. Such uniformity has not always characterized American society. There is fairly convincing evidence, for example, of ethnic differences in the role that schools have played in promoting occupational mobility. Studies of European ethnic groups show that during this century all of them made substantial increases in occupational status, but that they did so in rather different ways. The children of Russian immigrants (which means Jews for the most part) completed more years of school, on the average, than children from other groups. In addition, educational attainment had a much stronger relationship to the later occupational attainment of these children than it did for children from other groups—which probably means that a disproportionate number of Jews went into occupations which had substantial educational requirements. Not all nationalities had the same experience; Italian and Polish children, for example, tended to complete fewer years of school than those of some other groups. But for Italians and Poles educational differences were not in themselves an important influence as far as later occupational status was concerned.

The history of ethnic variations in the importance of schooling suggests in turn the underlying differences in the avenues that various ethnic groups have taken to achieve higher social and economic status. . . . But the important point is that to the extent that schooling is made an unavoidable requirement for occupational entry or advancement, it may close off genuine cultural differences in occupational values, and irrationally stifle alternatives which might otherwise flourish. To the extent that success in a homogeneous system of schooling becomes the sine qua non of entry to occupations, cultural diversity in conceptions of success and worthy work may be diminished. It is hard to think of any good which could possibly come from that situation.

In a sense, however, all the attention to the relative status of occupations is misleading. It is easy to understand why intellectuals might be obsessed with the question, but it is important in the discussion of meritocracy only because of the assumption that jobs which require brains wield more power than jobs which don't. If it turned out that people with high IQs did not really have more power than ordinary folks, there wouldn't be very much left for one to argue about.

Normally when intellectuals write about this question they bemoan the fact that people like themselves have *little* power and influence. Indeed, they have mourned this situation for so long that most Americans who read what intellectuals write probably concluded long ago that anyone who has power is either a knave or a fool. As a result, it comes as something of a surprise to hear that intellectuals are in danger of having too much power. But if holding political office, for instance, is an index of power, it is hard to see any cause for alarm, for there certainly is no evidence of an undue concentration of raw IQ among the ranks of government officials. Indeed, it is hard to imagine why anyone would think government officials should have unusually high IQs. After all, the motives which lead men and women into public life probably have more to do with the desire for power, or money, or recognition, than with the need to exercise a restless and powerful intellect.

Politics, however, is only one of the several sources of power and influence in America; great wealth is another. Here again, it should come as no great surprise to learn that a high IQ is not the main requirement for having lots of money. People with more schooling do tend to have somewhat higher incomes, but the relationship between the two is not even as strong as the relationship between schooling and occupational status. Partly this is due to the fact that lots of jobs with rather high status—preaching, teaching,

and the like—don't come with cushy salaries, and lots of jobs with rather low status, like being a plumber or a machinist, do. There also is the fact that spending decades in school is a condition of employment in most of the high status but low paying jobs, but not a condition of tenure in the others. And finally, doing well in school is not yet a prerequisite for inheriting money. . . .

Finally, anyone who imagines that "experts" with high IQs have a great future in public life ought to visit his nearest government agency and see how it works. Most important government business turns not on the technical skills that experts do monopolize, but on ethical and political considerations. Experts have had to relearn this lesson every few years since the progressive era.

Let us try to summarize, in general form, the conclusions of all this.

First, America is not a meritocracy, if by that we mean a society in which income, status, or power are heavily determined by IQ. All the evidence suggests that IQ has only moderate impact on adult success, and that this impact is exerted only through the schools.

Second, America seems on balance not to have become more meritocratic in the course of the 20th century. All the evidence suggests that the relationship between IQ and income and status has been perfectly stable. While opportunity has opened up for great segments of the population, the criteria for advancement seem to have involved many things in addition to, and other than, IQ.

Third, something we often incorrectly identify with IQ—namely schooling—seems to be a much more important determinant of adult success than IQ. If getting through school is a mark of merit, then America is moderately meritocratic. But then, in a society in which education is an increasingly universal experience, such a conception of merit begins to lose its meaning.

And finally, among all the many factors which lead to a situation in which some people are poor or hold low-status jobs, lower intellectual ability is not a terribly important one. Being stupid is not what is responsible for being poor in America.

12. WORKING-CLASS FAMILY LIFE-STYLES AND SOCIAL ALIENATION

LEE RAINWATER

Reprinted from "Making the Good Life: Working-class Family and Life-styles," by Lee Rainwater in Blue Collar Workers: A Symposium on Middle America, *Sar A. Levitan, ed., (New York: McGraw-Hill, 1971). Lee Rainwater is Professor of Sociology at Harvard University.*

■ The poor are regarded as a problem in society because they don't fit very well into our ideal picture about how society operates, and because they seem disproportionately involved in other kinds of problems (crime, welfare costs, etc.). But surely the great working class, which is not poor and which provides the backbone of the nation, should not *also* be regarded as a problem. Yet from time to time the elite—intellectuals and society's managers alike—regard as problematic the attitudes and behavior of the broad class of blue-collar and gray-collar (service) workers. Exactly how the problem is diagnosed depends on the politics and ideology of the diagnostician. Some of radical persuasion will hold that the working class is counterrevolutionary, and in communist nations it may be held that the working class is not properly appreciative of what the leaders of society have accomplished for them. Where the persuasion is more conservative, the complaint may be that the working class is too assertive and greedy in its struggle for higher wages and other kinds of benefits.

In the late 1960s the liberal-to-center person who identified himself with the Democratic Party was most sorely tried by the working class. The strong showing of Governor George Wallace of Alabama in his first presidential bid in 1964, and even more in 1968, brought home to these people the "reactionary" potential of the working class. White working-class resistance to Black advances in housing and school desegregation represented a further problem. In the first years of the Nixon Administration, Republican Party workers encouraged working-class resentment which achieved its symbolic apotheosis in the "hard-hat" phenomenon wherein construction workers attacked bearded peace marchers to demonstrate their disapproval of the lack of patriotism among hippies and college youth.

In this article I try to put into the context of the styles of life and adaptive pressures of working-class life the undoubted disdain of many working-class people for the symbols of libertarian commitment. The article exemplifies the necessity to go behind the attitudes and behaviors one may regard as "a problem" if one is to understand the sources and depth of whatever is defined as an interference with preferred strategies of social action. A great deal of working-class response can be understood more as resentment of the rhetoric by which the elite conduct politics than as disagreement with the basic equalitarian program the liberal elite seeks to advance. In the few years since the height of concern about working-class reaction (around 1970), we have seen the birth of a new populism that seeks to pull together the liberal preferences of the elite with the needs and equalitarian sentiments of both majority and minority working- and lower class people. Whether that effort will succeed in reestablishing or moving beyond the older Democratic coalition is still an open question, but it does suggest that the panic occasioned by working-class alienation of the late 1960s and early 1970s was a response to a pseudo-problem rather than a real one.

A number of studies provide useful background for understanding the working-class situation, in particular Mirra Komarovsky, *Blue Collar Marriage* (New York: Random House, 1964); and Herbert J. Gans, *The Urban Villagers* (New York: Free Press, 1962). An excellent review of data on the contemporary political attitudes of working-class people is found in Richard F. Hamilton, "Black Demands, White Reactions, and Liberal Alarms," in *Blue Collar Workers: A Symposium on Middle America*, ed., Sar A. Levitan. The other chapters in that book cover a range of working-class and blue-collar situations, attitudes, and institutions, and the impact of various kinds of public policies on them. A useful book dealing with some of the same issues is Patricia Cayo Sexton and Brenden Sexton, *Blue Collars and Hard Hats: The Working Class and the Future of America Politics* (New York: Random House, 1971). An influential analysis of working-class attitudes toward the goals of liberty and equality is Robert E. Lane, *Political Ideology* (New York: Free Press, 1962). ∎

WORKING CLASS OR MIDDLE CLASS?

PERHAPS THE MAJOR SUCCESS STORY of the post-World War II decades has been the steadily increasing level of prosperity and security of the average American working-man and his family. Although there is no evidence of significant redistribution of income from the top to the bottom half of the population, the working class's share of the rapidly rising GNP has resulted since 1947 in a near doubling of family income in dollars of constant purchasing power. A combination of government policy and individual family choices has resulted in an investment of much of that dramatically increasing purchasing power in a similarly dramatic increase in homeownership and suburban dwelling among the working class.

This good news has been celebrated all along the way by governments, by business, by the party in power ("you never had it so good"), and, not least, by working-class people themselves, who have always been ready to testify as to how much more comfortable and secure their lives are than their parents' were.

The increases in income experienced by the working class and the investment of these increases in a wide range of mass-market products have also led from time to time to premature celebration of the "middle classification" of the working class. Commentators representing business and government perspectives have time and again pointed toward the gradual disappearance of differences between blue-collar- and white-collar-based groups. For example, at the end of the Eisenhower years, the

Labor Department celebrated the disappearance of the distinctive working-class way of life, arguing that "the wage earner's way of life is well nigh indistinguishable from that of his salaried co-workers." In fact, however, studies by sociologists of the life-styles of the stable working class during the late 1950s and into the 1960s suggest that for all the tremendous change in life wrought by affluence, urbanization, and suburbanization, working-class life-styles continue to be relatively distinctive compared to lower middle class life-styles. For one thing, working-class people do not want to be carbon copies of the lower middle class that they know. Moreover, the lower middle class itself has changed so that even when working-class people adopted life-style traits characteristic of the lower middle class, the latter had shifted enough in life styles to retain class distinctions.

The invention of the Silent Majority made working-class world views, attitudes, and political action an issue of establishment concern. The results of public-opinion polls and the apparent auguries from various recent elections suggested that somehow the American economic miracle of working-class affluence and security was no longer believed in by its beneficiaries. No doubt from the late 1940s through the early 1960s working-class people had thought of themselves as the beneficiaries (to be sure, by dint of their own hard work) of the great American nation, which, through its democratic genius and technological creativity, was managing to pay off most handsomely for the average man. Now it seemed that the working class (and not they alone) had begun to feel that the American golden goose was losing its touch. Somehow it was no longer able to make things work right, and therefore the Democratic, Eastern-dominated establishment that had been in charge of the goose should be replaced by political forces that might get the country back on the right track again.

Our concern . . . [here is] to show how the constraints of working-class reality may work upon that way of life to produce the social and political attitudes that have lately become a source of concern of liberals and of joy to rightists.

COMFORT AND SECURITY FOR THE FAMILY

The central life goal of the stable working class is the creation of a comfortable and secure place for oneself and one's family. Once this is achieved, there is then room for efforts to make life more and more pleasurable by engaging in activities which are more playful and less earnest than' those directed to assuring family comfort and its continuation.

This goal of making the good life has both positive and negative referents. The negative referents are perhaps the more powerful. Working-class couples are centrally concerned with getting away from or staying away from the disorganized and frightening world of poverty and the slums. For many working-class people who moved out of such a world either in adult life or as they were growing up, the morally frightening and socially degrading lower class world is an ever-present centrifugal reference point. Others have not known that world personally but view it as a possibility, perhaps more mythical than actual, representing "what could happen" if economic sufficiency somehow failed.

A less prominent but nevertheless important negative reference point—particularly as working-class families move above what might be regarded as the minimum level for sustaining a working-class life-style—is the quieter and more constrained circumstance of just managing to get by, of having so little in the way of resources that one can just barely feed, shelter, and clothe one's family. This image of penury also haunts many working-class people who know of it from personal experience, from growing up in depressed families, or being told and retold family stories about the Great Depression. Here the danger is not that of moral survival as in the slum's threat to family respectability, but rather the survival of a fully human rather than stunted spirit. As we will see, working-class people are constantly aware of the need to exercise great self-control and care in spending their money; but they see a world of difference between the self-control needed to maintain a comfortable and gratifying standard of living, and the desperate control and care needed just to keep body and soul together.

The life-style of the working class, then, is constructed to ward off such negative but realistic possibilities. In addition, of course, the central strivings that motivate the working-class life-style have positive elements that involve a reaching out for known or imagined positive potentialities. Working-class people are deep believers in the possibilities of (though not overly sanguine about the inevitability of) a personally gratifying and meaningful existence. They tend to define these potentialities in terms of the amenities which a productive, technological society can provide, and in terms of the round of life that can be constructed with those amenities as the building blocks. The operating imagery of the good life is "the mainstream." Working-class people construct from many sources (people around them, more-favored relatives, mass media, advertising) a conception of a standard package of consumer goods and services which allow one to operate in, consider himself a part of, and be considered by others a part of the mainstream of American life. Living in the mainstream reassures you both that you have escaped the moral threat and human constriction of poverty and the slums and that you are enjoying a fair share of the good things that your world has to offer. One of the reasons that working-class people do not become middle class as their standard of living rises is that they reinterpret the mainstream consumer package in terms of their own goals and values. When they are able to afford a given object, they do not necessarily buy it for the same qualities that had attracted the middle class people who were the former principal users of it. For example, while a middle class woman is likely to value a dishwasher so that she can get out of the kitchen more quickly, a working-class woman is more likely to value it for the time and effort it allows her to invest in some other kitchen activity, or just for the lesser effort she will have to expend on her house-wifely chores. Owning a dishwasher does not make her more interested in becoming a clubwoman like her middle class sister.

The social capital needed to make the good life is, in working-class logic, perfectly straightforward. In order to enter the main-stream, you simply make a family by com-bining a man who is a good and faithful provider with a woman who is a sensible, responsible, and loving housewife-mother. All other things (such as economic conditions and personal health) being normal, this com-bination and the children the man and the woman have are assumed to produce a family that enjoys the good American life by dint of applying hard work and good sense. Children in this imagery are relatively passive objects, more products than subjects of the family unit. More emphasis is placed on what the parents can do for and to children in forming them into eventual adults like them-selves than on what the children contribute to the family's life. This construction of what the family is all about is simpler than in the middle class. Middle class parents are more likely to emphasize the children as interacting units in a whole family system which to-gether establishes its particular style of life. The tendency to see children either as pas-sive products of well-intentioned parents or, when something goes awry in that plan, as destructive and uncontrollable ("bad seed") makes for an inevitable conflict between the parents' definition of children as passive and their children's, particularly adolescents', natural assertiveness; this is traditionally handled by segregating children's activities from adult surveillance and by a tacit agree-ment of adults not to pry too fully into what adolescents are doing. Intensive media attention to the rebellious activities of youth has shattered this fiction of youth's passivity. Traditionally, these conflicts within working-class families and neighborhoods were mini-mized because young men and women termi-nated adolescence at a much earlier age than today by going to work. Now that working-class youths leave school later, their parents are under increased pressure to accommodate to "youth culture."

WORKING-CLASS WORLD VIEWS

The working-class family's method of achieving the good life reflects several charac-teristics of their orientations toward them-selves and the world around them. Working-class men and women resolutely regard them-selves as middle class. When given the option of designating themselves as working or mid-dle class, the great majority of them choose the former label. They recognize the distinc-tion in life station between white-collar and their own blue- or gray-collar worlds; yet they are often ambivalent when contemplating their own or their children's chances of mov-ing into such a world.

They tend to regard their own class as generous and kindly compared to the selfish-ness of those above or below them in status. People of superior status are seen as selfishly devoted to their own ends or to their own small social circle. To them, the price of striving after career success is a loss of the comfortable virtues of family devotion and shared time with wife, children, and relatives. They view the lower classes as selfish in a different way: "not caring," being involved in personal pleasures to the detriment of one's responsibilities, and unwilling to work hard in order to support and care for a family. Thus, the selfishness of the lower classes stems from "weakness of character"; that of the higher classes is an unfortunate vice bound up with an otherwise admirable "strength of character." One of the reasons working-class people are ofter uninterested in moving up to middle class status is that they believe the price to be that of accepting a more formal and self-controlled way of life. This formality tends to be strongly disliked; there is often the feeling that a secure working-class life provides for an optimally comfortable and interpersonally easy existence.

The group sees itself, then, as the backbone of the nation. In pre-World War II days the working class tended to define itself as "poor but honest folks." The rapid increase in affluence since World War II has dropped the self-conception as "poor." On the other hand, working-class people find it hard to conceive of themselves as affluent since they still have a sense of effort and struggle to achieve and maintain the standard American consumer package. At the same time, that package itself is so impressive that they know they are not poor.

The central roles in the good life are those of the husband as provider and the wife as mother-homemaker. The conjugal tie generally receives less emphasis in the stable working-class family than in the middle class; more emphasis is placed on the spouses' roles as operators of a family than on the affective demands between them. Thus there tends to be a sharper division of labor between the husband and wife, and less sharing of interest in leisure time and activities. The deep family orientation of the working class is perhaps its principal characteristic. And the family is imbued with such heavy responsibility that sometimes pleasure (as opposed to meaningfulness) hardly seems compatible with it. Working-class men experience a sharp discontinuity between their premarital and early marital roles. Before marriage, the greatest meaning in their life comes from being one of the boys in the extended adolescent-to-youth peer group. Their relations with girls tend to be fairly distant and either constricted or exploitative. With marriage they must not only come to terms with conjugal relations with a "stranger," but also give up irresponsible ways and irresponsible peer group activity and settle down and become a provider of the good-life consumer package. Since early adulthood is also a time of low stability and earnings, the combined pressures of personal, interpersonal, and economic adjustment threaten the early years of working-class marriages. When the marriages survive, the husband and wife often have a sense of weary triumph over both themselves and adverse external circumstances.

Traditionally the working-class family orientation included a very heavy involvement with kin, extending over a wide generational range in working-class communities where there has not been a great deal of geographic mobility. Very likely, much of what has been heralded as the ethnic quality of working-class life is more properly regarded as simply an extended family orientation. With greater geographical mobility—particularly as the working class is more and more suburbanized—the kin-based social network tends to be attenuated. Working-class men and women often lament the fact that large family gatherings seem much less frequent than they used to be. Since much of the sense of social security that working-class people have traditionally felt has come from being enmeshed in a network of ties based on blood, it may well be that one of the prices of affluence and modernity is a greater sense of isolation and social anxiety.

Working-class people have no clearly established place for ties that reach wider than those of family or close friends toward whom one adopts a kinlike relationship. The middle class emphasis on community roles and responsibilities sits very uneasily in working-class identities. Working-class women are concerned mainly with their homes, and by some small extention perhaps with the school or church. They belong to few voluntary associations, because they are not sure that it would be right for them. Husbands are concerned with the outside world, but the only concern that is really taken for granted has to do with the world of work. Working-class men do not generally have much interest in assuming community roles or participating in civic activities. On the other hand, they have a strong sense of loyalty and patriotism to country, and they know that within their family it is their job to be concerned and informed citizens. It is they who must shoulder the burden of fighting wars, because they are in fact the backbone of the nation at such times, as they are in the area of economic production.

But the preferred world of the stable working class is one in which the individual minds his own business and avoids larger entanglements than those of work and family. They feel that the challenges and the energy required for working and family life are more than enough to ask of any man or woman. And what more can a nation ask of its citizens than that a man work and be productive and that men and women together raise a next generation that is also productive and responsible?

Middle class and working-class perspectives on a family's life cycle across the decades show a striking difference. Whereas the middle class tends to see family circumstances as progressively better as the breadwinner matures and progresses in his career, and as the family's position is consolidated socially, working-class couples tend to view life in the future as essentially a replica of life in the present. They perceive a plateau—with the ever-present danger of things getting worse, not better. The middle class family typically expects to be considerably better off in the later family stages than in the earlier ones by virtue of increased earning power of the husband (and wife, if it is a two-career family). The working-class family sees itself better off in the future only by virtue of what it may have accumulated and constructed for itself—by saving their money or increasing the number of hours worked (though there is some acknowledgment also that wages for all tend to rise with time and therefore the future should be somewhat better than the present).

The plateau conception subtly affects the working-class conception of later family years. Working-class men tend to look forward to the possibility of retiring at an age which middle class men would regard as the time for just getting into full swing of a career. If they begin their families in their late teens or early twenties and their children finish high school and perhaps a little college, and get married by the time the parents are in the mid to late forties, it makes good sense to want to retire and enjoy life at that time. If one's way of life has been modest, if a good deal of the expensive consumption which husband and wife have struggled so hard to afford has been for the benefit of "the family" (that is, the children), then early retirement —perhaps in a better climate—can be a well-earned reward.

While working-class families have always wanted to do well by their children, to bring them up to be respectable but at the same time to find some enjoyment in life, their child rearing orientation has apparently shifted over the last two or three decades in a direction that would previously have been regarded as middle class. That is, working-class families now frequently orient themselves toward "giving" their children the good things of life. They still want to do well by them, but they also want them to enjoy themselves as they are growing up. This is a relatively new conception of parental responsibility for the working class. It accompanies a more suburbanite orientation and a greater involvement of the husband in the home as opposed to his own male peer group. Working-class people themselves often comment on the change, contrasting their own behavior with their parents' more standoffish and removed style when they were growing up. Very likely this trend follows upon the greater equalization of roles of men and women which Goode has observed is characteristic of industrialized and industrializing societies. . . .

WORKING-CLASS MORALE

The outside observer, depending upon his mood, standards, and ideological ax to grind, can look at the life-style of working-class people and see several things. In the past many commentators, impressed by the well-being of the working class, have tended either to celebrate the affluence and ease of their lives or to lament the *embourgeoisement* of the workers. In the last few years as working-class men and women have given unmistakable political indications that they are not very happy about the state of the world, it has become fashionable to stress the struggle and frustration that go into making a prosperous working-class life. But these are fashionable observer stances and in all likelihood do not reflect the real conditions of working-class life.

The working-class way of life has its costs and rewards. Anxiousness and isolation are probably the principal costs perceived by working-class men and women. The anxiety is constantly present because the working-class couple do not know whether they will be able to sustain the income they need to remain in the mainstream. Unemployment and ill health are frightening dangers because there is little margin against them in the form of savings, pension rights, or insurance.

Less obvious, but more pervasive, is the effect of social isolation. The pursuit of the good life, by concentrating energies heavily on the family, tends to increase working-class people's isolation from the community around them. The husband who has two jobs in order to make enough money to launch his new home is not likely to be very much interested in what goes on at either workplace. The wife, for her part, is often isolated both physically and psychologically. Psychologically she is deeply committed to her children and her homemaking, and she regards other commitments as distracting and potentially dangerous because they may reduce her effectiveness at home. And when the working-class family manages to acquire the house in the suburbs, the wife finds herself physically isolated. The family can afford only one car, and a surprisingly large number of working-class women do not know how to drive anyway. Thus the wife may not be able to get away from the house during the day unless a relative or neighbor drives her. She does her shopping with her husband in the evenings and on weekends. All she sees is her house, her yard, and a little bit of the neighbors' houses and yards. With her family she visits relatives and sees their familiar houses. For the most part this is the way she wants life to be, but the sameness haunts her from time to time; and she has the feeling of being trapped, of being so much of service to others that there are no time and resources left for her own pleasures.

If working-class people have occasion to examine their lives, most of them can find reasons for joy or sadness, gratitude or recrimination, comfort or frustration. Working-class people generally prefer to look at their lives with measured and pragmatic optimism. They prefer to recall how well things have gone and how much they have accomplished; by reflecting on this, they sustain their optimism about a future of which they are never quite certain. They believe that one's chances of having a good life, of being successful, are compounded of (1) strictly individual events and (2) the odds for all people such as they. In the post-World War II period the working class's assessment of their odds has tended to be quite positive. Despite threats of unemployment on the one hand and inflation on the other, the general sense of prosperity and security in contrast to the pre-World War II period has sustained an optimistic view of the chances for achieving a good life. In the working-class logic it then rests with the individual whether he in fact achieves such a life. His own chances are maximized by working hard and having a little bit of luck. You can have bad luck by getting sick or having an accident. A woman can have bad luck if her husband turns out unaccountably to be an alcoholic. A man can have bad luck if his job disappears while employment is generally good for everyone else. But these are personal problems requiring individual adjustment and the assistance of the people around you. Similarly, good luck may improve upon the achievements of hard work—if one is lucky enough to fall in love with and marry a girl whose father is a housebuilder who presents the couple with a house for a wedding present, or if one finds his way into a high-wage union-protected job. Such good luck merits enjoyment but must not go to one's head.

When, however, being sorely pressed by one's situation is interpreted as an indication of a turn for the worse in the odds for people in similar circumstances, then the basis for a nonindividual (political) interpretation is present. In such a situation, the traditional bread-and-butter issues of working-class politics—unemployment, wage levels, inflation—become salient.

Working-class morale is also affected by one's estimate of whether one's children can live a more prosperous mainstream life. Even when working-class parents are reasonably satisfied with their participation in the mainstream, they may be anxious about whether their children will be able to continue that participation. Much of this anxiety seems to center around the role of education in achieving economic status. Working-class people fear that the educational price of admission to mainstream jobs is going to increase so that their children will not have a decent chance unless they go to college. Thus, college would become not just an avenue to mobility, but a necessary path to staying where the parents are. Because working-class people feel intimidated by the financial demands of college and are not sanguine about their children's desire to go to college, they are doubly worried. Working-class people feel pressured by the rest of society, which continually emphasizes the value, the desirability, the moral superiority of college education. They would prefer a situation in which high school graduation plus hard work would merit participation in the mainstream, and they are confused by the middle class emphasis on college for the masses. But if events decree that college is necessary to compete for those mainstream jobs, then they are prepared to encourage their children to go to college and, reluctantly, to bear some of the costs. Until now they have regarded college as for the mobile young man. Working-class people are no longer surprised that many persons from their group attend college. It is just that they prefer a world in which college education is not necessary for a decent life. In the context of these varied issues, the tremendous anger which working-class people have recently expressed toward youthful rebellion and exhibitionism can be understood. The anger accompanies anxiety that their children, too, may be weaned away by the dramatic and obviously gratifying, if immoral, activities of college kids. The most direct impact of youthful immorality upon their lives has to do with the apparent widespread use of drugs in high school (and now in junior high school)—a problem which for all their brave self-assurance that their children would not participate cannot but concern the working-class parent. Drugs stand as a near-at-hand symbol for all the other kinds of immoral activities into which their sons (and less likely, their daughters—college education for girls is not regarded as particularly valuable) might be seduced should they go to college. In a singularly dramatic and nightmarish way, college attendance—the former mark of an upper middle class existence—now represents to the working-class parent the same moral danger that his children would have faced had the family not been able to escape the slums.

Inflation is the most immediate pressure working-class couples feel—an endemic pressure which in the past few years has been raised to a much higher level. Working-class women are especially alert to inflationary surges, since they have to pay keen attention to how they spend their money. Whether or not the issue is being played up by the media or in political contests, they see inflation in the grocery store and (less regularly) at other stores. They convey their concern to their husbands, and before long the husbands are concerned too. Whereas unemployment is a disastrous threat to the relatively few people whom it affects, inflation affects all families in this class. The bread-and-butter issues of inflation and unemployment are by far the most potent political issues in the lives of the working class because such problems threaten in a direct and unambiguous way the central life goals of these families.

POLITICIANS, ESTABLISHMENTARIANS, AND THE WORKING CLASS

The currently fashionable diagnosis of working-class conditions, however, addresses itself not to these traditional economic issues but rather to a mood of social alienation and a rightward swing that some argue is characterizing middle America. The present analysis, however, suggests that anger over what Scammon and Wattenberg have called "the Social Issue," to the extent that it characterizes the working class these days, is a fairly superficial concern, probably reflecting more the dynamics and pathologies of politics and the mass media (amplified by the frustrating economic situation over the past three years) than any deep rightist trend. At the base of the White working-class reaction to crime, racial turmoil, and campus unrest is probably a sense of unwarranted invasion of the tranquility of their private lives. That is, working-class men and women assume a stance of detachment, if not outright ignorance, toward the larger social-political scene. Somehow, the events and the politics of the last five years have conspired to force working-class people to pay more attention to politics than they would prefer, a fact which may anger them even more than their disapproval of what is going on in the ghettos, on the campuses, and in the streets.

The fashionable diagnosis discovers an alienation of the working class from the establishment, but this alienation has always been present, and indeed properly so. The working class would be foolish not to be alienated from a group which possesses power and uses it in terms of its own interests and not necessarily in terms of the interest of the working class. Given their desire to ignore larger social and political issues, working-class suspicion of the powers that be represents one of the few defenses they have against those powers, even though it may not be a particularly effective one. It is a typical error of fashionable commentary to exaggerate the degree of alienation of the working class, much as the same fashionable commentary exaggerated the degree of militancy and alienation of poor Blacks who, for all the misery of their existence, continue to be strongly committed to the central values of American society (a fact that will continue to embarrass those who seek to lead the Black community in a revolutionary direction).

But working-class men and women have had to pay attention to a great deal that is going on in the larger world in the last few years. They have had to pay attention to a war which they do not understand and which they support (when they do) out of a sense of patriotic duty that wears thinner and thinner as time goes on. They have had to pay attention to riots and rising crime rates, consistently coupled with race problems by the mass media and by politicians. While working-class people have a great deal more sympathy for the disadvantages suffered by poor Blacks and Whites than they are usually given credit for, their values tend to emphasize the virtue of fortitude more than rebellion; coupled with their deep fear of Blacks, this has meant that they have felt that the rioting and the lawlessness must be stopped before any improvement in the situation of Blacks can take place.

Much the same kind of ambivalence—support for the legitimate demands of the disadvantaged but anger and puzzlement over those who "take the law into their own hands"—is apparent in working-class attitudes toward strikes by public service workers. Surprisingly, although they feel pressed by inflation, working-class people often concede that public service workers such as teachers and postmen deserve more pay, and feel that such demands are legitimate because they have been long denied. At the same time, they are bothered when public service workers strike despite laws that say they should not. In the end they tend to side with the workers for, despite the unlawfulness, the tactic is recognized and the demands are just. Because public service workers provide essential services to the public, working-class citizens feel that they as members of the public must be prepared to pay for the value received.

It is the particular tragedy of the race and poverty issues that the working class perceives no direct value received from the changes argued on behalf of these disadvantaged groups. The initial effort at sympathy that many working-class people were willing to extend toward the poor and (more grudgingly) toward Blacks was reversed as the

1960s wore on. Originally, the working class assumed that these groups were simply trying to shift the odds so that they would have a better chance to achieve a mainstream existence. They further assumed that this existence would be achieved by the same combination of personal hard work and good luck that they feel operates for themselves. These assumptions have shifted as a result of the liberal and radical rhetoric by which the establishment has argued the cause of the poor and the Blacks, as well as of the great drama of the riots. Though few would really argue that the odds are fair for those at the bottom of society, working-class people have the impression that the established are proposing to remove the necessity for hard work and personal luck and simply "give" the disadvantaged the advantages of the good life. They quite properly perceive that this is impossible, and they also feel that it is not moral. As time has passed, they have gotten the idea that they are supposed to be so guilty about the situation of the poor and the Black that they will accept such policies. The effort to make the working class feel guilty has boomeranged because working-class people have plenty of reasons to feel sorry for themselves. They ward off self-pity by their measured optimism most of the time, but the moment comparisons of how badly the world treats them are made salient, they do not find it at all difficult to concentrate on all the troubles they have and to adopt the attitude that at least they work for what they have, which is precious little. Then, too, the attack on the system which accompanies the effort to change things on behalf of the disadvantaged tends as it becomes more and more personalized (particularly in New Left rhetoric) to make working-class people feel that they have to make a choice between their country and something else. At that point the simple virtues of patriotism and sticking to their own take over.

In the face of these challenges, the normally high morale of working-class people is no longer a social psychological asset. If things are better and better for a person, then he ought to be responsive to demands that he sacrifice something for people who are less well off. A moral threat comes from accepting the definition of his stratum in society as lucky and affluent. Feeling sorry for himself and pointing to all his troubles is a way of warding off the demands of other people. This course is particularly easy if those issues come to the fore during a period of rapid inflation which does press a great many working-class families quite sorely.

As policymakers have become aware of some of these issues, they have tried to find areas in which the working class has not been equitably dealt with. It is argued that the working class believes that they are being ignored and that their just demands are being passed over in the interests of less deserving lower class folk. Yet the sense of being ignored is probably a secondary issue, more responsive to the need to defend against the unpleasantness occasioned by lower class demands than representing a genuine belief of there not being enough "programs" for middle Americans. Aside from the issues of health, disability, and unemployment, which have been issues for a long time, working-class people do not have a particular sense of an unfinished New Deal agenda. They are really better Keynesians than that, tending to count on the growth of the economy and the greater affluence of society as a whole as the source of continued progress for people like them. It is probably futile for governments to seek out programs (again aside from the three mentioned above) which somehow "reduce the alienation" of the working class.

It is hard to escape the judgment that the revolt of the alienated middle American (to the extent that it has any reality at all) is principally the result of an establishment's becoming enmeshed in its own rhetoric, ambitions, and incompetence rather than of any newly revealed conflict of vital interests between militant poor and Black classes and an overly bourgeois working class. In their all too apparent haste to placate the newly assertive Black community during the 1960s, those in power succeeded only in making many promises and fostering a pseudoradical rhetoric that angered and insulted the working class, while at the same time delivering no more than symbolic resources to Black people. (It should be noted that Black working-class attitudes in this area are in many ways not different from White ones, although not infused in the same way with racial feeling. That is, Black working- and middle class people can be as vehement and angry in their denunciation of "criminals" and "welfare chiselers" as the White working and middle class can.) Now a wide middle range of the population deeply believes that many things are being "given to" the poor and the Blacks who are not required to work to earn them, while in fact nothing of value has been given to the Black masses or the poor (although a new bureaucratic cadre has been created which provides some work and leadership possibilities for representatives of those groups). As the failure and dishonesty of those tactics became increasingly apparent in the late 1960s, opportunities for political aggrandizement were opened for those who wished to capitalize on the myths of the revolutionary militants, and of a gigantic giveaway to the undeserving lower orders.

For the future, however, it may be of some value to try to identify the basis by which working-class people might favorably evaluate initiatives designed to improve the conditions of those at the bottom of the social scale. It will be useful to distinguish here between goals, policies, and programs. Initiatives directed toward increasing equality in society, which is the only meaningful way of improving life for those at the bottom of the social scale, can be divided into equalitarian goals, equalitarian policies, and equalitarian programs. There is no evidence that working-class people will not support equalitarian goals. Working-class people repeatedly say that they believe in a society in which no one has to be below the mainstream level. One has either to believe that they do not mean what they say or to accept what they say as the statement of an ideal that they are willing to support. This does not mean, of course, that working-class people, any more than any others in society, can be expected to make great sacrifices for the achievement of an ideal by which they do not see themselves to be particularly advantaged. However, their acceptance of equalitarian goals does suggest that at least under certain conditions it would be possible to elicit working-class support for a movement toward these goals.

Equalitarian programs, on the other hand, are much more problematic. The tendency of government to try to deal with each problem of disadvantage by establishing a program that somehow directly gets at it is not only often self-defeating but politically inflammatory. Thus many of the equalitarian programs of the late 1960s had the appearance of giving people something for nothing, of not being contingent on the recipient's willingness to earn his way in the mainstream. For equalitarian programs to be successful and to receive broad and continuing support, they need to make sense to working-class people. These programs cannot be seen as violating the central values of earning what you get and of not asking for more than you are entitled to. To a very large extent, this is a matter of how the programs are presented, but it is probably also true that many of the problems of the lower class and disadvantaged cannot be attacked directly by programs that do not have this self-limiting quality. Thus, working-class people might be willing to support a very low guaranteed income on humanitarian grounds, but they would hardly support one that is high enough to put families within striking distance of the mainstream if it is not tied to work.

The way out of the rhetorical dead end of equalitarian programs lies with equalitarian policies, that is, standards of government operation which are informed by a commitment to equalitarian goals. All government policies should be systematically evaluated in terms of their contribution toward bringing about a society in which all able-bodied members can earn participation in the mainstream. Policies would be oriented toward bringing about the conditions which facilitate equalitarian goals in terms of the common values of the society. Such policies could limit the areas in which equalitarian programs are necessary to clean up the messes in the form of dependency and social pathology left by an inequalitarian society.

The working class should prove to be a strong source of support for equalitarian policies that offer the twin payoffs of achieving equalitarian ideals and at the same time using the productive potential of the poor to contribute to the welfare of everyone through the products of their labor.

In the long run, it is likely that the working class and much of the lower middle class will prove responsive to political programs along these lines rather than to the current rash of rightist rhetoric with which the group is being courted. Working-class people are much too tough-minded to see their enjoyment of respectable rightists such as Vice-President Agnew and George Wallace as other than a small self-indulgence justified by how sorely tried they feel by these times. They do not see such political leaders as people who will protect their vital interests or who foster the social and economic policies necessary to sustain them in the mainstream. In the long run they are much more available to political leaders like the late Robert Kennedy, who are able to cut through rhetorical and mass media provocations to deal instead with the basic facts that the working class and Blacks and others of the underclass share essentially the same life goals and have a common interest in governmental policies that facilitate the achievement of those goals by the broadest range of citizens.

13. HOUSING AND INEQUALITY

■ In the 1960s, a supposedly liberal decade, many of the policies that had been advocated over the past 30 years to solve problems of poverty and racial discrimination were given greater funding and more assertive leadership, particularly by the mayors of many large cities. By the end of the decade many of the favored solutions had demonstrated themselves to be inadequate, either because they did not work very well—like manpower training programs— or because they generated so much opposition on the part of nonbeneficiaries that it was nearly impossible to implement them.

The public housing program in the U.S. has had a long history as a liberal solution to social problems related to inequality. Its original impetus came from the combination of a concern with slum clearance and a concern for the provision of a better environment for poor people. It was part of the conventional wisdom of the time—informed by a misreading of the sociological evidence about slum communities—that the replacement of bad housing with good housing could effect a substantial improvement in the well-being, morale, and behavior of poor people. Public housing was regarded as a leg up for the downtrodden, who were expected to use the chance to live in decent quarters as a way of getting on their feet and moving on to a better life without further subsidy.

By the 1960s, however, public housing had to a large extent become minority housing, at least in the largest cities. For many, public housing provided a permanent home or as near permanent a home as they would know, given the exigencies of their life, so it turned out to have no rehabilitative effect on the problems associated with low income. Living in "the projects" came to carry a stigma both within and outside lower class communities. As time went on, more and more of the financial, human, and political problems associated with public housing coalesced into a clear-cut crisis that pushed numerous housing projects into bankruptcy.

The first article in this chapter discusses some of the sociopolitical dynamics that produce residential concentrations of lower-class people, particularly concentrations of lower-class Blacks, and some of the ways by which narrow planning and architectural approaches serve to exacerbate these tendencies. Then we consider the housing goals poor people actually have for themselves and the ways by which these goals are frustrated by the dangerous environment of the slum. I draw some of my examples from Pruitt-Igoe, an all-Black project in St. Louis that had the distinction of being the first public housing project in the country to be partially demolished because of its high vacancy rate and its intractable financial and social problems. The problems described afflict similar projects in every major city in the country, and because such a high proportion of public housing families are Black the tendency has been to define these problems as distinctive to the Black ghetto. In fact (as some projects in the city of Boston nicely illustrate) exactly the same kinds of petty crime and vandalism occur in consequently run-down project communities located in the middle of White areas and populated exclusively by Whites.

The second article, by Bernard J. Frieden, discusses the range of federal programs to subsidize housing for low-income people with the aim of improving the quality of their lives. Frieden considers evidence which suggests that the innovative programs of the 1960s have not produced much in the way of improved housing quality for the low income people who are supposed to benefit from them. Instead, the benefits seem to go (as is so often the case) to the economically powerful intermediaries.

Many issues associated with urban renewal and public housing programs are covered in a collection of articles by Jewell Bellush and Murray Hausknecht, *Urban Renewal: People, Politics, and Planning* (New York: Doubleday-Anchor, 1967). These and other problems of lower-class areas are dealt with in Bernard J. Frieden and Robert Morris, eds., *Urban Planning and Social Policy* (New York: Basic Books, 1968). A comprehensive collection of material is found in Jon Pynoos, Robert Schafer, and Chester Hartman, *Housing Urban America* (Chicago: Aldine, 1973). Herbert J. Gans also deals with many of these issues in his collected essays on urban problems and solutions, *People and Plans* (New York: Basic Books, 1968). ■

13a. THE SLUM AND ITS PROBLEMS

LEE RAINWATER

Reprinted from "Poverty, Race and Urban Housing," in The Social Impact of Urban Design, The University of Chicago, Center for Policy Study, 1971. Copyright by Lee Rainwater. Mr. Rainwater is Professor of Sociology at Harvard University.

HOUSING AND NEIGHBORHOODS—their quality and placement in the urban geography—represent important resources and amenities for citizens. If we want to understand the deprivation of these resources for the lower class, we must understand the ways in which social processes both within the lower class community and from other segments of the society influence the availability of these resources to lower class persons.

Let us start with the effects of lower class adaptations on the available physical housing facilities. The struggle for survival, the stripped-down organizations developed to adapt to their marginality, and the strategies of exploitation and manipulation their marginality encourages—all combine to produce a style of dealing with physical property that is conductive to poor maintenance and a great deal of destruction to property. In private slum housing janitors and landlords constantly complain of how hard lower class tenants are on housing. In turn, of course, landlords use this complaint to justify their putting only the most minimal investment in the maintenance of their property and, as a result, set up a vicious circle in which the property becomes more and more deteriorated. We are familiar enough with this phenomenon in private slum housing, but it is somewhat of a surprise to find much the same dynamic operating in public housing. In the Pruitt-Igoe public housing project in St. Louis, which with a number of colleagues I studied for six years, the tenants take reasonable care of the interiors of their apartments; but the exterior spaces, both within and outside the buildings, are subject to massive depredations by teenagers and smaller children and command only general indif-

ference from adults. The result is a property in an incredible state of disrepair. Some 12 years after it was first opened over $7 million were appropriated for rehabilitation. But, 16 years after the opening the vacancy rate, destruction and bankruptcy of the project resulted in the removal of buildings by dynamiting to reduce the density of the project—apparently also a futile effort to keep the project functioning.

Conversely, in stable working-class neighborhoods, where the vicious effects of economic marginality and weak community structures are not nearly so persuasive, several researchers have documented the degree to which residents invest energy and money in designing for themselves and maintaining a habitable environment. (Such areas often are also regarded as slums because the middle class professionals who apply this label have different standards for appropriate levels of maintenance and visible order in a neighborhood or house.) The classic research of Herbert J. Gans in Boston's West End and, more recently, of Gerald Suttles on the near west side of Chicago have demonstrated that a relatively small abating of pervasive economic marginality can produce neighborhoods in which even very old physical structures are preserved and maintained rather than hurried along on their way to falling apart. Suttles points out, for example, that property in such an area is kept most effectively when the landlords themselves live in the neighborhood and when a complex relationship that involves both business and more sociable elements is developed so that landlords can rely on their tenants to exercise more circumspection about the property than would someone who was "just a renter." When this com-

148

plex tie is lost, as when an ethnic neighborhood begins to change its composition so that landlord and renter are of different ethnic groups, it becomes very difficult for the landlord to maintain his marginal enterprise and at the same time maintain his property.

By far the most powerful effect on the lower class urban environment is that of the concerns and decisions of the cities' political elites. These elites massively influence the nature of the lower class Black ghetto and the housing available to its inhabitants through their decisions on such mundane matters as zoning, highway construction, building codes, and the like, or on more dramatic matters such as how much public housing to build, where, and with what concentration, or on urban renewal programs. By the same token, the size, distribution, and quality of the Black ghetto and its amenities are primarily decided on by various elite interest groups whose decisions clearly have little to do with the needs and aspirations of those who live in the ghetto.

At the national level the role of political elites has been perhaps even more significant in its effect on the housing and neighborhood options available to the lower class. The image of the slum's unsightliness combined with the general federal predilection for special services as ameliorative devices has resulted in urban programs that tend to be heavily impersonal in their impact, designed to affect geographic areas and physical structures more than to improve the situation of lower class families as sets of individuals. The line of development of federal urban programs, from slum clearance to public housing to urban renewal to urban rehabilitation to model cities, in interaction with local political conditions, has had the effect of further concentrating lower class Blacks and further exacerbating their situation as special, deviant members of the society.

The social processes involved in the professionalization of urban design—in development of the professions of architecture and urban planning—has also had an effect on the space and amenities available to the lower class. It has been a small effect, dwarfed by that of the political elite, but to some extent professional designers have played a role in translating and legitimizing the impact of political forces. In this respect the design ethos has until quite recently served the function of mystification of urban housing issues.

As planner Roger Montgomery has observed, in order to make a positive contribution to improvement of the situation of lower class ghetto inhabitants, planners and architects would have to shift their focus from physical design to the fighting out of "battles over density, location, and segregation through political action not architecture. . . ." Instead, the dynamics of professionalization have encouraged architects and planners to turn inward on their own fields to find standards of excellence and success, perhaps as a way of avoiding a too-close confrontation with the scant impact their skills have had in improving the lives of those for whom they design. Montgomery observed that "the dissociation of an architect's professional status from the functional success of his building will continue to block a socially responsible environmental art. Unless persons concerned with urban design understand this, improvement will be difficult. Behavioral scientists can open the issue, but to resolve it, designers must reject the role of decorative artist and seek a self-regulation focus on human habitat."

Perhaps the most pernicious of the design aberrations inflicted on the lower class is the preference for large-scale development, whether in the form of high-rise buildings where no need for high-rise buildings exists, as in St. Louis, or in the form of perference for the development of maximum-sized plots of land rather than attention to smaller scale, scattered developments. Both of these design considerations, of course, stem from traditional professional interests within architecture, but they also play into the general political preference for concentrating and warehousing lower class people, particularly Blacks, and they serve to cover over this raw political goal with an aesthetic mystification.

The energy and expense that go into the development of attractive public spaces, suitable for impressive photographic treatment in *The Architectural Forum* or in the local newspapers, in place of careful attention to provision of the most in private indoor and less obvious spaces, are another example of the comfortable fit between the design standards important within the profession and the political needs of those who hire designers.

Although socioeconomic forces and their psychological effects are primary in influencing the styles of living by which lower class people adapt to their situation, physical design can facilitate or interfere with the ease and constructiveness of adaptation. Designs do sometimes affect how people pursue their goals and how much trouble they have in achieving them. Good design ought to facilitate the constructive adaptations that people are trying to make. However, the design parameters likely to do this are generally quite basic ones that involve more in the nature of planning choices than in design refinements.

For example, in Young and Willmott's classic study of the effect of moving from the lower class slum of Bethnal Green in London to housing estates outside the city, quite important changes in the style of life of the lower working-class families were observed, but these changes were the result of movement from a crowded, intimate slum area with a long history to a new suburbanlike housing estate. Because the men and women no longer had available the amenities of the slum—the pubs, the mother living next door, lifelong friends—they changed their way of life quite dramatically and focused their energies much more sharply on their homes and on jointly pursued family life, much less on the separate activities that husband and wife participated in with their sexsegregated peer groups. They were lonelier in the housing estates, which bothered Young and Willmott, but on balance they seem to have found their new lives more satisfying than the slum life of Bethnal Green. One cannot hope to achieve such major changes in style of life without comparably major differences in the milieus the community design provides.

Much the same order of difference between city and suburban life is suggested by Herbert Gans' study of Levittown. Here most of the inhabitants find more meaningful lives in the splendid isolation of their mass-produced suburban houses, no matter how much consternation this adjustment provides urbane social critics. However, teen-agers in the Levittown environment seem to suffer because they can do little with their isolation; they need the heavy and easy interaction that can be obtained only in a community that has a physical focus that brings many similarminded people together. Perhaps the new planned suburban communities that provide more in the way of community facilities— clubhouse, swimming pool, and the like—may resolve the teen-agers' problems as they allow the adults the isolation they insist on.

Social science research on the slum and the ghetto has cast the discipline in the odd role of alternately seeming to defend slums and argue for their abolition. One set of studies (represented most centrally by Herbert Gans' and Marc Fried's studies of Boston's West End) strongly defends the slum and the style of life that existed there before it was renewed out of existence. The principal finding of such studies is that in their desire to dress up the city governing elites may through urban renewal destroy functioning, satisfying communities of working-class people who feel no overriding desire for something "better." Where renewal has had this effect, it has generally been because the city fathers wanted to do away with what they saw as an embarrassing slum and replace it with middle class housing. The social science attack on urban renewal has served a very important purpose in making it more difficult for city governments to take advantage of workingclass people in order to benefit middle class people. This is not to say that a great deal of new middle class housing need not be built in central cities if they are not to become purely lower class enclaves. It is to say, however, that no social justification exists for placing so heavy a burden on stable working-class neighborhoods in achieving that goal. From the planning point of view the major contribution of this kind of research has been to abolish the notion that "deteriorated housing" is to be defined by relatively superficial indexes of the extent to which a neighborhood's exteriors seem unattractive or not "nice."

The apparent contradictory line of social science argument has involved a strong attack on the ghetto as a disorganized and pathological system. But here it has become clear, as more and more research has been done, that the problem basically is not the housing or other physical characteristics but, rather, the effects of a vicious socioeconomic system on the lives of the individuals who live there. The ghetto is simply a convenient physical representation of the destructive social system that operates within its borders. Part of that destructive social system is indeed the existence of economic arrangements that confine people to dangerous and inferior housing, but the housing per se is not the cause of their problems. As the nation has discovered, to its chagrin, public housing does little to improve the quality of lives of the people who reside there. This is not surprising since we now know that the quality of housing available to the ghetto is not really central to the troubles people had, but was more a result of those troubles. Because of inadequate income and discrimination ghetto dwellers are confined to the least desirable housing in the cities.

Research in ghettos demonstrates that as lower class people talk about housing the overriding concern is that it shelter them from the dangers that abide in their world, that it provide them with "defensible space." In the stable working and middle class, danger is less salient both because it is assumed that housing will shelter from inevitable physical threats and because, having more resources available to them, people at these levels are able to worry about putting together a home that expressively elaborates their conception of a pleasant and respectable place to live. But lower class people put first things first and are concerned with having a home to

which they can retreat, and in which they can feel secure from the troubles that abound outside.

Let us examine, first, the nature of these troubles and then consider some of the design implications for providing housing for lower class people. However, before doing so we should remind ourselves that addressing this as a design problem already represents a second-best solution to the basic difficulties of the lower class. It would be far better to devote the energies of social planning to helping lower class people find for themselves environments in which the concern with security would not have to be such a pressing order of business.

The dangers of the ghetto world have two immediate sources, human and nonhuman; the consequences feared from these sources usually represent a complex amalgam of physical, interpersonal, and mortal damage to the individual and his family. Let us look first at the various sources of danger and then at the overlapping consequences feared from them.

There is nothing unfamiliar about the nonhuman sources of danger. They represent a sad catalog of threats apparent in any journalist's account of slum living. That we become used to the catalog, however, should not obscure the fact that these dangers are very real to many lower class families. Rats and other vermin are ever-present companions in most big-city slums. From the sense of relief that residents in public housing often experience on this score, it is apparent that slum dwellers are not indifferent to the presence of rats in their homes. Poisons may be a danger, sometimes from lead-based paints used on surfaces that slum toddlers may chew. Fires in slum areas are not uncommon, and even in a supposedly well-designed public housing project children may repeatedly burn themselves on uncovered steampipe risers. The tenant who supplies his own heating could have a very cold apartment if he had no money, or, indeed, he could freeze to death (as we were told by one respondent whose friend fell into an alcoholic sleep without turning on the heater). Insufficiently protected heights, as in one public housing project, may lead to deaths when children fall out of windows or adults fall down elevator shafts. Thin walls in the apartment may expose a family to more of its neighbors' goings-on than is comfortable to hear. Finally, the very cost of the dwelling itself can represent a danger in that it leaves too little money for other things needed to keep body and soul together.

That lower class people grow up in a world like this and live in it does not mean that they are indifferent to it, nor that its toll is only that of possible physical damage in injury, illness, incapacity, or death. Because these potentialities and events are interpreted and take on symbolic significance, and because lower class people make some efforts to cope with them, they inevitably affect interpersonal relationships and moral conceptions of self and world.

The most obvious human source of danger involves violence directed by others against oneself and one's possessions. Lower class people are concerned with being assaulted, damaged, drawn into fights, beaten, raped. In public housing projects in particular it is always possible for juveniles to throw or drop from windows things that can hurt or kill, and if this pattern takes hold it is a constant source of potential danger. Similarly, people may rob anywhere—apartment, laundry room, corridor.

Added to this kind of direct violence is the more pervasive, ever-present potentiality for symbolic violence to the self and what is identified with the self—by verbal hostility, shaming, and exploitation expressed by the others who make up one's world. A source of such violence may be and often is within one's own family—from children, spouse, siblings, parents. It seems very likely that crowding tends to encourage such symbolic violence to the self, but certainly crowding is not the only factor since we also find this kind of threat in uncrowded public housing quarters. Most real and immediate to lower class people, however, seems to be the potentiality for symbolic destructiveness by their neighbors. Lower class people seem ever on guard

toward their neighbors, even ones with whom they become well acquainted and would count as their friends. This suspiciousness is directed often at juveniles and young adults, whom older people tend to regard as almost uncontrollable.

Symbolic violence on the part of caretakers (all those whose occupations bring them into contact with lower class people as purveyors of some private or public service) seems also endemic in slum areas. Students of the interactions between caretakers and their lower-class clients have suggested that a great deal of punitiveness and shaming commonly is expressed by the caretakers in an effort to control and direct their clients' activities.

Outsiders also present in two ways the dangers of symbolic violence as well as of physical violence. Using the anonymity of geographic mobility, outsiders may come into slum neighborhoods to con and exploit for their own ends and by virtue of the attitudes they maintain toward slum dwellers they may demean and degrade them. Here we would have to include also the mass media, which can and do behave in irresponsibly punitive ways toward people who live in lover class areas.

Finally, the lower class person's world contains many attractive alternatives to the pursuit of a stable life. He can fear for himself that he will be caught up in these attractive alternatives and thus damage his life chances, and he may fear even more that those whom he values, particularly in his family, will be seduced away from him. Thus wives fear that their husbands will be attracted to the life outside the family, husbands fear the same of their wives, and parents always fear that their children will somehow turn out badly. Again, that you may yourself be involved in such seductive pursuits does not lessen the fear that these valued others will be won away while your back is turned. In short, both the push and the pull of the human world in which the lower class people live can be seen as a source of danger.

Having looked at the sources of danger, let us look at the consequences lower class people fear from these dangers. The physical consequences are fairly obvious in connection with the nonhuman threats and the threats of violence from others. They are real and ever present: one can become the victim of injury, incapacitation, illness, and death from both nonhuman and human sources. Even the physical consequences of the symbolic violence of hostility, shaming, and exploitation, to say nothing of seduction, can be great if they lead one to retaliate in a physical way and, in turn, be damaged. Similarly, being caught up in alcohol and drug subcultures has physical consequences.

There are three related interpersonal consequences of living in a world characterized by these human and nonhuman sources of danger. The first relates to the need to form satisfying interpersonal relationships, the second to the need to exercise responsibility as a family member, and the third to the need to formulate an explanation for the unpleasant state of affairs in your world.

The consequences that endanger the need to maintain satisfying interpersonal relations flow primarily from the human sources of danger. That is, because the world seems to be made of dangerous others, at a very basic level the choice of friends carries risks. A friend may turn out to be an enemy, or his friends may. The result is a generalized watchfulness and touchiness in interpersonal relationships. Because other individuals represent not only themselves but also their families, the matter is further complicated since interactions with, say, neighbors' children, can have repercussions in the relationship with the neighbor. Because human agents stand behind most of the nonhuman dangers, one's relationships with others—family members, neighbors, caretakers—are subject to potential disruptions because of those others' involvement in creating trash, throwing objects, causing fires, or carrying on within thin walls.

In the exercise of responsibility, we find that parents feel they must bring their children safely through childhood in a world that both poses great physical and moral dangers and seeks constantly to seduce them into a way of life the parent wants them to avoid. Thus childrearing becomes an anxious and uncertain process. Two of the most common results are a pervasive repressiveness in child discipline and training, and, when that seems to fail or is no longer possible, a fatalistic abdication of efforts to protect the children. Because parents are not able to protect the child from many unpleasantnesses and even from himself, he loses faith in his parents and comes to regard them as persons of relatively little consequence.

The third area of effect on interpersonal relations is concerned with the search for causes of the prevalence of threat and violence in their world. We have suggested that to lower class people the major causes stem from the nature of their own peers. Thus a great deal of blaming others goes on and reinforces the process of isolation, suspiciousness, and touchiness about blame and shaming. Similarly, landlords and tenants tend to develop patterns of mutual recrimination and blaming, making it very difficult for them to cooperate with each other in doing something about either the human or the nonhuman sources of difficulty.

Finally, the consequences for conceptions of the moral order of one's world, of one's self, and of others are very great. Although lower class people may not adhere in action to many middle class values about neatness, cleanliness, order, and proper decorum, it is apparent that they are often aware of their deviance, wishing that their world could be a nicer place physically and socially. The presence of nonhuman threats conveys in devastating terms a sense that they live in an immoral and uncontrolled world. The physical evidence of trash, poor plumbing and the stink that goes with it, rats, and other vermin deepen their feeling of being moral outcasts. Their physical world is telling them they are inferior and bad just as effectively perhaps as do their human interactions. Their inability to control the depredation of rats, hot steam pipes, balky stoves, and poorly fused electrical circuits tells them that they are failures as autonomous individuals. The physical and social disorder of their world presents a constant temptation to give up or retaliate in kind. And when lower class people try to do something about some of these dangers they are generally exposed in their interactions with caretakers and outsiders to further moral punitiveness by being told that their troubles are their own fault.

A great deal of lower class life involves the organization for defense and survival in this dangerous world. Where lower class people have the option, they use space and barriers to further their defense against these various dangers. The first line of defense, of course, is the house. Here there is the wish that the house be isolable from its immediate surroundings—at the most primitive level that it have a lock that works, but also that its door not be so close to public circulation as to give the feeling of only a thin wall separating the home from the dangers outside. For example, one of the design problems in the Pruitt-Igoe housing project is that the apartment doors mostly open directly on very small landings of stairwells that serve as the major routes of circulation. Therefore, the doors prove inviting to children and teen-agers, who run up and down the stairwells, pounding, defacing, and trying to jimmy the locks.

In multiple-dwelling buildings, the building itself can serve as a barrier when the building has a front door lock. When freedom of entrance is limited to authorized persons, safety is increased; when, however, as in the Pruitt-Igoe project, no limitation restricts who may or may not circulate freely through the stairwells and elevators of the building, the sense of vulnerability is increased. A serendipitous event in the rehabilitation of some of the Pruitt-Igoe buildings provides a dramatic example. When a contractor was redoing a building that had been emptied out for that purpose, he built around it a high cyclone fence with locked gates to protect his materials. When the rehabilitation was completed and tenants began to move in, the contractor was ready to tear down the fence, but the tenants objected and persuaded the Housing Authority to leave the fence up so that they might have a better chance to control who had access to their building. This happened in several of the rehabilitated buildings in the

project. The way of using the fence varied, however. In one building a retired man informally assumed the role of doorman. He kept the keys to the fence and allowed strangers in only after checking their purpose. However, the degree of organization this control required was possible in only one building. In the other buildings the tenants were not able to organize themselves well enough to keep the fence locked; therefore the protection it afforded was much slighter, affecting somewhat the circulation of children through the area but not preventing any more determined person from entering the premises.

Many of the same concerns apply to larger areas, whether it be the block or the neighborhood. The concept of "turf" has become widely known in connection with juvenile gangs, but the sense of neighborhood space as belonging to some identifiable group is much broader than that. As Gerald Suttles shows in his study of a near west side area in Chicago, this sense of control over the block and sets of adjacent blocks is very important to the sense of security and comfort that people have in their neighborhoods. The control, however, must be informally managed since by and large lower class people have few skills, or resources, for organizing and maintaining formal social controls.

The designer who must concern himself with housing in a lower class location can best meet the needs of those who will use his housing if he pays serious attention to the desire for a "defensible space." This means he will provide as much private space as is feasible—a small enclosed patio or balcony for each apartment is much more desirable than attractive large playgrounds and green space. He will buffer the individual units from surrounding circulation space to minimize the traffic that bounces off the front and back doors. He will break up a large project into smaller identifiable units around which the residents can organize their own sense of turf. He may plan something like the fence, rather than discover by accident that the tenants have need for it. And he will minimize spaces that "belong" to no one, limiting them to areas that some formal authority will control.

If, then, housing must be designed for the ghetto, if we must reconcile ourselves to being unable to markedly change the social forces that produce the world of danger that lower class people experience, then the designer can make some small contribution by at least facilitating people's wishes to defend themselves against those dangers. For example, as an exercise a student of architecture at Washington University took the problem of providing defensible space for some 3,000 dwelling units on the 57-acre Pruitt-Igoe site, and he developed a plan for the site that might avoid some of the dangers the high-rise project itself had. First he discovered that it was possible to put the same number of units on the tract in a low-rise, four-story format. The 33 11-story buildings had covered only 10 percent of the land. The four-story units could be placed on the site in such a way as to provide ample outdoor play and sitting space and yet at the same time provide each unit with an outdoor walled patio or balcony and several other amenities that heightened its sense of separation and security from neighborhood traffic. Cost estimates revealed that the project could have been built in this way for somewhat less in construction cost than the high-rise structures. In short, a careful focus on the needs of the potential lower class tenants rather than on conventional wisdom about public housing, or conventional preferences for large, impressive structures, might have resulted in a community less terror-stricken than the one that eventually developed.

The immediate concern lower class people have for defensible space is matched by another, more desired but also more wishful goal of being able to achieve security from the dangers of the lower class ghetto by moving out of that world altogether. This is, after all, the traditional way that lower class people who have become more prosperous (and have been aided by such government programs as FHA) have resolved the difficulties the lower class community presents for them. Dispersion from the ghetto, then, offers a much more lasting solution to its problem than does the effort to make every home a fortress. It should be noted that from the point of view of ghetto inhabitants themselves, motivation is not so much a desire to move *toward* integration as to move away from the destructiveness of the ghetto. Dispersion from the ghetto would mean not so much an ideal of integration, in which every block had its proportionate share of Black residents, as it would mean the interspersing of small neighborhoods, in which perhaps most of the inhabitants were Blacks, with what are now lily-white neighborhoods. For the planner and urban specialist, this kind of dispersion seems a goal more worthy than that of assisting lower class people in the perfection of defensible space. Yet nowadays the goals of dispersion are somewhat overshadowed in professional thinking by the confusion of the collectivity with the individuals.

This confusion has been particularly apparent in connection with housing and urban development programs, and now is increasingly apparent with various kinds of community action programs. The human collectivity or the geographic area is confused with the lives of the individual people. Its earliest manifestation was in the slum clearance program. Here the emphasis was on clearing the slums rather than on solving the problems of the people who lived in the slums. Later with urban renewal, now with model cities, the tendency on the part of functionaries has been to concern themselves with the city as a physical place and with making it look nice, and to believe that thereby, somehow, the problems are solved. Mayors and others at the local level naturally are most concerned with the appearance of things, since these are the visible aspects of the community most available for making judgments about whether or not anything has changed.

With various kinds of community action programs, augmented by the new militancy of some in the Black and other minority communities, there is a great temptation to reify the community group to an almost physical object much like "the city." Much of the community action and new militant rhetoric leads one to suspect an ideological strain toward exalting a conception of the group (whether it be the neighborhood or the Black ghetto as a whole) over the highly varied needs, aspirations and hopes of the individual people and families who make up that collectivity. In some ways our oversophistication about the dynamics of social life—with emphasis on the ethnic ascendancy of immigrants in the 19th-century city or on the interdependence of interest groups in a social system—tends to distract from the much more ordinary and less dramatic goals of individual families who are concerned not so much for community self-determination as simply for *family* self-determination. It is seldom recognized that as economically weak families are just as vulnerable to exploitation and mistreatment at the hands of a supposedly self-governed neighborhood or ghetto as they are at the hands of city hall. The hope that the self-governing neighborhood will be less likely to exploit and mistreat is a thin basis for confidence from the point of view of the family that wants to make its own decisions and set its own priorities. Families in such a situation cannot avoid the impression that only the poor are subject to more than a modicum of such community leadership, and only the poor do not have the option of picking up and moving elsewhere if they do not like the kinds of decisions their self-governing community makes.

The importance of dispersion to a sense of security and self-reliance in lower class ghetto dwellers can hardly be overestimated. We know that dispersion that produces some degree of integration in the schools results in a greater amount of learning in school, in access to better community facilities of all kinds, and even in greater access to jobs. Economist John F. Kain has estimated that housing segregation in the 1960s had on Black employment the net effect of depriving Chicago Blacks of several tens of thousands of jobs they might have had if their residential distribution had been more widely dispersed.

With this subject, of course, we are back to the issues Roger Montgomery raised for those who seriously want to address the problem of urban design. The public housing project as the major design effort to solve lower class housing problems has by now been demonstrated to be a failure. The dynamics of the bureaucratic and power relations among the elites, who decide on type and locale of public housing, produce projects with tremendous numbers of physical design problems, but even more important, the public housing project has become a symbolic problem—an inevitability, given its conception as providing housing only for low income people. Anselm Strauss has noted the tendency of cities to create various kinds of "icons," which represent the city to itself and others, which communicate in condensed fashion the "self-conception" of whole cities or segments of it. Classes have their symbolizing icons, too, and the corporate welfare approach of the nation over the past decades has created no more stigmatizing icon than the high-rise, public housing project, such as Pruitt-Igoe or the interminable buildings of South State Street in Chicago. From the city fathers' point of view such lower class icons are presentable, not eyesores. But the very factors that give the project identifiability for the exercise of civic pride and for the designers' professional gratification present, from the point of view of the lower class inhabitants themselves, a liability in that projects come to symbolize the dead-ended quality of their lives and their occupation in society of a special deviant position—that of persons who cannot meet their needs in the way ordinary citizens do but require, instead, special welfare services of the government.

This is but the particular expression in the area of housing of an overriding general problem with special services approaches to the problems of the poor. The difficulty arises because they are service programs for the poor, and for no one else. This characteristic creates political difficulties in the opposition of the nonpoor to spending their "tax dollars" this way, but, even more important, *that the services are only for the poor inevitably reinforces the stigma of poverty.* A person who makes use of such services by that very act labels himself as a socially inferior person. No matter how hard social workers and other protectors of the poor try to soften the invidiousness of that label, it remains, both in the eyes of the poor themselves and in the eyes of the larger society. The more elaborated the special services framework becomes, the more the poor person is locked into his stigmatized status.

This is not merely an abstract issue but is brought home to the poor person by the typical attitudes of the caretakers who man the special services institutions. These attitudes are most blatant in the old line agencies, such as the schools, the police, the sanitation services, the welfare department. Even in the newer and therefore still hopful agencies, such as the community action agencies, the caretaker constantly tempted to hold himself out as a superior, more worthy, and deserving person than are those he serves. It may be the housing project manager who berates tenants for not listening to him at a tenant meeting because, after all, he has given up his evening at home in order to help them, or it may be the poverty program official who sees the goal of the community action program as teaching poor people good habits of life; whoever it is, a constant strain is present in the contacts of middle class caretakers with lower class clients toward behavior and attitudes that are demeaning and degrading of the client. No amount of radical or Black power punitiveness toward caretakers is likely to markedly affect this dynamic of the cross-class relationship. Indeed, were militants over time to man the special services institutions they probably would be just as likely to develop derogating attitudes toward their charges as are conventional middle class people, though the rhetoric might well be different.

From these considerations it follows that an overriding design consideration in any effort to do something about the problems of lower class people would take as a primary caveat the avoidance of special forms of housing or neighborhood design. Instead an effort would be made to reduce the stigmatization of lower class people by providing them with amenities that are simple and ordinary and blend in with the larger community rather than mark them off from it. Such goals argue for the development of a market strategy that encourages the dispersion of individual lower class families and allows for the maximum exercise of taste and predilections rather than accepting fiat decisions about what amenities are to be available—decisions that inevitably follow from centralized planning and large project construction. . . .

13b. IMPROVING FEDERAL HOUSING SUBSIDIES

BERNARD J. FRIEDEN

Reprinted from Papers Submitted to Subcommittee on Housing, Part 2, *Committee on Banking and Currency, House of Representatives, 92nd Cong., 1st sess., June 1971 (Washington, D.C.: Government Printing Office). Bernard J. Frieden is Professor of City Planning at the Massachusetts Institute of Technology and Director of the Joint Center for Urban Studies of M.I.T. and Harvard. He has written extensively on housing and city planning. He is the author of* The Future of Old Neighborhoods *(Cambridge, Mass.: M.I.T. Press, 1964), and has recently completed a book on the operation of the Model Cities Program.*

OUR STUDY OF FEDERAL HOUSING programs has been concerned with the ways in which subsidies are made available to low and moderate income families, and with the effectiveness of these subsidy arrangements in helping families to live in decent housing. Many of the defects in present housing programs result from the circuitous routes by which subsidies reach the families for whom they are intended. A review of existing programs suggests that these defects are serious enough to warrant congressional attention.

In evaluating the nature of subsidies under the various federal housing programs, it is important to recognize that these programs reach relatively small numbers of people and only a small proportion of families even at low income levels. (In fiscal 1968, 5.4 percent of nonfarm renter families were living in federally assisted housing.) As a result, even if these programs worked perfectly, they would not bring quick solutions to national housing problems. The relevant issues, however, are whether the subsidy programs are reasonably efficient, equitable, and satisfying to the clients they are intended to serve. A related issue of obvious significance—the physical quality of housing provided under the various subsidy programs—was beyond the scope and resources of this study.

THE COST OF INTERMEDIARIES

Federal housing aid to low and moderate income families typically passes through several intermediaries before it reaches the consumer. Public housing assistance flows through local housing authorities and requires local government approval. Rental housing aid under section 236 and homeownership aid under section 235 pass through the hands of local housing sponsors and FHA offices. Rent supplements require additional approval by local government. Rehabilitation loans and grants generally flow through local urban renewal agencies. Although these arrangements offer certain advantages, they also result in the diversion of a significant share of the subsidy dollars to the intermediaries, and they restrict the choices available to low income families in a number of significant ways.

To estimate the diversion of funds to the intermediaries, we obtained data on those federal programs that are used in the city of

TABLE 13b.1
ALLOCATION OF FEDERAL HOUSING SUBSIDIES TO TENANTS AND INTERMEDIARIES, BOSTON, 1970

Program	Total Annual Cost	Rent Assistance (Percent)	Federal and Local Administration (Percent)	Federal Tax Loss (Percent)
Public housing— conventional	$1,560	83	6	11
Public housing— Turnkey 1	1,380	83	17	10
Public housing— leasing existing units	732	78	22	0
Public housing— leasing rehabilitated units	1,872	31	9	61
Public housing— leasing new units	996	58	16	26
Rent supplements— new units	1,464	82	5	13
Rent supplements— rehabilitated units	1,944	62	4	35

An additional $140 per unit per year for local administrative costs is paid for out of tenant rents. This would be equivalent to an additional 9 percent of the total annual cost for conventional public housing, and an additional 10 percent for Turnkey 1.

Boston. (Cost allocations differ from one locality to another.) In most of these programs, we estimate that between one-fourth and one-half of the total federal subsidy does not reach the residents, but goes for federal and local administrative expenses and for tax benefits to investors (see Table 13b.1.). In one instance, that of rehabilitation grants and loans in code enforcement areas, the city's administrative expenses during the past one and a half years actually equaled two-thirds of the total value of loans and grants made to homeowners. The proportion of federal expenditures reaching the resident family varies among the different programs. The most efficient, in terms of this criterion, are the much-maligned public housing program, public housing leasing of existing units, and rent supplements in new housing.

LOCATIONAL RESTRICTIONS

The extensive use of intermediaries not only adds to the cost of federally aided housing but also restricts the choices open to client families in several unfortunate ways. Where intermediaries are required, consumers can obtain federal housing subsidies only by living in communities where the intermediaries exist and are active. In the case of public housing (conventional or leased), these are localities that have established a housing authority and have decided to sponsor additional housing. This requirement for local government action has resulted in a situation in which public housing is concentrated disproportionately in large central cities. As of 1967, nearly half of all low-rent public housing (47 percent) was located in 51 major cities with populations over 250,000. Public housing has been conspicuously unsuccessful in providing subsidized housing in the suburbs, close to expanding employment centers.

Two newer housing programs with requirements for local government action—221(d) (3) and rent supplements—have also been blocked in the suburbs. (This requirement was dropped from the 221 [d] [3] program in 1969.) When the question of whether low income families will have opportunities to live in a community is subject to a political decision, the record indicates that suburbs will exercise their veto freely. Yet when older housing becomes available on the private market at prices that low income families can afford, they have been able to move to the suburbs in substantial numbers. Eliminating the role of local government as an intermediary would therefore seem to be a way of offering low income families a degree of choice in subsidized housing comparable to the choice available in the private market.

The major programs authorized in 1968—section 235 homeownership and 236 rental housing—have taken the forward step of omitting a requirement for local government approval. Nevertheless, housing subsidies under these programs are not available wherever eligible families are or may wish to be. The programs normally depend on nonprofit or limited-dividend sponsors, many of whom had previously been organized in the central cities. Further, the emphasis is on newly built housing, which often requires zoning changes or other government action in the suburbs, thus opening the door once again to informal vetoes. Where 236 housing is combined with rent supplements, the formal requirement for local approval still applies.

Nevertheless, it was widely expected that the 235 and 236 programs could operate successfully in the suburbs, where land and construction costs tend to be lower than in the central cities, where job prospects are likely to be better, and where earlier subsidy programs had often been excluded. The Department of Housing and Urban Development seems to have no systematic information available on the suburban-central city distribution of its housing under these new programs. The HUD estimates made available to us, however, are that as of late 1970 less than 30 percent of the section 235 units completed or under way in metropolitan areas were located in the suburbs, and less than 15 percent of the section 236 units. The HUD data are based on field office estimates which in some cases include older suburbs within the "central city" definition. Even with allowances for definitional inconsistencies, the results seem disappointing.

While housing subsidy programs have been generally unable to operate in the suburbs, families with low and moderate incomes have been able to enter the suburbs on their own. As of 1967, Census Bureau estimates were that 1 million of the 2.6 million metropolitan area families with incomes below the poverty line were living in the suburbs. Many of these families live in inadequate or overcrowded housing, and constitute an important group that should be able to benefit from federal subsidies. Under the present requirements, they are largely unable to do so for lack of the required intermediaries or because of local government inaction in their own communities

Just as the reliance on intermediaries influences the location of federally assisted housing in suburbs and central cities, it also influences the distribution of subsidized housing to the different regions of the country. The presence or absence of aggressive housing authorities, and of experienced sponsors, will generate a greater volume of requests for housing assistance from some areas than from others. Other factors also influence regional distribution patterns, including building cost differences, the policies of local lending institutions, and federal allocation procedures. But we believe that the initial flow of applications from intermediaries is one of the most important factors. A recent analysis of the distribution of rental assistance programs (including public housing) has revealed little correspondence between the number of low income families in a region and the volume of federally subsidized housing there. In fact, most low income states are undersupplied in relation to need while high income states are oversupplied. If families in need of housing aid are to have equal opportunities to get it wherever they may live, the present system is clearly inefficient in reaching this goal.

The use of intermediaries to administer subsidy programs also limits consumer choice within local communities. Since subsidies are available only in designated projects, and the demand far exceeds the supply, the low income family has little choice of neighborhood or even housing type. Research into the relocation of people displaced by urban renewal has demonstrated the critical importance of neighborhood location to many low income families. For many, the choice of neighborhood is even more important than the condition of the house. When this choice is restricted narrowly, subsidized housing may interfere seriously with a family's other needs.

INTERMEDIARY DECISIONS AND HOUSING COSTS

Further, the locational choices and building decisions of sponsors may work counter to the goals of housing programs. Two recent studies of housing rehabilitation in Boston have noted connections between the sponsor's decisions and purposes and the characteristically high cost of subsidized rehabilitation. Renovation undertaken in connection with urban renewal projects, in particular, tends to reflect the mixed motives of the intermediaries as well as the results of restricted choices of buildings to improve. Urban renewal agencies seldom have as their main goal the provision of good housing for low income people. Their objective is often the conflicting one of attracting moderate and high income families to a neighborhood by undertaking substantial and costly improvements. Thus they influence developers and homeowners to rehabilitate to relatively high standards. Further, since they want to improve an entire neighborhood, they will encourage the renovation of many marginal buildings that cost-conscious sponsors would otherwise avoid. In contrast to this experience, several philanthropic groups that have been able to operate in locations of their own choice have succeeded in buying cheap housing that can be renovated at moderate cost for resale to low income families. In a subsidy system that provided the low income family with wider options, a different choice of buildings and of rehabilitation standards could well yield satisfactory housing at lower cost.

Charles Abrams' study of Philadelphia housing revealed still another way in which the heavy hand of intermediaries tends to raise housing costs and limit consumer choices. Abrams found that some Philadelphia neighborhoods had a good supply of older row houses in move-in condition which could be bought for $2,000 to $5,000. In his view, these houses could have made it possible for many low income families to become homeowners, particularly if federal mortgage assistance had been available. Instead, the Philadelphia Housing Authority bought and renovated many of these houses, and made them available for renting. In the process, the total cost per house rose to more than $12,300. Abrams did not understand why the houses had become too expensive for low income buyers.

I sought the reason for the $12,300 cost of houses and found it in some twenty-six pages of Housing Authority specifications. A good oil heater, for example, had to be replaced by a gas heater; all wallpaper had to be removed irrespective of its condition; unless walls were crack free, new plastering was mandatory; drywall was unacceptable; roofing had to be renewed and existing shingle roofs reshingled, even if recently redone; all wood trim had to be of one type or style; kitchen and bathroom floors had to be covered with asphalt tile free of irregularities, even when there was good vinyl. In short, each house had to be gutted, regardless of its condition. The result was a permanently subsidized, permanently supervised, and permanently dependent tenantry.

The families who benefit from federal housing programs are dependent upon intermediaries not only in matters having to do with the initial decisions about project location and design but also for continuing management decisions. The range of managerial functions does not differ much from that of conventional private landlords: tenant selection, maintenance, provision of normal services, and decisions on renovation from time to time. But there is an important difference. A tenant in private housing can move elsewhere without great loss if he is dissatisfied. The tenant in a federally assisted development—whether under public or private management—must give up his subsidy if he leaves, since the subsidy is linked to a specific house rather than to the family. Thus the tenants of federally aided projects are particularly dependent and vulnerable. This special vulnerability helps account for the bitter disputes that have arisen between public housing tenants and management.

To reduce the friction between tenants and local housing authorities, HUD and some local communities have taken a number of useful steps. These include clarifying tenant rights, instituting grievance procedures, requiring tenant involvement in renovation decisions, appointing tenants as authority members, and experimenting with tenant management. Measures such as these may well make management decisions more responsive to tenant wishes. To normalize these relations still further, however, would call for a more drastic revision of the subsidy system that would give tenants the option of moving elsewhere without losing their financial aid.

INTERMEDIARIES AS FAMILY ADVISORS

In calling attention to the ways in which intermediaries limit the choices open to residents by making decisions on their behalf, we do not mean to imply that low income families have no need of intermediaries to help them cope with housing problems. There are a number of circumstances in which families are very much in need of help from people who are more expert than they in negotiating the housing system. This need is especially clear when a family is involved either in renovating their home or in buying a house. In the case of renovation, the family typically needs technical help in deciding what renovation work to do, drawing up specifications, choosing a contractor, and inspecting the work to be sure that it has been done properly. In buying a house, a family needs advice on the condition of the building, whether it complies with zoning codes and other local regulations, how to handle the sale transaction, and how to arrange for the most advantageous financing.

Despite the abundance of intermediaries involved in federal housing programs, this technical assistance is seldom provided in a satisfactory way. A recent study of federally aided rehabilitation in Boston has indicated that the technical advice provided by the urban renewal agency was far from adequate. First, there were often conflicts between renewal agency personnel and resident families over the level of rehabilitation to be done. Agency officials frequently wanted to do more rehabilitation work than the family thought was necessary. In some instances the additional work may have been essential for reasons of health or safety, but in many others the rehabilitation advisers were operating on the basis of middle class housing standards that did not suit the more modest life-style of low income owners. In other cases, there were reasons to question the competence of the individual rehab specialists. Further, the renewal agency did not consider itself an advocate of the residents in their dealing with contractors. Agency personnel did not furnish adequate advance information on the quality of work done by different contractors, their inspections of work in progress tended to be superficial and infrequent, and they took the position of a mediator rather than a consumer advocate in disputes between residents and contractors.

The recent investigation of the section 235 program released by the House Committee on Banking and Currency points to similar conclusions. Low income home buyers clearly did not get reliable advice on the quality of work in the houses they bought, and in some cases they were unaware of violations of local zoning and building regulations. FHA staff were involved as intermediaries, but they did not serve resident interests effectively. Appraisals by mortgage lending institutions were also deficient. We do not interpret the results of this investigation as a repudiation of the concept of low income home ownership, but rather as evidence that the present intermediaries fail to provide competent building inspections and legal advice for buyers. To our knowledge, none of the abuses cited in the investigation involved programs in which nonprofit organizations provided these services.

SUBSIDY FORMULAS

Each federal housing program operates under a subsidy formula that determines which families are eligible for aid and how much aid will be supplied. These formulas thus bear directly on issues of equity in the provisions of federal subsidies. Although our review does not deal with the range and depth of subsidies, it is worth noting briefly that the income eligibility provisions and the amounts of subsidy supplied do not provide comprehensive coverage of all families whose incomes are too low to permit them to live in sound housing. The major new programs, sections 235 and 236, serve mainly families with incomes above $5,000. Public housing and rent supplements reach families with lower incomes, but even they do not reach the very lowest income groups. While it may not be necessary for every program to reach families at all income levels who need assistance, we believe that gaps in coverage at low income levels are particularly inequitable. Further, the clear desirability of providing families with reasonable choice of housing would argue for a subsidy system in which every family would be eligible for more than one type of housing.

We believe the formulas for individual programs should make subsidies available on a progressive scale with respect to income level and family size. That is, families that are poorer or larger should not be required to spend as high a proportion of their income for decent housing as families that are wealthier or smaller. The lower a family's income, or the larger its size, the more income it needs to devote to food, medical care, and other expenses. The subsidy formulas for public housing, rent supplements, section 235, and section 236 do incorporate this principle of progressivity by allowing deductions from income for minors in the family before calculating the percentage of income required to be spent for housing.

In some important respects, however, the subsidy formulas are regressive. In the case of section 235, families are required to spend 20 percent of their income for mortgage payments, taxes, and insurance. The cost of heating and utilities is not included in this calculation, however. In cold areas, these costs can be substantial, requiring low income families to spend more than one-fourth of their income for housing. Further, these costs are fairly constant and not directly related to income. Thus they require a greater proportion of the income of poor families than of wealthy ones.

A more striking regressive feature of the section 235 and 236 formulas has to do with the cost of housing for which individual families are eligible. The section 235 provisions illustrate how both formulas work. Twenty percent of the family's income must be sufficient to cover mortgage payments at an interest rate of 1 percent, plus taxes and insurance. Thus the higher a family's income, the more expensive the house they can afford under this program. But the more expensive the house, the greater the subsidy payment for which they are eligible. Our calculations, based on typical costs under the 235 program, show that a family of 5 with a gross income of $5,000 is confined to housing with a maximum purchase price of $8,700, while a family of 5 with an income of $7,000 can purchase a house up to a maximum value of $13,000. If these families buy houses at the maximum price permitted and receive the maximum subsidies allowed, the family with an income of $7,000 receives a federal subsidy 1½ times greater than the family with an income of $5,000.

Similarly, larger families are limited to lower purchase prices. As a result, a family of 5 with an income of $7,000 is eligible to receive twice the subsidy available to a family of 8 with an income of $5,000. These inequities help explain why the 235 program has been serving primarily small families with incomes above $5,000, many of whom could probably afford to pay for decent housing on the private market.

These regressive features, as well as the gaps in income groups served by housing subsidy programs, result directly from the basis on which subsidies are calculated. Subsidies are not based primarily on family income and size, but rather on the production cost of housing. Federal subsidies cover the debt service on local housing authority bonds, in the case of public housing. The debt service in turn reflects the capital cost of building the housing. In 235 and 236 housing, the federal subsidy is based on the difference between actual carrying charges at market interest rates and the cost of servicing a 1 percent mortgage. Within these basic allocations, adjustments in rent or ownership payments are made according to income and family size. As we have noted, these adjustments cannot meet the tests of comprehensive coverage, equity, and progressivity for all families that need help.

Subsidy formulas could meet these objectives if they were based primarily on family income and size, without having to conform to limits set by construction cost. Some of the current limits, such as a 1 percent mortgage, appear arbitrary in any case. If the subsidy were calculated on the basis of family characteristics, a large, low income family might pay the equivalent of an interest-free mortgage or might pay only enough to cover all or part of the operating expenses without contributing to financing charges.

In part, subsidy formulas have been tied to construction costs because federal policy has been to promote new construction or substantial renovation through the housing assistance programs. To do so, however, it is not necessary to base the subsidies on the capital costs. Eligibility for subsidies could be limited to families living in new or renovated houses, while the amount of subsidy could be based on family income and size. Recent amendments to the public housing legislation in fact move precisely in this direction. The special federal contributions to local authorities on behalf of elderly, displaced, unusually large or unusually poor families represent family-based subsidies, as do the provisions for federal payments to reduce rents in excess of 25 percent of a family's income. Existing programs can be modified in this way without altering their orientation to production and renovation, but family-based subsidies will, of course, require additional appropriations.

ARE HOUSING ALLOWANCES THE ANSWER?

The logic of our argument so far leads toward a conclusion that a housing allowance would be preferable to the present forms of federal housing subsidies. If housing assistance took the form of direct payments to low income families which they could apply toward their housing expenses, most of the problems resulting from the present dependence on intermediaries would be resolved. Families receiving help would no longer be limited to designated projects or locations. If the housing allowance plus their own income reached a reasonable level, they could exercise the same choices that middle income families now do. Within the limits set by available housing, they could make their own decisions on where to live and in what type of housing, whether to rent or buy, and how much renovation to do. Eligible families would not be denied aid because they happen to live in a community or a region where housing authorities or developers are not making use of federal-aid programs. Further, they would be able to move from central cities to suburbs without local government interference, as older homes come on the market at moderate prices. When families need the services of appraisers or lawyers, they would arrange for them privately.

From the federal government's point of view, housing allowances would constitute a relatively efficient form of subsidy, since the funds appropriated would reach the clients for whom they are intended without a major share being diverted to intermediaries. Presumably the federal administrative costs could be kept low, and there would be no need for local administrative agencies. In addition, the problem of gaps in the coverage of families at different income levels could be avoided by using a simple formula to provide housing

subsidies across a wide range of incomes, rather than tying the subsidy to the cost of particular housing units. And the design of the allowance formula could easily avoid the regressive features we have noted in some existing programs.

Although our evaluation of present subsidies points toward a housing allowance as a more promising approach, we recognize that there are many uncertainties about how effective a housing allowance would be in helping low income families to live in decent housing. Predicting the results of an untried program is very hazardous. In order to estimate what these results might be, we undertook a brief review of the one existing program that most closely approximates a housing allowance. This is the public welfare program, which provides recipients with cash income of which a portion is intended to cover housing expenses. In dollar terms, this is actually the largest of all federally subsidized housing programs. But it is not usually thought of as a housing program, and to our knowledge, the welfare experience has not previously been analyzed from the perspective of what it can tell us about how a housing allowance might operate. . . .

What we know about the housing conditions of families that receive direct housing subsidies through public assistance prompts us to question whether a system of housing allowances would be an effective replacement for the present federal subsidy programs. [A] national survey suggests that the source of income, as well as the level of a family's income, may influence the kind of housing a family can get. [A] Baltimore study and [a] New York [study] suggest that landlords often discriminate against welfare families, and that those who rent to welfare families do not maintain their properties in good condition. A number of other explanations are also plausible. Buildings in which welfare tenants are concentrated may not yield enough rent to provide for proper maintenance; or the owners of such buildings may find it difficult to get financing needed for renovation. Conceivably a large number of welfare recipients may have been living in substandard housing before they began to receive welfare, and simply continued to live where they were before. Or perhaps welfare families tend to cause more damage to the places where they live than do other families.

The process by which welfare families become housed in substandard conditions is not well understood. But until we understand it better, there is a great risk that major federal commitments to a housing allowance will not provide an adequate solution to low income housing problems. As a result, we believe that the wiser course of action is to undertake a series of more limited experiments with housing allowances and to study the results carefully before determining how best to administer housing allowances and before establishing large-scale programs of this kind.

RECOMMENDATIONS: A SHORT-TERM STRATEGY

Although we believe it would be premature for the federal government to undertake a large-scale program of housing allowances at the present time, we also believe that it is timely to test this concept and to redesign present programs so that they evolve toward housing allowances. If this short-term strategy begins to produce favorable results, more decisive steps can be taken in the near future. If problems become apparent, corrective action can be taken and a plan for the sound administration of housing allowances can be formulated on the basis of actual experience.

Our analysis of the present subsidy system has indicated a number of serious weaknesses in it. Reliance on a large number of intermediaries diverts a high proportion of federal funds away from low income families, distorts the allocation of aid so that it does not reach equal proportions of families in need in different regions and communities, prevents programs from operating in the suburbs, restricts the choices open to low income families, and leads to conflicts between families and intermediaries. Further, it fails to provide the kind of technical and legal assistance that many families need. The subsidy formulas them-

selves contain regressive features and leave certain gaps in the income levels that are covered. Remedial action can be taken to reduce the severity of all these problems; such action would at the same time move the present aid system closer to one providing housing allowances.

To reduce the number of intermediaries, and to limit the extent to which they control the nature of housing programs, we recommend the following.

1. Remove the requirement for local government approval of rent supplements. Eliminating this requirement would facilitate the provision of rent supplement units in additional communities, particularly in the suburbs. The impact of this step would be felt in the 236 program, as well, in those projects in which sponsors wish to reach lower income families by combining rent supplements with 236 aid.

2. Remove the requirement for local government approval of public housing leasing programs. Local housing authority approval is necessary in any event, and the requirement for separate action by local government creates an additional obstacle. Particularly in the case of short-term leasing, where no local tax abatement is involved, there seems to be no justification for allowing a local government veto.

3. Where there are suitable vacancies in local housing markets, federal policy should encourage the use of public housing leasing. Where housing supplies are tight, federal policy should encourage the use of turnkey programs and contracting for private management of projects.

4. To make it possible for tenants in public housing projects to have a greater voice in management decisions, the federal government should fund tenant organization activities and encourage experiments such as tenant involvement in maintenance, tenant patrols, and tenant management.

5. Provide funds for the services of intermediaries who would act as advocates for low income families using the 235 program and rehabilitation grants and loans. Nonprofit or-

ganizations should be given federal grants to offer inspection and legal services and technical advice to low income homeowners. Where it is not feasible for nonprofit groups to provide these services, a small fund should be created to allow low income families using these programs to pay for inspections and legal advice.

6. Replace the costly tax benefits now offered to developers and rehabilitation sponsors with more direct incentives, such as development fees or higher returns on equity.

7. Appropriate funds for the experimental housing allowance program authorized in the Housing and Urban Development Act of 1970. It will be important to provide for a careful evaluation of the results of these experiments. These results should also be compared with the outcome of other federal housing subsidies, and particularly with program modifications that move toward a housing allowance approach. In the housing allowance experiments, we recommend that the formula provide greater subsidies for larger and poorer families, and that the subsidy be based in part on the family's own housing expenditure rather than constituting a lump-sum grant.

To make the distribution of housing subsidies more equitable, we recommend the following.

1. Federal policy should aim at achieving a regional and community distribution of housing subsidies based on the distribution of need; that is, the number of low income families living in substandard or overcrowded housing or forced to spend more than a reasonable proportion of their income for housing. Regional and community allocations should reflect an estimate of need. HUD and FHA field offices should be given a mandate to encourage additional applications for funds in areas of high need, and to disapprove applications in areas where the needs are not as great.

2. Subsidy formulas should be revised to eliminate presently regressive features and to offer greater aid to lower income and larger

families. Subsidies should not be tied to the cost of housing, but rather to family income and size. In the case of 235 and 236 housing, this approach would mean permitting low income families to contribute less than the carrying charges on a 1 percent mortgage. In the case of public housing, rent formulas should be made progressive, and additional federal contributions should be provided to cover operating costs in excess of rent receipts.

To permit greater freedom of choice for families using federal subsidy programs, we recommend the following.

1. Allow greater use of existing housing for the 235 and 236 programs. The present ceiling of 30 percent on existing housing should be increased. In addition, families using section 235 should be permitted greater freedom of choice in buying multifamily buildings for their own occupancy plus rental income. Present restrictions prevent the use of a large number of three- and four-family buildings which could lend themselves to resident ownership.

2. To permit low income families a realistic opportunity to be owners as well as tenants, the 235 program should make special provision for several circumstances. Additional borrowing should be permitted on 235 mortgages to pay for emergency repairs, and a special reserve should be established to cover mortgage arrears for a grace period of several months. It would also be desirable to allow low income families who already own their houses to refinance them under section 235 to pay for rehabilitation.

If the results of the housing allowance experiments and these program modifications are encouraging, several existing programs could be extended still further in the direction of housing allowances. Families could be permitted to apply for rent supplements and for 235 and 236 assistance in any new or rehabilitated housing that falls within established cost ceilings, for example. Or, if market conditions are appropriate, these subsidies could be permitted in existing housing, as well. If the availability of funds makes it necessary to limit the size of these efforts, eligibility could be restricted to certain categories of families that have particularly pressing housing needs, such as families displaced from their previous houses by public action and very large families who are difficult to accommodate within existing programs.

TOWARD A LONG-TERM STRATEGY

Many of the weaknesses we have identified in present subsidy programs result from the fact that they have been designed to work toward two different objectives: increasing the production of housing, and providing financial aid to low income families. These objectives are often in conflict, and the programs that attempt to achieve both simultaneously constitute uneasy compromises. They assign a large role to intermediaries because the intermediaries are needed as agents of production; but the intermediaries then absorb a large share of the subsidy dollars and restrict the choices open to low income families. The subsidy formulas have been designed to spread federal assistance to as large a number of newly built or newly renovated units as possible; but as a result these subsidies often fail to reach families that are large or that have very low incomes.

Most of our proposals involve limiting the role of intermediaries or providing greater subsidies and subsidies tailored primarily to family income and size. These proposals, however, would reduce the volume of housing produced under federal-aid programs for any given level of appropriations. A housing allowance would probably work still further in the direction of reducing production in order to give more effective financial aid to families in need.

The desirability of sacrificing production goals to family assistance goals depends directly on the state of the housing market. When the total volume of housing production is high enough to increase the supply of vacant housing in good condition, a shift of goals in the low income programs away from

production and toward more adequate assistance would be most appropriate. In most parts of the country, however, the housing market today is very tight. Decisive moves to sacrifice production under the low income programs, therefore, could have unfortunate effects. . . .

As long as the volume of unsubsidized housing starts remains small, it is difficult to argue that federal-aid programs should sacrifice production in order to provide deeper subsidies and wider choices. To be sure, if federal housing funds were used for direct family allowances or similar approaches, they would lead to some growth in production and renovation by increasing the demand for housing at moderate cost levels. But the response of housing producers would almost surely be slower and less certain than is now the case through production-oriented subsidy programs.

The reforms we have recommended, as well as a more drastic shift to housing allowances, would be most effective as part of a different long-term strategy. This strategy would call for combining a high level of housing production with a high level of assistance of low income families. If unsubsidized new construction once again begins to produce a surplus, federal assistance funds can help low income families to afford the cost of housing that becomes available. Production itself would no longer need to receive high priority in the subsidy programs. . . .

The federal government can encourage a high volume of housing starts by using some production-oriented subsidy programs for middle income families who would otherwise be unable to afford new houses. . . . Home ownership and rental programs could extend the market for new construction by giving additional purchasing power to families whose incomes fall just below the level needed to pay for new construction.

Aids for the production of middle income housing would pose few of the problems we have found in reviewing present low income subsidies. The subsidy per family would not need to be very great, since the family's own income would almost suffice to pay for new housing. Families would be less restricted by the choices of housing sponsors, since they would have many alternatives open to them in existing houses. Middle income housing would produce far less opposition in the suburbs than would low income housing. Thus the chances for getting access to open suburban land would be much improved. And the success of such programs would help lower income groups by releasing a stock of older central-city and suburban housing now occupied by middle income families, which these groups could afford if aided by housing allowances.

We make this suggestion with some hesitation, however; for we believe there is a danger that middle income programs could divert attention and resources away from housing assistance for the poor. We wish to emphasize that aid for middle income production is justifiable only as part of a total strategy, and adopting this part of the strategy by itself offers little promise for a better national performance than we have had in the recent past.

14. HEALTH AND INEQUALITY

■ Surely the most fundamental chance *in* life is the chance *for* life. Antonovsky's examination of historical and current data on variations in life expectancy and mortality for different groups in the class system shows clearly that inequalities in even so basic a matter as how long one lives have not been eradicated by the tremendous advances in medicine and medical organization over the past century, although some evidence suggests that differentials between classes have narrowed. My own article discusses the situation of low income people in relation to health, illness, and their bodies, and its effect on their attitudes toward health institutions and professions.

In the period after World War II a large group of sociologists began to study health and medicine, especially the organization of medical services—physicians, nurses, medical schools, and the interrelations among the various specialties within the health professions. Much research also was devoted to the sociological and social-psychological aspects of the population's health and of the demand for health care.

Those who have sought to ensure decent care for low and middle-income people have had considerable reason to be encouraged by the rapid growth of private health insurance plans since World War II and by the 1965 passage of the medicaid and medicare programs. Medicare, which provides hospital medical insurance for the elderly, covered 20.4 million persons by 1970. Medicaid covers the cost of medical care for welfare recipients and the medically indigent (the aged, the blind, the disabled, and families with dependent children).

Background data about the health insurance issue are usefully summarized in the Brookings Institution's *Setting National Priorities: The 1973 Budget*. There we discover that while in 1950 two-thirds of health care costs were covered by direct private payments, by 1971 only slightly over one-third of the payments were made in that way. The slack had been taken up by private insurance payments and public expenditures; the private insurance share of the nation's medical bill increased by one-quarter in the 1960s, and the public share by 65 percent. Variations among income groups in private health insurance coverage were marked, however. In 1968 the proportion of people under 65 covered by private health insurance was 36 percent of those with incomes under $3,000, 57 percent of those with incomes of $3,000-$5,000, but up to 92 percent for those with incomes of $10,000 and over. Health insurance coverage also differs by income even for those who have insurance; higher income people are more likely not only to have some kind of health insurance but also to have a better kind in terms of coverage and payments.

In the early 1970s Congress was considering several different versions of national health insurance that would cover not just the elderly, as with medicare, but everyone in the country. However, experience with medicare made all advocates of health insurance—liberal as well as conservative—considerably more cautious. Inflation in the cost of medical care turned out to be such a severe problem that it threatened in the end either to wash away any reasonable level of benefits or to gobble up increasingly large proportions of the Gross National Product.

The ordinary citizen has long been aware that physicians in hospitals are in an extremely strong bargaining position in determining how much to charge for their services. In the U.S., this has resulted in health care costs that are markedly higher than in other nations. Insurance further strengthens the positions of the health care professionals and institutions because the consumer has even less incentive to resist high charges for services he may or may not need. Those involved in health care therefore have little incentive to resist cost increases or to organize the delivery of services in the most economical and efficient way.

As the rising affluence of the whole population has increased demands for good health care for all citizens, so has the government increased pressure on health care institutions to organize themselves more efficiently. Current efforts to slow the rate of rise in costs are directed partly toward enlarging the supply of physicians but mainly toward enlarging the supply of other health care professionals and

toward encouraging the development of organizations that make efficient use of a wide range of medical skills so that the highly paid physician can free himself from much of the less skilled work. The so-called "health maintenance" or "group practice" plans are expected to bring the cost-cutting benefits of rational organization to the chaotic medical care system. In addition, any national health insurance program eventually enacted probably will include a significant coinsurance feature requiring individuals to pay a portion of their medical costs and thus giving them an incentive to restrain their health care suppliers as much as they can.

An extremely useful integration of the wide range of sociological research on medical care —one that takes the role of inequality as an explicit organizing principle—is found in Eliot Friedson, *Professional Dominance: The Social Structure of Medical Care* (Chicago: Aldine, 1970), and in Friedson's *Profession of Medicine: A Study of the Sociology of Applied Knowledge* (New York: Dodd, Mead, 1970). A useful review of the implications of medical sociological research for mental health policy is found in David Mechanic, *Mental Health and Social Policy* (Englewood Cliffs, N.J.: Prentice-Hall, 1970). Among the central studies in medical sociology have been August B. Hollingshead and Frederick C. Redlich, *Social Class and Mental Illness* (New York: Wiley, 1958), and Jerome K. Meyers and Bertram H. Roberts, *Family and Class Dynamics in Mental Illness* (New York: Wiley, 1959). Just as inequality has its impact on life expectancy so it has an impact on the manner of dying; Barney G. Glaser and Anselm Strauss, *Awareness of Dying* and *Time for Dying* (Chicago: Aldine, 1965 and 1968), and David Sudnow, *Passing On* (Englewood Cliffs, N.J.: Prentice-Hall, 1967).

Discussions of current health insurance issues can be found in the Brookings Institution study cited above, in Mark V. Pauly, "An Analysis of Government Health Insurance Plans for Poor Families," *Public Policy*, Summer 1971, pp. 489 ff, and in a pair of articles by Joseph P. Neuhouse and Vincent Taylor and by Martin S. Felstein under the title "The Health Care Muddle," *The Public Interest*, Spring 1971, pp. 78-105. ∎

14a. CLASS AND THE CHANCE FOR LIFE

AARON ANTONOVSKY

Reprinted from A. Antonovsky, "Social Class, Life Expectancy and Overall Mortality," Milbank Memorial Fund Quarterly, vol. 45, no. 2 (April 1967), by permission. Aaron Antonovsky is Senior Research Associate at the Israel Institute of Applied Social Research in Jerusalem.

RECALLING WHAT HAPPENED when an "unsinkable" trans-Atlantic luxury liner, the *Titanic*, rammed an iceberg on her maiden voyage in 1912 . . . The official casualty list showed that only 4 first class female passengers (3 voluntarily chose to stay on the ship) of a total of 143 were lost. Among the second class passengers, 15 of 93 females drowned; and among the third class, 81 of 179 female passengers went down with the ship.

Death is the final lot of all living beings. But, as the tragic experience of the *Titanic* passengers dramatically illustrates, the time at which one dies is related to one's class. The intent of this paper is to examine the evidence which bears upon the closeness of this relationship, ranging as far back as the data will allow. It will first focus on the question of life expectancy at birth, and subsequently turn to that of overall mortality.

STUDIES OF LIFE EXPECTANCY

The average infant born today in the Western world can look forward, barring unforeseen events and radical changes in present trends, to a life span of about 70 years. That this has not always been the case for the human infant—and still is not for by far most infants born today—is well known. Whatever the situation prior to the era of recorded history, for the greater part of this

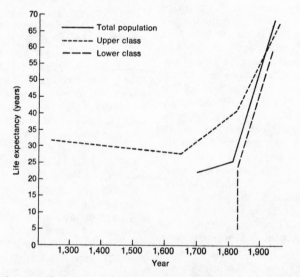

Data are derived from specific studies cited in the text and are plotted at the midyear of each time period. The values for the last five years for the total United States population are from *The Facts of Life and Death*, Public Health Service publication no. 600, revised 1965, p. 21.

FIGURE 14a.1
MODEL OF CLASS DIFFERENCES IN LIFE EXPECTANCY AT BIRTH IN
VARIOUS POPULATIONS.

era—that is, until the 19th century—most men lived out less than half their Biblical span of years.

In what is probably the first study of a total population, Halley, using data for the city of Breslau, Germany, for 1687 to 1691, calculated an average life expectancy at birth of 33.5 years. Henry's estimate for the expectation of life of Parisian children born at the beginning of the 18th century was 23.5 years. Half a century later, in the Vienna of 1752 to 1755, of every 1,000 infants born alive, only 590 survived their first year, 413 their fifth year, and 359 their 15th year. Henry further cites an estimate, which he regards as "too pessimistic," 28.8 years for the total French population toward the end of the Ancien Regime.

In the 19th century, Villerme, in a careful firsthand study, reported a life expectancy at birth for the total population of the city of Mulhouse, France, of 7 years and 6 months, based on the period 1823 to 1834. However, he also cites Penot's data for Mulhouse, from 1812 to 1827, which show an average life expectancy of 25 years. Ansell found a life expectation at birth for the total British population in 1874 of about 43 years. At about the same time, the reported figures for Italy were somewhat lower: 35 years (1871 to 1880); 36.2 years for males, 35.65 years for females (1881-1882).

Whatever the discrepancies and unreliabilities of these various sets of data, they consistently paint a picture of the Western world up to recent centuries which is quite similar to that of the world of presently "developing" societies until the last decade or two. Moreover, in the period of recorded history prior to the 18th century, no sizable increment had been added to the average life span. But if, from Greco-Roman times through the 18th or perhaps even the 19th century, the mythical "average" infant could anticipate living some 20 to 30 years, does any evidence indicate that dramatic class differences existed? Though the evidence is perforce limited, the answer would seem to be no. . . .

In other words, given a society which, though it manages to survive, does so at or near what might be called a rock-bottom level of life expectancy, one is not likely to find great differences among the strata of that society.

The data suggest the possibility that the trend in the 19th century, and perhaps even earlier, was toward a substantial widening of class differences. No report is available comparing the life expectancies of social strata of the population prior to the 19th century. . . .

Can any conclusion be drawn from these data, most of which are admittedly tenuous and not overly reliable? A crude picture, as represented in Figure 14a.1, could be inferred which indicates the following. The bulk of recorded history was one of high birth and high death rates, which offset each other and led to at most a very small increase in population. During the first 16 centuries of the Christian era, world population increased from about ¼ to ½ billion people, an annual growth rate of about .005 percent. Conceivably, throughout this period, no substantial differentials in life expectancy could be found among different social strata of the population. From 1650 to 1850 world population again doubled, most of the increase being in the Western world, representing an average annual increase of .05 percent. These two centuries would seem to mark the emergence of an increasing class gap in life expectancy, starting slowly but gathering increasing momentum and reaching its peak about the time Malthus made his observations. On the one hand, the life expectancy of the middle and upper strata of the population increased at a rapid rate. On the other, the lowest strata's life expectancy may have increased much more slowly or, conceivably, even declined as an industrial proletariat emerged. At some time during the 19th century, probably in the latter half, this trend was reversed, and the class gap began to diminish. This is reflected in the doubling of the world's population, again mostly in the West, this time in the 80 years from 1850 to 1930. In recent decades, the class gap has narrowed to what may be the smallest differential in history, but evidence of a linear gradient remains, with a considerable differential, given man's life span.

This supposition—not claimed to be more than that, since Figure 14a.1 is no more than a very crude representation—seems to be of more than historical interest. It is, for two important reasons, most germane to the concern of this paper. In the first place, the scientist, no less than the lay person, often seems, in considering the question of the relationship between class and health, to be beset by a 19th century notion of perpetual progress. Ideologically committed, in this area, to the desirability of the disappearance of the class gap, he tends to assume, with or without data, that the historical picture is unilinear; the history of mankind, in his view, shows steady progress in this respect. The realization that this may well be an inaccurate image, that the relationship is more complex, suggests a more cautious orientation. Such an orientation would suggest various possibilities: a narrowing gap being transformed into one which is widening; differing positions, on any given index of health, of differing strata of the population at various times.

The second reason for stressing the possibility of a curvilinear relationship between class and life expectancy over time is that such a relationship may help in forming an adequate idea of the relationship between class and health, and, more broadly, an adequate theory of disease. Once the search begins for explanations of why, in a given period, one stratum seems to be making more health progress than another, and less so in another period, factors are uncovered which must be integrated into a theory of disease.

Thus, for example, McKeown and Brown, arguing that the increase in the population of England in the 18th century was overwhelmingly due to the decline in mortality, attribute that decline to improvements in the environment (housing, water supply, refuse disposal, nutrition) rather than to any advances in medical care. Supposedly, such improvements first appeared in the upper strata of society, and only slowly percolated downward. This would explain the increasing class differences in life expectancy. Once the environmental sanitation gap began to narrow, some reversal in the trend could be expected which, however, might soon be offset by other factors—e.g., the malnutrition of poverty. The point is that a very careful collection of data over time and the search for ups and downs may serve to pinpoint the various factors, and their modes of interaction, which influence overall mortality or the course of any specific disease.

CLASS DIFFERENCES IN MORTALITY BEFORE WORLD WAR II

Twentieth century investigators have by and large focused on class differences in mortality rates. Chapin's study of Providence, Rhode Island, probably provides the earliest relevant information. Using census and tax records of 1865, he located all but about 200 of the 2,000 taxpayers, covering a total of 10,515 individuals. Every deceased person in that year was assigned to either the taxpayer or nontaxpayer group. Chapin then calculated the death rates per thousand in each group. The crude annual death rate of the latter (24.8 per 1,000 living) was more than double that of the taxpayers (10.8). . . . This disparity is found in all but the 5- to 9-year age cohort, and is greatest in the productive years (30 to 49) and in the 70 and over cohort. Since the nontaxpayer group includes more than 80 percent of the population, had Chapin been able to make a finer class breakdown he presumably would have found even greater differences between the top and bottom strata.

Collins, in an early review of socioeconomic mortality data, cites an 1887 paper by Humphreys on mortality in Dublin in 1883-1885, which shows a higher mortality among the poor, but presents no data. The earliest data presented by Collins refer to Danish mortality rates from 1865 to 1874, the 1870 census having been used to obtain denominator information. Individuals were assigned to high, middle, or poor classes on the basis of the head of household's occupation. The top category includes capitalists, professionals, wholesale dealers and higher officers. The middle group contains master mechanics, petty officers, teachers, clerks and small shopkeepers. The poor class is made up of workmen, servants and those in almshouses. . . . The data show that class differences are greater in Copenhagen than in provincial towns, and greater among males than among females. More significantly, although the rates show primarily an inverse class gradient, the differences between the high and middle classes are relatively small compared to the gap between them and the poor class. . . .

The first of many ecological studies was Rowntree's well-known survey of York, England, in 1899. Rowntree divided the wage-earner areas of the city of York into three levels. The overall death rates per thousand persons (not age-standardized) he reports for 1899 are: highest, 13.5; middle, 20.7; poorest, 27.8 (ratios of 100:153:206). In this case, unlike the earlier Danish data, the inverse gradient is quite regular.

In a paper focusing on later data, Britten calculates overall death rates for 1900 in the nine states and the District of Columbia, which then comprised the death registration area. He compared white-collar rates to those for the "laboring and servant" class in three age groups. Taking the white-collar death rate as 100, the ratios for the lower class group were: for ages 15-24, 151; for ages 25-44, 165; and for ages 45-64, 159.

As a prologue to her analysis of 1950 death rates, Guralnick presents, without analysis, the full set of data upon which Britten evidently based his calculations, as well as similar data for 1890. . . . For the employed male population as a whole, in both years, professionals have a somewhat higher mortality rate than do other white-collar workers or those in industry, most of whom are presumably manual workers. Conceivably this may be explained by the fact that the rates are not age-standardized, and professionals might be an older group. The age-specific rates do show professionals as having a lower than average rate in the younger age groups and somewhat above average in the

higher groups. The most striking fact about these data is the very sizable difference, at all ages, between the "laboring and servant" class and all other groups. In both 1890 and 1900, the ratio of this class is higher in ages 25-44 and 45-64, somewhat lower at ages 15-24, and lowest—though still relatively high—in the 65 and over category. An interesting pattern is shown by the clerical and official group: in the youngest age category its ratio is quite high, in 1900 approaching that of the lowest class; in each successive age category its ratio goes down, so that in the 65 and over category it has by far the lowest mortality rate.

Szabady, reporting the data (non-age-standardized) for the total population of pre-World War I Hungary, divides the nonagricultural population into nonmanual and manual groups. For all persons, the death rates per thousand in 1900 were, respectively, 15.1 and 25.1; in 1910, the gap had narrowed, with both rates having fallen to 13.8 and 20.9. That differences in infant mortality contributed considerably to class differences in overall mortality is shown by considering only the rates of earners. In 1900, the nonmanual death rate was 13.6, compared to 17.5 for manual earners. By 1910, the difference had nearly disappeared, the rates being 15.0 and 15.9 per thousand. . . .

Whitney's study using 1930 data was the first large-scale American study following the pattern which had been set by the British Registrar General. Death certificate data were obtained from 10 states: Alabama, Connecticut, Illinois, Kansas, Massachusetts, Minnesota, New Jersey, New York, Ohio and Wisconsin. These states contained 39 percent of the gainfully employed. The 1930 census was used to obtain denominator information. Analysis was limited to males aged 15 to 64, in an attempt to limit the unreliability introduced by retirement. Age-standardized data are presented within the social-economic classification developed by Edwards and used standardly by the United States Census.

As can be seen in Table 14a.1, mortality rates vary inversely with class in the total

TABLE 14a.1

ANNUAL DEATH RATES PER 1,000 GAINFULLY OCCUPIED MALES, AGED 15 TO 64
YEARS (AGE-STANDARIZED) BY AGE GROUPS
ACCORDING TO SOCIOECONOMIC CLASS, 1930

| | | | Age Groups* | | | | | |
| Socioeconomic Class | 15-64 | | 15-24 | | 25-44 | | 45-64 | |
	Rate	Ratio†	Rate	Ratio	Rate	Ratio	Rate	Ratio
All gainfully employed males	9.1	100	3.2	100	5.5	100	17.9	100
Professional men	6.7	74	2.3	72	3.5	64	16.2	90
Proprietors, managers, and officials	7.9	87	3.1	97	4.2	76	15.8	88
Clerks and kindred workers	7.8	86	2.3	72	4.1	74	16.5	92
Skilled workers and foremen	8.3	91	3.0	94	4.9	89	17.1	96
Semiskilled workers	10.1	111	3.2	100	6.1	111	20.8	116
Unskilled workers	14.5	159	4.7	147	9.6	174	24.8	138

*The age-standardized figures for the age group 15-64 are based on the 53 occupational groups with 500 or more deaths (Whitney, Table 8, p. 32). These cover 79 per cent of the gainfully employed. This set of data was selected as more reliable than the figures for all deaths, given by Whitney in Table 1, p. 17. The trends in the two sets of data are very similar. The age-specific data are only available in Whitney's Table 1, and cover the entire surveyed population.
†Rate for all gainfully employed males = 100.

age group of 15-64. Only the proprietor group is out of line. If retail dealers, whose rate is 8.4, are excluded from this category, the rate would be 7.0, making a linear relationship. The curve, however, is not smooth, as can be seen clearly from the ratios presented in the table. The largest difference is found between unskilled and semiskilled workers, with a sizable difference between the latter and skilled workers. Beyond this level the differences, although existent, are relatively small.

The same general pattern appears in each of the three age-specific sets of data. The spread, however, is greatest in the 25-44 age group and least in the oldest group. In the latter, differences among the four occupational categories from skilled workers and up are almost nonexistent. This study indicates, then, that class is most intimately related to mortality rates among the unskilled and secondarily among the semiskilled workers, and during middle age.

Sheps and Watkins sought to overcome the weakness of ecological studies by utilizing information obtained in careful sociological study which grouped areas in New Haven, Connecticut, into "natural areas." The boundary lines of these areas were such that information about census tracts could be used for purposes of setting denominators and standardizing for age. The seven resulting

areas for which death rates for 1930 to 1934 were calculated contained from 10,000 to 51,000 people. A total of 8,201 deaths were recorded during this period. The seven areas were ranked from best to worst, based on a composite of factors including rental, delinquency rates, social standing and financial dependency. All data were age-adjusted.

Taking the average annual death rate over the five-year period of the best area (8.0 per 1,000 persons) as 100, the ratios of the other six areas, going down the socioeconomic scale, were: 111, 110, 128, 136, 145, 148. Other than the fact that the rates for the second and third highest areas are almost identical, a clear inverse linear relationship is found. When the authors combined the seven areas into three, the range was substantially narrowed (100:114:134). The strongest relationship between mortality rates and economic level were found at ages 0-5 and 25-64. . . .

WORLD WAR II TO THE PRESENT

. . . By the 1950s, the number of studies of socioeconomic mortality differentials had increased considerably. . . . Tayback divided Baltimore's 168 census tracts on the basis of the 1950 median tract rentals, grouping them into equal-sized population quintiles. . . . In overall terms, a clear inverse class gradient is seen, the male slope being somewhat steeper than the female slope, with very few figures being out of line. The gap tends to be quite large in the younger age groups, where the death rate is low. Class differences in middle age (35-54) are very sizable. At this age, the major differences seem to be at the top and bottom, between the highest and next highest and between the lowest and second lowest economic levels. Differences remain considerable at ages 55-64, but tend to become much smaller thereafter.

Ellis conducted a very similar study in Houston. The index used to rank census tracts was a modification of the index of social rank developed by Shevky and Williams, which utilizes measures of education, occupation, and median family income. Tracts were grouped into quintiles, each of which contained 12 or 13 tracts. . . . Although class differentials do appear, they differ from those in other studies. The range of differences is smaller, though still substantial. The two top groups of tracts, for males, and the three top, for females, are quite similar in their death rates. Most puzzling, perhaps, is the fact that males in the lowest tract level have a lower rate than do those in the adjacent level. Ellis suggests as a possible explanation the availability of free medical treatment for the lowest group. Group 4, not having such an advantage but having a limited income, may utilize funds for the females, who do have a lower rate than the females in group 5, whereas the males go on working and refrain from using such funds for themselves. . . .

Since the British Registrar General system of social classification is the richest source of data on mortality differences over time among different socioeconomic levels, a number of attempts have been made to construct a comparable ranking in the United States. Breslow and Buell, using the 1950 census for denominator data, classified all deaths of California males, aged 20-64, from 1949 to 1951, in one of five occupational classes. . . .

For the entire age group, a rough inverse gradient is seen between class and mortality. . . .

A more ambitious attempt along the same lines was conducted by Guralnick, who analyzed all male deaths in age group 20 to 64 in the United States in 1950. In view of the fact that one primary purpose was to compare the United States data with the British, Guralnick collapsed classes II to IV to make this intermediate group comparable in the two countries. The data are presented in Table 14a.2. For the entire age group, the picture is quite similar to that presented in the California study: a linear inverse gradient, with the intermediate occupational level being closer to class I, and the major gap occurring between class V and the intermediate group. Another publication by Guralnick, in which standard mortality ratios are given separately for the five classes, presents figures almost identical with the California figures. The standardized mortality ratios for all United States males aged 20-64, in 1950, from class I to class V, are: 83, 84, 96, 97, 120. These ratios are for Whites only, except for class I, which contains a few non-Whites. Once again classes I and II do not differ, nor do classes III and IV.

Examination of the age-specific rates in Table 14a.2 shows the largest class gap to lie in the 25 to 44 age group, with classes II to IV being closer to class I than to class V. A considerable gap remains at ages 45-54, but it is substantially narrowed by ages 55-64.

Guralnick also analyzed the same 1950 data along more traditional American lines, using the occupational classification developed by Edwards for the United States Census. This scheme seeks to rank occupations by socioeconomic levels. The standardized mortality ratios for White males aged 25-59, show an inverse gradient, but one which does not distinguish among all of the eight occupational groups. The lowest ratios are found among the top three groups; they are followed closely by sales and skilled and semiskilled workers, whose ratios are identical. Service workers fare substantially poorer, and, finally, laborers have a considerably higher mortality ratio.

TABLE 14a.2

ANNUAL DEATH RATES PER 1,000, AND RATIOS, WHITE MALES, BY AGE AND MAJOR OCCUPATION GROUP, UNITED STATES, 1950

Major Occupation Group	25-29 SMR†	20-24 X	20-24 Y*	25-29 X	25-29 Y	30-34 X	30-34 Y	35-44 X	35-44 Y	45-54 X	45-54 Y	55-59 X	55-59 Y	60-64 X	60-64 Y
All occupations	93	1.7	100	1.6	100	2.0	100	3.9	100	10.1	100	19.4	100	28.8	100
Professional, technical, kindred	82	1.2	73	1.2	70	1.5	76	3.2	81	9.4	93	18.9	98	29.2	101
Managers, officials, proprietors, nonfarm	85	1.5	86	1.3	79	1.5	76	3.3	85	9.5	94	18.9	98	28.9	100
Clerical, kindred	83	0.9	54	1.3	78	1.5	76	3.3	86	9.6	95	18.2	94	26.9	93
Sales	94	1.1	62	1.1	66	1.7	82	3.6	94	11.0	109	21.7	112	31.8	110
Craftsmen, foremen, kindred	94	1.8	103	1.6	97	2.0	99	4.0	102	10.1	100	20.8	107	32.1	111
Operatives, kindred	94	1.8	106	1.8	108	2.2	107	4.1	106	10.3	102	19.4	100	28.6	99
Service, except private household	116	1.2	72	1.6	98	2.4	117	5.1	133	13.8	136	22.4	116	29.2	101
Laborers, except farm and mine	131	2.6	149	2.8	171	3.6	178	6.5	167	14.5	144	23.8	123	34.9	121

*X = death rate per 1,000. Y = ratio, computed on the basis of rate for all occupations in each age category = 100.

†Standardized mortality ratios are computed on the basis of the entire population. Since non-White are excluded in this table. SMRs can fall below 100.

This pattern does not hold in all age groups. Prior to age 30, only the roughest gradient appears, though laborers fare markedly worst. A clear gradient appears in the 30-34 groups, which is maintained in the next 10-year cohort. In both cases, the ratios of the top three occupational groups are nearly identical. This pattern holds in ages 45-54 and 55-59 in part. Three mortality levels can be distinguished in these groups, which do not conform to the socioeconomic ranking: nonmanual workers except sales workers; sales and skilled and semiskilled workers; and service and unskilled workers. In the oldest age category, only laborers continue to differ from all other groups. . . .

A problem which has consistently bedeviled those who seek to study socioeconomic differentials on mortality by use of death certificates and census records is the frequent noncomparability of data in the two sources, which leads to overestimation of the denominator in some occupations and underestimation in others, or difficulty in making any calculations. The nature of the problem has been explored, theoretically and empirically, by several writers. Among these, Kitagawa and Hauser have sought to overcome the difficulties by individual matching of 340,000 death certificates from deaths occurring in the United States from May through August, 1960, with census information recorded for these individuals in the 1960 census. In addition, personal interviews were conducted with individuals knowledgeable about 94 percent of a sample of 9,500 of the decendents.

A preliminary analysis of the data using education and family income for White persons has been reported, though not yet published. Consideration of the education variable, which is broken down into four levels of completed education by persons 25 and older, shows an inverse gradient of mortality rates by amount of education for both sexes in ages 25 to 64. Interestingly enough, this gradient disappears for males 65 and over, but remains quite strong for females of this age.

The latest mortality study available is Tsuchiya's presentation of standardized mortality ratios for an occupational-industrial categorization of Japanese males, age 15 and over, in 1962. No clear occupational gradient emerges from the data. The ratios, ranked from low to high, are: "management," 58; "clerks," 67; "mechanics and simple," 88; "sales," 89; "professional and technical," 92; "transporting and communicating," 135. . . .

Viewing the data for England and Wales in overall terms, class differentials in mortality in the 20th century both have and have not declined. On the one hand, the differentials between the middle levels (among whom mortality rates differed little even in the earlier years) and class I have more or less disappeared. On the other hand, class V is still strikingly worse off than the rest of the population. Though indications are that its relative position improved in the earlier decades of the century, this does not seem to be the case between 1930 and 1950.

CONCLUSIONS

This statistical examination clearly provides no basis to reject the inference drawn from the figures of the Titanic disaster. Despite the multiplicity of methods and indexes used in the 30-odd studies cited, and despite the variegated populations surveyed, the inescapable conclusion is that class influences one's chance of staying alive. Almost without exception, the evidence shows that classes differ on mortality rates. Only three such exceptions were found, indicating no or almost no class difference. Altenderfer, comparing 1939-40 mortality rates of 92 United States cities classified into 3 mean income groups, shows a relatively small difference among them. Szabady, comparing nonagricultural manual and nonmanual workers in Hungary in 1959-60, shows the same. In both cases, the classification is so gross as to minimize differences which a finer analysis might reveal. Only DeWolff and Meerdink's study in Amsterdam in 1947-52 can legitimately be regarded as strongly contradictory of the link between class and mortality. Their data, however, must be seen in the context of a population which has just about the lowest death rate ever recorded. This is not to dismiss the importance of their findings. On the contrary, it suggests the extremely important hypothesis that as the overall death rate of a population is lowered, class differentials may similarly decline.

This hypothesis finds support in an overall trend reflected in the studies reported. In the earlier studies, the differential between the mortality rates of extreme class groups is about a 2:1 ratio, but later studies show a narrowing of this differential, so that by the 1940s, a 1.4:1 or 1.3:1 ratio is much more typical. As can be seen from studying the death rates, these years witnessed a progressive decline in the overall death rate. At the same time, a cautionary note must be exercised. Despite an undoubted overall decline in mortality in the past three decades, the trend in the earlier decades of the century toward the closing of the class gap has been checked, if not halted.

This indication focuses on the differences between mortality rates of the lowest class and other classes. A more accurate picture of the overall pattern would be to suggest that what has happened is a blurring, if not a disappearance, of a clear class gradient, while class differences remain. On the basis of the existent data—using, for the sake of convenience, a fivefold class distinction, this being the most popular—it is difficult to conclude whether classes I to IV now no longer differ in their mortality rates, or whether classes I and II have the lowest rates, and II and IV have higher rates, though not necessarily substantially so. What seems to be beyond question is that, whatever the index used and whatever the number of classes considered, almost always a lowest class appears with substantially higher mortality rates. Moreover, the differential between it and other classes evidently has not diminished over recent decades.

At this point discussion of the complex question of explanations for such patterns would not be appropriate. A possibility could be suggested, however. The truly magnificent triumphs over infectious diseases have been crucial in both narrowing the overall class differentials and in nearly eliminating differentials among all but the lowest class. In recent decades, however, access to good medical care, preventive medical action, health knowledge, and limitation of delay in seeking treatment have become increasingly important in combating mortality, as chronic diseases have become the chief health enemy in the developed world. In these areas, lower class people may well be at a disadvantage. As such factors become more and more important, as the historical supposition presented in the first pages of this paper suggests, increasing class differentiation may occur. This approach does not necessarily preclude consideration of genetic selection and what has commonly come to be called "the drift hypothesis."

The data reviewed lead to a further conclusion. With amazing consistency, the class differentials are largest in the middle years of life. This is no less true in the latest than in the earliest studies. Over and over again, the greatest gap is found in young and middle adulthood. The predominant pattern characterizing class differentials by age is that in which class differences are moderately high in the younger ages, rise to a peak at ages 30 to 44, begin to decline at that point and tend to disappear beyond age 65. Where a given set of data varies from this pattern, it is in one of two directions: in the former cases, class differentials are lowest in the younger and older groups; in the latter, the decline in class differentials only begins in late middle age.

This pattern of greatest class differences in middle adulthood may be linked to the two historical suppositions which have heretofore been presented. To hypothesize in more general terms, when mortality rates are extremely high or extremely low, class differences will tend to be small. In other words, when men are quite helpless before the threat of death, or when men have made great achievements in dealing with this threat, life chances will tend to be equitably distributed. On the other hand, when moderate progress is being made in dealing with this threat, differential consequences are to be expected. The crucial idea that may be involved here is that of preventable deaths, at any given level of knowledge, technique, and social organization. Where and/or when such deaths are concentrated, class differentials will be greatest, unless appropriate social action is taken. This differential is not inevitable.

Much more, of course, could be said in summary, with reference to both substantive and methodological issues. Needless to say, consideration of patterns of class differences by cause of death is essential for a full understanding of this relationship. But this would have extended the paper into a book.

14b. THE LOWER CLASS: HEALTH, ILLNESS, AND MEDICAL INSTITUTIONS

LEE RAINWATER

Reprinted from Among the People: Encounters with the Poor, *edited by Irwin Deutscher and Elizabeth J. Thompson (New York: Basic Books, 1968).* © *1968 by Mrs. Meiling Weiss. Lee Rainwater is Professor of Sociology at Harvard University.*

Our concern is with ways in which the characteristics of lower class persons influence their behavior in connection with the issues of health, illness, and the utilization of medical services. The group characterized below constitutes some 25 to 30 percent of the population of the country. It includes that segment of the society usually referred to by the term " lower lower class" or "lower working class" (some 15 percent of the population) and a portion of the stable working class just superior to them in social status. A considerable body of research suggests that this group at the bottom of the social-status, occupational, income, and educational hierarchy has certain distinctive ways of looking at the world and of relating to it, as well as distinctive problems of adaptation to the world. Inevitably, these distinctive world views and modes of adaptation influence the ability of working-class people to take advantage of the standard services of the society, whether these be in the private or public sector.

The particular institutional activities considered in this chapter, those of medical care, represent but a very small part of the total adaptive activity of individuals. In the case of the lower class, we must at all times remain aware that lower class ways of coping with different kinds of problems are much less subject to the elaborate systems of specialized role behavior and concomitant cultural techniques that are so characteristic of the middle class. Lower class people find it much less easy or sensible to maintain different ways of coping and reacting to different situations and are more likely to bring to any one situation much the same approach that they bring to any other.

The lower class person's experience of himself and his world is a highly distinctive one in our society. It is distinctive for its qualities of pain and suffering, hopelessness, and concentration on the deadly earnest present. It is distinctive for its problem and crisis-dominated character—as S. M. Miller has commented, "Lower class life is crisis-life constantly trying to make do with string where rope is needed." Having many problems at any one time and being constantly either going into a crisis, trying to manage during a crisis, or coming out of a crisis mean that for lower class people any one misfortune does not stand out sharply and does not tend to call forth a focused effort at combating the misfortune. Thus, any one problem that lower class people have (which as middle class persons we believe should be solved immediately, if not sooner) appears to them as simply one among many fires that must be put out or controlled, or maybe just lived with.

This means that lower class people (often with a considerable amount of realism on their side) will be inclined to slight health difficulties in the interest of attending to more pressing ones, such as seeing that there is food in the house, or seeking some kind of expressive experience which will reassure them that they are alive and in some way valid persons. The same kind of medical problem will stand out much more sharply to the middle class person because he tends to conceive of his life as having a relatively even and gratifying tenor; his energies are quickly mobilized by anything which threatens to upset that tenor. (Studies of more stable working-class people who do not have the same chronic crisis situations suggest that the view of life as made up of a series of difficulties just barely coped with is not too far removed from their own impressions of the world they live in. While the overt character of daily life may seem quite stable, there is a constant theme of unease in stable working-class people, a constant sense that the world holds many potentialities for pushing them back into an unstable, highly punishing kind of existence.)

In the sections which follow we will take up particular aspects of the world view, belief system, and life-style of the lower class. But it is important to keep in mind that behind any one particular orientation discussed is the problematic character of lower class existence. This pervasive characteristic tends to make unreal the careful, meticulous, and solicitous attitude toward health which is held out by the health professions, and which is by and large subscribed to by the middle class and perhaps by an increasing proportion of the better-off parts of the working class. Such concerns will often seem empty and minor to lower class people, who feel they have much more pressing troubles.

Another very general characteristic of the lower class situation relevant to its crisis character is that these households are much more often "understaffed" than are stable working class or middle class households. That is, the complement of persons who normally maintain and run a household in our society, including at least a husband and wife, is much more often reduced. First off, households in which both husband and wife are present are less common in the lower class than in the middle and stable working class. For example, while in the St. Louis metropolitan area only 8 percent of the White children under 18 years of age do not live with both of their parents, 41 percent of Negro children are in this position. If one looks at the census tracts inhabited mainly by poor Negroes, we find that well over half of the children under 18 do not live with both of their parents. While marital dissolution among lower class Whites is perhaps not so common as it is among Negroes, it is certainly a great deal more common than in the White middle and stable working class. The understaffed households which result from this factor have many problems of coping with the normal pressures of daily living. Even when both the husband and wife are present, the typical patterns of lower class marital relations have the result that husbands tend to be much less involved with what goes on in the home and to contribute less in the way of labor to maintain the family enterprise. Even when the household takes the form of a stem family in which there is some other relative present, our research suggests that the most frequent pattern is one in which one adult ends up having almost all of the internal family-maintenance responsibilities; the other adults see their role as either that of provider or of grown-up child who has a right to spend her time away from home engaged in activities for her own amusement.

This pattern of understaffed households in a situation of considerable family stress means that each individual's health receives relatively little preventive attention; when someone is sick, it is more difficult to care for him; and when the main adult is sick, she or he will be in a very poor position to care for herself properly or even to find the time to seek medical help. The attitude toward illness (even when it becomes chronic) in this kind of situation is apt to be a fairly tolerant one. People learn to live with illness, rather than use their small stock of interpersonal and psychic resources to do something about the problem.

THE LOWER CLASS AND THE BODY

In many ways lower class people are heavily preoccupied with their bodies — a fact apparent in their heavy consumption of patent medicines, in the folk beliefs which researchers have documented as being common at this class level, and in the cultivation of various kinds of substances (alcohol, drugs) and activities (dancing, fighting) which have as one goal a heightened awareness of physical existence. Also frequently noted is that lower class people tend to express their psychic difficulties somatically. It might be more correct to say that lower class people do not differentiate psychic and somatic components of stress symptoms. For example, in our sample of some 50 intensively studied families, as many as a third indicated that at one time or another one member of the household had a "nervous" condition. It is usually apparent from the context that respondents are talking about some kind of undifferentiated state of unease which manifests itself both psychically, in terms of anxiety and confused feelings and cognition, and somatically, in terms of physical discomfort or other kinds of physical symptom. Considering all this, then, it would not be surprising to find lower class people heavily preoccupied with issues of health and illness, and in a certain sense, they are. However, we know that rather seldom do lower class people organize their lives around being ill, as in hypochondriasis; or, on a more constructive level, organize themselves instrumentally toward doing something about poor health.

Lower class people perceive the world as a dangerous and chaotic place. This very primitive level of existential comprehension also carries with it a tendency to see the body as dangerous, or as potentially so. Thus, lower class people seem fairly readily to think of their bodies as in some way injuring or incapacitating them. They view the body as mysterious, as not rationally understandable, and there is a tendency to relate to it in magical rather than in instrumental ways. When they talk about illness, lower class people sometimes communicate a sense of alienation from their own bodies, a sense of distance from the illness processes going on in their bodies. They do not, like middle class people, identify with their bodies and work toward a cure of physical difficulties in much the same way that they would work toward some lack in knowledge by discovering an appropriate solution to a problem.

This tendency to see the body as mysterious and potentially dangerous carries with it a rather poor differentiation of bodily parts and function. For example, in a study of how lower class men and women think about the process of reproduction and about the bodily parts relevant to sexual relations, we found a rather low differentiation of the female sexual organs on the part of both men and women. A majority of lower class respondents had very poor notions of the process of conception. This was found to be quite closely related to their inability to understand or trust chemical methods of contraception or feminine methods such as the diaphragm.

Another very general characteristic of lower class persons is their tendency to have a low self-evaluation, to have as a chronic problem difficulties in maintaining a secure sense of self-esteem. Much lower class behavior that appears flamboyant or deviant to middle class people can be seen as an effort to compensate for lowered self-esteem. The reasons for this chronic lower evaluation of self are complex, involving a lifelong interaction between the symbolic communications others make and the more direct experiences of failure, punishment, and impotence that lower class people have in striving to adapt to the harsh world in which they live. Lower class people thus develop an attitude toward themselves characterized by a sense of being unworthy. They do not uphold the sacredness of their persons in the same way that middle class people do. Their tendency to think of themselves as of little account is readily generalized to their bodies.

This is in sharp contrast to middle class attitudes, which emphasize the intrinsic value and worth of the self and of the body. For the middle class person, lowered body functioning is readily taken as an insult to both the body and the self, an insult which is intolerable and must be remedied as quickly as possible. For lower class people, a body which does not function as it should, which has something wrong with it, simply resonates with the self that has these same characteristics. Just as lower class people become resigned to a conception of themselves as persons who cannot function very well socially or psychologically, they become resigned if necessary to bodies that do not function very well physically. This is probably particularly likely to happen as lower class people grow older and increasingly face a sense of failure because some of the adaptive techniques they have used to ward off a negative self-image begin to play out. Related to these interactions between self-concept and body image is a finding reported by Bernice Neugarten that lower class people believe they become middle aged at a much earlier chronological age than do working- and middle class people. Thus, lower class persons are likely to accept impaired functioning in the thirties as a natural consequence of aging, whereas working- and middle class people are less likely to see impaired functioning at this, or even later ages, as "natural." Rosenblatt and Suchman's characterization of blue-collar attitudes toward the body takes on a special significance when related to the differential notions of aging that the classes have.

The body can be seen as simply another class of objects to be worn out but not repaired. Thus, teeth are left without dental care, and later there is often small interest in dentures, whether free or not. In any event, false teeth may be little used. Corrective eye examinations, even for those people who wear glasses, is often neglected, regardless of clinic facilities. It is as though the white-collar class thinks of the body as a machine to be preserved and kept in perfect functioning condition, whether through prosthetic devices, rehabilitation, cosmetic surgery, or perpetual treatment, whereas blue-collar groups think of the body as having a limited span of utility: to be enjoyed in youth and then to suffer with and to endure stoically with age and decrepitude. It may be that a more damaged self-image makes more acceptable a more damaged physical adjustment.

The low "body esteem" which lower class people have applies by extension to the persons under their care, including their children. Lower class persons tend to develop rather negative images of their children as "bad" and/or "unsuccessful." This seems inevitable, given their conceptions both of themselves and of the nature of the world. The low esteem in which others are held as social beings easily extends to a minimal exercise of protectiveness and solicitude toward their physical needs and states. Thus we observe lower class parents seemingly indifferent to all kinds of obvious physical illnesses their children have—particularly infections, sores, colds, and the like. Greater tolerance by their parents for children's physical disability or malfunctioning means that medical professionals cannot count on the parents to exercise careful observation or supervision of children's illnesses. And any program of treatment which does count on this is much more likely to fail than in the middle class case.

The acceptance of something short of good health has implications both in terms of the care of people who are already ill and in terms of preventive medicine. Lower class parents are much less likely to carry out a consistent preventive regimen in the way the household is maintained and the children's activities controlled. The much higher accident rate among lower class individuals, particularly children, is not only a result of the greater objective danger of their environment (more broken bottles around, more dangerous housing) but also results from the lack of consistent circumspection on the part of parents.

Low body esteem carries an important secondary gain. If one can regard one's body as in some sense not working right, then one has a legitimate extenuating circumstance for many failures to live up to one's own standards and those expressed by others. We have noted in our work with lower class families that an enormous number of health complaints come up both in participant observations of daily living and in interviews. While these complaints are obviously related to many of the factors discussed in this chapter, one important function or consequence of the developing conception of oneself as not in tip-top physical condition is that of warding off allegations of irresponsibility or failure based on "not caring."

At the risk of unnecessarily proliferating role terms, it may be worth while to distinguish here between the "sick role," the "patient role," and the "disabled role." As used by Parsons and others, the sick role involves basically a notion of withdrawal from all normal responsibilities because of physical incapacity; the "patient role" is superimposed when the individual brings himself within the purview of healing agents. It may be true, as some researchers have suggested, that higher status persons find it easier to accommodate themselves to these two roles, whereas lower status persons champ at the bit to shed the sick and patient roles. However, it is also clear that lower class people much more commonly regard themselves as in minor or major ways disabled from functioning "normally" — disabled in the sense of their physical condition not allowing them to function as fully active adults. We would suggest that the difficulties of coping with situations in such a way that self-esteem can be maintained tempts lower class people to assume the role of the partially disabled. This assumption of the disabled role was described in its most dramatic form by Halliday in his discussions of the psychosomatic diseases of English workers during the depression. We also see it in a more moderated but chronic form in lower class individuals, particularly women, where the connection with unemployment and the possibility of compensation is not at all in question. Once impaired functioning is defined as a "normal" state of the body and self, expectations of what one can and cannot do are greatly modified. It is possible for the individual to counter claims on the part of other individuals by pointing to his physical condition. To the extent that the disabling condition is thus defined as "normal," the individual's motivation to seek treatment is considerably lowered. Self-medication can then become a ritual which symbolizes the disabled state.

THE LOWER CLASS AND MEDICAL TREATMENT

The implications of most of what has been said so far for the kind of treatment regimen that will be maintained, and the likelihood of seeking medical treatment in the first place, are fairly obvious. Here we will simply focus the discussion on concepts of causality and initiative in connection with health and illness.

Lower class notions of how things happen attribute a very great importance to good or bad luck—to "the way things are"—and tend to deemphasize one's ability to affect importantly the course of future events by self-directed action. These beliefs, plus the deep commitment to self-maintenance in a difficult present, mean that lower class people concern themselves relatively little with the long-term aspects of their problems. They do not plan for the future (how can they?), but rather live from day to day or, at most, from week to week. Such future-oriented plans as they do develop tend to be held much less tenaciously and are much more readily dropped under the impact of immediate crisis. Lower class people tend to feel that the difficulties they encounter are the result of bad luck, rather than of failing to take proper care—indeed, the extent to which by taking proper care lower class people can significantly affect their life-chances is a very open question. The intense preoccupation with the immediate maintenance of the self in a given and difficult world makes it very hard to take out of this system energy for planful action toward some future goal. The readiness with which lower class people are distracted by immediate dangers or prospects for immediate gratification reduces the likelihood of their carrying out carefully tailored regimens of treatment and sharply limits preventive activities directed toward the future goal of avoiding an illness.

Health and illness, therefore, tend to be dealt with in terms of crises. That is, when the impairment of functioning becomes so great or so obvious in the immediate situation that the individual feels this problem stands out above the rest, some action is likely to be taken. Until that time, the illness problem recedes into the background as more pressing issues are dealt with. The immersion in the immediate situation also probably accounts for the difficulties lower class people have in observing schedules of all kinds. It is difficult for them to keep appointments because something that seems more important is always going on. Clearly, any program that requires lower class people to be as observant of highly time-bound schedules as middle class people are capable of being is going to have only modest success.

The lower class is motivated to obtain medical care when there is a breakdown of bodily functioning such that a crisis is presented and essential activities cannot be carried out. Therefore I would generalize a bit from Rosenblatt and Suchman's statement:

For the blue-collar workers, with their greater distance from the whole medical-care system, illness is related to dysfunction in work, primarily related to incapacitating symptoms. Symptoms which do not incapacitate are often ignored. For the white-collar groups, illness will also relate to conditions which do not incapacitate but simply by their existence call forth medical attention.

In the middle class, any symptom that is obvious incapacitates because it takes away from the kind of more perfect person the middle class individual likes to think of himself as being. The lower class person cannot afford this conception of himself; he attends to physical symptoms, if at all, only when they pose a crisis in carrying out those activities he considers necessary.

THE LOWER CLASS AND MEDICAL INSTITUTIONS

Lower class people tend to have mixed feelings about physicians. On the one hand, because of their involvement with their bodies as in some sense mysterious and unpredictable, they would like to be quite dependent on physicians and to have physicians behave in paternalistic, nurturant, and solicitous ways. On the other hand, the physician, representing middle class views and a detached instrumental approach to problems, can be quite intimidating and difficult to understand.

Just as lower class people tend to personalize all relationships, they tend to seek highly personalized relationships with physicians in private practice. Women of the stable working class often develop close and trusting relationships with their private physicians, and are both heavily dependent on them and quite responsive to what the physicians tell them to do. This is less likely to be the case in the lower class. Persons here often must use public medical facilities, where it is difficult to form a relationship with one physician. In addition, the lower class individual's distrust and uneasiness in dealing with middle class persons often gets in the way of establishing the kind of dependent relationship he would like. Even so, despite the frequent difficulties lower and working-class people have in paying high medical bills, we have found that seldom do women express hostility toward their own physicians as overcharging them or being unreasonable about payment.

It seems likely that the ability to form a trusting and dependent relationship with physicians increases as lower class people grow older and feel a greater need for a nurturant figure because of increasing failure in managing themselves and their lives. In any case, even when dealing with private physicians, where the structure of the relationship allows greater personalization, it would seem that lower class men and women have a good deal more difficulty in being really attentive to their physicians and in carrying out the regimens which the physicians prescribe.

The ability to form a close, trusting relationship with the physician is greatest in connection with the lower class person's own medical needs. It would seem to be a great deal more difficult to develop this closeness when the patient is a child rather than the parent. The preoccupation with oneself and the touchiness that lower class parents exhibit about somehow having failed their children make it difficult for them to sustain a relationship with a helping third party who is an authority and may make negative judgments about how one has behaved. In these situations, physicians need to be very careful that they do not alienate parents and make contact so uncomfortable that the parents cease to come back. For this reason, relationships with general physicians are much easier for lower class people to sustain, since they count on the physician to treat both their problems and the problems of their children. Relating to pediatricians, uninterested as they are in the health needs of adults, will be much more difficult for the lower class family.

When one shifts the focus of inquiry from the context of private practice to that of the large medical institution, the negative possibilities increase sharply. Many lower class people are used to dealing with medical personnel only in the context of the large institution, and have had little opportunity to develop the kind of more personalized relationships that they would like to have with physicians. They are often inured to receiving poor service in low cost or charity clinics and hospitals. They expect to have to wait long hours in order to receive medical service and to be shabbily treated by those with whom they deal. Because this is their experience and expectation, they tend to be rather docile and impassive in the face of such difficulties, but one should not be misled into thinking that these kinds of experiences have no effects. The lower class person who must journey by public transportation for an hour to reach a public facility and then wait for several hours before receiving service is going to think two or three times before going for such service. The difficulty of receiving care serves to reinforce the tendency to seek it only when a crisis situation is reached. Clinic personnel who force patients to wait long hours in order to weed out the "poorly motivated" only deepen these tendencies.

One of the problems lower class people have with bureaucratic organizations is that they are used to dealing with people in nonsegmentalized ways. They expect a superior or someone with special knowledge to be able to cope with whatever problem is presented him, and they neither understand nor are tolerant of the great division of labor that obtains in such institutions. They want *someone,* rather than a *team,* to take care of them. It takes them quite a while to sort out the various functions represented by a team— whether this be a team of physician specialists or the nurse-physician-technician team.

While it is true that the middle class has a greater understanding of a division of labor, it should also be noted that because of their ability to purchase services they are better able to have someone inside the system represent them to the whole system. That is, middle class people will turn to their own private physician to sort out any difficulties they have with the different specialties represented in the hospital. For the person who can afford his services, the private physician functions to moderate the impersonality of the medical division of labor. The lower class person, in contrast, often feels he has no one person to whom he can rightfully turn with his gripes and have them listened to. In addition, middle class people much more readily establish personalized relationships with many specialists, and can find pride and pleasure in having "my internist," "my pediatrician," "my obstetrician," and "my ophthalmologist." It takes a great deal of psychosocial energy for someone to form such relationships; lower class people have enough trouble forming a trusting relationship with one middle class professional, let alone several.

As many observers have noted, there are tremendous problems of communication between middle class professionals and lower class clienteles. One of the most striking aspects of this communication is the amount of derogation and hostility that is covertly (and often overtly) expressed by the middle class professionals. From the professionals' point of view, lower class people are by definition "problem" people. It seems that over time professionals build up a considerable store of hostility and blaming attitudes toward such persons. The understanding that middle class professionals develop of the peculiar characteristics of their lower class clientele seems more often used as a way of avoiding blame for failure than of gaining insight into problems of dealing with this clientele and developing techniques that allow them to be more successful at their jobs. When lower class people perceive the middle class professional as blaming, derogating, or hostile toward them, they withdraw quickly into an adaptation of resentful docility, and are then much less available for any real communication or learning. While a few lower class people develop an amazing ability to manipulate these situations toward their own ends, most simply retreat and get out of the situation as quickly as possible.

Lower class people appear particularly prone to a sense of pervasive anxiety during hospitalization. They do not know what is going on nor on whom they can count for help. As patients, they also are likely to feel quite isolated. Their families' realistic difficulties in visiting them are often great, and the family ties may be weak enough so that, despite the best intentions, relatives just do not manage to make frequent visits. Thus hospitalization can be a painful experience for the lower class person who spends most of his time alone in a situation in which he is frightened. There would seem to be a great need for facilities to be planned in such a way as to maximize the chance of establishing casual relationships with other patients. Also, visiting arrangements should be

flexible so that when visitors do turn up, even at inopportune times from the point of view of the hospital, they can visit the patient.

The connections between class-related life-style characteristics and medical settings are illustrated by Rosengren's study of obstetric patients.

Consider the blue-collar woman: the relative personal and social isolation in which she lives —isolated, at least, from the personal contacts and formal experiences by which one assimilates the meaning and significance of professional ministrations—the relatively minimal education she has achieved, and the life milieu in which she lives, where illness, incapacitation, and the like abound; and also the very real, heightened chances that either she or her baby may encounter either insult or accident during pregnancy—all of these factors and others combine to make the pattern of high sick-role expectations among this group particularly understandable. Considering also that the blue-collar woman is likely to be cared for in a clinic setting rather than by a private doctor, it is easy to see why she might regard herself as "ill." The middle-class woman chooses her own physician—normally, on the basis of word-of-mouth advice from friends and relatives. She appears for her prenatal care in a treatment setting which has little of the symbolism of sickness—a quite "living-room-like" waiting room, perhaps occupied by a nurse without a uniform. This is in dramatic contrast to the clinic-attending woman who experiences her treatment within the confines of a hospital, with ambulances going to and fro, with uniformed nurses and interns scurrying about, sometimes in apparent anxiety, with stainless steel, tile walls, and medicinal odors intermixed with medical machinery and equipment. Not only, then, does the life milieu and its attendant contingencies conspire to move the blue-collar woman toward the enactment of the role of the sick, but so, too, does the peculiar character of her obstetric-treatment episode.

The ecology of medical services can work to the disadvantage of the lower class person. Such persons customarily organize their use of the resources of the environment in such a way that they do not have to go far to get the necessities of living. They tend to shop close at hand for food, clothing, furniture, and other items. While they do not mind going far on rare occasions for entertainment or visiting, traveling around the city is generally costly, uncomfortable, and inconvenient. This is particularly true of women who typically have several children to care for and who seem to develop a very special kind of anxiety about the outside world, particularly as they grow out of the late-adolescent and young-adult period.

In addition, there is the very real problem of the expense of traveling. Some lower class people are so poor that even expenditures for carfare have to be carefully calculated. If emergencies seem to demand the use of taxis, there may just not be money available. For example, one woman in the housing project we are studying has a grandson with asthma. When he has attacks, she often has to spend precious time finding someone to drive her to the hospital or loan her money for cab fare. She cannot understand why the well-baby clinic across the street from her building will not provide the necessary service at times like this. Again, middle class people are often in a much better position to deal with the same problem. They have the money that allows them to travel (to own a car, call a cab, call an ambulance), and their demand for medical services is such that they are more likely to have the decentralized services of a suburban clinic or a medical office near them. . . .

15. WHO NEEDS ORGANIZED FAMILY PLANNING SERVICES?

FREDERICK S. JAFFE, JOY G. DRYFOOS, and GEORGE VARKY

Reprinted with permission from Family Planning Perspectives, *Vol. 3, No. 3, July 1971, pp. 22-32. Copyright 1971 by Planned Parenthood Federation of America, Inc. Frederick Jaffe is Director of the Center for Family Planning Program Development of Planned Parenthood-World Population; Joy G. Dryfoos is Planning Director of the Center; and George Varky is Research Economist in the Planned Parenthood Research Department.*

■ Man's ability to control his own fertility has come close to being complete in the past few decades. Modern contraceptive techniques, particularly when we include among them sterilization and abortion, provide a wide range of methods by which people can bring the number of children they have into line with their desires. But if people are to tailor their situations to their wishes and needs, family planning services are a crucial resource. Several studies of family planning and fertility in the 1950s and 1960s thoroughly documented the greater degree of access to birth control services and techniques that higher class couples had relative to those of lower status. These studies also pretty much destroyed the old myth that lower class people want large families or are not particularly concerned about family size. Instead, it was found that lower status people want families no larger than those of people of middle and higher status. In fact, if they had full control over fertility, persons at lower income levels probably would want families *smaller* than those at middle and higher levels.

However, access to family planning resources has been available in the United States principally through the private health care market. Therefore, lower income families have found it difficult to learn about and avail themselves of modern contraception. The importance of family planning services as an antipoverty device became clear early in the War on Poverty. Equity would require that all families have the resources to control so basic an aspect of their life chances as the size of their families. Certainly the costs of children bear more heavily on persons with low income potentials than those with high. Throughout the 1960s, therefore, various individuals and organizations argued for broad family planning service programs oriented toward the "poor" or "medically indigent."

At first the goals of the family planning movement involved simple establishment of the appropriateness of government intervention in this area and the laying to rest of pseudo-moral barriers to this kind of medical service. There was indeed a long symbolic distance between President Eisenhower's assertion in the 1950s that the government should not involve itself with birth control matters and President Nixon's 1969 message to Congress on population, which stated that "no American should be denied access to family planning assistance because of her economic condition. I believe therefore that we should establish as a national goal the vision of adequate family planning services within the next five years to all who want them but cannot afford them."

Once such a goal has been accepted, there remains the problem of defining the population to be served with enough specificity that the required level of budgeting and organization can be known. In the following article Jaffe and his colleagues apply the techniques of demographic analysis and their understanding of family planning clinic operation to the development of a national projection of the size and family characteristics of the target population for family planning services. Such projections are one of the most important ways in which social science techniques are applied to public policy matters in day-to-day operation. The article, therefore, is of interest both for its particular subject matter and for what it shows us of scientific methods applied to program operation.

The broad range of issues in fertility and family planning are discussed in Commission on Population Growth and the American Future,

Population and the American Future (New York: Signet Books, 1972). A useful summary of knowledge about family planning is found in Westoff and Westoff, *From Now To Zero* (Boston: Little, Brown, 1971). Survey research on family size desires, family planning, and contraceptive use is carried out periodically in "national fertility studies"; the 1965 study is reported in Norman B. Ryder and Charles F. Westoff, *Reproduction in the United States, 1965* (Princeton, N.J.: Princeton University Press, 1971), and the 1970 study has been completed and is in the process of publication. Additional analysis of family planning issues can be found in a background paper prepared for the Commission on Population Growth and the American Future: Frederick Jaffe, "Family Planning Services in the United States" (Washington, D.C.: Government Printing Office). ∎

RESEARCH STUDIES HAVE provided much information about the fertility attitudes and behavior of U.S. couples, and their findings provide a basic planning framework for family planning programs. Yet important factors affecting the ability of couples to control their fertility remain poorly understood. Although Americans have adopted contraception to a greater extent than citizens of most other nations, most births nevertheless are unintended or unwanted. U.S. married couples who *intended* no more children comprised two-thirds of all married couples; nearly three-quarters of them reported that they already had had at least one timing failure or unwanted birth. While birth planning failures are more common among the poor and less educated who have least access to effective contraception and safe abortion, a significant proportion of nonpoor and better educated couples also report number or timing failures. Indeed, two-thirds of married couples with college educations who intended no more children reported such failures.

These current patterns of birth planning failures are associated for some couples with lack of access to a health system providing effective medical contraception. Some other couples who have access to the health system nevertheless face difficulties in securing contraceptive help adequate to enable them to control their fertility successfully. In prin-ciple, failures could be reduced if all couples had access to the most effective contraceptive services, including instruction, continuing supervision and educational reinforcement. A family planning program, whose primary purpose is to assist couples to avoid unwanted pregnancies, should address itself to identifying the barriers which prevent couples in all socioeconomic groups from successfully controlling their fertility, and to developing activities aimed at overcoming these barriers. The individuals for whom such a program should be developed include all fecund persons who find themselves unable to realize their own preferences for the number and spacing of their children. This article seeks to estimate, in a very approximate way, the numbers and characteristics of individuals who comprise this universe of "need" for assistance in avoiding birth planning failures. . . .

THE UNIVERSE OF NEED

Two basic groups comprise the universe of "need" for assistance in obtaining family planning services:

1. Married and unmarried persons who cannot afford to purchase the family planning services they require—i.e., the "medically indigent"—and

2. Individuals who can afford to pay all or some of the cost of family planning services but experience other kinds of difficulties in securing and utilizing these services: the "other access" group. An important segment of the "other access" group includes nonpoor, unmarried individuals and, particularly, unmarried minors whose families are not poor.

A comprehensive nationwide family planning program should assist both groups. Public funds would subsidize the full cost of service for the "medically indigent" and part of the cost for those nonpoor who are likely to be deterred by cost factors from utilizing effective family planning services. In addition, some nonpoor persons might require the services of the program, even though they are able and willing to pay the full operating costs of the service. Some public funds might be needed to finance the start-up costs of establishing these services. Such a program for the organized delivery of these services is thus more extensive in coverage than a "subsidized" program since it is designed to serve both low income persons and others who are not able to secure the family planning services they require through unorganized general health delivery mechanisms.

While this analysis will seek to estimate the number of persons who constitute both groups in the universe of need, the starting point remains the estimated number of "medically indigent" persons in need of *subsidized* family planning services. It is necessary, therefore, first to review the estimates currently used and the methodology and assumptions on which they are based.

WHAT IS "MEDICAL INDIGENCY"?

In order to focus on a health service program which is to be utilized in large part by poor persons, it is first necessary for program planning purposes to define who are the "poor."

There is no generally accepted definition of the point or points in the income scale which separate the "medically indigent" from those who can afford to purchase medical care. In the one federal-state program which has necessarily involved a definition of "medical indigency"—Medicaid—differing standards have been set arbitrarily by the states, based strictly on the availability of funds. In addition, most people apply different criteria for deciding whether they can afford to pay for an elective health service such as family planning, than for such obligatory medical care as an emergency appendectomy. Over and above the question of an appropriate standard of medical indigency in general, therefore, is the need to establish a standard applicable to family planning which includes those individuals who would be deterred from utilizing this important elective service if they had to spend their own funds. Previous

studies of health services for low income Americans have confronted some of these issues. In the absence of definitive research, each study has been forced to adopt compromises based on available information.

THE 5 MILLION

The commonly used estimate of 5 million U.S. women who "need" subsidized family-planning services at any given time derives from two separate analyses: One was made by Arthur A. Campbell, Associate Director of the Center for Population Research (CPR), National Institute of Child Health and Human Development (NICHD); the other analysis was published by the Research Department of Planned Parenthood-World Population (PPWP) based on the Dryfoos-Polgar-Varky (DPV) formula. Both analyses use the Social Security Administration (SSA) "near-poverty" level to define "medical indigency." These two independent analyses made in the late 1960s yielded estimates ranging from 4.6 to 5.4 million women who at any given point in time comprised the prospective national caseload for subsidized family planning programs.

It is important to emphasize that both the Campbell and PPWP estimates were for the potential caseload *at any given time.* Instead of discussing the number of *women in need,* therefore, it would be more accurate to interpret the two estimates as defining 4.6 to 5.4 million *woman-years of service* as the target for the program. Since both methods deducted from the caseload women who at any given time were pregnant or seeking pregnancy, the *total number of individual women* to be served by the program during a 12-month period would necessarily be larger than the 4.6-5.4 million estimate, as some women passed through the childbearing cycle and returned to the group in need of contraception, as other women entered their childbearing years and began sexual activity, as still others became sterile or for other reasons did not need services over the entire year. For the Campbell and PPWP estimates, . . . the number of individuals to be served during a 12-month period are [approximately 5.4 million and 6.3 million, respectively].

CRITICISMS OF THE ESTIMATE

The 5 million estimate has been criticized by some observers as too high and by others as too low. Judith Blake maintains that the estimate is an exaggeration which fails to take into account the actual number of poor women at risk of conception, the proportion sterile or subfecund, those who object to contraception on religious grounds and those who already practice effective contraception. On the other hand, several family planning programs have stated that the DPV estimates for their communities are too low; they assert that the SSA near-poverty level is unrealistic as a criterion of medical indigency. Planned Parenthood of New York City, for example, has developed an estimate of need 60 percent higher than the DPV estimate, based on the criterion of medical indigency adopted by New York's official agencies. Apart from the issue of subsidy, an indicator that the near-poverty level does not adequately describe those who already utilize *organized* family planning services is the fact that in 1969 nearly 40 percent of new patients enrolled in Planned Parenthood clinics throughout the country had incomes *above* the near-poverty level.

Service statistics reported by family planning programs provide some empirical data with which to assess the validity of the estimate. For 1969, programs in 30 counties reported serving 70 percent or more of the DPV-estimated need in those counties. These programs continue to enroll new patients at a level higher than would be expected from the proportions of the estimated need already enrolled and are increasing their total number of active patients. This suggests that the DPV estimates have been fairly valid as a gross program planning tool in these counties, with a tendency to underestimate the actual need for subsidized family planning services.

FAMILY PLANNING AND POVERTY

A more fundamental criticism of the 5 million need estimate has been made by Phillips Cutright. He notes that one of the objectives of subsidized family planning programs is to assist couples to avoid poverty and dependency as a result of unwanted pregnancy. Rigid eligibility criteria based on existing poverty levels would tend to defeat this objective. Cutright points out that "if families cannot get access to the program *before* they are in poverty, then the program can do nothing to prevent their becoming poor due to increases in family size. Since the poverty line moves according to the size of the family, a small family with a moderate income cannot get into the program until it becomes large. Most *young* couples are, therefore, not eligible for the program."

The purpose of estimating need for family planning is not to define *eligibility* for the program but to approximate the *magnitude of services* required to meet national objectives. Nevertheless, the logic of Cutright's criticism applies even to the program planning concepts employed in determining the scope and direction of the program. A nationwide family planning program which seeks to help couples avoid poverty status by avoiding unwanted pregnancy will have to include as part of its potential caseload some people— particularly younger, less parous couples— whose incomes are above official standards defining poverty.

In retrospect, then, the 5 million estimate made in 1967 underestimated the potential caseload for a nationwide family planning program if one of its objectives is to help couples to avoid poverty. This analysis will attempt to correct for this underestimation.

THE LOW INCOME POPULATION IN 1969

A federal interagency committee adopted a governmentwide poverty standard in 1969 and discontinued the SSA near-poverty level

TABLE 15.1

WOMEN 15-44, BY POVERTY LEVEL AND MARITAL STATUS, 1969 (NUMBERS IN 1,000s)

Marital Status	U.S. Total	Below Poverty Level	Below 125% of Poverty Level	Below 150% of Poverty Level	Above 150% of Poverty Level
Married, living with spouse	25,387	1,445	2,382	3,694	21,693
Never-married, separated or not living with spouse, widowed, divorced	16,415	2,889	3,806	4,694	11,821
Total	41,802	4,334	6,188	8,388	33,414
Percent of Total	100.0	10.4	14.8	20.1	79.9

Source: Estimated from March 1970 Current Population Survey (CPS) special tabulations prepared for the Office of Economic Opportunity.

which had been the basis for approximating a national standard of medical indigency. In lieu of the near-poverty level, the Census Bureau now makes available data on numbers of persons who fall below 125 percent and 150 percent of the poverty line. Table 15.1 shows the distribution of women aged 15-44 by poverty and marital status for 1969, the latest year for which detailed data are available. . . . If the measures employed in the Campbell and PPWP analyses were to be maintained, the 125 percent of poverty income cutoffs would be used to define the universe of need for subsidized family planning services. This, however, would tend to negate the impact of the program in assisting couples to avoid poverty. A young couple with two children would be counted in the universe of need only if the family income was less than $4,651. Many couples with slightly higher incomes would not be so counted, and the program would not be designed to provide them with effective family planning services. They would, therefore, face a higher probability of incurring an unwanted pregnancy which could put them below the 125 percent level.

There are no definitive data available with which to determine how much above 125 percent of poverty the medical indigency level applicable to family planning ought to be. One approach would be to advance the cutoff for each family size by the difference in income for the next larger sized family. In terms of 1969 incomes, the cutoffs would range from about $3,051 for a 1-person fam-

ily to $8,239 for a family of 7 or more (Table 15.2). This is rather close to the schedule for 150 percent of poverty. Since some detailed Census Bureau data are available for those at 150 percent of poverty, this level will be used here to calculate an approxima-

TABLE 15.2

APPROXIMATE INCOME CUTOFF FOR PLANNING FAMILY PLANNING PROGRAM, BY FAMILY SIZE, 1969 (IN DOLLARS)

Family Size	Income Cutoff
1	$3,051
2	3,631
3	4,651
4	5,483
5	6,151
6	6,847*
7 or more	8,239*

*Adjusted to account for the fact that 150 percent of poverty cutoff in 1969 for a family of 7 or more members, as reported by the Census Bureau, actually is for a family of eight members.

tion of the *minimum* number of low income persons in the universe of need for subsidized family planning services. The approximate number of persons in need at any given time can be derived using either the Campbell or PPWP methods of estimation (see Table 15.3). Thus, in 1969 there were from 4.9 to 5.3 million woman-years of family planning service required to meet the needs of low income women. For purposes of this analysis, the average of the two estimates—5,110,000—may be taken as the minimum estimate of low income need. Ap-

TABLE 15.3

TWO ESTIMATES OF PROSPECTIVE FAMILY
PLANNING PATIENTS AT ANY GIVEN TIME,
1969, USING CAMPBELL AND PPWP
METHODOLOGIES

	Campbell	PPWP
Total number of women 15-44 below 150 percent of poverty, 1969	8,388,000	8,388,000
Not exposed to risk*	1,887,000	
or deduction for 15-17-year-olds†		1,300,000
Subtotal: Exposed to risk or women aged 18-44	6,501,000	7,088,000
Sterile	845,000	921,000
Subtotal: Fecund	5,656,000	6,167,000
Pregnant or trying to conceive	739,000	863,000
Subtotal: In need of family planning services	4,917,000	5,304,000

*The base for calculating those not exposed to risk are estimates of the never-married, widowed, and divorced from the March 1970 CPS.

†A special tabulation of the March 1970 CPS shows that in families below 150 percent of poverty, 15-17-year-old females constituted 15.5 percent of all females 15-44.

plying the same adjustment referred to above for age changes and reentry as women complete the childbearing cycle, the total number of individual women who needed service during the 12 months of 1969 was 5,979,000.

APPLICATION OF THE BLS LOWER MINIMUM BUDGET LEVEL

The above analysis, like earlier estimates of need for family planning services, derives basically from the SSA standards defining near-poverty (although correcting to include those who are nonpoor but who require family planning help to avoid becoming poor). Yet the near-poverty level is considered to be an unrealistic criterion for defining medical indigency in many communities. This consideration has led to evaluation of the Bureau of Labor Statistics (BLS) "lower minimum budget" level as an alternative basis for defining medical indigency for family planning programs. The BLS lower minimum budget

level was developed in 1967 in response to requests by public assistance agencies "for a measure that would be appropriate for evaluating the needs of families who were positioned at the low end of the income distribution." In 1969, based on a per capita daily food expenditure of $1.22, the BLS budgeted a pretax income of $6,567 as the minimum necessary for an urban family of four. . . .

Recent census data are not available in a form which permits the number of women aged 15-44 living in families with incomes below this BLS schedule to be determined precisely. Two methods have been used to approximate this number. In one a modified DPV formula was applied to Census Bureau estimates of the 1966 population in each county. This method yielded an estimated total of 12,330,000 women aged 15-44 with incomes below the BLS level, of whom, at any given time, 7,815,000 would constitute the potential caseload for a family planning program. The other method applied the estimated income-family size schedule, approximating the BLS standard, to the Census Bureau data on distribution of family income in 1969. This yielded an estimated total of 11,105,000 women aged 15-44 below the BLS level, of whom 6,738,000 would appear to constitute the prospective caseload at any given time. The average of these two estimates—7,276,000—may be regarded as an estimate of woman-years of service required to meet the needs of low income women based on the BLS schedule. Adjusting for age changes and reentry as women complete the childbearing cycle, 8,513,000 individual women, whose incomes were below the approximate BLS level, needed organized family planning services during the 12 months of 1969.

Some empirical support for the applicability of the BLS lower minimum budget level to estimating the need for organized family planning services is to be found in the utilization pattern of Planned Parenthood clinics. While, as noted above, nearly 40 percent of Planned Parenthood new patients in 1969 had incomes *above* the near-poverty level, an estimated 90 percent had incomes *below* the BLS lower minimum budget level. While many of these patients paid *something* toward the cost of the service, very few paid the full cost. In 85 large cities, some Planned Parenthood patients with incomes up to and even somewhat *above* the BLS level utilized an organized family planning service, at either full or partial subsidy.

The analysis above yields two alternative estimates of the number of woman-years of service which would have been required to meet the needs of low income women who needed subsidized family planning services in 1969. The lower estimate averaged 5.1 million, while the estimate approximating those below the BLS lower minimum budget level averaged 7.3 million. These could be viewed simply as minimum and maximum estimates of the number of woman-years of service needed for low income women for which the program should be planned.

In a sense, however, the concept of medical indigency itself sets up a false dichotomy between those who can and cannot afford to purchase medical care. More typically, there is a gradually increasing ability to pay some part of the cost of medical care as income rises above that level where the individual cannot afford to pay anything to where income is sufficient to enable the individual to pay the full cost of the service. Studies of low income families have shown that many families fluctuate below and above the cutoff points over relatively short periods of time because of the relative instability of their total income.

PROJECTING NEED AMONG LOW INCOME PERSONS FROM 1969 TO 1975

The discussion above is based upon estimates for 1969, the latest year for which Census Bureau data by poverty status are available. For planning purposes we will try to project these estimates through 1975. Any forward projection must be based on some assumptions about the probable course of the economy over the next five years and, derivatively, on the number and types of persons who will continue, year by year, to be below the 150 percent of poverty level, the BLS lower minimum budget level, or any other criterion selected as applicable. As the events of the last 18 months have amply demonstrated, this kind of economic forecasting can be hazardous. In 1970, the annual decline in the incidence of poverty which had prevailed since 1959 was reversed and there was, in fact, a 5 percent increase over 1969 in the numbers of persons below the poverty line.

No projections of the size and characteristics of the population in poverty between now and 1975 have been made which could be utilized here; and a definitive resolution of these issues is beyond the scope of this analysis. Since what is required here is an *approximation* of those who will need subsidized family planning services, this estimate would not be altered substantially by small changes from year to year in income: A couple which had no private physician and required the services of a subsidized program in one year would not, a year or two later, change that status fundamentally simply by increasing its income by several hundred dollars. (During and immediately following a period of recession, income distributions understate the size of the medically indigent group because they do not take into account the debts many people acquire as a result of unemployment and of underemployment during the recession.)

For purposes of this analysis, therefore, it will be assumed that the number of low income women aged 15-44, from whom the universe of need for family planning services is calculated, will remain a constant proportion of all women aged 15-44 from 1970 to 1975. In 1969, the group below 150 percent of poverty constituted 20.1 percent of all women aged 15-44. The same ratio will be utilized to calculate the minimum low income need for family planning through 1975. If economic conditions improve markedly, this procedure would have the effect of overestimating somewhat, during the later years of the projection, the number of women at the lower end of the low income spectrum in need of subsidized family planning services. This would in effect move the medically indigent line for family planning purposes somewhat closer to the BLS lower minimum budget level. The same procedure will be used to project the number of low income women whose incomes fall below the BLS lower minimum budget level. In 1969, approximately 11.1 million women fell into this category. They constituted 26.6 percent of all U.S. women aged 15-44. This ratio can be used to project an approximation of those below the BLS lower minimum budget level through 1975.

ESTIMATING NEED AMONG THE "OTHER ACCESS" GROUP

National fertility surveys show clearly that couples in all socioeconomic groups have been unable to control the number and timing of their children in accordance with their wishes. Although the incidence of number and timing failures is considerably higher among low income couples, it also occurs among those who are not poor: An estimated 15 percent of births to nonpoor couples from 1960 to 1965 were reported by their parents as unwanted at the time of conception (compared to 32 percent of births to poor and near-poor couples). These findings imply that, in addition to low income couples who have been denied access to effective fertility control because of their inability to purchase medical services, some proportion of nonpoor couples also have difficulties in securing and utilizing effective family planning services. These difficulties can be regarded as a kind of "access" problem, defining "access" here as ability to obtain adequate birth planning information and support as well as the ability to command a physician's services.

In seeking to determine the number of nonpoor persons who might need the services of a family-planning program, there is little empirical data with which to be guided. One might assume that the nonpoor, by definition, can afford the services of private physicians. However, there are noneconomic obstacles which the nonpoor may encounter in securing and utilizing effective fertility control services. These obstacles may be geographic, qualitative, cultural-moralistic or informational-motivational: In some cases, for example, the individual's physician may have religious objections, or he may lack the knowledge and experience to provide the quality of care required, or he may regard family planning as inappropriate in terms of the individual's age, marital or ethnic characteristics. The individual herself, although engaging in sexual relations, may have inadequate knowledge about the risks of pregnancy she is undertaking, or she may be deterred from seeking contraceptive help because of guilt or fear (what Cutright calls "the pseudo-moral barrier"). Nonpoor patients enrolling in organized clinics report these and other difficulties in explaining why they come to a clinic rather than go to their physician. But their incidence in the total population has not been adequately studied and, therefore, cannot be quantified with any certainty.

More careful investigations are needed of the barriers to effective family planning practice among nonpoor couples and of the effects of unwanted and unplanned pregnancies on their lives. Such studies would illuminate the ways in which organized family planning programs could overcome these barriers. The 1965 National Fertility Study (NFS) reports some findings on use of family planning methods which offer an approach to establishing the order of magnitude of need among nonpoor married couples. Two-thirds of all respondents under 45 in this national sample of married couples stated that they intended to have no more children, since they apparently regarded their families as completed. (Indeed, three-fourths of these couples had already had at least one timing or number failure.) With this fertility goal, they would be expected to use the most effective methods of fertility control available to minimize the risk of an unwanted pregnancy, had acceptable services and adequate information been available to them.* Yet 24 percent of nonpoor fecund couples who intended to have no more children were, at the time of the 1965 survey, using either douche, withdrawal, or other methods of doubtful effectiveness, or no method at all; and another 11 percent were using rhythm, thus increasing considerably their risk of having an unwanted pregnancy. It is difficult to believe that all these couples would have deliberately chosen *not* to use effective methods had a realistic choice (including adequate information) been available to them. It seems more likely that these couples experienced difficulties of one kind or another in securing effective contraception.

These data apply only to those nonpoor married couples who are "limiters"—i.e., who intend to have no more children. Comparable information on current contraceptive methods employed is also available for the remaining one-third of nonpoor married couples—the "spacers"—who need to practice contraception for purposes of timing the births of future wanted children. Other findings of the 1965 NFS (and other studies) indicate that limiters use more effective contraceptive methods, and use them more regularly, than spacers. These studies also show, however, that a very large proportion of couples have timing failures—i.e., they have been unable to space the arrival of their children in accordance with their wishes. Nearly 40 percent of all couples reported timing failures in the 1965 study, and 45 percent of all wanted births which occurred between 1960 and 1965 were reported by their parents as timing failures.

It would thus be expected that the use of less effective or no methods would be even greater among spacers than among limiters. The 1965 NFS data show that about 37 percent of fecund nonpoor spacers who were not currently pregnant or seeking a preg-

nancy were using either no method or were using less effective methods (and another 11 percent were using rhythm) increasing their risk of timing failures considerably.

This analysis thus yields two tentative quantitative measures of the "other access" group among nonpoor married couples who are not pregnant or seeking pregnancy: 24 percent of the limiters and 36.8 percent of the spacers. The first of these measures yields a *minimum* estimate of the need for organized family planning services among nonpoor married couples; while the sum of the estimates for limiters and spacers yields an alternative estimate. In 1969, there were approximately 20,008,000 married couples above the BLS lower minimum budget level. Applying the constants used earlier for desired pregnancy and sterility leaves 15,134,000 nonpoor married couples, of whom 10,089,000 were limiters who intended no more children, and 5,045,000 were spacers who needed effective contraception in order to time successfully the births of additional wanted children. Applying the above percentages (24 and 36.8), it may be estimated that between 2,421,000 and 4,278,000 nonpoor married couples at any given time in 1969 experienced access problems which prevented them from practicing family planning adequate to achieve their fertility preferences—problems which, in principle, might be solved by an organized family planning program. These estimates are for woman-years of service. The number of individual nonpoor married women who needed service during the 12 months of 1969 was, respectively, 2,542,000 limiters and 5,005,000 limiters and spacers (after the point-in-time estimates are adjusted for age changes and the reentry of women who complete the childbearing cycle).

PRACTICES CHANGE RAPIDLY

There is considerable evidence that U.S. family planning practices are changing rapidly, particularly as a result of more extensive experience with both the pill and the IUD.

---

* Twelve-month failure rates were estimated from 1965 NFS data as follows: pill, five percent; IUD, eight percent; diaphragm, 18 percent; condom, 19 percent; withdrawal, 23 percent; rhythm, 30 percent; foam, 32 percent. (N. B. Ryder and C. F. Westoff, "Contraceptive Efficacy in the U.S., 1965," presented at Western Hemisphere Meeting of International Union for the Study of Population, Mexico City, August 1970.)

These tentative measures must, therefore, be checked against comparable information from the 1970 NFS, when it becomes available, to determine how the current situation differs from 1965. For purposes of this analysis, however, there is little choice but to assume that the 1965 situation prevails and to use the estimates of the nonpoor other access group in 1969, calculated above from the March 1970 CPS, as the basis for a projection from 1970 to 1975. To accomplish this, the number of nonpoor couples falling into the estimated other access group in 1969 can be converted into proportions of all women aged 15-44, and these proportions can be applied to the projected number of women in these age cohorts in each of the succeeding years.

ESTIMATING NEED AMONG THE UNMARRIED NONPOOR

The analysis thus far has yielded two estimates of need for *subsidized* family planning services among women with low or marginal incomes (including unmarried persons,) and two estimates of need for *organized* family planning services among nonpoor married couples. To complete our estimate of the total need, it is necessary to estimate the proportion of *unmarried* nonpoor females aged 15-44 who are sexually active and do not have access to effective means of fertility control.

Estimating this component involves numerous difficulties, since there has been no adequate study in the last two decades of the extent of sexual activity among unmarried persons. The only available national data are from the Kinsey study in the 1940s of a nonrepresentative group of respondents, which revealed that half of all women and a much larger proportion of all men had some premarital sexual experience. This study has not been replicated in the intervening period, but it is generally believed that premarital sexual activity has increased during the last two decades. Out-of-wedlock births have increased; one-third of all first births and 18 percent of first births to married couples are conservatively estimated to be conceived premaritally; and there is evidence of a significant number of induced abortions—legal and illegal—among unmarried women. Nonetheless, there are few hard data from which to estimate the proportion of unmarried nonpoor individuals who are exposed to risk of unwanted pregnancy and, within this group, those who experience difficulties in securing access to effective means of fertility control.

Several approaches are possible, none very satisfactory. An arbitrary assumption could be made as to the extent of sexual activity among all unmarried persons, and this could be applied to the estimated number of nonpoor unmarried women aged 15-44. Alternatively, inferences could be drawn from fragmentary information. This was essentially the approach taken by Campbell when he assumed that 50 percent of unmarried low income women were regularly or occasionally exposed to risk of conception. He presented this as little more than an informed guess, based on a "train of tenuous assumptions." In the intervening four years, little has been added to our knowledge of U.S. sex practices which can be used to improve Campbell's estimate.

In 1969, there were 10,689,000 women aged 15-44 with incomes above the BLS level who were separated, not living with spouse, widowed, divorced, or never-married. For purposes of this analysis it will be assumed that half of them are either regularly or occasionally at risk of unwanted pregnancy: a total of 5,345,000. There are no national data on contraceptive practices among unmarried persons with which to estimate how many of these women experience difficulties in securing access to effective means of fertility control. Given current laws, policies, and mores which stigmatize sexual activity outside of marriage, and the resulting reluctance of many physicians to provide contraception to unmarried persons, it seems likely that a greater proportion of nonpoor *unmarried* women have access problems than of nonpoor *married* women. Since 37 percent

TABLE 15.4

PROJECTED NEED* FOR ORGANIZED FAMILY PLANNING SERVICES, AT ANY GIVEN TIME AND OVER 12-MONTH PERIOD, BY ESTIMATED NEED FOR CONTRACEPTION AND STERILIZATION, 1971-75 (NUMBERS IN 000s)

Group	FY 1971 U.S. Women 15-44	Need for Organized Services At Any Given Time	Over 12-Month Period Total	Contra-ception	Sterili-zation‡	FY 1972 U.S. Women 15-44	Need for Organized Services At Any Given Time	Over 12-Month Period Total	Contra-ception	Sterili-zation‡
Low Income (married and unmarried)	11,387	7,459	8,640	8,592	48	11,614	7,607	8,806	8,729	77
Below 150% of poverty level	8,605	5,240	6,073	6,037	36	8,776	5,344	6,189	6,131	58
From 150% of poverty to BLS "Lower minimum budget" level	2,782	2,219	2,567	2,555	12	2,838	2,263	2,617	2,598	19
Other Access (above BLS "lower minimum budget" level)	31,423	7,119	7,929	7,895	34	32,047	9,785	8,075	8,020	55
Married, living with spouse ('limiters')		2,476	2,576	2,559	17		2,525	2,624	2,596	28
Married, living with spouse ('spacers')		1,903	2,498	2,481	17		1,941	2,541	2,514	27
Separated, widowed, divorced, never-married		2,740	2,855	2,855			2,794	2,910	2,910	
Total	42,810					43,661				
Minimum		5,240	6,073	6,037	36		5,344	6,189	6,131	58
Maximum		14,578	16,569	16,487	82		14,867	16,881	16,749	132

*For Puerto Rico a crude estimate of low income need can be projected from the average of the two 1970 estimates. The number in need at any given time (woman-years) would be: FY 1971, 237,500; FY 1972, 240,000; FY 1973, 243,000; FY 1974, 246,000, and FY 1975, 249,000. The number in need over a 12-month period would be: FY 1971, 276,000; FY 1972, 279,000; FY 1973, 283,000; FY 1974, 286,000, and FY 1975, 290,000.

FY 1973					FY 1974					FY 1975				
U.S. Women 15-44	Need for Organized Services				U.S. Women 15-44	Need for Organized Services				U.S. Women 15-44	Need for Organized Services			
	At Any Given Time	Over 12-Month Period				At Any Given Time	Over 12-Month Period				At Any Given Time	Over 12-Month Period		
		Total	Contra-ception	Sterili-zation‡			Total	Contra-ception	Sterili-zation‡			Total	Contra-ception	Sterili-zation‡
11,853	7,853	8,987	8,879	108	12,101	7,926	9,173	9,038	135	12,355	8,093	9,366	9,200	166
8,957	5,455	6,317	6,235	82	9,144	5,568	6,448	6,346	102	9,336	5,685	6,582	6,457	125
2,896	2,398	2,670	2,644	26	2,957	2,358	2,725	2,692	33	3,019	2,408	2,784	2,743	41
2,708	7,410	8,241	8,162	79	33,391	7,564	8,411	8,314	97	34,094	7,724	8,588	8,468	120
	2,577	2,677	2,637	40		2,631	2,733	2,684	49		2,686	2,790	2,729	61
	1,981	2,594	2,555	39		2,022	2,647	2,599	48		2,065	2,703	2,644	59
	2,852	2,970	2,970			2,911	3,031	3,031			2,973	3,095	3,095	
,561					45,492					46,449				
	5,455	6,317	6,235	82		5,568	6,448	6,346	102		5,685	6,582	6,457	125
	15,263	17,228	17,041	187		15,490	17,584	17,352	232		15,817	17,954	17,668	286

alculated to reach in 1975 an incidence of contraceptive sterilizations of 15 percent of *married* women aged 15-44 in each compo-
of need. For example, approximately 55 percent of all women in the below 150 percent of poverty category are estimated to be
ried and this proportion served as the base for the calculation of the number of sterilizations which will be performed by 1975 for
group. In each category it was assumed that eight percent had contraceptive sterilizations by FY 1971. The number of tubal liga-
(and/or vasectomies on the spouses) assumed for 1971 was subtracted from the number projected for 1975, to yield an estimate
he number which will need to be performed over the five-year period. This estimate was distributed from year to year approximate-
proportion to the anticipated growth of the program.

of nonpoor married spacers appear to have access problems, a conservative assumption would be that half of the unmarried women at risk have such problems. Thus, a gross estimate of the number of nonpoor unmarried women needing the services of an organized family planning program in 1969 would be 2,672,000. This is a point-in-time figure, denoting woman-years of service required. Adjusting for age changes (but not for childbearing) yields an estimate of 2,806,000 individual unmarried nonpoor women who needed service during 1969. This estimate will be converted into a proportion of all women aged 15-44 for purposes of projection through 1975.

It should be emphasized that this tentative estimate is put forward only to provide a very gross approximation of the number of nonpoor unmarried women who would utilize the services of organized family planning programs if these were available to them. Program planning for family planning services will have to depend on such inadequate approximations until the actual incidence of sexual activity among unmarried persons is determined through definitive special research. . . .

1970-75 PROJECTION

For 1970-75, the number of women in their fertile years (aged 15-44) will increase significantly each year, as a result of the "baby boom" of the 1950s. In each of the next 5 years, the number of women in this age group will increase by between 800,000 and 1,000,000. Application of the proportions of all women aged 15-44 who are believed to be in each component of the universe of need for organized family planning services in 1969 to the total number of women aged 15-44 projected for the next 5 years will result in modifying the yearly estimate for the changing age composition of the female population.

[From] Census Bureau . . . projections [of] the number of women aged 15-44 from 1970 to 1975, . . . the number of women who would constitute the prospective group in need of a nationwide family planning program can be projected (Table 15.4) . . . During the 5 years of the projection, the estimate ranges from 6 million low income persons to nearly 18 million in all socioeconomic groups, depending on the interpretations placed on available research findings and the program assumptions which are made. It should be emphasized that these are only preliminary estimates intended to suggest the magnitude of need for more effective family planning services among all Americans. Since the policy implications of this range are significant, research certainly needs to be undertaken to determine more definitively the extent of need for family planning services, the health and social consequences of unwanted and unplanned pregnancies and the ways in which American couples can best be assisted to control the number and timing of their children in accordance with their desires. . . .

16. TAXES AND INEQUALITY

JOSEPH A. PECHMAN

Reprinted from "Alternative Sources of Federal Revenue" by Joseph Pechman in Charles L. Schultz, Edward R. Fried, Alice N. Rivlin, and Nancy H. Teeters, Setting National Priorities: The 1973 Budget, *copyright © 1972 by The Brookings Institution in Washington, D.C. Joseph A. Pechman is Director of Economic Studies at the Brookings Institution. He is a leading expert on tax policy and has pioneered in developing the empirical foundation for evaluating the impact of taxes on different kinds of families. His research in collaboration with his colleagues at Brookings has had a major impact on public policy discussion about taxes, income redistribution, social security, and similar issues.*

■ Most Americans assume that inequalities in the distribution of income are significantly reduced by the operation of the tax system. Even when they do not know the specifics, most people believe that taken altogether taxes are "progressive"—that people with higher incomes pay a higher proportion of their income in taxes than do those with lower incomes, so that resources are distributed more equally after taxes than before.

This situation actually is just barely true of the present U.S. tax system. As is apparent in Pechman's article, the current federal income tax system is progressive, but not so progressive as many people believe or as suggested by the marginal tax rates most citizens notice when they fill out their tax forms. Families with incomes below the median pay 5 percent or less of their income in federal income tax. In the broad range of $15,000 to $50,000, tax rates differ little, and even for those who make more than $1 million per year the effective tax seems to be only about one-third of their income.

But these rates are only part of the story. Taxes other than the federal income tax are *regressive* in their incidence: lower income people pay a higher proportion of their incomes than do those at higher levels. Adding all taxes together, Robert Lampman has shown, for example, that in 1965 people in the lowest income quintile paid 22 percent of their incomes in one kind of tax or another; those in the middle quintile paid 25 percent, and those in the highest quintile paid 33 percent. Those in the second, third, and fourth quintiles paid almost identical proportions of their income even though people in the fourth quintile had incomes that averaged twice as much as those in the second. Thus the seemingly dull and

technical economic issues of income tax versus sales tax versus property tax have important implications for the patterns of inequality of our society.

The growing capacity of social scientists to be specific and clear about the effects of public programs on different members of the society has had its effect on the definition and salience of social problems. Taxes, after all, are generally a favorite subject of complaint, but these complaints tend to be more chronic than effective because the issue of who pays what taxes and what is a fair share has been so difficult to grasp. The technical advances that Pechman and his associates at Brookings were able to achieve in the 1960s fueled the debate on inequity of taxation with much more precise data than had been possible before. The detailed level at which the Brookings analysis could be carried out served to sharpen both the definition of taxes as a social problem and the debate on tax reform alternatives.

The principal technical innovation the Brookings group used was the "MERGE" file of 30,000 family units, which was created by combining computerized data from a 1967 Census Bureau population survey with a computer file of income tax returns from households. This file made possible, first, a detailed description of what kinds of persons pay how much of various kinds of taxes, and then a simulation of the effects on particular kinds of families of proposed changes in the taxes. Thus it was possible to test ahead of time, rather quickly and relatively inexpensively, the likely effects of even the most minute change in the tax laws—effects in terms of the revenue that would be generated or lost and in terms of what kinds of families would pay for or benefit by the changes. Tax costs and effects now can be analyzed with the same sociological methods used to analyze voting behavior or public opinion or attitudes.

Taxes bear on central issues of class and equality in another sense as well. It is sometimes argued that even if the tax system is not notably progressive, the effect of shifting consumption from the private to the public sectors is to reduce inequality. That is, the public goods that taxes provide are so much more equally distributed than the private income which has been taxed that the resulting distribution of all resources is more equal than it would otherwise have been. We have seen that this argument often is made for educational expenditures, and we saw in the Weisbrod and Hansen study (Selection 11a) an example of how things don't work out the way policymakers expect. Educational benefits actually go disproportionately to people at higher income levels, and somewhat the same kind of analysis can be made about public expenditures in other areas—highways, parks and recreational services, cultural services, even pollution control. Thus the faith of liberals and Fabian socialists that increasing the size of the public sector somehow has automatic equalitarian effects has been seriously challenged. The knowledge that government benefits are not so heavily weighted toward the have-nots as people may think fires the debate over the tax system's fairness and centers attention even more sharply on the net joint effects of the tax system and the benefits of tax-supported programs.

More details of the distributional impact of federal income taxes can be found in Joseph A. Pechman and Benjamin A. Okner, "Individual Income Tax Erosion by Income Classes," in *The Economics of Federal Subsidy Programs, A Compendium of Papers Prepared for the Use of the Joint Economic Committee,* 92d Cong., 2d sess., 1972. Pechman's earlier study, which considers all forms of federal, state, and local taxes, is *Federal Tax Policy,* 2d ed. (Washington, D.C.: Brookings Institution, 1971). A recent study of the changing economic beliefs and ideologies sometimes called the Keynsian Revolution is Herbert Stein, *The Fiscal Revolution in America* (Chicago: University of Chicago Press, 1969). A broad study of the macroeconomic and distributional effects of taxes is Lester C. Thurow, *The Impact of Taxes on the American Economy* (New York: Praeger, 1971). Robert J. Lampman discusses changes in income redistribution by means of taxes and transfers in *Ends and Means of Reducing Income Poverty* (Chicago: Markham, 1971), pp. 90-103. ■

TAXES INEVITABLY GENERATE political controversy because no one likes to pay them. Taxpayers may recognize intellectually that taxes are the "prices" they pay for public services, but they seem to resent taxes far more than other prices—presumably because they see no immediate connection between the taxes they pay and the services they receive. When someone pays for an automobile or a steak dinner, however much he may complain about high prices, he can see that the payment produced some tangible benefit to himself. When he pays taxes to support federal programs to equalize educational opportunity or increase national security, the benefits seem intangible, diffuse, and unrelated to his individual tax payment. Hence, while private transactions are normally viewed as a two-way street—one pays money and receives a good or service—taxes are more often seen as purely negative. At best they are a necessary evil.

Moreover, tax decisions inevitably pit one group against another. The particular set of taxes chosen will determine how the cost of government is shared among different groups, and almost everyone feels that others could more fairly be called on to bear a larger share of the total burden.

There are no totally objective ways of distinguishing "good" taxes from "bad" taxes or saying who ought to pay the most. However, at least four questions should be raised in evaluating an existing or proposed tax.

1. *Is the tax equitable?* Most people would agree that "equity" implies among other things that people in the same economic circumstances should pay the same amount of tax. Some violations of the equity principle are obvious—for example, when local property tax assessors place different values on houses in the same neighborhood that turn out, when sold, to have the same market value. Other inequities are more controversial

—for example, those resulting from differing federal income tax treatment of individuals or business firms whose economic circumstances are basically similar. Is it equitable to tax income earned as wages or salaries differently from income earned as interest on a municipal bond and still differently from income earned as capital gains on the sale of property or securities—as federal income tax laws now do?

2. *Who bears the burden?* Taxes may be distinguished according to the burden they place on different income groups. A "progressive" tax is one that takes a larger proportion of the income of a rich person than of a poor person; a "regressive" tax takes a higher proportion of the income of the poor. Most people would agree that the tax system as a whole ought to be progressive. Taxes on the poor cause hardship because they reduce the ability of the poor to pay for the basic necessities of life. Taxes on higher income persons cut into luxuries rather than necessities. Problems arise, of course, in judging precisely how progressive a tax system ought to be and whether new taxes should make it more or less progressive than it already is.

It is also far from obvious how progressive or regressive a particular tax actually is unless one knows whose real income is ultimately reduced by the tax (the "incidence" of the tax). The person who writes the check to the government for the tax may not be the one who really bears the burden. Is the tax on property borne by the landlord, or does he pass it on to the tenant through higher rent? Is a tax on corporate profits borne by stockholders, or is it passed on to consumers in the form of higher prices?

Economists are fairly certain about the final incidence of general sales taxes and income taxes. In general, the burden of personal income taxes is borne directly by the individual taxpayers. The present federal income tax is progressive, despite numerous provisions that benefit mainly high income persons. General sales taxes fall on consumers because retailers pass along the full tax in higher prices. Since low income persons spend higher proportions of their income on consumption, sales taxes tend to be regressive.

With respect to corporate income taxes and property taxes, however, there is considerable disagreement among economists as to the ultimate incidence of these levies. Opinion is divided on how the burden of the property tax is shared between landlord and tenant and how the burden of the corporate tax is shared between owners of corporations and consumers of their products. To the extent that the corporate tax falls on owners of capital, it is progressive, since ownership of capital is concentrated among upper income groups. To the extent that it falls on consumers, it is regressive.

3. *What are the economic effects of the tax?* Progressive taxes are generally thought to accord more fully with ideas of fairness; but to what extent would an increase in progressivity impair incentives for work and for investment? If tax rates applying to those in upper income brackets are very high, do they penalize thrift, risk-taking, and investment? No one has the answers to these questions, but the argument that high tax rates reduce work incentives was used to justify reducing the top bracket rate under the federal individual income tax from its peak of 94 percent in 1945 to its present 70 percent level. Another economic aspect of taxation is the extent to which it distorts the allocation of resources in the economy. Excise taxes on particular commodities or services tend to penalize their production and consumption relative to those of untaxed goods and services. These penalties may be thought desirable in the case of such "harmful" products as liquor and tobacco, but in general, it seems preferable not to interfere with consumer choices.

4. *Is the tax hard to collect or administer?* In the United States, which has an amazingly good record of taxpayer compliance, this question is not as important as it is in some other countries where tax evasion is rampant and the mere passage of a tax law in no way guarantees that the taxes imposed will be collected. Sales and income taxes, however, are generally considered to be far easier to administer than are property taxes,

which often involve difficult judgment about property values.

THE CURRENT FEDERAL TAX SYSTEM

Compared with taxes in other industrialized countries, U.S. taxes impose a comparatively light burden on the economy. Because different levels of government perform widely differing functions in different countries, it is necessary to combine all receipts—federal, state and local—in comparing tax burdens among countries. On this basis, aggregate receipts amounted to 32 percent of the gross national product of the United States in 1969. In the same period, receipts in Norway, the Netherlands, and Sweden exceeded 40 percent of GNP, and in six other countries the total ranged between 35 and 40 percent of GNP. Taxes as a percentage of GNP for the United States and 14 other countries are shown below.

Country	Taxes as Percent of Gross National Product
Sweden	48
Norway	43
Netherlands	42
United Kingdom	39
France	38
Germany	38
Austria	37
Denmark	37
Canada	35
Belgium	34
Italy	33
United States	32
Switzerland	28
Spain	22
Japan	21

Source: Organization for Economic Co-operation and Development, *National Accounts Statistics, 1953-1969.* Data are for 1969, except for Sweden, Austria, and Canada, which are for 1968.

Roughly 60 percent of total U.S. taxes are collected by the federal government and the rest by state and local governments. Tax receipts of all levels of government have grown over the years, but in different ways. State and local governments rely heavily on sales and property taxes, and the federal government relies mainly on direct income taxes. . . . Major shifts have occurred in the last few years in the relative importance of various types of federal taxes. Excise taxes have been steadily reduced and many of them eliminated in the past two decades. Cuts in corporate profits taxes have also drastically reduced the importance of this source of income to the federal government.

Since the individual income tax is progressive, it could have been expected to rise in importance because it tends to grow faster than other taxes as national income rises. In the past several decades, however, this tendency has been offset by periodic individual income tax cuts—in 1954, 1964, 1969, and 1971. As a consequence, in 1973 revenues from the individual income tax will be about the same percentage of total revenue as they were 20 years ago, despite a more than threefold rise in personal income over the period. Employment (or payroll) taxes, on the other hand, have been rising steadily. Increases in tax rates and in the maximum amount of wages subject to tax have increased the yield of these taxes from 10 percent of federal revenues in 1954 to 29 percent in 1973. Over the past two decades, therefore, the reliance of the federal government on individual income taxes has remained roughly unchanged, while the decreased reliance on corporate income and excise taxes has been balanced by a large increase in payroll taxes.

In considering possible sources of additional federal revenue, some types of taxes can be ruled out. Estate and gift taxes, for example, while badly in need of reform, cannot be counted on to provide significant amounts of new federal revenue. Excise taxes tend to be regressive; they distort relative prices, interfere with consumer choice, and generate considerable political opposition from both producers and consumers. For these reasons, most of the excise taxes introduced during the Second World War and the Korean war have been gradually abandoned; except for the taxes on liquor and tobacco, the remaining federal excises are mainly user charges, such as the tax on gasoline. This trend away from excise taxation is unlikely to be reversed.

Another set of taxes that may be ruled out as a source of increased general revenues are payroll taxes, which are traditionally earmarked for social security and unemployment compensation and are not generally regarded as appropriate sources of revenue for other government programs. Indeed, because of its regressiveness, there are strong reasons to believe that reliance on the payroll tax is already too heavy and that future social security benefits should be financed more out of general revenues and less out of the payroll tax, or that a major restructuring of the tax should be undertaken. The social security payroll tax is in most cases divided into two parts. Half is paid by the employee and half by the employer. Most economists believe that the part paid by the employer is ultimately borne by the worker; his wages are lower than they would be if the employer did not have to pay the social security tax for him. Moreover, the payroll tax at present is levied on only the first $9,000 of wages or salaries, and, unlike the individual income tax, it has no exemptions or deductions. Hence, it is a regressive tax whose burden falls most heavily on low and moderate income workers. Those with earnings over $9,000 pay a lower proportion of their income in social security tax.

Among existing taxes, the individual income tax and corporate income tax are the most promising sources of sizable amounts of additional federal revenue. The possibilities of raising more revenue from these taxes are discussed in more detail below.

If the federal government were to seek a new tax source, it would probably have to turn to some kind of general consumption tax. General consumption taxes are used extensively in other countries and by 45 of the states in the United States, but not by the federal government. The present administration has raised the possibility of such a tax in a slightly different context. It has under consideration a value added tax—essentially a tax on consumer expenditures—whose proceeds would be used to replace the local residential property taxes now devoted to the support of schools. . . .

STRUCTURAL REFORMS OF THE INCOME TAXES

The revenues yielded by individual and corporate income taxes depend not only on the tax rate, but also on the tax base—the income to which that rate is applied. Over the years, the Congress has made frequent changes in the bases of the individual and corporate income taxes—sometimes to enlarge them but far more frequently to reduce them.

The federal tax bases have been reduced—or eroded—in two major ways. First, certain kinds of income have been excluded from taxation or are taxed at preferential rates. The first $100 a taxpayer receives in dividends is excluded from taxable income; income from oil, gas, and other mineral-producing activities is accorded special treatment through generous depletion allowances; capital gains realized from the sale of assets are subject to a lower tax rate than is ordinary income; and interest on state and local government bonds is completely exempt from taxation. Second, taxpayers have been allowed special deductions from their income for certain kinds of personal expenditures. For example, property taxes, gasoline taxes, medical expenses, and charitable contributions are all deductible in computing taxable income.

These base-reducing provisions were designed to benefit particular groups or industries or to encourage certain activities that are deemed desirable from the national viewpoint. The exemption of interest on state and local government bonds, for example, makes state and local security issues more attractive to investors and lowers the cost of borrowing for these governments. The preferential treatment of mineral industries has been defended in part on national security grounds as a means of stimulating development of domestic mineral resources. The deductibility of charitable contributions provides an incentive for private philanthropy.

However worthy the motives, such provisions reduce federal revenues and enable large numbers of persons, primarily in higher income brackets, to pay less tax than they otherwise would. . . .

Joseph A. Pechman and Benjamin A. Okner have estimated that at 1972 income levels, an additional $77 billion could be raised from the individual income tax alone with present tax rates and exemptions if the tax base were broadened to include all economic income and if most deductions and all preferential tax rates and credits were eliminated. Alternatively, the present yield of the individual income tax could be raised from the broadened tax base with rates that are 43 percent lower, on the average, than the present rates, which begin at 14 percent and rise to a maximum of 70 percent.

Besides cutting into revenues, the erosion of the tax base has the effect of making the personal income tax far less progressive than it would otherwise be. Under existing law, the marginal tax rates (the tax paid on additional dollars earned) rise quite steeply from 14 percent in the lowest bracket up to 70 percent. The schedule of marginal rates makes the tax appear highly progressive. When one looks at average effective rates for each income level, however, one sees that the tax is not really so progressive: the average effective rate now rises from less than 1 percent on incomes under $3,000 to 10.5 percent on incomes of $15,000 to $20,000. In the $20,000 to $50,000 range, there is little change in average effective rates as incomes rise, and even for incomes over $1,000,000 the average effective tax rate is not much above one-third.

The major factor reducing the progressivity of the income tax is that rich people benefit from preferential tax treatment far more than do those with low incomes. Indeed, in 1970, more than 100 individuals with adjusted gross incomes of more than $200,-000 were nontaxable.

Reducing tax preferences therefore would have the double result of increasing federal revenues and making the tax structure more progressive. The Congress, however, is hardly likely to sweep away all the special provisions in the tax laws at one time. The pressures for retaining most of them are strong, and progress typically is made only haltingly. Moreover, some of the tax preferences that constitute major elements in the $36 billion and $77 billion estimates presented above benefit a wide range of average taxpayers, not just the rich. An important example is the ability of homeowners to deduct interest and property taxes from their income as "business expenses" while not being required to pay taxes on the "imputed" income derived from ownership of a home.

Those who support tax reform as a means of raising additional revenue usually do not include *all* the elements of economic income that go untaxed, but confine their attention mainly to those of particular benefit to relatively small groups of taxpayers, principally those in upper income categories. But even here, the actual accomplishments of tax reform legislation in recent years are modest. The revenue raised as a result of changes in the Tax Reform Act of 1969 amounted to only $3.3 billion a year, and this occurred in a year when tax reform was a popular issue. The Revenue Act of 1971 introduced new tax preferences of $370 million, not including the revenue lost from the adoption of more liberal depreciation allowances and the reinstatement of the investment tax credit.

Three different packages of possible revenue-raising reforms are shown in Table 16.1. They include (1) increasing from 50 to 60 percent the portion of realized capital gains subject to tax; (2) reducing or eliminating some of the allowable deductions from income, such as state gasoline taxes, real estate taxes, and charitable contributions; (3) eliminating the current exclusion from taxable income of the first $100 of dividends; (4) reducing the preferential tax treatment of income from oil, gas, and other mineral-producing activities; and (5) increasing the special tax on all forms of preference income. These would be regarded by most experts as rather substantial revisions and doubtless

TABLE 16.1

REVENUE EFFECT OF VARIOUS STRUCTURAL REFORMS OF THE INDIVIDUAL INCOME TAX
UNDER ALTERNATIVE PACKAGES, 1972 INCOME LEVELS (BILLIONS OF DOLLARS)

Reform Provision	Package 1	Package 2	Package 3
Remove maximum tax on earned income	0.1	0.1	0.1
Include 60 percent of realized capital gains in adjusted gross income and remove alternative capital gains tax provision	1.5	1.5	1.5
Eliminate deduction of gasoline taxes	0.5	0.5	0.5
Eliminate deduction of real estate property taxes	. .	. .	2.3
Remove dividend exclusion	0.4	0.4	0.4
Eliminate 50 percent of excess depletion advantages	0.2	0.2	0.2
Place 3 percent floor on charitable contribution deductions	. .	1.9	1.9
Tax unrealized capital gains in excess of $5,000 transferred by gift or bequest at capital gains rates	. .	. .	0.6
Remove $25,000 exemption allowed for excess investment interest deduction	. .	. .	1.2
Revise preference income base*	0.5	. .	. .
Revise preference income base* and raise tax rate on revised base from 10 to 20 percent	. .	1.1	. .
Revise preference income base* and tax at one-half the regular income tax rates†	. .	. .	2.4
Total revenue effect‡	3.1	5.6	10.2

Source: Based on the Brookings MERGE File of 30,000 family units for the year 1966 with incomes projected to 1972 level.

*Revision of preference income base involves inclusion of state-local bond interest as a preference item and removal of deduction for current-year taxes paid.

†That is, tax the revised base at 7 percent to 35 percent—half the regular rates, which range from 14 percent to 70 percent.

‡The total revenue effect of each package is not equal to the sum of the components because various provisions interact with one another.

would be strongly opposed by those taxpayers who would be affected. Most of the changes would not significantly affect the average low and middle income taxpayer. The one exception is the group of reforms that limit personal deductions for gasoline and property taxes; these would impinge on a very large number of persons at all income levels. Nevertheless, package 3, which contains the largest number of reforms, would raise only $10.2 billion a year. Most of these reforms would not affect corporations, but those that did would probably increase 1972 revenues by $3.2 billion. These include $800 million from eliminating the alternative tax on long-term capital gains, $400 million from removal of half the excess depletion advantages, and $2 billion from the revision of the tax on preference income. Together, these reforms would raise $13.4 billion, or $1.4 billion more than the $12 billion needed

to increase full employment revenue by 5 percent.

As may be seen in Table 16.2, package 3 would make the income tax considerably more progressive than it is now. Effective tax rates would rise only slightly for low and middle income persons, but the rise would be steep for those with incomes over $500,000. . . .

A NEW REVENUE SOURCE: TAXING CONSUMPTION

In the United States, the federal government has confined its taxation of consumption to excise taxes, which apply only to selected commodities. But taxation of consumption through the general sales tax is widespread among state and local governments. General consumption taxes are also

TABLE 16.2

CURRENT EFFECTIVE INDIVIDUAL INCOME TAX
RATES AND RATE INCREASES WITH A $13.4
BILLION TAX REFORM PACKAGE,* BY INCOME
CLASSES, 1972 INCOME LEVELS (INCOME
CLASSES IN THOUSANDS OF DOLLARS; OTHER
NUMBERS IN PERCENT)

Income Class	Effective Rate, Current Law	Increase in Effective Rate from Reform Package
0-3	0.5	0.3
3-5	1.7	0.1
5-10	5.1	0.2
10-15	8.6	0.4
15-20	10.5	0.6
20-25	11.8	0.7
25-50	13.9	1.2
50-100	22.2	3.0
100-500	31.0	8.4
500-1,000	32.8	16.3
1,000 and over	34.2	19.0
All classes†	11.0	1.1

Source: Based on the Brookings MERGE File of 30,000 family units for 1966 with incomes projected to the 1972 level.

*$3.2 billion of the revenue raised by this reform package would come from the corporation income tax; the tax burden shown in this table arises from the $10.2 billion of revenues derived from the individual income tax as outlined in Table 14.2, package 3.

†Includes negative income class not shown separately.

used in other countries, where income taxation is less well developed. A general sales tax was seriously considered by the U.S. Congress in 1932 and during the Second World War, but the legislation was decisively defeated in 1932 and was never brought to a vote during the war.

There are two major kinds of general consumption taxes: (1) a *sales tax* levied on the sales of final goods and services, and (2) a *value added tax* (VAT) levied on the difference in value between a firm's sales and its purchases. The latter tax is now used extensively in Western Europe.

A truly general sales tax would apply uniformly to all goods and services purchased by consumers. In practice, however, food, rent, and medicine are often excluded from the sales tax base to moderate its impact on low income families. If the same exclusions and rates are used, a VAT will generally have the same economic effect as a sales tax. For example, the $400 retail price of a

color television set is made up of increments added by a large number of firms at various stages in the production process. Mining companies, the manufacturer, the wholesaler, the trucking firm, and the retailer each add some value to the set as it passes along the production and distribution chain. The government could either collect a 3 percent sales tax on the $400 set from the retailer or assess the 3 percent against the value added by each firm along the way. The end result, for all practical purposes, is the same. In both cases the ultimate consumer pays the same amount of tax.

Sales and value added taxes can produce large amounts of revenue because the base to which these taxes apply is large. For example, in 1972 the base of a national sales or value added tax would be about $560 billion if rents and the rental value of owner-occupied homes were exempted from the tax and about $400 billion if food consumed at home and medicine were also exempted. Thus, each percentage point of tax would raise $5.6 billion if levied on the broader base and $4 billion on the narrower base. To raise the illustrative $12 billion and $24 billion of revenue at 1972 levels, it would be necessary to levy sales or value added taxes at about 2.2 or 4.3 percent rates on the broader base and at 3 and 6 percent on the narrower base.

There is little reason to prefer the VAT over the sales tax, particularly in a country like the United States, where tax compliance is generally good. For countries with compliance problems, the VAT may be preferable because it is collected in smaller amounts than the sales tax as products flow through the production and distribution process, even though the final consumer pays the same amount of tax in the form of higher prices. This advantage might be extremely important in countries where there are large numbers of small retailers who are not good record-keepers. In the United States, most retail business is done through firms that may be expected to keep adequate records and to comply with the tax laws. Moreover, with general sales taxes already in existence in

45 states, retailers should have little trouble in accommodating themselves to a national sales tax. On the other hand, state and local government officials might well resent intrusion by the federal government into the retail sales tax area, which is one of their major revenue sources.

To adopt either a general sales tax or a VAT would require difficult decisions about the kinds of transactions to be included or excluded. Should services—dry cleaning, entertainment, automobile repairs—be taxed? What about legal and medical services or private and parochial schools? What about the sales of (or value added by) publicly owned utilities, such as municipal water systems and electric power companies? Major political pressures and controversies would be generated by questions of this kind.

General sales and broad-based value added taxes are regressive because the poor spend a higher percentage of their income on consumer goods than do the rich. The choice between sales taxes and income taxes for raising additional revenues depends primarily on the relative weight to be placed on protecting work and investment incentives as against the need to avoid placing higher taxes on low income families. Some believe that income tax rates are already too high and that any increase would discourage extra work effort and incentives to invest. Others point out that the top federal income tax rates have been brought down sharply since the end of the Second World War and that it is unwise social policy to place additional burdens on the poor and the near poor.

As was pointed out above, one way to lessen the regressiveness of retail sales taxes is to exempt food, medicine, and other necessities. Another way of moderating the burden of a consumption tax on the poor and the near poor would be to provide a credit against income taxes for the amount of value added taxes paid by families below a certain income level. The credit would be an estimate of the average amount of value added tax that families of different sizes and income levels would be likely to pay. A table showing the credits for families of various

sizes at each income level could then become part of the income tax form. Poor families that pay no income tax would receive a refund each year equal to their VAT credit. For example, a 100 percent credit for value added taxes paid could be given to families of 4 with incomes up to $5,000, with the cutoff appropriately scaled up or down for families of other sizes. As incomes rose to $20,000, the credit could be gradually phased out. A family of 4 with an income of $12,500 would receive a credit equal to 50 percent of its estimated VAT. Families with incomes of $20,000 or more would receive no credit. The rate of the VAT would, of course, have to be increased to make up for the revenue lost by the low income credit. And the further up the income scale the credit applied, the higher the value added tax rate needed to obtain a given amount of revenue.

The value added tax rates needed to raise $12 billion are as follows: (1) A 2.2 percent rate would be required if the tax were levied on a *broad base,* including all consumer expenditures except rent; (2) a 3 percent rate would be needed if the tax were levied on a *narrow base,* excluding not only rent but food and medical outlays; and (3) a 3.25 percent rate would be needed if a broad base were combined with the *low income credit* described above.

COMPARING THE ALTERNATIVES

Five possible ways of raising additional federal revenue . . . seem worthy of serious consideration: (1) structural reform of the individual and corporate income taxes—increasing the tax base by reducing preferential treatment of particular sources of income; (2) raising income tax rates by imposing a surcharge; (3) raising income tax rates by a certain number of percentage points; (4) enacting a value added tax with exemptions for rent, food, and medical care; and (5) enacting a value added tax with a low-income credit but no exemptions.

Each of the five methods would have different effects on the distribution of income, even if they were to raise approximately the same amount of revenue. Table 16.3 shows how effective tax rates would be increased for families at various income levels if approximately $12 billion were raised by increases in *individual* taxes under each method. The changes in effective rates are also shown in Figure 16.1 (except for the tax reform alternative).

When the alternatives are compared, it is clear that the tax reform package is by far the most progressive at the high end of the income scale. The reform package would increase average effective rates by less than 1 percentage point for families with incomes below $25,000; it would raise effective rates for those in the $50,000 to $100,000

range by 3 percentage points; and it would raise effective rates by 19 percentage points for families with incomes of $1 million or more. The income tax surcharge would be the next in order of progressivity, with the increase in effective rates ranging from less than 1 percent in the lowest income group to 4.1 percent for those with incomes of more than $1 million.

Despite the exemption of rent, food, and medical care, the narrow-base value added tax would be regressive along the entire income scale, increasing taxes for the poor much more heavily than for the rich. The broad-base value added tax, with the low income credit described above, would have a progressive incidence not very different from

TABLE 16.3

CURRENT EFFECTIVE INDIVIDUAL INCOME TAX RATES AND RATE INCREASES UNDER VARIOUS METHODS OF RAISING ADDITIONAL REVENUE, BY INCOME CLASSES, 1972 INCOME LEVELS (INCOME CLASSES IN THOUSANDS OF DOLLARS; OTHER NUMBERS IN PERCENT)

| | | | Increase in Effective Rate* | | | |
| | | | $12 billion tax increase | | | |
Income class†	Effective rate, current law	$10 billion tax increase Income tax reform‡	Income tax surcharge§	Percentage point income tax increase¶	Broad-base value added tax with credit**	Narrow-base value added tax††
0-3	0.5	0.3	0.1	0.1	0.1	1.8
3-5	1.7	0.1	0.2	0.3	0.6	1.5
5-10	5.1	0.2	0.6	0.8	0.8	1.5
10-15	8.6	0.4	1.0	1.2	1.1	1.4
15-20	10.5	0.6	1.3	1.5	1.7	1.4
20-25	11.8	0.7	1.4	1.6	1.9	1.3
25-50	13.9	1.2	1.7	1.6	1.7	1.2
50-100	22.2	3.0	2.6	1.8	1.1	0.7
100-500	31.0	8.4	3.5	1.6	0.8	0.5
500-1,000	32.8	16.3	3.9	1.3	0.4	0.2
1,000 and over	34.2	19.0	4.1	1.3	0.2	0.2
All classes‡‡	11.0	1.1	1.3	1.3	1.3	1.3

Source: Based on the Brookings MERGE File of 30,000 family units for the year 1966 with incomes projected to 1972 level.

*Tax as percent of income.

†Income is equal to the sum of adjusted gross income, transfer payments, state and local government bond interest, and excluded realized long-term capital gains.

‡Tax reform package 3 outlined in Table 16.1.

§Surcharge of 11.8 percent on 1972 income tax liabilities.

¶2.5 percentage point increase applied to each bracket rate.

**Broad-base value added tax at 3.25 percent with full credit up to $5,000 for a 4-person family; credit is phased out completely at $20,000.

††Narrow-base value added tax at 3 percent.

‡‡Includes negative income class not shown separately

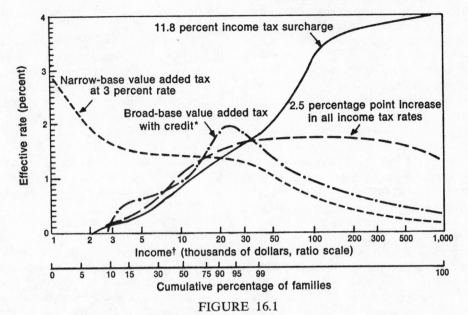

FIGURE 16.1

Effective Rates of Individual Income Tax Increases and Value Added Taxes Each Yielding $12 Billion, by Income Classes, 1972 Income Level

Source: Based on the Brookings MERGE File of 30,000 family units for 1966 with incomes projected to the 1972 level.
* Rate of 3.25 % with full credit up to $5,000 for a 4-person family; credit is phased out completely at $20,000.
† Income is equal to the sum of adjusted gross income, transfer payments, state and local government bond interest, and excluded realized long-term capital gains.

that achieved by a constant percentage point increase in all income tax rates on incomes up to about $17,000. For families with incomes between $17,000 and $40,000, the VAT with a credit would increase tax liabilities by somewhat more than the percentage point income tax increase, but for those with incomes above that level the reverse would be true.

The bottom scale in Figure 16.1 shows the proportion of families with incomes at or below the levels shown in the figure. From this scale it is possible to note that for the 75 percent of families whose incomes are below $17,000, the surcharge, the percentage point increase, and the VAT with low income credit would impose approximately the same additional burden. It is the 25 percent of families with incomes above $17,000 for whom these three alternatives would have quite different impacts.

SUBSTITUTION OF A VALUE ADDED TAX FOR THE PROPERTY TAX

The value added tax has also been suggested as a partial substitute for the local property tax, which is now the major source of revenue for financing elementary and secondary education in the United States. Since property is unequally distributed among communities, the financial resources available for education are also unequally distributed. The courts in several states have recently ruled that this method of financing leads to unequal educational opportunities for individuals and is unconstitutional. The U.S. Supreme Court has not yet ruled on these cases, but there is substantial public agreement that the present system of financing public education should be drastically modified. . . .

Replacement of the residential property tax

by a VAT for financing education would substitute a nationwide tax on consumption for a host of locally established taxes on property. Such a shift would help to reduce the differential burdens of taxation on property in different communities that now prevail because neighboring communities often have quite different property tax rates and assessment practices. Even within a single community, assessment practices are often so variable that levies on properties with the same market value are widely divergent. Such differentials tend to distort land use and planning and have sometimes placed excessive tax burdens on properties in urban areas.

Unfortunately, the distributional effect among those in different income classes of replacing part of the property tax with a consumption tax is particularly difficult to measure. As was pointed out above, economists are not agreed as to whether the owner of the property or the person who pays for the services the property renders ultimately bears the burden of the property tax. The tax on real estate may be thought of in two parts—a tax on the value of the land itself and a tax on the value of buildings and other improvements on the land. With respect to the tax on land, it is generally agreed that the landowner bears the tax and cannot pass it on. But land constitutes, on the average, only about 25 percent of the value of residential property subject to tax. Improvements form the major part of property values, and there are at least two distinct views as to who pays the tax on improvements.

The traditional view of the incidence of the property tax has been that renters pay the tax on residential buildings through higher rent payments and consumers in general pay the property tax on commercial and industrial property in the form of higher prices for the goods they buy. This view assumes that property taxes initially reduce the rate of return to investors in property improvements and that the lower rate of return slows the flow of new investment over time, thereby driving up the prices of business services provided by such assets until the old rate of return to the owners has been restored.

Renters and consumers thus end up paying the taxes.

An alternative view is that the initially lower rate of return on property improvements diverts investment into untaxed (or more lightly taxed) areas of the economy, but does not affect the *total level* of investment. This lowers returns on other kinds of investment generally, until a point is reached at which all owners of capital receive a lower rate of return because of the property tax. Under this view, a property tax is ultimately borne in a general way by all owners of capital.

Since there is no consensus on the incidence of the property tax, estimates of its distributional effect have been prepared on the basis both of the traditional assumptions and alternative ones. The two sets of assumptions yield very different conclusions about the burden of the property tax at various income levels. (See Table 16.4) If the property tax is borne by all owners of capital, it takes a high percentage of income at both the bottom and the top of the income scale. At the low end of the income scale is a large concentration of retired people who own their homes. Hence the property tax takes a relatively high proportion of the income of these low-income persons who own capital in the form of residential property. Those at the high end of the income distribution tend to own large amounts of capital of all types, and consequently the tax burden is also a sizable proportion of their income. In the middle of the income distribution, where most income is derived from wages and salaries, the burden of the property tax is much lighter.

Based on the traditional view—that property taxes on improvements are passed on in the form of higher rents and prices—the property tax is similar to a consumption tax, with a particularly heavy emphasis on the consumption of housing services. As a percentage of income it is highest for the very poor, and declines steadily as income rises.

In 1972, total state and local property taxes will amount to almost $46 billion. Even those who favor reducing property tax bur-

TABLE 16.4

EFFECTIVE GENERAL PROPERTY TAX RATES*
UNDER ALTERNATIVE INCIDENCE ASSUMPTIONS,
BY INCOME CLASSES, 1972 INCOME LEVELS
Income classes in thousands of dollars;
other numbers in percent

Income class‡	Effective property tax rate† assuming that the tax on improvements is borne by	
	Capital§	Renters and consumers§
0-3	7.2	13.0
3-5	5.4	8.0
5-10	3.6	5.9
10-15	2.6	4.9
15-20	2.9	4.7
20-25	3.7	4.4
25-50	5.7	4.4
500-100	14.1	3.7
100-500	22.4	3.5
500-1,000	24.5	3.0
1,000 and over	18.2	2.1
All classes††	5.0	5.0

Source: Based on the Brookings MERGE File of 30,000 family units for the year 1966 with incomes projected to 1972 level.
* Includes all property taxed by state and local governments such as automobiles; livestock; commercial, industrial, and residential real property; and so forth.
† Tax as percent of income.
‡ Income is equal to the sum of adjusted gross income, transfer payments, state and local government bond interest, and excluded realized long-term capital gains.
§ The tax on land is assumed to be borne by landowners. See text for explanation of the distribution of the taxes on improvements.
†† Includes negative income class not shown separately.

dens do not argue for replacing all property tax revenues by a tax on consumption; rather, the suggestion has been made that only the residential property tax devoted to education be replaced. This view has been supported by various court cases in which there has been a ruling against financing education from property taxes and by recent efforts to provide tax relief to aged homeowners.

The simple replacement of residential property taxes by a nationwide federal tax would create massive problems concerning the distribution of federal assistance among states and among school districts within a state. But there is also a question as to what such a substitution would imply for the distribution of tax burdens among families in different income classes. Residential property taxes

devoted to education currently total about $12 billion. In Table 16.5 combined estimates are shown of the distribution by income classes of the tax burden imposed by $12 billion of revenues raised in three different ways: a federal broad-based value added tax (with low-income credit), an individual income tax surcharge, and a general property tax on residential real estate. The estimates reflect an *average* tax burden in each income class; they do not take into account the tremendous variation in property taxes paid by people in different states and in different communities within states. In effect, the calculations assume a property tax levied at the same rate on all residential property in the nation. And, again, because of the lack of consensus regarding the incidence of the property tax, these calculations were made under the two sets of assumptions described above.

On the assumption that the property tax on improvements is borne by owners of capital, substitution of a *value added tax* (with a low-income credit) for residential property taxes would reduce tax liabilities for families with incomes under $5,000 and for those with incomes of $50,000 and above; families in the $5,000 to $50,000 income range would pay the same or higher taxes. On the assumption that the property tax on improvements rests on renters and consumers, the change in tax liabilities for most income classes would be relatively small, but families with incomes below $15,000 and over $500,000 would pay somewhat lower taxes after the substitution, while those between $15,000 and $500,000 would find their tax liabilities somewhat increased.

Assuming that the property tax on improvements is borne by all owners of capital, replacement of residential property taxes by a personal *income tax surcharge* would reduce tax liabilities at income levels below $10,000, increase them between $10,000 and $50,000, and reduce them for families with incomes above $50,000. If the property tax on improvements is paid by renters and consumers, taxes would be reduced for families with incomes below $15,000, remain unchanged for incomes between $15,000 and

TABLE 16.5

THE BURDEN OF $12 BILLION OF TAX REVENUE RAISED FROM TAXES ON RESIDENTIAL
PROPERTY, A VALUE ADDED TAX WITH A CREDIT FOR LOW-INCOME FAMILIES, AND
AN INCOME TAX SURCHARGE, BY INCOME CLASSES, 1972 INCOME LEVELS
Income classes in thousands of dollars; other numbers in percent

	Effective rates of tax*			
	Residential real property tax assuming tax on improvements is borne by		Value added tax with credits§	Income tax surcharge††
Income class†	Capital‡	Renters and consumers‡		
0-3	0.9	3.5	0.1	0.1
3-5	1.0	2.0	0.6	0.2
5-10	0.8	1.5	0.8	0.6
10-15	0.6	1.3	1.1	1.0
15-20	0.7	1.3	1.7	1.3
20-25	1.0	1.2	1.9	1.4
25-50	1.5	1.1	1.7	1.7
50-100	4.2	0.6	1.1	2.6
100-500	7.1	0.6	0.8	3.5
500-1,000	7.8	0.5	0.4	3.9
1,000 and over	5.8	0.4	0.2	4.1
All classes‡‡	1.3	1.3	1.3	1.3

Source: Based on the Brookings MERGE File of 30,000 family units for the year 1966 with incomes projected to 1972 level.
* Tax as percent of income.
† Income is equal to the sum of adjusted gross income, transfer payments, state and local government bond interest, and excluded realized long-term capital gains.
‡ The tax on land is assumed to be borne by landowners. See text for explanation of the distribution of the taxes on improvements.
§ Broad-base value added tax at 3.25 percent with full credit up to $5,000 for a four-person family; credit is phased out completely at $20,000.
†† Surcharge of 11.8 percent on 1972 income tax liabilities.
‡‡ Includes negative income class not shown separately.

$20,000, and be increased for those above $20,000.

Thus, replacing residential property taxes with a VAT would alleviate tax burdens somewhat at the very low end of the income scale, because of the full credit for low-income families used in these computations. But it would also reduce tax burdens substantially at the upper end of the income distribution. In contrast, substituting an income tax surcharge for residential property taxes would greatly increase progressivity for incomes up to $50,000, regardless of what assumption is made about the incidence of the property tax; and it would reduce progressivity for families with incomes above $50,000 only if the property tax on improvements rested entirely on all owners of capital.

These conclusions are only a first approximation. It is not feasible simply to substitute a nationwide federal tax for local property taxes in each locality on a dollar-for-dollar basis because of the inequities this would create among different states and communities. Any realistic plan of substitution would also require significant changes in taxation at the state level, leading to some increases in statewide property or other taxes. After this chain of events took place, tax burdens would be changed again. The ultimate consequences for individuals at different income levels would depend on precisely how the tax laws of each of the states were modified. Nevertheless, Table 16.5 does give some indication of the initial impact on the relative distribution of tax burdens by income class.

III.

INEQUALITIES

OF STATUS

ONE CAN ARGUE that as a result of industrialization and the ever more elaborate division of labor in modern society, the kind of social inequality that has the greatest impact on the lives of individuals and their families is that connected with economic resources, with income and with various kinds of entitlements to goods and services—the so-called "new property" such as social security, health insurance, paid vacations, and the like. However, membership in status groups continues to be important in American society, though perhaps less important than it was several generations ago. By "status situation," Weber referred to the "typical components of the life fate of men that were determined by a specific positive or negative social estimation of honor." Weber understood that class distinctions are linked in complex ways with status distinctions. Even so, he believed, it was important to look separately at status differentiations and how these affect the lives of individuals.

In American society the two principal kinds of status distinctions that affect the privileges and access to self-realizing possibilities of individuals are racial and (to a lesser extent) ethnic, group membership and sex. Therefore we examine in this Part several sociological studies dealing with racial and sexual inequality in access to resources. We consider something of the attitudes of Whites toward Blacks and of relationships between the racial groups. We also focus on the extent to which there have been important changes in the pattern of inequality of rewards between Whites and Blacks. Turning to sex, we consider first the complex issues posed by different models of sexual equality (in the article by Alice Rossi), and then consider one of the specific problems raised in the recent drive for greater equality for women—the issue of publicly-supported day care. Finally, we look at the other major group oppressed by virtue of "ethnic" difference, the Mexican-American.

215

17. BLACK UNREST IN THE 1960s

THOMAS F. PETTIGREW

Reprinted from Thomas F. Pettigrew, Racially Separate or Together? *(New York: McGraw-Hill, 1971), with permission of McGraw-Hill Book Company. Thomas F. Pettigrew is Professor of Social Psychology at Harvard University. He is a specialist in the social psychology of race relations and has carried out extensive research on the impact of racism on American Blacks and on discriminatory behavior by Whites. He has served as a consultant and director of research studies in connection with numerous civil rights issues and has functioned as a race relations adviser to state and federal governments.*

■ That Blacks in the 1960s should become assertive in their quest for rights long denied them came as a surprise to most social scientists. The conventional wisdom of race relations held that so long as Blacks were making slow but perceptible gains in their situation, the likelihood of vigorous and "inflammatory" pressure on their part was small, particularly in the South. Instead, it was expected that continued pressure from liberal Whites, emphasizing the irrationality of discrimination, would lead to the gradual erosion of Jim Crow attitudes and other kinds of barriers. Instead, younger Blacks in the late 1950s and early 1960s—with Martin Luther King as their preeminent spokesman and involving hundreds of Black college students—seized leadership in the Black civil rights movement. This protest generated considerable national action and then, as protest became more violent in the riots of the mid- and late 1960s, a second round of change was produced in the Black situation in cities of the North and South.

At the same time, once data from the 1960 census became available, celebrations of Black progress in the previous decade became numerous; it was noted, for example, that the average Black family had a higher income than the average White Canadian famliy. Pettigrew takes up this apparent paradox, between the improvement in the Black situation and the rising tide of protest that followed that improvement. He makes use of a central concept in the social-psychological exploration of social change—the concept of relative deprivation—and he shows that over the years, Blacks have consistently been impressed by the gap between where they stand and where comparable White people stand in terms of life chances. The knowledge of an artificial barrier between them and the better life they could expect

as Americans informs, on the one hand, their sense of being unjustly treated and, on the other hand, has consistently contributed to an optimism that somehow, with pressure, the future will be better for them than was the past. According to this view, the events of the 1960s were not remarkable but were rather to be expected. Pettigrew's analysis suggests that Black unrest will persist, though waxing and waning from time to time in public visibility and sharpness of focus, until Blacks enjoy equal status with Whites.

Detailed studies of Black attitudes toward their situation in the 1960s can be found in W. Brink and L. Harris, *The Negro Revolution in America* (New York: Simon & Schuster, 1964), and W. Brink and L. Harris, *Black and White: A Study of Racial Attitudes Today* (New York: Simon & Schuster, 1967). Pettigrew has summarized earlier research on the Black American situation in *A Profile of the Negro American* (New York: Van Nostrand, 1964). A useful collection of readings on the development of Black Americans is Nathan I. Huggins, Martin Kilson, and Daniel M. Fox, eds., *Key Issues in the Afro-American Experience* (New York: Harcourt, Brace, Jovanovich, 1971). The classic survey of race relations in the United States in the 1930s is Gunner Myrdal, *An American Dilemma* (New York: Harper, 1944). A useful collection of articles dealing with the 1950s and early 1960s is Talcott Parsons and Kenneth Clark, *The Negro American* (Boston: Houghton Mifflin, 1966). ■

BLACK AMERICANS HAVE BEEN oppressed for 350 years, first by a unique system of slavery, then by de jure and so-called de facto racial segregation. And they have protested their plight from the very beginning. Yet the question remains why these protests culminated so forcefully and nationally in the sweeping demonstrations of the 1960s. Why did they not burst forth after Reconstruction? Why not during the Great Depression? Why not decades from now? Why the 1960s?

Actually, the protests of the 1960s provide an almost classic case of *relative deprivation* as an explanation for popular uprisings. According to Davies' model for revolution, the characteristic pattern, repeated throughout history, is a relatively long period of objective economic and social development followed by a short period of sharp reversal. The first portion of the cycle is now underway in the United States; the ominous second stage may be near at hand.

Davies' model appears to fit history well because *improving* conditions typically set off four processes which lead to unrest. Thus, economic progress (1) frequently leads to faster improvement for the dominant group or elite than for the subordinate group, (2) typically creates expectations that rise more rapidly than actual changes, (3) generally leads to widespread status inconsistencies, and (4) often causes a broadening of comparative reference groups.

Living standards of Negro Americans have improved dramatically in absolute terms over the past generation. Indeed, relative to previous gains, the past generation has witnessed the most rapid economic and social advances of any generation of Negro Americans. But these advances have typically not closed the gap between standards of living of Whites and Blacks.

Thus, in each interrelated realm—health, employment, business, income, housing, voting, and education—the absolute gains of the 1950s pale when contrasted with current white standards. Numerous spokesmen for the status quo have boasted of the present status of the Negro in glowing international comparisons. Negroes in the United States today, goes one boast, have a consumer buying power comparable to that of similarly populated Canada. And a larger percentage of Negroes, goes another, attends college than residents of the British Isles. But such glittering statements must not blind us to the fact of greatest psychological importance. Negro American standards have their psychological

meaning relative to the standards of other Americans, not of Canadians or the British. The Negro American judges his living standards, his opportunities, indeed, even judges himself, in the only cultural terms he knows—those of the United States and its "people of plenty."

All four of the conditions which set off revolts by improving objective standards were present for Negroes in the United States in the 1960s. First, as was just noted, living conditions of the dominant group are improving more rapidly in a number of realms than living conditions of Negroes. Present discrimination is not necessary to create this situation. Past deprivations handicap many Negroes and deter them from seizing new opportunities: the runner with an initial distance handicap needs more than an equal chance if he is to make a race of it.

Second, the expectations of Negroes have climbed faster than actual changes. Even as early as 1954, the year the Supreme Court ruled against de jure segregation of public schools, these rising expectations became evident. A large probability sample of Americans was asked by Stouffer in 1954: "On the whole, do you think life will be better for you

TABLE 17.1
1954 OPTIMISM FOR THE FUTURE

	Percentage that believe "Life will be better . . . in the next five years"		
	National Negro Sample	National White Sample	White Control Sample*
Total sample	64	61	53
By occupation			
Laborer	63	46	. . . .
Other blue collar	66	62	. . . .
White collar	79	71	. . . .
By education			
Grammar school	58	46	. . . .
High school	72	66	. . . .
College	78	74	. . . .
By region			
South	66	55	. . . .
Non-South	60	64	. . . .

Source: T. F. Pettigrew, *A Profile of the Negro American* (Princeton, N.J.: Van Nostrand, 1964), p. 185.
*The White control sample is equated with the Negro sample in terms of age, sex, occupation, geographical region, and years of education.

or worse in the next few years than it is now?" Table 17.1 shows that, among those with an opinion, 64 percent of the Negro respondents felt life would soon be better, as compared with only 53 percent of a White control sample roughly equivalent to the Negro sample in region of residence, sex, age, years of education, and occupation. Indeed, just as relative-deprivation theory predicts, this heightened optimism of Negroes, relative to that of comparable Whites, was especially marked among the most deprived segments of the Negro population: the greatest relative optimism was expressed by Negroes who were laborers, or had only a grammar school education, or resided in the South.

Cantril provides data from a national survey on his "self-anchoring-ladder" questions for 1959 and 1963. Though the figures for Negroes in Table 17.2 are based on relatively small samples, a number of the results are suggestive. While personal ratings by Negroes are all lower in 1963 than in 1959, note the sizable shift in 1963 between the past and future personal ratings. This trend is even stronger for the 1963 ratings of the United States by Negroes. The sharp alterations of the data for Negroes, in contrast to the stable data for Whites, are partly a function of the larger sizes of the White samples; but the remarkably high hopes of Negroes in 1963 for national progress in the future appear to represent a definite racial difference. In response to open-ended questions about national and personal hopes and fears, Negroes cite far more social goals and aspirations for their nation than Whites. On the personal level, White respondents report more hopes concerning health and family, whereas Negroes report more economic hopes.

Another national survey made by Brink and Harris in 1963 questioned only Black Americans. It asked: "Thinking ahead to five years from now, if you had to say right now, do you feel in [your work situation, your housing accommodations, your pay, being able to get your children educated with White children, being able to eat in any restaurant, or being able to register and vote] you will be better off, worse off, or about the same as you are right now?" Table 17.3 again shows the high aspirations of Negro Americans. Note, too, that only 1 to 3 percent considered a slip backward likely. In response to open-ended queries, many Negroes made it clear that they expected to be better off in five years because of reduced racial discrimination.

Consistent with these expectations, 73 percent of this national Negro sample expected in 1963 that attitudes of Whites toward Negroes would be better in 5 years, and only 2 percent anticipated that they would be worse. Also, 73 percent thought Whites would

TABLE 17.2

1959 AND 1963 MEAN LADDER RATINGS*

"Where do you [does America] stand . . . ?"								
	5 Years Ago		At Present		5 Years From Now		Future-Past Diff.'s	
	1959	1963	1959	1963	1959	1963	1959	1963
Personal								
Negroes	5.9	4.6	5.3	5.2	7.3	6.6	+ 1.4	+ 2.0
Whites	6.0	5.7	6.7	6.3	7.9	7.5	+ 1.9	+ 1.8
National								
Negroes	6.6	5.3	6.3	6.6	7.2	7.7	+ 0.6	+ 2.4
Whites	6.4	6.3	6.7	6.7	7.6	7.3	+ 1.2	+ 1.0

*These ratings can vary from a low of 1 to a high of 10. For a full description of this ingenious technique, see H. Cantril, *The Pattern of Human Concerns* (New Brunswick, N.J.: Rutgers University Press, 1965), p. 43.

TABLE 17.3
1963 NEGRO OPTIMISM FOR THE FUTURE*

| | "... five years from now, do you feel ... you will be ..." | | | | |
	Better Off	Worse Off	About the Same	Not Sure	Total
Pay	67%	2%	14%	17%	100%
Work situation	64%	3%	15%	18%	100%
Housing accommodations	67%	2%	14%	12%	100%
Being able to get children educated with White children	58%	1%	21%	20%	100%
Being able to eat in any restaurant	55%	1%	31%	13%	100%
Being able to register and vote	42%	1%	48%	9%	100%

*Adapted from Brink and Harris, *The Negro Revolution in America* (New York: Simon & Schuster, 1964), p. 238.

accept racial change without violence; 33 percent expected "a lot" of integration in the next 5 years; and 85 percent wanted to own a private house. Though only 23 percent reported that they held white-collar jobs in 1963, 47 percent wanted such jobs and considered themselves qualified. Not surprisingly, then, Brink and Harris find that 51 percent felt in 1963 that "progress on Negro rights" was "too slow."

As uncovered by the analysis of the Coleman Report, a key variable in this process is the Negro's sense of environmental control. Shomer shows that only self-attributed gains lead to higher aspirations. If advances of Negroes in recent decades were perceived as paternalistically "given" by Whites, these advances would presumably have had far less psychological impact than they have had in fact—since they are typically seen as "won" by Negroes whose control over their fate is expanding.

A third consequence of rising standards is an increase in status inconsistency. In one sense, status inconsistency increases by definition as gains in education, employment, and income are made by Negroes. At least in Lenski's and Jackson's procedures, the Negro's racial status in America is regarded as low, and all Negroes of high educational, occupational, or income status are classified as "status inconsistents." And . . . this par-

ticular type of inconsistency—low ascribed status combined with high achieved status— is precisely the pattern of inconsistency, among both Whites and Negroes, that is associated with strong desires for political change.

But status inconsistency among Black Americans is increasing in a more fundamental sense. Census data show that as far back as 1940 educational attainment of Negroes had already exceeded their attainments in employment and income. This form of status inconsistency has increased much further in the past generation. From 1940 to 1960, census data reveal larger percentage gains in years of education for non Whites than for Whites; while over the same years percentage gains for non Whites in occupation and income have not kept pace with the gains for Whites. Though simple "years of education" has different quality meanings for Negroes and Whites, and absolute educational gains at the higher levels of education have been greater for Whites than Negroes, the rising amount of *status* inconsistency between, on the one hand, education and, on the other, occupation and income is still an important characteristic of Negro America.

The fourth product of long-term prosperity and advances is a broadening of comparative reference groups. Studies in the North and South and on Negroes and Whites repeatedly find a more differentiated view of the social stratification system among those of higher status. One has to be reasonably elevated before he can view the entire social terrain. But how have the objective social gains of the past generation altered the referents for Negro Americans? In what senses do White Americans become relevant referents, and under what conditions?

The processes involved in selecting referents are obviously complex. At the extremes of Negro life, White referents can be so strongly employed for evaluation that exaggerated behavior can result. Frazier maintains that a zealous adoption of White upper middle class referents as a positive reference group helps explain some of the exaggerated behavior he describes as characteristic of a segment of the expanding Negro middle class. And Lincoln maintains that a zealous adoption of White Christian referents as a *negative* reference group helps explain some of the anti-White and anti-Christian beliefs and behavior of the Black Muslims. The complexity of the problem is further illustrated by the Black Muslims' successful efforts to inculcate middle class values in its members. Speculations, at least, are possible. It seems reasonably certain that the living conditions and other external attributes of White Americans serve as comparison levels for Black Americans more today than formerly. This is not to imply that White comparisons did not serve an evaluative function previously; but White comparisons are now perceived as the appropriate standards to which Negroes are entitled as American citizens. The anchors of the distribution of American prosperity are less fixed now; and, as the social-comparison experiment by Thornton and Arrowood demonstrates, this shift means that divergent referents are more informative than similar referents.

Note that this subtle shift in the use of levels of Whites as standards for comparison could be occurring without any significant increase in contact as equals between Negroes and White. Indeed . . . data for such

realms as segregation of urban housing suggest that racial separation since 1940 has actually increased. Turner maintains that when evaluations are made using only external attributes of the referent, as in estimating satisfaction or social standing, "taking the role" of the referent is not necessary. The shift does require greater knowledge by Negroes since 1940 of the external attributes of White Americans; and this condition appears to be met through the somewhat higher social positions of many Negroes as well as the explosion in White-oriented mass communication since 1940.

Runciman's distinction between "egoist" and "fraternalist" deprivation, between one's deprived status within the group and the deprived status of the group in the wider society, is useful here. In Table 17.2 the differences between personal and national hopes for the future in the data for Negroes show that fraternalist aspirations are actually higher than egoist aspirations. In other words, Cantril's results suggest that many Negroes in 1963 expected major gains for their group's status in the total American society during the following five years, but they had somewhat more modest expectations for their own rise in status. Clearly, fraternalistic hopes for an improvement in the entire group's status must of necessity employ White Americans as referent; but it may well be that egoist hopes are typically made relative to similar Negro referents within the larger context of the total group's position. Research is obviously needed on these points, and such work could benefit from the use of Runciman's two types of evaluations.

Popular uprisings are not generally started and led by the most objectively deprived. Relative-deprivation theory leads one to predict that relatively upper-status individuals will initiate protests. They are the people elevated enough to judge the discrimination against their group; they are the ones who have received the most gains within the group and have thereby experienced the most severe status inconsistencies. Moreover, upper status individuals are secure enough to hold out hope for a better life—an essential ingredient in any movement for social change. Brinton observes:

The revolutionary movements seem to originate in the discontents of not unprosperous people who feel restraint, cramp, annoyance, rather than downright crushing oppression . . . [They] are not worms turning, not children of despair. These revolutions are born of hope, and their philosophies are formally optimistic.

The sit-ins led by college students provide an excellent illustration of upper status Blacks initiating protest. Matthews and Prothro present data on Negro college students and their participation in sit-ins and other protest demonstrations during the early 1960s. Not only are college students a high status group within the Negro community, but those students who take part have particularly high status. Only one-fourth of the students sampled report personal participation; 85 percent approve of the demonstrations. This active fourth, when compared with other Negro students, are more often from large cities and relatively high income families whose heads hold white-collar jobs. They are more likely to be either juniors or seniors who major in a "prestige" subject (humanities, natural sciences, or social sciences) rather than a practical subject (vocational, teaching, or business administration). Moreover, the activists are more likely to attend a better quality private institution, located in a southern area with a low percentage of Negroes in the population. Activists also differ from the other students in their racial attitudes. While more likely to rate race relations in the South as extremely bad, they nevertheless hold out more hope for change. They *less* often agree that "all White people are prejudiced against Negroes," less often think that half or more of White southerners favor "strict segregation," and less often feel that their home community is worse than the South as a whole. These results are consistent with those of Gore and Rotter, who find that the Negro college students willing to participate in protest possess a greater sense of environment control.

But what of the future? Race relations in the United States, it seems, remain perpetually in a state of crisis. Yet Davies' model predicts that a particularly critical time will occur whenever there is a period of sudden and sharp reversal in the Negro's struggle for full participation in American society. In some ways, 1966 to 1970, years of slowed civil rights activity and progress, suggest that such a time may be near at hand. Much depends on the duration of the war in Vietnam and the domestic decisions made at its close. Recall that some of the nation's most tragic racial conflicts have occurred during wars or just after their close—the so-called draft riots of 1863, the bloody summer of 1919, and the race riots in Detroit, Harlem, and Los Angeles in 1943 are a few examples. This relationship seems to hold true for several reasons: wartime prosperity in jobs and wages, combined with wartime domestic shortages, often raises relative-deprivation levels drastically; the nation's attention becomes so internationally fixed that such domestic concerns as civil rights receive little attention; and at a war's close, there is often an economic recession and too loose a labor market to absorb the veterans who reenter the labor force.

The close of the war in Vietnam need not repeat this sad history; moreover, the forms that protests assume will be significantly shaped by the circumstances of the national situation at the time.

Why Black unrest in the 1960s? The data reviewed . . . support the view that a strong feeling of *relative deprivation* has supplied the basic psychodynamic behind the Negro push for racial change. But it remains to put this theory in the context of competing theories; and we need, too, to raise further questions, such as these: Why was this unrest channeled into urban rioting in the middle and late 1960s? What altered this pattern of mass rioting at the close of the decade?

In their useful compilation of explanations for civil disorders, Masotti and Bowen contend that all the major theories reduce to four basic themes. The first two of these themes center on the individual level, and both were employed in the view just presented. One theme stresses deprivation, both absolute and relative. For it to operate, inequality must be perceived and must be considered unjust. As we have noted, both of these conditions were met by Blacks in the 1960s. The second theme emphasizes high expectations of a restless minority, the so-called want-get ratio. This notion differs from relative deprivation only in that the perceived inequality is a difference between what you have compared with your previously established expectations rather than with a relevant reference group. In real life, of course, this fine theoretical distinction is generally lost; the first two explanations, then, blend to form the theory put forward in this chapter.

The remaining two themes have to do with broader social levels. One focuses attention upon group conflict and struggles for power. It emphasizes sharp social cleavages, rather than social bonds; it therefore applies with special force when two or more significant cleavages correlate highly. For example, the high association in the United States between skin color and social class should according to this theory, create the conditions for an especially severe power conflict. The theory would further predict that as the Negro middle class grows in numbers, the struggle would subside, because the cross-racial ties of mutual class interest would naturally expand. This idea under certain conditions conflicts with predictions based on relative-deprivation theory, and it does not fit with the fact that the Negro middle class has furnished most of the leadership of the drive for change in recent years.

Masotti and Bowen call their fourth theme the "systemic hypothesis." It places civil disorders on a broad canvas and sees them as the logical consequence of a breakdown of consensual norms and the inability or unwillingness of agencies of social control to restore these norms. This systemic explanation points to sweeping social trends in industrialization, urbanization, and modernization, argues that these trends create new classes of citizens with conflicting perceptions and life-styles, and maintains that anomie and alienation are the necessary results of these alterations in the social fabric. This theory, then, would pay special attention to the mass migration of Black Americans out of the rural South since 1915. Indeed, we have already seen how many of these broad societal trends fit with the relative-deprivation explanation, though anomie and alienation do not appear to set in until the high hopes for the future within the system are dashed over an extended period.

Within this broader context, we can now pose questions about the pattern of urban rioting into which Negro unrest spilled. Why urban riots? And why did this pattern seem to shift by the end of the decade?

Masotti and Bowen again provide an important framework for considering these queries. They maintain that riots and rebellion are both civil disorders in that they challenge the civil and political order. Race riots, they insist, are not merely magnified crime or an undirected libidinal release, for neither of these popular explanations explain the directly *racial* targets of these urban disturbances. Yet since both forms are civil disorders, older theories of rebellion should still apply to riots.

But why did Black frustrations in the 1960s culminate in mass urban rioting and not in open rebellion? Masotti and Bowen supply three answers. First, despite rhetoric to the contrary from the New Left, the perceived legitimacy of the *national government* among Black Americans remains high; but the perceived legitimacy of *local* officials is often low. The low esteem in which the urban police are held by Negroes . . . is fundamental to the suspicion in which local officials are held. Second, riots rather than rebellion result when the capacity of the system for force as well as reform is perceived to be high. And, finally, the legacies of history affect forms of protest. The United States has had a long and bloody history of racial rioting, most of it violence by Whites against Negroes; but revolutionary movements have been rare on the American scene since the successful initial one in the 18th century.

This plausible explanation for the pattern of urban riots heightens interest in why the pattern began to break up by 1969-70. Considerations of relative deprivation provide a partial answer. Richard Milhouse Nixon was not the choice of Black Americans in the presidential election of 1968: well over nine-tenths of all Negro voters cast their ballots for Hubert Humphrey, the candidate of the Democratic Party; in fact, Black votes constituted one-fifth of Humphrey's total—the highest percentage they ever comprised of a major presidential candidate's total. Nixon ran on a so-called southern strategy (better termed a segregationist strategy), and, true to his word, behaved accordingly once in the White House. Negro Americans understandably expected little of him or his administration; and they were not disappointed. This has had the effect of lowering Black expectations for short-term racial gains, though several studies in 1970 indicated that long-term personal and group aspirations remained high. Relative-deprivation theory predicts that such a trend would temporarily cool racial protests and disturbances. This is not to argue that Negro Americans were more satisfied during such a time, or that they accepted with equanimity such inevitable results of the southern strategy as the blatant murders of Negroes by the police in Jackson, Mississippi, and Augusta, Georgia, in May of 1970. But it can reasonably be argued that riots are less likely during a period of low expectations combined with fear of national repression against Negroes in general.

Related explanations of the decline in large-scale urban rioting since 1968 emphasize the negative consequences of mass violence to the Black community itself. The victims of the pattern of ghetto rioting from 1965 to 1968 were overwhelmingly Negro. Once a Black area had suffered a destructive riot, it was not rich soil for another. "How many times can you burn down the same building?" is the popular statement of this point. The potency of this idea is suggested by the fact that during the 1960s the same ghetto never endured two major disturbances. Consequently, smaller cities, which had not previously known the agony of widespread violence, tended to be those involved in the comparatively few riots from the summer of 1968 through the remainder of the decade. And to the extent the pattern persists into the 1970s, it will center in smaller cities and in the South, where riots have been less prevalent.

Two possible alternatives for violent expression could replace this pattern. One would involve rioting in predominantly White areas well outside the ghetto. The other would involve avoiding mass participation and focusing instead on types of guerrilla action. But either of these alternatives would surely trigger swift counteraction, quite possibly indiscriminate repression against Black Americans in general. For some years now, the often-voiced fear in the ghetto has been that politicians and police officials motivated by fear would initiate a wave of repression against Black Americans, even to the point of mass internment camps tragically modeled after those for Japanese Americans during World War II. This can hardly be dismissed as collective Black paranoia when officials of Mr. Mitchell's Justice Department themselves hint at such possibilities.

Various patterns of racial violence, as well as other expressions of unrest, will persist in our cities for some time, waxing and waning to reflect both the national scene and local scenes. Yet the pattern of mass urban rioting which swept the nation in the 1960s is not likely to be replicated in the 1970s. In addition to the reasons just cited, there is a popular opinion among Negro Americans that the riots of the past decade served their purpose in "waking up White America," in attracting attention to the true conditions and feelings which exist in the bowels of the ghettos. Most Negroes deplored the riots, yet felt that they "did more good than harm" to the cause of achieving racial justice in America. And the dominant Black opinion, as surveys throughout the country repeatedly show, is that the positive functions of mass rioting have been served and further reenactments would prove largely counterproductive. Even the tough-talking Black Panthers argue for different strategies, especially efforts in coalition with young Whites. Without widespread community willingness to tolerate rioting, the typical mass disturbances of the 1960s would be difficult to mount.

Preventing urban race riots, however, should not and cannot be the chief national goal in American race relations. Affirmative, structural programs directed at the root causes of the unrest are clearly necessary.

18. THE 1960s: DECADE OF PROGRESS FOR BLACKS?

REYNOLDS FARLEY and ALBERT HERMALIN

Reprinted from Demography, *Vol. 9, No. 3, August 1972, pp. 353-367. Reynolds Farley is Professor of Sociology at the University of Michigan. He and Albert Hermalin are Research Associates at the University of Michigan Population Studies Center. Farley is the author of an authoritative study of the demography of Black America,* Growth of the Black Population: A Study of Demographic Trends *(Chicago: Markham, 1970).*

■ In their article, Farley and Hermalin systematically assess the evidence available from 1960 and 1970 census data that bear on the question of the extent to which the absolute and relative position of Black Americans has changed during the decade. Their findings fully support Pettigrew's argument about relative deprivation of Blacks during the decade of the 1960s.

Almost all the indicators Farley and Hermalin examine suggest that Blacks progressed to a significant extent. But almost all of the indicators also show that a large gap persists between Whites and Blacks. In measuring income we find the paradoxical result that because of rapid economic growth, the absolute gap between Whites and Blacks increased, while the relative gap declined somewhat.

The authors observe that the U.S. Black population is large, that 25 million Blacks constitute a population larger than that of some of the major nations of the world. Variability in the situations of Blacks is great, and the overlap between Whites and Blacks on any characteristic of interest is so great that the complexities of describing how Blacks fare relative to Whites are considerable. Why the differences persist is an even more complex question. Nevertheless, it is clear from the data that the time when racial differences in resources will have disappeared is not yet in sight. Given the performance of the past decade and the rate at which the gap between Whites and Blacks is closing, one cannot with any confidence predict that there will be equality between Whites and Blacks even by the end of the century, unless marked changes occur in the public policies that currently maintain these differences.

The consequences of the patterns of inequality that Farley and Hermalin discuss have been documented over the years by numerous sociological studies. One of the earliest such studies is that by a great Black sociologist, W. E. B. DuBois, *The Philadelphia Negro: A Social Study* (New York: Schocken Books, 1967). The northern big city ghetto of the 1930s is described in a classic study by St. Clair Drake and Horace Cayton, *Black Metropolis* (New York: Harper & Row, 1962). Studies of various urban ghettoes in the 1960s are found in Kenneth B. Clark, *Dark Ghetto* (New York: Harper Row, 1965); Elliot Liebow, *Tally's Corner* (Boston: Little, Brown, 1967); Ulf Hannerz, *Soulside: Inquiries into Ghetto Culture and Community* (New York: Columbia University Press, 1970); and Lee Rainwater, *Behind Ghetto Walls* (Chicago: Aldine, 1970). ■

THIRTY YEARS AGO Gunnar Myrdal argued that the most important changes for Blacks in this country would be changes in the values and beliefs of Whites. He contended that Blacks would make progress if and only if Whites accepted Blacks as equals and treated them in accord with democratic ideals. . . .

If the attitudes of Whites have changed, we would anticipate reductions in racial differences on a number of dimensions. In this paper we examine in some detail racial differentiation in income, occupation, and education, focusing on trends during the 1960s. . . . The analysis here is based on annual publications of the Bureau of the Census and decennial census material. Whenever possible, data for Negro and White populations have been used, but for some of the earlier dates statistics are available only for the White and non-White populations. In 1960, 94 percent of the non-White population identified themselves as Blacks.

INCOME TRENDS

FAMILY INCOME

Income is a crucial determinant of one's lifestyle and living arrangements; so we look first at change in income. The 1960s were a prosperous period, and most measures of income show gains during this period. For instance, median family income (before taxes) in the United States rose from $5,400 in 1959 to $9,400 in 1969. A portion of this increase represents inflation, and to eliminate this factor we express income trends in terms of the purchasing power of the dollar in 1969. Controlling for inflation, we still find that median family income rose between 1959 and 1969, from $6,800 to $9,400. This represents a real increase in purchasing power and means that families are able to buy more goods and services than they were a decade ago.

Rises in family income were greater among Blacks than among Whites. Median family income among Whites rose about 25 percent, while that of Blacks went up 40 percent, and as an outcome, the ratio of non-White to White income rose. These trends are illustrated in Table 18.1, which shows the median income of families by color, the ratio of median incomes, and two other measures of the similarity or equality of income distributions, delta and the Gini index. The ratio of median incomes is shown as dollars of Negro or non-White income per $100 of White income. Delta, or the index of dissimilarity, is useful for comparing two groups which are distributed among categories such as income levels. Suppose there were no racial difference in income. Then if 10 percent of all Whites were in a specific income class, we would expect that 10 percent of the Blacks would be in the identical class. If this were the case for every income category, delta would equal zero, indicating no racial difference in income distributions. If, on the other hand, all Blacks were concentrated at certain income levels and Whites at others, delta would equal 100, implying no overlap in the distribution of Whites and Blacks by income. This index ranges from 0 to 100 and high values indicate racial differentiation.

The Gini index is a Lorenz curve measure which has been widely used to assess inequalities in the distribution of income. Its range is from —1.0 through 0.0 to +1.0 or, as used here, from —100 to +100. A Gini index of +100 indicates that there is no overlap of the income distributions of the two races and that *all Whites* have higher incomes than *any Blacks*. A value of 0 indicates complete overlap and no racial differentiation in income, while a value of —100 means there is no overlap, and *all Blacks* are at higher income levels than *any Whites*.

Turning once again to Table 18.1, gain in Black income relative to that of Whites appears quite dramatic during the 1960s com-

TABLE 18.1
INCOME OF WHITE AND NON-WHITE FAMILIES, IN 1969 DOLLARS, AND MEASURES OF INCOME EQUALITY

Year	Median Income			Measures of Income Equality	
	White families	Non-White families	Ratio of Non-White to White	Delta*	Gini*
1947	$5194	$2660	51	36	45
1959	7106	3661	52	35	45
1961	7361	3913	53	33	41
1963	7841	4165	53	33	42
1965	8424	4666	55	33	40
1967	9086	5641	62	28	35
1969	9794	6191	63	27	34

*Delta and Gini indexes computed from current dollar distributions using 10 categories.
Source: U.S. Bureau of the Census, Current Population Reports, Series P-60, no. 75 (12-14-70), Table 8.

TABLE 18.2

INCOME OF WHITE AND NEGRO FAMILIES, IN 1969 DOLLARS, BY TYPE OF FAMILY AND AGE OF HEAD

Family type and age of head	Income in 1959					Income in 1969				
	Median income			Measures of income equality		Median income			Measures of income equality	
	White families	Non-White families	Ratio of Non-White to White	Delta*	Gini*	White families	Negro families	Ratio of Negro to White	Delta*	Gini*
Husband-wife families										
Head < 35	$7150	$4564	64	33	42	$ 8677	$7100	82	14	18
35-44	8657	5411	63	36	45	11691	8785	75	25	33
45-64	8435	4659	55	34	45	11515	7356	64	31	38
65+	4011	2317	58	25	32	4827	3154	65	21	31
Total	7672	4577	60	33	41	10241	7329	72	23	29
Families with female heads										
Head < 35	2599	1838	71	18	18	3171	2842	90	13	13
35-44	4116	2376	58	26	29	5450	3951	72	25	20
45-64	5415	2477	46	32	40	6748	3597	53	31	41
65+	4638	2052	44	32	40	5699	2511	44	31	39
Total	4457	2184	49	30	37	5500	3341	61	25	31

*Delta and Gini indexes computed from current dollar distributions using 10 categories.
Source: U.S. Bureau of the Census, Census of Population: 1960, PC(1)-1D, Table 224; Current Population Reports Series P-60, no. 75 (December 14, 1970), Table 17.

pared to the earlier period, as measured by the delta or Gini indexes or the ratio of non-White to White income. For each of these measures, the gain in the 4-year period from 1965 to 1969 was greater than that for the 18-year span from 1947 to 1965. (Comparable data are not available prior to 1947, so longer trends on these measures cannot be computed.) At the same time, it must be noted that Black income in 1969 was lower than that of Whites 10 years earlier, and that the absolute dollar gap between the two races has been quite constant at about $3,500 throughout the 1960s.

Family income varies systematically depending upon who heads the family and his or her age. To further analyze recent trends, we show, in Table 18.2, changes in family income by type of family and age of head. Husband-wife families, of course, include a married couple both of whom may be working. The woman in families with a female head has been widowed or divorced, lives apart from her spouse, or, in a few cases, has never been married.

There were increases in real purchasing power among both types of families and for every age group of heads. The measures of racial differentiation imply that the income distributions of White and Black families have become more alike. If we look at tabulations by age of head, we see that the most dramatic relative gains were made by Black families with heads in the younger age categories. By 1970, Black husband-wife families with heads under 35 had median incomes 82 percent as great as similar White families. Black families headed by a woman under 35 had incomes 90 percent as great as similar White families. Among families with older heads, there was some diminution of the racial difference, although it was quite small. As a result, black families of each type were more differentiated by age in the extent to which they approached White family income in 1969 than in 1959.

Problems of deprivation must be particularly acute in Black families headed by women. These families had a median income in 1969 of $3,300 and about one-third of them received less than $2,500. They included an average of 2 children under 18, while White female-headed families included an average of 1 child. Since 1960, the number of Negro families headed by a woman has grown more rapidly than the number of husband-wife families; and by 1970, female-headed families accounted for 28 percent of all Black families.

The regional data in Table 18.3 show that the ratio of Black to White family income increased most rapidly in the South from 1959 to 1969, although it was lower there than in the other sections of the country. This regional pattern of change in family income differs somewhat from that found in examining the regional trend in personal income of males and females shown in Tables 18.4 and 18.6. A number of factors are operating to account for these differences. First, the income of Black men relative to that of Whites increased more in the South than in the other

TABLE 18.3

RATIO OF NEGRO TO WHITE FAMILY MEDIAN INCOME BY REGION, 1959 AND 1969 AND PROPORTION OF FEMALE HEADED FAMILIES, BY RACE AND REGION, 1960 AND 1970

Region	Ratio of Negro Family Median Income to that of Whites		Proportion of Families Headed by Females			
			Negro		Whites	
	1959	1969	1960	1970	1960	1970
Northeast	69	67	24%	32%	9%	10%
North Central	72	76	21	27	7	8
South	46	57	22	27	8	9
West	70	75	20	27	8	9

Source: U.S. Bureau of the Census, Census of Population: 1960, PC(1)-1D, Tables 247,266; PC(2)-1C, Table 14; Census of Population: 1970, PC(1)-B1, Table 58; Current Population Reports, Series P-60, no. 75, Table 37.

regions, as shown in Table 18.4. Since male income is the predominant factor in family income, the regional pattern in Table 18.3 more closely resembles the racial pattern of male income than of female. A second change worth noting is the differential rate of growth by region of female-headed families. The proportion of Black families headed by women increased in every region, a factor which limited gains in average family income since female-headed families report smaller incomes than families headed by a man (see Table 18.2). The increase in the proportion of Black female-headed families was lowest in the South, as shown in Table 18.3, and this also contributes to the more rapid improvement in average Negro family income in that region.

INCOME OF PERSONS: MEN

In this section the focus is on racial differences in personal—not family—incomes in 1959 and 1969. Table 18.4 presents the median income for men of each race and measures of income equality and similarity for a number of characteristics—age, region of residence, occupation, and education— known to be associated with income differentials.

Between 1959 and 1969, the median income of each group of men rose, and with few exceptions the increases were greater for Blacks than for Whites. We can be certain that it was not just young Blacks, Blacks outside the South, those with college educations, or those with professional jobs who improved their economic position. Rather purchasing power rose and racial differentiation in income declined among almost all groups.

There are differences in the relative rates of improvements. If we look at age data, we observe that the largest reductions in racial differentials occurred among the youngest groups. Black men 20 to 24 in 1970 had median incomes 91 percent as large as White men in the same age span. At the other end of the distribution, there is no evidence that the racial gap diminished among men 65 and over.

We can make an abbreviated cohort analysis from data in Table 18.4. Men 25 to 34 in 1960—when the information concerning 1959 income was obtained—were 35 to 44 in 1970. Similarly, we have two readings on the cohorts of men who were 35 to 44 and 45 to 54 in 1960. When we compare the same cohorts with regard to income in 1959 and 1969, we observe very small relative improvements for Blacks. In most cases Black and White men had similar percentage increases in income, and the measures of income distribution declined very little.

This analysis suggests that a primary reason why Black men improved their income in the 1960s was that young men entering the labor market obtained incomes more nearly equal those of young White men. Apparently, even during the prosperous 1960s, there was not much relative improvement in income for Black men who were 25 and over in 1960.

We wondered if the relative improvements in income experienced by Black men during the 1960s were similar to improvements experienced by Black men during the 1950s. To explore this matter, we calculated ratios of median incomes for the youthful age groups for the three most recent census years, as shown in Table 18.5. (The income figures used are for the year preceding the date shown.)

These ratios indicate that during the 1950s, young Black males did not gain on young Whites. However, between 1960 and 1970, the ratio of non-White to White income rose, and this implies that the 1960s differed from the previous decade in terms of the progress made by Blacks who were entering the labor force.

During the 1960s racial differences in the income of men decreased in all regions. The South remains distinctive because of its low income level and the very large racial differences in income. Incomes went up at all educational attainment levels, and racial differences diminished. In both years, the racial differentiation in income was greater among men with extensive educations than among men who had only grammar school

TABLE 18.4

INCOME OF WHITE AND NEGRO MALES, IN 1969 DOLLARS, BY AGE, REGION, EDUCATION, AND OCCUPATION, 1959 AND 1969*

Selected Characteristics	Income in 1959					Income in 1969				
	Median income			Measures of income equality		Median income			Measures of income equality	
	White men	Non-White men	Ratio of Non-White to White	Delta§	Gini§	White men	Negro men	Ratio of Negro to White	Delta§	Gini§
Age										
20-24	$3408	$2183	64	23	29	$3822	$3466	91	8	7
25-34	6349	3667	58	38	49	8311	5558	67	34	44
35-44	7156	4050	57	41	53	9399	5810	62	36	49
45-54	6708	3543	53	39	51	9001	5117	57	40	52
55-64	5797	2833	49	35	46	7576	4263	56	34	41
65+	2307	1213	53	26	34	2941	1491	51	32	42
Total†	5464	2919	53	30	38	6765	3935	58	26	32
Region‡ (for men 14 and over)										
Northeast	5824	4190	72	27	30	7055	5339	76	19	22
North Central	5701	4369	77	21	23	7133	5907	83	20	17
South	4440	2070	47	35	42	5841	3133	54	32	37
West	6013	4277	71	24	26	7255	5312	73	19	20

Education (for men 25 and over)

Elementary < 8	3422	2300	67	18	24		3613	2973	82	14	16
8	5031	3667	73	20	24	n.a.	5460	4293	79	17	18
High school 1-3	6313	4120	65	31	41		7309	5222	71	25	31
4	6972	4713	68	34	43		8631	6144	71	30	39
College 1-3	7682	5089	66	33	44		9575	7051	74	30	35
4	9791	6150	63	35	43		12437	8567	69	30	35

Occupation (for year-round, full-time workers only)

Professionals	8952	5254	59	n.a.	11860	8606	73	n.a.
Managers	8842	4725	53		11157	6598	59	
Clerical	5602	5380	96		8032	7263	90	
Craftsmen	6660	4498	68		8905	6488	73	
Operatives	6262	4485	72		7525	5824	77	
Service	5401	3515	65		6671	4865	73	
Laborers	5448	3893	71		6278	5328	85	

*Data refer to men reporting income in 1959 or 1969. Median income figures shown in 1969 dollars.
†Includes some men under 20 who report income.
‡Data for regions in 1960 refer to Negroes.
§Delta and Gini indexes computed from current dollar distributions using 10 categories.
Source: U.S. Bureau of the Census, Census of Population: 1960 PC(1)-1D, Tables 219 and 262; PC(2)-5B, Table 7; 1960 Census of Population and Housing, One in One Thousand Sample of the Population; Current Population Reports, Series P-60, no. 75, Tables 45, 47, 50, and 59.

TABLE 18.5
RATIO OF MEDIAN INCOME OF NON-WHITE
MEN TO WHITE MEN, FOR SELECTED AGES,
1950, 1960, AND 1970*

| Year | Ratio of non-White male income per $100 White male income | | |
	Total males	Males 20-24	Males 25-34
1950	52	65	56
1960	53	64	58
1970	58	91	67

*Data for 1970 refer to Blacks.
Source: U.S. Bureau of the Census, Census of Population:
1950, P-C1, Table 139; Census of Population, 1960, PC(1)-
1D, Table 218; Current Population Reports, Series P-60,
no. 75, Table 45.

educations. This trend has accentuated from 1959 to 1969, as measured by the ratio of Black to White income.

Despite the improvements in income, racial differences remain, and Black incomes lag far behind those of White men. The figures in Table 18.4 present income statistics for 23 different groupings of men. In 20 of the 23 groups, the median income of Blacks in 1969 was less than the median income of Whites a decade earlier.

INCOME OF PERSONS: WOMEN

Table 18.6 presents income information for women classified by their age, educational attainment, and region of residence. Among women, as among men, incomes rose during the 1960s, and racial differences diminished. These trends were operative for all age groups, at all educational attainment levels, and in each region.

There are several important sexual differences in income trends. First, the gains in income by Black women, relative to White women, seem more pervasive and extensive than those of Black men. Median incomes rose 60 percent for Black women, only 35 percent for Black men. If we perform a cohort analysis, we find that Black women who were 25 and over in 1960 gained on their White peers, but this was generally not the case among Black men.

Second, we find that by 1970 the median income of several groups of Black women exceeded that of comparable White women, and the Gini indexes demonstrate that Black women were concentrated at higher income levels. In all regions except the South, the median incomes were higher for Black than for White women. This was also the case among women who had completed secondary school. For instance, among college educated women, the median income of Blacks was 20 percent greater than that of Whites in 1969.

One might speculate that this occurs because Black women work more hours per week or weeks per year. We do not have data which would permit an adequate test of this hypothesis. Nevertheless, at the aggregate level, there seem to be only small racial differences in the time women spend at work. In 1969, for example, 39 percent of the non-White and 41 percent of the White women in the labor force worked full time for at least 50 weeks. In 1959, there was a similarly small difference in the number of hours or weeks worked.

Two factors may account for the higher incomes of Black women. Labor force participation rates imply that Black women work for a greater proportion of their lives than White women. It is possible that Black women often have greater seniority and experience than White women of a similar age. Second, since their husbands earn relatively little, Black women may seek the most lucrative jobs available. White women may feel less need for income, and when they seek jobs they may consider factors such as the place of employment or timing of the working day.

INCOME AND EDUCATION

Many discussions of contemporary racial inequalities point out that Blacks with a given education or holding a specific job receive lower incomes than Whites with similar occupations or educations. The nature of this inequality can be gauged, in part, from the data already presented in Table 18.4. In 1960, Black men with a college education had a median income lower than that of White

TABLE 18.6

INCOME OF WHITE AND NEGRO FEMALES, IN 1969 DOLLARS, BY AGE, REGION, AND EDUCATIONAL ATTAINMENT, 1959 AND 1969*

Selected characteristics	Income in 1959					Income in 1969				
	Median income			Measures of income equality		Median income			Measures of income equality	
	White females	Non-Whites females	Ratio of Non-White to White	Delta§	Gini§	White females	Negro females	Ratio of Negro to White	Delta§	Gini§
Age										
20-24	$2286	$1136	50	24	29	$2629	$2031	77	12	14
25-34	2522	1631	65	17	19	2985	3024	101	15	—1
35-44	2765	1646	60	20	24	3303	2862	87	13	5
45-54	2986	1273	43	30	36	3740	2256	60	21	24
55-64	2201	1042	47	27	33	2990	1493	50	23	28
65+	1009	783	78	18	19	1432	1050	73	22	28
Total†	1902	1159	61	17	20	2182	1840	84	9	9
Region‡ (for women 14 and over)										
Northeast	2202	2172	99	13	4	2422	2993	124	13	—6
North Central	1755	1707	97	10	4	1969	2322	118	9	—4
South	1659	922	56	25	29	2147	1327	62	18	20
West	2031	1944	96	11	5	2215	2481	112	10	—6
Education (for women 25 and over)										
Elementary 8	1081	914	85	11	13	1303	1195	92	5	7
8	1435	1222	85	9	9	1688	1320	78	12	13
High school 1-3	2131	1506	71	16	18	2355	2268	96	10	5
4	2809	2182	78	12	13	3234	3257	101	12	—2
College 1-3	3060	2729	89	9	6	3427	4247	124	12	—10
4	4745	4625	97	19	1	5707	6747	118	23	—16

*Data refer to persons who reported income in 1959 or 1969. Median income figures shown in 1969 dollars.
†Includes some income recipients under age 20.
‡Data for regions in 1960 refer to Negroes.
§Delta and Gini indexes computed from current dollar distributions using 10 categories.
Source: See Table 4.

males with one to three years of high school. Even after the progress of the 1960s, a college educated Black man had a lower median income than a White secondary school graduate in 1969. These differences do not exist between Black and White females, since their incomes for the identical educational level are much more nearly equal, as reported in Table 18.6.

OCCUPATIONS AND EMPLOYMENT

OCCUPATIONS OF EMPLOYED WORKERS

Discussions of the manner in which people earn their livelihood can be focused around, first, the occupations pursued by workers and, second, the labor force status of adults. In this paper we will analyze occupational trends. Table 18.7 shows the distribution of employed men and women at dates between 1950 and 1970. Cautious interpretations of these data are appropriate since they are drawn from two different sources. The 1950 and 1960 data were gathered by decennial censuses, while the more recent figures come from the Census Bureau's Current Population Survey, a monthly sample of 50,000 households.

Considering males first, the delta index comparing the occupational distributions of Whites and non-Whites shows that there were decreasing racial differences in the 1960-70 decade as contrasted with practically no change in the previous decade. More specifically, the relative gains for Blacks appear to have occurred since 1966, and the change since then far exceeds that of the prior 16 years. From 1966 to 1970, the White occupational distribution has remained almost constant, while among Blacks a gradual upgrading is in evidence. Before 1966, a trend toward higher status occupations was in evidence for Whites and Blacks with little consequent change in the degree of racial differentiation.

A look at recent changes in the *number* of men employed at white-collar jobs or as craftsmen (data not shown in this paper) reveals much greater percentage increases for non-Whites than for Whites. At several of the higher occupational levels, Black males were employed in large numbers for the first time during the 1960s. Despite this progress, large racial differences in occupational structure remain. Only 13 percent of the Black men are professional or managerial workers compared to 30 percent among Whites; 17 percent of Blacks, in contrast to 6 percent of Whites, work as laborers.

Substantial changes have occurred in the occupational distribution of non-White women in the last 20 years. In 1950, over half of the employed non-White females worked as domestic help or on farms. This proportion declined, and presently fewer than 20 percent of the non White women hold such jobs. There have been sharp rises, during the 1960s, in the proportion of non-White women working at professional, clerical, and service jobs.

In an effort to understand what happened during the 1960s, we compared the 1960 and 1970 occupational distributions of women. We found that there was very little change in the distribution of Whites, but among non Whites there was a substantial shift during the decade. The fastest growing occupations were the more prestigious ones and, as a result, the racial difference in occupations of women decreased. The delta index, comparing Black and White women on occupational distributions, shows that, unlike the male situation, growing similarity between the races was not confined to the 1966-70 period. Some diminution of racial differences is evident from 1950 to 1960; the change became more rapid during the 1960s and roughly proportional across the decade.

EDUCATIONAL ATTAINMENT

During the 1960s, the educational attainment of the adult population increased. Among Black men, for example, the rise in median school years completed was from 7.9 to 9.8, while among Whites, the change was from 10.6 to 12.2 years. Similar increases

TABLE 18.7
OCCUPATION OF EMPLOYED PERSONS BY RACE AND SEX, 1950-1970*

Occupation	Non-Whites					Whites				
	1950	1960	1966	1968	1970	1950	1960	1966	1968	1970
Males										
Total percent	100	100	100	100	100	100	100	100	100	100
Prof., managerial	4	5	9	10	13	20	23	28	29	30
Clerical, sales	4	7	8	9	9	14	15	13	13	13
Craftsmen	8	11	11	13	14	20	22	20	21	21
Operatives, service	36	43	44	43	41	25	26	26	25	25
Laborers	24	22	20	18	17	7	6	6	6	6
Farmers, farm labor	24	12	8	7	6	14	8	7	6	5
Delta comparing occupations of Whites and non-Whites†	37	38	36	33	31					
Females										
Total percent	100	100	100	100	100	100	100	100	100	100
Prof., managerial	7	9	10	12	13	18	19	20	20	20
Clerical, sales	5	10	16	19	22	40	44	44	44	44
Craftsmen	1	1	1	1	1	2	1	1	1	1
Operatives, service	34	36	41	41	44	32	30	29	29	29
Pvt. household workers	42	39	28	24	18	4	4	4	4	4
Laborers	2	1	1	1	1	1	·	·	·	·
Farmers, farm labor	9	4	3	2	1	3	2	2	2	2
Delta comparing occupations of Whites and non-Whites†	53	47	38	33	30					

*Figures for 1950 and 1960 refer to the week preceding the census enumeration. Data for other years refer to April of each year.

†These indexes are computed from a detailed distribution of 11 occupational categories.

Source: Daniel O. Price, Characteristics of the Negro Population (Washington: Government Printing Office, 1969) Table IV-3; U.S. Bureau of Labor Statistics, Employment and Earnings, vol. 13, no. 11 (May 1967), Table A-17; vol. 14, no. 11 (May 1968), Table A-17; vol. 16, no. 11 (May 1970), Table A-19; U.S. Bureau of the Census, Census of Population: 1960, PC(1)-1C, Table 88.

are evident for the female population. This occurred primarily because young people are remaining in school longer, reflecting the secular trend toward more education. In this section we report on the number of school years completed. We note at the outset that this may not be a satisfactory indicator of intellectual achievement. Several studies, for example, suggest that when Blacks and Whites who have completed the identical number of school years are compared, Blacks tend to score lower on certain standardized tests.

Table 18.8 shows the median educational attainment in 1960 and 1970 for different age groups and two measures of educational equality—Gini and delta. For most of the age groups, attainment was greater in 1970 than in 1960; and the values of the delta and Gini indexes declined, meaning that the White and Black educational distributions became more similar.

Perhaps more interesting are the cohort changes which can be discerned by looking at different age groups. For instance, no more than 15 to 20 percent of the Black men who were teenagers in the 1920s completed secondary school, and their median attainment was about eight years. They lagged very far behind their White age peers in attainment. Among Black males who were teenagers in the 1960s, over 60 percent completed secondary school, and their median attainment exceeded 12 years.

Reading down the columns of delta or Gini indexes in Table 18.8, one generally finds progressively larger values. Over time then the increases in attainment have been greater among Blacks than among Whites; and, as a result, racial differences in educational attainment are smaller among the young than among the old. This indicates that the 1960s were not unique; rather there has been a long-run trend toward smaller racial differentiation in attainment.

Traditionally, Black women have completed more years of schooling than Black men, while among Whites, the sexual difference in education has been much smaller. Some changes appear to be occurring, and

the median education of Black males and Females has become approximately equal. However, the proportion who are high school or college graduates remains higher among young Black women than among men.

Even though racial differences in attainment are smaller now than they used to be, it is not obvious that they will disappear in the near future. On the one hand, if racial differences in attainment among young people continue to be small, the overall racial difference will diminish, because young people will be replacing older cohorts in which the racial differences were much greater. On the other hand, there are still substantial racial differences in enrollment rates and, hence, in the attainment of young persons. Table 18.8 shows that among people 20 to 24 in 1970, the proportion who graduated from high school was 15 or 20 percentage points greater for Whites than for Negroes.

When enrollment rates are scrutinized more carefully, we observe sharp increases, from 1960 to 1970, in the proportion of Blacks 18 to 21 attending school. By 1970 about one-quarter of the Blacks of college age were enrolled in colleges and universities. This is approximately the proportion of the same age range of Whites who were enrolled in colleges in 1960.

Among Whites, increases in enrollment at ages 18 to 21 were as great as among Blacks, while at ages 22 and over, the increases were sharper among Whites. These changes in enrollment suggest that racial differences through the completion of high school are being reduced but are not yet eliminated. However, at college ages racial differences in enrollment seem to be growing because of the recent jump in the enrollment rate of Whites. There will continue to be racial differences in attainment, and the proportion having a college education is likely to be much greater among Whites than Blacks.

CONCLUSION

The data presented in this paper touch upon a number of different aspects of race

TABLE 18.8

INDICATORS OF EDUCATIONAL ATTAINMENT AND MEASURES OF EDUCATIONAL EQUALITY BY AGE, SEX, AND COLOR, 1960 AND 1970

Sex and age	1960						1970					
	Percent HS graduate		Median years completed		Measures of educ. equality		Percent HS graduate		Median years completed		Measures of educ. equality	
	White	Non-White	White	Non-White	Delta†	Gini†	White	Non-White	White	Non-White	Delta†	Gini†
Males												
20-24	65%	39%	12.4	10.9	25	32	83%	62%	12.8	12.3	22	30
25-29	63	36	12.4	10.5	26	33	79	54	12.7	12.1	25	34
30-34	56	30	12.2	9.7	25	35	74	43	12.6	11.4	33	38
35-44	53	24	12.1	8.6	29	41	66	39	12.5	10.7	27	34
45-54	38	14	10.3	7.1	38	47	60	29	12.3	9.1	31	40
55-64	26	9	8.7	5.8	39	47	44	18	10.9	7.6	36	42
65+	17	7	8.2	4.4	37	43	27	8	8.5	4.0	45	52
Total*	41	20	10.6	7.9	30	36	57	32	12.2	9.8	28	33
Females												
20-24	68	45	12.7	11.5	24	26	83	67	12.7	12.3	15	21
25-29	65	41	12.3	11.1	24	27	76	58	12.5	12.2	19	20
30-34	61	35	12.3	10.5	26	30	74	56	12.5	12.1	18	22
35-44	56	27	12.2	9.2	30	37	67	44	12.4	11.4	24	26
45-54	53	16	10.8	8.0	34	43	63	29	12.3	9.4	34	39
55-64	31	11	9.0	6.7	37	43	48	16	11.6	8.1	35	46
65+	22	7	8.5	5.1	39	45	32	10	8.8	6.0	40	44
Total*	44	23	11.0	8.5	26	32	58	34	12.2	10.3	22	27

*Total refers to population age 25 and over.
†Delta and Gini indexes calculated from distributions showing seven educational attainment categories.
Source: U.S. Bureau of the Census of Population: 1960, PC(1)-1D, Table 173; Current Population Reports, Series P-20, no. 207 (November 30, 1970), Table 1.

relations, some quite directly and others tangentially. We structure this summary and conclusion in terms of a number of questions and answers, starting with those which can be answered quite directly and proceeding to others which, we feel, can be discussed only speculatively and generally.

1. HAVE BLACKS MADE SOCIAL AND ECONOMIC PROGRESS DURING THE 1960s?

The answer here, on the basis of our data, is unambiguously yes. Poverty was substantially reduced among Blacks between 1959 and 1969, and on a number of key socioeconomic characteristics, such as income, occupation, and education there was a significant upward shift of Blacks. In each case, differentials between Whites and Blacks narrowed. A diminution of racial differences was evident in most demographic groups, but progress was more rapid for some Blacks than for others. In particular, gains for Black females appeared more substantial than for Black males; young Blacks gained more rapidly than the old.

2. HAS PROGRESS DURING THE 1960s BEEN MORE RAPID THAN PREVIOUSLY?

With some qualification, the answer would seem to be yes. In a number of instances we have noted that gains from 1960 to 1970 far exceeded those of the previous decade. Information over longer time periods is not readily available; so we cannot determine whether the 1960s represent a significant shift to a level of more rapid progress. Also, rates of progress will depend on the precise time periods chosen; it is likely that in certain past time periods, probably during World War II, progress among Blacks was as rapid as that we have noted for the 1960s. With these reservations in mind, however, it does appear that certain important racial differences narrowed notably during the past decade.

3. DOES THE PROGRESS OF THE 1960s SIGNIFY AN END TO RACIAL SOCIOECONOMIC DIFFERENTIATION IN THE NEAR FUTURE?

Though the progress of the sixties appears rapid in a number of respects, it does not, in our opinion, presage a shortrun end to racial differences in income, occupation, or education. Overall differences between Blacks and Whites, particularly among males, in 1970 were still substantial, and, on a number of measures, Blacks in 1970 were still behind the status that Whites reached 10 years earlier.

The progress among the young is noteworthy in a number of respects: progress here appeared rapid in comparison to previous decades, and differentials between races were relatively small for this age group. As this cohort ages, one may expect differentials at the older ages to diminish from those we now observe; furthermore, the children of these younger Blacks can be expected to increasingly show higher status distributions on income, education, and occupation, on the basis of what we know about the influence of parental education and occupation. . . . But it must be noted that these developments, however encouraging they may be, are implicitly rather long range—of a generation or two in length. Furthermore, the differentials in higher education enrollment and attainment among the young further lengthen the time horizon for achieving racial equality.

4. DO THE TRENDS OF THE 1960s IMPLY THAT OUR SOCIETY IS BECOMING RACIALLY INTEGRATED?

Improvements in the social and economic status of Negroes do not necessarily mean that racial integration is occurring. It is possible for Black incomes to rise, occupations to be upgraded, and educational attainment to advance without there being any racial integration of workshops or offices, in the neighborhood or in schools. In brief, economic improvements and racial integration are different dimensions of race relations.

Although the Kerner Commission study warned that we were becoming a polarized society, few empirical studies of racial integration have been conducted in recent years. Several investigations of racial integration in neighborhoods indicate that there was no decline in segregation during the early 1960s. Another study discovered that the public schools of this nation's largest cities in 1967 were highly segregated, the segregation level being similar to that of residential areas. Preliminary results from the census of 1970 indicate a continued outmigration of Whites from numerous central cities while their suburban rings contain relatively few Blacks.

Our tables indicating racial differences in income and occupation suggest that Blacks made particularly great advances after 1966. For this reason, it is possible that a detailed study of residential segregation carried out at present would show some increase in integration as compared to the early 1960s. On the other hand, it may be that the conditions for such a change are only now taking place, as growing numbers of Whites are coming into contact with fellow employees who are Black. One possibility is that as Whites have contact with Blacks as peers on the job, their attitudes may be altered and barriers to neighborhood integration may lessen. This is in keeping with Stouffer's findings regarding attitude change. If this is the case, future analyses may show declines in neighborhood and school segregation.

5. WHAT IMPLICATIONS DO THESE TRENDS HAVE FOR GOVERNMENTAL POLICY?

To answer this question there must be an accurate measurement of exactly what role governmental policies played in the changes we have described. Unfortunately, we cannot provide this analysis. We can identify three different views of the impact of federal policies during the 1960s.

One can point to a cluster of governmental actions that may have contributed to Black socioeconomic gains in the 1960s, among them civil rights legislation; governmental prodding of employers, especially those under contract for goods and services; and federal, state, and local employment of Blacks. With regard to the latter factor, Price reports that increasing governmental employment was one of the major reasons why the occupational distribution of Blacks was upgraded prior to 1960, and this trend may have continued in the past decade. Insofar as one gives salience to such factors, governmental policy would be viewed as a direct contributor to Black socioeconomic advance.

An opposing view would contend that federal activities, including the civil rights legislation, merely reflect changing attitudes. Rather than being an instigating factor, the government's policies may be trailing behind the actions of employers, administrators, and local officials. Myrdal detected a growing awareness, on the part of Whites, that Blacks were not treated in consistency with our fundamental principles. Such an awareness may have increased in the 1960s and may explain some of the progress which we have described.

A third view would be that federal economic policies rather than civil rights actions are the key variable. We have alluded to several investigations which demonstrate that Blacks began to "catch up" with Whites during World War II. Studies of labor force trends indicate that during the Korean war, Black workers were employed at rates approaching those of Whites; but during the recession of the late 1950s and early 1960s, the racial difference grew wider. The late 1960s were a booming period with rapid expansion of employment, sharp increases in the revenues received by local governments, and a high rate of new constructions of both homes and buildings. During this period, young people—both Black and White—found growing educational and social service facilities and a very favorable job market. In brief, the government's decision to simultaneously maintain a burgeoning domestic economy and dramatically expand military activities in Southeast Asia may account for the progress made by Negroes.

A further assessment of federal policies is needed to establish their role in effecting the changes of the 1960s and for developing future programs. With regard to future policy, it is our opinion that such programs should reflect recent progress as well as existing needs; mere continuation of older programs may not be in order. For example, the socioeconomic gains described suggest that many Blacks are able to afford housing in middle class suburbs. Recent presidential statements on suburban and school integration seem to overlook these developments and may hinder integration at levels commensurate with socioeconomic gains. Though specification of governmental actions must be carefully worked out, we do feel that current opportunities and needs require more than a policy of "benign neglect."

6. WHAT IS THE CONSEQUENCE OF THIS PROGRESS FOR THE ATTITUDES OF BLACKS AND WHITES?

Our answer to this must also be speculative. Turning to Blacks, we do not know what attitudes will become popular, but we can isolate three possible outcomes. First, Franklin Frazier argued that Negroes were rapidly accepting the norms and values of white society. He, along with DuBois and numerous other commentators, described the large size of the middle class Black population and foresaw growth of this group. If there is a continuation of economic gains by Blacks, this may lead to a fairly conservative Black population, one which accepts the traditional ideals of American society. Racial accommodation may be the end result.

Second, a very different trend may emerge. We have noted that while Blacks made gains they are still far behind Whites. The racial gap in the purchasing power of families was as great in 1969 as a score of years earlier. Racial differences with regard to income are greatest among those at the higher educational levels. It may be that as Blacks make progress, they will become increasingly aware of the gaps which separate them from Whites. Blacks may become more insistent in demanding equality, and if it is not forthcoming, they may increasingly favor militancy or turn to violence.

Third, it may be that Negroes will pursue a separatist course. Apparently we still have many ethnic residential enclaves and numerous church, school, and social organizations which cater to an exclusive ethnic group. We can imagine the development of similar institutions for the Black population, and economic gains will place Blacks in a stronger position to establish and maintain these organizations.

The Black population of the United States is large. Its 25 million make it as numerous as some of the major nations of the world. Blacks are heterogeneous with regard to social background, region, religion, and political affiliation. There is no reason to expect that one set of attitudes will become predominant among Negroes. Surveys indicate a wide differentiation in the attitudes of Blacks, and it appears to us that each of these three positions will be espoused by large numbers of Blacks.

Finally, we turn to possible changes in the attitudes of Whites. Two trends may produce more accommodating attitudes on the part of Whites. First, educational attainment continues to increase, and since attainment is generally associated with more egalitarian views of racial issues, this augurs for a diminution of prejudice. Second, we have speculated that there is a growing frequency of interracial contact on the job and perhaps in schools. This also may reduce prejudiced attitudes held by either Whites or Blacks.

On the other hand, we do not know the extent to which the attitudes of Whites depend upon general economic conditions. A fairly large proportion of Whites, in the late 1960s, favored equal treatment for Blacks on the job and supported better schools and welfare services for Negroes. In a time of affluence, it may cost Whites very little to aver these views. At a different time, when jobs are scarce, tax revenues in short supply, and better homes unavailable, Whites may be distinctly less amenable to the advances of Negroes.

19. ATTITUDES TOWARD RACIAL INTEGRATION

ANDREW M. GREELEY and PAUL B. SHEATSLEY

An original article published by permission of Andrew M. Greeley and Paul B. Sheatsley. Reprinted by permission. Andrew Greeley is Professor of Sociology and Program Director at the National Opinion Research Center, University of Chicago. Paul B. Sheatsley is Director of the Survey Research Service of the National Opinion Research Center. Each has written extensively on White attitudes towards Blacks as these have changed over time and in response to the racial turmoil of the 1960s. Greeley has also written extensively about the contemporary situation of American ethnic groups.

■ The racial events of the 1960s seemed so much more the product of Black assertiveness than of change in White attitudes that it is easy to ignore the extent to which White attitudes may show a continuing decrease in prejudice and acceptance of integration. In this selection the authors show a long-term increase in favorable White attitudes toward integration in a wide range of areas of life, and they note the convergence of southern with northern attitudes.

Racial attitudes are, of course, complex and deeply imbedded in people's personalities. Even so, it is possible to chart major trends in attitudes using opinion questions, although given sufficiently negative attitudes certain issues of racial equality cannot be raised at all. In many ways what we have seen during the 1960s, is the burial of official and established policies of racial segregation and separateness. In their place are the more complex processes that continue to maintain distance and inequality between the races. Greeley and Sheatsley also show how attitudes favoring "going slow" on integration may well have grown during the latter part of the 1960s as a reaction to the apparent pace and violence of the Negro movement.

Studies such as this often demonstrate that in terms of public attitudes policymakers have more leeway than they like to believe. While the public may respond adversely to the rhetoric used in connection with policies designed to achieve equality in line with official norms, there has, in fact, been a good deal of support for civil rights policies designed to assure Blacks of their rights, particularly in the North. But, for all the change, it is important to recognize also that a preference

for status inequality is still strong for many Americans. Thus even in 1970 one-third of the respondents in the NORC study apparently would object to dining at home with a Black and 50 percent seem to want laws against racial intermarriage and believe that Whites have the right to keep Blacks out of their neighborhoods.

We can summarize these shifts in White attitudes, in the context of the continuing inequalities discussed in the previous two selections, by saying that the 1960s saw the disintegration of a heavily institutionalized caste system of race relations. (We need to remember that in the 1950s many places of public accommodation in the North still continued quite openly to refuse their facilities to Blacks.) In place of the caste system we have institutionalized mechanisms that continue to preserve inequality and deny full human acceptance to Blacks, but these mechanisms are less clear-cut and formally structured. Some have argued that this institutional racism is somehow worse than the old caste system because discrimination and prejudice then were much more open. But the possibilities for change and for individual achievement in the more fluid racial patterns of the present are certainly greater. It may well be that one of the effects of changes in White attitudes and institutional realities will be an increase of inequality within the Black group, while increasing numbers of Blacks manage to achieve positions of some reward and respect in the larger society.

Paul Sheatsley has analyzed White attitudes toward Blacks as of the early 1960s in his contribution to Talcott Parsons and Kenneth Clark, eds., *The Negro American* (Boston:

241

Houghton Mifflin, 1966). For research probing shifts in White attitudes in the last half of the 1960s, see Angus Campbell, *White Attitudes Towards Black People* (Ann Arbor: University of Michigan, Institute for Social Research, 1971). ■

A YEAR AGO WE presented in the pages of the December 1971 issue of *Scientific American* the results of the National Opinion Research Center's (NORC) end-of-the-decade survey of White attitudes toward racial integration. The article reported that despite the turbulence of the sixties White attitudes toward racial integration continued to become more favorable in the years between 1963 and 1970 just as they had in the previous seven years.

NORC now monitors these attitudes every year. Because of two notable developments since 1970 we herewith present this report of NORC on changing racial attitudes.

1. Despite the fierceness of the controversy around the busing issue, White acceptance of racial integration has grown as much in the last two years as it did in the previous seven years.

2. Much of this change has taken place in the South. If the trend continues (as it has for 30 years), within a very brief period of time there will be no difference between the racial attitudes of White southerners under the age of 45 and those of their northern counterparts.

Table 19.1 shows the percentage of White Americans taking prointegration attitudes on five items of NORC's eight-item scale devised in 1963. It is noteworthy that three of the items on the original scale have been retired simply because virtually all Americans now accept without question integration in jobs, public transportation, and public facilities.

Between 1963 and 1970 there was an increase of 11 percentage points in sympathy for school integration and an increase of 12 percentage points between 1970 and 1972. Acceptance of a Negro at dinner increased from 49 percent in 1963 to 63 percent in 1970 and to 70 percent in 1972. There was a five percentage point improvement in sympathy for Blacks as neighbors between 1963 and 1970 and a seven point increase between 1970 and 1972. The percentage of American Whites who accept racial intermarriage was 36 percent in 1963, 48 percent in 1970, and 59 percent in 1972. Finally, the extreme item in the scale—reaction to the statement that Negroes shouldn't push themselves where they are not wanted—has behaved erratically: 27 percent took a prointegration attitude response in 1963, only 16 percent in 1970, and 20 percent in 1972.

TABLE 19.1

ATTITUDES ON INTEGRATION 1963, 1970, AND 1972

PERCENT PROINTEGRATION

Item	1963	1970	1972
"Do you think White students and Negro students should go to the same schools, or to separate schools?" ("Same schools")	63	74	86
"How strongly would you object if a member of your family wanted to bring a Negro friend home to dinner?" ("Not at all.")	49	63	70
"White people have a right to keep Negroes out of their neighborhoods if they want to, and Negroes should respect that right." ("Disagree slightly" or "Disagree strongly.")	44	49	56
"Do you think there should be laws against marriages between Negroes and Whites?" (No.")	36	48	59
"Negroes shouldn't push themselves where they're not wanted." ("Disagree slightly" or "Disagree strongly.")	27	16	22

TABLE 19.2
PROINTEGRATION SCALE BY REGION

	1963	1970	1972	Change 1963-70	Change 1970-72	Change 1963-72
Non-South	2.45	2.88	3.16	.43	.28	.71
	(887)	(911)	(1010)			
South	1.11	1.47	2.17	.36	.70	1.06
	(331)	(352)	(342)			

By assigning to each respondent to the survey a score ranging from five to zero, depending on the number of prointegration responses he gave, we can readily compute the average scores for various subgroups of the population. The five items form what is known as a Guttman scale. If a person rejects one item on the scale, the odds are extremely high that he will reject all items below it. For example, someone opposed to integrated schools is not likely to welcome the presence of a Negro at his dinner table, and even less is he likely to approve of integrated neighborhoods or racial intermarriage. Thus, a person with a score of 4 can be assumed in the great majority of cases to take a prointegration stand on the first four items of the scale.

We have said that much of the change that has occurred in the last two years has been concentrated in the South. Indeed, we observe in Table 19.2 that the movement toward sympathy for racial integration in the South between 1970 and 1972 is as extensive as that in the North between 1963 and 1972. White southerners still lag behind in support for integration, but in 1963 the typical White southerner was just barely willing to accept integration in the schools. In 1972 he is willing to accept integration in the schools and a Black at the family dinner table, and has made some progress toward accepting the right of Negroes to live wherever they wish.

Much of the change in racial attitudes in the past has been concentrated among the young. White people under age 25 have always had racial attitudes more tolerant than those of their elders, and between 1963 and 1970 this generation gap was increasing. (Table 19.3) But since 1970 the largest gains on the prointegration scale have been registered by the two groups of people aged 25-44 and 45-64. Thus not only is the South "catching up" with the North but these data also suggest that the middle-aged are now beginning to "catch up" with the young.

TABLE 19.3
PROINTEGRATION SCALE BY AGE

	1963	1970	1972	Change 1963-70	Change 1970-72	Change 1963-72
Under 25	2.38	3.26	3.62	.88	.36	1.24
	(218)	(121)	(161)			
25-44	2.32	2.71	3.16	.39	.45	.84
	(545)	(453)	(515)			
45-64	1.93	2.27	2.69	.34	.42	.76
	(400)	(402)	(474)			
Over 65	1.53	2.05	2.19	.52	.14	.66
	(184)	(281)	(199)			

TABLE 19.4
PROINTEGRATION SCALE BY REGION AND AGE

		Non-South				
	1963	1970	1972	Change 1963-70	Change 1970-72	Change 1963-72
Under 25	2.93 (80)	3.76 (82)	3.78 (123)	.83	.02	.85
25-44	2.66 (401)	3.11 (341)	3.39 (399)	.45	.28	.73
45-64	2.26 (283)	2.66 (283)	2.91 (347)	.40	.25	.65
Over 65	1.90 (120)	2.41 (201)	2.55 (138)	.51	.14	.65
		South				
	1963	1970	1972	Change 1963-70	Change 1970-72	Change 1963-72
Under 25	1.37 (37)	2.23 (39)	3.08 (38)	.86	.85	1.71
25-44	1.19 (131)	1.52 (112)	2.37 (116)	.33	.85	1.18
45-64	1.06 (107)	1.36 (119)	2.08 (127)	.30	.72	1.02
Over 65	.82 (56)	1.11 (80)	1.34 (61)	.29	.23	.52

Among the young the greatest change is taking place in the South. Table 19.4 shows the prointegration score by both region and age group. One can see that in the last two years there has been little or no change in attitudes among young northerners but striking changes among those in the South under age 45. If the years between 1972 and 1974 show continuing changes of the magnitude registered during the past two years in both North and South, there will be virtually no difference in sympathies for racial integration between southerners under 45 and their northern counterparts. We could project that by 1974 both northerners and southerners under age 25 will have a score close to 4.0 on the scale, which means that both groups will accept school, residential, social, and marital integration. For typical White Americans between age 26 and 45 we could project a score somewhere between 3.0 and 4.0, which means that in the North and South alike, typical Whites in that age group will be able to accept educational, social, and neighborhood integration.

Even if we grant that NORC's integration scale is, like all survey instruments, an imperfect device and that it may to some extent measure what people think they ought to say instead of what they are in fact prepared to accept, nonetheless, the change in these expressed racial attitudes in the South over the past decade must still be classified as one of the most impressive social accomplishments of modern times. Given the South's past and the immense resistance to integration that once existed there, the changes reported in Table 19.4 and not unreasonably projected into the future would not have seemed possible 10 years ago.

If changing racial attitudes in the past two years have been particularly concentrated in the South and especially among younger southerners, they have also been mostly likely to occur among better educated Whites who have graduated from college (Table

TABLE 19.5
PROINTEGRATION SCALE BY EDUCATION

	1963	1970	1972	Change 1963-70	Change 1970-72	Change 1963-72
Grammar school	1.32	1.69	1.98	.37	.29	.66
	(335)	(281)	(238)			
Some high school	1.88	2.23	2.50	.35	.27	.62
	(315)	(242)	(247)			
High school graduate	2.32	2.57	2.98	.25	.41	.66
	(376)	(413)	(453)			
Some college	2.73	3.06	3.32	.33	.26	.59
	(193)	(189)	(245)			
College graduate	3.15	3.48	3.97	.33	.49	.82
	(130)	(135)	(168)			

19.5). Prointegration attitudes have always been highly correlated with education, but since 1963 the college graduate group has shown by far the highest rate of change. This finding has important implications for the future, as the proportion of our sample reporting college graduation increased from 9 percent in 1963 to 14 percent in 1972. At the same time, the proportion who failed to complete high school, who are the least tolerant of Negroes, dropped from 49 percent of our sample to 36 percent over the same period. Again, should these trends continue, the average scale scores are bound to increase in future years.

When the influence of education and region on prointegration attitudes is considered simultaneously (Table 19.6), it is clear that the effects of education are consistent in the North and the South. In both regions it is the college graduates who have shown the greatest amount of change, in the last decade as well as in the last two years. The gains in the South vis-a-vis the North have come primarily from the high school graduates and those with some college. White southerners who did not graduate from high school still lag far behind their northern counterparts in acceptance of integration, and the gap has narrowed very little in the last decade.

To sum up, in the last two years changing attitudes toward integration have occurred most notably in the South among the young and the college educated. To the extent that there has been change in the North in the past two years, it has been most notable among those who have graduated from college.

Changes in racial attitudes have been more likely to occur in the smaller metropolitan centers under 2 million population (Table 19.7). However, the 10 largest metropolitan areas, where the largest numbers of Blacks are concentrated, are still most likely to be sympathetic to racial integration. The smallest change has been in rural counties, a pattern that has persisted these last two years as it did in the prior seven. Always least tolerant of integration, the rural counties are slipping even further behind the metropolitan areas in this respect.

Jews are still the American religious group most favorably disposed to racial integration; but there has been little change in the Jewish attitude between 1963 and 1972, while both Protestants and Catholics have changed substantially (Table 19.8). Among the major American ethnic groups (in the non-South), the greatest change in the last two years has been among Italian Catholics and among Irish Catholics whose sympathy for integration is presently only slightly behind the Jews (Table 19.9). Anglo-Saxons and Slavic Catholics have also increased their sympathy for racial integration more than the average northern increase. Scandinavian Protestants and German Catholics have increased less than the northern average, while German

TABLE 19.6
PROINTEGRATION SCALE BY EDUCATION AND REGION

	1963	1970	1972	Change 1963-70	Change 1970-72	Change 1963-72
		Non-South				
Grammar school	1.73	2.09	2.34	.36	.25	.61
	(207)	(176)	(155)			
Some high school	2.27	2.74	2.84	.47	.10	.57
	(208)	(164)	(186)			
High school graduate	2.60	2.85	3.14	.25	.29	.54
	(263)	(311)	(358)			
Some college	2.99	3.36	3.51	.37	.15	.52
	(121)	(149)	(174)			
College graduate	3.48	3.77	4.09	.29	.32	.61
	(86)	(108)	(136)			
		South				
Grammar school	.68	1.03	1.31	.35	.28	.63
	(112)	(105)	(83)			
Some high school	1.01	1.17	1.64	.16	.47	.63
	(84)	(78)	(61)			
High school graduate	1.36	1.75	2.47	.39	.72	1.11
	(72)	(102)	(95)			
Some college	1.42	1.95	2.76	.53	.81	1.34
	(33)	(40)	(71)			
College graduate	2.00	2.33	3.12	.33	.79	1.12
	(30)	(27)	(32)			

TABLE 19.7
PROINTEGRATION SCALE BY SIZE OF MUNICIPALITY

	1963	1970	1972	Change 1963-70	Change 1970-72	Change 1963-72
10 largest metropolitan areas	2.73	3.06	3.43	.33	.37	.70
	(269)	(270)	(344)			
Metropolitan areas under 2 million	2.05	2.47	2.97	.42	.50	.92
	(475)	(493)	(553)			
Urban county	1.94	2.47	2.71	.53	.24	.77
	(217)	(216)	(221)			
Rural county	1.63	1.98	2.17	.35	.19	.35
	(257)	(284)	(234)			

TABLE 19.8
PROINTEGRATION SCALE BY RELIGION

	1963	1970	1972	Change 1963-70	Change 1970-72	Change 1963-72
Protestant	1.81	2.28	2.64	.47	.36	.83
	(878)	(783)	(804)			
Catholic	2.58	2.75	3.08	.17	.33	.50
	(344)	(335)	(393)			
Jew	3.61	3.79	3.67	.18	-.12	.06
	(36)	(24)	(54)			

TABLE 19.9
PROINTEGRATION SCALE BY ETHNICITY (NON-SOUTH ONLY)

	1970	1972	Change 1970-72
All northerners	2.88	3.16	.28
Anglo-Saxons	2.80	3.18	.38
	(220)	(148)	
German Protestants	2.81	2.70	-.11
	(137)	(142)	
Scandinavian Protestants	2.82	2.98	.16
	(29)	(65)	
Irish Catholics	3.06	3.46	.40
	(48)	(63)	
German Catholics	2.97	3.18	.21
	(41)	(44)	
Italian Catholics	2.65	3.14	.49
	(38)	(63)	
Slavic Catholics	2.45	2.76	.31
	(53)	(49)	
Jews	3.79	3.67	-.12
	(24)	(52)	

Protestants and Jews have declined somewhat in their sympathy for integration during the past two years. Jews remain, however, the most sympathetic of all ethnic groups, and the relatively small number of Jews in the sample make any speculation on the apparent slight decline in sympathy for integration inappropriate.

It should be noted that those groups which have the highest sympathy for racial integration—Jews and northern youth under age 25—have changed the least in the past two years. This suggests that at the present time there may be a "ceiling" for integration sympathy as measured by the NORC scale. It should be noted, however, that even though the scale does enjoy the properties of a Guttman scale, the fifth item, "Negroes shouldn't push where they are not wanted," represents much more of a social psychological attitude than it does a policy stance.

There is, then, a broad consensus in American society in favor of racial integration, but it does not follow that there is universal acceptance of policies advocated to achieve racial justice. One need only read the daily

TABLE 19.10

ATTITUDES ON BUSING AMONG WHITES (PERCENT IN FAVOR OF BUSING
NEGRO AND WHITE SCHOOL CHILDREN FROM ONE
SCHOOL DISTRICT TO ANOTHER)

Region		Religion	
South	6	Protestant	11
Non-South	15	Catholic	12
		Jew	24
Age			
Under 25	23	*Ethnicity*	
26-44	14	Anglo-Saxon	7
45-64	11	German Protestant	13
Over 65	9	Scandinavian Protestant	16
		Irish Protestant	9
Education		Irish Catholic	10
Grammar	11	German Catholic	11
Some high school	13	Italian Catholic	6
High school graduate	11	Slavic Catholic	9
Some college	13		
College graduate	20		
Graduate school	24		

newspapers to know how strong opposition to busing is even among those who are sympathetic to the general principle of racial integration (and among many whose children do in fact attend integrated schools). The strength of the opposition to busing is obvious from our Table 19.10. Only among 4 population categories does the percentage in favor of busing get over 20 percent: persons under 25, college graduates, those who attended graduate school, and Jews. But even in these four categories more than three-quarters of each group are not in sympathy with busing.

Neither is the Black attitude on busing at all unanimous (Table 19.11). While a little more than half of the Blacks in our sample (and the relatively small number of Blacks makes us cautious about generalization) are in favor of busing, almost half of the Black respondents are not in favor of it. The strongest support for busing among Blacks is to be found among the oldest and among those with only grammar school education. Perhaps the youngest and better educated Blacks are somewhat more in sympathy with the separatist positions taken by the recent Black political meeting in Gary, Indiana.

How can one reconcile the overwhelming

sympathy for integration with almost equally overwhelming opposition to busing? It is tempting (and not all observers have resisted the temptation) to dismiss the support for school integration as hypocrisy, indeed covert racism, unless it includes support for busing. However, such a simple solution may not do full justice to the complexity of social reality, and certainly it does not explain the lack of Black unanimity on the busing issue./

There are at least four possible explanations for opposition to busing:

1. Racism, explicit or implicit, which wishes to protect its children from attending school with Blacks.
2. Fear of danger or resentment of the inconvenience of busing.
3. Commitment to the neighborhood school as an important social institution.
4. Doubt as to whether "racial balance" would in fact achieve much improvement in the quality of education for Blacks.

It is not the purpose of this article to discuss the pros and cons of busing. However, it must be noted that on the last three

TABLE 19.11

ATTITUDES ON BUSING AMONG BLACKS
(PERCENT IN FAVOR OF BUSING NEGRO AND
WHITE SCHOOL CHILDREN FROM ONE
SCHOOL DISTRICT TO ANOTHER)

Region	
South	52
	(81)
Non-South	55
	(57)
Age	
Under 25	54
	(21)
26-44	51
	(42)
45-64	51
	(47)
Over 65	62
	(28)
Education	
Grammar school	60
	(52)
Some high school	48
	(19)
High school graduate	55
	(31)
College	52
	(15)

explanations the evidence to support or deny those objections seems to be inconclusive to most experts.

It may very well be that busing is absolutely essential to achieve racial justice in American society, but the evidence in favor of this position has not been made in such a way as to convince educational specialists. Hence one cannot, at least on a priori grounds, write off popular opposition to busing as pure racism. Unquestionably, there is racism involved in some of the opposition to busing, but with the tools presently available to us we are not able to sort out the purely racist opposition from opposition based on fear of the risks of busing and skepticism about its effectiveness.

The difference in attitudes on racial integration as a general principle and busing as a specific policy that would achieve an integration which is perceived as socially necessary illustrates what seems to us to be a decisive change in the racial issues that face us in the United States. Until relatively recently, a large segment of the American population was unwilling to accept the principle of racial integration even though that principle was an obvious deduction from the American creed and even though the nonacceptance of the principle created what three decades ago Gunnar Myrdal called "the American dilemma." Now, on the verbal level, the principles have been accepted, the creed is now honored in theory by most of the population, and the American dilemma has been resolved in theory.

The problem has shifted from the acceptance of the principle of racial integration to the question of the practical policies which most effectively will achieve racial justice. Contrary to opinions of a generation ago, there is now no question that segregated schooling enforced by law is a violation of the American creed, but there can still be considerable question as to what are the most effective means of achieving racial justice in education. In the last decade, a subtle shift has taken place from questions of general social principle to questions of concrete social policy. Necessarily, the latter issues are more complicated and less certain.

We suspect that if the elites in American society hope to obtain broad consensus for certain major social policy changes to achieve racial justice, they are going to have to demonstrate why a given social policy is absolutely necessary to implement the new theoretical consensus. Data presented in Tables 19.10 and 19.11 suggest that the overwhelming majority of Whites and a very substantial minority of Blacks have not yet been persuaded that busing is an indispensable prerequisite for racial justice.

The NORC integration scale does not have many years of life ahead of it. It will shortly be retired to pasture with the observation that as far as theoretical principles are concerned the overwhelming majority of Americans are committed to racial integration. New and more elaborate measures will then have to be devised to discover what policies for achieving racial justice are likely to obtain broad consensus and what kind of arguments in favor of these policies are likely to be the most effective. Not only are the social issues more complicated and less clear-cut, the problems for social researchers are going to be far more difficult than they were in the days when 70 percent of the American Whites were against school integration.

We emphasize that we are dealing only with expressed attitudes and that we are measuring these attitudes with very imperfect tools. It is quite possible that our respondents are giving the answers they think are socially desirable—although even that prointegration answers should become socially desirable represents a change of a sort. Furthermore, survey items are but crude indicators of a complex personality orientation involved in racial tolerance and racial bigotry.

Nevertheless, the data reported in NORC's monitoring of American racial attitudes amply documents the capacity of Americans to change. In 1952 only 30 percent of the population accepted school integration. In 1956 the figure had risen to 49 percent; in 1963 it was 63 percent; in 1970, 74 percent; and in the spring of 1972, 86 percent. To say that such change is a remarkable social accomplishment is neither to suggest that the American nation should rest on its laurels nor to conclude that the sin of racism has been exorcised from the land. If any pride is to be taken in the accomplishment of attitudinal change in the past three decades, it is the kind of pride which imposes an obligation to work for those policy changes which will be attuned to the new attitudes.

20. WHEN THE MELTING POT DOESN'T MELT

NATHAN GLAZER

Reprinted from The New York Times Magazine, *January 2, 1972. Copyright © 1972 by The New York Times Company, and reprinted by permission. Nathan Glazer is Professor of Education and Social Structure at Harvard University. He was an urban sociologist for the Housing and Home Finance Agency in the first years of the Kennedy Administration. He has written extensively on ethnic relations in the United States, on housing, and on other urban social policy issues, and has served as a consultant and adviser to numerous private and governmental organizations.*

■ U.S. cities have had complex patterns of openness and restriction in the ethnic separation of residential neighborhoods. To some extent this stratification has been a simple product of the different dates of arrival of each ethnic group. Ethnic succession has been a repetitive process in the early history of cities such as Chicago, where these patterns have been documented from the 19th century to the present. For Blacks, however, time and accident have had little to do with the patterns of segregation that have confined them to Black neighborhoods—almost always the least desirable neighborhoods in the city.

As residential patterns change, as Blacks move out from the edges of the ghetto and meet White resistance, it is sometimes difficult to separate racial feeling, ethnic preferences, and fear of lower class encroachment regardless of race and ethnicity. A major aim of recent public policy has been to foster racial and socioeconomic desegregation, a goal that has been argued forcefully in criticisms of federal and local housing practices that have tended to reinforce rather than break down racial and other barriers. Public housing programs turned out further to concentrate rather than reduce the concentration of Black and lower class populations, and the need for new housing strategies became obvious in the light of their failure.

New York City, chronically short of low income housing, for a long time managed to run a highly successful public housing program with only a few "problem" projects. But the problems associated with public housing and the stigma that came to be attached to the notion of a "project" suggested that other approaches should be tried. One new policy advocated by housing experts was scattered site housing—that is, small numbers of units scattered within neighborhoods of standard housing to prevent the development of large "federal slum" communities. Even this hope turned out to be vain, as experience with some of the newer subsidized programs in the early 1970s began to demonstrate. In addition, large housing authorities like the one in New York City transformed the notion of scattered sites outside ghetto and slum areas into a bureaucratic distortion of the original idea.

Nathan Glazer's article presents a case study of what happened when one such scattered site development was announced for the Forest Hills section of New York City. He describes with sympathy the feelings and concerns of the predominantly White area residents about what could (given the public housing population) only be expected to be a predominantly Black and Puerto Rican project. The political furor still in progress when Glazer wrote his article did not abate, and the Forest Hills project may never be built. In any case, it is clear that in building such a project the political costs to the mayor and others in the city administration are so great that few such projects are likely to be proposed in the future.

Recognition that housing projects can focus political conflict and can be vetoed by the groups affected has been a factor in convincing those interested in low income housing to favor the so-called "rent allowances," whereby the government gives poorly housed families the difference between what they can afford to pay for rent and what better housing would cost on the private market. These allowances are supposed to permit low income and minority families to find decent housing on their own so that, it is hoped, they are dispersed and thus reduce social and economic segregation. Whether this expectation is sound remains to be seen, but in 1972 several large-scale experiments with housing allowances were about to be fielded. The failure of so many programs to accomplish similar objectives made policy planners and political executives eager to secure some evidence that the new policies could actually produce the desired results before they initiated large-scale funding and before bureaucracies were created that would defend the programs regardless of how poorly they were accomplishing their goals.

The situation of ethnic groups in New York City is described in a classic study by Nathan Glazer and Daniel P. Moynihan, *Beyond the Melting Pot,* 2d ed. (Cambridge, Mass.: M.I.T. Press, 1970). The issue of housing desegregation in relation to urban patterns and growth is analyzed by Anthony Downs in *Urban Problems and Prospects* (Chicago: Markham, 1970). The classic lament on the decline of American cities is Jane Jacobs, *The Death and Life of Great American Cities* (New York: Random House, 1961). Several articles that deal with housing and local communities are found in Daniel P. Moynihan, *Toward a National Urban Policy* (New York: Basic Books, 1970). ■

THERE ARE MANY questions raised by the astonishing spectacle of the liberal, middle class Jewish community of Forest Hills fighting the building of a housing project. But the most serious question is whether the hope for an integrated America is a false one. Are we, as so many believe, an irretrievably racist society, one in which even the liberal will be proven a bigot when he is forced to accept Negroes into his own community? Unfortunately, this is what most people will conclude. It is certainly what the local NAACP chapters of Queens have concluded. It may end up being what the people of Queens who oppose the project conclude about themselves, too.

What makes the Forest Hills case so important is that it seems to rip away the last veil protecting Americans, en masse, from the charge of a vicious and all-embracing racism as the principal explanation for resistance to integration of White neighborhoods. Thus, in the past, when Whites have resisted Black movement into their areas, it has been pointed out that the resisters feared a decline in property values. Most Americans are homeowners, and their reaction to any proposed neighborhood change must take into account their investments in their houses. But the people of Forest Hills are largely apartment dwellers, and they need have no concern over the loss of value of resident-owned homes. In other cases of resistance, it has been pointed out that the resisters were members of closely knit ethnic communities, of limited outlook, with many fears, some justifiable. But the people of Forest Hills are well educated and vote liberal. Understanding as much as they do, is not their resistance simple racism—opposition to social intercourse with Blacks? In the context of the remarkable realities of New York City in 1971, this conclusion, evident as it may be to many, ignores some weighty facts.

Forest Hills is an amazing sight. The last major subway line to be built in New York City, in the thirties, ran through the area, which was then still, in large measure, empty lots and small communities of homeowners. Some apartment houses went up before World War II, but the great expansion of the neighborhood came after the war. The dominant building types shifted from the single-family home and the six-story apartment house to taller apartment houses. Queens Boulevard became lined with great apartment houses, stretching back from the subway. The standard of density was, by any theory of city planning, outrageous. The standard of amenity was, by any theory of city planning, equally outrageous. Enormous freeways reaching out to Long Island cut up the area, introducing a permanent roar and stench of traffic. There were no new parks built; the only remaining open space was some windswept, leftover corners. The schools were consistently overcrowded, as the inadequate system for school building in New York City failed to cope with the flood of apartment dwellers. The public transportation was among the worst in the city. The single subway line that had been built to serve a few hundred thousand now served a million. The sewers could not accommodate the heavy rains, and the area was regularly flooded.

With all this, people poured into Forest Hills from Brooklyn and the Bronx, which were less crowded, had better transportation, cheaper housing, less crowded schools, better drainage. Every site in Forest Hills that could be used for apartments was covered with them. Indeed, the 8½ acres on which 3 24-story buildings are now to be placed as a housing project had once been chosen as the site for privately built apartment houses—until the builders abandoned it as too swampy and expensive. . . .

If one had to give the predominant cause of the movement away from the older areas of Brooklyn, the Bronx and Manhattan, one would have to say it was the search for safety. Safety in the streets, safety in buildings, elevators, and corridors, safety in the schools.

There were, of course, other causes. Forest Hills was newer. One could hope to escape from roaches and broken plaster and old plumbing. Forest Hills, because it was growing, had new and better stores, instead of old ones with poor displays, broken windows and limited merchandise. Forest Hills, because it was in large measure Jewish, had new synagogues and temples, and one could hope to join a younger congregation than those that survived in the older parts of Brooklyn and the Bronx, which were made up predominantly of elderly people.

Forest Hills was particularly attractive to better-off conservative and orthodox Jews, who require special religious and cultural facilities, such as synagogues to which they can walk and day schools which teach Hebrew or religious subjects, in addition to the regular curriculum. Forest Hills became particularly rich in such facilities, which involve substantial investments. It has been argued that the day schools have grown so rapidly only because they provide an escape from integrated schools. But the fact is that these schools began to grow long before integration was an issue, and for reasons having nothing to do with integration. Indeed, in Forest Hills the public schools have relatively

few Negro students. Even in the public schools, there is less disruption and less crime, and the children, wonder of wonders, can listen to the teachers and one another in relative peace.

Again and again it comes back to the main issue, safety. The houses were better not only because they were newer, but because there was less regular damage by drug addicts and vandals; the stores were better because the operators had fewer broken windows to repair and did not have to defend themselves against regular robbery; the schools were better because they were safer.

No one can spend any time in New York City without discovering that this is the overwhelming concern of its citizens, rich and poor, educated and sophisticated as well as uneducated and unsophisticated, Negroes and Puerto Ricans as well as Jews, Italians, the Irish, and the WASPS. In the minds of many Whites, a dangerous but understandable confusion develops, leading to the conclusion that the presence of Blacks equals lack of safety. The confusion occurs in the minds of people who remember when they could walk the streets, needed only one lock on their apartment and did not fear for their children, in school; they also remember that this was a time when there were no or few Blacks in the area. Blacks came, and crime mounted. It is simple enough to conclude as some do, that Blacks cause crime, and to decide to move to a neighborhood where there are few Blacks. This will solve the individual family's problem, or at least mitigate it. But of course there is no simple equation between Blacks and crime. The Black citizens of New York are as desperately eager to flee from crime-ridden neighborhoods as the White, and if they can, they do—out of the city, to Westchester and Nassau counties, and, within the city, to whatever area seems to provide greater safety.

Fewer of them can afford to move—but more and more of them can, and more and more of them do. The populations of the worst Black slum areas—Bedford-Stuyvesant, Harlem, Brownsville, the South Bronx—keep on dropping, while the overall Black and

Puerto Rican population in the city rises. And the drops in population would be even greater if housing policies had not anchored so many of the Black and Puerto Rican poor into the areas with huge projects, which are simply too good a bargain to give up.

The equation "Black equals crime," if we put it that simply, is wrong. Poor Blacks, however, provide a breeding ground for crime—and anyone who values his safety, White or Black, is going to try to distance himself from a tangle of pathology. This may not be the noblest response. The nobleminded would undoubtedly seek to untwist the tangle through good works, or even, in more saintly fashion, to enter it, live in it, try by example to overcome it. But few of us are noble or saintly, White or Black. We have lives to lead, families to support, children to educate, and as we regularly hear that the best-informed and the most knowledgeable are themselves not quite sure just what policies will overcome the pathology, the wisest individual response is to move away, until it is overcome.

But if this action, which is not noble and certainly not saintly, is denounced as "racist," as so often happens, the danger is that the confusion in the minds of some, that Black *does* equal crime, which it is in the best interest of all to unravel and straighten out, becomes only deeper. If those who know truly that they search for safety are denounced for being racist, are they not to conclude that the only way *not* to be racist is to accept living with personal danger? Does not the confusion grow when liberals and Black organizations argue that the people escaping from crime are really trying to escape from the presence of Blacks?

I believe that in the response to painful conflicts such as we see in Forest Hills, this is just what is happening. . . .

Thus many forces come together to make ever stronger in the minds of the Whites of Forest Hills the equation, Blacks equals crime: Their own experiences with what happened to their neighborhoods as poor Blacks came in; the insistence of civil rights leaders that any effort to escape from crime is racist,

which, if the Whites believe it, will only confirm their experience—that Black does equal crime; and perhaps worst of all, the proud assertion that Black crime is Black protest, and that there should be, and will be, more of it—not less.

But, it is asked, why does a housing project bring in crime? Is it not racist to assume it does? The Housing and Development Administration points out there is less crime in projects than in the areas surrounding them. Moreover, 40 percent of the project will be allocated to the elderly, who commit no crimes. The rest will go to families who desperately need housing, often headed by women, who commit few crimes, and consisting of children, many of whom are too young to commit crimes. Is this not a false issue?

In some measure it is, and city housing and planning authorities, argue, properly, that there is no reason why this project, or any project, should turn out to be like the public's image of it. But it is also understandable that the word "project," and the reality of a project on such a large scale, evoke the worst image rather than the better one. The credibility gap exists at the city as well as the national level. Again and again we have seen fairly good urban renewal projects resisted because people remembered what the bad urban renewal projects were like. When neighborhood and way-of-life and security are at stake, it appears that most people find it hard to make fine distinctions. In the same way, after urban renewal was labeled "Negro removal," with some good cause, it was very hard to get Blacks to accept the possibility that some urban renewal would not involve "Negro removal."

But even if the reaction to the Forest Hills project is hysterical, one suspects, *in view of the kind of project it is,* that the people resisting it may be right, and the housing experts giving the assurances may be wrong.

The housing project in question is one of a group that is supposed to introduce "scattered sites" for public housing, so that, presumably, the concentration of the poor in huge projects will be reduced and more of them will be able to live in better-off neighborhoods where a stabler way of life will rub off. That is the theory. The fact is that New York City seems incapable of building true "scattered-site" housing on a large scale—that is, housing for the poor in relatively small clumps (perhaps 20 or 30 families), adjacent to, or in the same buildings with, full rent-paying families. The difficulty is that overhead work involved in starting a small project is almost as great as in starting a large project. There is the job of planning, site selection, government approval, fighting political opposition to the site, signing contracts and so on; once the project is built, it is relatively more expensive to administer. In a time when housing is desperately needed by the poor it is far more efficient to build 840 units in 3 24-story buildings than to rehabilitate older buildings or rent a few apartments or houses here and there. The small project on West 103rd Street in Manhattan, where a row of brownstone was rehabilitated for a few dozen families is a model—but it was expensive in terms of time commitment. For not much more time than that, the city administration can come up with a project for hundreds of families and thus show a much better political record.

"Scattered sites" originally seemed to mean housing that involved small numbers of the poor and that blended into the surrounding middle class areas. Ironically, the 24-story towers in the Forest Hills plan are far taller than anything in the area, and the density of 840 families on an 8½-acre site is greater than any planning theory accepts, or indeed, than is common in this very dense area. The issues are not simply architecture and crowding. One can be sure there would be no objection if 24-story towers were put up for luxury apartments for 840 families. People would be quite happy to have high-income families as neighbors, even if bulk and density broke neighborhood standards. Lewis Mumford would object (as he has to the airless, expensive apartments of Park Avenue), but the neighbors, we know, would not.

But the impact of low-income apartments is far, far greater than high-income apartments. The desperate need, we know, is for apartments to house large families. Inevitably, the 500 family apartments will house large families. Inevitably, some substantial portion of the families will be headed by females, and some substantial number "disorganized." Even if the children are young when they move in, large numbers will be adolescents. The chances of such a project bringing to the neighborhood in a very short time some 500 to 600 adolescents and young men and women are all too high. That they will be a burden to the neighborhood is probable, too. Many of them will extort money from children at school, beat them if they don't provide any, break the windows of the neighborhood stores, rob from them, attack the elderly for money or sport. These are simple facts which the Black and White people of Forest Hills are quite aware of. The placement of a housing project in middle class Jewish neighborhoods is not a new phenomenon. There are already such projects in various sections of the Bronx and Queens. The people of Forest Hills have seen that many of the residents of these projects have been a torment to their neighbors. And they will, apparently, quite willingly brave the charge of racist for the chance to spare themselves this torment. The history of neighborhood change is complicated, and undoubtedly the simple charge that public housing leads to neighborhood deterioration is too crude. But the unfortunate fact is that no one who is informed on these matters can say it is too crude to be serviceable.

When the city authorities argue there will be no such impact, they obscure the realities that have to be dealt with. They convince the people of the area that something is being put over on them, and increase their resistance.

In Manhattan, it is true that projects—or at least some projects—lie cheek-by-jowl with middle class neighborhoods. Perhaps the best examples are the two adjacent developments of General Grant Houses and Morningside Gardens, the first a low rent project and the second a middle income cooperative. In Morningside Gardens, however, the co-op owners have chosen, with full knowledge, to risk the dangers that might flow from a low income housing project, in exchange for getting an inner location in Manhattan. They may be different from the people of Forest Hills in various ways—more cosmopolitan, better aware of the city's inevitable dangers and more understanding of the causes of crime, without any hostage young children. Indeed, the planning for the General Grant and Morningside Gardens developments was almost simultaneous. The people applying to both knew what they were getting into.

The General Grant-Morningside Gardens complex argues on the one hand for the possibility that such placement of low income housing will work. On the other, it can be argued that the experiment's value is exaggerated. The presence of Morningside Gardens can hardly have had much effect on the people of General Grant. One hazards this conclusion simply because the numbers involved in General Grant are so enormous (more than 2,000 families) that the main characteristics of the project must be those given by the people within it, rather than by the middle class cooperative development on its borders. We might expect that the fact that General Grant is not entirely surrounded by the disorganized poor adds to its attraction for project residents who are as concerned about safety as the middle class. For this reason alone, there may be less crime and danger. The project may be more attractive to potential tenants, and if there are many tenants to choose from, the management may be able to impose some selectivity. But on the whole selectivity is very difficult in public housing. There is the constant danger of lawsuits from the army of young lawyers, who are paid by various federal and foundation programs, if the authorities try too egregiously to exclude families with juvenile delinquents, drug addicts, child molesters, and the like.

Even if one can make a case that the opposition to the Forest Hills project is not racist, even if one can point out that people much like those opposing the project seem quite content to live with middle class Blacks in such developments as Lefrak City, one has not gone very far toward a solution of the problems of housing the poor. One must acknowledge the fact that even though the level of danger in Forest Hills rises somewhat with the building of a housing project, the level of danger for those living in it will very like fall, compared to that in the areas they are leaving. If members of the middle class, White and Black, have the right to make choices that maximize their safety, do not the poor, White and Black, have that choice too? And even if danger is one consequence of the siting of a low income project, is not the location of this project in a middle class area on the whole a wise act of government, offering those who escape the ghetto not only better physical conditions but a greater measure of safety and, perhaps, some chance to gain the benefits of integration into a middle class area—a better mix in the schools, perhaps some marginal effects from the possibility of friendship and neighboring?

I believe that any fair estimate of the situation must agree that the placement of low income housing in middle class areas has considerable merit, that the transformation of areas like Harlem and Bedford-Stuyvesant into huge stretches of housing project is simply to concentrate social pathology, and that while we know little enough about conquering the disease, we know enough to condemn these massive concentrations. The best judgment of social scientists is that small mental hospitals are better than large ones, small jails better than large ones, halfway houses better than either hospitals or jails, small housing projects better than large ones, and that the distribution of the poor and the Black among the better-off and the non-Black is perhaps the best approach to our problems. For this reason we have seen added to the approach of building large, low income projects, which began in the early sixties, several new government tools for promoting better housing, including rent supplements, subsidies for home purchase by the poor, leased housing and private- and non-profit developer-built small projects with interest-rate subsidies.

We do have better alternatives than the large project. And 840 units, in 24-story buildings, is a large project—whatever the rhetoric of "scattered site." Perhaps what is saddest in the situation is that the authorities in New York have been so inadequate in their efforts to use the available tools and to mitigate the resistance of an edgy population.

Bad as they are, the government policies that people in Forest Hills are resisting are, perhaps, the best we can devise in view of the city's overwhelming social problems. It is easy to say that the city, even while making a laudable effort to integrate the poor into middle class neighborhoods, could have done a better job. I believe it could have. One sees no reason why the project should not have conformed, in terms of the number of stories, to the height that is common in the neighborhood. That would have reduced the units by half, even if one assumes that site coverage was doubled. One sees no reason why the instruments of rent supplements and leased housing might not have been used to distribute 500 poor families through the area, instead of concentrating them into the project. I believe these policies would have been preferable. Even in saying so, however, I am aware of the great difficulties involved. Reducing the project by half might have proved an embarrassment to a city administration that is trying to make a record for providing a great deal of housing for the poor. To distribute 500 families in groups of 20 and 30 through the neighborhood by the new methods would have raised the possibility of endemic resistance in 20 buildings. The costs of cutting the project in half include trying to find a site for a project as big somewhere else, and the cost of distributing the families throughout the area means an investment of political time the administration may not be able to afford.

The city administration would have had severe political handicaps even if it had carried out a more desirable policy. It already was looked upon with suspicion by the middle class Jewish residents. They did not have as strong an antipathy to it as the poorer Jews of Brooklyn and the Bronx, who believed the administration had done nothing to protect them, either during the massive riots in 1968 or in the period of guerrilla warfare against the Jewish storekeeper and the aged that followed the riots. But neither did the people of Forest Hills have the positive enthusiasm for the mayor in 1969 that could be found among the liberal wealthy Jews of Manhattan, who lived barricaded in their great apartment houses and who sent their children to private schools. Forest Hills was not antagonistic, but neither was it enthusiastic.

One thing that the Jewish community in many parts of the city felt was that the mayor would not tangle with the Italian, Slavic, and German homeowning areas, such as Woodhaven and South Ozone Park. The Jews were not expected to become physically violent. They so rarely did in the face of Black residential succession. They simply moved away. And the sense that this was what the mayor's strategy expected of them certainly played a role in the anger of Forest Hills Jews. The anger was expressed quite openly. And yet, having said this, who could expect the mayor to take on the Italians and others as well as the Jews with a policy that distributed the scattered-site housing in small areas throughout the city? That would have been undoubtedly the course of ineffectiveness—and political suicide. By concentrating on the softer neighborhoods, the mayor hoped, politically, to gain Black and Puerto Rican support without losing too much White working-class and middle class support.

The strategy will probably work. Even though there is local resistance to the project, there is a good deal of support based on resigned acceptance that this is the best the city can do, or on positive liberal commitment to racial and class integration. National Jewish organizations and their citywide branches, as well as leading rabbis in this area such as Ben Zion Bokser, also support the project. One wonders what one would do as a resident. Though no one can really place himself in someone else's shoes, I conclude that I, too, would join the supporters—with a mixture of resignation and hope.

Conceivably, the project will be reduced. But it is more likely that with the mayor and the Federal agencies all sticking to their guns on the importance of distributing low-income housing in middle-income areas, it will be built to its scheduled scale. The people of Forest Hills may be proven wrong about the amount of crime it will bring. Their fears may contribute to the decline of their neighborhood by convincing some people to flee. Or, as they believe, the burden of uncivil behavior placed on the neighborhood by the project will cause the decline. But when we review the alternatives, they are not easy. Yes, the city should have used more of the new tools that permit more even distribution of the poor in middle-income areas—but that would have meant, as we have seen, less housing and as much, or more, conflict.

Is there no relief then for the people of Forest Hills? In the short run, it is hard to see any. In the long run, there are possibilities. Thus, one reason why we find such a shortage of low-income housing in the city is that, on the one hand, our city policies prevent new private building and, on the other, the social pathology of the slums leads to the abandonment of still good housing in the older boroughs, particularly in Brooklyn and the Bronx. Policies that might provide a better measure of housing for the poor and a better measure of safety for the middle classes and the poor may be glimpsed—but they involve more political energy, courage and foresight than the administration has shown, and, in any case, it would be some time before they could come into play.

The flight of the poor from the crime- and drug-ridden older sections might be slowed if landlords were given assistance to maintain their buildings in the face of the assaults upon them, by means of subsidized rents and mortgages, as the New York City Rand Institute has suggested. Unfortunately, in view of the city's financial woes, these aids would have to come from the Federal Government.

It might be possible to find ways to expand the use of Section 235, the Federal program of subsidies for home ownership by the poor, to provide communities for the poor with lower density farther out from the inner city, without requiring a massive intrusion into middle-income areas. Expansion of subway lines—now proceeding, but very slowly—will open up new areas to housing for the poor, and make it economically feasible to reduce the requirement to build at the density of 100 families to the acre. The economic improvement we have seen in the Black community in the nineteen-sixties, if it could be maintained through the seventies, would raise a larger proportion of Blacks out of poverty and increase the Black middle class, thus permitting more of be relatively trouble-free integration of Black and White middle classes that is so common in New York City—in middle-income co-ops (for example, Rochdale Village) and in other middle-income neighborhoods.

In the long run one hopes the high level of crime and violence in New York and other cities will be reduced, in part through higher income and better living conditions. One must warn soberly that it is hardly likely this will happen while the mass media, the sophisticated and a good part of the Black leadership steadily engage in the justification of violence and criminal behavior. We cannot take lightly the now habitual abuse and robbing of White children in the public schools. All too many people—including those in positions to lead and to influence—do take such things too lightly. Certainly, one does not, while this goes on, have to reach out for elaborate explanations of racial prejudice to explain the White flight from poor Blacks.

In listing these policies that might help, one is not encouraged. They require political energy and courage and time. In the meanwhile, we all do what is easiest. The city builds huge projects wherever it can; the poor suffer bad housing and frightful neighborhood conditions; the upper classes rest behind barriers of doormen, private schools and taxis, or set out for distant suburbs. The middle classes fight where they are as best they can, as in the case of Forest Hills. What seems quite unfair is that in their fight for a hard-won security, they should be labeled racists.

21. SEX INEQUALITY

■ Clearly the most dramatic and powerful extension of the Black rights movement into the "New Egalitarianism" (see Selection 1) was the development of a new women's liberation movement in the late 1960s. The feminist campaigns of the 19th and early 20th centuries were presumably over, and indeed we had something like a cultural counterrevolution in the post-World War II period when women were urged to turn again to family, hearth, and home and away from the "imitation" of men in the larger world. For all that, more and more women were completing college although it was understood, by and large, that this education would equip them to be better wives and mothers, and maybe to do a little paid work on the side before the children came and after the children left home.

The ideal of the companion-in-marriage, of "togetherness," was solidly entrenched and legitimated by many intellectuals—both men and women—as well as by the mass media. Equality in this context meant equal respect for the properly different roles of each. It also meant a greater sharing in family chores than had been traditional; U.S. husbands were said to be a laughingstock to European men because they washed dishes. But this greater sharing only allowed the wife freer range for her femininity—a range that might include creative hobbies at home, community involvement and leadership, and participation in "appropriate" community activities.

Now it seems that beneath the surface changing habits were laying the groundwork for a radical change in cultural definitions of the appropriate roles for men and women. For example, the rapid increase in the proportion of women who worked during World War II produced a permanent increase in women's participation in the work force. Women without children had, for a long time, a high rate of participation in the labor force, but by the end of World War II 18 percent of all *mothers* were in the labor force. That proportion increased at a steady 3 percent per year through 1970, and by that year 42 percent of all mothers were in the labor force. The rate of increase was most dramatic for mothers with children under six: by 1947, 13 percent of such mothers worked, and that proportion increased by 4 percent per year so that by 1970, 32 percent were in the labor force. While the reigning values of the time held that these mothers were simply "helping out" or doing a little something to relieve the boredom of being tied to their children, looking back we can see that their participation had greatly eroded the previous neat separation of reality into a man's world and a woman's world. It also seems likely that the growing participation of middle class women in higher education built up an increasingly widespread frustration at the narrowness of even "modern" definitions of feminine roles.

Several histories of the women's liberation movement emphasize the moral outrage among women who sought to participate in civil rights, antiwar, and radical movements when they discovered that for all the words about freedom, liberation, and equality, the men in these movements consistently required them to play basically subordinate roles. Young women intellectuals increasingly applied the abstract logic of equality and freedom to their own situations and found themselves heavily oppressed by cultural definitions of what was appropriate for them and what they had a right to expect.

As women's liberation became a popular subject of discussion, as ideas about a new equality for women began to diffuse through society, a watering-down has taken place. In some ways this new feminism, much like the old, may strengthen traditional family relationships by giving them greater flexibility, thus disappointing some of the earlier leaders of the movement. Conversely, and also like the earlier feminist movement, the new liberation may ease the way for men and women who do not fit into the conventional mold because they will meet less pressure and stigmatization from the people around them.

Three issues have become the principal focus of specific policy initiatives by the movement's leaders. One is the issue of ending discrimination toward women in employment; a second is the legalization of abortion so that women can "control their own bodies"; the third is the provision of more broadly available day care centers, possibly at public expense, to free women from constant attention to their children. Here women's liberation has joined what might be called the "child development movement" and with those concerned about burgeoning welfare rolls and putting welfare mothers to work. These various forces have brought the issue of day care to sharp focus in the federal executive and in Congress, as well as in countless local communities across the country.

The work generally recognized as the first serious attempt to lay the intellectual groundwork for a new feminism is Simone DeBeauvoir, *The Second Sex* (New York: Knopf, 1953). It was followed 10 years later by a book that was a great popular success but was treated by many male reviewers more as a joke or curiosity than as a work on a serious subject; this was Betty Friedan, *The Feminine Mystique* (New York: Norton, 1963). The book that launched the women's liberation movement into broad public consciousness was Kate Millet, *Sexual Politics* (New York: Doubleday, 1970). Useful collections of writings about women's roles include Nancy Reeves, *Womankind: Beyond the Stereotypes* (Chicago: Aldine, 1971); Eileen Kraditor, ed., *Up from the Pedestal: Landmark Writings in the American Woman's Struggle for Equality* (Chicago: Quadrangle Books, 1968); and Constantina Safilios-Rothschild, ed., *Toward a Sociology of Women* (Xerox College Publishing, 1972). One of the most careful surveys of the need and demand for child care services can be found in Richard R. Rowe et al., *Child Care in Massachusetts: The Public Responsibility,* a study for the Massachusetts Advisory Council on Education. ∎

21a. SEX EQUALITY: THE BEGINNING OF AN IDEOLOGY

ALICE S. ROSSI

Reprinted with permission from The Humanist, *September/October, 1969. Alice Rossi is Professor of Sociology at Goucher College. She has made important contributions to the sociology of the family, and to studies of such policy issues as abortion and women's rights. She is National Chairman of the Committee on the Status of Women in Academe of the American Association of University Professors.*

It should not prejudice my voice that I'm
  not born a man
If I say something advantageous to the
  present situation.
For I'm taxed too, and as a toll provide men
  for the nation
    While, miserable graybeards, you,
      It is true
Contribute nothing of any importance
  whatever to our needs;
    But the treasure raised against the Medes,
You've squandered, and do nothing in
  return, save that you make
Our lives and persons hazardous by some
  imbecile mistake.
What can you answer? Now be careful, don't
  arouse my spite,
Or with my slipper I'll take you napping
  faces slapping
    Left and right.
    —Aristophanes, *Lysistrata,* 413 B.C.:

IT IS 2,400 YEARS SINCE Lysistrata organized a sex strike among Athenian women in a play that masked a serious antiwar opposition beneath a thin veneer of bawdy hilarity. The play is unique in drama as a theme of women power and sex solidarity, and takes on a fresh relevance when read in the tumultuous 1960s. Women in our day are active as students, as Blacks, as workers, as war protesters, but far less often as women qua women pressing for equality with men, or actively engaging in a dialogue of what such equality should mean. Until the last few years, women power has meant only womanpower, a "resource to be tapped," as the manpower specialists put it.

It has been exactly 100 years since John

Stuart Mill published his classic essay on "The Subjection of Women" in England, and the Seneca Falls Conference in New York State gave public recognition to the presence of women critical of the political and economic restrictions that barred their participation in the major institutions of American society. Thus, 1969 is a propitious year in which to examine what we mean by a goal of equality between the sexes, rather than to persist in the American penchant for tinkering with short-run "improvements in the status of women."

The major objective of this article is to examine three possible goals of equality between the sexes, while a secondary objective is to pinpoint the ways in which inequality on sex grounds differs from racial, ethnic, or religious inequality.

MEANING OF INEQUALITY

A group may be said to suffer from inequality if its members are restricted in access to legitimate valued positions or rewards in a society for which their ascribed status is not a relevant consideration. In our day, this is perhaps least ambiguous where the status of citizen is concerned: We do not consider race, sex, religion, or national background relevant criteria for the right to vote or to run for public office. Here we are dealing with a particular *form* of inequality—codified law—and a particular *type* of inequality—civil and political rights of an individual as a citizen. There are several other forms of inequality in addition to legal statute: corporate or organizational policies and regulations, and most importantly, those covert social pressures which restrict the aspirations or depress the motivation of individuals on the ascribed grounds of their membership in certain categories. Thus, a teacher who scoffs at a Black boy or White girl who aspires to become an engineer, or a society which uniformly applies pressure on girls to avoid occupational choices in medicine and law are examples of covert pressures which bolster racial and sexual inequality. *Forms* of inequality therefore range

from explicit legal statute to informal social pressure.

Type of inequality adds a second dimension: the area of life in which the inequality is evidenced. There are inequalities in the *public* sector, as citizens, employees, consumers, or students; and there are inequalities in the *private* sector as family, organization, or club members. Throughout American history, the gains made for greater racial and sexual equality have been based on constitutional protection of individual rights in the public area of inequality, as citizens, students, and workers. But precisely because of constitutional protection of privacy of home, family, and person, it is more difficult to remove inequalities rooted in the private sphere of life. Attempts to compensate for emotional and nutritional deprivation of preschool, inner-city children are through three-hour Headstart exposure to verbal stimulation and nutritious food from caring adults. We have yet to devise a means to compensate for the influences of parents who depress a daughter's aspirations to become a physician, while urging a son to aspire beyond his capacity or preference. In both instances, the tactics used tend to be compensatory devices in the public sphere (counseling and teaching in the schools, for example) to make up for or undo the effects of inequalities that persist in the family.

There is, thus, a continuum of increasing difficulty in effecting social and political change along both dimensions of inequality: by *form*, from legal statute to corporate regulation to covert and deeply imbedded social mores; by *type*, from citizenship to schooling and employment, to the private sector of family. Hence, the easiest target in removing inequality involves legal statute change or judicial interpretation of rights in the public sector, and the most difficult area involves changes in the covert social mores in family and social life. It is far easier to change laws which presently penalize women as workers, students, or citizens than it will be to effect social changes in family life and higher education which depress the aspirations and motivations of women.

An example of this last point can be seen in higher education. Few graduate schools discriminate against women applicants, but there are widespread subtle pressures once women are registered as students in graduate departments—from both faculty and male peers. In one graduate department of sociology, women represent a full third of the students, and, hence, the faculty cannot be charged with discriminatory practices toward the admission of women students. On the other hand, it was not uncommon in that department to hear faculty members characterize a woman graduate student who showed strong commitment and independence as an "unfeminine bitch," and others who were quiet and unassertive as "lacking ambition"—women who will "never amount to much." Since it is difficult to be simultaneously independent and ambitious but conventionally feminine and dependent, it would appear that the informal rules prevent many women from winning the game, although they are accepted as players.

Discrimination against women in hiring or promotion may be barred by statute and corporate policy, but this does not magically stimulate any great movement of women up the occupational status ladder. Progress on the legal front must be accompanied by compensatory tactics to free girls and women from the covert depression of their motivations and aspirations through ridicule and double-bind pressures to be contradictory things.

UNIQUE CHARACTERISTICS OF SEX INEQUALITY

Many women find an easy empathy with the plight of the poor, the black, and minority religious groups—not from any innate feminine intuition but simply because a subordinate group is sensitive to both unintended and intentional debasement or discrimination where another subordinate group is concerned. Women know from personal experience what it is like to be "put down" by men and can therefore understand what it is to be "put down" as a Black by Whites. But there are also fundamental differences between sex as a category of social inequality and the categories of race, religion, or ethnicity. I shall discuss three of the most important differences.

1. CATEGORY SIZE AND RESIDENCE

In the case of race, religion, and ethnicity, we are literally dealing with minority groups in the American population, whether Mexican, Indian, Jewish, Catholic, or Black. This is not the case for sex, since women are actually a numerical majority in the population.

While the potential is present for numerical strength to press for the removal of inequalities, this is counterbalanced by other ways in which women are prevented from effectively utilizing their numerical strength. The Irish, the Italians, and the Jews in an earlier period, and Blacks in more recent history, have been able to exert political pressure for representation and legislative change because residential concentration gave them voter strength in large urban centers. By contrast, women are for the most part *evenly distributed throughout the population.* Women can exert political pressure in segmental roles as consumers, workers, New Yorkers, or the aged; but not as a cohesive political group based on sex solidarity. It is inconceivable that a political organization of Blacks would avoid the "race" issue, yet the League of Women Voters does precisely this when it takes pride in avoiding "women's" issues.

2. EARLY SEX ROLE SOCIALIZATION

Age and sex are the earliest social categories an individual learns. The differentiation between mother and father, or parent and child, is learned at a tender, formative stage of life; and consequently we carry into adulthood a set of age and sex role expectations that are extremely resistant to change. Not only do girls learn to accept authority from the older generation and from men, but they learn this lesson in intense, intimate relationships. By the time they reach adulthood, women are well socialized to seek and to find gratification in an intimate dependence on men, and in responsible authority over children. They may be dominant and affirmative mothers with their own children, or as teachers in classrooms, but pliant and submissive as wives.

Sex role expectations tend to remain a stubborn part of our impulse lives. This is often not visible among young men and women until they become parents. Many young people are egalitarian peers in school, courtship, and early marriage. With the birth of a child, deeper layers of their personalities come into play. Since there is little or no formal education for parenthood in our society, only a thin veneer of Spock-reading hides the acting out of old parental models that have been observed and internalized in childhood, triggering a regression to traditional sex roles that gradually spreads from the parental role to the marriage and self-definition of both sexes.

As a result of early sex-role socialization, there is bound to be a lag between political and economic emancipation of women and the inner adjustment to equality of both men and women. Even in radical political movements, women have often had to caucus and fight for their acceptance as equal peers to men. Without such efforts on their own behalf, women are as likely to be "girl-Friday" assistants in a radical movement espousing class and racial equality as they are in a business corporation, a labor union, or a conservative political party.

3. PRESSURES AGAINST SEX SOLIDARITY

Racial, ethnic, and religious conflict can reach an acute stage of political strife in the movement for equality without affecting the solidarity of the families of Blacks, Whites, Jews, or Gentiles. Such strife may, in fact, increase the solidarity of these family units. A "we versus them" dichotomy does not cut into family units in the case of race, religion, or ethnicity as it does in the case of sex. Since women typically live in greater intimacy with men than they do with other women, there is potential conflict within family units when women press hard for sex equality. Their demands are on predominantly male legislators and employers in the public domain—husbands and fathers in the private sector. A married Black woman can affiliate with an activist civil rights group with no implicit threat to her marriage. For a married woman to affiliate with an activist women's rights group might very well trigger tension in her marriage. While there is probably no limit to the proportion of Blacks who might actively fight racial discrimination, a large proportion of married women have not combated sex discrimination. Many of them fear conflict with men, or benefit in terms of a comfortable high status in exchange for economic dependence upon their husbands. There are many more women in the middle class who benefit from sex inequality than there are Blacks in the middle class who benefit from racial inequality.

The size of a women's rights movement has, therefore, been responsive to the proportion of "unattached" women in a population. An excess of females over males, a late age at marriage, postponement of childbearing, a high divorce rate, a low remarriage rate, and greater longevity for women, all increase the number of unattached women in a society and therefore increase the potential for sex equality activism. The hard core of activists in past suffrage and feminist movements were women without marital and family ties: exwives, nonwives, or childless wives, whose need to support themselves triggered their concern for equal rights to vote, to work, and to advance in their work. The lull in the women's rights movement in the 1950s was related to the fact that this same decade saw the lowest age at marriage and the highest proportion of the population married in all of our history.

Since 1960, the age at marriage has moved up: the birth rate is down to what it was in the late 1930s; the divorce rate is up among couples married a long time, and more married women are in the labor force than ever before. These are all relevant contributions to the renascence of women's rights activism in the mid-1960s. The presence of older and married women in women's rights organizations (like the National Organization for Women) is also responsible for a broadening of the range of issues that concern women activists—from the civil, political, and economic concerns they share with feminists of an earlier day, to a host of changes affecting family roles: repeal of abortion laws, revision of divorce laws, community provision of child-care facilities, equal treatment under social security in old age, and a debunking of the clinging-vine or tempting-Eve image of married women that pervades the American mass media.

The point remains, however, that movement toward sex equality is restricted by the fact that our most intimate human relation is the heterosexual one of marriage. This places a major brake on the development of sex solidarity among women, a brake that is not present in other social inequalities, since marriage tends to be endogamous with respect to class, race, and religion.

MODELS OF EQUALITY

Courses in social stratification, minority groups, prejudice, and discrimination have been traditional fare in sociological curriculum for a long time. Many sociologists studied immigrants and their children and puzzled about the eventual shape of a society that underwent so massive an injection of diverse cultures. From these writings, we can extract three potential models that will be useful in sketching the alternate goals not only for the relations between ethnic groups, but for those of race and sex as well.

Three such models may be briefly defined, and then each in turn explored in somewhat greater detail:

1. *Pluralist Model:* This model anticipates a society in which marked racial, religious, and ethnic differences are retained and valued for their diversity, yielding a heterogeneous society in which it is hoped cultural strength is increased by the diverse strands making up the whole society.

2. *Assimilation Model:* This model anticipates a society in which the minority groups are gradually absorbed into the mainstream by losing their distinguishing characteristics and acquiring the language, occupational skills, and life-style of the majority of the host culture.

3. *Hybrid Model:* This model anticipates a society in which there is change in both the ascendant group and the minority groups—a "melting-pot" hybrid requiring changes not only in Blacks and Jews and women, but White male Protestants as well.

PLURALIST MODEL OF EQUALITY

It is dubious whether any society has ever been truly pluralist in the sense that all groups which comprise it are on an equal footing of status, power, or rewards. Pluralism often disguises a social system in which one group dominates the upper classes (White Anglo-Saxon Protestants) and minority ethnic, religious, or racial groups are confined to the lower classes. The upper classes may ceremonially invoke the country's cultural heterogeneity and delight in ethnic food, art, and music, but exclude the ethnic members themselves from their professions, country clubs, and neighborhoods. Bagels and lox for breakfast, soul food for lunch, and lasagna for dinner; but no Jews, Blacks, or Italians on the professional and neighborhood turf! Pluralism has been a congenial model for the race segregationist as well, rationalizing the confinement of Blacks to unskilled labor, and segregated schools and neighborhoods.

In the case of sex, the pluralist model posits the necessity of traditional sex role differentiation between the sexes on the grounds of fundamental physiological and hence social differences between the sexes. This is the perspective subscribed to by most behavioral scientists, clinical psychologists, and psychoanalysts, despite the fact that the women they have studied and analyzed are the products of a society that systematically *produces* such sex differences through child-rearing and schooling practices. There is no way of allocating observed sex differences to innate physiology or to sociocultural conditioning.

Freudian theory has contributed to the assumption of innate sex differences on which recent scholars in psychology and sociology have built their case for the necessity of social role and status differentiation between the sexes. Freud codified the belief that men get more pleasure than women from sex in his theory of the sexual development of the female: the transition from an early stage in which girls experience the clitoris as the leading erogenous zone of their bodies to a mature stage in which vaginal orgasm provides the woman with her major sexual pleasure. Women who did not make this transition were then viewed as sexually "anaesthetic" and "psychosexually immature." Psychological theory often seems sterner and more resistant to change than the people to whom it is applied. It is incredible that the Freudian theory of female sexuality was retained for decades despite thousands of hours of intimate therapeutic data from women, only recently showing signs of weakening under the impact of research conducted by Masters and Johnson and reported in their *Human Sexual Response*, that there is no anatomical difference between clitoral and vaginal orgasm.

Implicit in both psychological theory of sex differences and the Freudian vaginal-orgasm theory was a basic assumption that women should be exclusively dependent on men for their sexual pleasure, hiding from view the realization that masturbation may be different from, but not necessarily less gratifying sexually than sexual intercourse. Much the same function has been served by the strong pressures to disassociate sex from maternity. Physicians have long known that nursing is associated with uterine contractions and have noted that male babies often have erections while nursing, but no one has suggested that the starry-eyed contentment of a nursing mother is a blend of genital as well as maternal pleasure. The cultural insistence upon separating sex from maternity, as the

insistence that vaginal orgasm is the only "normal satisfaction" of a mature woman, serves the function of preventing women from seeing that they can find pleasure and fulfillment from themselves, other women, and their children and do not have to depend exclusively upon men for such gratification.

Coupled with this is the further assumption, peculiar to American society, that child-rearing is the exclusive responsibility of the parents themselves, and not a community responsibility to assure every child a healthy physical and social development (as it is, for example, in East European countries, Israel, and Sweden). This belief keeps women tied closely to the home for the most vigorous years of their adulthood. The "new" look to a woman's life span, now institutionalized by over 100 centers for continuing education for women in the United States, does nothing to alter this basic assumption, but merely adapts to our lengthened life span. Women are urged to withdraw from outside obligations during the childbearing and rearing years and to return for further training and participation in the labor force when children reach an appropriate mature age. The consequences of such late return to active work away from the home are lower incomes, work at levels below the ability of the women, and withdrawal for the very years all studies show to be the peaks of creativity in work, their twenties and thirties.

Why does American society persist in maintaining erroneous myths concerning female sexuality, contrary to research evidence, as it does in urging women to believe their children's development requires their daily attendance upon them, again contrary to research evidence? I believe the answer lies in the economic demand that men work at persistent levels of high efficiency and creativity. To free men to do this requires a social arrangement in which the family system serves as the shock-absorbing handmaiden of the occupational system. The stimulation of women's desires for an affluent style of life and a bountiful maternity—to be eager and persistent consumers of goods and producers of babies—serves the function of adding continual pressure on men to be high earners. The combination of pronatalist values and aspirations for a high standard of living has the effect of both releasing and requiring men to give heavy psychic and time investment to their jobs, and requiring women to devote their primary efforts and commitments to homemaking. As a result, the broad sweep of many an American woman's life span is caught by the transitions from Bill's daughter to John's wife to Johnny's mother and Billy's grandmother.

Behind the veneer of modern emancipation is a woman isolated in an apartment or suburban home, exclusively responsible for the care of young children, dependent on her husband for income, misled to believe that sex gratification is only possible via a vaginal orgasm simultaneous with male ejaculation, and urged to buy more and more clothes and household possessions, which she then takes more time but little pleasure in maintaining. Complementing the life of the woman in the pluralist model of sex roles, the American male is prodded to seek success and achievement in a competitive job world at the emotional cost of limited time or psychic energy for his marriage or his children, tempted by the same consumption-stimulating media and promises of easy credit, expected to uproot his family if a move is "good for his career," and ridiculed as "unmanly," if he seeks to participate more extensively in home and child care.

The odds are heavily stacked against the pluralist model of society as a goal in terms of which racial, ethnic, or sex equality can be achieved.

ASSIMILATION MODEL OF EQUALITY

This model anticipates that with time, the minority groups will be gradually absorbed into the mainstream of society by losing their distinguishing characteristics, acquiring the language, educational attainment, and occupational skills of the majority host culture. Concern for inequality along ethnic or racial lines is concentrated on the political,

educational, and economic institutions of society. Little sociological interest or political concern is shown once men in the minority group are distributed throughout the occupational system in roughly the same proportion as mainstream males.

Feminist ideology is but one variant of the assimilation model, calling upon women to seek their place with men in the political and occupational world in sufficient numbers to eventually show a 50-50 distribution by sex in the prestigious occupations and political organizations of the society. The federal government has served as a pacesetter for the economy in urging the appointment and promotion of competent women to the highest civil service posts and encouraging private employers to follow the federal example by facilitating the movement of women into executive posts.

The feminist-assimilation model has an implicit fallacy, however. No amount of entreaty will yield an equitable distribution of women and men in the top strata of business and professional occupations, for the simple reason that the life men have led in these strata has been possible only because thir own wives were leading traditional lives as homemakers, doing double parent and household duty, and carrying the major burden of civic responsibilities. If it were not for their wives in the background, successful men in American society would have to be single or childless. This is why so many professional women complain privately that what they most need in life is a "wife"!

The assimilation model also makes an assumption that the institutional structure of American society developed over decades by predominantly White Protestant males, constitutes the best of all possible worlds. Whether the call is to Blacks or to women to join White men in the mainstream of American society, both racial integration and a feminist ideology accept the structure of American society as it now exists. The assimilation model rejects the psychological theses of innate racial or sex differences implicit in most versions of the pluralist model, but it accepts the social institutions formed by the ascendant group. This is precisely the assumption numerous Blacks, women, and members of the younger generation have recently been questioning and rejecting.

HYBRID MODEL OF EQUALITY

The hybrid model of equality rejects both traditional psychological assumptions and the institutional structure we have inherited. It anticipates a society in which the lives of men and of Whites will be different, not only [those of] women and [of] Blacks. In fact, it might be that this hybrid model would involve greater change in the role of men than of women, because institutional changes it would require involve a restructuring to bring the world of jobs and politics to the fulfillment of individual human needs for both creativity and fellowship. From this point of view the values many young men and women subscribe to today are congenial to the hybrid model of equality: the desire for a more meaningful sense of community and a greater depth to personal relations across class, sex, and racial lines; a stress on human fellowship and individual scope for creativity rather than merely rationality and efficiency in our bureaucracies; heightened interest in the humanities and the social sciences from an articulated value base; and a social responsibility commitment to medicine and law rather than a thirst for status and high income. These are all demands for social change by the younger generation in our time that are closer to the values and interests women have held than they are to the values and interests of men. They represent an ardent "no" to the image of society projected by the new crop of male technitronic futurists—a machine- and consumption-oriented society that rewards technological prowess in a "plasticWasp9-5america."

Because women have tended to play the passive, adaptive role in the past, they have not been prominent as social and political critics of American institutions. In fact, the traditional roles of women confined them to the most conservative institutions of the society—the family, the public schools, and the church. Women deviant enough to seek greater equality with men in professional, business, and academic life have tended to share the values of their masculine colleagues, while professional women who did not share these values have been quiet, either because they distrusted their own critical bent as a vestige of unwanted "womenliness," or because they feared exclusion from the masculine turf they have precariously established themselves on.

But there is a new groundswell in American society, which is a hopeful sign of a movement toward the hybrid model briefly sketched here. One finds it in Women's Liberation groups across the country, particularly on the university campus. I would predict, for example, that these young women, unlike their professional older sisters, will not bemoan the fact that academic women have been less "productive" than men, but will be critical of the criteria used to assess academic productivity. Up to now these criteria have been such things as "number of publications," "number of professional organization memberships," and "number of offices held in professional organizations." The new breed of women will ask, as many young students are now demanding, that the quality of teaching, the degree of colleagueship with students, the extent of service to both an academic institution and its surrounding community, become part of the criteria on [the basis of] which the productivity of an academic man or woman is evaluated. No one has conducted research on academic productivity with this enlarged net of criteria, and it is a moot point whether men would show greater productivity than women if such criteria were applied. Though it will be a difficult road, with all the money and prestige pulling in the opposite direction, this thrust on the part of the young, together with like-minded older humanist scholars and critics, creative artists, natural and behavioral scientists, has the potential of developing oases of health and sanity in many educational, welfare, and cultural institutions in American society.

CONCLUSION

A *pluralist* model of social equality is implicitly a conservative goal, a descriptive model that accepts what exists at a given point in time as desirable and good. The *assimilation* model is implicitly a liberal goal, a Horatio Alger model that accepts the present structure of society as stable and desirable, and urges minority groups to accept the values and goals of the dominant group within that system as their own. The *hybrid* model is a radical goal which rejects the present structure of society and seeks instead a new breed of men and women and a new vision of the future. Applied to the role of women, these models may be illustrated in a summary fashion as follows: the pluralist model says the woman's nurturance finds its best expression in maternity; the assimilation model says women must be motivated to seek professional careers in medicine similar to those pursued now by men; the hybrid model says, rather, that the structure of medicine can be changed so that more women will be attracted to medical careers, and male physicians will be able to live more balanced and less difficult and status-dominated lives.

An analysis of sex equality goals may start with the reality of contemporary life, but soon requires an imaginative leap to a new conception of what a future good society should be. With the hybrid model of equality one envisages a future in which family, community, and play are valued on a par with politics and work for both sexes, for all the races, and for all social classes and nations which comprise the human family. We are on the brink not of the "end" of ideology, but its "beginning."

21b. WOMEN'S RIGHTS AND THE DRIVE FOR DAY CARE

CHARLES L. SCHULTZE, EDWARD R. FRIED, ALICE M. RIVLIN, and NANCY H. TEETERS

Reprinted from C. L. Schultze et al., Setting National Priorities: The 1973 Budget, *copyright © 1972 by The Brookings Institution, Washington, D. C. The authors are all senior fellows at The Brookings Institution in Washington, D.C. Before joining Brookings, Mr. Schultze was director of the U.S. Bureau of the Budget; Mr. Fried was a senior staff member of the National Security Council; Mrs. Rivlin was Assistant Secretary of Health, Education, and Welfare for Planning and Evaluation; Mrs. Teeters was a fiscal economist in the Bureau of the Budget.*

. . , TRADITIONALLY IN THE UNITED STATES, the responsibility for the care and supervision of children has rested squarely with parents. Only when a child reached age six did society at large take a major hand by insisting that he attend school and by providing schools at the taxpayers' expense. But even at school ages, public concern is limited primarily to the child's intellectual development and to a few hours a day on school days. What happens to the child the rest of the time is his parents' business. Society intervenes only if he is severely abused or neglected or runs afoul of the law.

Public services offered to help parents with their responsibilities for children have been far from comprehensive. Some health services are provided—well-baby clinics, measles vaccine, medicaid for some poor families—but there is no comprehensive program for meeting the health expenses of children comparable to medicare for the aged. Many communities, though not all, provide free public kindergarten for five-year-olds, but few provide public nursery school for the three- and four-year-olds or any kind of infant care, except in emergencies. The mother who needs or wants to take a job normally has to make her own arrangements for child care without public help. Indeed, welfare programs have been designed to reduce the need for women to go to work, by paying them to stay at home and look after their children if there is no male breadwinner in the household.

Until recently, this division of labor between the family and the public was widely accepted as being in the best interest of all concerned. That mothers stayed home and cared for their children before school age and after school hours was considered good for children, good for mothers, and good for society at large. But now this division of responsibility is being challenged from several directions at once. Pressure for public provision or subsidization of day care and preschool programs of various sorts arises from at least three concerns.

1. *Concern with reducing welfare rolls by enabling welfare recipients to work.* The number of mothers and children receiving public assistance has grown rapidly in recent years, causing widespread interest in ways of reducing the welfare rolls. Some believe that mothers on welfare should be required to work; others think that they should simply be encouraged to work. In either case, lack of day care facilities for their children is seen as one of the major impediments to increasing the employment of welfare mothers.

2. *Concern with the children of working mothers generally.* The number of mothers at all income levels who are in the labor force is rising rapidly, causing concern about the large number of children who need care while their mothers work. Little is known about how these children are cared for now, but there is reason to believe that the care is not adequate—that "latchkey" children, left to their own devices, may get into trouble and that low quality day care may be harmful to children. The women's liberation movement is arguing more and more vocally that the public has a responsibility to provide adequate child-care arrangements so that mothers will have a genuine choice between staying at home and going to work.

3. *Concern with early childhood development, especially for low income children.* Children develop intellectual skills and capacities very rapidly at early ages. By age three, poor children on the average already lag behind children from more affluent homes. These observations have led to the hope that early intervention could reduce the handicaps of the poor and might increase the capabilities of all children.

These different concerns all point in the direction of wider public responsibility for children outside the usual school hours and ages and have greatly increased the pressure on the federal government to provide new and expanded day care and preschool programs.

In considering how the federal government should respond to these concerns—if at all—at least three sets of issues need to be resolved.

1. *What kinds of programs are desirable?* The possibilities include "custodial" day care, aimed primarily at keeping children from harm; child development services, including preschool education, nutrition, and health care (in day care settings or elsewhere); and parent education in nutrition, health, and child development.

2. *What should be the government's role?* The government could confine itself to setting standards; it could subsidize parents by giving them vouchers or tax relief for child care; or it could finance or even operate programs directly.

3. *Who should benefit?* Government-supported child care programs could be made available to everyone or limited to the needy. If the latter course is chosen, the problem becomes one of defining who is "needy." . . .

THE DEMAND FOR DAY CARE

If consideration is being given to a large-scale day care program, the first question is:

TABLE 21b.1

LABOR FORCE PARTICIPATION RATES OF MOTHERS, BY AGE OF CHILDREN, 1940, 1950, 1960, AND 1970

Year	All mothers	Mothers with children 6 to 17 years only	Mothers with children under 6 years
1940	9*	n.a.	n.a.
1950	22	33	14
1960	30	43	20
1970	42	52	32

Sources: 1940; U.S. Department of Labor, Women's Bureau, *Women as Workers: A Statistical Guide* (1953), p. 74; other data, from Women's Bureau as given in *Child Care Data and Materials,* Senate Committee on Finance, p. 19.
n.a. Not available.
* Estimate.

What is the demand for various kinds of day care? The answer depends on how many children are likely to need care because their mothers work, on what kind of child care arrangements parents want, and on what they are willing to pay.

Available information indicates (1) that the proportion of young children with working mothers is rising rapidly and seems likely to continue to do so whether the government provides day care or not; (2) that most working mothers arrange to have their children cared for in their own homes or someone else's and that they do not pay much for child care; and (3) that the demand for more elaborate and educational forms of day care appears to be very sensitive to price. Hence, if the government were to offer an expensive variety of day care, it would also have to provide a large subsidy to parents, or they would not enroll their children.

THE INCREASE IN WORKING MOTHERS

In this generation a dramatic change has taken place in American family life. Two or three decades ago, it was unusual for mothers to work outside the home, especially if they had young children. (See Table 21b.1.) Now it is not unusual. More than half the mothers of school age children are in the labor force, and about one-third of those with children under six. In the past decade, the rise in labor force participation has been especially rapid among mothers of very young children—those

with children under six or even under three years old. (See Table 21b.2.) This increase is not a reflection of the breakup of families; it has occurred mainly among wives living with their husbands. Separated, widowed, and divorced women bringing up children on their own have had relatively high labor force participation rates for some time. This group is increasing, but it is not large and does not account for the increased labor force participation rate of mothers.

Mothers are much more likely to be in the labor force if they are Black than if they are White, and the difference is not attributable to the fact that Black women are more likely to head families. Labor force participation rates of Black mothers living with their husbands are also high and have increased markedly in the past decade among those with young children. (See Table 21b.2.)

Some working mothers work part time, but a majority have full-time jobs. (See Table 21b.3.) Also some work only part of the year. It follows that the proportion of mothers who seek work at some time during a year is higher than the proportion in the labor force at any one time. As is shown in Table 21b.3, in a March 1970 survey, 44 percent of all wives with preschool children and 58 percent of those with school age children reported that they had worked during the previous year. Comparable figures for Black wives were 63 percent for those with children under 6 and 73 percent for those with school age children.

TABLE 21b.2
LABOR FORCE PARTICIPATION RATES OF MOTHERS* BY AGE
OF CHILDREN, COLOR, AND MARITAL STATUS, MARCH 1960 AND MARCH 1970

Age of children, and color	All ever-married mothers		Married, husband present		Widowed, divorced, or married, husband absent	
	1970	1960	1970	1960	1970	1960
All ever-married mothers	42.0	30.4	39.7	27.6	60.6	55.5
Children 6 to 17 years only	51.5	42.5	49.2	39.0	67.3	66.2
Children under 6 years	32.2	20.2	30.3	18.6	50.7	39.8
Children 3 to 5 years, with none under 3 years	39.2	27.4	37.0	25.1	58.8	51.7
Children under 3 years	27.3	16.5	25.8	15.3	43.6	32.4
Non-White	53.8	n.a.	53.4	n.a.	54.9	n.a.
Children 6 to 17 years only	62.0	n.a.	62.6	52.6	60.8	n.a.
Children under 6 years	47.2	n.a.	46.9	27.0	48.1	n.a.

Sources: Elizabeth Waldman and Anne M. Young, "Marital and Family Characteristics of Workers, March 1970," U.S. Bureau of Labor Statistics. Special Labor Force Report 130 (1971: processed), Table F; Jacob Schillman, "Marital and Family Characteristics of Workers, March 1960." Bureau of Labor Statistics, Special Labor Force Report 13 (1961: processed), Tables G, K.
n.a. Not available.
*Mothers who have children under 18 years of age and who are or have been married.

TABLE 21b.3
WORK EXPERIENCE IN 1969 OF MARRIED WOMEN WITH HUSBAND PRESENT, BY AGE OF
CHILDREN, AND COLOR, MARCH 1970

Age of children, and color	Percentage of civilian non-institutional population with work experience	Percentage distribution of wives with work experience				
			Worked at full-time jobs			Worked at part-time jobs
		Total	Total	50 to 52 weeks	1 to 49 weeks	
All wives*	50.4	100.0	69.5	40.8	28.8	30.5
With children under 18 years	51.0	100.0	64.5	32.5	31.9	35.5
Under 6 years	44.3	100.0	63.8	21.9	41.9	36.2
Under 3 years	41.9	100.0	66.3	15.6	50.7	33.7
6 to 17 years only	57.5	100.0	65.0	40.6	24.3	35.0
White*	49.2	100.0	69.0	40.8	28.3	31.0
With children under 18 years	49.5	100.0	63.1	31.9	31.2	36.9
Under 6 years	42.3	100.0	62.0	21.0	40.9	38.0
Under 3 years	40.2	100.0	64.8	15.0	49.8	35.2
6 to 17 years only	56.3	100.0	63.8	39.6	24.2	36.2
Black*	64.3	100.0	74.2	40.3	33.8	25.8
With children under 18 years	66.9	100.0	75.8	36.6	39.2	24.2
Under 6 years	62.6	100.0	75.0	26.2	48.8	25.0
Under 3 years	57.9	100.0	75.5	17.9	57.6	24.5
6 to 17 years only	73.0	100.0	76.7	49.3	27.4	23.3

Source: Elizabeth Waldman and Kathryn R. Gover, "Children of Women in the Labor Force," *Monthly Labor Review*, Vol. 94 (July 1971), p. 21. Figures are rounded and may not add to totals.
*Includes wives with no children under 18 years.

The chances that a mother will be working are related not only to her race, her marital status, and the ages of her children, but to several other factors. The chances are higher if she: (1) has more education; (2) lives in a city; (3) has a small number of children; (4) believes her family needs the money. At any level of education, mothers are more likely to work if the rest of the family's earnings are low than if they are high; and wives are more likely to work if their husbands are unemployed. Indeed, when asked why they work, most mothers give economic reasons.

REASONS FOR THE INCREASE

Although differences exist among population groups in the extent to which mothers work, the striking fact is that the proportion of working mothers is rising in all groups. Mothers may say that they work for money, but family incomes have never been higher, so explanations for the increase must lie elsewhere. At least six sets of reasons may be offered, though all of them seem as likely to be results of the phenomenon as causes of it.

1. *The declining birth rate.* The two- and three-child family has become typical, while larger families are becoming rarer. A mother with fewer children has less housework to do and is more likely to be able to earn enough to cover the cost of buying child care outside the home. Moreover, even if she drops out of the labor force until her children reach school age, a mother with two children is likely to have many more years left for working than has a mother of six. The longer work span makes it more worthwhile for the mother of two to invest in the education and on-the-job learning that make work remunerative.

2. *Changing technology in the home.* Taking care of children in the home requires a full-time adult presence but does not require the complete attention of the adult all of the time. So long as mothers have other economic activities to perform at home (cooking, cleaning, canning, laundry), they can look

after children at relatively low extra cost. Laborsaving devices and convenience foods, however, have made it far less necessary for women to stay in the home for reasons other than child care and have made it more important to earn income to cover the cost of these conveniences. Thus, women have greater incentives to seek employment outside the home, even if they have to purchase child care from someone else.

3. *Changing technology outside the home.* The mechanization of manufacturing and the growth of service industries have reduced the proportion of jobs for which physical strength is required and have greatly increased job opportunities for women, albeit usually at lower wage levels than men. Many occupations traditionally considered almost exclusively "women's jobs" (teaching at the elementary and secondary school level, nursing, secretarial work) have expanded dramatically in recent years.

4. *Increasing educational levels of women.* Young mothers have substantially more education now than they did a generation ago. Hence, the economic cost to a mother of staying home—the wages she gives up by not entering the labor market—are appreciably higher than they used to be.

5. *Changing attitudes toward "woman's place."* Although attitudes may not be changing fast enough to suit the more militant leaders of the women's liberation movement, the idea that women should be individuals with lives and careers of their own—not exclusively wives and mothers—is clearly gaining ground, especially among the young.

6. *Changing attitudes about what is good for children.* To an increasing extent, kindergarten and nursery school are considered—by educators and parents alike—to be desirable experiences for children, even if their mothers do not work. Most children now go to kindergarten, and preschool enrollment of three- and four-year-olds is rising rapidly, especially among middle and upper income groups. In 1970, nearly half of the three- and four-year-olds from families with incomes over $10,000 in 1969 were enrolled in some sort of preschool program (compared with 23 per-

cent from families with incomes under $3,-000).

Since all of these factors seem likely to continue operating in the same direction, there is every reason to expect a continuing increase in the proportion of mothers who work—even if no major new day care programs are undertaken by the government. If the proportion of mothers in the labor force increases at the same rate in the 1970s as in the 1960s, one would expect that about 59 percent of all mothers will be in the labor force by 1980—51 percent of those with preschool children and 63 percent of those with school age children, and even higher percentages will work at least some time during the year. Increased availability of subsidized day care would probably increase these proportions somewhat and enable some mothers to shift from part-time to full-time work. Nevertheless, a substantial proportion of mothers, especially those with young children, will continue to choose not to work, so one would not expect these proportions to approach 100 percent. Hence, the main effect of more subsidized day care is likely to be not an increase in the proportion of mothers working, but a change in the kind of care available for children whose mothers have decided to work.

CHILDREN OF WORKING MOTHERS: WHAT HAPPENS NOW?

A mother who works can arrange for the care of her children in a variety of ways, depending on their ages, her income and the hours she works, her family situation, and where she lives. Perhaps her husband, an older child, or another person living in the household can take over while she works. She may have a relative with whom she can leave the children or who can come to her home to look after them. If she thinks the child is old enough, she can let him look after himself, perhaps asking a neighbor to keep an eye on him. If she can afford it, she can hire a maid or a sitter, or she can find a woman who earns money by taking care of other people's children in her home. Or she can enroll her child in a day care center if there is one within feasible commuting distance of where she lives or works.

Of the 70 million children under age 18 in 1971, 26 million had mothers in the labor force. Of these, nearly 6 million were under 6 years old. Another 18 million were between 6 and 14, presumably in school but requiring some kind of supervision after school or on nonschool days. When one considers the large number of children involved, it is remarkable how little is known about what happens to them. Several recent surveys agree, however, on the main outlines of the situation.

The most striking fact is that most children of working mothers are cared for in their own homes or someone else's; only a small proportion are in day care centers. A government survey of child care arrangements of working mothers in 1965 revealed that about half the children under six were cared for in their own homes, usually by their father or another relative, less often by a nonrelative, such as a sitter or a maid. (See Table 21b.4.) Some were looked after by the mother while she worked, presumably in a small business or on a farm. About 30 percent were cared for in someone else's home, about half by a relative, and the rest by a nonrelative, a situation often described as "family day care." A very small group, only about 6 percent, were in day care centers. For school age children the predominance of home and family arrangements was even greater. Roughly two-thirds were cared for in their own homes, and a substantial proportion were described as looking after themselves.

A survey made by the Westinghouse Learning Corporation in 1970, while not entirely comparable, confirmed these general findings. Westinghouse found somewhat greater use of day care centers than did the earlier survey, perhaps reflecting the growth of public programs for low income children. Nevertheless, the survey found only 10 percent of the preschool children—and a negligible proportion of school age children—enrolled in day care centers.

TABLE 21b.4

PERCENTAGE DISTRIBUTION OF CHILD CARE ARRANGEMENTS OF WORKING MOTHERS, BY
AGE OF CHILDREN, 1965 AND 1970

| | Age of children | | | |
| | Under 6 years | | 6 to 14 years | |
Child care arrangement	1965*	1970†	1965*	1970†
Care in own home	48.0	49.9	66.0	78.7
By father	14.4	18.4	15.1	10.6
By other relative	17.5	18.9	22.6	20.6
By a nonrelative	15.3	7.3	6.8	4.5
Mother worked during child's school hours	0.8	5.2	21.5	42.9
Care in someone else's home	30.7	34.5	9.2	12.6
By a relative	14.9	15.5	4.7	7.6
By a nonrelative	15.8	19.0	4.5	5.0
Day care center	5.6	10.5	0.6	0.6
No special care‡	15.7	5.0	24.3	8.3
Total	100.0	100.0	100.0	100.0

Sources: 1965, Seth Low and Pearl G. Spindler, *Child Care Arrangements of Working Mothers in the United States*, U.S. Children's Bureau and U.S. Women's Bureau (1968), pp. 15, 71, 72; 1970, Westinghouse Learning Corporation and Westat Research, Incorporated, "Day Care Survey—1970: Summary Report and Basic Analysis," Prepared for Evaluation Division, Office of Economic Opportunity (1971); processed), pp. 175, 178-80. Figures are rounded and may not add to totals.
* When several kinds of care were used for the same child, the predominating and most recent child care arrangement is given.
† Child care arrangements on the last day the mother worked.
‡ Includes child looked after self, mother looked after child while working, and other.

Since so many of these arrangements are within the family, it is not surprising that few mothers pay much for child care. Indeed, most get it free. The 1965 survey estimated that only 21 percent of the arrangements for care of children under 14 and 34 percent for children under 6 involved a money payment.

While most mothers do not pay, those who do, pay widely differing proportions of their income. As may be seen in Table 21b.5, families with higher incomes tend to pay higher dollar amounts, but some low income families pay significant proportions of their income for child care. The figures in the table are for *each* child, and some families have several children needing care. . . .

WHAT MOTHERS WANT

When asked if they are "satisfied" with their child care arrangements, most working mothers reply that they are. More probing questions, however, frequently turn up serious problems, complaints, and anxieties. Some mothers are concerned about abuse and neglect of their children, especially by baby-

sitters or day care homes. Some worry about the safety of children left alone or with siblings. There are many complaints about the high cost of day care, about the difficulty of making satisfactory arrangements for children under three years old, about the problem of transporting children to distant locations for care and picking them up after work, about the inflexible hours of day care centers and homes and the refusal of many of them to take care of even mildly ill children.

Surveys indicate that more mothers would use good day care centers if they were available at an acceptable cost. On the other hand, substantial numbers of mothers appear to prefer care in their own home or in another home in the neighborhood. Transporting children long distances lengthens the mother's working day and is tiring for both mother and child. There is evidence that mothers place a large premium on closeness to home when choosing child care arrangements. When a Massachusetts survey asked parents whether they would prefer day care next door at $15 a week (for all children) or free care one-half hour away, 58 percent said they would prefer to pay for the care next door.

Surveys to determine what parents are seeking in child care arrangements indicate that they give high priority to convenience and to the child's well-being and social development (getting along with each other) and generally lower priority to educational aspects. The Westinghouse survey found that users of day care centers tended to rate education higher than other mothers do.

Some nonworking mothers say they would work if cheaper or better day care were available, but it is not clear how seriously these statements should be taken. In the Westinghouse survey, 18 percent of the nonworking mothers said they did not work because they could not find satisfactory day care or could not earn enough to pay for it. When asked what kind of care they would prefer if they went to work, more than half the mothers said they would prefer care in their own home or in another's home, but 27 percent indicated they would prefer day care centers. Preferences for day care centers were substantially higher among Blacks than Whites, possibly because Blacks are already heavy users of day care centers and are more familiar with this kind of arrangement.

It is clear from the surveys that the demand for day care is highly sensitive to price. The Westinghouse study asked working mothers with children under age 10 and annual incomes under $8,000 what they would be willing to pay for the kind of day care arrangements they would most like to have. Sixteen percent said they could pay nothing. Of those who would be willing to pay something, the median response was $10

a week. Less than one-fourth of all the families responding said they could pay more than $13 a week, and only 7 percent said they could pay as much as $23 a week per child. There was particular reluctance to pay for care of school age children.

On the basis of survey evidence, Mary P. Rowe has concluded: "It can be expected that fewer than 5 percent of all families in all ordinary populations will pay over $20 per week per child and fewer than 1 percent of all such families would now pay $40 per week. As [a rule] of thumb, families ordinarily will not pay more than 20-30 percent of family incomes for child care for all children."

In sum, information about the demand for day care suggests the following: (1) the number of working mothers seeking care for their children is likely to increase; (2) many mothers would like "better" day care for their children—more convenient, more reliable, more conducive to the child's educational development and well-being; (3) some of these mothers would prefer day care centers to their present arrangement; (4) most mothers, especially those at low income levels, are unwilling or unable to pay much more than they are now paying. Hence, more expensive forms of day care would have to be subsidized if they are to be used by families in the lower and middle income groups. These results are hardly surprising. If large numbers of families were willing to pay more for day care than they are now paying, the private market would surely have responded to this unsatisfied demand.

TABLE 21b.5

PERCENTAGE DISTRIBUTION OF CHILDREN FOR WHOM SOME PAYMENT FOR CARE WAS MADE, BY FAMILY INCOME AND AMOUNT PAID PER YEAR, 1964

Family income (dollars)	Total	Amount paid per year* Under $250	$250-$450	$500 and over
Under 3,000	100	47.2	28.1	24.7
3,000-5,999	100	26.0	43.2	30.7
6,000-9,999	100	20.9	46.1	33.0
10,000 and over	100	17.1	30.0	52.9

Source: Seth Low and Pearl G. Spindler, *Child Care Arrangements of Working Mothers in the United States,* p. 106. Figures are rounded and may not add to totals.
*The amount paid is per child in the family.

SUPPLY OF DAY CARE

Shifting the focus from demand to supply raises the question, What would it cost to supply various types of day care if the federal government were to undertake to do so? Combing the day care literature for answers to the question "What does day care cost?" yields answers ranging from $300 a year per child to $3,000. On closer examination, however, it appears that these widely divergent estimates are actually answers to different questions. To give a useful answer to the question "What does day care cost?" it is necessary to specify (1) how many hours a day one is talking about—half day, full day, after school, and so on; (2) whether the program is carried out in a home or in an institution, such as a day care center; (3) what kinds of services are to be provided—custodial care, an educational curriculum, or a full range of developmental services that include psychological testing, health examinations, social work counseling, and so on; (4) whether the costs to be measured are the operating costs of an existing program or the startup costs of a new program; and (5) whether a relatively small program operating now is at issue or a major national program operating in the future that might be expected to raise the wages of day care workers.

Despite these difficulties of definition, however, two major facts about day care costs are clear. First, day care, however defined, is a process in which adults look after children. Hence, the cost of day care per child depends primarily on two factors: (1) the ratio of adults to children and (2) the wages paid to these adults. The wage level in turn depends mainly on the educational background and training required for the staff. College graduates, certified teachers, and specialists in child development obviously command higher wages than do nonspecialists with lower educational qualifications.

Second, the cost of child care depends in part on whether it is regarded as a by-product of the ongoing operation of households, or whether it is a separate economic activity whose full costs must be met. So long as the care of children of working mothers is kept largely within the family, as it is now, the additional costs are low. It involves the labor of mothers and other family members who would have stayed at home anyway and the use of a facility (the home) that is being used also for other purposes. Once day care becomes a separate economic activity, staffed by people who must be paid what they could be earning in other jobs outside the home, and located in facilities devoted solely to day care, costs tend to rise. The higher wage and facility costs of institutional day care, however, may be more than offset by higher ratios of children to adults. . . .

A study by Abt Associates was based on the actual budgets of 20 day care centers offering educational and developmental as well as custodial services and recognized as "among the better centers of their kind in the country." Model budgets derived by Abt from this study gave an annual cost per child of $2,349 in a center of 25 children, $2,223 for a center with 50 children, and $2,189 for a center with 75 children. In other words, economics of scale were modest and were possibly offset by impersonality and a decline in "warmth" in the larger centers. The high cost was due to low ratios of children to total staff, not to high salaries. The day care teachers were assumed to earn $6,000 a year.

Another set of cost estimates was prepared [in 1972] for the Office of Economic Opportunity (OEO) by David Weikart for a proposed experiment to test the effect on children of various staffing ratios and the extent of training of staff. Weikart divided day care into two basic types: "inexplicit," in which staff time was devoted primarily to care of children, not to teaching, and "explicit," in which staff members had more training in early childhood education and devoted 40 percent of their time to teaching. A basic cost of $295 per child for health, social services, and related items was assumed in all categories. Salaries were taken from the Abt study. The following are the cost estimates (in dollars per child per year) made in the Weikart proposal:

Type of program and staff child ratio	Inexplicit	Explicit
Day care home 1:6	2,351	2,656
Day care center 1:6	2,247	2,552
Day care center 1:10	1,784	2,039
Day care center 1:15	1,553	1,783

The impression that emerges from these studies is that $2,000 per child per year is a typical estimate of the cost of full-day care in a center with an education curriculum and moderate medical and other developmental services. Costs might be less if lower ratios of staff to children were assumed, but they might also be appreciably higher if more elaborate services were provided or if wages and salaries of day care workers should rise appreciably above the levels now paid in the better day care centers. If the salaries of day care teachers, for example, were to rise to the public school level, costs would be increased appreciably.

These typical estimates do not support the notion that carrying out such a program in day care homes rather than day care centers would save money. They assume that the lower wages paid to caregivers in day care homes would be offset by the lower ratio of children to adults.

SHOULD DAY CARE BE SUBSIDIZED?

If these studies are correct, full-day "developmental" day care for preschool children outside their own homes may be expected to cost about $2,000 per child per year, or $40 a week. Most families are not paying this much at present—indeed, few are paying as much as $20 a week—nor could they afford to do so. It follows that substantial subsidies would be required to make developmental care available to the majority of working mothers. . .

Both welfare benefit levels and day care costs differ from state to state, but in general if a mother has more than two children, it is

unlikely that the taxpayers will benefit, at least in the short run, by paying day care costs rather than welfare benefits to the mother. This of course does *not* mean that encouraging work and day care is a bad idea. It means only that such a policy has to be justified on grounds other than saving money —for example, on the grounds that day-care is beneficial to children. . . .

Preschool for four- and five-year-olds appears to have some immediate positive results, and it certainly has not been shown to do children any immediate or lasting harm. By itself, however, it may not be a particularly good investment if the objective is to increase children's ability to function well in school. It is still an open question whether funds should be concentrated on preschool education, on improving the schools themselves, or on other programs—income maintenance, housing, public employment, parent education—that would improve the child's home environment.

Moreover, if the primary motive is to provide preschool education and child development services for disadvantaged children, it is not necessary to go to the expense of providing a full-day program. Half-day programs would meet the needs of the children, though such programs would be less convenient for working mothers. Television programming, visiting nurses and "teachers" and special education for mothers might also be effective and less costly ways of providing preschool stimulation for low income children. . . .

Many who favor subsidizing day care believe that the subsidies should not be limited to the poor, but should be extended to middle and upper income groups as well. Some argue for making day care freely available at public expense to everyone, and others for a sliding scale of payments based on income that would extend at least a partial subsidy to families well above the median income level.

The case for making day care free to all income groups is similar to the case for free public schools. First, it is argued that children benefit from good quality day care, but that parents—even middle and upper income parents—may not understand how valuable the experience is to the child and may not be willing to pay for it. . . .

Second, it is contended that society at large, not just the children, benefits if children have a satisfactory preschool experience. It is argued that a good child development program can reduce failures in school—which may cause problems for others than the ones who fail—and can avert health or psychological difficulties that would be costly to others later on. . . .

Both kinds of benefits—those to children and those to society at large—are very difficult to assess. Their magnitude, however, is likely to be much greater for the poor than for the nonpoor. . . .

Finally, it is alleged that the only way to achieve real equality for women is for society to take over the financing of child care for those who want to work outside the home. If this does not happen, women will either have to stay at home to take care of their children or feel guilty about subjecting their children to the inferior care that all but the rich must make do with in the private sector. Men do not have to make this choice. They can pursue careers while their wives worry about the children, and the argument is that women should have equal freedom.

The primary argument against subsidizing day care for everyone is its tremendous expense. Providing day care costing $2,000 a year per child for all children under 6 would cost $28 billion, even if one-third of them did not participate. It seems extremely inefficient to subsidize all families when a substantial proportion could afford to buy the service for themselves. Of course, the same argument could be made about public schools and public kindergartens. In effect, society has decided that sometime about the age of five the case for a universal subsidy outweighs the case against it. There is no magic about the age of five, and universal day care advocates are asking, "Why not at four, or three, or even at birth?"

Another argument against a universal subsidy for day care, especially for the very young, is that it might encourage people to have more children at a time when there

is a fairly general belief that a lower rate of population growth would be in the national interest. At present, most of the responsibility, financial and otherwise, for rearing children in the first five or six years of life falls on parents, and this may deter many people from adding to their families. If free day care and preschool for infants and toddlers were available to all parents, they might be less cautious about having more children. . . .

ISSUES TO BE DECIDED

It is difficult to defend subsidizing day care solely on the grounds that it would save taxpayers money by enabling welfare mothers to work. If a mother has little education or work experience, or if she has more than two children, the training-work-day care option may be more costly than paying her to stay home. For this group, a day care subsidy has to be defended either on the grounds that there are noneconomic benefits to the mother —such as the self-respect she gains from holding a job—or to the child. The benefits to poor children of developmental day care, in turn, are difficult to assess. Many persons would weigh heavily the immediate benefit to the child of being in a safe, attractive environment, getting attention from adults who consider his well-being their job, eating balanced meals, and receiving routine medical attention. Others believe that a subsidy can be justified only on the basis of long-run benefits, such as permanent increases in IQ or reading scores. At the moment, there is little reason to hope that preschool education *alone* will yield these permanent benefits. Whether preschool plus improved education in elementary school would constitute a permanent breakthrough for low income children is an open question.

If a decision is made to subsidize developmental day care for the poor in general (not just to ration it to a minority as at present), serious questions arise about the treatment of moderate-income families. As we have seen, day care charges for families in the $4,000 to $12,000 range could be adjusted to income. If, however, the charges rose steeply as income increased in this range, middle income parents would either seek less costly alternatives in the private sector—presumably resenting the fact that better care was available to the poor—or would make less effort to increase their earnings. On the other hand, if charges rose gradually as income increased, the public cost would mount, rapidly approaching the cost of universal free day care.

If the developmental day care option is chosen, it seems likely that the costs will be large because political pressure to extend the subsidy in the middle income range will be heavy. Some would argue that these costs to the taxpayer are fully justified. Others would argue that developmental day care should not be subsidized, even for the poor, but that emphasis should be placed on less costly ways of reaching low income children, either in their own homes or in whatever day care arrangements their mothers choose to make for them. Options that have been suggested include more educational television programming for preschool children, educational programs for mothers and family day care providers, and visiting nurse arrangements. . . .

22. COLONIALISM: THE CASE OF THE MEXICAN AMERICANS

JOAN W. MOORE

Reprinted from Social Problems *17(4) (Spring 1970) by permission of the Society for the Study of Social Problems. Joan W. Moore is Associate Professor of Urban Affairs and Sociology at the University of Southern California at Los Angeles. She is co-author of the principal sociological study of Mexican-Americans (J. W. Moore, and A. Cuellar, Mexican Americans, Englewood Cliffs, New Jersey: Prentice-Hall, 1970).*

■ The attention—both scholarly and popular—given to the persistent and pervasive patterns of discrimination and oppression of Blacks in the United States has tended to obscure the fact that there are other minorities subjected to very similar treatment. Most of these minorities have been small, or hidden away in relatively unpopulated areas (like Indians); some have been successful enough in socioeconomic terms so that the minority problem seems to be resolved (Japanese-Americans). By the early 1960s popular understanding of the situation of minorities in the United States seemed to suggest that only for Blacks was there still a "major" problem of inequality based on ethnic differences. By the end of the 1960s, however, events brought sharply to public attention the existence in the United States of a large minority of Spanish-speaking origin. This issue came to the fore first in the East, with the large migration of Puerto Ricans to New York, and later to other Eastern and Midwestern cities. To some extent it was defined as a "minorities problem" like the racial issues between Blacks and Whites and partly as a problem of discrimination against and adaptation by first generation immigrants, an old and familiar matter.

Meanwhile, rising group consciousness and assertiveness on the part of Mexican-Americans in the Southwest and in California focused attention on a group that had been present in the United States for a long time and could hardly be considered simply as new immigrants. While many Mexican-Americans were indeed recent arrivals, many others came from families that had been present for as long or longer than the Anglos who held most of the power and economic resources in these areas. Thus the paradigm of "colonialism" seemed particularly useful in coming to an understanding of the situation of the Mexican-American minority vis-à-vis the rest of our society.

In this article, the author examines the utility of this paradigm by considering the central facts of Mexican-American experience in its light.

Other discussions of the situation of Mexican-Americans in the United States can be found in Nancie L. González, *The Spanish Americans of New Mexico: A Distinctive Heritage,* Advance Report 9 (Los Angeles: University of California, Mexican American Study Project, 1967); Leo Grebler, et al., *The Mexican American People* (New York: Free Press, 1970); and George I. Sanchez, *Forgotten People* (Albuquerque: The University of New Mexico Press, 1940). ■

AMERICAN SOCIAL scientists should have realized long ago that American minorities are far from being passive objects of study. They are, on the contrary, quite capable of defining themselves. A clear demonstration of this rather embarrassing lag in conceptualization is the current reassessment of sociological thought. It is now plain that the concepts of "acculturation," of "assimilation," and similar paradigms are inappropriate for groups who entered American society not as volunteer immigrants but through some form of involuntary relationship.

The change in thinking has not come because of changes within sociology itself. Quite the contrary. It has come because the minorities have begun to reject certain academic concepts. The new conceptual structure is not given by any academic establishment but comes within a conceptual structure derived from the situation of the African countries. In the colonial situation, rather than either the conquest or the slave situation, the new generation of Black intellectuals is finding parallels to their own reactions to American society.

This exploration of colonialism by minority intellectuals has met a varied reaction, to say the least, but there have been some interesting attempts to translate these new and socially meaningful categories into proper academic sociologese. Blauner's (1969) article in *Social Problems* is one of the more ambitious attempts to relate the concept of "colonialism," as developed by Kenneth Clark, Stokely Carmichael, and Elridge Cleaver, to sociological analysis. In the process, one kind of blurring is obvious even if not explicit—that is, that "colonialism" was far from uniform in the 19th century, even in Africa. In addition, Blauner (1969) makes explicit the adaptations he feels are necessary before the concept of colonialism can be meaningfully applied to the American scene. Common to both American internal colonialism of the Blacks and European imperial expansion, Blauner argues, were the involuntary nature of the relationship between the two groups, the transformation or destruction of indigenous values, and, finally, racism. But Blauner warns that the situations are really different: "the . . . culture . . . of the [American Black] colonized . . . is less developed; it is also less autonomous. In addition, the colonized are a numerical minority, and furthermore, they are ghettoized more totally and are more dispersed than people under classic colonialism."

But such adaptations are not needed in order to apply the concept fruitfully to America's second largest minority—the Mexican Americans. Here the colonial concept need not be analogized, and, in fact, it describes and categorizes so accurately that one suspects that earlier "discovery" by sociologists of the Mexican Americans, particularly in New Mexico, might have discouraged uncritical application of the classic paradigms to all minorities. The initial Mexican contact with American society came by conquest, not by choice. Mexican American culture *was* well developed; it *was* autonomous; the colon-

ized *were* a numerical majority. Further, they were—and are—less ghettoized and more dispersed than the American Blacks. In fact, their patterns of residence (especially those existing at the turn of the century) are exactly those of "classic colonialism." And they were indigenous to the region and not "imported."

In at least the one state of New Mexico, there was a situation of comparatively "pure" colonialism. Outside of New Mexico, the original conquest colonialism was overlaid, particularly in the 20th century, with a grossly manipulated voluntary immigration. But throughout the American Southwest where the approximately 5 million Mexican Americans are now concentrated, understanding the Mexican minority requires understanding both conquest colonialism and "voluntary" immigration. It also requires understanding the interaction between colonialism and voluntarism.

In this paper I shall discuss a "culture trait" that is attributed to Mexican Americans both by popular stereotype and by social scientists—that is, a comparatively low degree of formal voluntary organization and hence of organized participation in political life. This is the academic form of the popular question: "What's wrong with the Mexicans? Why can't they organize for political activity?" In fact, as commonly asked both by social scientist and popular stereotype, the question begs the question. There is a great deal of variation in three widely different culture areas in the Southwest. And these culture areas differ most importantly in the particular variety of colonialism to which they were subjected. In the "classically" colonial situation, New Mexico, there has been in fact a relatively high order of political participation, especially by comparison with Texas, which we shall term "conflict colonialism," and California, which we shall term "economic colonialism."

NEW MEXICO

An area that is now northern New Mexico and parts of southern Colorado was the most successful of the original Spanish colonies. At the beginning of the war between the United States and Mexico, there were more than 50,000 settlers, scattered in villages and cities with a strong upper class as well as a peasantry. There were frontier versions of Spanish colonial institutions that had been developing since 1600. The conquest of New Mexico by the United States was nearly bloodless and thus allowed, as a consequence, an extraordinary continuity between the Mexican period and the United States period. The area became a territory of the United States, and statehood was granted in 1912.

Throughout these changes political participation can be followed among the elite and among the masses of people. It can be analyzed in both its traditional manifestations and in contemporary patterns. In all respects it differs greatly in both level and quality from political participation outside this area. The heritage of colonialism helps explain these differences.

On the elite level, Spanish or Mexican leadership remained largely intact through the conquest and was shared with Anglo leadership after the termination of military rule in 1851. The indigenous elite retained considerable strength both in the dominant Republican Party and in the state legislature. They were strong enough to ensure a bilingual provision in the 1912 Constitution (the only provision in the region that guarantees Spanish speakers the right to vote and hold office). Sessions of the legislature were—by law—conducted in both languages. Again, this is an extraordinary feature in any part of the continental United States. Just as in many Asian nations controlled by the British in the 19th century, the elite suffered little—either economically or politically.

On the lower class level, in the villages, there was comparatively little articulation of New Mexican villages with the developing urban centers. What there was, however, was usually channeled through a recognized local authority, a *patron*. Like the class structure, the *patron* and the network of relations that sustained him were a normal part of the established local social system and not an ad hoc

or temporary recognition of an individual's power. The political participations on both the elite and the lower class levels were outgrowths of the existing social system.

Political participation of the elite and the *patron* system was clearly a colonial phenomenon. An intact society, rather than a structureless mass of individuals, was taken into a territory of the United States with almost no violence. This truly colonial situation involves a totally different process of relationship between subordinate and superordinate from either the voluntary or the forced immigration of the subordinate—that is, totally different from either the "typical" American immigrant on the eastern seaboard or the slave imported from Africa.

A final point remains to be made not about political participation but about protopolitical organization in the past. The villages of New Mexico had strong internal organizations not only of the informal, kinship variety but also of the formal variety. These were the *penitente* sects and also the cooperative associations, such as those controlling the use of water and the grazing of livestock. That such organizations were mobilized by New Mexican villagers is evidenced by the existence of terrorist groups operating against both Anglo and Spanish landowners. Gonzalez (1967) mentions two: one functioning in the 1890s and one in the 1920s. Such groups could also act as local police forces.

Let us turn to the present. Political participation of the conventional variety is very high compared to that of Mexican Americans in other states of the Southwest. Presently there is a Spanish American in the United States Senate (Montoya, an "old" name), following the tradition of Dennis Chavez (another "old" name). The state legislature in 1967 was almost one-third Mexican American. (There were no Mexican American legislators in California and no more than 6 percent in the legislature of any other Southwest state.) This, of course, reflects the fact that it is only in very recent years that Mexican Americans have become a numerical minority in New Mexico, but it also reflects the fact that organized political participation has remained high.

Finally, New Mexico is the locus of the only mass movement among Mexican Americans—the *Alianza Federal de Mercedes*, headed by Reies Tijerina. In theme, the *Alianza*, which attracted tens of thousands of members, relates specifically to the colonial past, protesting the loss of land and its usurpation by Anglo interests (including, most insultingly, those of the United States Forest Service). It is this loss of land which has ultimately been responsible for the destruction of village (Spanish) culture and the large-scale migration to the cities. In the light of the importance of the traditional village as a base for political mobilization, it is not really surprising that the *Alianza* should have appeared where it did. In content the movement continues local terrorism (haystack-burning) but has now extended beyond the local protest as its members have moved to the cities. Rather than being directed against specific Anglo or Spanish landgrabbers, it has lately been challenging the legality of the Treaty of Guadalupe Hidalgo. The broadening of the *Alianza's* base beyond specific local areas probably required the pooled discontent of those immigrants from many villages, many original land grants. It is an ironic feature of the *Alianza* that the generalization of its objectives and of its appeal should be possible only long after most of the alleged land-grabbing had been accomplished.

TEXAS

Mexican Americans in Texas had a sharply contrasting historical experience. The Mexican government in Texas was replaced by a revolution of the American settlers. Violence between Anglo-American settlers and Mexican residents continued in south Texas for generations after the annexation of Texas by the United States and the consequent full-scale war. Violence continued in organized fashion well into the 20th century with armed clashes involving the northern Mexican *guerilleros* and the U.S. Army.

This violence meant a total destruction of Mexican elite political participation by conquest, while such forces at the Texas Rangers were used to suppress Mexican American participation on the lower status or village levels. The ecology of settlement in south Texas remains somewhat reminiscent of that in northern New Mexico: there are many areas that are predominantly Mexican, and even some towns that are still controlled by Mexicans. But there is far more complete Anglo economic and political dominance on the local level. Perhaps most important, Anglo-Americans outnumbered Mexicans by five to one even before the American conquest. By contrast, Mexicans in New Mexico remained the numerical majority for more than 100 years after conquest.

Texas state politics reflect the past just as in New Mexico. Mexican Americans hold some slight representation in the U.S. Congress. There are two Mexican American Congressmen, one from San Antonio and one from Brownsville (at the mouth of the Rio Grande River), one of whom is a political conservative. A minor representation far below the numerical proportion of Mexican Americans is maintained in the Texas legislature.

It is on the local level that the continued suppression is most apparent. As long ago as 1965 Mexican Americans in the small town of Crystal City won political control in a municipal election that electrified all Mexican Americans in Texas and stirred national attention. But this victory was possible only with statewide help from Mexican American organizations and some powerful union groups. Shortly afterward (after some intimidation from the Texas Rangers) the town returned to Anglo control. Some other small towns (Del Rio, Kingsville, Alice) have recently had demonstrations in protest against local suppressions. Small and insignificant as they were, the demonstrations once again would not have been possible without outside support, primarily from San Antonio. (The most significant of these San Antonio groups have been aided by the Ford Foundation. The repercussions in Congress were considerable and may threaten the future of the Ford Foundation as well as the Mexican Americans in Texas.)

More general Mexican American political organizations in Texas have a history that is strikingly reminiscent of Negro political organization. (There is one continuous difference: Whites participated in most Negro organizations at the outset. It is only very recently that Anglos have been involved with Mexicans in such a fashion. In the past, Mexicans were almost entirely on their own.) Political organization has been middle class, highly oriented toward traditional expressions of "Americanism," and accommodationist. In fact, the first Mexican American political association refused to call itself a political association for fear that it might be too provocative to the Anglo power structure; it was known as a "civic" organization when it was formed in Texas in the late 1920s. Even the name of this group (LULAC or the League of United Latin American Citizens) evokes an atmosphere of middle class gentility. The second major group, the American G.I. Forum, was formed in an atmosphere of greater protest, after a Texas town had refused burial to a Mexican American soldier. In recent years, increasing politicization has been manifested by the formation of such a group as PASSO (Political Association of Spanish Speaking Organizations). But in Texas, throughout the modern period the very act of *ethnic* politics has been controversial, even among Mexican Americans.

CALIFORNIA

The California transition between Mexican and American settlement falls midway between the Texas pattern of violence and the relatively smooth change in New Mexico. In northern California the discovery of gold in 1849 almost immediately swamped a sparse Mexican population in a flood of Anglo-American settlers. Prior to this time an orderly transition was in progress. Thus the effect was very much that of violence in Texas: the indigenous Mexican elite was almost totally excluded from political participation. A generation later when the opening of the railroads repeated this demographic discontinuity in southern California the Mexicans suffered the same effect. They again were almost totally excluded from political participation. The New Mexico pattern of social organization on a village level had almost no counterpart in California. Here the Mexican settlements and the economy were built around very large land holdings rather than around villages. This meant, in essence, that even the settlements that survived the American takeover relatively intact tended to lack internal social organization. Villages (as in the Bandini rancho which became the modern city of Riverside) were more likely to be clusters of ranch employees than an independent, internally coherent community.

In more recent times the peculiar organization of California politics has tended to work against Mexican American participation from the middle and upper status levels. California was quick to adopt the ideas of "direct democracy" of the Progressive era. These tend somewhat to work against ethnic minorities. But this effect is accidental and can hardly be called "internal colonialism," coupled as it was with the antiestablishment ideals of the Progressive era. The concept of "colonialism," in fact, appears most useful with reference to the extreme manipulation of Mexican immigration in the 20th century. Attracted to the United States by the hundreds of thousands in the 1920s, Mexicans and many of their U.S.-born children were deported ("repatriated") by welfare agencies during the Depression, most notably from California. (Texas had almost no welfare provisions; hence no repatriation.) The economic expansion in World War II required so much labor that Mexican immigration was supplemented by a contract labor arrangement. But, as in the Depression, "too many" were attracted and came to work in the United States without legal status. Again, in 1954, massive sweeps of deportations got rid of Mexicans by the hundreds of thousands in "Operation Wetback." New Mexico was largely spared both waves of deportation; Texas was involved primarily in

Operation Wetback rather than in the welfare repatriations. California was deeply involved in both.

This economic manipulation of the nearly bottomless pool of Mexican labor has been quite conscious and enormously useful to the development of California extractive and agricultural enterprises. Only in recent years with increasing—and now overwhelming—proportions of native-born Mexican Americans in the population has the United States been "stuck" with the Mexicans. As one consequence, the naturalization rate of Mexican immigrants has been very low. After all, why relinquish even the partial protection of Mexican citizenship? Furthermore the treatment of Mexicans as economic commodities has greatly reduced both their motivation and their effectiveness as political participants. The motivations that sent Mexican Americans to the United States appear to have been similar to those that sent immigrants from Europe. But the conscious dehumanization of Mexicans in the service of the railroad and citrus industries in California and elsewhere meant an assymmetry in relationship between "host" and immigrant that is less apparent in the European patterns of immigration. Whatever resentment that might have found political voice in the past had no middle class organizational patterns. California was structurally unreceptive and attitudinally hostile.

Thus in California the degree of Mexican political participation remains low. The electoral consequences are even more glaringly below proportional representation than in Texas. There is only one national representative (Congressman Roybal from Los Angeles) and only one in the state legislature. Los Angeles County (with nearly a million Mexican Americans) has no supervisor of Mexican descent, and the city has no councilman of Mexican descent. Otherwise, the development of political associations has followed the Texas pattern, although later, with meaningful political organization a post-World War II phenomenon. The G.I. Forum has formed chapters in California. In addition, the Community Service Organization, oriented to local community political mobilization, and the Mexican American Political Association, oriented to statewide political targets, have repeated the themes of Texas' voluntary association on the level of the growing middle class.

How useful, then, is the concept of colonialism when it is applied to these three culture areas? We argue here that both the nature and the extent of political participation in the state of New Mexico can be understood with reference to the "classical" colonial past. We noted that a continuity of elite participation in New Mexico from the period of Mexican rule to the period of American rule paved the way for a high level of conventional political participation. The fact that village social structure remained largely intact is in some measure responsible for the appearance of the only mass movement of Mexicans in the Southwest today—the *Alianza*. But even this movement is an outcome of colonialism; the expropriation of the land by large-scale developers and by federal conservation interests led ultimately to the destruction of the village economic base—and to the movement of the dispossessed into the cities. Once living in the cities in a much closer environment than that of the scattered small villages, they could "get together" and respond to the anticolonialist protests of a charismatic leader.

Again following this idea, we might categorize the Texas experience as "conflict colonialism." This would reflect the violent discontinuity between the Mexican and the American periods of elite participation and the current struggle for the legitimation of ethnic politics on all levels. In this latter aspect, the "conflict colonialism" of Texas is reminiscent of Black politics in the Deep South, although it comes from different origins.

To apply the colonial concept to Mexicans in California, we might usefully use the idea of "economic colonialism." The destruction of elite political strength by massive immigration and the comparative absence of local political organization meant a political vacuum for Mexican Americans. Extreme economic manipulation inhibited any attachment to the reality or the ideals of American society and indirectly allowed as much intimidation as was accomplished by the overt repression of such groups as the Texas Rangers.

To return to Blauner's use of the concept of "internal colonialism": in the case of the Mexicans in the United States, a major segment of this group who live in New Mexico require no significant conceptual adaptation of the classic analyses of European overseas colonialism. Less adaptation is required in fact than in applying the concepts to such countries as Kenya, Burma, Algeria, and Indonesia. Not only was the relationship between the Mexican and the Anglo-American "involuntary," involving "racism" and the "transformation . . . of indigenous values," but the culture of the Spanish American was well developed, autonomous, a majority numerically, and contained a full social system with an upper and middle as well as lower class. The comparatively nonviolent conquest was really almost a postscript to nearly a decade of violence between the United States and Mexico which began in Texas.

The Texas pattern, although markedly different, can still be fitted under a colonialist rubric, with a continuous thread of violence and suppression and adaptations to both in recent political affairs.

The Mexican experience in California is much more complicated. Mexicans lost nearly all trace of participation in California politics. Hence, there was no political tradition of any kind, even the purely negative experience in Texas. Then, too, the relationship between imported labor and employer was "voluntary," at least on the immigrants' side. The relationships were much more asymmetrical than in the "classic colonial" case.

If any further proof of the applicability of the idea of "colonialism" were needed, we have the developing ideology of the new *chicano* militants themselves. Like the Black ideologies, *chicanismo* emphasizes colonialism, but in a manner to transcend the enormous disparities in Mexican American experience. Thus one of the latest versions of the ideology reaches out to a time *before* even Spanish colonialism to describe the southwestern United States as "Aztlán"—an Aztec term. "Aztlán" is a generality so sweeping that it can include all Mexican Americans. Mexican Americans are the products of layer upon layer of colonialism, and the overlay of American influence is only the most recent. That the young ideologues or the "cultural nationalists" (as they call themselves) should utilize the symbols of the first of these colonists, the Aztecs (along with Emiliano Zapata, the most "Indian" of Mexican revolutionaries from the past), is unquestionably of great symbolic significance to the participants themselves. But perhaps of more sociological significance (and far more controversial among the participants) is the attempt to legitimate *chicano* culture. This culture comes from the habits, ideas, and speech of the most despised lower class Mexican American as he has been forced to live in a quasi-legal ghetto culture in large southwestern cities. These symbols are all indigenous to the United States and are neither Mexican, nor Spanish, nor even Aztec. But they *do* offer symbols to all Mexican Americans, after a widely varying experience with Americans in which, perhaps, the ideologues can agree only that it was "colonialist."

IV.

INEQUALITIES OF POWER

WE HAVE SEEN in Selection 5 that power can be considered the basic principle of stratification. We can paraphrase Lenski's observation as "In the beginning, there was power inequality," and particular patterns of economic and status inequality can exist only to the extent that they are supported by power inequality. Just as the division and specialization of economic activity has increased almost geometrically with the rise of industrialization, so has the division and specialization of power. Accordingly, to define an individual's position in the stratification of power is a complex task, since he deals with so many representatives of institutions with power.

We examine in this Part issues of political inequality involving the right of ordinary citizens to vote, the ability of neighborhoods to affect local government activity, and the success of a particular policy (the government regulatory agency) designed to deal with the social problem of overweaning business power. Then we examine a subject many observers have characterized as the most important problem of American society: increased Presidential power linked with increased military power. In one case the issue is the use of secrecy and the free range of Presidential initiative to pursue the war in Vietnam; next is the somewhat broader issue of the "military-industrial complex" as a factor in encouraging the very rapid growth of American military institutions. Finally we shift to a much less obvious area of power but one that is likely to be of a growing importance in our society: the power to define what is "culture" in a society like ours where the mass media are highly varied and very popular.

23. EQUALITY OF VOTING

WALTER DEAN BURNHAM

Reprinted from "A Political Scientist and Voting Rights Litigation: The Case of the 1966 Texas Registration Statute," in the Washington University Law Quarterly, *Vol. 1971, No. 2, 1971 by permmission. Walter Dean Burnham is Professor of Political Science at Massachusetts Institute of Technology and the author of* Critical Elections and the Mainsprings of American Politics *(New York: Norton, 1970).*

■ In many countries the proportion of eligible citizens who vote is higher than in the United States; comments on this observation generally imply that U.S. citizens are less interested in politics and perhaps less grateful for their democratic privileges than citizens of other nations. The selection by Walter Dean Burnham reviews evidence suggesting that the lower turnout in this country may instead be principally a product of an effort by those in control of governments and legislatures to limit the number of citizens who vote. In most democracies the central government assumes responsibility for registering all citizens so they may vote. In contrast, registration in the United States is left completely up to the citizen who often encounters roadblocks like those used openly in the southern states to discourage Black voting and somewhat less obviously to discourage poor White voting.

Burnham's article is interesting both because it presents a thorough analysis of the effects of voter registration statutes and because it is an example of social science research applied to public policymaking in a very concrete way. His research was prepared as the basis for his testimony as an expert witness on behalf of the plaintiffs in a Texas challenge of Jim Crow laws. This use of social science research in policy formation is increasingly common, one of the earliest and most dramatic examples of which is the evidence marshaled in the early 1950s to support the argument that de facto school segregation is inherently unequal. NAACP lawyers made use of a wide range of psychological and sociological research that bore on the issue, and the Supreme Court in its decision cited this evidence as demonstrating that it was impossible to meet the Constitution's equal protection requirement with a segregated school system no matter how "equal" the facilities might be. The Court also seems to have found in the testimony of Burnham and other social scientists convincing evidence that the effect of a registration system

such as that in Texas is discriminatory. With the growth of various kinds of advocacy on behalf of the poor, the consumer, and minorities, we can expect social science evidence to be brought before the courts and the legislatures in increasing quantity.

Additional readings on voting and equality can be found in D. Rae, *The Political Consequences of Electoral Law* (New Haven, Conn.: Yale University Press, 1967). Burnham has dealt more generally with voter participation in *Critical Elections in the Mainsprings of American Politics* (New York: Norton, 1970). Supreme Court involvement in election and voting law is analyzed in R. Claude, *The Supreme Court and the Electoral Process* (Baltimore: Johns Hopkins Press, 1970). ■

A VERITABLE REVOLUTION in the public law of voting rights has been underway in this country since the early 1960s. Not so very long ago, it was almost universally accepted doctrine that the states had nearly plenary power to regulate the conduct of elections, the qualifications of voters and the apportionment of legislative district boundaries within their borders. This sweeping power, for all intents and purposes, was circumscribed only by the requirement that the states not discriminate in too crude a way against racial minorities. Since World War II this very broad state discretion has undergone erosion, and this erosion has been immensely accelerated during the past decade. Even the most cursory review of the development of legal doctrine in this area must conclude that the hitherto ascendant "American suffrage medley" has been increasingly subjected to central authority. As a consequence of both judicial and congressional action, a considerable degree of nationalization or standardization of suffrage and apportionment has come into being. . . .

For at least the past century, the balance between central and local control of electoral process at any given time has been largely determined by the level of national tolerance of racism in our political life. The national commitment to juridical equality for all American citizens which has emerged over the last generation has inevitably subjected all sorts of exclusionist southern electoral management devices to a devastating attack from the center. But with this movement has also come a much wider sensitivity to the more subtly discriminatory nature of many state-prescribed "rules of the game" which have little obtrusive relationship to race or region.

It is not the purpose of this commentary to deal at length with the evolution of judicial doctrine and legislative action affecting voting rights. Rather, I shall attempt a sketch of two things here: the background and implications of a recently decided case in which a state's personal-registration statute was struck down by a federal court, and my own involvement in the case.

Between 1890 and 1908, all 11 of the ex-Confederate states adopted without effective federal challenge an interlocking network of legal devices whose primary purpose was to purge Blacks from their electoral processes. This is now a matter of common knowledge, even knowledge of the special sort subject to official—and especially judicial—cognizance. But it is perhaps less apparent that these control devices were paralleled in a less extreme form elsewhere by the introduction at the same time of such devices as literacy tests, contrived malapportionments and personal registration statutes which initially were applied solely against the populations of major cities. There are certain broad themes which link the origins of all such legislation together. To a very great degree, it was motivated by racism—in the North, directed against the "newer races" immigrating from eastern and southern Europe—and by fear of the considerable potential for political radicalism during an era of transition to industrial-capitalist hegemony over the political economy. To this should be added more than a dash of old middle class reformism directed against state and city "machines" and their ethnic clienteles. Perhaps most important was the influence of a broad, if very ambiguously defined, consensus that voting was rather more a privilege the individual had to prove himself worthy to exercise than a right which was an attribute to adult citizenship.

The peculiarities of such American suffrage-regulating mechanisms as personal registration statutes are best appreciated in a comparative context. During the same transitional period, virtually every other Western democratic polity—including Canada to our north—made public authority, not the individual, legally responsible for the burden of voter registration. Virtually everywhere outside the United States, government is charged with the duty of compiling and updating registers of qualified electors. This might seem to be a small enough matter of technical detail, were it not for the demonstrated fact that personal registration qualifications *impose a sociologically differential barrier to the exercise of the franchise.* The United States has incomparably the steepest class differentials in voting participation to be found in any western nation. Turnout among blue-collar strata is normally hardly more than half of the rate of participation among professional managerial people. There is no doubt that the reasons for this are complex, but two considerations emerge which are relevant to this discussion. In the first place, personal registration statutes produce a measurable and substantial depressing effect on lower class participation. Secondly, before about 1900 class differentials in American voting participation, at least outside the South, were extremely small—probably not much if any greater than in Germany or Sweden today.

Perhaps most remarkable of all, the adoption of personal registration statutes appears to have met with practically no effective resistance in the 1890-1910 period. Moreover, a perusal of the literature of political science down until well after World War II reveals only the most limited awareness of the political sociology involved. Indeed, the entire question was virtually invisible to scholars and political elites alike; the device was simply accepted by something approaching unanimous consent. Such unquestioning acceptance of this form of electoral bookkeeping can, I think, be explained only on the ground that the individual responsibility value premises on which the legislation rested conformed admirably to the larger postulates of an individualist liberal political culture at a time when these postulates had not been brought under effective critical review, either in academic or other elite circles.

The voting rights revolution has changed a good deal of this. Perhaps more precisely, this revolution is itself an artifact of a changing and much more self-conscious awareness by judges, lawyers, and academics about the nonobtrusive social costs of a traditional American politicolegal pattern. One result is that political scientists like myself are now being asked to contribute position papers to party commissions concerned with expanding and equalizing the franchise, and also depositions in cases challenging the constitutionality of certain kinds of personal registration statutes.

There is a sense in which the creation of new ranges of constitutional doctrine can sometimes be said to flow from a "dialectic of extremes." This was particularly obvious in the decisional background of *Brown* v. *Board of Education* which laid down the general doctrine that "separate educational facilities are inherently unequal." For the Supreme Court had been sensitized over a number of years to the sociological realities of educational segregation by a series of *law school* cases extending from *Missouri ex rel. Gaines* v. *Canada*, 305 U.S. 337 (1938) to *Sweatt* v. *Painter*, 339 U.S. 629 (1950). As lawyers, the Justices could see from their own experience and knowledge that "separate" was not only far from being "equal" in the field of legal education, but that racial segregation itself fundamentally denied equality of opportunity or of access to the larger benefits of professional status to the Blacks

involved. From this point in 1950, it required rather little more for the Justices in the 1954 segregation cases to reach their famous reformulation of the relationship between racial separation and equality in education generally.

Of course, it would be most premature to assume that the public law of personal registration statutes will follow the same pattern even though alternative procedures for voter enrollment exist elsewhere which minimize the severe class bias in voter participation so conspicuously associated with personal registration. Indeed, there seem to be specific difficulties in the way of such a doctrinal evolution from "extremes" to general principles in this field. First, the profound national consensus about the utility and equity of these procedures has only very recently been significantly challenged even by professional students of the American political process. It can be assumed that challenges directed at the substantive sociological effects of such statutes as a general class of regulation of the franchise will be rather long in coming and even longer in being accepted by courts. Second, the equal protection questions involved in this area seem to lead further away from the original close relationship between race and voting rights litigation. This requires the establishment of a quite discrete array of empirical evidence which, related to the more diffuse class implications of registration statutes, has power to persuade courts; and this, too, will take time. Third and not least important, changes in the personnel of the U.S. Supreme Court produce the likelihood—at least in the short run—that a more or less "conservative" majority, a majority of Justices whose decision-shaping values may not include sensitivity to such empirical demonstrations, will control the court's decisions.

Nevertheless, we may be on our way. An extreme case which highlights a more general problem has emerged in Texas. This case is of particular interest, both because it sets a precedent involving judicial scrutiny of personal registration statutes and the requirements they establish for individual access to the polls, and because of the court's heavy reliance in its opinion upon the testimony and quantitative data presented by political scientists.

Before 1966, Texas was one of the few states which still imposed a poll tax as a prerequisite for voting. The paid-up poll tax receipt was used by election officials as the equivalent of personal registration. Such receipts had to be collected and the tax paid not later than January 31 of the year in which the election was to take place. After judicial invalidation of the poll tax prerequisite, the Texas legislature drafted a personal registration statute which was in essence a reenactment of the old poll tax law with the $1.75 left out. The 1966 statute had two leading features which worked to depress turnout about as much as possible without including a money charge for voting. First, it provided for closing the registry books as of January 31 of the year of election. Second, it provided for a system of *periodic* personal-registration—i.e., the individual was required to reregister in person every year.

In February 1970, one Jimmy F. Beare of Corpus Christi attempted to register, but was turned away by local officials because the January 31 cutoff date had passed. Suit was brought in federal district court to challenge the constitutionality of the 1966 Texas registration statute. Along with several other political scientists, I was contacted by attorneys for the plaintiff in the spring of 1970 and asked to provide answers to certain questions of fact in my capacity as a professional student of voting behavior. The interrogatories and my answers to them follow in an appendix to this discussion.

On January 7, 1971, a three-judge federal district court unanimously invalidated both the statute and a parallel provision of the Texas constitution as being in violation of the Equal Protection Clause of the Fourteenth Amendment. In his opinion for the court, Judge Singleton followed his preliminary statement of the controversy by a forceful assertion of the right to vote as a fundamental social and political value in the United States. The opinion goes on to observe that "It is beyond doubt that the pres-

ent Texas voter registration procedures tend to disenfranchise multitudes of Texas citizens otherwise qualified to vote." This conclusion was based on the court's estimate that at least 1 million Texans were effectively disenfranchised by the onerous requirement of annual registration, and that about 1 million Texans were also disenfranchised by the cutting off of registration more than nine months before the date of the general election. In turn, these estimates are wholly based on the testimony given by political scientists, particularly by Professors Allen Shinn of the University of Texas, Stanley Kelley, Jr., of Princeton University, and myself. One of the most enlightening features of Professor Shinn's presentation was the determination that turnout increases at a rate of about 2.7 percent for each month of an election year as one approaches the date of the general election—a fairly precise statement of the familiar generalization that many people tend to become motivated to vote by exposure to the issues and individuals of a political campaign, not months before the candidates actively take the field.

The court then reviewed the state's claim that it had a predominant state interest in the maintenance of these procedures. It first concluded that annual registration was hardly compellingly necessary to avoid electoral corruption or fraud: elections in the overwhelming majority of states which have permanent rather than periodic registration are clean enough for the most part. The court then turned to an argument made by the state which brilliantly discloses the profound significance of this case.

One such interest suggested by the state as compelling which the provisions in question are said to promote is the purity of the ballot. In other words, the state contends that those who overcome the annual hurdle of registering at a time remote to the fall elections will more likely be better informed and have greater capabilities of making an intelligent choice than those who do not care enough to register. This is a claim which cannot be accepted. . . . A state may not dilute a person's vote to give weight to other interests, see, e.g., *Reynolds* v. *Sims,* 377 U.S. 533 (1964), much less deny it completely to thousands of

Texans who fail to comply with the existing registration statutes.

Here, in 1971, we are confronted with a fundamental issue of political philosophy and values. The Texas argument here is—couched in modern form—the proposition that voting is less a universal right than a privilege to be confirmed, if possible, to the *melior pars* of the citizenry. The theory which animated the original poll-tax legislation still dominates the thinking of the state's officials; it represents one side of an ancient controversy. The key issue in this controversy is simply this: is there, or ought there to be, a social stratum which should be accepted as "weightier" than the rest of the citizenry because of some supposed virtue, and hence be given *legally-prescribed preference* over the rest? This is the kind of question to which, broadly, only a yes or a no is a possible answer; and the answer defines the respondent's political philosophy. Conflict over which answer to this question is to prevail can be easily traced back to the debates on enfranchisement in the Massachusetts and New York conventions of 1820 and 1821, and beyond into the colonial period. But it is ultimately traceable to a still earlier if not primordial set of debates: those conducted at Putney by members of Oliver Cromwell's army in the years 1647-49, and especially a justly memorable colloquy between General Ireton and Colonel Rainborough.

Lest it be said that this is very ancient history indeed, let us examine the antiphonies involved, not only within each "debate" but between the two, separated as they are by more than three centuries. First, the exchange between Rainborough and Ireton concerning voting and representation:

Rainborough: . . . For really I think that the poorest he that is in England hath a life to live, as the greatest he; and therefore truly, sir, I think it's clear, that every man is to live under a government ought first by his own consent to put himself under that government; and I do think that the poorest man in England is not at all bound in a strict sense to that government that he hath not a voice to put himself under. . . .
Ireton: . . . Give me leave to tell you, that if you make this the rule I think you must fly for refuge to an absolute natural right, and you must

deny all civil right; and I am sure it will come to that in the consequence. . . . I think that no person hath a right to an interest or share in the disposing of the affairs of the kingdom, and in determining or choosing those that shall determine what laws we shall be ruled by here—no person hath a right to this, that hath not a permanent fixed interest in this kingdom, and those persons together are properly the represented of this kingdom, and consequently are to make up the representers of this kingdom, who taken together do comprehend whatsoever is of real or permanent interest in the kingdom.

Then, in 1970-71, came the case of *Beare* v. *Smith*. The argument made by Texas to justify its procedures has already been stated as paraphrased by the court: it asserts a compelling state interest in ensuring that only the intensely political survivors of its multiple procedural hurdles will be admitted to the active electorate. By such tests, apparently, such voters will have demonstrated that they have a "permanent fixed interest in this kingdom," now that poll taxes may no longer be levied. The court's answer to this is a remarkably unambiguous statement of the opposite view:

At the outset, it must be said that the right to vote is a right which is at the heart of our system of government. . . . That government should derive its powers from the consent of the governed is one of the basic tenets of the Declaration of Independence. This right is one which has been jealously guarded by the judiciary over the years.

Later in his opinion, Judge Singleton incorporated with approval the following commentary by an outside observer:

Participation in decisions affecting one's life and the community contributes to the growth of the individual and tends to promote the stability of the political system by enhancing its legitimacy. In this day and age, with many explosive forces at work, we should pay more attention to the stability acquired by justly giving to all qualified citizens easy access to the ballot.

Admitting that Rainborough was obviously committed to the political fate of the little man, while the author quoted approvingly by the court is more preoccupied with stabilizing the political system, the resonance thus achieved with the utterances of a man dead more than three hundred years is nonetheless striking.

The issue presented here is of the most cardinal importance in determining what "free government" actually means in concrete terms. For those of us who may have thought that this issue had become largely academic in the United States, Texas' Iretonian argument of 1970 comes as a pointed reminder that it is not academic at all. Still more, it reveals with unusual clarity that this primordial question of political value has never been conclusively resolved in this country down to the present day. If it be true that this is an extreme case, and that Texas' argument was expressed in exceptionally explicit if not crass terms, it seems to me equally true that personal registration requirements as such survive because the United States has yet to accept without ambiguity the elementary proposition that voting in elections is an attribute of adult citizenship, and not a reward for good behavior or some superior virtue.

So far as the district court's reliance on social science evidence is concerned, of course, no new ground was broken here. The growing complexity of society long ago brought the realization to lawyers and judges that expert testimony was required for rational decisions in many fields where judicial decisions were to be made. It was after all at the turn of this century that the Goldmark-Brandeis brief, with its heavy emphasis on sociological data relevant to legal problems, was developed; and as early as 1908 that the Supreme Court's decision in a major case was informed by the data in such briefs. The precedent here is substantive, not methodological:

Courts are now involved in exploring a major "gray area" of voting rights, though how far they move into it—or even whether they remain in it—must ultimately rest on what the Supreme Court does in the years ahead. Even so, one further note about method should be added. The quantitative behavioral revolution in the study of voting has permitted political scientists to develop increasing precision in their statements about the effects of electoral laws on electorates. We are in a far better position than even five years ago to provide concrete information which should be useful to courts as they evaluate the right to vote on one hand and the "compellingness" of state interest in suffrage regulations on the other.

The process of egalitarian standardization of voting requirements in the United States will, I think, prove irreversible in the long run. Our self-consciousness about supposedly neutral "rules of the game" has almost certainly undergone irreversible expansion. That new-found consciousness alone will make it difficult for a number of traditionally sanctioned practices to survive indefinitely. Moreover, individuals who are subject to complex procedural restrictions on their right to vote will be increasingly likely to file suits challenging the constitutionality of such restrictions. Both the volume of this litigation and the pressure engendered by it to change legal doctrine and formulate universalistic norms will correspondingly increase. And thus the involvement of voting behavior specialists in the judicial process—a properly peripheral but not insignificant involvement—will probably not cease with *Beare* v. *Smith*. (The following appendix, pages 294-298, gives information concerning *Beare vs. Smith*.)

APPENDIX
[Abridged]
IN THE DISTRICT COURT OF THE UNITED STATES
FOR THE SOUTHERN DISTRICT OF TEXAS
CORPUS CHRISTI DIVISION

JIMMY F. BEARE, ET AL.   X

VS.   X   CIVIL ACTION NUMBER 70-C-42

PRESTON SMITH, ET AL.   X

ANSWERS TO INTERROGATORIES

BY: WALTER DEAN BURNHAM, PROFESSOR OF POLITICAL SCIENCE, WASHINGTON UNIVERSITY, ST. LOUIS, MISSOURI 63130.

Has your research shown any relationship between personal registration systems and class bias and voter participation? Yes, although as a professional student of electoral processes, I should at some point emphasize that there are many variables which enter into a truly comprehensive evaluation of the influence of registration as such on class stratification in American electoral participation. It seems evident to me, however, that such relationships exists.

If so, what is that relationship? The analytical argument in favor of the relationship is simple enough, and is essentially taken from Anthony Downs' volume, *An Economic Theory of Democracy.* Putting the matter most simply, it can be said that any personal registration system imposes costs of access to the polls on individual voters to some extent. These costs are legally identical but sociologically sharply differentiated; that is, people of lower socio-economic status will tend to find the additional hurdle of personal registration more of a barrier (in terms of expenditure of scarce time resources, the costs of transportation to central places of registration, etc.) than will people in the middle classes. The extreme case can be found in the dense network of hurdles which were set up by the Southern states in the period 1890-1904—including in many cases extremely laborious and inconvenient registration procedures. Such hurdles were explicitly set up to achieve complete disfranchisement of Negroes, of course, but they clearly worked to disfranchise considerable parts of the poor-white population of these states as well.

Further discussion of comparative class stratification in voter participation will be left to the answer to the question on class bias. At this point, several ranges of data can be presented. (1) Prior to the introduction of personal registration statutes, the turnout in a number of states was so high as to make it virtually certain that lower-class people participated about as fully as did middle and upper class people. Thus, for example, the turnout in the 1880-1896 period can be found in several selected states with considerable urban populations (see Table 23.1). There are, as mentioned above, a number of explanations for the much lower turnout in these states today than in the 1880-1896 period; but among these, personal registration costs of access to the polls seem of considerable significance. It seems evident on the face

TABLE 23.1

PERCENT TURNOUT OF ESTIMATED POTENTIAL ELECTORATE

	1880	1884	1888	1892	1896	Mean, 1952-68
Illinois	89.9	84.4	82.9	86.0	95.7	73.9
Indiana	94.4	92.2	93.3	89.0	95.1	74.5
New Jersey	95.4	88.6	91.9	90.3	88.4	69.7
New York	89.3	87.5	92.3	86.3	84.3	65.6
Ohio	94.4	93.4	91.9	86.2	95.5	67.6

of the data that in this earlier period there must have been virtually no differential in turnout along class lines in these states.

(2) The existence of profound class bias in actual participation is easy to detect in the United States at the present time. It can, I think, be categorically stated that this bias is sharper by far in the United States than in any other Western democratic political system.

Annex V [not reproduced here] presents correlation data drawn from intensive aggregate analysis of Baltimore, 1952-1968, resting ultimately on the precinct level. The simple correlation array at the top of the page sets out in sharp relief the extremely sharp class-related basis of electoral participation in that city. There is also a substantial negative correlation between turnout and the nonwhite population, as could be expected. What is doubly significant, however, is that when class is controlled for in the multiple correlations, at the bottom of the page, the racial-ethnic correlations virtually disappear. Indeed, the percentage Negro and the percentage turnout is actually positively correlated, once the former is controlled for by two classifications of lower-class percentages in the 1960 male labor force. This further reinforces the point that, untangling racial-ethnic variables, class remains clearly the strongest predictor of turnout and that there is a systematic relationship between the two. This can be summarized more simply by the assertion that, on balance, the ratio between upper-middle class and lower-class turnout in Baltimore is approximately 2 to 1. . . .

Finally, it seems extremely likely that, granted the systematic differences in voter participation in areas with personal registration systems and in areas without, the class bias of participation is markedly less strong in non-registration areas (those which correspond functionally to European politics where registration is assumed by the state) than in areas which, like Baltimore City, impose this additional cost of access to the polls on the individual voter.

What is a periodic registration system? A periodic registration system is one in which, in addition to the requirements of personal registration, the individual voter is also required to register in person, usually before each election.

Has your research shown any relationship between periodic registration systems and electoral participation in general? On the whole not, since such systems have tended to become unusual in the United States. I am able, however, to cite two points in tests by leading American political scientists; these are referred to immediately below.

If so, what is that relationship? It is, again, perfectly clear to me that the additional imposition of a requirement that individual voters re-register in advance of each election will further depress turnout above and beyond what might be expected from the effects of personal registration systems generally. One authority for this view is that of *The American Party System*, 3rd. (1940) edition, by Charles Merriam and Harold F. Gosnell. These two scholars, both of the University of Chicago, were among the leading experts on American politics a generation ago. They comment as follows (p. 385): "When personal registration was adopted in the large cities of this country, it was felt that it should be periodic. The requirement of a new personal registration at frequent intervals would automatically clear the lists of those who had died or moved away. Registration was made annual in New York and a number of states, while it was made biennial or quadrennial in other states. *There is no question that the periodic systems of registration are burdensome upon the voters and virtually disfranchise many qualified persons. . . .*" [emphasis added]

The requirement imposed by the New York legislature whereby voters in New York City, and only such voters, were required to register annually was particularly notorious as a bone of contention between the city and the upstate areas which controlled the legislature. The late V. O. Key, Jr.—the undisputed dean of students of American politics during his lifetime—had the following to say about the New York case in his text, *Politics, Parties and Pressure Groups* (New York: Crowell, 1958—4th edition) at pp. 677-678, footnote 8: "Nonpersonal registration is used in over half the election districts in upstate New York. In 1950 registration in ten of the 57 upstate counties of New York exceeded the numbers of citizens 21 and over as reported by the census. In another 11 counties registrants numbered between 90 and 100 percent of the citizenry of voting age. In New York City, with personal [and at the time periodic—WDB] registration, only 53.5 percent of the citizens 21 and over were registered; in the state outside the city the percentage was 79.8." The periodic-registration requirement for New York City was at last abolished by the state legislature in 1957, and a permanent registration substituted for it.

A very rough estimate on my part would be that—assuming that, as in New York, periodic reregistration was permitted up to a few weeks before election day—such as additional burden on the voter would depress turnout by between 10 and 20 percent from what might be expected from a permanent registration system fairly and non-discriminatorily administered. . . .

Does class bias exist in registration systems used outside the United States in countries whose cultures and traditions are somewhat cognate to our own? This question is put a little inaccurately. We may begin with the point that throughout Western Europe and in Canada, the responsibility for developing registers of qualified voters and keeping them up to date is borne entirely by governmental authority, delegated in some cases (such as Great Britain and Canada) to Electoral Officers with powers to punish for noncompliance by individuals with their surveys of the resident population. By definition, therefore, such systems preclude class bias in the registration procedure, except in the very limited sense that people of the very lowest social classes may be difficult to locate at fixed addresses. If one asks, however, what class bias tends to exist in European or Canadian voting *turnout* at elections, the answer is somewhat more varied. In general, it can be surmised that a moderate class differential in participation *may* exist in Canada and Great Britain, though I have no data which

bears directly on this. It seems certain that even here, the class bias in turnout is immeasurably less than it is in the United States, if it indeed exists to any significant extent.

Voting turnout in Continental Europe is much more nearly *invariant along class lines,* and is also much higher, than it is in the United States. In general, it can be said that in historical perspective, class bias in which middle-class persons participated more than working-class persons was more frequently encountered in European political systems before World War II and especially before World War I, but that: (a) in the past quarter-century such bias has virtually disappeared; and (b) there are numerous cases even in the earlier period of high mobilization of all classes in the population. (See Annexes . . . VIII and IX.)

Requiring individuals to re-register for each election with a terminal date falling months before the actual election is particularly onerous. People become interested in elections during the campaign, not months before it; and it is my considered view that having a January 31 cutoff date for periodic registration guarantees a low turnout; indeed, a turnout which is probably about as low as possible short of a reimposition of the poll tax.

In 1968 (I assume under the registration law now under attack), almost exactly one-half of the potential electorate of Texas voted for presidential electors. I believe that a permanent registration system—provided that it permitted registration up to a few weeks or days before primary and general elections, as is now common in this country—would permit Texas turnout to increase from 50 percent to between 65 and 70 percent. In 1968, the estimated potential electorate of Texas was approximately 6,180,000. Of these, only 3,078,917 actually voted in the presidential election. An increase of turnout to 65 percent would be equivalent to adding about 940,000 voters to the presidential electorate. If the turnout reached 70 percent, this would involve an addition of about 1,250,000 persons who did not actually vote in 1968 in Texas. Even if the periodic-registration requirement was responsible for only one-half of this difference, it is evident that hundreds of thousands of potential voters are involved.

Were Texas to eliminate its personal registration system and place the burden of registration on the government, the probable result would be to increase electoral participation to a maximum of about 80 percent of those potentially qualified—a rate significant-

ly below that of many European countries, but approximately that found in high-stimulus election years in countries such as Canada, Great Britain and France. This would add about 1,850,000 more actual voters than came to the polls in 1968. Presented in tabular form, the approximate results of changes in electoral law (these are maximum results, assuming that no other intervening variables in Texas turnout exist) would appear as shown in Table 23.2.

TABLE 23.2
ACTUAL VOTING IN 1968 COMPARED WITH POTENTIAL
VOTING UNDER CHANGES IN ELECTORAL LAW

Category	Vote 1968	Increase over Actual
Existing statute	3,079,406	...
Permanent personal registration: lower limit	4,020,000	+941,000
Permanent personal registration: upper limit	4,328,000	+1,249,000
Governmental maintenance of registry	4,947,000	+1,868,000
Potential electorate, 1968 (approximate)	6,184,000	...

ANNEX VIII A.
SWEDEN: VOTER PARTICIPATION BY SEX AND
BROAD OCCUPATIONAL CATEGORY, 1960*

Category	Electoral Participation in %, 1960			N. of Cases
	Men	Women	Total	
Non-Agricultural:				
Employers and Professional Workers				
Office Employees (Salaried)	91.1	90.6	90.8	18,371
Salaried Service Employees	90.9	90.4	90.7	15,722
(Including governmental)	93.8	91.3	92.5	8,493
Other Salaried Employees	90.0	88.0	88.6	13,335
Foremen and Craftsmen	93.2	93.5	93.3	4,084
Workers	88.0	87.0	87.5	60,064
Independent, Members of Families	78.1	72.9	75.5	23,275
Agricultural:				
Farmers & Farm Managers	90.4	86.4	88.4	19,890
Farm and Other Workers	80.9	84.1	82.5	6,834
Total, 1960	87.6	85.5	86.6	163,339

*Based on a 1/30th sample of the total voting-age population.
Source: *Statistisk Arsbok for Sverige,* 1964, p. 380.

ANNEX VIII B.
UNITED STATES: VOTER PARTICIPATION BY SEX AND
BROAD OCCUPATIONAL CATEGORY, 1968*

Category	Electoral Participation in %, 1968		
	Men	Women	Total
Non-Agricultural:			
Professional & Managerial	81.4	82.7	81.8
Clerical, Sales & Kindred Workers	79.0	76.5	77.4
Manual Workers:	63.5	56.9	62.3
Craftsmen, Foremen, etc.	68.6	69.3	68.6
Operatives & Kindred Workers	60.3	56.0	58.9
Laborers, except Farm & Mine	54.8	54.3	54.8
Service Workers	67.6	60.2	62.7
Agricultural:			
Farmers, Farm Managers	82.3	66.5	81.6
Farm Laborers & Foremen	42.4	62.1	50.6
Total USA, 1968	71.4	70.6	71.1

* Source: U.S. Bureau of the Census, Current Population Reports Series P-20, No. 192 (December 2, 1969), *Voting and Registration in the Election of November 1968*, p. 22.

ANNEX IX
AVERAGE (MEAN) ELECTORAL PARTICIPATION IN
TWENTY WESTERN NATIONS, 1945-1969

I. Countries with Compulsory Voting

Country	Mean Turnout
Australia	95.5
Belgium	92.3
Italy	92.4

II. Countries with Non-Compulsory Voting

Country	Mean Turnout
Austria	94.9
Canada	76.3
Denmark	85.0
Finland	78.9
France	79.0
Germany (West)	85.6
Iceland	90.4
Ireland	73.8
Israel	82.3
Luxemburg	91.1
Netherlands	94.7

II. Countries with Non-Compulsory Voting (Cont.)

Country	Mean Turnout
New Zealand	90.7
Norway	79.7
Sweden	82.6
Switzerland	69.0
United Kingdom	79.2
United States	59.9

III. Composite Averages

Category	Mean Turnout
Compulsory-voting nations	93.4
All others except United States	83.3
English-speaking countries except Australia and United States	80.0
Nations of Continental Europe + Israel	84.4
United States	59.9
(Texas, 1948-1968:	40.8)

24. COMMUNITY ACTION AND NEIGHBORHOOD CONTROL

■ The disparity of power between citizens and their government becomes ever more salient as government assumes a larger and larger role in providing the resources that individuals and families need to pursue their goals. In a nation where the public sector is small, as in the United States before the 1930s, these issues could not loom so large as they have in the 1960s and 1970s. Big bureaucracy has taken its place alongside big business and big labor as an important area of concern to those who worry about inequalities of power.

When one considers communities of the poor, and even more communities of poor Blacks or other minorities, the disparity between public servants—the "caretakers," to use Herbert Gans' word—and their disadvantaged clientele are especially striking. Social scientists who studied lower class communities in the 1950s and early 1960s developed a particular point of view about these power inequalities and argued that one of the most important changes to improve the situation of the disadvantaged would be to give them more power to affect the disposal of the resources that government made available for their presumed benefit. This concern meshed with the rising activism of the civil rights movement and with the new kind of political consciousness represented in the founding of Students for a Democratic Society and expressed in their initial statement of program. From all these sources came an emphasis on "community action," on "maximum feasible participation" of the poor in poverty programs, and the later insistence that "clients" be represented on governing bodies of all kinds of organizations—the public on corporate boards of directors, students on university boards of trustees, and so on.

Lipsky argues in the following selection that to make urban services responsive to the needs of citizens (and therefore efficient) currently centralized urban service organizations need to be decentralized. In the next selection, I assess the prospects of neighborhood action as a tactic in lower class communities.

General discussions of power in several urban contexts are found in Robert Dahl, *Who Governs?* (New Haven, Conn.: Yale University Press, 1961), and in Nelson Polsby, *Community Power and Political Theory* (New Haven, Conn.: Yale University Press, 1963).

The first systematic strategy of local community organization is described by Saul Alinsky in *Reveille for Radicals* (New York: Random House, 1969). A concrete example of the Alinsky method in action is reported in Charles Silbermann's *Crisis in Black and White* (New York: Random House, 1964). A useful case study of the development of a local community organization is in William W. Ellis, *White Ethics and Black Power: The Emergence of the West Side Organization* (Chicago: Aldine, 1969). Experience with community action and participation by the poor has been analyzed by Peter Marris and Martin Rein in *Dilemmas of Social Reform*, 2d ed. (Chicago: Aldine, 1973); by Daniel P. Moynihan in *Maximum Feasible Misunderstanding* (New York: Free Press, 1969); and by Alan Altschuler in *Community Control: The Black Demand for Participation in Large American Cities* (New York: Pegasus, 1971). An interesting study of the effects on the participants of membership on community action boards is found in Lewis Zurcher, *Poverty Warriors: The Human Experience of Planned Social Intervention* (Austin: University of Texas Press, 1970). ■

24a. RADICAL DECENTRALIZATION

MICHAEL LIPSKY

Reprinted from The Second International Symposium on Regional Development, *Tokyo, Japan, September 17-19, 1968. Michael Lipsky is Associate Professor of Political Science at Massachusetts Institute of Technology. He has conducted research dealing with aspects of urban politics, urban bureaucracy, and the role of protest in local and national politics. He is the author of* Protest in City Politics *(Skokie, Ill.: Rand McNally, 1972).*

ONE OF THE PROBLEMS in the United States today, and one of the major sources of conflict in American cities, is the allocation of authority over public programs in the cities. I want to deal with the problem of "radical decentralization," which in large part developed out of the Black power movement in the United States. I hope that my discussion will illuminate some of the problems of planning and administrative decentralization which more generally characterize the organization of industrial societies. The reasons that demands for radical decentralization arise may provide significant insight into the potential and limitations of democratic planning.

The words "radical decentralization," in most general terms, refer to a distribution of authority over programs and institutions which, to the maximum extent possible, would place authority in the hands of the people who are most directly affected by the institutions or programs. This may relate to control of schools by parents, control over housing policies by area residents, and control over police policies by residents of the area. Many Negro politicians in the United States advocate development of Negro-controlled businesses and the allocation of grants to individual neighborhoods for community development programs which are not controlled by the national or city governments. Such a plan, for example, has been started in Columbus, Ohio, where a single neighborhood has been incorporated as a foundation with significant capital to plan programs for the area. The term "radical decentralization" embraces such common terms as *community control, neighborhood development,* and *neighborhood self-help.*

Before going further, it is important to distinguish radical decentralization from what I call conservative decentralization. Radical decentralization refers to placing authority to the maximum extent possible in the hands of those who are affected by institutions or programs. In distinction, conservative decentralization merely refers to distributing authority in governmental units below the national level—to states, to counties, cities or other subdivisions.

Now the extent to which authority is decentralized has been a theme in American politics throughout the country's history. Political controversies frequently have been fought over the appropriate level of government to formulate policy. In a sense, the American Civil War was fought over this issue. Current concerns over desegregation also relate to which unit of authority will ultimately make policy.

The debate over radical decentralization differs from other decentralization controversies in that it focuses on: (1) attempts to establish the legitimacy of a neighborhood, community or ethnic group as a legitimate entity to which power is allocated. and (2) attempts to solve the problems of program effectiveness through establishment of a fundamental unity between power, responsibility and impact.

This essay will be divided into three parts. First, I will describe some of the developments which have led to advocacy of radical decentralization. Second, I will discuss a number of significant dilemmas of radical decentralization which must be explored further. And third, I will demonstrate the consistency between radical decentralization and some recent thinking of social scientists.

I am one of those who think that social scientists have something to say to planners.

Let me mention some developments in American politics which have led to support of radical decentralization as a political movement. First, the civil rights movement. Many of the civil rights organizations which developed in the 1960s were wary of problems of organizational rigidity which accompany organizations as they grow older and more powerful. The leaders of these civil rights organizations, and leaders of White radical student organizations, also developed the theory that creating viable indigenous organizations among people who are traditionally apathetic toward organizational participation requires new organizational structures. An ideology developed which suggested that all people should participate in decision making. This would be an alternative to elite democracy in which representative leaders make decisions from positions somewhat remote from the people. These leaders hoped, perhaps in a Trotskyist sense, that there would be a constant renewal of the organization through leadership turnover and full involvement of members in the organization's decision-making structures.

At the same time critics of American urban development programs began to recognize that community participation in decision making would have to become more central in the planning process. This realization stems from many unhappy experiences with urban program planning. This is illustrated in the urban renewal program in the United States, for example, which has often been criticized as amounting to "Negro removal," since this seemed to be the major impact of the urban renewal programs on the residents of the areas to be renewed. Although urban renewal programs promised to assist slum residents, public housing construction has been very inadequate.

In response to criticisms along these lines, some programs and some government agencies have made halfhearted attempts to introduce greater representation of community groups into the planning process. But these programs essentially have been tokenistic.

They did not recognize the unity between responsibility and power. In other words, citizen participation was encouraged, but critical decisions were not made at the level that citizens actually participated.

These criticisms have been paralleled by substantive criticisms of existing government programs. In cases where existing programs fail to benefit the Negro population, radical decentralization is advocated as a residual solution. It is argued that "since current arrangements and reforms seem incapable of substantially improving program performance, communities ought to try to run the programs. The situation cannot get much worse than it is." Furthermore, it is argued, community involvement in program planning will provide the essential element of commitment which is so lacking in the Black ghettoes. It is further argued that the problem with previous government social planning is that it was viewed by the community as alien. With radical decentralization community projects would no longer be considered foreign and people might take the kind of interest necessary for successful program implementation.

It is these criticisms that have led theorists of city planning to develop the "advocate planning" orientation. These theorists reject notions of comprehensive community planning and recognize that comprehensive planning benefits various interest, and that the planning mechanism itself may represent a strategy in which conflict over urban political decisions is removed to an area where elites make decisions while minimizing pressures from community groups. Advocate planners—that is, people who accept this theory—in contrast to central agency planners want to associate themselves with community groups and develop plans which embody the values of the community. These plans would then represent alternative strategies for community development. Neighborhood groups could then debate the merits of *alternative* proposals rather than merely react to a plan presented to them by a government agency.

Supporting all of these trends are certain trends in political theory. Radical decentralization is consistent with concepts of direct democracy, decentralization, and the importance of neighborhoods that Americans highly value. Radical decentralization finds support among American conservatives, and is also attractive to liberals who recognize that legislative coalitions are necessary to obtain massive federal financing without which meaningful programs will not emerge.

There are three reasons that radical decentralization is attractive to conservatives. First, the stress on community development in proposals for radical decentralization suggests that there will be an increase in the number of Black capitalists, Black entrepreneurs and Black homeowners. This is a development consonant with belief in and support of the free enterprise system. Second, radical decentralization conforms to the widely honored premise that Black Americans should be able to fit into American patterns of upward mobility. These patterns of upward mobility are held in front of the American Negroes because of the accepted belief that immigrant groups in previous periods in American history bettered their conditions through group solidarity and growth. Third, as pointed out above, radical decentralization deflects pressure for racial integration. Public housing in Black neighborhoods is clearly more attractive to the majority of Whites than is location of public housing projects in White neighborhoods where Blacks would share White facilities.

Let me turn now to some dilemmas of radical decentralization which illustrate some of the difficulties of changing existing systems. These difficulties should be regarded as problems in need of solution rather than barriers to trends in radical decentralization.

First, where will resources come from? Advocates of radical decentralization do not advocate decentralizing the financial base of the American government. On the contrary, advocates of radical decentralization expect that financing will continue to be centralized at the same time that authority over programs will be decentralized. Clearly funds must continue to come either through government mechanisms of redistribution or through direct private investment. Yet, Black politicians must recognize that if funding comes from outside sources so a measure of power will remain outside community control. Furthermore, if communities try to build an economic base in order to become self-sufficient, they will come under pressure from groups in the community which advocate short-run, consumer-oriented programs. You cannot make long-run investments, in other words, if you are spending money for short-run popular programs.

The second major problem is the maintenance of standards. Historically, certain functions of city and federal government were developed in response to the need for regulations to ensure minimum health and welfare. The federal, city, and state governments have developed standards on which the society depends. In the areas of land use, health, and levels of public service, these standards are the fruit of earlier reforms periods. They have been developed at much cost and effort, and should not be easily given away or modified.

Let me give you some examples. Minimum educational standards for teachers have been developed to ensure a certain level of education in schools and to protect teachers through a civil service mechanism. Currently these standards are being questioned in Black neighborhoods on at least three grounds. First, the standards may inhibit or limit the quick development of increases in the number of Black teachers. Second, Black teachers whose backgrounds are similar to those of their pupils are likely to be more effective than White teachers who may have difficulty either understanding their Black students or serving as "role models" for their students to emulate. Third, in some circumstances progressive educators in the United States feel that people without formal education may play creative roles in low income school districts.

The question is: to what extent should community boards of education, empowered to have authority over school policies, be able to change or modify these standards? Community school boards may want to discharge teachers for various reasons, which would abridge teachers' former rights. What kinds of teacher protections are necessary to attract talented teachers to the schools? If strict teacher education is abandoned as an inflexible standard, what standards will be substituted? Some standards surely are necessary to ensure teacher morale. These problems are currently at issue in New York and in a number of other cities where efforts at school decentralization are being discussed.

These problems are resolvable. There are a number of ways in which general standards could be assured. These standards might include establishing annual review procedures of administrative agencies, monitoring performance on a constant basis, establishing a system of spot-check inspections, and so forth. We have in the United States many ways to ensure performance standards. These problems could be solved with serious and rational debate.

The third major dilemma is designating the critical population. Some procedures must be developed to designate specifically the population which would exercise control over community programs. The available options include the following. First, designation by geographic boundary—the usual procedure for creating governmental subdivisions. Current district boundaries, or a new districting procedure, might be used. A demographic dimension might be added. Clearly Black people are asking for control over certain kinds of institutions and radical decentralization would be meaningless if apportionment designed to keep Blacks in the minority was tolerated. A third way of designating the population might be to accept a conception of a clientele. This is the model adopted by the poverty program in the United States. Elections for membership on councils making certain decisions over the poverty program are based in part on a franchise for the poor within a given neighborhood.

Proceeding in an ad hoc manner, using the notion of clientele, would probably be most profitable in the short run. Geographic boundaries for city services already are designated, in many cases (e.g., police precincts).

Additionally, this approach is most consistent with the characteristic incrementalism of American politics.

A fourth major dilemma includes problems of priorities. Liberal critics of radical decentralization are alarmed by the impact of Black power on other programs which they support. For example, it is difficult to advocate continued integration of public housing projects if Blacks now argue that they want to remain in the ghetto with increased control over the neighborhood. These arguments also can be dealt with by pointing out that liberal reforms and Black power are not inconsistent. Radical decentralization of authority over programs and full freedom and opportunity for all Americans are not incompatible.

A significant problem in regard to this, however, is that radical decentralization may hurt the centralized national social welfare system which has been responsible for initiating social security and welfare programs, public housing programs, social medicine programs, and so on, however inadequately conceived and executed these developments have been. Without the federal redistributive instrument it would be increasingly difficult to find money to finance social welfare and development programs. Advocates of radical decentralization would be well advised to support federal spending programs in social welfare areas, regardless of the means of program implementation.

Let me now turn to some developments in social science theory related to these questions. I have suggested some significant problems with radical decentralization dilemmas, but it would be hasty to conclude that the problems are so complex that they should not be considered seriously. For a long time American students of metropolitan affairs have expressed concern with the development of suburbs and metropolitan areas. They lament the fact that the fragmentation of governmental jurisdictions created by suburban growth hurts plans for creating metropolitan governments whose jurisdictions would be congruent with the scope of metropolitan area problems. Since the late 1950s, however, most political scientists have recognized that increases in suburban fragmentation are not merely unhappy accidents which might be corrected if public opinion were alert to the harmful effects of such developments. Rather, political scientists have recognized that urban development and jurisdictional fragmentation serve the interest of suburban residents by ensuring that they live in a jurisdiction with economic privilege.

Metropolitan fragmentation may be viewed as a means to ensure inequality. In contrast, the central city cannot provide the services, amenities, and protections for the economic interest of the middle class. This is because of the redistributive nature of providing public services in the city. Metropolitan fragmentation from this perspective is a reflection, then, and insurer, of economic inequality.

These insights direct attention toward questions relating to the functions and interests served by central city organization. If suburban fragmentation serves the interest of suburban residents, perhaps we should think of central cities as serving the interests of groups within cities to maintain dominance over city affairs. Comprehensive planning in regional development also has been usefully criticized as planning for the benefit of specific interests in the name of "the public interest" or "the common good." The centrality and relative remoteness of urban government planning also sets the ground rules for conflict to the detriment of some subgroups in the population.

Now, some people may think that these observations are inappropriate. They may point out that American cities provide protection against exploitation and deprivation which the urban poor suffer. They may argue that to fragment the central city further would be to remove the remaining incentives for middle class citizens to live in the cities. But these objections, I believe, are unimaginative. They fail to allow for the variety of solutions which might be derived for the problems of city decentralization. They also fail to allow for the possibility that city governments might delegate authority in the

same manner that states delegate authority to cities without losing ultimate jurisdiction.

These insights also suggest that neighborhoods may serve important functions which are obscured by contemporary city government organization. Historically many United States cities were governed by coalitions of immigrant groups generally referred to as "machines." The machine was substantially based on coalitions of neighborhood groups because immigrants tended to segregate themselves when they first arrived in the cities. The decline of the machine has been accompanied perhaps by a decline of cohesive subcommunities within the cities. These subcommunities may have important effects on an individual's sense of well-being, on an individual's interest in the relationship to government, and his ability to secure amenities within the city system. This has been suggested by such scholars and writers as Robert Merton, William F. Whyte, and Jane Jacobs. It may be desirable to consider ways to reestablish the sense of community and the sense of representation of community interests that are now important to the Negro community and are becoming more important at a time when these considerations are less relevant to other ethnic groups.

Political scientists have been increasingly interested in analyzing the relationship between actual government performance and the stated or intended purpose of government programs. This perspective, applied in the United States to such areas as urban planning, police practices, administration of justice, and low income housing policies, require analysis of government performance at the neighborhood or consumer level.

I suggest that assessment of policies must be undertaken at the point where programs actually affect people's lives. Radical decentralization is supportive of this view. It suggests that because government services must be assessed at the point of impact, authority to make decisions about those services should rest in the hands of those people who are affected by the services.

Finally, political scientists are interested in participation in the political process. We are concerned with the impact of expanded Negro voting, and are concerned with trying to explain why people riot and otherwise act outside the conventional political system. In a similar way, Japanese academics are also interested in knowing why students choose to act outside the conventional political system.

Scholars interested in participation have suggested that there is a positive relationship between participation and the availability of meaningful alternatives, between participation and the clarity of the link between participation and outcome, and between participation and the availability of information. These three propositions in the literature of participation are affirmed by political scientists with some feeling of confidence.

There is reason to think that these conditions for political participation can best be satisfied with political concerns at the neighborhood levels. The proximity of issues to people's concerns is likely to be high when they can see the nature of the programs. And information can be transmitted easily about events of which people are aware. What is usually lacking in political conflicts at the neighborhood level is any significance to decisions that are made. This lack of significance is related to the lack of power at the neighborhood level to effect public policies. This may explain a great deal of the relatively low participation in neighborhood elections in the United States compared with elections for "higher" offices. People in the United States vote at a greater rate in presidential elections than in municipal elections. This may be because the decisions that are made at the national level are more visible and much more salient than the decisions that are currently made at the local level.

Radical decentralization might change these conditions by placing authority over community institutions in the hands of the community. Such authority would be accompanied by responsibility for high standards of performance. It would be a real responsibility, where citizens would have increased capacity to effect their own lives. Parents who have control over their schools would have more incentive to keep their children in the school. Residents of a neighborhood scheduled to be renewed might cooperate with government agencies because they participated in shaping the renewal plan. This is at the heart of Japanese student discontent, insofar as I understand it, and it certainly is at the heart of American student discontent where students have virtually no power to effect significant institutional policy. In terms of democratic theory it is difficult to ask students to be responsible in a rational way under circumstances where they have no power.

Let me conclude by mentioning some implications of these remarks for the American federal structure. Advocacy of radical decentralization represents a rejection of present distributions of authority, and it represents the failure of contemporary planning mechanisms. Black people are beginning to dominate some American cities numerically just at the point that cities are least able to provide for the poor. Legislative and judicial advances that were achieved in recent years have not matched the legitimate expectations of Negroes that their status will be radically altered and that the fact of equality will be realized. Under such conditions concepts of self-development and group development through "Black Power" have emerged around which Black people now rally. Radical decentralization not only represents a demand for group authority over institutions but it also represents a demand that cities return to a distribution of authority when ethnic communities exercise greater control over relevant city services. Contemporary planning mechanisms are rejected by the advocates of radical decentralization because contemporary planning has neglected the poor and has not sufficiently involved those in whose name planning takes place. Planning in the United States has been most often at the expense of poor people. Neighborhoods are renewed for the benefit of downtown merchants and major taxpayers. Automobile travel is given high priority when the poor require cheap mass transportation.

It is not that planning is currently highly centralized in the United States. Rather, the ways in which planning is decentralized tend to exclude relatively poor communities from the critical decision-making processes and tend to exclude them at the critical points in the planning process sequence.

The next stage of development in the movement toward radical decentralization will be government sponsorship of limited decen-tralized experiments. Some developments in this area are already taking place. As I have tried to point out, some important questions remain to be addressed. As an alternative to current planning policies these questions deserve being raised by thoughtful scholars of American urban affairs. They deserve to be considered rationally, and with the kind of commitment to find answers that the American urban crisis demands.

24b. LOWER CLASS LIFE-STYLES AND COMMUNITY ACTION

LEE RAINWATER

Reprinted from John B. Turner, ed. Neighborhood Organizations for Community Action *(New York: National Association of Social Workers, 1968). Copyright © 1968 by Lee Rain-water. Mr. Rainwater is Professor of Sociology at Harvard University.*

GOALS OF THE LOWER CLASS

WHATEVER THE REALITIES of lower class life, a good deal of the strategy of neighborhood action groups will ordinarily be oriented to the goals that lower class people have for themselves. The most important issue here is whether from the perspective of lower class people the goal of a decent life is to be pursued mainly on an individual or group basis. If lower class people define the solution to their problems as a group effort, then organization will inevitably make more sense as an avenue to the end goals.

The evidence is strong, however, that lower class people, again like most Americans, tend to think of the most direct route to a decent life as one that is pursued along highly individual lines. In essence, each individual is supposed to have a right to make it on his own. Families often take the view that their best chance of getting what they want will come from disassociating themselves from those around them, not from combining forces with them. A decent life is defined most basically in terms of income. One needs an income in order to be able to live in a "decent neighborhood." Not only is neighborhood important for the adults to have a reasonably secure and gratifying life, but it is also important for the further mobility of the children. Thus, "moving out to a decent neighborhood" is seen as the way to give the children a chance at a better life than their parents have had.

The high rate of spatial mobility that characterizes lower class individuals and families has two bases. The first is related to survival problems: people move in order to have a chance to earn some money, or to find a slightly better place to live, or to escape from situations in which debts are piling up, the rent cannot be paid, and so on. The second source is more directly related to social mobility. Slum neighborhoods are often seen by their inhabitants as way stations on the way to the goal of living in a decent house in a decent neighborhood. This is probably more true of Whites than Negroes because of the greater opportunities available to even un-skilled and uneducated Whites for employment at the wage levels that might allow one to move into a stable working-class neighborhood. For example, Harwood found in a study of the uptown area of Chicago (which had been chosen as an area for much community action because it was believed that poor southern Whites lived there) that the southern White migrants in the area had little interest in the community because they regarded it simply as a point of entry into the city and as a place in which to accumulate enough resources to move out into more stable working-class areas. There was little interest in the community action efforts directed toward providing better social and community services, or even in those directed toward employment opportunities in the city.

One can assume, therefore, that except when lower class people feel trapped in their nighborhoods by low income and unemployment or by discrimination they will not be available for neighborhood organizations. Even when there is this sense of being trapped, the preferred route of mobility is individual; lower class people will often have difficulty in seeing a strategy of organized groups as really relevant to their own needs and wishes.

Group goals of a better or better-served neighborhood will prove attractive, on the other hand, in certain kinds of marginal working-class neighborhoods, which are sometimes mistakenly considered by middle class organizers to be slum neighborhoods. People live in these neighborhoods by preference— they like the community and may well be amenable to a neighborhood improvement approach. However, because the residents of such neighborhoods are attached to their communities, they tend to see no particular problem with them, although they will organize themselves when they feel that they are not receiving adequate city services or are being interfered with by redevelopment authorities, highway planners, and so on.

ORGANIZATIONAL PARTICIPATION

The most pervasive fact about lower class people as organizational participants is that they are not socialized either within the family or in their outside lives to work toward the solution of their problems on the basis of organization. This is, of course, to a large extent true of working and middle class people as well. After all, most activity in American society is pursued on a private and individual basis. However, in the middle class, organizations have assumed an important if highly restricted role in dealing with group and community problems. If the most spontaneous American solution to any problem is to "pass a law," the second most popular solution is to "form an organization." Thus, middle class Americans tend to be socialized from childhood into the ways of organizational participation. From the Boy and Girl Scouts to the various forms of student committees and governments in elementary school, high school, and college, middle class Americans are taught that one way to achieve one's goals is through participation in an organization of like-minded people.

On the other hand, the extent to which voluntary organizations play a central role in the lives of all but a few of the middle class should not be exaggerated. Organizations, including a great many political organizations, probably function more as entertainment and leisure-time activities than as serious mechanisms for attaining one's central life goals. Even organizations like the American Legion are, for the vast majority of their members, sources of entertainment, of a sense of belongingness and ideological indulgence, rather than a major avenue to the solution of problems of adaptation. Therefore, when the tremendous difficulty lower class people experience in using organizational action to cope with their basic problems of poverty, discrimination, and powerlessness is discussed, it should not necessarily be assumed that the same kind of organizational strategy has proved effective for middle class people.

Given these considerations, it is doubtful that many of the difficulties connected with organizing lower class people are as central as one is likely to believe. That is, it is possible that if lower class people were as skilled and ready for organization as middle class people are believed to be, they would still not be able to achieve their goals by organizational action.

Nevertheless, if an organizational strategy is chosen for dealing with lower class problems, then some of the typical characteristics of lower class people and their background of experience with organization present impediments to building viable action groups. To the extent that lower class people have had experience with organization, that experience tends to make them not at all sanguine about the likelihood of rewards from participation. To the extent that they come into contact with organizations and associations, lower class and even working-class people tend to experience a good deal of exclusion. When they are allowed to participate they tend to find that participation rather uncomfortable, to feel looked down on and treated as special. Participation in these organizations is perceived as highly competitive and they feel that they are left out by their inability to dress well, to speak correctly, and so on. Thus, the accumulated wisdom of the lower class concerning organizations is hardly optimistic. Lower class people expect to be manipulated, looked down on, and exploited by organizations. Thus, any community organizer will find he has a heavy load of suspicion to overcome before he can begin to establish any kind of rapport with those he wishes to organize.

Perhaps the main complaint organizers make about lower class organizations is that lower class people tend to be apathetic. Apathy is a kind of shorthand that serves to summarize the organizer's perspective on at least three different kinds of situations.

1. The *lower class people involved are not interested for quite valid reasons.* Thus, Harwood's study of southern rural migrants in the uptown area of Chicago suggests that both the more traditional community organizers and the Students for a Democratic Society organizers totally misperceived the situation of the people they were trying to serve. From the point of view of the organizers the migrants were a depressed and exploited group trapped in poverty and in the plight of migrants to the big city. From the point of view of the migrants themselves, the city provided them many opportunities that they were exploiting as vigorously as they could. The migrants found work opportunities readily available and intended to move out as quickly as they accumulated sufficient resources. They were quite optimistic about their future and did not see their lives as "filled with problems" in the same way the organizers did.

2. *The lower class people involved may not view organization as a potential solution to their problems.* Here it is not a question of an incorrect diagnosis by the organizers of the troubles of the target group. There may be complete agreement between the organizers and the people involved that they have numerous problems they do not have ways of solving. The disagreement is about the treatment. The organizers believe that group action will make some progress toward solving the problems; the people involved do not. If the organizers are reasonably congenial and unthreatening to the group, the lower class people involved may tolerate them, develop considerable affection for them, and enjoy participating in some of the activities they stimulate, but they will not put forth a great deal of effort in the ways the organizers want and they are likely not to respond to dangers and challenges that the organizers themselves see as crucial. The organization becomes an avenue for various kinds of expressive gratifications, much as other kinds of peer group activities are, but the organizers are frustrated because they do not get any sense of movement or concentration of the power that they believe to be potentially present in the group. Organizations that have difficulty in moving from "gripe sessions" to concerted action might be thought of as illustrating this tendency.

3. *Finally, apathy sometimes means, "I have too many other problems to take all this seriously."* The widespread accusations of apathy made about lower class people—rang-

ing from their failure to take advantage of available services (such as health or special educational services) to their failure to take grass-roots organization seriously—mean simply that so much of the energy available to lower class people is taken up in day-to-day survival that there is little left over for organization. Efforts to encourage them to take some of their time and emotional energy for organizational purposes are viewed as an unrealistic imposition. If lower class parents find it difficult to put together the energy and other resources necessary to take their children regularly to clinics for treatment or to organize their meager income in such a way as to buy food stamps—all activities that pay off immediately—it should not be surprising that they find it difficult to make a commitment to a neighborhood action group that can only promise a problematic gain in a much more distant future.

In the project workshops held for lower class groups, these people exhibited a tendency to operate as a committee of the whole and with ad hoc subcommittees, but without more clear-cut permanent organization; this is probably to some extent the result of the ideology of the organizers, but is also in line with the attitudes many lower class people have toward organization. The low structuring of relationships within the group facilitates expressive behavior and provides maximum chances for everyone to be the center of the stage from time to time. As Gans observed concerning his Italian West-Enders in Boston, lower class peer groups emphasize egalitarian relationships in which everyone has a chance to assume the center of the stage while the others make up an appreciative audience for him. More bureaucratic structures of relationships tend to inhibit this. As with Gans's West-Enders, lower class people generally are suspicious of leadership and of the monopoly of expressive gratification that leadership tends to encourage. Thus, only highly charismatic leaders are tolerated or given loyalty for very long, because only they are sufficiently rewarding to make the participants give up their right to their own turn as the center

of attention. In short-run crisis situations in which everyone knows what the problems are and in which the strategy is a fairly straightforward one of protest, this organization can function quite effectively. Over the long run, however, organization along these lines tends to run down, and even those who are most insistent about creating an open participatory pattern are likely to lose interest on the grounds that nothing is being accomplished.

ORGANIZATIONAL GOALS AND LOWER CLASS PERSPECTIVES

As noted before, from the lower class individual's perspective his most pressing goals do not generally seem amenable to an organizational solution, but only to solutions that involve individual mobility of some kind or another. Therefore, lower class people come to organizational settings with little optimism that an organization will really be able to make much difference in their lives. This would seem to be especially true when the organization is neighborhood based. Neighborhoods contain a variety of people with quite different life circumstances, and it is only in an abstract sense that it is possible to speak of the common interests deriving from their neighborhood situation. Thus, the neighborhood is in sharp contrast with, say, the workers in a factory. The workers have a concrete community of interest in terms of their wages and job security. While one can always move out of a "bad neighborhood" if one has enough money, workers who know that wages are pretty much the same for their kind of work everywhere can have recourse only to collective bargaining. This points up the general fact that in our kind of society economic status is much more fixed than the consumer statuses that derive from the expenditure of income. All of this is not to deny that non-work-related status is important in organization, but only to emphasize that organization needs to have some concrete and important payoff if it is to be successful. One of the most striking successes of organizational action in recent times is the organization of the Mexican-American farm workers in California. Their ethnic status was an important element in the success of the organization, but the direct relevance of work and collective bargaining around wages was certainly crucial to its success. One may expect, given these considerations, that efforts to organize people on welfare would also meet some success because of the clear salience of the goal of doing something about welfare "wages" and "work conditions." Since from the point of view of most people on welfare individual mobility is no longer a possible resolution to their difficulties, the relevance of an organizational approach is relatively straightforward for them.

PROSPECTS FOR SOCIAL CHANGE

Given these various considerations concerning lower class characteristics in relation to organizational action, what are the prospects for some of the more important strategies implicit in various neighborhood action groups? What kind of payoff can be expected from community action toward the common end goal of bringing about the conditions necessary for people to live decent lives, for doing away with deprivation and exclusion?

Some neighborhood action groups have modest goals indeed; they simply seek to improve slightly the quality of life of people who seem condemned to poverty and discrimination. Other action groups have much more ambitious goals; they look forward to altering society through organizational action. Three kinds of strategies currently seem most popular among those involved in community action: *power, self-help,* and *communication.* with the larger society. A fourth, and little used, strategy is that of *political power.*

POWER STRATEGY

The strategy of power has received a great deal of attention both in the writings of those involved with poverty and civil rights action and in the mass media. When taken at the neighborhood level, the power strategy often seems highly unrealistic since it implies that if those in the neighborhood can somehow assume power they will then be able to influence decisions in such a way as to change their lives markedly. This is seldom true because the forces that maintain deprivation and exclusion are generally not ones that operate most significantly within the context of the neighborhood or even the community, but ones that operate nationally. Even a highly solidary neighborhood action group could probably obtain little for its people from the community power structure. When there is little profit in slum housing, when local businessmen (even when they cheat their customers) make small profits, when local communities are practically bankrupt, it is unlikely that powerful neighborhood groups could pay off very well for their constituents. And given the fact that they cannot pay off, they would quickly lose their power even if they could for a short while achieve a solid power base.

In the long run, on the other hand, in situations in which the deprived and excluded are in a majority, as with Negroes in some part of the South and increasingly in areas of major cities, the strategy of power has some long-run importance. However, the time dimension becomes crucial. It is not so much a question of organizing to change things today or in the near future, but building over time a viable and resilient organization that can gradually wield more and more influence in the community. Crisis-oriented organizations will simply not do the trick because the resources available to the power structure are such that they can readily fend off any attack that will play itself out in a month or two. Power strategies in this long-run perspective assume importance to the extent that they are directly oriented to assuming political power; they will therefore be discussed in more detail later.

SELF-HELP STRATEGY

Self-help strategies have a great deal of attractiveness for those who are concerned about the poor and to the larger indifferent community. "Cleanup campaigns" are perhaps the simplest expression of this view. Yet the experience with self-help approaches suggests that they have little effect on the quality of life of the community. The forces that produce things that people want to do something about are simply too tenacious and too pervasive to be overcome by volunteer efforts. Also, as Kenneth Clark has noted, cleanup campaigns have the negative effect of seeming to place the responsibility for what needs to be cleaned up on the poor and excluded themselves, rather than on the system that puts them in the position in which they find themselves. Further, efforts to regenerate the community either physically or socially (as in the case of delinquency prevention) have the negative effect over time of increasing the amount of ingroup aggression since those who deviate from the new standards of a clean or well-behaved community are made to feel even more attacked and alienated than before.

Another kind of self-help involves not so much the effort to change the community as to help individuals get out of the community. These mobility projects are a different matter. As with the old settlement houses, to the extent that they provide services to individuals that enable them to change their position in society and move out of the lower class world, they have a constructive effect. This is no solution to the basic problem, since only a few people can be helped in this way, but it is a kind of "rescue work" that can constructively affect the lives of a few.

COMMUICATION STRATEGY

Strategies of forceful communication with the larger society have as their implicit goal not so much directly improving the quality of life of the lower class or even of acquiring direct power for them; rather, the emphasis is on communicating to the larger society the problems and desperation present in the lower class situations in such a way as to bring about eventual change. The civil rights revolution in the South has functioned mainly in this way. Seldom have Negroes acquired sufficient direct power to bring about the changes that were desired. But by raising an awful fuss they have brought about situations in which the power structure has felt compelled to act in order to maintain civil order. Systems of deprivation and exclusion depend for their smooth operation on a good deal of selective inattention to the effects of this exclusion. The rest of society pulls apart from the lower class; there is a cushioning effect of low communication between people in lower class situations and the rest of society. This low communication is maintained by mutually ignoring what goes on "on the other side of the tracks," and by the development of elaborate etiquettes that mask and conceal the actual facts of exploitation. One strategy of community action, then, is to break the conspiracy of silence that maintains the system and to expose as publicly and as repetitively as possible what is actually going on.

In this strategy the important considerations are not so much those of the power or solidarity of the action group as of public appearance and impression management. Thus, the civil rights movement in the South managed to communicate an image of much broader and deeper grass-roots involvement than actually existed; this image of involvement was important in bringing about the changes that took place.

When the strategy is that of communication it becomes much less important that there be in some sense full participation on the part of the lower class people in the action group. What is necessary is only that there be sufficient public participation to make credible the claim that the action group represents the people. This might be called "symbolic participation." The problem of credibility is a complex one. Obviously, if 20 people picket city hall they cannot credibly maintain that they represent the anger of the ghetto. If 500 or 1,000 pickets appear, the claim becomes much more credible, although in fact they still represent only a drop in the bucket in terms of the group they represent.

POLITICAL STRATEGY

Finally, there is *the strategy of political power*. The political strategy has proved remarkably uninteresting to most of those involved in community action. That is, outside the South, and to a surprising extent even there, those who engage in this kind of action seem to have relatively little interest in developing viable political organizations that can elect their own people to office and bring their points of view to bear in the political decision-making process. Perhaps nothing is more naively American in the new action movement than the belief that politics is a dirty and meaningless business.

The characteristics of the organizers seem to operate against political involvement. Professional social workers who become involved in community action work tend to define themselves as relatively apolitical, and in any case are more oriented to bureaucratic and therapeutic roles than they are to political ones. One the other hand, the young radicals who have been attracted to community action work would tend to regard participation in the political system as a kind of "finking out." The intellectual gratification of attacking the system is much too beguiling. For both groups the long-term commitments that are necessary to build both political organizations and political careers are ones that these by and large highly mobile individuals are not willing to make. Actual commitments to a political career (either elective or as a "political boss") would require for many of them a kind of downward mobility they are unwilling to tolerate.

The strategy of political organization is probably effective only when the lower class group involved is Negro or of another minority group. It is likely that the White poor are so dispersed in working- and even middle class constituencies that the chances of building a political power base among them is relatively small. On the other hand, for Negroes and other minority groups there is real potential here. The effective strategy is probably not so much to build independent parties (except under certain circumstances when an independent party can be a formalization of a block vote) as it is to build highly independent units within one of the traditional parties.

It is not so much that those involved in organizational action have refused to take advantage of traditional political styles; these probably are inadequate to the task. Rather, all of the energy and inventiveness of the past 10 years has gone into the invention of a-political organizational styles rather than into the invention of new political organizational approaches that would plug in fairly directly to the way governments are organized in this country. The pattern in most northern cities seems to have been to leave the structure of ward committeemen, aldermen, state representatives, state senators, and congressmen to old-style Negro and other minority politicians rather than to seek to change the political systems of the slum in such a way that candidates are elected who are ideologically committed to the needs of their constituents rather than to traditional political careers.

Thus, we still await a time when there can be a creative synthesis of the new action styles, which could achieve great impact if it combined the power and the communication of symbolic participation models with political organization styles. The fact that so much of the money for neighborhood action comes from the government itself perhaps plays a role in this. Obviously, the money for building new political organizations cannot come from the government, at least not openly. To the extent that action organizations are manned by people who derive their income from the organizations it seems unlikely that these organizations will move in a political direction. It is unfortunate that a fair amount of money is available to do things that can make little or no difference in terms of the long-range goal of achieving a decent life for people who live excluded and deprived lives, but that so little money seems to be available for doing the things that could make a difference.

25. POWER AND SYMBOL IN ADMINISTRATIVE REGULATION

MURRAY EDELMAN

Reprinted from The Symbolic Uses of Politics *(Urbana, Ill.: The University of Illinois Press, 1967).* Murray Edelman is Professor of Political Science at the University of Wisconsin. He has specialized in the study of political bureaucracy and of political impact on public policy. He is the author of The Politics of Wage Price Decisions; American Politics: Public Policy, Conflict and Change; *and, most recently,* Politics as Symbolic Action: Mass Arousal and Quiessence.

■ The first major efforts to curb the power of business and industry during the late 19th and early 20th centuries often were implemented by means of regulative commissions. Government regulation of business to ensure fairness, honesty, and equity, to preserve competition, and so on, was an important public policy invention that in the two or three decades before World War I appealed to reformers as a way of disciplining and humanizing the impact of business on society. The New Deal period of the 1930s saw the establishment of additional regulatory groups, particularly in industrial relations. As time has gone on, political analysts have come to be increasingly pessimistic about the ability of government regulatory agencies to achieve the official goals set for them. Nevertheless, they are an important locus of power in our society, as attested by the vigor with which affected interests struggle to be represented in administrative units, bureaus, and agencies, and to dominate their thinking.

Murray Edelman, who has for many years studied the functioning of regulatory agencies, presents here a general model of the actual operation of administrative regulation and of the role of administration as symbol in preserving rather than moderating power inequalities.

Edelman's most recent book, *Politics as Symbolic Action: Mass Arousal and Quiessence* (Chicago: Markham, 1971), discusses the role of symbolism in government in the context of modern political events, particularly those connected with mass conflict in society, whether that conflict is related to race, poverty, or industrial relations. He is particularly interested in the role of ritualization as a basic function of politics in preserving social inequalities.

The standard view on the operation of the administrative system to which Edelman refers is developed by Herbert A. Simon, et al. in *Public Administration* (New York: Knopf, 1950). Another approach to modern political bureaucracy is Anthony Downs, *Inside Bureaucracy* (Boston: Little, Brown & Co., 1967); see also Theodore Lowi, *The End of Liberalism* (New York: Norton, 1969). Two basic modern sociological anaylses of bureaucracy are found in Michael Crozier, *The Bureaucratic Phenomenon* (Chicago: Univ. of Chicago Press, 1964), and in Peter Blau, *Dynamics of Bureaucracy* (Chicago: University of Chicago Press, 1965). ■

TO CONTROL automobile speeding within a 65-mile-an-hour limit or to enforce a $1.15 minimum wage provision are concrete administrative objectives. In these and similar cases the administrator's problem is to maximize compliance and cooperation, for there will always be resistance, footdragging, and some overt defiance. If there were no resistance, there would be no need for the administrative program at all; and if it were impossible to increase the frequency of compliance through governmental action, there would equally obviously be no reason for administrative action.

Both the supporters and the defiers will, however, be clear as to what they are supporting or defying. They will talk and act with respect to the same concrete issue, and they can rationally choose behaviors which will further their objectives (though probably not in optimal fashion). In this kind of situation an administrator will try to achieve a satisfactory degree of compliance by increasing the material, moral, sunk, or other costs of defiance or by rewarding compliance.

Concrete legal objectives are ordinarily pursued as though administrators and potential defiers were involved in a game with rather clear rules. The basic rule is that a fairly large proportion of the instances of noncompliance will not be detected or penalized. Automobile drivers and policemen are both aware that most speeders will not be caught or fined, and both adapt their behavior to this assumption: drivers speed when the chance of being caught is slight or considered worth taking. Policemen stop some but not all violators, and let some of these off with a warning. As long as the game is played in this way, both drivers and policemen accept the order of things fairly contentedly: drivers paying occasional fines complainingly but without massive political protest, policemen noticing a certain amount of modest surpassing of the posted limits without further action. Similarly, employers accept health, safety, child labor, and minimum wage laws on the assumption that inspectors will appear at the plant only once in a while, and that if they are caught in violations on *these* occasions, a fine may have to be paid. The game of taking calculated risks in filing income tax returns is so clearly understood and so universally played that it needs only to be mentioned here.

Fortunately for scholarship and for "constitutional" government, we get just enough administrators ignorant of this rule of the game to serve as an object lesson in the disaster that its violation brings and in the wholly new symbolic relationship that then occurs. Officer Muller of the Chicago police force dismayed and pained his superiors some years ago by systematically ticketing every good citizen who took advantage of the long-standing practice of parking in a no-parking zone near city hall. After high state and city officials and received this treatment, the conscientious Mr. Muller was assigned to a remote beat. It was never assumed by either the police department or the public that enjoyed the story in the newspapers that such substitution of ordinances for the game could be allowed to continue. Similarly, national and local automobile organizations protest and citizens grow righteously irate when a village creates a speed trap and really penalizes every violator. Victor Thompson has described in detail and with rare political insight the battle that occurred inside the World War II OPA Rationing Division between some lawyers determined to read legal language literally and catch every chiseler and the administrators determined to play the only game that would permit OPA to survive.

Each legal offense or administrative enforcement program is a separate game with its own stakes, penalties, and ploys, and these vary enormously from one such game to another. Not the size of the stakes or the penalties, but rather the meaning of the offense to enforcers and possible violators is what determines whether a game or a dogma is involved. Even murder falls into the game class in our society, though as a kind of limiting case. Here the stakes and the penalties are high; but the rules prescribe many avenues for avoiding detection and even more for avoiding conviction if detected. If we really regarded murder as an unacceptable and unforgivable act, as we pretend to do, we would certainly put more of our resources into its detection, and we would not write into the laws a long series of acceptable excuses, from insanity to self-defense (usefully ambiguous terms, serving in practice to allow juries, lawyers, and judges to play the game). Our equivocation in these matters no doubt reflects quite faithfully the ambivalence we feel about murder and our occasional temptations to indulge in it ourselves. Such widespread personal ambivalence or shared role-taking very likely underlies all substitution of game playing for unequivocal legal enforcement. The popular response to television programs that treat crime and law enforcement as a game of wits is another clue to our deep-seated feelings about the matter.

What distinguishes a game from other forms of competition? The essential agreement on rules which fix or shape obstacles, stakes, and penalties; agreement to accept the result for each round of play; and inability to play at all unless your opponent plays, too, either because there is then nothing to win or because the victory is empty and unrewarding if it is won without opposition. The keynote in these rules of a game is mutual dependence, and in every one of these respects legal regulation meets the test of a game and not the test of an all-out, no-holds-barred strike for booty.

What happens psychologically when law is enforced as if it were a command rather than a virtuous generalization around which a game can be played? Instead of a trial of wits, it becomes a trial of force. Where law is treated as dogma, defiance becomes heresy; and this formulation states exactly the change in social roles and in symbolic interplay that takes place. Where enforcement is played as a game, none of those involved pretends that the offense is virtuous; but all recognize, through mutual role-taking, that there are temptations, that there is a shared interest in resisting them; and that, within the rules, offenders caught under specified conditions shall pay the specified penalties. . . .

We may sum up this part of the argument by noting that so far as the great bulk of law enforcement is concerned "rules" are established through mutual role-taking: by looking at the consequences of possible acts from the point of view of the tempted individual and from the point of view of the impact of his acts upon the untempted. The result is a set of unchallenged rules implicitly permitting evasions and explicitly fixing penalties. Administrators are thereby able to avoid the sanctions of politically powerful groups by accepting their premises as valid; while at the same time they justify this behavior in the verbal formulas provided in the rules.

The other, less common, mode of law enforcement involves the establishment of rules asserting the exclusive validity of a belief-disbelief system which is challenged by a heresy. The function of these rules being to defend a dogma under attack, they provide for no evasions but rather for stamping out deviation through both verbal incantation and physical intimidation. Such an overt threat to the opposition produces resistance, further repression, and the social and personal pathologies that perceptions of strong threat

evoke. Symbolically, the two kinds of law enforcement amount to the difference between mutual threat (the command) and mutual role-taking (the game).

Because the term "mutual role-taking" is fundamental to this analysis of administrative enforcement of rules, it deserves close attention. It derives, of course, from George Herbert Mead's emphasis upon the significance, both for social action and for the creation of the self, of "taking the role of the other." It is only by continuously trying to look at one's own actions from the perspective of the "significant other" person that anyone acts at all. . . .

Role-taking is action. It is behavioral and observable. And, as Mead brilliantly demonstrates, it is through role-taking that significant symbols are created. If the normative political philosopher asks whether the choice of one role rather than another does not depend upon a value hierarchy, we can answer, with Mead's work and the many empirical studies based upon it as our evidence, that it is role-taking that creates the symbols in terms of which we rank values. Or, to put it another way, the ranking of values is the rationalization of our behavior: an aftermath of it and not a cause. . . .

Politics always involve group conflicts. For the individual decision maker group conflict means ambivalence, and ambivalence can be described in behavioral terms as the concomitant taking of incompatible roles. Here is the key to the "game" theory of law enforcement just discussed. Enforcers and "enforced" alike assume both the role of the potential violator and the role of his victim. Out of their responses to such mutual role-taking come the rules as actually acted out: the specification of the loopholes, penalties, and rewards that reflect an acceptable adjustment of these incompatible roles. We know how "acceptability" is determined from many empirical studies of policymaking. It is a function of the sanctions available to the groups involved. Where one of the groups is organized, the rules, as enforced, are likely to be rigged so as to favor it disproportionately. Those who administer the rules in such cases become in effect part of the management of the organizations they regulate, through role-taking.

An interesting special case often occurs in local police agencies. From Lincoln Steffens' time to our own we have heard repeatedly of policemen in league with criminals, sometimes by accepting bribes in return for immunity, sometimes by actively helping in thefts. If we view administrative regulation as role-taking, it becomes quite understandable that policemen should occasionally choose this role. They are forced by their jobs to involve themselves closely both with the organization for which they work and with the one they regulate. Their every official act involves a calculation of its consequences for both organizations and for themselves. As this fact is clear to the criminals, too, some mutually understood rules of behavior are certain to emerge. It would be surprising indeed if these rules did not sometimes include understandings about bribery, looking the other way, and even joint enterprises. Although the ethics and the stakes may be different, the mutual role-taking is very much like what happens when staff members of regulatory commissions become part of the organizations of *their* clienteles.

It would be a mistake to believe that only individual delinquency and not organizational behavior is involved in such cases. The local police department that makes a great show of picking up lone offenders and amateur delinquents but leaves organized syndicates very much alone apart from occasional token actions is not uncommon. Even the FBI has consistently concentrated on the dramatic capture of the Dillingers, while making little headway against nationally organized gambling and other crime syndicates. The "ten most wanted criminals" device has been the dramaturgical core of FBI publicity and claims of effectiveness in its law enforcement work.

Once the pattern of role-taking is established within an administrative agency it becomes self-fulfilling and self-reinforcing. This result occurs through the operation of a number of devices that students of organization have often observed; but they can be seen now as tied together through their joint function of maintaining the organization's course in line with its established role. First, there are clear value biases in hiring, in job applications, and in staff separations. This practice need not be deliberate, as it was in the TVA and NLRB of the thirties, both of which quite explicitly used adherence to the philosophy of their respective programs as a screening device. Many staff members voluntarily left the NLRB after the enactment of Taft-Hartley because of restiveness over the new promanagement role of the agency. Civil libertarians and criminologists interested chiefly in the rehabilitation of offenders are unlikely to apply for jobs at the FBI, or to be accepted or advanced if they do apply. Richard Nixon left the wartime OPA at one stage of his career because he was uncomfortable in the liberal climate that prevailed in its offices, and many liberals sought or accepted jobs at OPA for the same reason.

A second consequence of the establishment of a clear pattern of role-taking is value contagion within the agency. Each staff member who works on a case is strongly tempted to emphasize or to soft-pedal premises in line with what he knows will please or displease the people scheduled to get the docket after him. This tendency of the group to encourage conformity has been established in experimental research, and it is observable in the agencies themselves as well by every employee or observer sensitive to it.

A certain number of staff members of every agency can expect to end their careers as employees or officers of the firms they are regulating, and the possibility occurs to every staff member. In some agencies, as in the FCC, government service is recognized as probably the best and most common training ground and channel for some kinds of private employment in the industry. Such an expectation is, of course, wholly compatible with the role-taking we are discussing, and inevitably reinforces it. Not only is the individual likely to assume the role of the group into which he eventually hopes to graduate; in a section or bureau in which such expectations are widely held, the work group will further encourage conformity to the group's values.

The status dysfunctions Barnard has cataloged and analyzed contribute to the same pattern. The major consequence of these dysfunctions for decision making is that they lead subordinates to hesitate to call attention to premises that suggest the advisability of change in established policy. As the specialists most familiar with the relevant facts are likely to be hierarchical subordinates, the result is a bias in favor of continuing to apply established policies. Anxieties of superiors stemming from their awareness of their growing incompetence as specialists may lead them to ever more rigid insistence upon uncritical adherence to the roles and policies they know.

New premises disturbing to established roles may also be screened out by time-consuming routine. When every staff member finds his day taken up in checking case dockets for routine problems and premises, there is likely to be no place in the organization as a whole for innovation. March and Simon refer to this phenomenon, familiar to every bureaucrat in an old-line agency, as a Gresham's Law: ritualistic routine minimizing the likelihood of energetic search for more satisfactory solutions.

Backing up all of these organizational supports of accepted roles are the agency's constituencies. We may take it as the key feature of any constituency that it can cripple or kill an agency. A congressman's constituency can fail to return him to office. Similarly, every administrative agency is at the mercy of specific groups which, given sufficient provocation, can hurt or scuttle them. Occasionally, a private group is formally given such power; labor and management organizations showed that they had it by using it several times against the War Labor Board and Wage Stabilization Board. More often Congress, the President, and the courts are the only formal constituents of administrative agencies, and it is a rare bureaucrat who does not bear the fact constantly in mind. Once he has found a pattern of action which is not disturbing to these constituents and lets them turn their attentions elsewhere, he will vigorously resist any change in the pattern, for he knows where survival lies. . . .

Administrative agencies are to be understood as economic and political instruments of the parties they regulate and benefit, not of a reified "society," "general will," or "public interest." At the same time they perform this instrumental function, they perform an equally important expressive function for the polity as a whole: to create and sustain an impression that induces acquiescence of the public in the face of private tactics that might otherwise be expected to produce resentment, protest, and resistance. The instrumental function of administrative agencies, as defined here, has been observed, demonstrated, and documented by every careful observer of regulatory agencies. This literature has nonetheless never successfully been used to challenge the widely held view and remains an esoteric facet of the study of economics and political science. . . .

Few if any norms are more deeply embedded in our culture, as verbal abstractions, than the two repeatedly cited as guiding administrative refereeing of conflict: that the weak should be protected from the strong and that conflict should be settled peacefully. Yet administrative surveillance over rival groupings commonly facilitates one of two quite different results: (a) aggrandizement by an organized group in the wake of symbolic reassurance of the unorganized . . . ; or (b) an alliance of the ostensibly rival groupings at the expense of "outside" groups. In neither case does the regulatory agency restrict claims backed by sanctions or referee a conflict. In both cases it becomes a psychologically and organizationally effective *part* of a political constellation which possesses potent private weapons already. Specifically, it becomes that instrument of the constellation whose function it is to allay outside political protest: to provide a setting of stability and predictability within which the organized groups involved can use their weapons with minimal anxiety about counterattack. It can perform this function better than any "private" group can do it because, as a public agency, it inevitably manipulates and evokes the myths, rituals, and other symbols attaching to "the state" in our culture.

Implicit in this formulation is the view that the creation of an administrative agency in a policy area signals the emergence of a changed relationship between the groups labeled as adversaries. The agency, the regulated groups, and the ostensible beneficiaries become necessary instruments for each other while continuing to play the role of rivals and combatants. Careful examination of the nature of the change in their strategic positions clarifies the sense in which this proposition holds true. The establishment of a National Labor Relations Board, Interstate Commerce Commission, Federal Communications Commission, Office of Price Administration, or utilities commission constitutes assurance that none of the groups directly involved can push any temporary or permanent bargaining advantage to the point of eliminating the other. Certain messages are implicitly but clearly conveyed by the very creation and continued functioning of the agency, and the messages are solace for very anxious people. Unions will continue to exist as part of the American economic scene. Radio stations, railroads, airlines, and utilities will not be nationalized. Negroes will be protected in their use of economic and other weapons. Consumers are assured that the majesty of the state will protect them from the threat posed by powerful economic concentrations and sellers. In short, existing institutions are legitimized, permitting them to utilize their bargaining weapons to the full, if they have any, and to survive and comfort themselves if they have not.

To see vividly this function of an administrative agency it is helpful to consider the alternative: the situation prevailing before an agency is established in a policy area, or the situation that would prevail if an existing agency were magically abolished. We have had enough case studies of the political origins of regulatory agencies to be well aware of what is involved. A group with oligopolistic or other economic weapons at its disposal maximizes its gain, testing to learn how much

the traffic will bear. This strategy creates adverse interests and anxieties: tensions and a need for their resolution on the part of both the predatory group and of its victims. Both need a definition of the situation: a legitimizing act which will remove uncertainty and the more serious anxieties in precisely the fashion I have just posited that administrative agencies do.

If the Interstate Commerce Commission, for example, were suddenly abolished, its function of maintaining and raising rates and legitimizing mergers and abandonments of service would have to be performed by the private carriers themselves. Potential customers would fear sudden and substantial changes; and the carriers themselves would fear strong public protest. Anxieties on both sides and anticipatory protest would create a degree of instability and tension that would have to be eliminated, very likely by the creation of an agency much like the ICC. . . .

For the unorganized the administrative activity brings a change from the role of potential victims to the role of the protected: ostensible sharers with the regulated industry in the economic benefits together with a powerful showering of symbols suggesting that the new role is secure.

For those not immediately involved the same meaning is conveyed. Once it is assumed that an agency assures service and fair rates for consumers, protection of the industry against loss or destruction becomes a tactic in the protection of the industry's clients as well. A rate increase that would be rather obvious exploitation of these clients in a setting of economic infighting unrestrained by government is magically converted into help for the customers as well as the industry. Where the agency's functioning constitutes legitimizing of a claim on the national product, the same functioning symbolically involves both adversary parties as supporters of the claim. The commuter or airline passenger needs his transportation, and, by definition, the industry cannot now exploit him.

A rather more interesting symbiosis takes place where both adversary parties are organized, as in labor-management relations.

Here the blood and thunder of battle, the charges and countercharges that the other group is behaving unfairly, the more or less incessant invocations of stereotyped images of the others' great strength and predatory habits, the occasional well-publicized resort to boycotts, sit-ins, and other economic and social weapons all serve to underline in the public mind the reality of the rivalry and the incompatibility of the rival interest.

It is true that there was a real effort by each adversary to crush the other for the first several decades after the industrial revolution came to the United States. Labor created such syndicalist or socialist organizations as the IWW and the Knights of Labor. Management used terrorism, espionage, its incomparably greater economic strength, and its psychological controls over judges and other public officials to break unions. This history of all-out warfare remains symbolically a part of the relationship between labor and management; but rivalry between management and labor in the go-for-broke sense disappeared at about the time administrative agencies were established in the field and was replaced by a common interest in a larger share of the national product to split between them. The new institutions did not neatly or completely replace the old ones everywhere, and the continued skirmishing effectively blinded practically everybody to the significance of the change for a long time. No group was more thoroughly blinded than those labor economists of the postwar years who had been drawn to the field in the first place by the picturesque and ideologically clean-cut infighting of the thirties and therefore had a large emotional stake in the thesis that the battle was real.

A major function of much union-management bargaining in the late fifties and sixties has been to provide a ritual which must be acted out as a prerequisite for the quiescent acceptance of high prices and higher wages by those not directly involved. Nor is it surprising that the rite is most formalized precisely in the industries in which the bargaining and the speculation about the likelihood of a strike are most widely publicized:

steel, autos, meatpacking, heavy machinery, electronics. In these cases union-management bargaining has come close to joining such foreign institutions as codetermination and national economic councils or such domestic ones as the agreed bill process as virtual giveaways both of the game and of the gross national income. The symbiosis could hardly be clearer.

In this case, as in many others, the claims made on each other by the groups involved are such that they can be satisfied by larger claims on outside groups. This drama has now been repeated so often in the industries named that its social function is manifest. . . .

Administrative activity is effective in inducing a measure of wide acceptance of all the objectives symbolized by the agencies only because the mass public that does the accepting is ambivalent about these objectives. Its responses to events and speeches manifests both a recognition of the value of each function and anxiety about the self-seeking and predatory intentions of the economic groups profiting from them. The personification of the elements in such psychic tension, and resolution of the tension through an acting out of the contending hopes and fears, has always been a common practice in both primitive and advanced societies. To let the adversary groups oppose each other through the workings of an administrative agency continuously resolving the conflicts in "decisions" and policies replaces tension and uncertainty with a measure of clarity, meaning, confidence, and security. This is precisely the function performed in more primitive societies by the rain dance, the victory dance, and the peace pipe ceremony, each of which amounts to an acting out of contending forces that occasion widespread anxiety and a resolution that is acceptable and accepted. . . .

The administrative system is in fact a rather sensitive instrument for highlighting those political functions that are widely, if ambivalently, supported. It has time and again been necessary to change the hierarchical locus of a function precisely to facilitate such highlighting, even though there was no reason to suppose that the locational change meant a shift in policy direction or in the relative influence of interested groups. The intense lobbying in the 19th century by farm, business, and labor groups for their "own" cabinet departments is one expression of this phenomenon, even though in each instance the new departments at first did little or nothing not done by a bureau before, and there was even a bit of scrambling to find things for them to do. The current pressure for a department of urban affairs to take over what is already being done in various other departments is another example. . . .

The forms benefits take also focus attention on a widely approved function rather than on the distribution of benefits to organized economic groupings. The administrative proceeding is so structured that benefits are perceived in relation to a symbolically potent and widely shared abstract objective and not in relation to their very material recipients. What we have here is a fascinating application of a well-known psychological phenomenon: that we screen percepts and interpret them in relation to a preconceived organization of reality. In administrative activity the organizing conception is very plainly presented and reiterated. It is given first in the very name of the agency. More important, it is reiterated and continuously emphasized as both proponents and opponents of specific policies justify their positions in the name of the same objective or organizing principle: a smoothly functioning transportation system or power system or communications system, rendering maximum service; the most effective defense posture; equality of management-labor bargaining power; fair trade practices; and so on.

Finally, the structure of the administrative system eliminates practically every opportunity to consider these various symbolic objectives at the same time, as rival claimants on the national product. As policy questions arise within each agency, decisions are justified in relation to the objective or organizing concept of that agency. An attack on the value of that organizing concept could come only from outside: from a different interest cluster. But this never happens in a setting in which any significant public attention to the attack could occur. It can happen only in congressional appropriation committee considerations, and there only to a slight degree and in a setting guaranteeing minimal weighing of the comparative values of alternatives even by the committee members, let alone the uninvolved public. The organizing principle retains its pristine potency.

The most valuable tangible benefits distributed by the federal government of the United States are certainly defense contracts. The form in which these become conspicuous to the uninvolved public is in defense appropriations, which highlight the universally approved defense function. That the appropriations mean high profits for the contractors is rendered inconspicuous by the political structures and modes of communication utilized. Administrative form both serves to confer an important benefit and legitimizes it through its presentation as a means of meeting a universal popular demand. There is no necessary implication here that the appropriations are not really needed for defense; only that the mode of structuring the benefit legitimizes it and makes its continuation probable whether or not it serves its ostensible instrumental function.

This form of benefit is probably feasible only if the instrumental objective to be served is potent and widely shared: defense, postal service, airmail service, road construction, and so on. Where the objective is less widely shared, the form of benefit characteristically changes. A classic example is agricultural subsidies, which are so structured as to highlight a virtuous abstraction: parity. The formula by which parity payments are computed is a periodically manipulated resultant of group bargaining, and the payoffs have disproportionately gone to large and commercial farming establishments; but the administrative organization symbolizes the creation of parity.

Though parity is practically a household word to newspaper readers, its dynamics are a mystery. Congress has required at one or another time that interest, taxes, freight rates, and wages be added to the formula for computing the index of prices paid by farmers. Before 1950 there were 170 items in the index; since 1950 there have been 337. It includes 48 agricultural commodities, each given its own weight. This weighting, inclusion, and exclusion is, of course, the real determinant of the benefit, not the abstraction "parity."

Another example of subsidies hidden under the guise of a popular objective are the large federal payments to publishers and advertisers in the form of second-class mail rates far lower than is necessary to cover the costs of delivering magazines and hard-sell blurbs. Again, the subsidy may or may not be justified, depending on the observer's values, but administrative structuring has a continuing influence on the process.

Where the benefits are not to come from the public treasury at all, but rather from a grant of official permission to charge higher rates for goods or services, the administrative form is still different; but it again amounts to a ritual emphasis upon a symbolically potent objective. Benefits are still offered so that they are perceived in relation to the abstract objective and not in relation, to their material recipients. Thus administrative decision makers on the regulatory commissions function in a setting in which they become in effect part of the management of the industry they are to regulate. They are forcefully and regularly bombarded with statements of the various costs confronting the industry and with its business problems; they associate formally and often informally with its top officers, learning their perspectives and their values. At the same time they are kept intensely aware of the sanctions that await them and the agency if these business and organizational considerations are ignored: congressional displeasure, public attacks, probable displacement at the end of their terms of office. Even more obviously, their careers and prestige are now tied to the industry. As the industry grows, so does their function and importance; if the industry dies, so does the agency. Symbiosis ripens into osmosis and digestion. There is no significant difference between this situation and that of the corporation officers themselves. . . .

The administrative system, as symbol and ritual, thus serves as legitimizer of elite objectives, as reassurance against threats, and sometimes as catalyst of symbiotic ties between adversaries. It should not be surprising that we find these larger social functions of the administrative system mirrored inside each of the agencies as well, in the gathering and choice of premises upon which decisions are based.

Simon and others have demonstrated that complete rationality in decision making is never possible in any case: because knowledge of the consequences of any course of action is always fragmentary, because future values cannot be anticipated perfectly, and because only a very few of the possible alternative courses of action ever come to mind. By observing how administrative staff members are themselves guided in their work by the compelling symbols the system serves, we can go a considerable way toward defining the particular biases or policy directions which these limits upon rationality take. We can, that is, hope to observe some systematic patterns in departures from administrative rationality.

26. THE VIETNAM WAR AND PRESIDENTIAL POWER

DANIEL ELLSBERG

Reprinted from "The Quagmire Myth and the Stalemate Machine," Public Policy No. 2, Vol. 19, Spring 1971. Daniel Ellsberg is Senior Research Associate at the Center for International Studies, Massachusetts Institute of Technology. He was an official in the Defense and State departments and for eight years was with the RAND Corporation, a principal private contractor for social science research applied to defense policy.

■ The events that most dramatically demonstrate the power of the President of the United States are the same events that more than any other demonstrate the destructive potential inherent in the office in modern times. The maximum use of the power of that office has involved its greatest failures also. The failure of United States policy in Indochina and the immense destructiveness it has brought about is one matter; the light shed by those events on the power of the President compared with all other centers of power in American society (including the power of the public) is great indeed.

In this paper, a kind of prelude to the famous "Pentagon Papers" expose, Daniel Ellsberg tries to show how four presidents consistently used their power, while concealing their goals, to stabilize their own political positions by escalating United States involvement in Southeast Asia. Ellsberg was one of several social scientists with Defense Department experience who were assigned by the then Secretary of Defense Robert McNamara to compile a history and collection of documents detailing the course of U.S. involvement in Indochina. The full study, now published by the Government Printing Office, takes up approximately 3,000 pages of narrative history compiled by the social science staff and more than 4,000 pages of appended documents—47 volumes in all, covering the period from World War II to May 1968. Ellsberg released copies of almost all this material, which was officially classified as secret, to *The New York Times* as a way of dramatizing the discrepancy between the manner in which our presidents presented our involvement in Vietnam and what the Pentagon Papers demonstrated in fact to be the case.

An ability to keep secret the President's intention and to control information about what was planned proved to be crucial to the conduct of U.S. Indochina policy. The most dramatic example of the difference between public stance and internal policy decisions occurred in the fall of 1964 when President Johnson was running for election against Senator Barry Goldwater, who was advocating full-scale air attacks on North Vietnam and who because of his stance on escalating the war (among other reasons) was not faring well in the campaign. President Johnson took a public stance against bombing in the North and against any major commitment of U.S. troops—but within a year he had done both. The Pentagon Papers suggest that at the very time he was campaigning on a platform committed to limiting U.S. involvement, his staff was planning the escalation. Part of these plans included efforts to provoke the North Vietnamese into activities that the administration could then publicly define as providing good grounds for escalation if they wished.

In this article Dr. Ellsberg seeks to show that Indochina was not a quagmire into which American presidents "stumbled," one after another but that their actions can be understood as rational choices, given their political strategies for remaining in office and for furthering their conceptions of America's role as "the most powerful nation on earth."

The major information contained in the Pentagon Papers is well condensed in Neil Sheehan et al., *The Pentagon Papers as Published by the New York Times* (Phantom Books, 1971). The classic analysis of presidential power is Richard Neustadt, *Presidential Power* (New York: Wiley, 1960). Aaron Wildavsky has analyzed the relationships between President and Congress in "The Two Presidencies," *Transaction,* December 1966, in which he argues that presidential power is greatest when directing military and foreign policy, at least in the domestic arena. In the Vietnam War the President's power so exceeded Congress's constitutional and traditional role that even some conservative legal scholars believe the war was technically unconstitutional; see, for example, Alexander M. Bickel, "The Constitution and the War," *Commentary*, July 1972. An anguished view of Congress's impotence before the President is offered by Senator J. William Fulbright in *The Arrogance of Power* (New York: Penguin Books, 1970). An inside view during the Kennedy and early Johnson years by one who adheres to the "quagmire" theory is Arthur Schlesinger, Jr., *The Bitter Heritage*, (Fawcett Books, 1968). A useful collection of material representing many points of view from the establishment of the United States to the present is in Robert S. Hirschfield, ed., *The Power of the Presidency*, 2d ed. (Chicago: Aldine, 1973). ∎

THE STALEMATE MACHINE

. . . ALTHOUGH THE DATA . . . are adequate decisively to reject the Schlesinger "quagmire model" of the generation-long process of U.S. involvement, they do not point conclusively to an alternative. . . .

What follows is a discussion of a particular "decision model"—in the form of "presidential decision rules in Vietnam crises"—that does, given actual perceptions and premises of Washington decision makers, imply policy choices and executive performance conforming in considerable detail to those actually obtaining at major escalation points between 1950 and 1968. (Presidential decisions significantly escalating the nature of U.S. involvement have occurred, in fact, only in crisis situations of impending failure.) That is all I can say for it, at this point. I cannot prove, or even feel sure, that any particular president has actually seen his decision problem and constraints in just this way. . . .

One of these characteristics happens to be the striking impression of the *sameness* of the bureaucratic debate, in substance, tone, and agency position, and of its relation to presidential choice, at decision points throughout the 20-year period. This is in itself a surprising, if subjective, datum, given the differences in circumstances—e.g., the steadily rising level of prior U.S. involvement—and in the character of the several presidents.

The obvious differences between administrations do not, after all, seem to have made much difference in Vietnam policy; at least, so far as concerns a determination to stay in Vietnam, to do what was necessary at any given time to avoid losing, and not, at that time, much more. (As Morton H. Halperin has pointed out, this does not mean that a permutation of the sequence of actual presidents would have made no difference at all; for example, if Lyndon Johnson—or still more, Richard Nixon—had come earlier than he actually did, escalation might well have started sooner and gone further.) This sameness suggests that a single, perhaps complex, hypothesis might cover the whole set of decisions with more validity than a set of purely ad hoc explanations. (To this degree, one sympathizes with Schlesinger's approach.)

In any case, it appears that an appropriate abstraction of elements of the initial 1950 decision to intervene—despite the lack of major prior commitment or involvement—fits very well all the major subsequent decisions to escalate or to prolong the war, at least through 1968 and probably beyond. . . .

One presidential ruling at work both in 1950 and 1961 [was]: *This is a bad year for me to lose Vietnam to Communism."* Along with some rules on constraints (see below), this amounts to a recursive formula for calculating presidential decisions on Vietnam realistically, given inputs on alternatives, anytime from 1950 on. The mix of motives behind this judgment can vary with circumstances and presidents, but since 1950 a variety of domestic political considerations have virtually always been present. These have been sufficient underpinning in those years when (unlike, say, 1961) "strategic" concerns were not urgent.

In brief: A decade before what Schlesinger calls Kennedy's "low-level crisis" in South Vietnam, the right wing of the Republican Party tattooed on the skins of politicians and bureaucrats alike some vivid impressions of what could happen to a liberal administration that chanced to be in office the day a red flag rose over Saigon.

Starting in early 1950, the first administration to learn painfully this "lesson of China" began to undertake—as in a game of Old Maid—to pass that contingency on to its successor. And each administration since has found itself caught in the same game.

Rule 1 of that game is: *"Do not lose the rest of Vietnam to Communist control before the next election."*

But the rules do not end with that. There is also—ever since late 1950, when Chinese Communists entered Korea—Rule 2, which asserts among other things: *"Do not commit U.S. ground troops to a land war in Asia, either."*

Breaking Rule 2 (which has some further clauses) will not expose one to the charge of treason, but otherwise the political risks—loss of electoral support, loss of Congress, loss of legislative program, loss of reputation—are about the same. And many of the very same pursuers who would be howling and pointing at the scent of a violation of the first rule would be among the pack chasing a president who proposed to ignore the second.

It so happens that a factional attitude within Congress or the public of intense appreciation of U.S. stakes in a non-Communist Southeast Asia does *not* go with a willingness politically to support costly or risky or domestically unpopular measures to protect those stakes. On the contrary, it tends to be coupled precisely with a determination to oppose and punish many such measures (in company with those who do not believe the stakes are all that important), because it is typically part of a philosophy asserting such efforts to be both unnecessary—to a patriotic and resolute administration willing to rely on Asian allies and the threat or use of U.S. airpower—and dangerous to the economy.

Suppose, then, an administration fears attack by or needs the support of the particular faction that holds these attitudes (which is suspected of being able to mobilize a much larger following on these issues in a crisis). What if the President is informed that he cannot avoid enraging that faction by losing part of Southeast Asia in the near future to Communist control, except by antagonizing other major groups (and perhaps it as well) by committing troops, or mobilizing reserves, or risking war with the Soviet Union or China?

In that case, the President is in a bind. The Indochina Bind.

That dilemma is all the more certain to recur because of some other politically derived premises that constrict policy. One of the sacred beliefs, inherited from the late 1940s, that any U.S. official must appear to share (and probably does share) is that toleration of an overt Communist Party in a less-developed country or a provisional or coalition government including Communists, must inevitably lead to total Communist domination. Any prospects of these developments, then, are proscribed under Rule 1.

But that means that acceptable U.S. long-run aims for South Vietnam must be quite ambitious: the total exclusion from national power of the Communist Party; the assurance indefinitely of a totally non-Communist regime.

These were internally stated U.S. goals until at least 1969; lest they appear too ambitious or interventionist, they were rarely spelled out publicly, and the public position was ambiguous. It is not clear yet—and appears doubtful—whether recent changes in public formulas correspond to genuine operational changes in the outcomes perceived as "tolerable."

U.S. intelligence analyses have generally recognized that in the face of the actual strength of the Communist Party of Vietnam, such goals could not be achieved—without major U.S. involvement indefinitely—by the sort of narrow, conservative, foreign-oriented, anti-Communist, authoritarian regime (supported mainly by Catholics, the army, bureaucrats, and the rich) that alone among Vietnamese political elements was willing to pursue such an aim. Hence, for the long-run goal of an acceptable outcome at an acceptable cost to the U.S., civilian analysts have regularly stressed "reform" and "broadening" of the Saigon regime.

But this runs into another sort of bind. For even proponents of those political changes admit that such a "broadened" government, or even U.S. pressures to achieve it or to reduce the influence of the army, would increase to some degree the risk in the short run of "instability"—coups, chaos, military weakening, governmental paralysis—and thus quick Communist take-over. Thus any measures—U.S. "leverage," political strategies, genuinely "revolutionary" social-political approaches, broad-based regimes—to achieve such long-run aims conflict directly with Rule 1, and perhaps with Rule 2 as well. The rules have always won out.

It follows that in those periods when major U.S. policy innovations have actually been determined, long-run success at acceptable cost, if attainable at all, has been perceived to depend either on U.S. military measures that involved high domestic risks—unless they were sure to be quickly successful, which could not be guaranteed and which presidents tend to doubt—or upon political strategies in Vietnam that posed the equally high domestic political risks of short-run instability and failure in Vietnam.

The standard resolution at such moments has been simply to turn away from long-run aims and the measures associated with them, to concentrate almost exclusively upon the aim of minimizing the short-run risk of non-Communist collapse or Communist take-overs. To this end the policy relies heavily on means that do not raise domestic apprehension and opposition, but it also includes those types of instruments "restricted" under Rule 2 —their acceptability roughly in the order listed below—judged by the President minimally necessary to this short-run aim.

Rule 2 (extended): *Do not, unless needed to satisfy Rule 1:*

1. Bomb North Vietnam;
2. Commit U.S. combat troops to Vietnam;
3. Commit U.S. combat troops to Laos or Cambodia;
4. Mobilize reserves;
5. Destroy major cities in North Vietnam;
6. Institute wartime domestic controls;
7. Take major risks of war with Soviet China or Communist China;
8. Invade North Vietnam;
9. Use nuclear weapons.

Strong political inhibitions against initiating such "restricted" measures are revealed by the prolonged unwillingness of any administration to introduce any of them until needed to sustain Rule 1: i.e., to prevent defeat in Vietnam before the next election. The President himself must be persuaded that they are essential for that purpose; this is usually long after their use has been urged by others. Indeed, most of these measures have never yet been used. Although most of them have been considered or recommended at various times, often on the more-or-less plausible grounds that they were essential, or highly important, to achieving real "success," presidents have not, in fact, been willing to adopt any one of them unless and until it was judged essential to avoiding short-run defeat: i.e. to restore a stalemate.

A general presidential tendency to preserve flexibility, or to focus on or value only short-run consequences, or to economize on means could not explain the strength and specificity of these inhibitions. Nor have presidents been strictly indifferent to longer-run prospects, or to the possibility of "victory." The chosen policy usually employs far more in the way of "nonrestricted" instruments than is needed merely to avoid defeat. These include: non-U.S. ground forces; commitments and assurances to allies, warnings to opponents; clandestine activities; economic and military aid; advisers; combat, logistic, mobility, and air support (even to allied invasion forces).

Moreover, once a "restricted item" is first used to avoid defeat, its use may be greatly expanded in pursuit of ultimate "success": thus, Johnson's use of U.S. ground troops in South Vietnam and bombing of "military targets" in North Vietnam and Laos, after they had been introduced in 1965 to avoid imminent defeat. Yet even in the optimistic mood of 1967 and despite the urgings of his military commanders that new means could bring a "win," Johnson resisted going further down the list—e.g., to drop all White House controls on the target list in North Vietnam, or to invade Laos or Cambodia, or mobilize reserves—in the absence of an urgent need to avert failure.

After March, 1968, de-escalation was subject to limits similar to those earlier for escalation; again, choices had the desired effect of avoiding short-run collapse, in this case, on the U.S. domestic front: in other words, once more "buying time" rather than winning or losing; buying stalemate; prolonging the war.

Many of the paradoxical features of U.S. escalating decisions as seen from the inside—the "discrepancies" noted earlier between chosen policies, on the one hand, and internal predictions, recommendations and long-run aims on the other—can thus be seen to reflect conflict between domestic political requirements on outcomes and domestic political constraints on means.

A peculiar effect of a strong domestic political ingredient in policymaking is greatly to enhance the salience and importance of short-run considerations. There are always a legislative program and presidential appointments to get through Congress this year, and congressional elections no later than next year, even when a presidential election is not close at hand.

It so happens that in Vietnam policy alternatives have not allowed a subtle adjustment of long-term and short-term considerations, which appear in sharp conflict. The President is challenged, in effect, to pursue one or the other. Thus, the long-run aim of a self-sufficient and relatively democratic South Vietnam not entirely dominated by Communists seems to demand an approach—e.g., a regime based on Southern, civilian, nationalist, and non-Catholic religious leadership, drawing peasant and union support—that poses relatively high risks in the short run of government collapse or of "accommodation" to Communists. To decide that short-run interests are very important is to bias policy almost entirely toward a short-run orientation: away from such approaches as that above, whatever their long-run merits, toward policies whose only advantages lie in their higher degree of U.S.

control and security against short-run "disaster."

Thus, among the consequences of applying Rules 1 and 2 to policy choices, as officials have perceived the alternatives in Vietnam, are several of the patterns observed earlier.

1. Chosen policies appear from the inside as oriented almost exclusively to short-run considerations; evidently ignoring or trading off very large differences in predicted long-run costs, risks, benefits, and probability of success in pursuit of small reductions in the short-run risk (tacitly, of "losing" South Vietnam prior to the next election).

2. Chosen programs are predicted internally to be inadequate—or at best "long shots"—either to "win" or even to avert defeat in the long run (in contrast to public statements, and to some recommended policies that pose higher short-run domestic risks).

3. Actual policies emphasize predominantly military—rather than political—means, aims, considerations, and executive responsibility, on both the Vietnamese and American sides, for reasons of short-run security.

4. The U.S. supports—intervening as necessary to instate or maintain—a narrow-based, right-wing, anti-Communist, "pro-American," authoritarian (since 1963, essentially military) regime in Saigon, with heavy Northern and Catholic influence: despite its inability to win wider support for long-run self-sufficiency.

All of these features combine to give American policy its peculiar appearance, seen from inside, of being dedicated to preserving a stalemate, at ever-increasing levels of violence.

Moreover, at least three other characteristics of U.S. government performance, not discussed earlier, correspond to the implications of this decision model: lack of "leverage," lying, and self-deception. Let us examine these in turn.

The notable weakness of U.S. influence on the policies, either political or military, of its principal ally—first the French and then the GVN—despite near-total dependence of the ally on U.S. support to pursue the war, follows directly from the U.S. political imperatives.

Rules 1 and 2 together led us, from 1950 to 1965, to accept the role continuously of adviser and supporter to another government carrying the responsibility for administration and fighting—even when our limited role seemed to risk imminent defeat of the non-Communist efforts. From time to time in those 15 years, administration leaders would point out publicly of the ally we were supporting: "It is, after all, *their* fight." But these officials' private perceptions would have been better expressed: "In view of our strategic (and domestic political) interests, it is *our* fight, all right, but they have got to fight it for us; because if they don't, we might have to, and that would be nearly as bad as losing."

Given the domestic political constraints embodied in Rule 1, U.S. leaders saw the avoidance of Communist take-over of all of Vietnam as of very considerable importance, both internationally and domestically. Yet for the same reasons as reflected in Rule 2, they had to hope urgently they could induce others to do the fighting, and take the responsibility for the failures and the casualties, leaving us only with the burden of dollars, material, and advice.

This "bargain"—first with the French, then with the GVN—has always seemed in danger of breaking down, facing the current administration with the loss of South Vietnam or with a necessity to take over the combat ourselves. Hence, our officials rarely felt they could afford to strain the bargain by "pressuring" our ally into fighting better or differently, or into taking political measures to which it was, in fact, adamantly opposed, even when we suspected that such changes were critical to success. In effect the U.S. had no leverage to use, despite the intelligence perception that the military-political challenge of the Communist-led forces would almost surely grow, and the ability of the ally (French, then the GVN/RVNAF) to meet it would decline, unless these changes did occur.

Meanwhile, as an essential part of the bargain with our ally—serving to keep it in power, fighting—high U.S. officials provided verbal and symbolic encouragement and evidence of U.S. concern and commitment. This came "cheap" in terms of current demands on the U.S. public. But it was making ever more certain the provision of U.S. combat forces if that became essential to holding Vietnam.

To convince the GVN (and its Vietnamese critics and rivals)—in lieu of sending U.S. troops immediately—that we would do "whatever necessary" to support them, the administration had to say so publicly, and to assert that major U.S. interests were at stake; likewise, to warn Hanoi's leaders and deter them from pressure.

On the other hand, to get sizable enough sums of money out of Congress, these officials had to say, again, that major U.S. interests were at stake, implying that even major commitments would be justified; but at the same time suggest that there was very little likelihood that these programs would lead to U.S. combat involvement. The only way in which these requirements could be harmonized was to profess, at any given time, great optimism for the results of the GVN's performance if the U.S. aid were sent (combined with pessimism, and the prospects of major losses for the United States, if it were not).

Here, then, is the explanation for . . . news management . . . Deceptive games with Congress and public are played for serious stakes. The President's resolution of the conflicting demands and constraints upon him called for suppressing any indications of possible inadequacy of the programs he proposed. The penalty for frankness could be to ally against his programs those who might conclude these were not worth attempting at all, and those who would condemn him for not doing much more. Yet the latter could be expected to oppose him if he did ask and do much more, unless he won quickly, which he did not expect; and the former would desert him if he took their advice, and lost Vietnam. Honesty, it appeared, would only earn him opposition whatever he did, and sooner than otherwise.

But in this case, internal analyses, estimates, reports, planning, recommendations, all indicated that in a whole variety of ways these programs were inadequate. Thus all these documents and opinions had to be concealed, by secrecy and deception.

In short, the public is lied to: about what the President's decision is, what advice he rejects, what he was told to expect, what he foresees and intends for the future.

When he decides to go slow and small, as in November 1961, the fact that much more was considered and recommended is suppressed lest doubts be raised on the meaningfulness of the program. James Reston's remark at the outset of the Taylor mission that Taylor was not a man who would "blithely" recommend committing U.S. combat units to a jungle war was presumably right; likewise Taylor's own comment that "any American" would be reluctant to do so "unless absolutely necessary." Nevertheless, that is what Taylor did recommend. The fact that he did so, therefore, carried an important message about the seriousness of the situation, and the prospects of the lesser course the President chose. To suppress the fact of this recommendation, as the President chose to do, was to conceal this information. And for officials to lie to reporters about Taylor's views—which were shared by Rostow and the JCS, and initially at least by McNamara and Gilpatric —was to convey the opposite, untrue impression.

By the same token, when a president finally decided to go in big, the schedule and total commitment were concealed, with increments —actually programmed in advance—being announced as if based on a sequence of ad hoc decisions on "small steps," lest public fears be aroused on the costs of the program, and the ultimate risks and commitment. This was the nature of the "public information" program associated with the early bombing campaign against North Vietnam, the buildup of troop levels to 75,000 in the spring of 1965, and the open-ended buildup of troops to 175,000 and beyond, determined in July 1965 (the latter after an announcement of mobilization had been tentatively decided on and drafted—by me, for one—then abandoned).

One pertinent effect of this information policy was that it considerably distorted the public view, then and later, of what the President thought he was getting us into, what he thought of the chances and the relevant goals, and just what was in the inner pages of the contracts Congress and the public were being asked, implicitly, to sign.

From such a mistaken understanding of this and the other choices, bad predictions and prescriptions must follow. It leads to wrong questions and wrong inferences about presidential motives, and about what changes in his calculations and in the pressures on him might influence his choices. It could lead, for example, to the inference that "the only thing we have to fear is (presidential) hope": when, in truth, unrealistic presidential hopes were not a prominent factor in any major decisions to press onward.

Thus those who keep secret the past condemn us to repeat it.

ESCALATION, PHASE B: THE QUAGMIRE MACHINE

Both of the deceptive practices noted above bear on the question: Why is the quagmire model, flawed as it is, so plausible to the public eye?

Part of the answer is that presidents choose to foster to a misleading degree impressions that their Vietnam decision making is subject to a "quicksand process." They do this despite a number of unfavorable implications: "inadvertence"; ignorance; inattention; lack of presidential control; lack of realistic planning; lack of expertise; overambitious aims for means used; overoptimistic expectations. They choose to encourage, ultimately, these particular criticisms because either a different substantive policy or a more accurate public understanding of their actual policy seems to them to pose even greater disadvantages and risks.

All very calculated, this. But, it turns out, this posture of secrecy and deception toward Congress and the public, maintained over time, takes its internal toll. Ironically, one price is that all of the above imputed flaws and limitations increasingly do characterize the executive decision-making process. And for a number of reasons, as the chosen policy begins to be implemented, internal operational reporting, program analyses, and high-level expectations do gradually drift in the direction of the public optimism expressed constantly from the outset.

Thus real hopes—ill-founded hopes—follow hard upon the crisis choices, eventually replacing phony and invalid optimism with genuine invalid optimism.

Again, the aftermath of the November 1961 decision is typical. Schlesinger reports it well: the striking move to optimism in official expectations in 1962, a reversal which the public misread as vindication of earlier estimates. U.S. combat troops, it was now appearing, had not been "essential" after all. (If the President had, indeed, suspected that earlier, he was the only one who seemed vindicated.) But no recriminations blossomed in this atmosphere; only mutual congratulations that the long shot was paying off.

Roger Hilsman reports a meeting in Honolulu in April 1963, at which,

General Harkins gave us all the facts and figures —the number of strategic hamlets established, number of Viet Cong killed, operations initiated by government forces, and so on. He could not, of course, he said, give any guarantees, but he thought he could say that *by Christmas it would be all over.* The Secretary of Defense was elated. He reminded me that I had attended one of the very first of these meetings, *when it had all looked so black—and that had been only a year and a half ago.*

Why the fast turnaround? For several reasons, none peculiar to this case. First, the new programs had been accompanied by new officials directed to carry them to success. Ignorant of past estimates and current realities in Vietnam, they had no strong reason to assume that the tasks they had been given were infeasible with the means at hand. And they quickly learned that Washington tended to rely on reporting up through the chain of operational command; which is to say, their performance in their jobs would be evaluated by their own reports of "progress" in their respective fields. As an American division commander told one of his district advisers, who insisted on reporting the persistent presence of unpacified VC hamlets in his area: "Son, you're writing our own report card in this country. Why are you failing us?"

Even when this did not lead to conscious dishonesty at the higher levels in Saigon, it created a bias toward accepting and reporting favorable information from subordinates and Vietnamese "counterparts," neither of whom failed to notice.

Thus, it was more mechanism than coincidence that in 1962 and early 1963,

the strategy of unconditional support of Diem combined with the military adviser system seemed to be working—or so at least the senior American officials in Saigon assured the President.

Such assurances said nothing more nor less than that the two officials themselves were "working"—succeeding—in the precise two programs they had been sent by Kennedy respectively to manage.

Ngo Dinh Nhu made the strategic hamlet program his personal project and published glowing reports of spectacular success. One might have wondered whether Nhu was just the man to mobilize the idealism of the villages; but Ambassador Nolting and General Harkins listened uncritically to his claims and passed them back to Washington as facts, where they were read with elation.

One might also have wondered—but no one ever seemed to—whether Nhu was just the man uniquely to report upon "his personal project"; or whether Nolting was just the man to report the effects and value of reassuring Diem and Nhu, or Harkins the success of the military adviser system, their own respective personal projects.

But to emphasize exclusively subordinate bureaucratic influences in this process of internal self-deception would be greatly to underrate the impact of the President himself, and of his high-level appointees. They, too, like Nolting, Harkins, or Nhu, had their "personal projects," larger ones, on which they reported to those who controlled their budgets and their tenure: Congress and the public. And they too, thanks to the security system and executive privilege, "wrote their own report cards": with a little help from their subordinates.

Precisely as at lower levels, but with enormously broader impact, the needs of the President and the Secretaries of State and Defense to use "information" to reassure Congress and the public had its effect on the internal flow of information up to the President. Reports and analyses that supported the administration's public position and could be released or leaked to that end were "helpful" and welcome, while "pessimism" was at best painful, less "useful," if not even dangerous to have down on paper. Executive values like these (vastly sharpened in 1966-1968, when skeptics and critics were louder and had to be refuted) translate into powerful incentives at lower levels to give the Chief what he so obviously wants.

Thus—granted human wishfulness, as well, as a factor at all levels—pessimism regarding an ongoing policy is a fragile, unstable phenomenon within the government. Ironically, even the VC and the GVN (earlier, the Viet Minh and French) played their role, too, in providing indicators of allied "progress" and intervals when things "seemed to be working." In 1951, 1956, 1962, and 1965, bureaucratic pressures toward optimism were catalyzed by actual effects of the new programs on allies and opponents in the desired direction. But "in the field" these effects proved very temporary, whereas our reading of them did not. As Kennedy had predicted, the effects of a "small drink" on friend and opponent faded quickly. What he may not fully have foreseen was the far more lasting afterglow in our own system.

In each case, the aftermath of escalation was an increased emphasis on military factors, and an accompanying alteration of mood from pessimism to great optimism. Thus, when U.S. combat units flooded into Vietnam from 1965 on, the pessimism of later 1964 gave way increasingly to buoyant hopes, by 1967, of an essentially military victory. But this had had its counterpart as early as 1951, after U.S. materiel and American liaison teams had made their way to Tonkin to join a failing French effort.

Meanwhile, the Viet Minh, and later the VC, had a characteristic response to a new

U.S./GVN strategy or a scaling-up of our involvement that further encouraged our switch to unbounded optimism. After suffering initial setbacks, it has been their practice to lie low for an extended period, gather data, analyze experience, develop and test new adapted strategies, then plan and prepare carefully before launching them. (Nothing, our Vietnam experience tells us, could be more un-American.)

Since so great a part of U.S. and GVN knowledge of enemy activities comes from operational contacts, there seems to be an irresistible tendency for U.S. operators to believe that data concerning contacts reveals enemy capabilities—i.e., that lessened VC combat operations indicate lessened capability. Another mechanism, then: U.S. optimism grows during VC "inactivity"—periods when VC activities are of a sort we do not observe —reaching a peak, ironically, when extreme VC quiescence is due to intense preparations for an explosion.

Crisis periods, then, are typically preceded by high points in U.S. official expectations. Thus, peaks of U.S. optimism occurred in late 1953 (just before Dienbienphu), 1958 (when guerrilla warfare was about to recommence), early 1963 (the VC had been studying the vulnerabilities of the strategic hamlet program, and meanwhile infiltrating massively), and late 1967 (during last-minute recruiting and preparations for the Tet offensive, including feints at the borders).

If a fever chart of U.S. expectations— say, anticipations of success—could be drawn meaningfully for the last 20 years, it would have a recurrent saw-tooth shape: an accelerating rise of optimism just before an abrupt decline (Fig. 26.1 is a conceptual sketch of such a graph). Our perceptual and emotional experience in Vietnam can be regarded as a sequence of two-phase cycles, in which Phase B—optimism—evolves causally in large part from decisions that follow Phase A, a crisis period of pessimism.

(The B-phases in Fig. 26.1 have been drawn with a reverse S-shape, signifying three subphases: an initial period in which the VC suffer real reverses and the GVN stabilizes on

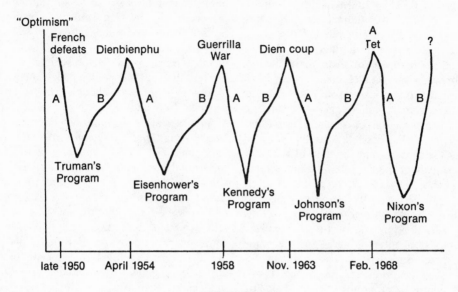

FIGURE 26.1

the basis of new programs; then a period in which, in reality, the VC have adapted and the GVN is declining, but U.S. expectations remain at a plateau rather than being reduced; finally, the VC begin quietly preparing for a major offensive, causing U.S. hopes to soar.)

If major escalating decisions qualitatively increasing our involvement had actually been made during Phase B's, that would be the quagmire model. It has never been the case.

However, during the B-phases, although no new major policies or commitments are introduced, U.S. aims may change significantly in the atmosphere of optimism, especially in the last stage, going beyond the avoidance of defeat—dominant aim in Phase A and the early Phase B stage—to achieving a victory. At the same time, real optimism leads officials to be much less cautious in public aims and predictions; to give commanders more leeway; to monitor operations less closely; and to indulge in operations that are costly (in many terms) and of low effectiveness but may speed the coming win. All of these responses lead to toleration of rapidly rising costs, and hence to a feeling, when a new crisis brings the return of Phase A, that the stakes, the investment, the commitment have become still

higher than before, the need to avoid "defeat" being now even greater.

Nevertheless, this postescalation euphoria, or "quagmire phase" of the cycle seems to play no essential role in the escalation process. It simply reinforces the presidential tendency to escalate if and as necessary to avoid a short-run "defeat" or "loss of all Vietnam to Communists." As Leslie Gelb has put it: "Each administration was prepared to pay the costs it could foresee for itself." Political, along with strategic, motives underlying that tendency were already strong enough in 1950 to induce the initial U.S. commitment without any prior or current period of American optimism. And they almost surely were felt strongly enough in subsequent years to have induced much greater escalation than occurred if that had appeared both necessary and effective in the short run.

Consciously oriented as escalating decisions actually were, when chosen, to the defensive aim of averting short-run Communist take-over, *each of these decisions of the past two decades can be said to have achieved its initial, internal aim.*

In Gelb's phrase: "The system worked." In fact, these presidential policies and tactics, in sequence, had the effect of holding South Vietnam out of Communist hands "cheaply" —i.e., without sizable numbers of U.S. combat troops—for 15 years, from 1950 to 1965.

Whether efforts and sacrifices, by Americans and Vietnamese, of even these limited but increasing magnitudes could easily have been justified to various parts of the electorate in terms of such limited aims—in starkest terms, the restoration of stalemate, and the postponement of a possible Communist takeover in Vietnam beyond the date of the next U.S. election—is another question. No administration chose to find out. To publicize more idealistic or strategically decisive goals, as they all did, was to forego credit for meeting successfully the limited short-run objectives that each—it is inferred here—privately accepted. More seriously, it was to incur the likelihood of suffering an appearance of recurrent failure of programs to meet their announced aims, and failure of administration predictions or "hopes" to be confirmed. But these impressions of failure, however embarrassing politically, each administration since 1950 has preferred either to the risks of candor on its private aims and expectations or to the risks of accepting the "loss of Vietnam" during or soon after its term in office.

In these respects, too, the policies "worked." Until 1968, at least, each president avoided the kinds of political costs related to Vietnam that his tactics were meant mainly to avert. In fact, up to the present, no president has had to face a political penalty for losing South Vietnam. Not even LBJ will be blamed in history for that, although he is blamed for other things.

Yet the earlier "cheap victories," year by year from 1950 to 1965, were purchased at a long-term price, one not yet paid in full. Presidential policies and tactics actively sustained and encouraged over that period a high estimate of U.S. strategic stakes in the conflict within the U.S. executive branch and the military, the Congress, and the public. Meanwhile they failed—as was highly likely, in the light of earlier internal estimates— either to strengthen adequately non-Communist Vietnamese efforts; to modify Communist aims; to deter or prevent an increase in Communist capabilities; or, of course, to induce the acceptance by Hanoi's leaders or revolutionary forces in South Vietnam of the U.S. role, presence, or aims in South Vietnam, or of the U.S.-supported Saigon regime.

Thus these presidential policies and tactics locked together with these other factors to produce, from the perspective of most of that 15-year period, *a high probability that U.S. troops would end up fighting in South Vietnam, and U.S. planes bombing throughout Indochina: i.e., high probabilities that they would be sent if necessary; and that they would be necessary.*

This is the future that three U.S. presidents failed to resist: indeed, knowingly cooperated with and prepared. Not, of course, that any president liked, wanted, or hoped for the darker developments that actually emerged— the deaths, the costs, the disruptions—only that they preferred the risk of these, and later the certainty, to certain other prospects they saw as alternatives. Thus the first three presidents determined the reality of large-scale war that the next two accepted and sustained. That is a generation of presidents: all the presidents within the lifetime of a recent college graduate.

Will the tradition end with the current president? How many more could it encompass? Nothing in the generalizations we have abstracted in this paper from experience of the last two decades gives a clear hint of a definite breaking-point, or a foreseeable change in basic motives and values either for the Communist-led forces or the U.S. government. On its face, that is simply a limitation of the analysis, a characteristic— perhaps a defect—of the model suggested.

Or perhaps it is a property of reality.

If so, it is a human and political reality, and humans can, in principle, change it. But change would not be easy. Rule 1 has deep roots in politicians' fears and motives, and in public responses, that have been powerfully influential for 20 years, through some hard times and challenges. There is little indication yet that it will not speak commandingly to presidents after this one. (Of its authority for the present one, there can be no real doubt.)

Improved presidential foresight—even the awareness that might be attained from this analysis—would not probably supersede Rule 1. If anything, it might serve to relax the constraining influence of Rule 2.

In the spring of 1965 President Johnson is reported to have received calls almost daily from one of his closest advisers telling him (what no one had to tell him): "Lyndon, don't be the first American president to lose a war."

It is true that such advisers omitted warnings of other deadly errors. They neglected to caution him: "Don't, over more than one or two years, lie to the public; or mislead and bypass Congress; or draft and spend and kill and suffer casualties at the rate your military will propose; or abort negotiations: or, even once, allow your generals to describe the enemy as defeated on the eve of their major offensive."

But if they had, and if he had seen the cogency of their warning: Would he then have decided to lose the war? Or would he, mindful of the time constraints, have acted to win it within them?

The same question applies to earlier presidents; and later.

THE FACES OF THE QUAGMIRE

Why is the quagmire model so often pressed? And why is it so widely accepted?

Looking at where their policies and tactics have brought us so far, it is easy to understand why the past four presidents would want, before and after, to conceal and deprecate their own foreknowledge and intentions. And it is no harder to guess why—perhaps unconsciously—participant-observers of one of these administrations or another have promoted the same interpretation of foresight and purpose, values and priorities, influence and responsibility, respecting their past colleagues within and outside government. Indeed, they make no secret of the conclusion they wish to convey by the quagmire metaphor and model

concerning the responsibility of individuals and groups.

Thus, Townsend Hoopes, acutely and perceptively critical of the policies under Johnson and earlier presidents, extends what Richard Falk has called "the circle of responsibility" widely indeed, in explicit purpose to relieve the burden of those seemingly at its center. Traumatized by a lunch with two reporters from the *Village Voice* who suggested that he himself, as Assistant Secretary of the Air Force under Johnson, might have been guilty of war crimes (their subsequent article was titled: "The War Criminals Hedge Their Bets"), Hoopes has published several rejoinders and discussions of the problem of responsibility. In the first of these, after describing his chief concern in the disturbing luncheon conversation as having been "The broad question of how the *entire nation* had stumbled down the long slippery slope of self-delusion into the engulfing morass," Hoopes concludes:

The tragic story of Vietnam is not, in truth, a tale of malevolent men bent upon conquest for personal gain or imperial glory. It is the story of an entire generation of leaders (and an entire generation of followers)....[Johnson's] principal advisers were, almost uniformly, those considered when they took office to be among the ablest, the best, the most humane and liberal men that could be found for public trust. No one doubted their honest, high-minded pursuit of the best interests of their country, and indeed of the whole noncommunist world, as they perceived those interests.

Arthur Schlesinger, Jr., less generous in his appreciation of some civilian Johnson lieutenants, is no less reluctant to single them or their Chief out as "guilty" in any special way for their role in our vast national undertaking. In the "quagmire" (literally, "morass") passage so often cited in this paper, he asserts:

It is not only idle but unfair to seek out guilty men. . . . we find ourselves entrapped today in . . . a war which no President, including President Johnson, desired or intended. The Vietnam story is *a tragedy without villains*. No thoughtful American can withhold sympathy as President Johnson ponders the gloomy choices which lie ahead.

One can read some of these passages as reflections of the sentiment Hoopes expresses: "What the country needs is not retribution, but therapy. . . ." (It is just possible that both are needed, at this point, in the interests of our country and of others.) He completes the sentence, plausibly, "therapy in the form of deeper understanding of our problems and of each other"; but in all of these passages and the larger arguments in which they are embedded, one senses that the drive for sympathetic therapy is setting back the cause of understanding.

Both the substance of the tentative conclusions in this paper and my experience of the heuristic process that gradually pointed toward them warn that a deeper analytical understanding of these well-guarded data and controverted events will not be likely to be reached by a searcher committed and determind to see the conflict and our part in it as "a tragedy without villains": war crimes without criminals, lies without liars, a process of immaculate deception.

The urge in these former officials to defend American institutions and legitimate authority (and surely some former administration leaders and colleagues, if not themselves) from the most extreme charges and sanctions ("Lyndon Johnson, though disturbingly volatile," Hoopes remarks, "was not in his worst moments an evil man in the Hitlerian sense") leads them as analysts to espouse and promulgate a view of process, roles, and motives that is grossly mistaken—as should be known to them from their own experience and access to information as officials.

Thus, an effort to defend against perceptions or charges of "immorality," in alleged pursuit of "objective judgment," leads in this case to historical and analytical error. And it has political consequences: it underwrites deceits that have served importantly a succession of presidents to maintain support for their substantive policies of intervention in Vietnam.

Of course, to promulgate a view is not necessarily to have it accepted. But this one has a powerful appeal. Earlier we asked, "Why is the quicksand model accepted by so

many?" and offered some cognitive answers. But we can suspect that an image speaks to deeper, more emotional concerns when it is presented regularly in the broad strokes of political cartoons in mass-circulation newspapers. That is what happened on the nation's editorial pages during the Cambodian invasion.

That week, while photographs on the front page showed unwonted images of *blitzkrieg*—tanks in formation driving across fields trailing plumes of dust, and locust swarms of American armed helicopters moving across new borders—and while reporters offered verbal pictures of the Cambodian village of Snoul being destroyed and looted, the drawings on the editorial pages were of Uncle Sams and GI Joes engulfed, bemused, floundering from a swamp marked "Vietnam" to one marked "Cambodia." Images, curiously, of impotence, passivity: ironically contrasting both with the news and the photographs of what Americans in southeast Asia were actually doing and with the President's announced intent to expunge notions of America as a "pitiful, helpless giant."

One cartoon, reproduced in *Time,* left the quagmire symbol to show the "U.S. citizen" in tatters on a raft, confronting three enormous, wide-mouthed whales, labeled: Vietnam, Cambodia, and Laos.

Whales?

The imagery, pressed too far, reveals its key. The scale, and the menace, have simply been reversed. The actual role of America and Americans in and toward Indochina is distorted, to a staggering degree, in the very process of suggesting that it be reconsidered.

Looking back to the quicksand cartoons, one sees their self-pity, their preoccupation with Uncle Sam's predicament, and one finally asks: Where are the Asians? Where are the Cambodians, the Lao, the Vietnamese in these drawings?

Presumably—there is no other sign—they are the particles of the bog, bits of the porridgey quagmire that has seized GI Joe and will not free him. . . .

It is not, after all, only presidents and

Cabinet members who have a powerful need and reason to deny their responsibility for this war—and who succeed at it. Just as presidents and their partisans find comfort and political safety in the quicksand image of the *President-as-victim,* so Americans at large are reassured in sudden moments of doubt by the same image drawn large, *America-as-victim.* It is no more real than the first, and neither national understanding nor extrication truly lie that way.

To understand the process as it emerges in the documents behind public statements, the concerns never written that moved decisions, the history scratched on the minds of bureaucrats: to translate that understanding into images that can guide actions close-related to reality, one must begin by seeing that it is Americans, our leaders and ourselves, that build the bog, a trap much more for other victims: *our* policies, our politics the quagmire in which Indochina drowns.

27. AMERICAN MILITARY POLICY AND ADVANCED WEAPONS

JAMES R. KURTH

This selection is from a slightly revised version of "A Widening Gyre" in Public Policy, *No. 3, Vol. 19, September 1971. James R. Kurth is Assistant Professor of Government at Harvard University.*

■ Power means the ability to call on resources. In this respect one of the most powerful organizations in the world is the U.S. Department of Defense. The ability of the military establishment to command a large portion of the national product increased dramatically during the 1950s and 1960s. Before World War II defense spending accounted for 1 percent of the Gross National Product, and when it leveled off just after World War II, the figure had risen to 5 percent. After the Korean war in the mid-1950s, defense commanded 10 percent of the Gross National Product, and in the early 1970s the defense budget amounted to about 7 percent. Those who steward the power of the military are obviously determined to keep the percentage at that level against the increasing determination of others to lower the proportion of GNP committed to defense.

The military establishment's ascendency in society is maintained through the complex of political, organizational, and technological activities involved in the procurement of advanced weapons. Spending for weapons does not represent the major proportion of the defense budget which goes for personnel, just as in an insurance company. However, complex weapons provide a central symbol in the rationale for defense demands on the GNP. It is the weapons that make the personnel more productive in providing defense, and weapons procurement, of course, provides the link between the military and the part of the business world that makes up the private sector of the "military-industrial complex." In this article, James Kurth systematically compares several theories that social scientists have offered about the formulation of American military policy. By careful assessment of evidence of the changes in weapons procurement policies over time, he suggests which of these theories he believes best fits the facts.

The various explanations of American military policy analyzed by Kurth can be found in Thomas C. Schelling, *The Strategy of Conflict* (Cambridge, Mass.: Harvard University Press, 1960); Henry A. Kissinger, *Nuclear Weapons and Foreign Policy* (New York: Harper, 1957) and *The Necessity of Choice* (New York: Harper, 1961); Herman Kahn, *On Thermonuclear War* (Princeton, N.J.: Princeton University Press, 1960) and *On Escalation* (New York: Praeger, 1965); Ralph E. Lapp, *Arms Beyond Doubt: The Tyranny of Weapons Technology* (New York: Cowles, 1970); Herbert York, *Race to Oblivion: A Participant's View of the Arms Race* (New York: Simon & Schuster, 1970); Samuel P. Huntington, *The Common Defense* (New York: Columbia University Press, 1961); Warner R. Schilling, Paul Y. Hammond, and Glen H. Snyder, *Strategy, Politics and Defense Budgets* (New York: Columbia University Press, 1962); John Kenneth Galbraith, *How to Control the Military* (New York: New American Library, 1969); and Gabriel Kolko, *The Roots of American Foreign Policy* (Boston: Beacon Press, 1969). Bruce M. Russett in *What Price Vigilance? The Burdens of National Defense* (New Haven, Conn.: Yale University Press, 1970) has analyzed in some detail the shifts in national spending brought about by the military establishment's increasing claims on the GNP, and has made a comparative analysis for Western nations of the impact of defense on the distribution of resources. ■

THE MAKING OF MILITARY POLICY: A THICKET OF THEORIES

IN THE WAKE OF the Vietnamese War and under the threat of a costly and dangerous Soviet-American arms race, basic questions are being asked about the making of American military policy. Why does the United States buy a costly antiballistic missile system (ABM), despite expert testimony that it will not work and despite urgent pleas to "reorder national priorities" toward domestic problems of the 1970s? Why does the United States deploy multiple independently targeted reentry vehicles (MIRV), despite expert testimony that they will re-create "the reciprocal fear of surprise attack" and "the delicate balance of terror" of the 1950s and despite a Senate plea to postpone their deployment? And what will be the consequences of such weapons systems for U.S. strategic doctrines?

The problem with questions about the making of military policy, and also about the making of foreign policy, is not that there are no answers but that there are too many answers. Around ABM, or around MIRV, or around nearly every significant military policy, there has grown up a cluster of competing explanations, a thicket of theories, which prevents us from having a clear view of the making of that policy. For example, does MIRV result from rational calculation about Soviet threats, or from reckless pursuit by weapons scientists of technological progress for its own sake, or from resourceful efforts by weapons manufacturers and by their allies in the military services to maintain production and profits, or from some combination of these factors? Today men debate and denounce each other over such competing explanations of military policies.

Of course, some would quickly prune away some explanations as obviously being mere brambles. They might say of the effect of a hypothetical cause what Robert Dahl has said of the power of a hypothetical act.

Suppose I stand on a street corner and say to myself, "I command all automobile drivers on the street to drive on the right side of the road"; suppose further that all the drivers actually do as I "command" them to do; still most people will regard me as mentally ill if I insist that I have power over automobile drivers to compel them to use the right side of the road.

But when we turn from traffic to politics, as we know from Dahl's own efforts to analyze power, the difference between madmen or mad theories and rules of the road or rules of political behavior is no longer so obvious to so many objective observers.

COMPETING EXPLANATIONS OF MILITARY POLICIES

Let us distinguish five major competing explanations of American military policies: the strategic, the technocratic, the bureaucratic, the democratic, and the economic.

1. *The strategic theory.* This explanation emphasizes the international system and America's security and status within it as the determinant of military policies. Until recently, this approach probably was the most common among scholars: Balance of power theory, game theory, bargaining theory, and analyses of the reciprocal dynamics of arms races are all variations on the strategic theme. Leading strategic theorists of American military policies are Thomas Schelling, Henry Kissinger, and Herman Kahn. And, of course, strategic arguments remain the chosen rationales of policymakers, for example in presentations to Congress by the current administration, such as President Nixon's "U.S. Foreign Policy for the 1970's" and Secretary of Defense Laird's annual "Defense Report."

2. *The technocratic theory.* This explanation emphasizes the technical interests of weapons scientists as the determinant of military policies. It argues that a weapons system is developed becaues, as J. Robert Oppenheimer put it about an H-bomb design, it is "technically so sweet." Leading technocratic theorists are Ralph Lapp, and, for the most part, Herbert York. Among policymakers, the Defense Department's Director of Science and Engineering, John Foster, has asked, "By what mechanisms does our society select the goals and opportunities which our research and development community will pursue?" His answer: "Many are pursued because they are possible or because they are exciting."

3. *The bureaucratic theory.* This explanation sees military policies as the outcomes of

competition between bureaucracies, especially the army, navy, and air force. As such, it is a form of interest group theory, with a shift in locus from Congress to the executive and a shift in content from "low politics" to "high politics." Leading bureaucratic theorists of American military policies are Samuel Huntington, Warner Schilling, and, for the most part, John Kenneth Galbraith. Closely related to this explanation from bureaucratic politics is the explanation from bureaucratic process; this explanation sees military policies as the outputs of processes and standard operating procedures *within* bureaucracies. Graham Allison's work is an explicit illustration of the bureaucratic or organizational process explanation as well as the bureaucratic politics explanation.

4. *The democratic theory.* Another possible explanation of military policies would emphasize the political system as the determinant. Here, congressional and presidential elections would be central and, relatedly, pork-barrel politics and corporate campaign contributions. At present, however, no one has systematically emphasized electoral politics as the major determinant of military policies, although Bruce Russett has done statistical analysis along these lines, and many journalists have made fragmentary observations.

5. *The economic theory.* This explanation emphasizes the economic system as the determinant of military policies, for example, the role of industrialism, capitalism, and the great corporations. In a less sweeping but more frequent formulation of the economic theory, the emphasis is on one section of the economy, the aerospace industry. Leading economic theorists of American military policies are Gabriel Kolko, Harry Magdoff, and the late Paul Baran.

The bureaucratic and economic explanations in combination yield, of course, the theory of the military-industrial complex, which in its pure form argues that the military and industry are roughly equal in their influence on policy outcomes. This argument has often been advanced by journalists. Some give equal weight to a third element in the complex, the major military committees of Congress.

In normal times, this rather dry recital of competing explanations of military policies would have only descriptive value; at the present time, however, when men debate "the need to reorder national priorities" and fear the risks and burdens of a new arms race, the different theories hav different implications for action, have prescriptive value.

Let us imagine men who find fault with American military policies and who hope to contribute to their correction. For them, each of the major theories or explanations has a different prescriptive implication.

1. The strategic theory: individual reasoning with the leading policymakers.
2. The technocratic theory: procedural reform of research and development.
3. The bureaucratic theory: bureaucratic reorganization.
4. The democratic theory: electoral or constitutional reform.
5. The economic theory: industrial reorganization or even social revolution.

Consequently and generally, the prescriptive implications become successively more radical. Each theory permits but does not prescribe the corrective or preventive prescription of the theories listed before it in the above order; given one particular theory, the preceding prescriptions may be helpful but will not be sufficient for the correction or prevention of a military policy. Conversely, assuming norms of economy of effort and economy of effect, each theory proscribes the prescriptions of the theories listed after it; given one particular theory, the succeeding prescriptions will not be necessary for the correction or prevention of a military policy. In brief, each theory precludes the sufficiency of the ones before it, and each precludes the necessity of the ones after it.

Given this array of competing explanations and the corresponding array of correcting prescriptions, how should we choose among them? . . .

Today many men seem to resolve the question of selection by a leap of faith. We probably are entering into an era of multiple and competing explanations of U.S. military policy, or of any U.S. policy, each rooted in faith and each immune from being disproven by evidence or by logic. In this situation, the process of argument and the fuel of passion probably will lead to reinforcing and rigidifying the competing theories rather than dissolving them in a great empirical and pragmatic consensus. . . .

This essay is an effort to cut away at the thicket of theories. In it, we will examine the four major cases of American weapons procurement of the 1960s and 1970s—that is, of the period covering the Kennedy, Johnson, and Nixon administrations. These are (1) the massive buildup of Minuteman and Polaris missiles; (2) MIRV; (3) aircraft procurement, in particular the F-111 fighter-bomber, the C-5A jumbo transport, and the B-1 large bomber; and (4) ABM.

THE MISSILE BUILDUP: QUANTITATIVE CHANGE

The first important case of American weapons procurement in the 1960s was the massive buildup of Minuteman and Polaris missiles from 1961 to 1964. This case is also the simplest to examine and explain: a decision was made during a relatively limited time and for a merely quantitative change.

Because Minuteman and Polaris were invulnerable and thus second-strike weapons, they had a generally stabilizing impact on the strategic balance between the Soviet Union and the United States. As such, a strategic explanation of the U.S. buildup, focusing on international stability, might seem quite sufficient. However, even Secretary of Defense McNamara in 1967 retrospectively criticized as excessive the *degree* of the U.S. expansion and its effect on the Soviets.

Our current numerical superiority over the Soviet Union in reliable, accurate and effective warheads is both greater than we had originally planned and more than we require. . . . Clearly,

the Soviet buildup is in part a reaction to our own buildup since the beginning of the 1960s.

Why did the United States deploy as many missiles as it did? McNamara's own explanation, like almost all official explanations, is a strategic one; but it stresses his lack of accurate information.

In 1961 when I became Secretary of Defense, the Soviet Union possessed a very small operational arsenal of intercontinental missiles. However, they did possess the technological and industrial capacity to enlarge that arsenal very substantially over the succeeding several years. We had no evidence that the Soviets did plan, in fact, fully to use that capability. But, as I have pointed out, a strategic planner must be conservative in his calculations; that is, he must prepare for the worst plausible case and not be content to hope and prepare merely for the most probable.

Since we could not be certain of Soviet intentions, since we could not be sure that they would not undertake a massive buildup, we had to insure against such an eventuality by undertaking ourselves a major buildup of the Minuteman and Polaris forces. Thus, in the course of hedging against what was then only a theoretically possible Soviet buildup, we took decisions which have resulted in our current superiority in numbers of warheads and deliverable megatons. But the blunt fact remains that if we had had more accurate information about planned Soviet strategic forces, we simply would not have needed to build as large a nuclear arsenal as we have today.

Let me be absolutely clear. I am not saying that our decision in 1961 was unjustified; I am saying that it was necessitated by a lack of accurate information.

But McNamara's account does not explain why the U.S. ordered a massive buildup all at once instead of ordering part of the buildup at first and delaying the rest of it until more information became available.

An alternative explanation emphasizing bureaucratic politics is given by Schlesinger in his account of the drawing up of the Kennedy administration's first full defense budget in the fall of 1961.

The budget . . . contemplated a sizable increase in missiles; and the White House staff, while favoring a larger Minuteman force than the original Eisenhower proposal, wondered whether the new budget was not providing for more missiles than national security required. But the President, though intimating a certain sympathy for this view, was not prepared to overrule Mc-

Namara's recommendation. As for the Secretary, he did not believe that doubling or even tripling our striking power would enable us to destroy the hardened missile sites or missile-launching submarines of our adversary. But he was already engaged in a bitter fight with the Air Force over his effort to disengage from the B-70, a costly, high-altitude manned bomber rendered obsolescent by the improvement in Soviet ground-to-air missiles. After cutting down the original Air Force demands considerably, he perhaps felt that he could not do more without risking public conflict with the Joint Chiefs and the vociferous B-70 lobby in Congress. As a result, the President went along with the policy of multiplying Polaris and Minuteman missiles.

A similar account is given by David Halberstam, one which, however, emphasizes more the power of Congress.

In 1961 some White House aides were trying to slow the arms race. At that point the U.S. had 450 missiles, and McNamara was asking for 950, and the Chiefs were asking for 3,000. The White House people had quietly checked around and found that in effectiveness the 450 were the same as McNamara's 950.

"What about it, Bob?" Kennedy asked.

"Well, they're right," he answered.

"Well, then, why the 950, Bob?" Kennedy asked.

"Because that's the smallest number we can take up on the Hill without getting murdered," he answered.

In summary, the massive buildup of Minuteman and Polaris missiles resulted from a decision made for a merely quantitative change and during a relatively limited time. It is best explained by bureaucratic politics: bargaining among different actors within the executive branch over the share and degree of incremental change, with allies within Congress playing a supporting role. But . . . the missile buildup also can be fitted into a broader economic analysis.

MIRV: INNOVATIVE CHANGE

The Minuteman and Polaris buildup was the first important case of American weapon procurement in the 1960s. But the most important case, because of its potentially destabilizing impact on the strategic balance between the Soviet Union and the United States, was MIRV.

With its high accuracy in targeting, its high number of warheads, and its high immunity to aerial surveillance, MIRV readily and reasonably can provoke a Soviet fear of an American first-strike against Soviet land-based, even hardened, missiles, and it will provoke the Soviets into acquiring their own MIRV's, perhaps leading again to "the reciprocal fear of surprise attack" and "the delicate balance of terror." In the face of these foreseen strategic risks, the procurement of MIRV seems both momentous and dangerous.

Why did the United States develop and deploy MIRV? The official explanation is again a strategic one, and the usual argument has been that MIRV is needed to penetrate Soviet ABM systems. But this does not explain why highly accurate, as opposed to merely multiple, warheads are needed. Nor does it explain why the U.S. continued to develop MIRV in the mid-1960s after the Soviets limited their development of ABM. A more accurate strategic explanation, suggested by the following censored congressional testimony, would argue that MIRV was developed in order to increase the U.S. capability to destroy Soviet missiles, and, in effect, to give the U.S. a first-strike capability.

Question (by Senator Mike Mansfield, D.—Mont.):

Is it not true that the U.S. response to the discovery that the Soviets had made an initial deployment of an ABM system around Moscow and probably elsewhere was to develop the MIRV system for Minuteman and Polaris?

Answer (by Dr. John S. Foster, Director of Defense Research and Engineering):

Not entirely. The MIRV concept was originally generated to increase our targeting capability rather than to penetrate ABM defenses. In 1961-62 planning for targeting the Minuteman force it was found that the total number of aim points exceeded the number of Minuteman missiles. By splitting up the payload of a single missile (deleted) each (deleted) could be programmed (deleted) allowing us to cover these targets with (deleted) fewer missiles. (Deleted.) MIRV was originally born to implement the payload split-up (deleted). It was found that the previously generated MIRV concept could equally well be used against ABM (deleted).

Although McNamara had rejected a first-strike targeting doctrine, the Air Force commanders, formally his subordinates, had not. They preferred a first-strike doctrine, with its double implication that the United States could *win* a war with the Soviet Union and that the Air Force would have the prime role in doing so, to a second-strike doctrine, which implied that the U.S. could only *deter* a war and that the Air Force would be only an equal of the Navy in the task. Against McNamara, the Air Force commanders could not achieve an official first-strike targeting doctrine for the United States; with MIRV, however, they could achieve a real first-strike tageting capability for the Air Force.

The research and development of MIRV was, of course, highly classified, so that knowledge of it would be kept from the Soviets. But the effect was also to keep knowledge of MIRV from Congress and the public. Nor, in the early phases of the program, did Defense officials have any need to build support in Congress and the public for large expenditures of funds. As a result, the MIRV program faced no political opposition, and it progressed in accordance with technical and bureaucratic procedures of research and development internal to different organizations within the Defense Department. By the time the existence and implications of MIRV became public knowledge, it had already been tested, the production of Minuteman III and Poseidon missiles had already commenced, and the conversion of Polaris-launching submarines into Poseidon ones had already begun. Given this momentum generated by initial technocratic interests and by internal bureaucratic processes, the MIRV program could have been brought to a halt after 1968 only if the President or leading members of Congress had been willing to expend an extraordinary amount of political capital. Further, once the United States had successfully tested MIRV, the Soviets could not be sure that the United States had not also deployed it. The Soviets probably then felt themselves compelled to test and deploy their own MIRV; the Soviet program, in turn, reinforces the pressures behind the American one.

In summary, MIRV resulted from developmental procedures for an innovative change, over a relatively lengthy time, but within a relatively limited circle of organizations. It is best explained by bureaucratic processes: bureaucratic doctrines, bureaucratic standard operating procedures, including in this case normal procedures for the research and development of technocratic interests, and bureaucratic programs for organizational preservation and growth. But, again, as we shall see in the next section, MIRV also can be fitted into a broader economic analysis.

AIRCRAFT PROCUREMENT: RENOVATIVE CHANGE

In contrast to missile procurement, the two major cases of manned aircraft procurement in the 1960s were less important strategically but more debated politically. These were the F-111 fighter-bomber and the C-5A jumbo transport. Both aircraft became famous, even notorious, because of financial troubles ("cost overruns"), mechanical failures, and Congressional investigations. Further, in June 1970, the Air Force awarded a contract to produce prototypes of a new, large, manned bomber, the B-1, which begins anew the numbering of the bomber series and which would go into operational deployment in the late 1970s. By that time, given the efficiency of strategic missiles and antiaircraft missiles, the new B-1 would seem to be about as useful and about as obsolete as the first B-1 of the 1920s.

Why did the United States buy such aircraft? There are, of course, the official, strategic explanations: the F-111 is needed for a variety of tasks, such as tactical bombing, strategic bombing, and air defense; the C-5A is needed for massive airlifts of troops and supplies; and the B-1 is needed for strategic bombing and postattack reconnaissance. But these explanations neglect the fact that the respective tasks can be performed by a variety of ways and weapons, and that these particular manned aircraft are not clearly the most cost-effective (to use McNamara's own proclaimed criterion) way to do so.

There are, also, the possible bureaucratic explanations: the F-111 was needed by the Tactical Air Command to preserve its power and prestige within the overall balance of the military bureaucracies; the C-5A was needed similarly by the Military Aircraft Command; and the B-1 is desired by the aging commanders of the Air Force and of the Strategic Air Command within it, who look back with nostalgia to their youth and to the manned bomber in which they rode first to heroic purpose and then to bureaucratic power. But these explanations are not fully satisfactory: neither the Tactical Air Command nor the Military Airlift Command is the strongest organization within the Air Force (the strongest is the Strategic Air Command), and probably neither of them could achieve such expensive programs as the F-111 and C-5A without allies. And even the powerful commanders of the Air Force and the Strategic Air Command could not achieve the B-1 on the basis of nostalgia alone, especially in a period of unusually sharp criticism of military spending and after the predecessor of the B-1, the B-70, had been canceled as obsolescent by McNamara several years before.

An alternative explanation, more economic in emphasis and more general in scope, can be constructed by drawing some relations between two variables for the period since 1960: (1) aerospace systems which are military or military-related (i.e., military aircraft, missiles, and space systems) and (2) aerospace corporations which produce such systems.

AEROSPACE SYSTEMS

The major military aerospace systems produced at some time during the period since 1960 have been the following: the B-52, B-58, and B-70 large bombers; the Minuteman and Polaris missiles and their MIRV successors or follow ons, Minuteman III and Poseidon; the F-111 and F-4 fighter-bombers; and the C-130, C-141, and C-5A transports. In addition, there has been the military-related Apollo moon program. Major military aerospace systems presently planned for production in the mid or late 1970s include the B-1, which can be seen as a long-delayed follow on to the canceled B-70; the Undersea Long-Range Missile System (ULMS), which will be a follow on to Poseidon; the F-14 and F-15, which will follow the F-4; and the military-related space shuttle program.

These various aerospace systems can be grouped into five functional categories or production sectors: (1) large bombers, (2) missile systems, (3) fighters and fighter-bombers, (4) military transports, and (5) space systems.

AEROSPACE CORPORATIONS

At the beginning of our period, in 1960, a large number of aerospace corporations produced military aircraft, missiles, or space systems. Four stood out, however, in the sense that each received in fiscal year 1961 military and space "prime contract awards" of some $1 billion or more: General Dynamics, North American, Lockheed, and Boeing.

During the decade after 1960, each of these four corporations continued to normally receive each year $1 billion or more in military and space contracts, although Boeing's awards occasionally dropped below that amount. McDonnell, a minor contractor at the beginning of the decade with contracts of $295 million in FY 1961, greatly expanded its military sales, primarily with the F-4 Phantom. In 1967, McDonnell merged with Douglas, another minor contractor; during the remainder of the decade, the merged corporation of McDonnell Douglas normally received each year contracts of $1 billion or more.

Thus, in the 1960s, five major aerospace corporations produced military aircraft, missiles, or space systems and normally received $1 billion or more in military and space contracts each year. Further, we can analytically split Lockheed, which was normally the largest military contractor, into its two main military divisions, Lockheed-Missiles and Space, located in California, and Lockheed-Georgia. There were thus six major production lines.

We can then chart the major military and military-related aerospace systems according to the production line to which the United States awarded the contract and according to the years when major development or production phased in or out or is scheduled to do so. Some interesting patterns result. (See Table 27.1.)

About the time a production line phases out production of one major government contract, it phases in production of a new one, usually within a year. In the cases of new aircraft, which usually require a development phase of about three years, the production line normally is awarded the contract for the new system about three years before production of the old one is scheduled to phase out. In the cases of new missiles, the development phase usually is about two years. Further, in most cases, the new contract is for a system which is structurally similar while technically superior to the system being phased out—i.e., the new contract is a follow on contract. (An exception is Apollo, but even here North American was NASA's largest contractor before the Apollo contract was awarded; in the case of the B-1, the follow on is one step removed from the B-70.)

At the end of the 1960s, a seventh major production line emerged. Grumman at the beginning of the decade was a minor production line with annual military and space sales of some $300 million. In the early 1960s, it was awarded two large subcontracts, one for the aft fuselage of the F-111 and one for elements of the Apollo moon program. In 1968, Grumman neared $1 billion in annual military and space sales. As the phaseout of the two large subcontracts approached, the navy awarded Grumman in January 1969 the prime contract for the F-14, with a prospective value of $9 billion.

A large and established aerospace production line is a national resource—or so it seems to many high officers in the armed services. The corporation's managers, shareholders, bankers, engineers, and workers, of course, will enthusiastically agree, as will the

area's congressmen and senators. The Defense Department would find it risky and even reckless to allow one of only six or seven large production lines to wither and die for lack of a large production contract. There is at least latent pressure upon it from many sources to award a new, major contract to a production line when an old major contract is phasing out. Further, the disruption of the production line will be least and the efficiency of the product would seem highest if the new contract is structurally similar to the old, in the same functional category or production sector—i.e., is a follow on contract. Such a contract might be seen as a renovative change: it renovates both the large and established aerospace corporation that produces the weapons system and the large and established military organization that deploys it.

This latent constraint or rather compulsion imposed on weapons procurement by industrial structure might be called the follow on imperative and contrasted with the official imperative. The official imperative for weapons procurement might be phrased as follows. If strategic considerations determine that a military service needs a new weapons system, it will solicit bids from several competing companies; ordinarily, the service will award the contract to the company with the most cost-effective design. The follow on imperative is rather different. If one of the seven production lines is opening up, it will receive a new major contract from a military service (or from NASA); ordinarily the new contract will be structurally similar to the old—i.e., a follow on contract. Relatedly, the design competition between production lines is only a peripheral factor in the award.

The follow on imperative would have predicted and can perhaps explain the production line and the product structure of eight out of the nine major contracts awarded from 1960 to 1970: (1) Minuteman III follow on to Minuteman, (2) Poseidon follow on to Polaris, (3) C-141 follow on to C-130, (4) C-5A follow on to C-141, (5) F-14 follow on to F-111 major subcontract, (6) F-15 follow on to F-4, (7) F-111 after B-58—a

TABLE 27.1.

MILITARY AEROSPACE SYSTEMS AND MAJOR PRODUCTION LINES

	General Dynamics	North American Rockwell	Boeing	Lockheed-M & S	Lockheed-Georgia	McDonnell Douglas
1960	B-58	B-70	B-52 Minuteman	Polaris	C-130	F-4
1961		Apollo d. in	Minuteman build-up	Polaris buildup	C-141 d. in	
1962	B-58 out F-111 d.in		B-52 out			
1963						
1964		B-70 out			C-141 p. in	
1965					C-5A d. in	
1966	F-111 p. in	Apollo p. in	Minuteman III d. in	Poseidon d. in		
1967						
1968			Minuteman out Minuteman III p. in	Polaris out Poseidon p. in	C-141 out C-5A p. in	
1969						F-15 d. in
1970		B-1 d. in				
1971						
1972	F-111 out	Apollo out			C-54 out	F-4 out
1973	?	B-1 p. in	Minuteman III out Super-MIRV or SST in ?	Poseidon out ULMS in ?	?	F-15 p. in

d. = development; p. = production

somewhat less certain case, (8) B-1 delayed follow on to B-70. In regard to the ninth contract, Apollo, North American might have been predicted to receive the award, because it was already NASA's largest contractor.

The imperatives of the industrial structure are reinforced, not surprisingly, by the imperatives of the political system, as would be suggested by a democratic explanation. Four of the production lines are located in states which loom large in the Electoral College: California (Lockheed-Missiles and Space and North American Rockwell), Texas (General Dynamics), and New York (Grumman). The three others are located in states which in the 1960s had a senator who ranked high in the Senate Armed Services Committee or Appropriations Committee: Washington (Boeing, Henry Jackson), Georgia (Lockheed-Georgia, Richard Russell), and Missouri (McDonnell division of McDonnell Douglas, Stuart Symington).

It might be said, however, that one should expect most contracts to be follow on contracts. Production of the original system should give an aerospace corporation a competitive edge in technical experience and expertise which will win for it the next system awarded in the same production sector. But in at least three major cases, the Source Selection Board on technical grounds chose a different corporation than the one already producing a similar system; the contract became a follow on contract only when the board was overruled by higher officials. With the F-111, the original, technical choice was Boeing rather than General Dynamics; with the C-5A, it was Boeing rather than Lockheed; and with Apollo, it was Martin rather than North American. More importantly, it is not always obvious that there should be any new system at all in an old production sector.

The table indicates that there has been considerable pressure on the Nixon administration. In 1969-70, the administration confronted two impending phaseouts, the F-4 Phantom program of the McDonnell division of McDonnell Douglas, which was expected to phase out in 1972, and the Apollo program

of North American Rockwell, whose funding was scheduled to decline sharply after the first two or three manned landings on the moon. The administration resolved the problem in the easiest and most incremental way, by a follow on contract, the F-15, to the McDonnell division in December 1969 and by a delayed follow on, the B-1, to North American Rockwell in June 1970. Seen in this perspective, the other competitors for the F-15 (Fairchild Hiller and North American Rockwell) and for the B-1 (General Dynamics and Boeing) were never really in the running.

In summary, the F-111, C-5A, and B-1 each resulted from a contract cycle of small but successive decisions made for a renovative change, over a relatively lengthy time, and among a relatively large circle of actors. These cases of aircraft procurement are best explained by bureaucratic-corporate alliances, otherwise known as military-industrial complexes.

The table also indicates that the pressure on the Nixon administration will be especially intense in the future. In the next year or two, two other production lines will open up—General Dynamics and Lockheed-Georgia. The latter is the largest industrial enterprise in the southeastern United States. How will the administration fill the contract gap?

The problem becomes especially acute because of the recent evolution of the five functional categories or production sectors. The aerospace systems within them or follow on contracts are, of course, becoming progressively more complex and expensive, but they are also becoming progressively more dangerous strategically (MIRV), or operationally (F-14 and C-5A), or at best dubious (B-1, F-15, and the space shuttle).

In confronting its contract dilemmas, the Nixon administration seems to have chosen a combination of half-measures and extreme measures. For a stopgap and the short run, Lockheed and General Dynamics have been awarded new but smaller contracts in other production sectors, such as antisubmarine warfare. But for a cureall and the long run, the Nixon solution for the plight of the aerospace industry might be those endlessly expensive contracts in that endlessly expansive production sector of missile defense—the ABM.

ABM: REDISTRIBUTIVE CHANGE

The ABM is, in many ways, the superlative case among our four cases of weapons procurement. In regard to the probable cost of the completed system, at least $10 billion, it is the most expensive. In regard to the length of time that the system has been an issue (programs date back to 1955), it is the most extensive. In regard to the scope of actors participating in the decision-making process, it is the most inclusive. And in regard to the heat of the public debate over procurement, it is the most intensive.

Why did the United States buy the ABM? More specifically, why did the Johnson administration in September 1967 propose the Sentinel ABM, and why did the Nixon administration in March 1969 and since propose the Safeguard ABM? The official, strategic explanations have been many and varied. McNamara in 1967 argued that the ABM was needed to protect cities from China. Nixon and Laird in 1969 argued that it was needed to protect Minutemen from the Soviet Union. More recently, they have extended the proposed protection to some cities again. All of the justifications have been questioned by many strategists, scientists, and congressmen; the most decisive refutation is simply the argument that the ABM will not work, especially given the ease with which the Soviets could overload the system with a dense attack.

Bureaucratic explanations are possible but not very plausible. The army sees the ABM as its way to get again into missile programs, from which it has been excluded while the air force has had Minuteman and the navy has had Polaris and Poseidon, and thus as its way to restore the bureaucratic balance of power. But this had been the case for almost a decade before 1967. Little had come of it, although Congress in 1966 had voted funds to prepare ABM production, which the Johnson administration had refused to spend. Further, within the army, the air defense and missile defense organizations are not the dominant organizations; the large-scale deployment of ABM will redistribute bureaucratic power within the army.

A democratic explanation is also possible, and, for the 1967 decision, more plausible. President Johnson feared being vulnerable in the approaching election to charges from the Republicans that he has neglected the nation's security. John Kennedy in 1960 charged a "missile gap;" Lyndon Johnson in 1967 feared an "ABM gap." But in 1969, the Nixon administration faced quite different political problems. The next presidential election was far away, Congress had to be pressured by the administration to approve ABM, the reverse of the situation two years before (in the Senate in 1969, an amendment to prevent deployment was defeated by only two votes), and within the public there was much more criticism of ABM. Why, then, did the Nixon administration go ahead with ABM, albeit under a different rationale and under a different name?

What about economic explanations? One argument would be that Nixon was aware of impending difficulties in the aerospace industry and that he saw ABM contracts as increasing his options and instruments with which to manage these difficulties. The initial contract for the main missile of the ABM system, the Spartan, had been awarded to the healthiest of the production lines, McDonnell Douglas. But as the ABM system is expanded, major subcontracts could go to other production lines as they open up and when contracts are needed: to General Dynamics as it phases out the F-111, to Lockheed-Georgia as it phases out the C-5A, and perhaps to Boeing, as it phases out Minuteman III and is unable to phase in the SST. Such thoughts were suggested in the preceding discussion of the follow on imperative.

Another economic argument would be that Nixon was aware of impending difficulties not only in the aerospace industry but in the economy generally and that he saw ABM contracts as increasing his options and instruments with which to manage this larger recession. The ABM will benefit not only many aerospace firms but also corporations beyond the aerospace sector of the economy. Major ABM contracts have been awarded to corporations whose major production is not aerospace, such as Western Electric, a subsidiary of AT&T, and General Electric; the large-scale production of ABM will redistribute economic benefits from military contracts within the economy just as the large-scale deployment of it will redistribute bureaucratic power within the army. And, to some extent, it will be redistribution upward. The five major aerospace corporations (Lockheed, General Dynamics, Boeing, McDonnell Douglas, and North American Rockwell) normally rank between 20th and 50th (by annual sales) in the *Fortune* Directory of the 500 largest industrial corporations. But Western Electric and General Electric are normally among the top 10.

Thus, a new aerospace production sector, missile defense, is being created and added on to the five sectors already established. At the same time, new aerospace production lines, Western Electric, General Electric, and perhaps others, are being created and added on to the seven lines already established. The ABM might be used to resolve the current dilemmas of the aerospace industry or of the general economy, but it would do so only by expanding the number of production lines and thus only by insuring that the next set of dilemmas would have to be resolved on an even grander and more expensive scale.

More generally, the above discussions of aircraft procurement and the ABM suggest that the early 1970s will see expansion in the number of production sectors, in the number of production lines, in the costs of weapons systems, and in the dangers and damages that they bring; weapons procurement will feature wider and wider scope, higher and higher costs, greater and greater risks, and less and less control by the President, by Congress as a whole, and by the people they are supposed to represent. "Turning and turning in the widening gyre, the falcon cannot hear the falconer."

MODES OF CHANGE AND MODES OF CAUSATION

Can we find any general pattern in these four cases of weapons procurement? The preceding accounts have suggested four modes of change—quantitative, innovative, renovative, and redistributive—and four modes of causation—bureaucratic politics, bureaucratic processes, bureaucratic-corporate alliances, and the economic system. In this section, we will review these modes of change, putting the quantitative last so as to make the order analytical rather than historical.

1. *Innovative change.* An innovative change is the development, production, and deployment of a weapons system in which both the technical advances and the strategic implications are unfamiliar and far-reaching. Indeed, the strategic implications will seem strange and fearsome. MIRV has already been discussed under the heading of innovative change, but ABM is an innovative change along with being a redistributive one. Other major innovative changes since the Second World War have been the H-bomb, the ICBM, and the Polaris missile system. In the case of MIRV, the innovative system was not only unfamiliar; in the early stages of research and development, it was also inexpensive.

Because an innovative change is unfamiliar and sometimes inexpensive, it normally begins not in a decision at the higher levels of policymaking and budgetmaking but in technical and organizational procedures for research and development. At this initial point, some sort of technocratic explanation seems best. The Director of Defense Research and Engineering, John Foster, has described the process as follows.

Now most of the action the United States takes in the area of research and development has to do with one or two types of activities. Either we see from the field of science and technology some new possibilities, which we think we ought to exploit, or we see threats on the horizon, possible threats, usually not something the enemy has done but something we have thought ourselves that he might do, we must therefore be prepared for. These are the two forces that tend to drive our research and development activities.

Thus, a strategic consideration of a rather remote sort is also present. Once the new weapons system reaches a later phase, a stronger strategic imperative enters into the picture. It will now seem plausible that the Soviet Union is also secretly developing the system. At the same time, there is not yet any certainty about how the system will work and what it will do. A Defense Department planner will think that he must be, in McNamara's words, "conservative in his calculations; that is, he must prepare for the worst plausible case and not be content to hope and prepare merely for the most probable." Such calculations, which are made in some degree about any weapons system, will be especially compelling when the system is both fearsome and cheap. Thus, there will be great pressure within the Defense Department to continue with its development.

During this phase, moreover, high secrecy and low expense continue to keep the system out of public debate, and it will face no significant opposition from Congress or even from other bureaucracies until development is near or at completion. Bureaucratic momentum, propelled by procedures for weapons testing and programs for bureaucratic growth, is sufficient to bring the innovation to full development. To reach this point, an explanation emphasizing bureaucratic process seems best.

Bureaucratic momentum alone, however, does not seem sufficient to explain the expensive jump from research and development to production and deployment. The combination of bureaucratic momentum and strategic fears may be sufficient to do so, although the evidence is unclear. The four innovative systems that have been widely deployed and strategically crucial—H-bomb, ICBM, Polaris, and MIRV—have been not only technically and strategically innovative, but also bureaucratically and economically renovative. More generally, as an innovative change moves beyond development to production and deployment, it follows one of two paths and

becomes a change that is either renovative as well as innovative or redistributive as well as innovative. The following discussions of renovative change and redistributive change suggest the characteristics of each path.

2. *Renovative change.* The pure form of renovative change is the production and deployment of a weapons system whose technical characteristics are generally familiar, whose strategic implications are generally minor, whose production renovates an established aerospace corporation, and whose deployment renovates an established military organization. Good examples are the F-111, C-5A, B-1, F-14, and F-15.

Weaker forms of renovative change lack one or more of the features of the pure form. The most relevant is a form we have already suggested, a combination of innovative and renovative change: the development, production, and deployment of a weapons system whose technical characteristics and strategic implications are generally unfamiliar and far-reaching, whose production renovates an established aerospace corporation, and whose deployment renovates an established military organization. The best example is MIRV: Here, the reentry vehicles or MIRVs proper are innovative, while the carrier vehicles or Minuteman III and Poseidon are renovative. Other examples, which fit the category less perfectly, are the H-bomb, ICBM, and Polaris.

Because a renovative change, by definition, involves large-scale production and deployment, economic costs will be relatively high. If the strategic threat posed by similar Soviet weapons is relatively low, as it is in the pure form of renovative change, then the combination of high cost and low threat forces the nurturing military organization to mobilize its allies in the congressional committees and the aerospace corporations in order to make the jump from research and development to production and deployment. At the same time, the high economic cost—i.e., large contract awards—invites these allies in their own interest to push for the renovation. Such bureaucratic-corporate alliances for renovation, or military-industrial complexes, become even more natural, if not powerful, in times of budgetary stringency.

In contrast, if the strategic threat and associated strategic fears are high, as they are in the form of renovative change which is also innovative, then these fears can be a substitute for allies under certain conditions; bureaucratic-corporate alliances can be rendered unnecessary by bureaucratic-strategic anxieties. Whether this happens seems to be a function of the relative bureaucratic power of the nurturing military organization.

If the organization is the dominant one within a military service (for example, the Strategic Air Command within the air force), then the combination of bureaucratic momentum and strategic fears will be sufficient to propel the jump from research and development to production and deployment. The ICBM and MIRV are examples of innovative changes that smoothly moved into renovative ones, and they did so under the shelter of SAC. If, however, the organization is a subordinate one within a military service (for example, the submarine forces within the navy and the Air Defense Command within the army), a jump to large-scale production and deployment will also be a redistribution of relative bureaucratic power within the military service, and additional forces will be needed to propel the jump. The critical variable now seems to become the organization's allies in Congress and in the corporations.

If the major contractors for the new system are established aerospace corporations, among the seven major production lines (for example, Lockheed for the Polaris missile), then the combination of (subordinate) bureaucratic momentum, strategic fears, and corporate influence will be sufficient to propel the jump, although only after considerable bureaucratic conflict and delay. The Polaris is an example. If, however, the major contractors are corporations whose main production is not aerospace (for example, Western Electric and General Electric for ABM), a jump to large-scale production and deployment will be not only a redistribution of relative bureaucratic power within the military

service but also a redistribution of relative economic power within the economic system, and still more forces will be needed to propel the jump. This brings us to a discussion of redistributive change proper.

3. *Redistributive change.* A redistributive change is the production and deployment of a weapons system whose production redistributes the relative economic rewards among industrial sectors. Such changes are rare. The ABM has been the only major example since the Second World War, although the war itself brought several redistributive changes, including the buildup of the military aircraft industry and the A-bomb. Moreover, such changes are complex. In the case of the ABM, the cost of the program is unusually high, the scope of its consequences unusually wide, and the variety of plausible explanations unusually rich.

Given the historical rarity and the analytical complexity of redistributive change, any effort to determine its causes and conditions would be more speculative than conclusive and in any case would be beyond the scope of this essay. I shall confine myself to a few suggestions.

In redistributive change, the critical forces needed to propel the jump from research and development to production and deployment have to be both unusual in kind and general in scope, although not necessarily so unusual and so general as the Great Depression and the Second World War, which had so much to do with earlier redistributive changes such as the buildup of the military aircraft industry and the A-bomb. For the contemporary period, there seem to be two possibilities.

Presidential elections. As already suggested, a president will fear being vulnerable in an approaching election to charges of neglect of the nation's security. Kennedy in 1960 charged a "missile gap"; Johnson in 1967 feared an "ABM gap." Electoral considerations probably were the major cause of the Johnson administration's Sentinel ABM system, announced in September 1967. In general, presidents will seek to avoid a gaptrap.

Economic recessions. Policymakers could try to blunt a recession and to manage the economy with large-scale and widespread military contracts, which might be redistributive in nature. Or they could try to prevent the collapse of several failing aerospace corporations, turning the redistributive change toward a renovative one, but one in multiple form. Economic considerations probably were the major cause of the Nixon administration's Safeguard ABM system.

4. *Quantitative change.* A quantitative change is the simplest change of all, a mere change in the numbers of a highly familiar weapons system.

Each military service wants more of what is already has or is scheduled to get. The services compete with each other and with other bureaucracies over their share of the budget. The particular quantity bought of a weapons system will be the outcome of a complex bargaining process of negotiating, logrolling, and trading, such as the trade-off between the Minuteman buildup and the B-70 cancellation. Quantitative disputes, being about merely numerical changes and highly familiar weapons, are especially amenable to bargaining and to precise compromises and tradeoffs. The bargaining ordinarily takes place among actors within the executive branch; it is, as Huntington long ago pointed out, "executive legislation." Although each service has its own allies in Congress and among the corporations beyond, these normally play only a supporting role.

Yet, in a sense, quantitative change is the extreme, simplest form of renovative change: With more of the same produced and deployed, both the military organization and the aerospace corporation enjoy renovation with a minimum of unsettling innovation. It would seem natural, then, for bureaucratic-corporate alliances to form and push for quantitative changes as well. And in a period of opposition to the military among members of Congress and of more stringent budgetmaking within the executive, such alliances for quantitative changes will be more natural and more necessary than before.

THE FUTURE OF AMERICAN WEAPONS PROCUREMENT

What are the implications of this analysis of past military policies for future ones? The internal dynamics of the aerospace industry and of the general economy may move weapons procurement in a widening gyre, but perhaps congressional opposition or public opinion will impose limits on movement in this direction and encourage alternative paths. Congress has already rejected the Nixon administration's proposal to continue the SST program. However, it will probably accept the administration's proposal that the federal government guarantee $250 million in bank loans to Lockheed.

In the debates over military policies and changing priorities, several alternative paths for the major production lines have been proposed.

1. Convert production lines from aerospace to nonaerospace production. Mass transportation and waste disposal systems are the alternatives most often proposed. The normal experience of aerospace corporations with such conversions, however, has been quite limited in scope or in success, and their executives generally take a pessimistic view of the possibilities. Significant progress down this path in the 1970s is unlikely.

2. Convert production lines from military aerospace to nonmilitary aerospace production. Here, commercial aircraft is the alternative. Again, the actual experience with such conversions is not encouraging, and even suggests that the cure is worse than the disease.

Thus, General Dynamics in the early 1960s entered the commercial aircraft market with the Convair 880, only to lose so much money that the F-111 contract was needed to save the corporation from bankruptcy. Similarly, Lockheed in the early 1970s entered the market with the L-1011, only to drive Rolls Royce into bankruptcy and consequently Lockheed itself into a position in which only government guarantees of bank loans would save it from bankruptcy. If Congress rejects the Nixon administration's proposal for such guarantees, however, it will greatly increase the probability that the administration will award a large-scale, follow on contract for the ULMS to Lockheed, which produces Poseidon in California as well as the L-1011. It is most unlikely that Congress will refuse to approve such an important weapons system. Similarly, Congress's cancellation of the SST program greatly increases the probability that the administration will award a large-scale, follow on contract for a super-MIRV, now being planned, to Boeing, producer of Minuteman III as well as the SST. Again, it is most unlikely that Congress will refuse to approve.

There seem to be structural limits on conversion to nonmilitary aerospace production. The number of major production lines for commercial transports seems to be limited to two (Boeing with its 700 series and McDonnell Douglas with its DC series); improvements which are both economically sound and ecologically safe seem to be limited to the airbus (the Boeing 747 and the McDonnell Douglas DC-10). Significant progress down this second path in the 1970s is also unlikely.

3. Collapse production lines from seven into a smaller number. A persuasive case can be made that the United States needs only three production sectors for new aerospace systems (missile systems, particularly submarine-launched ones, fighter-bombers, and perhaps space systems) and two for carrying on existing systems (military transports and commercial transports). If so, then the United States needs only three or four major production lines.

The most attractive candidates for preservation would be Boeing (strong in missile systems and commercial transports), McDonnell Douglas (fighter-bombers and commercial transports), and one of the two Lockheed lines, either Lockheed-Missiles and Space (submarine-launched missile systems) or Lockheed-Georgia (military transports). Consequently, the other Lockheed plant would be shut down, as would be the General Dynamics plant in Fort Worth, Texas. North American Rockwell would shrink from a major to a minor production line, specializing in a mini-

mal space program, and Grumman would return to being a minor production line.

Yet, Lockheed-Georgia is the largest industrial enterprise in the Southeastern United States. As for Lockheed in California, President Nixon has said,

We need a strong airframe producer like Lockheed in Southern California. And if we can save the company and frankly help it toward better management, we will do so.

And a year or so from now, he will probably say the same thing about General Dynamics in Texas. More generally, the shutting down of any one of the major production lines would mean the direct liquidation of some 50,000 jobs and a local economic depression. It probably would mean also the bankruptcy of the corporation, the liquidation of hundreds of millions of dollars in loans from the major U.S. banks, and the risk of a credit crisis and stock market decline comparable to that of May and June of 1970. The shutting down of any two of the major production lines, not far apart in time, probably would generate one of the biggest shocks to the American financial system since the Great Depression. Given these costs and risks, it is unlikely that any administration will permit the shutting down of two production lines or even one, if it can prevent it. Further, given the ease with which an administration can point to a Soviet strategic threat and the ease with which it can embarrass a congressman who fails to perceive it, it is unlikely that Congress will reject administration proposals for strictly military systems.

4. Constrict production lines from $1 billion or more each in annual weapons sales to a smaller amount. Relatedly, a major weapons system would be shared between production lines, much as, in the case of the F-111, General Dynamics produced most of the airframe, but Grumman produced the rear fuselage. This approach, which is the most promising of the four, would permit Congress to decrease the funding of weapons procurement by the incremental method which is so congenial to it. And to some extent, constriction is already being carried out, with

employment at some production lines in 1971 having declined 15-30 percent since the peak year of 1968. Of course, this approach would permit incremental increases in funding too, and the bases for powerful bureaucratic-corporate alliances and for renewed expansion of weapons procurement in the future would remain.

Whatever the possibilities of control of weapons procurement in the coming decade, there is a need to control the strategic consequences of missile and aircraft procurement in the decade that is past. An incident during the Six Day War of 1967 suggests the problems in strategic control, the ease of strategic escalation, and the size of the strategic stakes. Israeli forces mistakenly attacked the *Liberty*, a U.S. Navy communications ship. Several months later, Secretary of Defense McNamara testified about the incident: "I thought the *Liberty* had been attacked by Soviet forces. Thank goodness, our carrier commanders did not launch directly against the Soviet forces who were operating in the Mediterranean at the time."

In the years to come, there will be deployed MIRVs and super-MIRVs along with bombers and fighter-bombers. They may some day mean fears or fire for many men. But, for now, they mean jobs for workers, profits for businessmen, and power for bureaucrats. And to weapons engineers and scientists, they mean problems that are "exciting" and solutions that are "technically so sweet."

28. THE POLITICS OF CULTURE IN AMERICA

HERBERT J. GANS

Reprinted from Communications *(Paris), No. 14, 1969. Copyright by Herbert J. Gans. Professor Gans was introduced in the headnote for Selection 1.*

■ Power is not always exercised only in such consequential matters as war and peace, how firmly business is to be regulated, or which political party controls the government; it is also brought to bear on some of the less obviously consequential aspects of society. Power is at issue in the ideas and ideologies that are encouraged and discouraged, that flower and wither in a society. Public life centers on various kinds of cultural events, on television's nightly fare, performances at the big-city concert hall, the offerings of the local movie house. Some people have strong feelings about what kinds of culture or entertainment should be supported, approved, and allowed. In democratic societies the various social classes wage a struggle for living space and ascendency, for the right to enjoy culture in line with their interests, world views, and values.

Herbert Gans analyzes this improbable political struggle for resources and for ascendency in the cultural market place among cultural creators and audiences. We are accustomed to the politics of cultures and ideas in societies where firmer political control is exercised over what creators may offer and what audiences may receive, but the value of freedom of speech in the U.S. does not do away with these issues here.

Gans discusses other aspects of popular culture in America in his contribution to Howard Becker, ed., *Social Problems*, 2d ed. (New York: Wiley, 1972). Many of the ideas in this paper are developed in more detail in his *High Culture and Popular Culture* (Basic Books, 1973). A range of views on the role of mass culture is found in Bernard Rosenberg and David M. White, eds., *Mass Culture: The Popular Arts in America* (New York: Free Press, 1957), and in Norman Jacobs, ed., *Culture for the Millions* (New York: Van Nostrand, 1961). Various aspects of high culture are analyzed in *The Arts in Society*, ed. Robert N. Wilson

(Englewood Cliffs, N.J.: Prentice-Hall, 1964). See also Pauline Kael, *Kiss, Kiss, Bang, Bang* (Little, Brown, 1968) and Norman Podhoretz, *Making It* (Random House, 1967). ■

CULTURE IS USUALLY CONSIDERED a form of spiritual expression, and is therefore thought to be "above" such worldly concerns as politics. This view of culture is naive, however, for politics concerns the distribution of resources, power, and prestige in society, and culture plays a role in determining that distribution.

My analysis of the politics of culture must begin by defining the term *culture*. As translated from the German word *Kultur*, the term refers to the aesthetic standards, activities and products of "serious" artists and intellectuals who create for "cultivated" audiences, but I use culture in a broader sense, to mean the aesthetic standards, activities, and products of any human group, a definition that encompasses both high culture and popular (or mass) culture.

Culture affects the distribution of resources, power, and prestige in at least two ways. First, culture is transmitted by institutions such as television networks and schools, and such institutions participate in the governmental or party politics of almost every society. Second, culture provides people with symbols, myths, values, and information about their society. Every cultural "product," whether a serious play or a light novel, offers some social commentary about today's society, and often some political commentary as well. Because culture has influence on the members of society—although not as much as is often thought—the determination of what culture and what sociopolitical commentary is to be created and distributed has

353

political implications. For example, even the most impartial television documentary about income redistribution would create some political support for this issue, partly because some viewers might now favor redistribution as a result of having watched the documentary, and partly because the mere fact that the subject is presented on a mass medium gives it some political strength. But even a light comedy about family life has some political implications, for it must inevitably comment on the rights and privileges of parents and children, and can thus affect, however slightly, the struggle between the generations over the allocation of power within the family.

The question of what sociopolitical commentary is to be distributed is particularly important because in any modern society just as a number of classes, ethnic and religious groups, age groups, and political interests struggle for control over the society's resources, they also struggle for the power to determine or influence the society's values, myth, symbols, and information. Every group seeks to persuade the mass media to transmit its values and to exclude competing ones, for whichever group can have its values legitimated as the values of the nation obtains considerable political advantage. For example, many working-class and lower middle class Whites are attempting to persuade America of the values of "law and order" to justify the repression of the protesting Black population, and they—or their political representatives—would like to see the mass media present mainly their point of view.

This type of struggle is most intense in films and television, for because of the limited number of television channels and movie theaters only a few of the potentially infinite number of cultural products can be distributed. Consequently, the decision as to what will be shown on the screen must inevitably be political, involving considerations that go beyond the merit of the cultural product in question. It should be emphasized, however, that the participants in these cultural struggles are rarely conscious either of the conflict or of its political implications,

for the struggles are usually fought over whether a particular cultural product has artistic merit or commercial appeal. For example, I doubt that the producer and director of a recent Hollywood film (neither of them Catholic) which portrayed the happy life of a family with 18 children ever realized that their film might be relevant to the public debate about birth control.

In Europe, where government plays an important role in the creation and distribution of culture, the politics of culture often takes place within the formal political institutions, but in the United States, the politics of culture takes place largely in the world of commerce, although government officials are sometimes asked to regulate the commercial media in behalf of one or another class or interest group. Moreover, the major issues in the politics of culture are different in America and Europe. In Europe, where high culture has considerable power and prestige, the question of how much high and popular culture are to be distributed by the mass media is a major issue. In America, high culture is politically too weak to appear in the mass media, and the major cultural-political struggles take place within popular culture, particularly over erotic and quasi-erotic material. The producers of films, television programs, etc., are under considerable pressure from older, conservative audiences and from their elected representatives and church and school officials to censor such material, and under commercial pressure to provide it, reflecting the demand for erotic material from younger, more liberal audiences. Since the assassinations of Martin Luther King and Robert Kennedy, the reduction of violence in television entertainment and the role to be played by Blacks as performers and characters in popular culture have also become major issues.

Formal censorship plays only a minor role in America's politics of culture. The United States Supreme Court has severely limited the power of the federal government to censor, although it can still refuse permission for the import of foreign culture. Most formal censorship is practiced by local governments, particularly in the conservative rural areas of the country, but the Supreme Court decisions have also reduced this in recent years. Informal censorship and precensorship still abound, however; church and civic group pressures impose a taboo on overt eroticism in Hollywood films, and films with a left-wing point of view have been persecuted so harshly by right-wing "patriotic" organizations that they had practically disappeared until the recent wave of "underground" films—but these are shown only in a handful of cities and on college campuses. There was no censorship, formal or informal, of violence until the recent political assassinations.

An analysis of the patterns of cultural politics in America is best carried out by comparing it with governmental or party politics. Since U.S. party politics is rarely concerned with questions of culture—the political parties do not have ideological positions on culture—and since government plays such a minor role in the creation and distribution of culture, the politics of culture takes place largely in commercial institutions devoted to culture, and in the complex relationship between the *distributors,* the owners, and managers of the media which distribute culture, high or popular, and the artists, writers, directors etc., who are the *creators* of culture, and the *audiences* who consume it. For purposes of comparison, the distributors and creators may be described as *cultural politicians;* the audience, as their *cultural constituencies.* The cultural politicians are engaged in providing culture to their constituencies with the purpose of achieving their own goals and also satisfying their constituencies. Thus they face the same problem as the governmental politician, how to appeal to a constituency whose wants cannot easily be predicted in advance, and which actually consists of a number of subconstituencies with conflicting or different wants.

These subconstituencies are not organized groups; they are aggregates of people with similar tastes, and may therefore be called taste constituencies or *taste publics,* who share a taste subculture or *taste culture.* A society as heterogeneous as the United States contains many taste publics and cultures, each culture having its own preferred types of art, music, literature, theater, architecture, etc., its own media, distributors, creators and critics, and, of course, its own definitions of beauty and aesthetic standards. For the purpose of this analysis, I will describe only the most important taste publics and cultures: high, upper middle, lower middle and low.

High taste culture (or high culture) needs little discussion; it is the culture of "serious" art, music, literature, etc., and its public is made up largely of affluent, university-educated persons, many themselves creators or critics of culture.

Upper middle taste culture resembles and often borrows from high taste culture. It is "sophisticated" but not "serious," for its aim is to provide appreciation and enjoyment rather than the intellectual and emotional insight sought by high culture. Its public is the upper middle class of the United States, the college-educated professionals, executives, and managers. They are rarely creators of culture; they are consumers, which is why the culture seeks to provide enjoyment. Among its more important media are the *New York Times, Harper's Magazine,* Broadway theater, "educational television," and the national symphony orchestras—whose products differ significantly in content and tone from such high culture media as *Partisan Review, The New York Review of Books,* the off-Broadway theater, and chamber music groups.

Lower middle and low taste culture are generally described as popular or mass culture; they shun both seriousness and sophistication, and perhaps their main identifying characteristic is literalness and concreteness. *Lower middle taste culture* appeals to middle class people in semi-professional and white collar jobs, who have graduated from high school and have perhaps attended a state or community college. The major media of this taste culture are Hollywood movies, commercial television, magazines such as *Life* and *Reader's Digest,* the Broadway musicals, and today, the pseudorealistic novels, for example, *Valley of the Dolls,* which become best-sellers.

Low taste culture is pursued by people with less than a high school education, mainly blue-collar workers and the poor. Low taste culture differs from lower middle taste culture by its yet greater literalness and by its emphasis on "action," as found in adventure stories, melodramas, and violent sports such as boxing and football. Because the low taste public is not affluent and is therefore unattractive to advertisers, it has to obtain much of its culture from the media that cater to the lower middle taste public; comic books, confession and fan magazines, and tabloid newspapers are about the only purely low culture media still in existence today.

These descriptions are quite superficial, and a more detailed analysis would have to indicate subdivisions and factions within each taste culture and public. For example, each culture has traditional, progressive and avant-garde factions, and age-graded subdivisions as well. In almost all taste cultures, adolescent publics have tastes in music vastly different from those of adults; today the former prefer rock and roll, acid rock, folk-rock, and folk music with social protest lyrics, which are rarely popular among adults. Moreover, the boundaries between taste cultures are very diffuse, and much popular culture tries to appeal to several taste publics at once. For example, some parts of *Life* magazine are written for upper middle taste publics, others for lower middle publics. The recent film *Bonnie and Clyde* was successful partly because it appealed to many publics, although for different reasons; the lower taste publics viewing it as a crime adventure film, the higher publics as a commentary on violence in American society. Some forms of culture cater to just one taste public; formal literary criticism is found mainly in high culture, boxing appeals almost entirely to the low taste public, and TV is created mainly for lower middle taste publics, although "educational TV," which is not really educational, seeks out educated audiences—that is, the upper middle taste public.

The hierarchy and characteristics of taste cultures and taste publics are quite similar to the hierarchy and characteristics of U.S. class structure. This is not coincidental, for the kind of taste a person develops depends very much on his class origins and particularly on the amount and quality of education he has received. In general, it is accurate to say that the better a person's education, the "higher" his cultural taste.

Moreover, the taste cultures often express the class concerns of their publics. For example, a considerable amount of high culture writing, fictional and nonfictional, consists of thinly veiled attacks on the middle and working classes for holding too much cultural power, and much lower middle and low taste culture fiction tells of heroes with traditional sexual norms who unmask as villains other characters with avant-garde sexual norms. The taste cultures do not, however, often express the class interests, in the Marxist sense, of their publics. Since the media of all taste cultures are owned by businessmen, these media are generally more conservative, at least on domestic policies, than many members of their publics. For example, low culture news media, which appeal to a working-class public, are probably even more opposed to socialism than are middle and high culture media.

Because the taste hierarchy reflects the class hierarchy, taste conflicts occur which are similar to class conflicts, with every taste culture critical of the standards and products of all others. Generally speaking, each taste culture criticizes those "above" it in status as being snobbish and dull, and those below it as being superficial or vulgar. High culture, of course, rejects all other taste cultures as being spurious and inauthentic. Indeed, the theory of mass culture has been developed as a major ideological tool with which high culture defends itself against the other, more powerful and popular taste cultures.

Since the various taste cultures and publics rarely meet on a common battleground, the conflicts between them are fought out by the critics, reviewers, and commentators who represent specific taste cultures. For example, a book reviewed favorably by high culture magazines may be criticized harshly by upper middle culture critics as being too abstract or scholarly, and it will probably be ignored entirely by low middle culture reviewers as uninteresting. Conversely, high culture reviewers normally ignore all popular books as too superficial to deserve attention, and no one reviews low culture books, for they are thought to be so violent, erotic, and poorly written that they cannot even be found in public libraries and regular book stores.

The politics of culture exists at every level of society, ranging from governmental conflicts over censorship to adverse comments people make about the cultural tastes of their neighbors. The most interesting phenomenon in America, however, is the political struggle between taste cultures over whose culture is to predominate in the major media, and over whose culture will provide society with its symbols, values, and world view. This struggle is fought not only over the merits of each culture but also involves the political and economic power of the various taste publics in the American class system and power structure.

High culture has the greatest prestige, of course, but because its public is numerically small—too small to justify even one television program that caters to it—the culture is relatively powerless. Low taste culture is also quite powerless because its public lacks purchasing power and political influence. As a result, the mass media rarely provide information or entertainment about working-class or poor people. Indeed, although Black characters have recently been introduced into movies and television entertainment, so far all of them are middle and upper middle class in status; characters modeled on typical ghetto residents have not yet appeared on the screen.

Most of the cultural power in the United States is held by the upper middle and lower middle taste publics. The former includes many of the affluent corporate decision makers, and is therefore most powerful in public cultural activities; members of the upper middle taste publics obtain government grants to establish cultural centers, and architects who reflect the style preferences of upper middle taste culture design many of America's public buildings (other than in Washington, where congressmen, most of whom come from and represent the lower middle taste public, vote for the traditional architecture still favored by this public). The power of lower middle taste culture is, of course, most visible in the mass media, which cater mainly to it. Its power is also enhanced by the public schools, which are run largely by lower middle class administrators and teachers, although they tend to favor a highly traditional, almost Puritan form of the culture, whereas students prefer a much more progressive form of the same culture. Indeed, as I have already noted, perhaps the major conflict in the culture of politics today is a power struggle between the traditional and progressive wings of lower middle class culture over the question of how much erotic material should be permitted in the mass media.

Another power struggle is now developing between traditional lower middle taste culture and progressive upper middle taste culture over the political content of the news media: whether or not news should express nationalistic and ethnocentric values, and whether events should be explained by a "morality play" theory of national and international heroes and villains or by a more "naturalistic" theory based to some extent on social science concepts. For example, conservatives from lower middle taste culture attacked the news media for "unpatriotic" reporting of the war in Vietnam, and for describing the causes of the ghetto rebellions of 1966 and 1967 as poverty and segregation rather than as the work of villainous revolutionaries.

Although these cultural-political issues are attracting a lot of attention, the most typical and frequent processes of the politics of culture take place within the media of the various cultures, particularly between the distributors and creators of culture. The creators are usually recruited on the basis of their ability and willingness to create for the particular publics to which a medium appeals, so that one rarely finds high culture advocates in television or low culture advocates in museum staffs. Because of this recruitment pattern, the creators of culture are normally free to create what they consider good; they are professionals who are allowed to use their professional judgment and their own aesthetic standards in their creative work.

Because creators are usually free to create what they consider best, what they create reflects their own taste culture, and as a result their products generally promulgate the values of their taste culture. For example, high culture creators are very much concerned about their position in a society in which popular culture is politically and culturally dominant, so that much recent high culture fiction has dealt with the relationship of the alienated individual to society. Similarly, adults of all taste levels are currently upset about adolescent youth culture, and as a result there are many films, television programs, and popular novels about adolescents, most of them reflecting their adult creators' misgivings about the "hippies" and other forms of youth culture.

Although distributors and creators for any given product tend to come from the same taste culture, they often have conflicting ideas. Creators have what might be called a *creator-oriented* view of their culture, while distributors are more *consumer-oriented*.

Creators want to create good or important or entertaining or tradition-breaking products; they are primarily concerned with improving their aesthetic techniques and with "educating" their audiences, trying to go to the fore of public demand, both in the mass media and in high culture. Distributors, on the other hand, are concerned first with attracting and satisfying not the largest possible audience but the largest possible audience from those taste publics which they define as their "market." Conflict takes place when the distributors demand changes in the creator's work that would make it attractive to an additional audience—for example, by inserting youthful characters into a screenplay to attract young audiences—and creators object because such a change would violate their creative purpose and destroy the unity of what they have created. If the creator has enough prestige

and a record of having created financially successful cultural products in the past, he is likely to be victorious in this conflict; if not, the distributor will win.

As I noted earlier, ideological or other political issues rarely enter into this process explicitly; the conflict between creators and distributors is usually about questions of artistic merit and commercial appeal. Even so, if distributors argue that a film should have a happy ending to make it commercially more attractive to lower middle and low taste publics, they are also arguing by implication that in the end society and individuals can solve their problems, and that the status quo can be preserved.

The constituents play an important but largely passive role in the political process by which culture is created. Their main role is to choose from among the cultural products available, and this choice, reflected, for example, in box office results and television ratings, is their "vote" for or against the distributors and creators. The outcome of this vote determines the prestige, power, and, in fact, the careers of the distributors and creators; the director of a successful film is overwhelmed with job offers; the director of an unsuccessful film may have difficulty in obtaining another job.

Because the careers of creators and distributors depend on their ability to attract their constituents, they try to create products which they think will appeal to their constituents. Distributors may do this deliberately, but creators usually create cultural products that appeal to them personally, hoping that the audience will feel as they do. Even so, both creators and distributors "represent" their taste public in the creation of cultural products, such as politicians represent their constituencies when they create legislation. In fact, some of the conflict between creators and distributors is over the question of which taste cultures and publics are to be represented in a cultural product. When creators and distributors come from different taste cultures or from opposing factions of the same culture, the conflict may end in the replacement of the creator by someone who shares the cultural allegiances of the distributor. Film directors are often replaced in the middle of a film for this reason.

Neither creators nor distributors have much direct contact with or knowledge of their constituents, and because past audience choices cannot predict future choices, culture is created amidst great uncertainty about its ultimate acceptance. If a creator or distributor does not know whether his next effort will be a success, and whether he can maintain his power and prestige, he tries to find ways of reducing the uncertainty and of obtaining a base of power that is independent of his creative efforts. Like government and party politicians, creators organize cliques that will support them in instances of failure; they put their friends into positions of power for the same purpose; and they even try to obtain "patronage," establishing jobs in their own organizations or elsewhere whose holders will be indebted to them and will support them. The "literary politics" of high culture and the internal bureaucratic struggles within the mass media are therefore quite similar; in both instances, creators (or distributors) use many of the same methods as the politician in government to stay in power.

These observations about the culture of politics apply to all taste cultures, high or low, for in America, at least, the "serious" artist of high culture must concern himself with distributors and constituents as much as the mass media artist, and perhaps more because the high culture audience is so much smaller than the mass media audience, and the occupational opportunities to work as a creator of high culture are so much scarcer.

Moreover, what I have written about the culture of politics applies not only to the arts and entertainment, but also to news and other "informational culture," for each taste culture has its own *Weltanschauung* which affects the kind of news and nonfiction it prefers, and even its attitude toward the social sciences. For example, lower taste publics are more interested in local news and "human interest" stories than in national and international news, and, as already noted, upper middle

taste culture is at least mildly interested in social science explanations of events. High culture still prefers to get its social analyses from literary sources, while the more progressive factions of lower middle culture are beginning to be interested in "popular sociology," although this is often created by journalists, with concepts and methods that bear only a slight resemblance to academic sociology, and with findings and generalizations that are often completely different from those of academic sociology.

The news media function much like the other media, with every newspaper or magazine appealing to only one or two taste publics. As already noted, the *New York Times* appeals largely to upper middle taste publics; tabloid newspapers to low taste publics. Although the style and complexity of news *writing* also varies depending on the educational level of the taste publics in a particular publication's audience, news *reporting* tries to ignore cultural differences by seeking "objectivity" through a highly logical-positivist philosophy of what facts are deemed to be news, and by "balanced" reporting which tries to provide information about all sides of every controversy. The complexity of reporting is adjusted to taste culture considerations, however; high and upper middle taste culture news media attempt to analyze and explain events as well as describe them, while the other news media place more emphasis on pure description.

My analysis of some aspects of the politics of culture has proceeded from the perspective of cultural relativism, an anthropological doctrine which assumes that all taste cultures are of equal worth. This perspective has some obvious normative implications, for it questions the traditional belief of high culture that it is superior to all other taste cultures.

My own normative position is close to the position implicit in the analysis. I do not believe that all taste cultures are of equal worth, but that they are of equal worth *to their publics*. Indeed, I would agree with the advocates of high culture that their culture is superior in quality because it provides greater, more intense, more diversified, and perhaps even more permanent aesthetic gratification.

Taste cultures are chosen by people, however, and therefore cannot be evaluated without taking their publics into consideration. The choice of taste culture is, however, a function of the class and educational level of the person who is choosing, and the ability to create and consume high culture requires an education of the highest quality and, almost always, a high income as well. Consequently, it would be unfair to expect or demand that people of lower educational levels and incomes choose high culture. Rather, I would argue, every person should be able to choose the taste culture that accords with his educational and class status; conversely, every taste culture should be considered as having equal worth *in relation* to the people who choose it, simply because all people are of equal worth, regardless of their class position. From this point of view, high culture cannot be considered as having superior worth unless and until society provides everyone with the education and income prerequisite to participation in high culture.

Until then, I would advocate the desirability of cultural democracy and cultural pluralism; the coexistence of all possible taste cultures in accordance with the distribution of taste publics in society, so that everyone may enjoy the kind of culture for which his education and class background has trained him. This does not prevent anyone from participating in any other taste culture, and it does not discourage political efforts to increase educational levels and change the class system so as to change the quality of taste cultures. (In fact, this has already happened in the United States on a laissez-faire basis; improvements in public education over the last 25 years have significantly reduced the number of people who prefer low taste culture, and they have also increased the aesthetic and intellectual

level of lower middle and upper middle taste culture.) I would limit cultural democracy only to the extent of excluding any taste culture, or elements thereof, that can be *proved* to be harmful to the individual or to the society, but so far I have seen no reliable evidence which proves that any culture is harmful, despite the claims by high culture that popular culture is intellectually and emotionally damaging.

The role of government in the politics of culture ought to be to maximize cultural democracy, to enable all taste cultures to exist, grow, and develop. This means that government should not censor or otherwise restrict any taste culture because politically powerful members of another taste public demand censorship; instead, government should aid the growth and development of taste cultures which are held back by economic and class inequality. In America, governmental efforts should not concentrate solely on subsidizing high and upper middle taste culture as is now the case, for their publics are affluent, and many private foundations are already providing subsidy. Instead, these subsidies should go primarily to low culture, for it cannot attract foundations or advertisers to finance the growth of the culture and the recruitment of more creative talent. The most needy group in America is probably the Black community; until recently, Black culture has been discouraged and even suppressed, and Black people have had to choose among films, television, fiction, and art created by, for, and about White people. Only Black music has flourished—but because it has been popular with Whites as well. Greater cultural democracy in the United States could best be achieved by aiding Black creators and distributors, financially and politically, to develop culture in all forms of art and entertainment that is relevant to the needs and wants of the Black community, and particularly of the poor Blacks in the ghetto.

V.

INTERNATIONAL STRATIFICATION AND INEQUALITIES

THOSE WHO DEFINE social problems have increasingly expanded their focus from the nation to the world. As the interdependency of nations increases, particularly the influence of advanced industrial nations on other parts of the world, people will take as problematic not just what goes on in their own country but the human condition more broadly conceived.

The issues of stratification among nations are particularly extreme with respect to patterns of inequality. The inequality within any advanced industrial nation is small compared to the inequality between the rich and the poor nations. Policies of foreign aid and assistance in economic and social development have become more and more institutionalized over the past generation, and we can expect that process to continue. In our selections we have not tried to represent the full range of issues of international stratification, but rather we have concentrated on issues that have particularly to do with the question of social inequality, and with the availability of resources in the poorer parts of the world.

29. THE THIRD WORLD IN INTERNATIONAL STRATIFICATION

IRVING LOUIS HOROWITZ

Reprinted from 'The Three Worlds of Development. Copyright © 1966 by Irving Louis Horowitz. Reprinted by permission of Oxford University Press, Inc. Irving Louis Horowitz is Professor of Sociology at Rutgers University and editor of Society. He has written extensively in the areas of the sociology of development, political sociology, the sociology of sociology, sociological theory, and the sociology of war.

■ As the United States sought a central world role in the post-World War II period, the dominant manner in official circles of interpreting events included the idea of two worlds—free and communist—with the United States leading one and the Soviet Union leading the other. All other nations were thought of as lined up, or about to line up, on one side or the other. From the American point of view, if you weren't with us, you were against us.

Many nations, loath to accept this neat dichotomy, began to assert a symbolic third principle against the two great powers. These nations spoke of themselves as "neutralist," as not wanting to take sides in the cold war, and even more important, as having their own problems and goals to worry about. Neutralism was led by such men as Yugoslavia's Premier Tito and India's Pandit Nehru.

The principal fact about the "Third World," as the United States and other industrialized countries viewed it, was and is that these countries are underdeveloped, or, euphemistically, "developing" nations. The complex interrelationships among the nations of the Third World and the First and Second Worlds, in Horowitz's terms, represent a playing out on a global scale of issues of inequality and stratification that share more than a few similarities with the inequalities within nations. In this selection from Horowitz's book, which seeks to define some of the essential issues of Third World dynamisms and at the same time to criticize much of academic theory about economic and political development, the author defines this newly self-conscious group of nations and shows something of the way in which inequalities of economic position, power, and status go into the definition of their world view.

Works that deal with the Third World Horowitz seeks to describe in his study include Gabriel A. Almond and James S. Coleman, eds., *The Politics of the Developing Areas* (Princeton, N.J.: Princeton University Press, 1960); Albert O. Hirschman, *Strategy of Economic Development* (New Haven, Conn.: Yale University Press, 1958); Richard Harris, *Independence and After: Revolution in Underdeveloped Countries* (New York: Oxford University Press, 1962); and Morris Janowitz, *The Military and the Political Development of New Nations* (Chicago: University of Chicago Press, 1964). Horowitz has examined one such country in detail in *Revolution in Brazil: Politics and Society in a Developing Nation* (New York: E. P. Dutton, 1964). Gunnar Myrdal deals with the Asian Third World experience in the context of planned development in *Asian Drama: An Inquiry into the Poverty of Nations* (New York: Pantheon, 1968). ■

AMERICAN POLITICAL THINKING generally focuses on choices between false alternatives. On one side we are deluged with propaganda informing us that peaceful coexistence is impossible between the United States and the Soviet Union. Even if coexistence were possible, it would be better for all concerned to be "dead than red" if coexistence were to lead to a Communist take-over. There are also the absurd "contrasts" between a "God-fearing people" and a "Godless atheistic state," between a two-party system and a one-party system, and between "free enterprise" and "state planning." As a response to these oversimplified versions of social systems, a new superradicalism is emerging which starts from the abstract notion that the architect of modern evil is the industrial system. Since both the United States and the Soviet Union are archetypes of this industrialization process, they reveal a common condition of dehumanization of labor, deprivation of historical conscience, and emphasis on the values of material giganticism over any other values. Beneath this *Sturm und Drang* romanticism lies a nostalgic faith in the past. And this longing for paradise lost has led to a drowning out of concrete historicity, of specific differences between capitalism and socialism, democracy and authoritarianism, development and stagnation, poverty and wealth, market anarchy and social planning.

What the nations of the Third World are continually searching for are specific ways in which some sort of "mixture" between the two giant social structures can be brought about without destroying either the vitality or integrity of national development as such. Perhaps the Third World cannot escape the problems of political eclecticism (not even by calling such problems "pluralism"). But it has made a powerful and largely successful effort to define itself over and against both the First and Second Worlds. This it has been able to do only by clearly separating the various reasons for the success offered by the United States and the Soviet Union—particularly those reasons based on technological innovation from those based on rejecting past colonial status.

We might say that the Third World is characterized by the following set of conditions. First, it tends to be independent of both power centers, the United States-NATO complex and the Soviet Warsaw Pact group. Second, the bulk of the Third World was in a colonial condition until World War Two. Third, it draws its technology from the First World while drawing its ideology from the Second World. Thus, the Third World is non-American, ex-colonial, and thoroughly dedicated to becoming industrialized.

The Third World is a self-defined and self-conscious association of nation-states. Definitions of the Third World position have been made at the Bandung Conference of Colored Peoples in 1955: the Belgrade conference of Non-Aligned Powers in 1961; the Congress of African States in Addis Ababa in 1963; and the Second Conference of Non-Aligned Nations held in 1964 at Cairo. The leading nations involved in formulating the politics and ideologies of the Third World at this point are India, Ceylon, United Arab Republic, Yugoslavia, Indonesia, and Ghana. This informal web of association extends to every continent, with a nucleus of membership in Africa, Asia, and Latin America. Marginal membership must be accorded such nations as Canada (a new arrival on the scene of Third World politics), China (which prefers to consider itself ['aligned" but "independent"), and Algeria (which although only recently independent is already a powerful voice in the formulation of policies for the Third World).

The very rise and maturation of the Third World points up the instability and schismatic propensities of this coalition of nations. These "underdeveloped" nations have traditionally been the playground for wider international rifts. The Third World sometimes mirrors the ideological disputes between the Soviet Union and China on strategic matters concerning "peace offensives" or "revolutionary actions." At the same time, difficulties in offering an exact definition of the Third World become apparent. In terms of economic and organizational problems, for example, China ranks as a prime member of the Third World. Yet, in terms of its own explicit rejection of the concept of nonalignment, and its own concern for carrying nationalist revolutions to socialist revolutions, China must be considered as outside the Third World on political and ideological grounds.

At this juncture, it is less important to determine where China "fits" than to consider the nations that define themselves as a part of the Third World. From this point of view, all nations not organically linked with the North Atlantic Treaty Organization or the Warsaw Pact are increasingly defining themselves as part of the Third World. The very polarization of the world into a military stalemate has made possible the redefinition of aims and functions of the smaller powers within the NATO and Warsaw Pact alliances. In the Soviet bloc, strong signs of independence are evident in Poland and Rumania. In the Western bloc the fissures are slower to appear because the control apparatus was weaker to begin with. Nonetheless, they can be found in the new attitudes of France and in the policies of Austria and Finland. Not only are former colonies caught in the crossfire of this organizational dissonance, but even some of the nonimperialist centers of Europe.

Within the bowels of capitalist Europe, Sewden anticipated the rise of a mixed economy. The Third Way of Sweden bears more than a superficial resemblance to the Third World of India. The *Force de frappe* of Gaullist France, however different in ambitions and traditions from the independent deterrent approach of a Maoist China, has a sympathetic relation with the corresponding search for political and military independence in the "inscrutable East." The Third World, is, however amorphous and unwieldy, an expanding entity.

Before going into the special features of the Third World, we ought to immediately point out that there is a Fourth World of undevelopment. That is to say, a world of tribal societies which for one or another reason are unconscious of alternatives to their own ways of life. The undeveloped society has no consciousness of being undeveloped. The Third World nations have a concept of emergence and characterize themselves as being developed socially and culturally, and of being *under*developed economically and technically. This gulf between *un*development and *under*development is thus central in relation to the definition of the Third World. We are dealing with mature peoples and backward economies.

Any definition of the Third World must account for the powerful psychological force of invidious comparison. To the degree to which a knowledge of differences in earnings and opportunities exists, to that degree there will be a competition in ideologies and orientations. The earning power of each citizen of the United States, measured by the gross national product per capita, is 10 times or more that of our "good neighbors" to the south in Brazil, Chile, Colombia, Mexico, Bolivia, and other nations in the hemisphere—outside of Argentina, Venezuela, Cuba, and

Uruguay—and at least 4 times higher than these "exceptional" high income nations. This is in itself a brute fact making for "thirdness."

This conscious awareness of difference is at its core an appreciation of invidious distinctions, what have euphemistically come to be called asynchronous forms of development. Ironically enough, this sense of difference is provoked by the competition of the First and Second Worlds. Through the inundation of propaganda in the form of films, books, periodicals, the peoples of the emergent nations are wooed for their political affections, and in this process they are made acutely aware of the riches of consumer affluence in the United States and the industrial-military complex built up over the past 50 years in the Soviet Union. The impulse for development is thus partly stimulated by these extrinsic features. It may be reinforced by women's magazines no less than political organs, by Hollywood films no less than by Soviet documentaries. However coated this passion for emulation is with slogans about folk identity and national culture, the economic and sociological demands for better living conditions and better credit terms are dictated by standards derived from the cosmopolitan centers. The consciousness of impoverishment gives an aura of frenzied immediacy to the process of social change. To catch up with "fully developed" societies becomes a definition of national purpose. To introduce doubt as to the value of this contest becomes a form of intolerable subversion. This is one primary reason why pluralistic and parliamentary politics have become increasingly scant in Third World nations. Controversy has itself come to be viewed as a luxury which only advanced nations can afford.

What are the character and scope of these asynchronous aspects in the developmental contest?

The developed regions grow rapidly because they are industrialized and sell finished commodities. The underdeveloped regions grow slowly because they are agriculturalized and sell primary products. The developed regions often determine conditions of production and also the price of primary goods.

The developed regions, in order to maintain their own privileged position, induce protective high-level tariffs, price-support programs, customs duties, etc., all of which create a sluggishness for the goods produced in the Third World. The underdeveloped world, for its part, cannot specify its own tariff arrangements without violating the terms of trade and financial loans.

The developed regions exhibit a relative evenness in their demographic patterns, production norms, and planning systems, which make scientific prediction of economic behavior possible. The underdeveloped nations exhibit extreme unevenness in these sociological factors of the economy and hence are disadvantagd in bargaining and negotiating.

These various abrasive features in the world system of invidious comparison are no longer in dispute. What remains open to question is what to do about them. Do these features represent "conflicts" or "contradictions"—items which can be removed without too much difficulty and without too much loss for either the developed or underdeveloped nations by mending, or only by revolution, by smashing? The selection between such alternatives rests on an article of faith, or rather, on contrasting strategies for stimulating social change. For some, contrasts between underdeveloped and fully developed nations can be removed through a concerted effort; that is to say, both "sides" can show long-range net gains by development. Former colonial powers make excellent contacts. The postcolonial status of England is often brought to bear in support of this argument. On the other side, there are those who insist that development and underdevelopment are defined in terms of each other; that underdeveloped nations can "emerge" only by the removal of imperialist economic relations and not simply colonial military occupations. They argue that former colonies make excellent economic partners instead of expensive status hobbies.

At one level, the designation Third World is a strategy for economic development rather than a type of economic or social structure. The "mix" in the Third World is ostensibly between *degrees of* (rather than *choices between*) capitalism and socialism at the economic level, and libertarianism and totalitarianism politically. It is not a new synthesis of political economy. One of the typical self-delusions of Third World nations is that they perceive themselves as developing new economic forms, when as a matter of fact this has not been the case thus far. There is little evidence that there will be any real new economic alternatives to either capitalist or socialist development in the immediate future. In the political sphere, however, the Third World seems to have added a new style if not a new structure.

The Third World is a mixture of different adaptations of capitalism and socialism but not an option to either of them at the economic level. The Third World is transitional. It is in a state of movement from traditional to modern society. It is the forms of transition which therefore have to concern us.

The fact that the First and Second Worlds are always in competition within a relative balance of power makes possible the exercise of Third World strategies in determining the role of foreign capital and aid, and not being determined by such capital. To be a member of the Third World, in short, is not to make a choice in favor of one political bloc or another. As a matter of fact, it is to be very conscious and deliberate about not making this decision for the present.

As might be expected, within the Third World there is a wide range of choices of economic methods. Thus it contains some very strange mixtures.

India and Brazil have more than 75 percent of their productive industries in the capitalist sector, while Algeria and Egypt are more than 75 percent nationalized. Yet all four nations belong to the emergent bloc. In other words, to be considered part of the Third World it is not necessary to limit the character of the national economic system. The political posture in relation to the main power blocs is central to defining conditions of "membership" in the Third World.

In addition to economic factors, there are politically compelling reasons why the Third World is likely to be expanded further. Nations such as Canada and Mexico in the Western hemisphere are developing sharply independent policies in connection with the United States. Similarly, Yugoslavia, Poland, and Rumania, which between 1945 and 1960 were designated, perhaps not improperly, as satellites of the Soviet Union, are now largely performing a role inside a Third World orbit and ideology. Nations which in the recent past were satellitic and even parasitic are now increasingly linking ideological arms inside an "integral" protective cover of Third World slogans. Paradoxically, at the very moment when the Third World is experiencing great difficulties in defining the scope and character of its economic mix, its political influence is becoming more sharply delineated. The political contraction of American and Soviet spheres of influence has proceeded so evenly that, although an equilibrium of a "delicate balance of terror" is maintained, a great deal is happening in the no man's land between the First and the Second Worlds. This is the widest possible definition of the Third World, but in the absence of clear political-economic guidelines it may turn out to be the only definition which is operationally meaningful.

Many Third World nations have achieved their sovereignty in the present century—and especially after World War II. The Latin-American states are exceptions in that they had at least their formal sovereignty for a longer period of time. They represent old states, and not simply new states evolved out of old nations. This formal sovereignty is primarily political and not economic. Thus the initial phase of entering the Third World bloc is the establishment of national state sovereignty. The swollen membership of the United Nations reflects this process. It has more than doubled its member states inside of 15 years. This tendency does not foreshadow the breakup of the nation-state for the sake of international government, but rather the development of the nation-state as a prelude to, and the organizing force in, the economic development process.

An essential factor about the international status of Third World nations is that they hold no dependencies. The First World drew political prestige and economic wealth from its colonial holdings. The Second World did likewise with its satellites. But the Third World cannot develop in terms of colonial holdings, since as ex-colonial nations they have neither such possessions nor do they have the possibility of developing colonial ambitions. The development of the Third World nation-state is not tied to foreign colonial expansionism, although it can stimulate what is called "internal colonialism." Third World nations do not compete for membership in the major power blocs. They generally form restricted regional organizations, such as the organization of Arab states, the organization of Pan-African unions, or the Latin-American union. The policy of nonalignment militates against entry into such organizations as NATO or SEATO or the Warsaw Pact. Therefore treaty membership for Third World nations is considered undesirable and is avoided wherever possible.

In primary exchange economies, where raw materials are exported and finished commodities are imported, the gap between the Third World and the First and Second Worlds is widening, not narrowing. Therefore competition between the Third World and First and Second Worlds becomes increasingly keen. Preferential rates and prices between highly developed nations are established; and preferential prices for finished commodities over raw materials are set. As a consequence there is a curbing or unevenness of economic growth.

Very few Third World nations have fully mobilized their industrial potential. As a general rule, when there is such a mobilization it is of a sectoral nature, usually benefiting elite groups within the Third World nation-state, and it differs widely according to class interest. Thus the gap between classes keeps the level of development low and uneven. Judged by real income per person, 90 percent of the Third World peoples are between the 400 and 500 U.S. dollar level, another 5 percent are between the 500 to 750 dollar level, and another 4 percent between the 750 and 1,000 dollar level. Not more than 1 percent earns over $1,000. This lag grows greater as the gap between falling prices for agricultural and mineral products confronts the rising costs of finished commodity production. This fact alone casts grave doubt on the theory that a "middle sector" will be the savior of the Third World, or at least save it from social revolution.

Often "uneven development" is considered erroneously as the antithesis of even development— or as it is more conventionally called, "balanced growth." But this theory of equilibrium as the ideal condition for development, while perhaps of some value for Western European models, is inappropriate for Third World nations—where there is nearly a complete *inelasticity* of demand due to low income levels. What is really at stake is not balanced growth versus uneven development—but the more modest and serious task of less uneven growth than what presently obtains. For example, in a nation such as Venezuela, petroleum accounts for approximately 90 percent of the exports but employs only 2 percent of the labor force. The bulk of Venezuelans continue to work in the unproductive agricultural sphere. The settlement is never going to be in terms of parity—90 percent of the labor force in petroleum production—but an expansion of the domestic economy can serve to offset the degree and extent of imbalance.

Unevenness of development is not a metaphysical curse. It reveals concrete components: money income and outlays above what is warranted by the capacity to produce for the purpose of satisfying consumer demands; imitation of patterns of industrial waste; high tariff restrictions for the purpose of taxing the foreign trade sector in place of a system of graded taxation; disinvestment in the domestic economy for the purpose of paying off purchases in foreign markets; low amounts received for raw materials and high costs for finished goods, etc. And while every economy in some profound sense is "uneven," the difference between developed and underdeveloped societies is the extent of imbalance.

Any sound theory of social change must indicate what development excludes; that is, how it distinguishes itself from such cognate concepts as industrialization, externally induced transformation, growth of population and of the economy.

First, development differs from industrialization in that the latter implies a series of technological, mechanical, and engineering innovations in forms of social production. Social development for its part implies transformation in human relations, in the economic and political status in which men relate to each other, irrespective of the level of industrialization. Industrialization does produce stress and strain in human relationships which in turn have a large-scale effect on the overall process of social development. But to identify industrialization with development is to run the grave risk of offering prescriptions for economic growth independent of social inequities.

Second, development differs from change in that the latter implies a continual adaptation through small steps and stages to an existent social condition. Development implies a genuine break with tradition—perceptible disruptions of the "static" equilibrium. Social development requires a new set of conceptual tools to explain "reality" whereas social change may leave intact old conceptual tools adapted to modified situations. Indeed, precisely what is modifiable is subject to change; while that which no longer contains the possibility of elasticity and plasticity is subject to development.

Third, development differs from externally induced transformation in that the latter implies a prime mover which is external to the developmental process. Thus, Caesarism, Stalinism, or simple old-fashioned imperialism may perform important functions with respect to the economic transformation of subject nations, but this is done for the prime, if not the exclusive, benefit of the mother country. Thus the building of a network of roads, communications systems, or the like is designed to expedite the shipment of raw materials to the home country. Similarly, the relationship of the urban complex to the rural regions may undergo similar transformations for the benefit of the city needs, of the needs of "internal colonialism," or of dominant minorities. Here, too, one cannot speak of development, despite the obvious stimulus such colonial contributions do make to long-run social development.

Fourth, development differs from growth in population or national wealth since, like the simple process of quantitative change, these do not call forth any new process, but are simply processes of adaptation. Furthermore, it should be noted that growth in "natural events" of a society may actually sap development—thus the rapid rise in population may in fact serve to lower the total financial reserves of a nation. In short, some types of growth may be dysfunctional with respect to the needs of a developing society.

Development thus implies a new technology which makes available consumer goods. New methods of production radically alter the position of labor with respect to management. New markets radically alter the position of empire nations to colonized nations. New sources of raw materials and energy supplies radically alter the balance of world commerce and trade, and new forms of social organization radically alter the position of old strata since they now must reckon with a new "technocratic" stratum in addition to their traditional rivals. It is precisely this revolutionary side of the developmental process that has come to characterize the Third World—and precisely this side which is most conveniently forgotten by developmental theorists in the West.

In the main, the Third World is a low industrial, goods-producing area no less than a high commodity-cost area. This affects the quality as well as the amount of foreign aid that they receive from the First and the Second Worlds. Disregarding the question of whether this aid is harmful or beneficent, with or without strings, the fact is that the Third World *receives* economic assistance, some kinds of funds, while the First and Second Worlds represent funding agencies for it. Thus national independence does not in itself guarantee an end to foreign domination. This distinction between nations receiving aid and nations rendering aid is central to a definition of the Third World.

The Third World supplies world markets with primary commodities, primary agricultural supplies, nonferrous base metals, etc. The First and Second Worlds basically export not primary commodities but manufactured goods. The Soviet Union has been more sensitive to the international imbalance between raw materials and finished products than has the United States. With the exception of wartime conditions, export of primary commodities is never as financially lucrative as export of manufactured goods. While it is true that without these primary commodities there can be no manufacture of goods, still the source of primary supplies is wider than imagined. Therefore, the First World has tended to maintain the imbalance between the fully advanced and the underdeveloped nations. Contrary to the rhetoric of foreign aid, the extent of First and Second World assistance to Third World development is not so much a question of direct fiscal support but rather of prices paid for raw materials, costs of importing goods, and control of international trade and money markets.

The question of setting market prices is generally allocated to the First and Second Worlds. That is, the Soviet Union can set the price on wool; the United States, along with its Western European cotton manufacturers, can set the price on cotton. This ability to set the price is a characteristic of monopolies in general, and this ability to monopolize prices is a characteristic of the First World. Monopolization is therefore a form for preventing price and wage fluctuation in the metropolitan areas. At the same time, by controlling the flow of vital parts, it is a way for preventing mass expropriation in the backward areas. Underdeveloped regions in the Third World suffer heavy price fluctuations and accentuated inflationary spirals, because they cannot control world markets, set or regulate prices, or expropriate property or resources when this is nationally desirable or feasible.

In the Third World the *formal* systems are nearly always and everywhere republican in character, while their *real* systems are nearly always authoritarian. They are neither monarchies nor total dictatorships. They are under the "rule of law"—that is, they have constitutions—but this lawfulness is deposited in the hands of the dynamic leader of the single party. They have an unchecked higher political directorate, a party charisma. There is neither a developed parliamentary system nor the kind of relatively stable multiparty groupings found in Western Europe and the United States. Where such parliamentary systems have been allowed to expand, they have been a conservative force which has served to fragment the political power of progressive social groups. Parliamentary rule is often present in older sectors of the Third World which already have achieved formal independence, as in Latin America. Here, for instance, the agricultural proletariat has been systematically excluded from effective participation, either directly through disenfranchisement, or indirectly through electoral frauds of various sorts. In such circumstances the legislative branch becomes the legal front for property ownership. In Africa, nations have avoided this situation by abandoning the multiparty system. Thus, in Ghana, Algeria, Tunisia, Kenya, Egypt, and Guinea, there has been the gradual erosion of parliamentary norms in the name of mass participation. The parliament has become an upper class forum, while the president has become the hope of the masses. This struggle is simply another way of describing the differences between formal and real political systems in emerging nations.

Given the great importance of this element, the revolutionary system is often identified in the minds of the mass with a particular party. Hence, Congress Party, however amorphous its organization may be, retains a virtual monopoly of the political apparatus in India. The same is true of the PRI in Mexico. Thus, even in nations which are traditionally identified with Western values of democracy and libertarianism, parliamentary norms are more formal than real. To achieve even a minimum rate of growth, to enter the "take-off" period, the Third World nations have had to recognize the need for central planning. And such high level planning is in itself a political act, necessarily under the aegis of the state system. The politics of this system, while often "benevolent" in character, cannot be said to be particularly concerned with the observance of parliamentary norms.

A parliament is a forum of conflicting and contrasting interests and opinions. As such, its ability to serve the "whole people" is subject to ridicule and, ultimately, to disrepute. In the cases of the Congo and Pakistan parliamentary rifts prevented the normal functioning of society. And only with the passing of such nominally democratic forums was social order maintained.

Parliamentary development can be afforded as a splendid luxury when time and history allow. This was the case for the United States in the 19th century. Whether there is a margin for parliamentary developments in the Third World depends on the role that parliaments perform in these nations. The case histories presently available are hardly encouraging. In Latin America they have tended to preserve the status quo and to retard the development of central planning. It is hard to imagine the new African states following such a model. Therefore, there is within the Third World a development of radical political orientations without many basic constitutional safeguards. This is one basic reason why Western social democratic ideology has found it extremely difficult to champion the Third World cause.

The authoritarian nature of the Third World has resulted from the rapid growth and consolidation of the one-party state. Yet, this rarely spills over into totalitarianism, into the control of the total social system. Technological advance and bureaucratic efficiency have not advanced to the point where this is possible. A verbal commitment to democratic values is retained. The democratic society remains a goal to be attained, while authoritarian solutions are considered temporary necessities. However, its governmental machinery is feared for its total control and the effect on the social system. Yet, almost every Third World nation has a written constitution and a formal legislative body. Oftentimes, these documents are tailored after those extant in the advanced countries. But generally these documents serve to legitimize bodies which act as rubber stamps. Actual political structures bear a much closer resemblance to the Second World of the Soviet orbit than to the First World.

The Third World is subject to a unique set of political circumstances. Nearly every industrial, highly developed society has emerged in the wake of political, economic, or religious conflicts reaching a point of open armed hostilities, and resolved by the play of internal forces with a minimum of external intervention or interference. This is illustrated by the English Revolution of 1640-88, the American Revolution of 1775-81, the French Revolution of 1789, the Russian Revolutions of 1905 and 1917, and even the Chinese Revolution of 1948-49. At present, however, the costs of development under circumstances of international conflict have become prohibitive. Development must now, more than ever, be a response to both international and national pressures. The fact is also that every one of these past revolutionary events resulted in part from the pressures exerted by a newly created working mass for participation in the political process. As much as anything else, these revolutions democratized politics by bringing about the participation of a vast, previously excluded public. These humanistically inspired revolutions were designed to transform the human species from masses into classes.

The Third World nations, as presently constituted, have attempted to develop military alternatives to the First and Second Worlds—not just political options to military power, but genuine large-scale military force. The most powerful Third World nations are nations that had popular revolutions, which means revolutions which have either crushed or eliminated the old elites, rather than just reshuffling power among them. It is no accident that nations such as Ghana, Algeria,

Cuba, India, and Yugoslavia are leaders of the Third World; they represent the nations which have had this fully developed "revolution from below." For this reason Mexico can probably be considered a more fully developed member of the Third World than Venezuela, because in the 1910-20 Mexican Revolution the old military caste was crushed. The old military caste was tied up with the feudal aristocracy and the landed nobility. The new military was at the outset a popular peasant militia.

In the Third World, where revolutions have been successful, the traditional military has either been crushed or fully absorbed into revolutionary actions. There has not always been an armed struggle between military groupings. Nevertheless, the national liberation front has been the major stimulus to successful popular reform and revolutionary movements in the Third World nations. The development of these nations in large measure is connected to the outcomes of these internal military conflicts.

Third World nations also cannot really operate with foreign military bases on their soil. Dependent colonial states have in general granted extraterritorial rights to imperialist or colonialist powers. When a nation has a foreign military base, it is almost axiomatic that it is not fully accepted into the Third World. Therefore, one would have to say that East Germany is not a member of the Third World any more than South Vietnam, for both these nations, irrespective of their radically different levels of development, are clear illustrations of regimes buttressed by the presence of foreign military bases, a presence which makes development, as I have defined it, exceedingly difficult.

Ethnic and/or religious differences are exceedingly important in the Third World. With the exception of Latin America, religions of Asia and Africa are neither Roman Catholic, Protestant, Jewish, or Greek Orthodox. They are, basically, Moslem, Shinto, Taoist, Confucian, Buddhist, Hindu, primitive. Even Latin-American Catholicism has always been special, often infused, as in Haiti and Brazil, with non-Christian sources of religious practice and ritual. Religious culture remains an element apart, as a cohesive factor for maintaining tradition in the Third World. The religious expression of the value of leisure over work, the sharp distinction between the sacred and the profane, and the separation between castes reinforces the fatalism often linked to ideas opposing development.

The Third World is an area where there are few competing religious institutions, since nationalism and patriotic ferver supercede linguistic and religious preferences. Whether Christian, Moslem, Hindu, or Hebrew, a national church often accompanies the national state. Where different religions coexist, there is usually strong conflict. The India-Pakistan partition was made inevitable by religious differences; and the Buddhist-Catholic rift in Vietnam is long-standing and severe. Many of the non-Christian religious organizations do not have established church hierarchies separate from the state bureaucracy. This is particularly true in the Middle East, and was true of prewar Japan and China. Also, since leadership in the Third World is more tied to ethnic values than to religious values as such, the "secularization" process appears more accentuated than it is in fact. The parochial nature of religions in the Third World tends to force the individual to choose between religious belief and nonbelief, rather than between competing religions. Socialist-atheist ideologies, rather than Western-Christian religions, compete with the established religions in Asia and Africa. And in a slightly modified sense, the same is true of Latin America—where Socialism is more tolerated than Methodism.

A large majority of the people in the Third World, prior to their independence, have very little, if any, primary or secondary school training. It is almost axiomatic that once the Third World nation passes through its first ordeal of development, the main push is toward cultivation of its people; at least the technical and primary training that a population needs in order to enter any socially developed world. There is a modifying factor to be considered. Prior to the achievement of national independence, there

is a heavy premium on ideological leadership. The new ruling class tends to be recruited from the political elite. In the second stage, once sovereignty and a level of primary education are also achieved, concern for technical proficiency promotes the demand for higher education for all, a new technical ideology replaces the conventional ideology of revolutionism. This took place in Russia. The first stage was experimentation and freedom followed by an emphasis on heavy industrial growth, which in turn slowly adapted revolutionary Marxism to technical needs—rather than developed a technological ideology as such. This same path seems to be pursued in such faraway places as Rumania and Cuba—where increasingly the political leadership is recruited from technical engineering sources.

This changeover within the Third World, from a militant ideological point of view to a technological point of view, is accompanied by large-scale cultural reorientations. Hence, in all Third World nations, one finds a continuing struggle between humanistic traditions and growing technical predilections between traditional values and scientific innovation. Each newly formed nation is working out the conflict between these "two cultures" that Charles P. Snow has described. As a general rule, the conventional revolutionary ideology lasts longer at the cultural level than at the economic level. Since Marxism, socialism, and the variants thereof represent a general way of life, an effort is made to rationalize technical change within the conventional ideology, rather than risk raising questions about the ideology. Hence, there is considerable disparity and lag between mass sentiments favoring the conventional ideology and technological demands for cultural innovation. This in itself can be an important factor in the emerging nations, as has been made plain in the cultural debates which have taken place in Cuba, almost without letup, since the Castro Revolution of 1959. Nonetheless, if the problem of two cultures is not quite resolved by the evolution of the Third World, thus far it has become a meaningful base for the reexamination of scientific and cultural integration.

"Natural" geographic and demographic

factors also directly affect the structure of the Third World. For example, many of the Third World areas have unfavorable climate and/or soil resources. Extreme heat, bacteriological infiltration of the soil, heavy rainy seasons, etc., seriously impede sustained and rapid growth. There is no question that technological advancements such as air conditioning and artificial irrigation can compensate for these natural deficits, but it would be foolish to deny the grave effects of geographical and ecological impediments in Third World areas. Indeed, such a natural phenomenon as water supply has played an immense part in the political and economic development of China, determining the character of political control, no less than who shall rule at any given time.

Complicating the tasks of development still further are the demographic imbalances that exist in the Third World. There is today a definite trend toward overpopulation in Asia, Africa, and, more recently, in Latin America. It is a vicious circle, in effect: an agricultural economy can sustain large populations, and large extended families are a requirement for the maintenance of an agricultural economy. The facts and figures on life expectancy rates, infant mortality, and per capita daily intake of calories are too well known to require elaboration. Yet, the demographic factor is complicated by the fact that medical and scientific innovation extends the life span, and in turn places a higher valuation on life. At the same time that mortality is steadily declining, there is no corresponding increase in family planning.

The problems created by the transition from rural to urban life styles leave no aspect of social life untouched. They affect everything from food tastes to cultural preferences. The impact of urban form—the first contact with foreigners and foreign ways—has profoundly shaped the attitudes of social classes in the Third World. People feel as strongly about mass leisure or political participation in Jakarta and Buenos Aires as they do in London or New York. The transitional process is of a special nature. The Third World nations generally have a single metropolitan

center, without either middle-sized cities or competing metropolitan centers within their boundaries. Thus they represent highly developed city-states, with a backward countryside surrounding them. This is particularly the case in Latin America. This promotes a great unbalance in migration patterns. Class and cultural dissonance becomes inevitable because of the gaps between country and city living, and the rapid and often difficult transition forced upon migrants who move to the city. In addition, the large urban centers of the Third World are parasitic rather than promoters of development. They tend to exploit, through the domestic bourgeoisie, the labor and produce of the countryside. And in turn, this parasitism is extended to the international sphere. The cities are not favorably located with respect to further industrialization of the nation, but are evolved in terms of their uses as import-export centers.

It is obvious that the broad outlines of the Third World are easier to define than the precise contours. The selection of variables is a critical factor in this latter task. Thus, if we select "non-alignment" with either the United States or the Soviet Union as the chief criteria, such nations as France and China might well fall within the Third World. However, if we select the character of the social system as central, then France is clearly aligned with the Western bloc, and China no less with the Eastern bloc.

If we try to simplify the definitional problem by asking the "showdown" question—i.e. where would the Chinese Communist regime or a Gaullist France stand in the event of military hostilities between the United States and the Soviet Union—some clarification is possible. From a showdown perspective, it is evident that France is as much a part of the First World as China is of the Second World. The likelihood of a shift at this level in any near future is indeed quite slim. The tensions in the United States and Soviet orbits alike are a consequence of the spread of thermonuclear power, of a general military affluence that has taken place. Thus, France may be considered not so much outside the American power bloc as attempting to set up a countervailing leadership in that bloc. Similarly, ideologically, institutionally, and politically, China remains dedicated to the ideals and principles of communism, and hence can scarcely afford to allow its criticism of Soviet *policies* to spill over into a general critique of the communist philosophy.

Nonetheless, the selection of other sets of variables would clearly make China in particular a leader no less than a member of the Third World. China has so many topographic, economic, and sociological features in common with the Third World that it must be said that the Chinese Communist regime seems just as concerned with achieving a directorate in the Third World as it has been in developing a leadership role within the international Communist movement. France for its part is not simply attempting to redefine the relationship between itself and the United States within the First World, but is also attempting to man the bastions of a fourth position—an orientation which sees a "United Europe" as equal in capacity and strength to a "United States." The dilemmas in the Chinese position are graver. China is committed to a socialist economic system built on standardized Marxist-Leninist positions (indeed, China's ideology is more dogmatic than that of any nation in the Soviet orbit), and thus its leadership pretensions are circumscribed by its ideological commitments.

It will be protested that in this discussion of the three worlds of development far too little emphasis has been given to the "re-emergence of Europe" in the past decade or so. Indeed, there is a new literature speaking of the "fall and rise of Europe," and various theorists turned enthusiasts now speak of the "New Europe." Perhaps it is a personal bias, grounded in little else than idiosyncrasy, but it seems that Europe, even while engaging in spectacular changes in social relations and scientific inventions, gives the appearance, as one writer put it, of an "antique shop" and a "well-protected aquarium." The continued outward emigration from Europe, its traditional, unimaginative politics (of both Left and Right), the way that the European culture has become a simple footnote to events

in either the United States or in the Soviet Union, the relative stagnation of the economies of England, Italy, and France—all these factors weaken the leadership potential of Europe. This is not to deny the role of Europe in East-West relations. But in a volume concerned with a "natural triad"—with the three worlds of development—Europe does tend to lose a pivotal function.

Nonetheless, one cannot negate the persistent influence of England and France (the "good colonialists") or of Belgium and Portugal (the "bad" colonialists") in Africa. There is also the persistent German influence in North Africa and in Latin America. To be sure, Western Europe continues to be the largest buyer of African produce. It is possible that the widening latitude of European commercial activities will have great bearing on the future forms of African development.

France, for its part, has adapted its archaic middle-sized capitalism to the possibilities of bureaucratic technological domination. Even if it were possible for France to continue its independent economic position, this could be done only through the sufferance and forbearance of the United States. United Europe is a dream; the United States is a reality—the French posture has confused dream and reality. It is scarcely likely that this will affect other European nations—which, if they are not satellites with respect to the United States, continue to remain seriously dependent economically. Even if Europe moves away from the United States, which it shows every indication of doing, the likelihood is that Europe will expend its energies forging a new economic synthesis between East and West. When this relatively short-run task is achieved, in some 10 to 20 years, only then will Europe be likely to have a deep impact on development in the Third World.

All of this is said not to minimize the theoretical difficulties posed by France or China. There are certainly new features at work which modify any definition of the Third World—but what is really underscored by these schismatic developments within capitalism and socialism is not so much the growth of new and alternative systems of political economy but alternative control agencies within each system. Whether capitalist or socialist economic organization is favored in the allocation of national resources for purposes of full industrial development, the new strategies are circumscribed by the social classes and political means used to exert control over the development process. Doctrines favoring the bourgeoisie and the working class are being rejected in favor of pragmatic appraisals of who can and will win leadership.

Humanitarian, authoritarian preferences are balanced against national needs and sacrifices to be made. As Third World nations are driven by the power struggle between the First and Second Worlds, they have to adopt such postures that enhance their own "freedom of movement." There is no one set of premises which can encompass this whole portion of the world. Perhaps the surest guide to the existence of a Third World view is its own perceived interest as a bloc, despite an exasperating range of variation.

30. WORLD POPULATION CRISIS

KINGSLEY DAVIS

Reprinted from "Population Policy: Will Current Programs Succeed?" Science Vol. 158, November 10, 1967. Copyright 1967 by the American Association for the Advancement of Science. Kingsley Davis is Professor of Sociology and Director of International Population and Urban Research at the University of California at Berkeley. He is a distinguished sociologist who has made major contributions not only in the field of demography but also to basic sociological theory, the sociology of the family, and social stratification theory.

■ In the 1950s, as interest in developing nations became a major concern of Western governments and social scientists, and as this concern achieved policy expression through national and United Nations programs, the problem of rapid population growth became an increasingly important subject of research and "remedial" efforts. Hampered by political and religious prejudices associated with "birth control," these programs got off to a very slow start, and only in the late 1960s were more than a handful of large-scale family planning programs operating in the underdeveloped world. During this time those involved with population growth problems were so single-mindedly concerned with making the contraceptive technology of the West available to people in underdeveloped countries that they seldom questioned their underlying premise: that when the services were available people would adopt them readily and population growth would promptly turn down. Kingsley Davis examines this premise in the following article and finds it dangerously naive. He suggests that no simple technical means will solve the problem of population growth, which must instead be understood as fed by important institutional and personal sources. Unless there are analyzed and taken into account, any worldwide effort to limit population is doomed to failure.

Works that deal with family planning in developing countries include Bernard Berelson et al., *Family Planning and Population Programs* (Chicago: University of Chicago Press, 1966); and the various publications of the Population Council in New York, including particularly the series, *Studies in Family Planning*. A useful introduction to world population issues is found in Ronald Freedman, ed.,

Population: The Vital Revolution (New York: Doubleday Anchor, 1964). ■

THROUGHOUT HISTORY the growth of population has been identified with prosperity and strength. If today an increasing number of nations are seeking to curb rapid population growth by reducing their birth rates, they must be driven to do so by an urgent crisis. My purpose here is not to discuss the crisis itself but rather to assess the present and prospective measures used to meet it. Most observers are surprised by the swiftness with which concern over the population problem has turned from intellectual analysis and debate to policy and action. Such action is a welcome relief from the long opposition, or timidity, which seemed to block forever any governmental attempt to restrain population growth, but relief that "at last something is being done" is no guarantee that what is being done is adequate. On the face of it, one could hardly expect such a fundamental reorientation to be quickly and successfully implemented. I therefore propose to review the nature and (as I see them) limitations of the present policies and to suggest lines of possible improvement.

THE NATURE OF CURRENT POLICIES

With more than 30 nations now trying or planning to reduce population growth and with numerous private and international organizations helping, the degree of unanimity as to the kind of measures needed is impressive. The consensus can be summed up in the phrase "family planning." President Johnson declared in 1965 that the United States will "assist family planning programs in nations which request such help." The Prime Minister of India said a year later, "We must press forward with family planning. This is a programme of the highest importance." The Republic of Singapore created in 1966 the Singapore Family Planning and Population Board "to initiate and undertake population control programmes."

As is well known, "family planning" is a euphemism for contraception. The family planning approach to population limitation, therefore, concentrates on providing new and efficient contraceptives on a national basis through mass programs under public health auspices. The nature of these programs is shown by the following enthusiastic report from the Population Council:

No single year has seen so many forward steps in population control as 1965. Effective national programs have at last emerged, international organizations have decided to become engaged, a new contraceptive has proved its value in mass application, . . . and surveys have confirmed a popular desire for family limitation. . . .

An accounting of notable events must begin with Korea and Taiwan. . . . Taiwan's program is not yet two years old, and already it has inserted one IUD [intrauterine device] for every 4-6 target women (those who are not pregnant, lactating, already sterile, already using contraceptives effectively, or desirous of more children). Korea has done almost as well . . . has put 2,200 full-time workers into the field, . . . has reached operational levels for a network of IUD quotas, supply lines, local manufacture of contraceptives, training of hundreds of M.D.'s and nurses, and mass propaganda.

Here one can see the implication that "population control" is being achieved through the dissemination of new contraceptives, and the fact that the "target women" exclude those who want more children. One can also note the technological emphasis and the medical orientation.

What is wrong with such programs? The answer is, "Nothing at all, if they work." Whether or not they work depends on what they are expected to do as well as on how they try to do it. Let us discuss the goal first, then the means.

GOALS

Curiously, it is hard to find in the population-policy movement any explicit discussion of long-range goals. By implication the policies seem to promise a great deal. This is shown by the use of expressions like *population control* and *population planning* (as in the passages quoted above). It is also shown by the characteristic style of reasoning. Expositions of current policy usually start off by lamenting the speed and the consequences of runaway population growth. This growth, it is then stated, must be curbed—by pursuing a vigorous family planning program. That family planning can solve the problem of population growth seems to be taken as self-evident.

For instance, the much-heralded statement by 12 heads of state, issued by Secretary-General U Thant on 10 December 1966 (a statement initiated by John D. Rockefeller III, Chairman of the Board of the Population Council), devotes half its space to discussing the harmfulness of population growth and the other half to recommending family planning. A more succinct example of the typical reasoning is given in the Provisional Scheme for a Nationwide Family Planning Programme in Ceylon.

The population of Ceylon is fast increasing. . . . [The] figures reveal that a serious situation will be created within a few years. In order to cope with it a Family Planning programme on a nationwide scale should be launched by the Government.

The promised goal—to limit population growth so as to solve population problems—is a large order. One would expect it to be carefully analyzed, but it is left imprecise and taken for granted, as is the way in which family planning will achieve it.

When the terms *population control* and *population planning* are used, as they frequently are, as synonyms for current family planning programs, they are misleading. Technically, they would mean deliberate influence over all attributes of a population, including its age-sex structure, geographical distribution, racial composition, genetic quality, and total size. No government attempts such full control. By tacit understanding, current population policies are concerned with only the *growth* and *size* of populations. These attributes, however, result from the death rate and migration as well as from the birth rate; their control would require deliberate influence over the factors giving rise to all three determinants. Actually, current policies labeled population control do not deal with mortality and migration, but deal only with the birth input. This is why another term, *fertility control,* is frequently used to describe current policies. But, as I show below, family planning (and hence current policy) does not undertake to influence most of the determinants of human reproduction. Thus the programs should not be referred to as population control or planning, because they do not attempt to influence the factors responsible for the attributes of human populations, taken generally; nor should they be called fertility control, because they do not try to affect most of the determinants of reproductive performance.

The ambiguity does not stop here, however. When one speaks of controlling population size, any inquiring person naturally asks, What is "control"? Who is to control whom? Precisely what population size, or what rate of population growth, is to be achieved? Do the policies aim to produce a growth rate that is nil, one that is very slight, or one that is like that of the industrial nations? Unless such questions are dealt with and clarified, it is impossible to evaluate current population policies.

The actual programs seem to be aiming simply to achieve a reduction in the birth rate. Success is therefore interpreted as the accomplishment of such a reduction, on the assumption that the reduction will lessen population growth. In those rare cases where a specific demographic aim is stated, the goal is said to be a short-run decline within a given period. The Pakistan plan adopted in 1966 aims to reduce the birth rate from 50 to 40 per thousand by 1970; the Indian plan aims to reduce the rate from 40 to 25 "as soon as possible"; and the Korean aim is to cut population growth from 2.9 to 1.2 percent by 1980. A significant feature of such stated aims is the rapid population growth they would permit. Under conditions of modern mortality, a crude birth rate of 25 to 30 per thousand will represent such a multiplication of people as to make use of the term *population control* ironic. A rate of increase of 1.2 percent per year would allow South Korea's already dense population to double in less than 60 years.

One can, of course, defend the programs by saying that the present goals and measures are merely interim ones. A start must be made somewhere. But we do not find this answer in the population policy literature. Such a defense, if convincing, would require a presentation of the *next* steps, and these are not considered. One suspects that the entire question of goals is instinctively left vague because thorough limitation of population growth would run counter to national and group aspirations. A consideration of hypothetical goals throws further light on the matter.

INDUSTRIALIZED NATIONS AS THE MODEL

Since current policies are confined to family planning, their maximum demographic effect would be to give the underdeveloped countries the same level of reproductive performance that the industrial nations now have. The latter, long oriented toward family planning, provide a good yardstick for determining what the availability of contraceptives can do to population growth. Indeed, they provide more than a yardstick; they are actually the model which inspired the present population policies.

What does this goal mean in practice? Among the advanced nations there is considerable diversity in the level of fertility. At one extreme are countries such as New Zealand, with an average gross reproduction rate (GRR) of 1.91 during the period 1960-64; at the other extreme are countries such as Hungary, with a rate of 0.91 during the same period. To a considerable extent, however, such divergencies are matters of timing. The birth rates of most industrial nations have shown, since about 1940, a wavelike movement, with no secular trend. The average level of reproduction during this long period has been high enough to give these countries, with their low mortality, an extremely rapid population growth. If this level is maintained, their population will double in just over 50 years—a rate higher than that of world population growth at any time prior to 1950, at which time the growth in numbers of human beings was already considered fantastic. The advanced nations are suffering acutely from the effects of rapid population growth in combination with the production of ever more goods per person. A rising share of their supposedly high per capita income, which itself draws increasingly upon the resources of the underdeveloped countries (who fall further behind in relative economic position), is spent simply to meet the costs, and alleviate the nuisances, of the unrelenting production of more and more goods by more people. Such facts indicate that the industrial nations provide neither a suitable demographic model for the nonindustrial peoples to follow nor the leadership to plan and organize effective population-control policies for them.

ZERO POPULATION GROWTH AS A GOAL

Most discussions of the population crisis lead logically to zero population growth as the ultimate goal, because any growth rate, if continued, will eventually use up the earth. Yet hardly ever do arguments for population policy consider such a goal, and current policies do not dream of it. Why not? The answer is evidently that zero population growth is unacceptable to most nations and to most religious and ethnic communities. To argue for this goal would be to alienate possible support for action programs.

GOAL PECULIARITIES INHERENT IN FAMILY PLANNING

Turning to the actual measures taken, we see that the very use of family planning as the means for implementing population policy poses serious but unacknowledged limits on the intended reduction in fertility. The family planning movement, clearly devoted to the improvement and dissemination of contraceptive devices, states again and again that its purpose is that of enabling couples to have the number of children they want. "The opportunity to decide the number and spacing of children is a basic human right," say the 12 heads of state in the United Nations declaration. The 1965 Turkish Law Concerning Population Planning declares:

Article 1. Population Planning means that individuals can have as many children as they wish, whenever they want to. This can be ensured through preventive measures taken against pregnancy.

Logically, it does not make sense to use *family* planning to provide *national* population control or planning. The "planning" in family planning is that of each separate couple. The only control they exercise is control over the size of *their* family. Obviously, couples do not plan the size of the nation's population, any more than they plan the growth of the national income or the form of the highway network. There is no reason to expect that the millions of decisions about family size made by couples in their own interest will automatically control population for the benefit of society. On the contrary, there are good reasons to think they will not do so. At most, family planning can reduce reproduction to the extent that unwanted births exceed wanted births. In industrial countries the balance is often negative—that is, people have fewer children as a rule than they would like to have. In underdeveloped countries the reverse is normally true, but the elimination of unwanted births would still leave an extremely high rate of multiplication.

Actually, the family planning movement does not pursue even the limited goals it professes. It does not fully empower couples to have only the number of offspring they want because it either condemns or disregards certain tabooed but nevertheless effective means to this goal. One of its tenets is that "there shall be freedom of choice of method so that individuals can choose in accordance with the dictates of their consciences," but in practice this amounts to limiting the individual's choice, because the "conscience" dictating the method is usually not his but that of religious and governmental officials. Moreover, not every individual may choose: even the so-called recommended methods are ordinarily not offered to single women, or not all offered to women professing a given religious faith.

Thus, despite its emphasis on technology, current policy does not utilize all available means of contraception, much less all birth-control measures. The Indian government wasted valuable years in the early stages of its population control program by experimenting exclusively with the "rhythm" method, long after this technique had been demonstrated to be one of the least effective. A greater limitation on means is the exclusive emphasis on contraception itself. Induced abortion, for example, is one of the surest means of controlling reproduction, and one that has been proved capable of reducing birth rates rapidly. It seems peculiarly suited to the threshold stage of a population control program—the stage when new conditions of life first make large families disadvantageous. It was the principal factor in the halving of the Japanese birth rate, a major factor in the declines in birth rate of East European satellite countries after legalization of abortions in the early 1950s, and an important factor in the reduction of fertility in industrializing nations from 1870 to the 1930s. Today, according to *Studies in Family Planning*, "abortion is probably the foremost method of birth control throughout Latin America." Yet this method is rejected in nearly all national and international population control programs. American foreign aid is used to help *stop* abortion. The United Nations excludes abortion from family planning, and in fact justifies the latter by presenting it as a means of combating abortion. Studies of abortion are being made in Latin America under the presumed auspices of population-control groups, not with the intention of legalizing it and thus

making it safe, cheap, available, and hence more effective for population control, but with the avowed purpose of reducing it.

Although few would prefer abortion to efficient contraception (other things being equal), the fact is that both permit a woman to control the size of her family. The main drawbacks to abortion arise from its illegality. When performed, as a legal procedure, by a skilled physician, it is safer than childbirth. It does not compete with contraception but serves as a backstop when the latter fails or when contracepitve devices or information are not available. As contraception becomes customary, the incidence of abortion recedes even without its being banned. If, therefore, abortions enable women to have only the number of children they want, and if family planners do not advocate—in fact decry—legalization of abortion, they are to that extent denying the central tenet of their own movement. The irony of antiabortionism in family planning circles is seen particularly in hair-splitting arguments over whether or not some contraceptive agent (for example, the IUD) is in reality an abortifacient. A Mexican leader in family planning writes:

One of the chief objectives of our program in Mexico is to prevent abortions. If we could be sure that the mode of action [of the IUD] was not interference with nidation, we could easily use the method in Mexico.

The questions of sterilization and unnatural forms of sexual intercourse usually meet with similar silent treatment or disapproval, although nobody doubts the effectiveness of these measures in avoiding conception. Sterilization has proved popular in Puerto Rico and has had some vogue in India (where the new health minister hopes to make it compulsory for those with a certain number of children), but in both these areas it has been for the most part ignored or condemned by the family planning movement.

On the side of goals, then, we see that a family planning orientation limits the aims of current population policy. Despite reference to "population control" and "fertility control," which presumably mean determination of demographic results by and for the nation as a whole, the movement gives control only to couples, and does this only if they use "respectable" contraceptives.

THE NEGLECT OF MOTIVATION

By sanctifying the doctrine that each woman should have the number of children she wants, and by assuming that if she has only that number this will automatically curb population growth to the necessary degree, the leaders of current policies escape the necessity of asking why women desire so many children and how this desire can be influenced. Instead, they claim that satisfactory motivation is shown by the popular desire (shown by opinion surveys in all countries) to have the means of family limitation, and that therefore the problem is one of inventing and distributing the best possible contraceptive devices. Overlooked is the fact that a desire for availability of contraceptives is compatible with *high* fertility.

Given the best of means, there remains the questions of how many children couples want and of whether this is the requisite number from the standpoint of population size. That it is not is indicated by continued rapid population growth in industrial countries, and by the very surveys showing that people want contraception—for these show, too, that people also want numerous children.

The family planners do not ignore motivation. They are forever talking about "attitudes" and "needs." But they pose the issue in terms of the "acceptance" of birth control devices. At the most naive level, they assume that lack of acceptance is a function of the contraceptive device itself. This reduces the motive problem to a technological question. The task of population control then becomes simply the invention of a device that *will* be acceptable. The plastic IUD is acclaimed because, once in place, it does not depend on repeated *acceptance* by the woman, and thus it "solves" the problem of motivation.

But suppose a woman does not want to use *any* contraceptive until after she has had four children. This is the type of question that is seldom raised in the family planning literature. In that literature, wanting a specific number of children is taken as complete motivation, for it implies a wish to control the size of one's family. The problem woman, from the standpoint of family planners, is the one who wants "as many as come," or "as many as God sends." Her attitude is construed as due to ignorance and "cultural values," and the policy deemed necessary to change it is "education." No compulsion can be used, because the movement is committed to free choice, but movie strips, posters, comic books, public lectures, interviews, and discussions are in order. These supply information and supposedly change values by discounting superstitions and showing that unrestrained procreation is harmful to both mother and children. The effort is considered successful when the woman decides she wants only a certain number of children and uses an effective contraceptive.

In viewing negative attitudes toward birth control as due to ignorance, apathy, and outworn tradition, and "mass communication" as the solution to the motivation problem, family planners tend to ignore the power and complexity of social life. If it were admitted that the creation and care of new human beings is socially motivated, like other forms of behavior, by being a part of the system of rewards and punishments that is built into human relationships, and thus is bound up with the individual's economic and personal interests, it would be apparent that the social structure and economy must be changed before a deliberate reduction in the birth rate can be achieved. As it is, reliance on family planning allows people to feel that "something is being done about the population problem" without the need for painful social changes.

Designation of population control as a medical or public health task leads to a similar evasion. This categorization assures popular support because it puts population policy in the hands of respected medical personnel, but, by the same token, it gives responsibility for leadership to people who think in terms of clinics and patients, of pills and IUD's, and who bring to the handling of economic and social phenomena a self-confident naiveté. The study of social organization is a technical field; an action program based on intuition is no more apt to succeed in the control of human beings than it is in the area of bacterial or viral control. Moreover, to alter a social system, by deliberate policy, so as to regulate births in accord with the demands of the collective welfare would require political power, and this is not likely to inhere in public health officials, nurses, midwives, and social workers. To entrust population policy to them is "to take action," but not dangerous "effective action."

Similarly, the Janus-faced position on birth control technology represents an escape from the necessity, and onus, of grappling with the social and economic determinants of reproductive behavior. On the one side, the rejection or avoidance of religiously tabooed but otherwise effective means of birth prevention enables the family planning movement to avoid official condemnation. On the other side, an intense preoccupation with contraceptive technology (apart from the tabooed means) also helps the family planners to avoid censure. By implying that the only need is the invention and distribution of effective contraceptive devices, they allay fears, on the part of religious and governmental officials, that fundamental changes in social organization are contemplated. Changes basic enough to affect motivation for having children would be changes in the structure of the family, in the position of women, and in the sexual mores. Far from proposing such radicalism, spokesmen for family planning frequently state their purpose as "protection" of the family—that is, closer observance of family norms. In addition, by concentrating on *new* and *scientific* contraceptives, the movement escapes taboos attached to old ones (the Pope will hardly authorize the condom, but may sanction the pill) and allows family planning to be regarded as a branch of medicine: overpopulation becomes a disease, to be treated by a pill or a coil.

We thus see that the inadequacy of current population policies with respect to motivation is inherent in their overwhelmingly family planning character. Since family planning is by definition private planning, it eschews any societal control over motivation. It merely furnishes the means, and, among possible means, only the most respectable. Its leaders, in avoiding social complexities and seeking official favor, are obviously activated not solely by expediency but also by their own sentiments as members of society and by their backgrounds as persons attracted to the family planning movement. Unacquainted for the most part with technical economics, sociology, and demography, they tend honestly and instinctively to believe that something they vaguely call population control can be achieved by making better contraceptives available.

THE EVIDENCE OF INEFFECTIVENESS

If this characterization is accurate, we can conclude that current programs will not enable a government to control population size. In countries where couples have numerous offspring that they do not want, such programs may possibly accelerate a birth-rate decline that would occur anyway, but the conditions that cause births to be wanted or unwanted are beyond the control of family planning, hence beyond the control of any nation which relies on family planning alone as its population policy.

This conclusion is confirmed by demographic facts. As I have noted above, the widespread use of family planning in industrial countries has not given their governments control over the birth rate. In backward countries today, taken as a whole, birth rates are rising, not falling; in those with population policies, there is no indication that the government is controlling the rate of reproduction. The main "successes" cited in the well-publicized policy literature are cases where a large number of contraceptives have been distributed or where the program has been accompanied by some decline in the birth rate. Popular enthusiasm for family planning is found mainly in the cities, or in advanced countries such as Japan and Taiwan, where the people would adopt contraception in any case, program or no program. It is difficult to prove that present population policies have even speeded up a lowering of the birth rate (the least that could have been expected), much less that they have provided national "fertility control."

Let us next briefly review the facts concerning the level and trend of population in underdeveloped nations generally, in order to understand the magnitude of the task of genuine control.

RISING BIRTH RATES IN UNDERDEVELOPED COUNTRIES

In 10 Latin-American countries, between 1940 and 1959, the average birth rates (age standardized), as estimated by our research office at the University of California, rose as follows: 1940-44, 43.4 annual births per 1,000 population; 1945-49, 44.6; 1950-54, 46.4; 1955-59, 47.7.

In another study made in our office, in which estimating methods derived from the theory of quasi-stable populations were used, the recent trend was found to be upward in 27 underdeveloped countries, downward in 6, and unchanged in 1. Some of the rises have been substantial, and most have occurred where the birth rate was already extremely high. For instance, the gross reproduction rate rose in Jamaica from 1.8 per thousand in 1947 to 2.7 in 1960; among the natives of Fiji, from 2.0 in 1951 to 2.4 in 1964; and in Albania, from 3.0 in the period 1950-54 to 3.4 in 1960.

The general rise in fertility in backward regions is evidently not due to failure of population control efforts, because most of the countries either have no such effort or have programs too new to show much effect. Instead, the rise is due, ironically, to the very circumstance that brought on the population crisis in the first place—to improved health and lowered mortality. Better health increases the probability that a woman will conceive and retain the fetus to term; lowered mortality raises the proportion of babies who survive to the age of reproduction and reduces the probability of widowhood during that age. The significance of the general rise in fertility, in the context of this discussion, is that it is giving would-be population planners a harder task than many of them realize. Some of the upward pressure on birth rates is independent of what couples do about family planning, for it arises from the fact that, with lowered mortality, there are simply more couples.

UNDERDEVELOPED COUNTRIES WITH POPULATION POLICIES

In discussions of population policy there is often confusion as to which cases are relevant. Japan, for instance, has been widely praised for the effectiveness of its measures, but it is a very advanced industrial nation and, besides, its government policy had little or nothing to do with the decline in the birth rate, except unintentionally. It therefore offers no test of population policy under peasant-

TABLE 30.1
DECLINE IN TAIWAN'S FERTILITY RATE,
1951 THROUGH 1966.

Year	Registered Births per 1,000 women Aged 15-49	Change in rate (percent)*
1951	211	
1952	198	−5.6
1953	194	−2.2
1954	193	−0.5
1955	197	+2.1
1956	196	−0.4
1957	182	−7.1
1958	185	+1.3
1959	184	−0.1
1960	180	−2.5
1961	177	−1.5
1962	174	−1.5
1963	170	−2.6
1964	162	−4.9
1965	152	−6.0
1966	149	−2.1

*The percentages were calculated on unrounded figures. Source of data through 1965, *Taiwan* Demographic Fact Book (1964, 1965); for 1966, *Monthly Bulletin of Population Registration Statistics of Taiwan* (1966, 1967).

agrarian conditions. Another case of questionable relevance is that of Taiwan, because Taiwan is sufficiently developed to be placed in the urban-industrial class of nations. However, since Taiwan is offered as the main showpiece by the sponsors of current policies in underdeveloped areas, and since the data are excellent, it merits examination.

Taiwan is acclaimed as a showpiece because it has responded favorably to a highly organized program for distributing up-to-date contraceptives and has also had a rapidly dropping birth rate. Some observers have carelessly attributed the decline in the birth rate—from 50.0 in 1951 to 32.7 in 1965—to the family planning campaign, but the campaign began only in 1963 and could have affected only the end of the trend. Rather, the decline represents a response to modernization similar to that made by all countries that have become industrialized. . . .

A plot of the Japanese and Taiwanese birth rates (Fig. 30.1) shows marked similarity of the two curves, despite a difference in level. All told, one should not attribute all of the post-1963 acceleration in the decline of Taiwan's birth rate to the family planning campaign. . . .

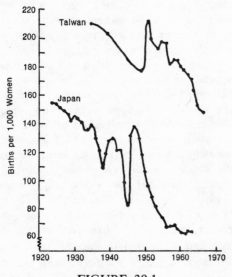

FIGURE 30.1
Births per 1,000 women aged 15 through 49 in Japan and Taiwan

The important question, however, is not whether the present campaign is somewhat hastening the downward trend in the birth rate but whether, even if it is, it will provide population control for the nation. Actually, the campaign is not designed to provide such control and shows no sign of doing so. It takes for granted existing reproductive goals. Its aim is "to integrate, through education and information, the idea of family limitation *within the existing attitudes, values, and goals* of the people" (italics mine). Its target is *married* women who do not want any more children; it ignores girls not yet married, and women married and wanting more children. . . .

Moving down the scale of modernization, to countries most in need of population control, one finds the family planning approach even more inadequate. In South Korea, second only to Taiwan in the frequency with which it is cited as a model of current policy, a recent birth-rate decline of unknown extent is assumed by leaders to be due overwhelmingly to the government's family planning program. However, it is just as plausible to say that the net effect of government involvement in population control has been, so far, to delay rather than hasten a decline in reproduction made inevitable by social and economic changes. Although the government is advocating vasectomies and providing IUD's and pills, it refuses to legalize abortions, despite the rapid rise in the rate of illegal abortions and despite the fact that, in a recent survey, 72 percent of the people who stated an opinion favored legalization. Also, the program is presented in the context of maternal and child health; it thus emphasizes motherhood and the family rather than alternative roles for women. Much is made of the fact that opinion surveys show an overwhelming majority of Koreans (89 percent in 1965) favoring contraception, but this means only that Koreans are like other people in wishing to have the means to get what they want. Unfortunately, they want sizable families: "The records indicate that the program appeals mainly to women in the 30-39 year age bracket who have 4 or more children, including at least two sons."

In areas less developed than Korea the degree of acceptance of contraception tends to be disappointing, especially among the rural majority. Faced with this discouragement, the leaders of current policy, instead of reexamining their assumptions, tend to redouble their effort to find a contraceptive that will appeal to the most illiterate peasant, forgetting that he wants a good-sized family. In the rural Punjab, for example, "a disturbing feature . . . is that the females start to seek advice and adopt family planning techniques at the fag end of their reproductive period." Among 5,196 women coming to rural Punjabi family planning centers, 38 percent were over 35 years old, 67 percent over 30. These women had married early, nearly a third of them before the age of 15, some 14 percent had 8 or more *living* children when they reached the clinic, 51 percent 6 or more. . . .

IS FAMILY PLANNING THE "FIRST STEP" IN POPULATION CONTROL?

To acknowledge that family planning does not achieve population control is not to impugn its value for other purposes. Freeing women from the need to have more children than they want is of great benefit to them and their children and to society at large. My argument is therefore directed not against family planning programs as such but against the assumption that they are an effective means of controlling population growth.

But what difference does it make? Why not go along for awhile with family planning as an initial approach to the problem of population control? The answer is that any policy on which millions of dollars are being spent should be designed to achieve the goal it purports to achieve. If it is only a first step, it should be so labeled, and its connection with the next step (and the nature of that next step) should be carefully examined. In the present case, since no "next step" seems ever to be mentioned, the question arises: Is reliance on family planning in fact a basis

for dangerous postponement of effective steps? To continue to offer a remedy as a cure long after it has been shown merely to ameliorate the disease is either quackery or wishful thinking, and it thrives most where the need is greatest. Today the desire to solve the population problem is so intense that we are all ready to embrace any "action program" that promises relief. But postponement of effective measures allows the situation to worsen.

Unfortunately, the issue is confused by a matter of semantics. "Family *planning*" and "fertility *control*" suggest that reproduction is being regulated according to some rational plan. And so it is, but only from the standpoint of the individual couple, not from that of the community. What is rational in the light of a couple's situation may be totally irrational from the standpoint of society's welfare.

The need for societal regulation of individual behavior is readily recognized in other spheres—those of explosives, dangerous drugs, public property, natural resources. But in the sphere of reproduction, complete individual initiative is generally favored even by those liberal intellectuals who, in other spheres, most favor economic and social planning. Social reformers who would not hesitate to force all owners of rental property to rent to anyone who can pay, or to force all workers in an industry to join a union, balk at any suggestion that couples be permitted to have only a certain number of offspring. Invariably they interpret societal control of reproduction as meaning direct police supervision of individual behavior. Put the word *compulsory* in front of any term describing a means of limiting births—*compulsory sterilization, compulsory abortion, compulsory contraception*—and you guarantee violent opposition. Fortunately, such direct controls need not be invoked, but conservatives and radicals alike overlook this in their blind opposition to the idea of collective determination of a society's birth rate.

That the exclusive emphasis on family planning in current population policies is not a "first step" but an escape from the real issues is suggested by two facts. (1) No country has taken the "next step." The industrialized countries have had family planning for half a century without acquiring control over either the birth rate or population increase. (2) Support and encouragement of research on population policy other than family planning is negligible. It is precisely this blocking of alternative thinking and experimentation that makes the emphasis on family planning a major obstacle to population control. The need is not to abandon family planning programs but to put equal or greater resources into other approaches.

NEW DIRECTIONS IN POPULATION POLICY

In thinking about other approaches, one can start with known facts. In the past, all surviving societies had institutional incentives for marriage, procreation, and child care which were powerful enough to keep the birth rate equal to or in excess of a high death rate. Despite the drop in death rates during the last century and a half, the incentives tended to remain intact because the social structure (especially in regard to the family) changed little. At most, particularly in industrial societies, children became less productive and more expensive. In present-day agrarian societies, where the drop in death rate has been more recent, precipitate, and independent of social change, motivation for having children has changed little. Here, even more than in industrialized nations, the family has kept on producing abundant offspring, even though only a fraction of these children are now needed.

If excessive population growth is to be prevented, the obvious requirement is somehow to impose restraints on the family. However, because family roles are reinforced by society's system of rewards, punishments, sentiments, and norms, any proposal to demote the family is viewed as a threat by conservatives and liberals alike, and certainly by people with enough social responsibility to work for population control. One is charged

with trying to "abolish" the family, but what is required is selective restructuring of the family in relation to the rest of society.

The lines of such restructuring are suggested by two existing limitations on fertility. (1) Nearly all societies succeed in drastically discouraging reproduction among unmarried women. (2) Advanced societies unintentionally reduce reproduction among married women when conditions worsen in such a way as to penalize childbearing more severely than it was penalized before. In both cases the causes are motivational and economic rather than technological.

It follows that population control policy can deemphasize the family in two ways: (1) by keeping present controls over illegitimate childbirth yet making the most of factors that lead people to postpone or avoid marriage, and (2) by instituting conditions that motivate those who do marry to keep their families small.

POSTPONEMENT OF MARRIAGE

Since the female reproductive span is short and generally more fecund in its first than in its second half, postponement of marriage to ages beyond 20 tends biologically to reduce births. Sociologically, it gives women time to get a better education, acquire interests unrelated to the family, and develop a cautious attitude toward pregnancy. Individuals who have not married by the time they are in their late twenties often do not marry at all. For these reasons, for the world as a whole, the average age at marriage for women is negatively associated with the birth rate: a rising age at marriage is a frequent cause of declining fertility during the middle phase of the demographic transition; and, in the late phase, the "baby boom" is usually associated with a return to younger marriages.

Any suggestion that age at marriage be raised as a part of population policy is usually met with the argument that "even if a law were passed, it would not be obeyed." Interestingly, this objection implies that the only way to control the age at marriage is by direct legislation, but other factors govern the actual age. Roman Catholic countries generally follow canon law in stipulating 12 years as the minimum *legal* age at which girls may marry, but the actual average age at marriage in these countries (at least in Europe) is characteristically more like 25 to 28 years. The actual age is determined not by law but by social and economic conditions. In agrarian societies, postponement of marriage (when postponement occurs) is apparently caused by difficulties in meeting the economic prerequisites for matrimony, as stipulated by custom and opinion. In industrial societies it is caused by housing shortages, unemployment, the requirement for overseas military service, high costs of education, and inadequacy of consumer services. Since almost no research has been devoted to the subject, it is difficult to assess the relative weight of the factors that govern the age at marriage.

ENCOURAGING LIMITATION OF BIRTHS WITHIN MARRIAGE

As a means of encouraging the limitation of reproduction within marriage, as well as postponement of marriage, a greater rewarding of nonfamilial than of familial roles would probably help. A simple way of accomplishing this would be to allow economic advantages to accrue to the single as opposed to the married individual, and to the small as opposed to the large family. For instance, the government could pay people to permit themselves to be sterilized; all costs of abortion could be paid by the government; a substantial fee could be charged for a marriage license; a "child tax" could be levied; and there would be a requirement that illegitimate pregnancies be aborted. Less sensationally, governments could simply reverse some existing policies that encourage childbearing. They could, for example, cease taxing single persons more than married ones; stop giving parents special tax exemptions; abandon income-tax policy that discriminates against couples when the wife works; reduce paid maternity leaves; reduce family allow-ances; stop awarding public housing on the basis of family size; stop granting fellowships and other educational aids (including special allowances for wives and children) to married students; cease outlawing abortions and sterilizations; and relax rules that allow use of harmless contraceptives only with medical permission. Some of these policy reversals would be beneficial in other than demographic respects and some would be harmful unless special precautions were taken. The aim would be to reduce the number, not the quality, of the next generation.

A closely related method of deemphasizing the family would be modification of the complementarity of the roles of men and women. Men are now able to participate in the wider world yet enjoy the satisfaction of having several children because the housework and child care fall mainly on their wives. Women are impelled to seek this role by their idealized view of marriage and motherhood and by either the scarcity of alternative roles or the difficulty of combining them with family roles. To change this situation women could be required to work outside the home, or compelled by circumstances to do so. If, at the same time, women were paid as well as men and given equal educational and occupational opportunities, and if social life were organized around the place of work rather than around the home or neighborhood, many women would develop interests that would compete with family interests. Approximately this policy is now followed in several communist countries, and even the less developed of these currently have extremely low birth rates.

That inclusion of women in the labor force has a negative effect on reproduction is indicated by regional comparisons. But in most countries the wife's employment is subordinate, economically and emotionally, to her family role, and is readily sacrificed for the latter. No society has restructured both the occupational system and the domestic establishment to the point of permanently modifying the old division of labor by sex.

In any deliberate effort to control the birth rate along these lines, a government has two powerful instruments—its command over economic planning and its authority (real or potential) over education. The first determines (as far as policy can) the economic conditions and circumstances affecting the lives of all citizens; the second provides the knowledge and attitudes necessary to implement the plans. The economic system largely determines who shall work, what can be bought, what rearing children will cost, how much individuals can spend. The schools define family roles and develop vocational and recreational interests; they could, if it were desired, redefine the sex roles, develop interests that transcend the home, and transmit realistic (as opposed to moralistic) knowledge concerning marriage, sexual behavior, and population problems. When the problem is viewed in this light, it is clear that the ministries of economics and education, not the ministry of health, should be the source of population policy.

THE DILEMMA OF POPULATION POLICY

It should now be apparent why, despite strong anxiety over runaway population growth, the actual programs purporting to control it are limited to family planning and are therefore ineffective. (1) The goal of zero, or even slight, population growth is one that nations and groups find difficult to accept. (2) The measures that would be required to implement such a goal, though not so revolutionary as a Brave New World or a Communist Utopia, nevertheless tend to offend most people reared in existing societies. As a consequence, the goal of so-called population control is implicit and vague; the method is only family planning. This method, far from deemphasizing the family, is familistic. One of its stated goals is that of helping sterile couples to *have* children. It stresses parental aspirations and responsibilities. It goes along with most aspects of conventional morality, such as condemnation of abortion, disap-

proval of premarital intercourse, respect for religious teachings and cultural taboos, and obeisance to medical and clerical authority. It deflects hostility by refusing to recommend any change other than the one it stands for: availability of contraceptives.

The things that make family planning acceptable are the very things that make it ineffective for population control. By stressing the right of parents to have the number of children they want, it evades the basic question of population policy, which is how to give societies the number of children they need. By offering only the means for *couples* to control fertility, it neglects the means for societies to do so.

Because of the predominantly profamily character of existing societies, individual interest ordinarily leads to the production of enough offspring to constitute rapid population growth under conditions of low mortality. Childless or single-child homes are considered indicative of personal failure, whereas having three to five living children gives a family a sense of continuity and substantiality.

Given the existing desire to have moderate-sized rather than small families, the only countries in which fertility has been reduced to match reduction in mortality are advanced ones temporarily experiencing worsened economic conditions. In Sweden, for instance, the net reproduction rate (NRR) has been below replacement for 34 years (1930-63), if the period is taken as a whole, but this is because of the economic depression. The average replacement rate was below unity (NRR = 0.81) for the period 1930-42, but from 1942 through 1963 it was above unity (NRR = 1.08). Hardships that seem particularly conducive to deliberate lowering of the birth rate are (in managed economies) scarcity of housing and other consumer goods despite full employment, and required high participation of women in the labor force, or (in freer economies) a great deal of unemployment and economic insecurity. When conditions are good, any nation tends to have a growing population.

It follows that, in countries where contraception is used, a realistic proposal for a government policy of lowering the birth rate reads like a catalog of horrors: squeeze consumers through taxation and inflation; make housing very scarce by limiting construction; force wives and mothers to work outside the home to offset the inadequacy of male wages, yet provide few child care facilities; encourage migration to the city by paying low wages in the country and providing few rural jobs; increase congestion in cities by starving the transit system; increase personal insecurity by encouraging conditions that produce unemployment and by haphazard political arrests. No government will institute such hardships simply for the purpose of controlling population growth. Clearly, therefore, the task of contemporary population policy is to develop attractive substitutes for family interests, so as to avoid having to turn to hardship as a corrective. The specific measures required for developing such substitutes are not easy to determine in the absence of research on the question.

In short, the world's population problems cannot be solved by pretense and wishful thinking. The unthinking identification of family planning with population control is an ostrich-like approach in that it permits people to hide from themselves the enormity and unconventionality of the task. There is no reason to abandon family planning programs; contraception is a valuable technological instrument. But such programs must be supplemented with equal or greater investments in research and experimentation to determine the required socioeconomic measures.

31. INEQUALITY AMONG NATIONS AND INTERNATIONAL REDISTRIBUTION

ERNST MICHANEK

Reprinted from "Leveling of Incomes . . . Not Always Upward," The World Development Plan: A Swedish Perspective (Stockholm: Almquist and Wiksell, 1971.) Copyright 1971 by the Dag Hammarskjold Foundation. Ernst Michanek has been Executive Chairman and Director General of the Swedish International Development Authority since 1964. Previously he was an advisor on domestic policies and Undersecretary of State at the Minister of Labor, Housing, Social Security, and Welfare. He served as Swedish delegate to the United Nations Economic and Social Council, as Chairman of the governing body of the International Labor Office, as Chairman of the U.N. Technical Assistance Committee, as delegate to the governing council of the U.N. Development Program, and as delegate to the U.N.E.S.C.O. general conference.

■ Modern governments, particularly in developing nations, generally make national development plans for five or ten year periods. These national plans represent an effort to bring together in one place an orderly presentation of national goals that have some realistic possibility of being achieved in a given period of time. They serve to inform decision-makers in particular areas of government and the economy about the over-arching goals toward which their more specific activities supposedly contribute. National plans are perhaps most notable for the extent to which their goals are not achieved, nevertheless they provide guidelines for the incredibly complex task of keeping a modern nation functioning in a way that satisfies the needs of its members.

In 1961 the United Nations, which in the previous two years had admitted 23 new member states, all part of the developing world, proclaimed the first "development decade." In his short essay Michanek assesses the extent to which this program achieved its goals and finds more reasons for pessimism than for optimism. He observes that the developing countries achieved the desired economic growth rate—5 percent per year in GNP—but that population growth all but wiped out the per capita gain this growth might have represented. He observes also that the distribution of income is even more distorted than before, both among and within nations; everywhere the gap between rich and poor has widened. He hopes the second United Nations development decade will prove more successful, because of increased technical knowledge about

development and because of clearer recognition of the goals toward which development should be directed.

In this selection Michanek brings together two concerns, one with equality and the other with the need to avoid ever-increasing environmental degradation. He draws from his assessment of these two issues some conclusions that will not be palatable to either the elites or the ordinary people of the developed nations. Indeed, the issue of achieving international equality without lowering the standard of living in the developed countries or hastening the time when environmental degradation will make human life untenable is so stark that until recently it has seldom been discussed even by those most concerned. ■

THE DEMAND FOR EQUALITY is politically and morally universal. The UN plan specifically states that its goals are applicable to *all* human beings. We must strive and work for employment and a reasonable income level for *everyone*, a good, well-equipped home, public health care and opportunities for recreational and cultural activities of a high standard for *everyone*. The gaps between rich and poor nations, and between rich and poor within each nation, must be narrowed. In Sweden we assume a rise in real incomes amounting to 3-5 percent annually, or a doubling of real income in the next 15-25 years. The UN plan settles for the goal of doubling the real income level of poorer peoples (and more than doubling it for the very poorest among them) within two decades. Most of us are likely to take it for granted that the leveling of incomes will be in an upward direction—i.e. that disadvantaged peoples will benefit without causing any absolute lowering of standards for those who now enjoy a normal income. In any case, no politician seems to be claiming that ordinary people must sacrifice part of their standard of living for the sake of income leveling.

We in Sweden would not have to raise our living standard much further to reach the present average level of consumption in North America. The 200 million inhabitants of the United States, who constitute 6 percent of the population of the earth, already consume one-third of the world's energy production, one-third of its steel, and one-half of its aluminum. It has been said (by Max Ways) that Americans are sheathed in a mass energy nimbus which produces paper, plastics, scrap, ash, soot, dust, sludge, slag and fumes, which exceeds by many magnitudes the individual's own bodily wastes. It has been estimated that 10 billion people without this nimbus of energy would produce no more wastes than the 200 million Americans are now doing. That is how large the multiplier effect of technology can be in the highly industrialized parts of the world.

If the current total energy production of the world were distributed using American standards, it would be enough for fewer than 600 million people or one-sixth of the current world population of 3.6 billion. At the American level of consumption, the world supply of fertilizers would suffice for 900 million people. The total industrial complex in the world today has a productive capacity which would not be enough for 1 billion people living at American levels of affluence. In order to raise the *entire* population of the world to *this particular* level of consumption, we would have to increase by many times over our removal of natural resources from the irreplaceable deposits of the earth, to say nothing of the consequent pollution of the environment. By the year 2000, a population of 50-70 percent in the United States and almost 100 per-cent in the world as a whole over the present numbers seems almost inevitable. On that presumption, the per capita consumption and waste production are about to reach levels so high that—*even without any leveling at all* between the richer and the poorer countries of the earth—they go far beyond what at the present time we can manage to achieve without a catastrophic plundering of the biosphere. The effects of environmental pollution on population growth cannot be predicted today.

Let us take another example. Imagine that the number of cars in relation to the population were on the same level in India as the present figure for Sweden, which is the highest outside North America. This would mean 150 million cars in India, in addition to the 500,000 or so at present in use there. The additional investment, the additional consumption and environmental pollution this number of cars would bring are almost beyond our power to imagine, in any case, beyond the power of anyone who is familiar with present-day India or who has seen Japan, a country where the density of cars seems likely to be exceeded soon only by the density of carbon dioxide in the air.

The conclusions we can draw from this reasoning are that a level of consumption such as that already reached in the West, and soon to be reached in Japan, is totally unrealistic as a basis for a far-reaching demand for equality embracing all humanity. The capacity of the biosphere can be calculated. Using examples like the ones mentioned above and building up a total balance covering all areas of consumption, we soon arrive at the conclusion that all talk of an international leveling of income to the standard enjoyed by a nation like the Swedish is pure nonsense.

TWO IRRECONCILABLE DEMANDS

This situation leads to a dilemma for anyone who advocates our active participation not only in formulating the world strategy, but also in putting it into practice. On the one hand, one may reveal the logical consequences of the ideology of full equality and risk losing the sympathy of those who feel that their own standard is being threatened, as well as of those who speak for the very poorest people in the developing countries. On the other, one may confine one's statements to what is called realistic. However, I will suggest the following compromise, which will probably not fit the views of any of the current political groupings in Sweden.

Anyone who advocates narrowing the gap between rich and poor nations, while at the same time envisioning, let us say, a continued 3-5 percent increase per year in real income for the bulk of the Swedish people, is supporting two irreconcilable policies. If he advocates both theses and predicts that both can be carried out simultaneously, he is either ignorant or mendacious.

The authors of the UN strategy for the 1970s sit on the fence. They propose a 3.5 percent annual growth rate in per capita production in the poorer countries. This is said to represent "at least . . . a modest beginning towards narrowing the gap in living standards between the developed and the developing countries." If the growth rate recommended for the poorer countries is to bring about any narrowing whatsoever of this gap during the 1970s, it actually requires the people of industrialized countries to accept a considerably lower rate of growth—a lower rate than they are accustomed to, and a lower rate than that of the less developed countries. It requires that they permit a considerable portion of their seemingly inevitable growth in production to be transferred to the poorer nations. The UN strategy does not mention this fact.

REALISM: CONFRONTATION

This fact was pointed out by a hundred of the world's most prominent development economists, representing all political persuasions and all continents, who gathered at Columbia University in February 1970 for a discussion of the Pearson Report. "A growth rate of 6 percent in GNP will not be ade-

quate to deal with the situation. In the Indo-Pakistan subcontinent, for instance, 6 percent growth until the turn of the century will still leave one and a half billion people with an average per capita income of only 200 dollars per year." The recommendations of the Pearson Report were accepted by these economists as a point of departure and nothing more. In their statement, the economists included a demand for massive increases in development assistance, which they saw as a necessary condition for rapid economic development. Their target was $400 a year as the lowest average income for all countries by the year 2000. (Four hundred dollars by the year 2000! In Sweden we are currently thinking in terms of raising our average income from more than $3,000 to somewhere close to $10,000 during the same period!) The economists called for unilateral measures to abolish trade barriers, and they demanded a number of economic and social reforms in developing countries. "Nothing is more unrealistic than the apparent realism of those who argue that the Pearson Report is fully adequate or even over-ambitious in terms of the future prospects," the economists concluded. There is every reason to believe that this statement is also applicable to the subsequently published UN strategy for the 1970s. "Such realism can only lead to growing confrontation between the developing and the developed countries of the world, and to growing misery and frustration for a majority of mankind."

What is needed, now that the idea of a global strategy has been accepted and a number of tangible development goals have been proposed by the international society, is a more exact estimate of costs and requirements. For this purpose, we need to draw up an international balance sheet. Many national models could serve as a basis. The UN Department of Economic and Social Affairs must be given resources for this task. The World Bank, the OECD and many other public and private agencies can be counted on to provide active cooperation. Substrategies must be worked out in a number of specialized fields and be included in a revised and expanded UN strategy. The balance sheet of world resources can be completed in time for the scheduled review of the UN strategy in 1975.

A country such as Sweden can, and should, contribute a great deal toward accomplishing this task. We should delegate financial resources and personnel, pursue an energetic and imaginative campaign in the UN and its specialized agencies and generously place funds at their disposal for the expansion of planning work. Equally important, we should give political weight to this international work in our own country, by introducing these issues into our centers of power—our large national organizations and our Parliament—and by directly involving our decision makers in international events.

We need an increasingly comprehensive world strategy, and eventually some kind of directorate for leading the work of carrying it out. We also need a national staff in Sweden that can take responsibility for our part in the general campaign. Why not present the entire UN strategy to the Swedish Parliament, not only to show that we have already done our share but to request parliamentary authority to continue working in the spirit of this international declaration of principles? The UN strategy is designed to cover the 1970s. Swedish development assistance programs have been planned through 1974-75, and we must now make plans for the years after 1975. We need substrategies for our own part of the international development effort as well.

It is not a question of trying to be nice to poor nations. It is a question of committing ourselves and others to devising a program that will focus attention on man and his environment, as we used to say in recent national election campaigns. More tangibly, it is a question of establishing a conscious, goal-oriented global population policy and similar policies on environmental protection, economic development, trade relations, and so on. All these components must be directed toward bringing about a realistic utilization of the resources of the biosphere, as we can estimate them, and a realistic distribution of these resources, which means the beginnings of a gradual redistribution.

VI.

CONFLICTS OF EFFICIENCY, CHOICE, AND EQUALITY

THE FOCUS ON problems of inequality in this volume has been sharp enough to prove misleading if it suggests that problems of inequality are distinct from other kinds of social problems. In the companion volume, dealing with *Deviance and Liberty,* we will see some of the intimate connections between social inequality and problems in which deviance appears as the central element. In this Part of Volume 1 we have included several selections that illustrate the connections between inequality and the issues of efficient use of resources with which any social system must cope.

In contemporary American society the issues of efficiency and wastefulness that stand out most particularly are those of pollution and environmental conservation, and what has sometimes been called "the urban crisis"—the degradation of the environment of the central cities and the growth of mammoth metropolitan areas, the so-called "megalopolis." Each of these issues also involves matters of inequality and justice.

In a very real sense the most important cause of the urban crisis is social inequality. George Sternlieb in his article, "The City as Sandbox," shows how efforts to maintain patterns of extreme social inequality based on economic status and race precipitate the crisis of the central city. Similarly, in his essay Barry Commoner highlights the relationship between economic affluence, which is so important in symbolizing class inequalities, and the environmental problems that threaten all members of society.

The two initial selections in this Part provide us with a conceptual framework for thinking about the interrelations between the seemingly uncontroversial issues of efficiency and prudent resource allocation and the more divisive issues of inequality. The paper by Nagel suggests with that such a separation is artificial, and Schelling shows us how in individualistic pursuit of their own ends people often end up worse off than if they had been less intent on seeking and preserving their advantages.

32. REASON AND NATIONAL GOALS

THOMAS NAGEL

Reprinted from Science, *Vol. 177, September 1, 1972, pp. 766-70. Copyright 1972 by the American Association for the Advancement of Science. Thomas Nagel is Professor of Philosophy at Princeton University.*

■ Often those who deal with public policy issues define them as if questions of equality were irrelevant—as issues only of efficiency or rationality or the common good. But policy analysts increasingly are pointing out that almost all issues have distributive implications. At the very least, the question of how decisions for the "general good" are made involves the relative equality of power in the hands of those who wish to affect those decisions, and in almost all cases the decisions also have an effect on the distribution of resources.

An assumption that equality problems are either absent or relatively trivial and easy is seen particularly in connection with issues related to the environment, national resources, knowledge and technology, and population growth. In this article Nagel examines that assumption and systematically shows how a concern with rationality that ignores questions of ethics or justice is self-deluding if not self-serving.

The National Academy of Sciences study to which Nagel refers is NAS Panel on Technology Assessment, *Technology: Processes of Assessment and Choice: Report to the House of Representatives' Committee on Science and Astronautics* (Washington, D.C.: Government Printing Office, 1969). The national goals study to which he refers is National Goals Research Staff, *Toward Balanced Growth: Quantity with Quality* (Washington, D.C.: Government Printing Office, 1970). ■

IT IS NOT SELF-EVIDENT that the subject of national goals is worth expending breath on, since the decisions that matter are really decisions about policies and programs, and too often the larger stated aims of these enterprises are purely rhetorical. Nevertheless, general ideas, whether expressed or not, appear to enter into the design of public policy in some way, and it might be worthwhile to attempt to make these ideas explicit and to discover whether or not they have any foundation.

A better understanding of these ideas is important for the policymakers themselves, who have nothing to lose from a better understanding of what is rational and what is irrational in their motives, as well as for those who urge programs and expenditures on the government or who cooperate in their design—the scientific community, the academic community, and the aerospace industry being prime examples. If one appeals to motives that are inadequately grounded or understood, one may find oneself suddenly abandoned in midair by a fickle government or public.

The entire basis of major national resource allocations is rarely probed in any depth. It is as important for a middle-aged nation to consider what, fundamentally, it wishes to do with its national life as it is for a middle-aged man to decide what his life is all about. Yet, if the recent report of the National Goals Research Staff, *Toward Balanced Growth: Quantity with Quality*, is any indication, the reflections are not likely to be fundamental enough. That document assumes that we know more or less what we want and do not want, and treats the problem as one of settling conflicts among different aims and designing the pursuit of those aims to avoid undesirable side effects. It assumes that a general set of goals for the nation is defined by an increase in the availability of certain generally accepted goods—education, housing, health, transportation, scientific research, and technological advance—and a reduction of certain generally accepted evils—poverty, pollution, and overcrowding. All of these are to be balanced against suitable demands in the areas of national security and space exploration.

The report does not discuss these last two areas. The initial list of goods and evils contains only one controversial item—technological advance. The report is justified in rejecting the current wave of antitechnological hand wringing, most of which comes from affluent, well-educated people who would cry bloody murder if they had to give up their dishwashers, air conditioners, dictaphones, nonstop jet flights, direct distance dialing, and so forth. Technological advance in this country has made it possible for many people to live a comfortable life without exploiting the remainder of the population. We need more and better technology to extend this possibility to more people and to improve the quality of such public services as transportation and waste disposal.

The report does stress the need, which everyone seems suddenly to have recognized, for assessing technological developments in advance—not just in relation to their stated aims, but also in relation to their unintended fallout and interaction with the total social and natural order. The problems of applying ecological model are discussed with great penetration in *Technology: Processes of Assessment and Choice*, a report prepared by a panel of the National Academy of Sciences for the House Committee on Science and Astronautics. Although it may not be easy to accomplish, preservation of the environment and reduction of the untoward side effects of technological progress can themselves be made high-priority technological goals. The problem is how to bring this about by new decision procedures, incentives, and regulations. To quote from the National Academy of Sciences report:

The objective of heightened sensitivity in technology assessment should, whenever possible, be achieved by structuring the incentives of individual decision-makers so that they are induced to alter their cost-benefit calculations to encompass wider concerns than have heretofore been given consideration.

It is clear that the external diseconomies of many activities and enterprises do not automatically receive their proper weight in current decision-making procedures. It is also clear that a program cannot be designed solely with reference to one goal, but must refer to a variety of considerations; in fact, the conception of goals, which one tries to reach, might profitably be replaced by a body of considerations thought to be important. Moreover, it is desirable to devote a certain amount of effort to the development of capacities not designed for any particular goal at all, on the grounds that general scientific and technical advance will be useful in meeting needs yet unformulated or will provide unexpected new methods of achieving old aims.

FOUR TYPES OF DESIRABILITY

All of these points are commonplace by now. The problems are not trivial, and they will arise in any complex, advanced society, even in the absence of doubt about its fundamental aims. The questions I am raising lie somewhat deeper. They concern the basis for regarding any given thing as a relevant consideration in the design of national policy.

It becomes important to adopt aims at a national level when something desirable cannot be achieved, or something undesirable prevented, by individual or local action—when either the motivation or the resources are lacking. It is immediately possible, however, to distinguish four different ways in which such an end may be desirable. Something may be desirable because (1) it is in the interest of individual members of the society; (2) it is in the interest of the nation, conceived as something more than its individual members; (3) it is in the interest of people generally, whether in this society or elsewhere; or (4) it is good in itself, rather than good *for* anyone or anything.

Often more than one of these categories is involved in a given aim, but it is instructive to distinguish them and discuss some of the problems peculiar to each, with an eye to drawing some conclusions about their relative importance in the deliberations of a modern society.

The first category is sometimes uneasily assumed to be the standard to which all government policies must be referred for justification. There exist elaborate defenses of the space program on the grounds of its contribution to the design of underwear, the development of new procedures for fitting artificial limbs, the dramatic increase in the number of churches in Huntsville, Alabama, and countless other benefits. Curiosities aside, however, there are various problems about how individual interests should be counted in the determination of public policy. I focus on three main questions. First, to what extent can individuals be relied on to know what their own interests are? This is the problem of paternalism. Second, to what extent is it permissible for the society to give special weight to the interests of some individuals rather than others? This is the problem of elitism. Third, how can the inevitably conflicting interests of millions of people be justly served by policies that do not serve all of them equally? This is the problem of distributive justice.

There are many other problems connected with individual interests—for example, whether the interests of future generations should be counted equally with those of the present population in determining present policy and whether there are certain interests, such as personal liberty, that must be accorded extraordinary weight or that should be regarded as rights. I shall concentrate, however, on the above three topics.

PATERNALISM

There are several areas in which government policies and regulations do not leave it up to individuals to decide what is best for them: one is medicine; another is sexual stimulation and gratification through publications, movies, prostitution, or nonstandard sexual practices; another is drugs; another is military security. In all of these cases the lawmakers, or the experts to whom they defer, establish policies or restrictions intended to benefit individuals in the society,

whether the individuals see them as beneficial or not.

There is little dispute over the legitimacy of paternalism based on expertise in the medical sphere. The other three areas are highly controversial; many people feel that paternalism in these areas should be eliminated or reduced. In the case of military security, of course, there must be a national policy—it cannot be left up to the individual. But it is an area of strong paternalism nevertheless. At present, general public opinion plays an insignificant role, compared to expert military and technical opinion, in determining what is an increase in military security and what is a decrease, how much should be sacrificed to obtain a certain position of military dominance, what level of deterrent capability is worth a vast increase in civilian casualties if a war should take place, and so forth.

Admittedly, many people submit in a docile fashion to paternalism in military affairs, although fewer are docile about less important but more personal matters such as pornography and marijuana. Nevertheless, I believe that there is a substantial general wariness of paternalism in this society—a wariness that is justified by some of the excesses of paternalism, but that may hinder its extension to other areas in which it might be valuable. If paternalism could be properly based on unbiased expertise, it might well be extended to new areas as they are opened up by technological advance. I recognize, however, that the "if" is a big one. As it is, the Food and Drug Administration relies on the drug companies for testing, the Public Health Service's monitoring and evaluation of the effects of underground nuclear tests is funded by the Atomic Energy Commission, and so on. Such facts do not encourage confidence in an extension of government paternalism to other areas of technology and consumer affairs. Such an extension may be necessary nonetheless, and it is important that people with the necessary expertise keep a sharp eye on how it is carried out.

It is important, whenever possible, to distinguish paternalism about values from paternalism about the methods by which certain valued aims may be achieved. In the case of medicine, for example, there is a presumed common aim of long life, good health, and physical comfort. Paternalism about methods of achieving this is unobjectionable and can be based on expertise. Paternalism about sexual conduct, on the other hand, is instituted precisely because certain basic values are not shared by everyone. It is therefore a far more fundamental interference with individual liberty than medical paternalism is. Still other cases cannot easily be classified as paternalism about ends or paternalism about means—for example, auto safety requirements, where the ends of safety, economy, and convenience are all assumed, and where the issue is how to trade them off against one another, in terms of specific requirements for design features.

ELITISM

This society appears to depart from equal treatment in two directions: compensatory programs for the underprivileged and elitism. I do not discuss the first, partly because it is not accurate to describe it as counting the interests of the poor and uneducated more heavily than the interests of those who are better off; even if the interests of both groups are given equal weight, the underprivileged are automatically in a less favorable position for securing those interests. (Admittedly, it has been urged that damage done by the society to a group in the past should be compensated for by exceptional treatment in the present. But such an argument is not required to justify exceptional attention to the interests of Blacks in the United States, for example.)

Elitism in national policies is very difficult to avoid, since those who are best endowed by nature and background and who have had the greatest advantages are in a stronger position to press their interests in determination of government policies than are the poor, the inarticulate, the ignorant, and the unimportant. Numbers by themselves do not overcome these disadvantages, and, although numbers

combined with organization can do so, organization is not easily achieved without antecedent power of some kind.

Elitism today takes the form of major investments of resources in pursuits that interest the highly educated, technologically sophisticated top layer of American society. These pursuits include higher education itself, basic scientific research, and the space program, among others. Admittedly all of these things might be defended in other ways—for example, in terms of benefits that are not individual, but national or international. Just as often, however, an attempt is made to defend clearly elitist programs on more democratic grounds, and this just obscures the issue. The obscurity can go further if, for example, the underprivileged population is sold on an interest in higher education on the grounds that those of their number who are qualified will now have an opportunity to go to college. This is elitism with the wrinkles ironed out.

It may be that the advancement of particle physics or the landing of men on the moon are in themselves goods of great magnitude, but it is simply untrue that they serve the interests of the average janitor, dishwasher, farm laborer, or laundress. On the other hand, such projects do serve the interests, both intellectual and economic, of hosts of scientists, technicians, managers, and investors. It may be claimed that the elitism is a side effect of other aims, but this would be a distortion. The nation often identifies its interests predominantly with those of its most powerful and "advanced" groups, even if those groups are a minority and their interests conflict with those of the majority. When the most powerful groups also have access to modern communications, public opinion of a wider scope can usually be marshaled in support of an effectively elitist position.

It is important to recognize this tendency in order to decide whether it is justified and whether the justification could be appealed to publicly. Certain interests are common to everyone. Other interests appear only at certain levels of cultural and educational sophistication, and this naturally means that fewer people are involved. A central problem in government support for scholarship, cultural activities, and pure science is whether they are justifiable solely in terms of the benefits to those directly affected, or whether they must be defended in terms of eventual fallout and spin-off that will benefit everyone.

This is similar to the issue posed by John Stuart Mill's attempt to include distinctions of value between higher and lower pleasures in a utilitarian system. Put this way, it seems improbable that such differential allocation of national resources could be justified solely on the ground that some people's interests are more important than others. Rather, such a justification will succeed only if it appeals to considerations of another type—namely, that certain activities and achievements are good in themselves, or good for the society that produces them—quite apart from their benefit to individuals.

DISTRIBUTIVE JUSTICE

The third, and probably most difficult, problem under the heading of individual interests is that of just trade-offs. People are apt to use a phrase like "the general welfare" without reflecting that it expresses an extremely obscure and probably ill-defined concept. Any government policy helps some people and hurts others, or at the very least yields a distribution of benefits different from that of an alternative policy. Where resources are limited, is there some quantitative measure of individual benefits that government policy should seek to maximize, or should it seek to equalize benefits over the affected population, or should it follow a subtler principle of distribution?

These issues come into focus over the question of how the least privileged members of a society should fare under its policies. Is it legitimate to improve the situation of those who are already affluent, or at least comfortable, while letting the poor stay where they are? The same question arises about the relation between benefits to the upper middle and lower middle classes. A society with a large system of public higher education dispenses benefits to the former without giving anything analogous to the latter—to say nothing of helping to make life easier for the clever than for the not-so-clever.

The question is whether social justice should be a fundamental goal in the determination of public policy designed to serve individual interests, in order that equitable distribution, rather than the maximization of benefits, assumes primary importance. One view of a suitable measure for distributive justice is the Difference Principle formulated by John Rawls. It states that social and economic inequalities have to be justified in terms of their benefit to everyone, in particular to the least privileged groups in the society. This means not only that we cannot justify enslaving some individuals to make life easy for others, but also that we cannot justify massive government investment in higher education or scientific research unless it can be argued that this contributes, through its effects on the economy, technology, and political life, to the needs of poorly paid, unskilled manual laborers.

While this is not a straightforwardly egalitarian view, it does require that socially imposed inequalities be strictly justified, and it is likely to seem an extreme position to many. The elitism of this society—of most societies —is very deep and very natural. It is taken for granted that public services will be better in well-to-do than in poor areas of town, and the recent decision of the U.S. Court of Appeals, Fifth Circuit, which challenges this assumption, must have come as a shock to many communities.

Few things are more important for this country than a determination of the role to be played by a principle of distributive justice in shaping the massive interventions of the federal government in the country's social and economic life. What that principle should be—specifically, how egalitarian it should be—is an issue that already underlies most debates about social policy. There is much to be gained by bringing out the issue of principle in abstract form, for that is where the deep divisions are to be found.

NATIONAL INTEREST

The idea of a national interest that is not merely a composite of antecedent, individual interests may strike some people as romantic. Perhaps it is, yet it plays a significant role in American politics and American policy formation. Prestige, dominance, not losing face, winning this or that technological race, being the most powerful country in the world—all of these goals are offered in justification of great sacrifices of life and wealth, often without any serious attempt to show how they serve the interests of individual citizens.

It may be argued that to be a citizen of the first country to land men on the moon is in itself a considerable benefit: if it justifies pride, it must be worth something. But even if such feelings of pride and vicarious accomplishment are significant motivations, is it rational to accord them the weight they would need to have to warrant such massive allocation of resources? My own view is that national prestige and national pride are not worth the sacrifice of any real goods—that is, benefits for individual people or things good in themselves. There is little reason to believe that citizenship of the first country to land a man on the moon is a substantial good, although it may seem so to many people. It is evident that men will do irrationally wasteful and self-destructive things to avoid losing face. Politicians are not immune to this weakness, and nations as a whole are continually behaving like the heroes and villains of grade-B westerns.

This creates a problem. One should avoid basing an appeal for support of a costly program on the grounds of national prestige or rarefied national interest if one is not genuinely convinced that these have objective importance. Yet the temptation to use arguments that will convince, even if they are not very good arguments, must sometimes be considerable. It can even lead to the construction of mission-oriented schemes that appeal to such interests, but whose real motive is to support more general research. Even more effective in producing legislative response than the appeal to national prestige is the appeal to national security, which has been widely employed by those seeking support for research and development.

The scientific and technological communities have reason to exercise collective restraint in these areas. It is very difficult, in appealing for funds, to disarm unilaterally while various other supplicants continue to use the full arsenal of arguments and persuasions, rational and irrational. If the scientific community were in some agreement as to the legitimate grounds for resource allocation and the relative importance of these grounds, they might be able to refer to most appeals for government support to those grounds alone. But this would require confidence that all parties would conform, and confidence may be difficult to achieve.

A strong conception of national interest clashes with those strongly individualistic assumptions of traditional political theory that still dominate our thought in this area. If national interest and prestige are to be useful in determining national goals, they must be defined by reference to other values whose independent validity is clear. This means that the justification for pursuing a goal can never be prestige per se, but only the independent value of whatever it is that confers prestige. For example, if national security means reduced likelihood or likely extent of military destruction, then it cannot be identified with an edge in the number of nuclear warheads. Another possible example is that national decency or justice, or an unwillingness to do what is inhumane even if it would be convenient, might be counted among the legitimate objects of national pride. But these things are valuable in themselves, and worth pursuing; otherwise, they could form no legitimate grounds for pride. As a general principle, the claims of national interest must be *shown* to be worth the sacrifices that they may require, and this is most effectively done by relating them finally to individual interests.

INTERESTS OF HUMANITY

It is not easy to say how a country should weigh the interests of individuals other than its own nationals in making policy: nor is it easy to describe the connection between rhetoric and reality in the current practice of the United States. With a few exceptions like the Marshall Plan, the greatest expenditures of American resources in the service of humanity have taken the form of massive military action. Currently, our altruism involves the systematic devastation of several countries and the massacre of civilians in large numbers. Even the rhetoric is beginning to sound peculiar: the President's repeated defense of various enormities, on the ground that they are necessary to save American lives, invites the question, "How many Asian lives is an American life worth?" It may be wise not to insist on an answer.

If things are as grim as this, careful analysis of the exact weight to be given internationalist sentiments has a flavor of unreality. The sense of detachment, which permits most people to regard the suffering of those unlike them as insignificant, does not seem to have been overcome by the vividness of modern techniques of communication. It may be that we are a fundamentally cruel and bloodthirsty species and that Freud is right when he says, "It is always possible to bind together a considerable number of people in love, so long as there are other people left over to receive the manifestations of their aggressiveness."

However, to assume that man is fundamentally cruel and bloodthirsty would be simply to reinforce the existing tendencies in that direction. Those who object to the communal barbarism that now governs international relations must pay attention to the eradication of its roots in individual psychology. If those engaged in public debate fail to question the total primacy of American interests in policy formation and appeal only to patriotism of the narrowest sort, the public at large will continue to think about these issues in the same terms, and it will remain politically dangerous to appeal to other considerations. If chauvinism and xenophobia can be reduced in any degree by the quality of public argument about government programs, it would be unfortunate to miss the opportunity.

Some might say that moral considerations are meaningless outside of a legal system, and the real problem is that we lack a system of international law. But the premise is in error for various reasons: (1) much of morality and the requirements of human decency are not covered by law, even within legally ordered societies; (2) antecedent moral judgments have to enter into the formulation, the interpretation, and the application of law; and (3) one of the many reasons international law has such difficulty finding acceptance is that people do not consider themselves part of a worldwide moral community, all of whose members share a basic human worth. The two systems, moral and legal, help to sustain one another. When a sense of moral community is lacking within a society, it creates serious problems for the viability of the legal system—as may be seen in the history of the American South, for example.

It is not clear what can overcome the weakness of most people's sense of an international moral community. But it is important that, when the occasion presents itself, consideration of the interests of humanity at large should be included in arguments about policy formation—and this should be done without apology and without further justification in terms of the national interest. What is required is no more than an extrapolation from the usual ethical demands on the interaction of individuals. It might seem that nothing would be easier, but evidently we must contend with powerful motives leading in a contrary direction.

GOODS IN THEMSELVES

The final category of desirable ends to be considered here is the most obscure, but it plays a very important, often submerged role, and it may offer the most significant justification for departing from the allocation of resources to benefit individuals.

One of the justifications for elitism is that certain accomplishments and activities are intrinsically finer, rarer, higher than others and that a society should be committed to excellence, even if only a few of its members can enjoy the achievement. Such an argument would, for example, defend the large investment needed for continued intensive work in high-energy physics, not because it serves the interests of the scientists involved or because it increases national security, but because an understanding of the basic constitution of matter is a fine thing for human beings to achieve. If it is a fine thing absolutely, then it is to the credit of a nation to have furthered the achievement.

There are many investments of national resources that can only be defended adequately in these terms. The preservation of natural beauty, even at the cost of making large areas almost inaccessible to most people, is an example. Support of advanced or esoteric work in the arts, in literature, or in scholarship; the general promotion of high culture that claims the devotion of only a small audience; the preservation of significant architectural achievements of the past, despite their lack of current utility—all of these belong to the same category. They are warranted not because the people whom these things interest are more deserving of satisfaction than other people, but because the loss of the most beautiful possessions and advanced achievements of a society would not be worth the savings to be made by giving them up.

The space program has to be defended primarily on such grounds, but it is not an easy task. The extent to which a society can afford to devote its resources to the advancement of knowledge and human achievement for no further purpose depends on the extent to which that society is capable of satisfying much more basic needs and meeting the minimal conditions of social justice. A country with a serious famine problem would not be justified in diverting large sums for the support of symphony orchestras and astronomical observatories. If the space program cost no more than a string of orchestras or a national park or several observatories, it would be easy for this country to justify. But it costs a good deal more, and, even in the relative economic prosperity of the United States, there are serious deficiencies and inequities that make it difficult to regard the expenditure as other than a luxury.

To a great extent, societies are measured by the best that they produce. Everyone has a sense of history; it is conditioned by an awareness of past societies that is gained through their art, literature, science, and exploration, rather than through their attempts to achieve broad prosperity and social justice. However, this is a distorting perspective, and if we apply it to ourselves, grandiosity is in danger of overcoming decency and common sense in the formation of policy.

A natural anthropocentric conceit leads people to regard it as a great event that members of our species have reached the moon of this planet. But it is dangerous to allow oneself to be motivated too strongly by considerations of cosmic significance. Nothing we do in this out-of-the-way corner of an unremarkable galaxy would be likely to have cosmic significance, if there were such a thing. The human race, which is in terrible shape, manages to remain in love with itself, and this is nowhere more evident than in the peculiar floods of self-congratulation that accompany each step into space.

SUMMARY

It has been argued that rationality, moral considerations, and a sense of proportion can be coherently applied in determining national policies. At present, the determination of policies, programs, and goals is often irrational, in that considerations under the four categories discussed—individual interests, national interests, the interests of humanity, and goods in themselves—receive more or less weight than they should.

Rationality is said to be increasingly under

attack at the present time. It has never been terribly popular, but certainly the sources of suspicion are new, for those who distrust reason currently include numbers of college students. There is an explanation for this. Mistrust of rational analysis in political discourse is evoked by the impoverishment of the terms in which questions are often posed for rational solution and by the restrictive frame of reference, common in political discussion, which can make it appear that reason excludes morality and humanity. The appeal to cool, rational analysis is too often an excuse for refusing to listen to the clear warnings of conscience or common sense.

There is no opposition between reason and ethics, however. If rational principles of decision produce results that seem obviously wrong in a particular case, then there is reason to suspect that the principles failed to take some factor into account properly.

There are no general principles at hand for the evaluation of public policy; even if there were, their application would not be obvious. This discussion attempts only to describe relevant considerations and to pose questions about their relative weight. Those individuals actually engaged in public debate over policy and resource allocation have to do the work of broadening the range of factors accepted as relevant and of making the understanding of such factors deeper and more systematic. The scientific, technological, and academic communities are in a position to further this work by the character of their appeals for public funds, and it is to be hoped that their important position as special-interest groups will not hinder them from doing so.

33. INDIVIDUAL ADAPTATION AND COLLECTIVE RESULTS

THOMAS C. SCHELLING

Reprinted from "On the Ecology of Micromotives," Discussion Paper No. 2, The Public Interest No. 25, Fall 1971. Copyright © 1971 by National Affairs, Inc. The original version of this paper was sponsored by the Harvard University Program on Technology and Society, as part of its project on The Corporate Society. The several papers comprising that project are in Robin Marris (ed.), The Corporate Society, Macmillan, 1973. Thomas C. Schelling is Professor of Economics and a member of the Faculty of the John F. Kennedy School of Government and Institute of Politics at Harvard University.

■ One solution to the problem of equality and efficiency is to try to assure a fair distribution of resources through political action, and then to rely on a free market of choices for allocating those resources among different individuals and groups. The competitive market provides the discipline that ensures that individuals pay the full cost of their actions and also that they get their money's worth. As government bureaucracies have grown larger, the problems associated with their rigidity in areas such as education, health institutions, and social service agencies have led to a renewed interest in market schemes even for goods distributed by the government. One such scheme is an educational system in which families could choose among schools that would compete for education "vouchers" which the government would issue to cover the cost of education. The rent allowance plans discussed in Selections 13a and 13b also depend for their success on the effectiveness of a competitive market.

In this paper Schelling raises some basic questions about market principles of allocation and suggests how the individual's freedom to pursue his own interests—even when equality of resources already exists—can result in everyone's being worse off. The necessity of regulating the high costs of allowing everyone to seek his own goals engenders many opportunities for the creation and perpetuation of inequalities. When inequalities already exist, an effort to limit this waste is likely to encounter strong opposition from those with the most resources. So the conflict between efficiency which is in everyone's interest, individual rights of choice, and equity is constant in public policy formation.

Schelling suggests that as time goes on, as populations grow and—even more important —as human activities multiply, this conflict will become sharper. If the great challenge of the last two centuries was conquering death and want, the great challenge of the next two will undoubtedly be that of learning to control man's behavior in his own interests as he protects and increases equality. It is the genius of Schelling's article that he shows us how all these issues are related to very mundane matters so that the abstract principles involved stand out sharply to command our interest. ■

The man who invented traffic signals, if there was such a man, had a genius for simplicity. He saw that where two streets intersected there was confusion and lost time because people got in each other's way; and he discovered, probably by personal experience, that self-discipline and good will among travelers was not enough to straighten them out. Even the courteous lost time waiting for each other, and some who mistakenly thought it was their turn suffered collision.

With magnificent simplicity he divided all travelers into two groups, those moving east-west and those moving north-south, ignoring differences in vehicle size or the personal qualities of travelers. He put the traffic into an alternating pattern. He needed neither tickets nor schedules, nor did he have to make any traveler apply in advance for a reservation to cross the intersection. All necessary instructions could be reduced to a binary code in red and green lights; all travelers within the scope of the plan could be reached by visual signals; and a single alternating mechanism could activate both sets of lights.

There was no need to plan the day in advance; neither the lights nor the travelers needed to be synchronized with any other activity. Nor was there need for enforcement: Once travelers got used to the lights, they learned that it was dangerous to cross against a flow of traffic that was proceeding with confidence. The lights created the kind of order in which noncompliance carried its own penalty. And there was impartial justice in the way the lights worked. Unable to recognize individual travelers and their merits, the lights could hurt no one's feelings by not granting the favoritism anyone might have expected from a more sophisticated system. The lights were arbitrary, though, only within the range of tolerance of the typical traveler; it was worth no one's while to appeal the lights' decisions or to seek special privilege in advance, because the benefits of privilege would be at most a few moments' time.

If the sluggard can be admonished to study the ant, the social planner is well-advised to study traffic signals. They remind us that, though planning is often associated with control, the crucial element is often coordination. People need to do the right things at the right time in relation to what others are doing. In fact, the most ingenious piece of planning ever introduced into society may have been our common scheme for synchronizing clocks and calendars. I do not set my watch at zero every morning on arising and let it run through the day on the decimal system; I have a watch just like yours, one that I coordinate with everybody else's at remarkably little cost. And I know nobody who cheats.

There is a great annual celebration of this accomplishment in early summer when we all set our watches ahead together for daylight saving. For the federal government to order us all to do everything an hour earlier would be an interference in our personal lives; it would confront everybody with discretionary decisions; we'd all have to check who had actually changed his schedule and who had not. But if we just set our watches ahead on the same night it all goes smoothly. And we haven't much choice. . . .

KEYBOARDS AND CALENDARS

Traffic signals and daylight saving both reflect the compelling forces toward *convergence* in many social decisions. Weights and measures, the pitches of screws, decimal coinage and right-hand drive are beyond the power of individual influence. Even for governments few such decisions are as easily manipulated as the one about what time we get up in the summer. Clock technology makes daylight saving markedly easier than switching steering posts and road signs to get all those cars on the other side of the road at the same moment. Coins circulate much more rapidly than screws and bolts; we'd be years working off the thread angles that we inherited in all of our durable hardware.

Decimal coinage and right-hand drive may be worth the heroic collective effort. Calendar reform would probably work. Spelling reform has been successfully organized; switching nationally to another language may require the extreme authority of a despot, the fervor of a religious cause, or polyglot confusion that leaves the focus of a new convergence open to manipulation.

The inertia of some of these social decisions is impressive and sometimes exasperating. The familiar English typewriter keyboard was determined before people learned to play the machine with both hands. Anyone who types could recommend improvements, and experiments have shown that there are superior keyboards that can be quickly learned. The cost of changing keys or even replacing machines would entail no great outlay, especially as typists on different floors of a building can type on different keyboards without disturbing each other. My children, though, apparently as long as they live, will use their ring fingers for letters more appropriate to the index. . . .

EXPRESSWAY SOCIETY

A strange phenomenon on Boston's Southeast Expressway is reported by the traffic helicopter. If a freak accident, or a severe one, occurs in the southbound lane in the morning, it slows the northbound rush-hour traffic more than on the side where the obstruction occurs. People slow down to enjoy a look at the wreckage on the other side of the divider. Curiosity has the same effect as a bottleneck. Even the driver who, when he arrives at the site, is 10 minutes behind schedule is likely to feel that he's paid the price of admission and, though the highway is at last clear in front of him, will not resume speed until he's had his look, too.

Eventually large numbers of commuters have spent an extra 10 minutes driving for a 10-second look. (Ironically, the wreckage may have been cleared away, but they spend their 10 seconds looking for it, induced by the people ahead of them who seemed to be looking at something.) What kind of a bargain is it? A few of them, offered a speedy bypass, might have stayed in line out of curiosity; most of them, after years of driving, know that when they get there what they're likely to see is worth about 10 seconds' driving time. When they get to the scene the 10 minutes' delay is a sunk cost; their own sightseeing costs them only the 10 seconds. It also costs 10 seconds apiece to the 3 score motorists crawling along behind them.

Everybody pays his 10 minutes and gets his look. But he pays 10 seconds for his own look and 9 minutes, 50 seconds for the curiosity of the drivers ahead of him.

It is a bad bargain. More correctly, it is a bad result because there is no bargain. As a collective body, the drivers might overwhelmingly vote to maintain speed, each foregoing a 10-second look and each saving himself 10 minutes on the freeway. Unorganized, they are at the mercy of a decentralized accounting system according to which no gawking driver suffers the losses that he imposes on the people behind him.

Returning from Cape Cod on a Sunday afternoon, motorists were held up for a mile or more, at a creeping pace, by a mattress that had fallen off the top of some returning

vacationer's station wagon. Nobody knows how many hundreds of cars slowed down a mile in advance, arrived at the mattress five minutes later, waited for the oncoming traffic and swerved around before resuming speed. Somebody may eventually have halted on the shoulder just beyond the mattress and walked back to remove it from the traffic lane. If not, it may still have been there the following Sunday.

Again there was no bargain. Failing the appearance of a driver in a mood to do good —not a common mood on a hot highway with hungry children in the back seat—somebody would have had to be elected to the duty or compensated for performing it. Nobody gains by removing the mattress after he has passed it, and nobody can remove it until he has passed it. . . .

PRIVATE CHOICE AND PUBLIC INTEREST

Both the curiosity on the Southeast Expressway and the urge to get home once the mattress has been passed illustrate universal situations of individual decision and collective interest. People do things or abstain from doing things that affect others, beneficially or adversely. Without appropriate organization, the results may be pretty unsatisfactory. "Human nature" is easily blamed; but accepting that most people are more concerned with their own affairs than with the affairs of others, and more aware of their own concerns than of the concerns of others, we may find human nature less pertinent than social organization. These problems often do have solutions. The solutions depend on some kind of social organization, whether that organization is contrived or spontaneous, permanent or ad hoc, voluntary or disciplined.

In the one case—pausing to look at the wreck—the problem is to get people to *abstain* from something that imposes costs on others. In the second case—yanking the mattress off the cement—the problem is to get somebody to take the trouble to *do* something that benefits himself not at all but will be highly appreciated.

Another distinction is that the first case involves *everybody,* the second *somebody.* We can easily turn the mattress case around and make it an act of carelessness that hurts others, not an act of good will for their benefit. Whoever tied the mattress carelessly may have considered the loss of the mattress in case the knot came loose, but not the risk that a thousand families would be late getting home behind him. So also on the expressway we can drop our prejudices against morbid sightseeing and just suppose that people are driving comfortably along minding their business. They are in no great hurry, but somebody behind them is, in fact a lot of people. It is worth a lot of time collectively, and maybe even money, to get the unhurried driver to bestir himself or to pick another route. He needn't feel guilty; he may even want something in return for giving up his right of way to people who like to drive faster; but without organization he may know nothing about the hurry they are in behind him, and care even less.

A good part of social organization—of what we call society—consists of institutional arrangements to overcome these divergences between perceived individual interest and some larger collective bargain. Some of it is market-oriented—ownership, contract, damage suits, patents and copyrights, promissory notes, rental agreements, and a variety of communications and information systems. Some have to do with government—taxes to cover public services, protection of persons, a weather bureau if weather information is not otherwise marketable, one-way streets, laws against littering, wrecking crews to clear away that car in the southbound lane and policemen to wave us on in the northbound lane. More selective groupings—the union, the club, the neighborhood—can organize incentive systems or regulations to try to help people do what individually they wouldn't but collectively they may wish to do. And our morals can substitute for markets and regulations in getting us sometimes to do from conscience the

things that in the long run we might elect to do only if assured of reciprocation.

What we are dealing with is the frequent divergence between what people are individually motivated to do and what they might like to accomplish together. Consider the summer brownout. We are warned ominously that unless we all cut our use of electricity in midsummer we may overload the system and suffer drastic consequences, sudden blackouts or prolonged power failures, unpredictable in their consequences. In other years we are warned of water shortages; leaky faucets account for a remarkable amount of waste, and we are urged to fit them with new washers. There just cannot be any question but what, for most of us if not all of us, we are far better off if we *all* switch off the lights more assiduously, cut down a little on the air-conditioning, repair the leaky faucets, let the lawns get a little browner and the cars a little dirtier, and otherwise reduce our claims on the common pool of water and electric power. For if we do not, we suffer worse and less predictably—the air conditioner may be out altogether on the hottest day, and all lights out just when we need them, when overload occurs or some awkward emergency rationing system goes into effect.

But turning down *my* air conditioner, or turning the lights out for five minutes when I leave the room, or fixing that leaky faucet can't do *me* any good. Mine is an infinitesimal part of the demand for water and electricity, and while the minute difference that I can make is multiplied by the number of people to whom it can make a difference, the effect on me of what I do is truly negligible.

Within the family we can save hot water on Friday night by taking brief showers rather than racing to be first in the shower and use it all up. But that may be because within the family we care about each other, or have to pretend we do, or can watch each other and have to account for the time we stand enjoying the hot water. It is a little harder to care about, or to be brought to account by, the people who can wash their cars more effectively if I let my lawn burn, or who can keep their lawns greener if I leave my car dirty.

THE SOCIAL CONTRACT

What we need in these circumstances is an enforceable social contract. I'll cooperate if you and everybody else will; I'm better off if we all cooperate than if we all go our separate ways. In matters of great virtue and symbolism, especially in emergencies, we may all become imbued with a sense of solidarity, and abide by a golden rule. We identify with the group, and we act as we believe or hope or wish to be the way that everybody acts. We enjoy rising to the occasion, rewarded by a sense of virtue and community. And indeed a good deal of social ethics is concerned with rules of behavior that are collectively rewarding if collectively obeyed (even though the individual may not benefit from his own participation). But if there is nothing heroic in the occasion; if what is required is a protracted nuisance; if one feels no particular community with great numbers of people who have nothing in common but connected water pipes; if one must continually decide what air-conditioned temperature to allow himself in his own bedroom, or whether to go outdoors and check the faucet once again; and especially if one suspects that large numbers of people just are not playing the game— most people may cooperate only halfheartedly, and many not at all. And then when they see the dribbling faucet from which the pressure is gone, or read that the electrical shortage is undiminished in spite of exhortations to turn off the air conditioners, even that grudging participation is likely to be abandoned.

The frustration is complete when a homeowner, stepping onto his back porch at night, cocks his head and hears the swish of invisible lawn sprinklers in the darkness up and down the block, and damns the lack of enforcement as he turns the handle on his own sprinkler, making it unanimous.

There is no inconsistency in what the man damned and what he did. He wants the ban enforced; but if it is not enforced he intends to water his lawn, especially if everybody else is doing it. He's *not* interested in doing minute favors for a multitude of individuals, most of whom he doesn't know, letting his lawn go to ruin; he *is* willing to enter a bargain, letting his lawn go to ruin if they will let theirs go the same way, so that they can all have unrestricted use of their showers, washing machines, toilets, and sinks. . . .

The trouble is often in making the bargain stick. Water meters capable of shifting gears at peak load times of day, with weekly water rates or water rations publicized through the summer, would undoubtedly take care of the problem. But fancy meters are expensive; fluctuating rates are a nuisance and hard to monitor; large families with lots of dirty clothes to wash will complain at the rates, while a childless couple can afford to wash its new car; and long before an acceptable "solution" has been devised and publicized, a wet, cold autumn ensues and the problem now is to devise a scheme of mandatory snow tires on select roads in time for that unexpected early snowstorm that snarls everything up because my car, skidding sideways on a hill, blocks your car and all the cars behind you. In waiting to get my snow tires at the after-Christmas sales, I was gambling *your* dinner hour against the price of *my* tires. . . .

Sometimes it won't work unless nearly everybody plays the game. Trash cans in our nation's capital say that "Every Litter Bit Hurts," but it is really the first litter bits that spoil a park or sidewalk. Ten times as much makes it worse, but not ten times worse. It takes only one power mower to turn a quiet Sunday morning into the neighborhood equivalent of a stamping mill; indeed, the speed with which a few timid homeowners light up their machines once the first brazen neighbor has shattered the quiet with his own 3-1/2 horsepower suggests that they expect no reproach once it's clear that it's beyond their power to provide a quiet Sunday by merely turning off one machine among several. . . .

There are the cases, though, in which not everybody gains under the social contract. Some gain more than others, and some not enough to compensate for what they give up. An agreement to turn off air conditioners, to make sure that electric lights and the more essential appliances can keep functioning, may be a bad bargain for the man with hay fever, who'd rather have a dry nose in darkness than sneeze with the lights on. A ban on outdoor uses of water may be a crude but acceptable bargain for most people, but not the man whose joy and pride is his garden. . . .

If participation requires unanimous consent, . . . it may be possible to compensate, . . . those to whom the advantages do not cover the costs. Compensation does complicate the arrangements, though, and when that man who loved his garden gets paid for seeing it wither, his neighbors may suddenly begin to discover how much they really loved their own gardens.

In economics the most familiar cases of this general phenomenon involve some resource or commodity that is scarce, inelastic in supply, but freely available to all comers until the supply has run out. Whales belong to no one until they are caught; they then belong to the people who catch them, who can sell them for money. If there is no limit on whaling and whalers, whaling activity will press on to the point where the sales price of whale products barely covers the cost of capture. But at that point nobody is benefiting from the abundant whales, because at this intensity of whaling, the whales are scarce. With rationing, a larger whale population might be harvested at smaller cost.

The most striking case may have been that of the buffalo, 20 or 30 million of whom roamed the plains west of the Mississippi at the end of the Civil War. As meat they were not marketable; rail transport of live animals had not reached the west. Their tongues were delicious and drew a high price, and for several years there was a thriving business in buffalo tongues, each of which left behind a thousand pounds of rotting meat. Then the hides became marketable and that was the end; 20 billion pounds of live meat was turned to rotting carcasses in the course of half a dozen years. Wagon trains detoured to avoid the stench of decaying buffaloes; and, roughly, for every five pounds of buffalo meat left on the ground, somebody got a penny for the hide. At any plausible interest rate the buffalo would have been worth more as live meat 15 years later, when marketing became feasible, but to the hunter who killed 50 a day for their hides, it was that or nothing now. There was no way that he could claim a cow and market his property right in her offspring 15 years later.

Whales and electricity, buffaloes and the water supply: scarce to the community but "free" to the individual as long as they last. In the small the same phenomenon occurs when half a dozen businessmen tell the waiter to put it all on a single check; why save $1.80 for the group by having hamburger, when the steak costs the man who orders it only 30 cents more? People drink more at a party where the drinks are free and everybody is assessed his fraction of the total cost afterward; it's a great way to get people to drink more than they can afford, and conviviality may recommend it, but the manager of a club would have to be out of his mind to propose that each month's long-distance telephone bill be merely divided equally among all the members.

THE CROWDED COMMONS

Congestion is what we call it when we'd rather swim in that water than sprinkle it on our lawns. A beach can be so crowded that we wonder whether the people can actually be enjoying themselves. They might not be there if they weren't, but that does not mean they are enjoying it *much*. And some find the beach so crowded that they'd be happier not to have come.

Economics illustrates congestion by the example of a road through the wilderness. Before the road, everybody who traveled made his way across the countryside. The new road is supremely attractive but lacks the capacity to accommodate everyone who wishes to use it. People flock to the road until traffic density reduces the attractiveness of the road to a point where people are indifferent between the old way, overland, and the new way, crammed together on a congested road. As long as the road is *any* better than the countryside, people will abandon the old way and join the crowd on the road. When the two modes of travel are just equalized, the smooth, dry surface and the moderate grades of the road being offset by overcrowding, the system will have reached "equilibrium." And what an equilibrium it is! Everyone using the road might as well, or almost as well for all he enjoys it, be picking his way through the wilderness.

With less traffic the value could have been substantial for those who got to use it. Making it freely available means that anyone who might have been excluded, under a scheme to limit the traffic, becomes privileged to share a useless asset rather than to envy the few who share a valuable one.

Traditionally this problem has been associated with common grazing grounds. If everyone has the right to graze his cattle on the common, and the common is small compared with the alternative forage available, the common will be crowded with cattle to the point where it no longer offers any advantage because so much grass is trampled, and the shares per cow are so small, that it is barely worth the daily round trip.

We can call this a shortage of grass or, alternatively, a congestion of cattle. The latter formulation has advantages. It is often the case with congestion that the scarce capacity is so misused by overcrowding that much of the value dissipates, perhaps all of it. And the term "congestion" reminds us that people who crowd each other in sharing some facility often impinge on each other in many ways, not alone in competing to consume the facility that attracted them. People using an overloaded switchboard not only complete fewer calls than they would like but spend time dialing busy signals or waiting for calls that cannot come in; and urgent calls often await the leisurely completion of idle conversations by callers who, once they get on the line, have it as long as they choose to keep it but know they cannot readily get it back.

The cattle on the common have their counterpart in the natural behavior of some species of wildlife. While some animal populations have apparently developed social practices that restrict population size relative to available food, others tend, when food supply is above the bare minimum for survival, to produce enough offspring to keep the numbers of mouths and stomachs increasing until the food supply, once able to sustain reproductive growth, just sustains survival. This is the tendency Thomas Malthus ascribed to the human race.

And indeed, as Garrett Hardin has recently pointed out, the earth itself, though compartmented against migration, is like an immense commons for whose husbandry no one is responsible. Individually and collectively we can deprecate an American population of 300 million by the end of the century, but we should probably not expect many mothers and fathers who want three or four children to stop at two (or who want one or two to do without, or who want five or six to stop at three or four) to help reduce the crowding for the other 299-odd million with whom their grandchildren will have to share the ground, the air, and the sunshine. . . .

THE DARK SIDE OF PLENTY

Pollution is a little like congestion: It is what you tend to have when there are too many people around, doing what people do—burning trash or gasoline, breathing, flushing toilets, doing their own laundry or sending it out, killing bugs, heating water to make steam and cooling steam to make a vacuum, and generally overusing that great heritage of natural disposal and dispersal systems, wind and running water. Unlike congestion, pollution rarely represents too much of a good thing. Not even the most frustrated librarian prefers to have no one ever read his books, but he may wish that none of his readers smoked.

Still, though a little pollution is rarely a good thing, there are kinds that are not bothersome until they reach some critical density. That may be why some problems of pollution were barely recognized as problems before they became intolerable or, worse, beyond remedy. . . .

In earlier times it was easy to believe that dirty streets, foul air, bad sanitation, and heaps of refuse were, like the other burdens and privations of life, transient manifestations of a standard of living that would eventually be superseded by greater wealth, ever-increasing productivity, and the ineluctable promotion of most people to income levels that were earlier enjoyed by only the few—income levels at which one could buy a clean environment or escape from a dirty one if he chose to spend his money that way. Now people are beginning to doubt it. Pollution, litter, noise, wastes, and unsightliness are being recognized as by-products of the very processes that were expected to bring about their abatement. We cannot leave the trash behind if we have no place to go. We cannot together get rid of it by dumping it in each other's neighborhoods. (It used to be said that we could not all get rich by taking in each other's wash; now it looks as though we cannot even get clean that way, detergents having become the newest kind of dirt.) We cool and clean the air with electricity, making rivers tepid and dirtying air with smoke in the process. And those of us old enough to remember when you could barely hear the music for the static on the radio have seen fidelity lose the race against energy, and nowadays cannot hear the music for the other fellow's radio. . . .

This idea that virtue brings its own penalty, that soap is its own kind of dirt, that goods are not consumed but merely converted into bads, and that we cannot forever dispose of waste over the back fence because someone lives there, does not mean that we have an unsolvable problem—just that we have a problem. It is disappointing to discover that material progress comes at a price; but the high price may be less the ineluctable concomitant of material progress than of social institutions that evolved before we were powerful enough to endanger our environment permanently. Our institutions developed when the problem was a scarcity of goods, not a plethora of bads. For most people that is still the problem. . . .

THE WORST THINGS IN LIFE ARE FREE

A history of economic institutions might be written as a history of property rights. Scarce resources have to be husbanded, crops have to be planted and herds accumulated, roads built and canals dug; people must be induced to come within reach of each other to exchange commodities, and the two sides to an exchange have to be separated in time by some recognition of debt or obligation. Johnny Appleseed left a legacy for strangers to enjoy in a later generation, and on the Appalachian Trail campers may leave kindling behind in return for what they found waiting; but in most human cultures people will not cultivate crops without a claim to the harvest, build houses that they can be crowded out of, or carry goods to market that will be pounced on as free for the taking. Seal cubs today like the buffalo a hundred years ago are a property that nobody owns, and if nobody owns it, anybody owns it.

But throughout most of history it has been the supply of *goods* that has been inelastic, not the supply of *bads*. True, vandalism has been made illegal (when it involves physical contact), and an elaborate law of torts has been developed for the cases in which one person can identify another who has done him harm. There are some property rights in God's bounty, but they are not well developed. (Some English buildings have "ancient lights" —access to the sky that may not be obstructed—and governments do ration radio frequencies.) But for the most part our institutions were developed to *help* us keep things, not to *make* us keep them; to economize scarce goods, not to suppress the bads; to keep others from removing what we wanted, not from leaving behind what they were through with. Medicines are proprietary, btu germs are free; I own the tobacco that I plant in my field, but you may have the smoke free of charge. I can have you arrested if you steal my electric amplifier, but help yourself to the noise.

There are two inadequacies in our inherited

institutions. First, though some among us care about the nuisances they generate, they do not *have* to care, because they are not accountable. If you leave your engine running, you pay for the gasoline but not for the exhaust. And, second, even if we care we may have no way of *knowing*. The hostess will occasionally tell me that my cigar is bothering another passenger; but I truly do not know how much my son's use of penicillin contributes to the evolution of penicillin-resistant bacilli.

We are going to need some new accounting systems. We are going to need ways of measuring the bads and comparing them with the goods. We are going to need ways to make people both *know* and *care* about the nuisances they commit, and not merely care in being concerned, but care in a way that guides them in a multitude of actions that are neither wholly bad nor wholly good. . . .

SORTING AND SCRAMBLING

Minor-league players at Dodgertown—the place where Dodger-affiliated clubs train in the spring—are served cafeteria-style. "A boy takes the first seat available," according to the general manager. "This has been done deliberately. If a white boy doesn't want to eat with a colored boy, he can go out and buy his own food. We haven't had any trouble."

Major-league players are not assigned seats and, though mixed tables are not rare, they are not the rule either. If we suppose that major- and minor-league racial attitudes are not strikingly different, we may conclude that racial preference in the dining hall is positive but less than the price of the nearest meal. Actually, though, there must be an alternative: Whites and Blacks in like-colored clusters can *enter* the line together and, once they have their trays, innocently take the next seats alongside each other. Evidently they don't; if they did, some scrambling system would have had to be invented. Maybe we conclude, then, that the racial preferences, though enough to make separate eating the general rule, are not strong enough to induce the slight trouble of picking partners before getting food. Or per-

haps we conclude that players lack the strategic foresight to beat the cafeteria line as a seat-scrambling device.

But even a minor-league player knows how to think ahead a couple of outs in deciding whether a sacrifice fly will advance the ball team. It is hard to believe that if a couple of players wanted to sit together it would not occur to them to meet at the beginning of the line, and the principle extends easily to segregation by color.

We are left with some alternative hypotheses. One is that players are relieved to have an excuse to sit without regard to color, and cafeteria-line scrambling relieves them of an embarrassing choice. Another, consistent with that one, is that most players can ignore, or accept, or even prefer, mixed tables but become uncomfortable or self-conscious, or think that others are uncomfortable or self-conscious, when the mixture is lopsided. Joining a table with Blacks and Whites is a casual thing, but being the seventh at a table with six players of opposite color, or the eighth where the ratio is six to one, imposes a threshold of self-consciousness that spoils the easy atmosphere and can lead to complete and sustained separation.

Middle class hostesses are familiar with the problem. Men and women mix nicely at stand-up parties until, partly at random and partly because a few men or women get stuck in a specialized conversation, some clusters form that are nearly all male or all female; and selective migration leads to the cocktail-party equivalent of the Dodgertown major-league dining hall. Hostesses, too, have their equivalent of the cafeteria-line rule: they alternate sexes at the dinner table, grasp people by the elbows and move them around the living room, or bring in coffee and make people serve themselves to disturb the pattern.

Sometimes the problem is the other way around. It is usually good to segregate smokers from nonsmokers in trains and planes and other enclosed public places; swimmers and surfers should be segregated in the interest of safety; and an attempt is made to keep slow-moving vehicles in the right-hand lane of traffic. Many of these dichotomous groupings are asymmetrical: Cigar smokers are rarely bothered by people who merely breathe; the surfer dislikes having his board hit anybody in the head, but there is somebody else who dislikes it much more; and the driver of a slow truck passing a slower one on a long grade is less conscious of who is behind him than the man behind is of the truck in front. . . .

These several processes of separation, segregation, sharing, mixing, dispersal—sometimes even pursuit—have a feature in common. The consequences are aggregate, but the decisions are exceedingly individual. The same is true, say, of marriage: hardly anyone picks a spouse according to a genetic plan, but because marital pairing is nonrandom, linguistic and cultural patterns persist. The family swimmer who avoids the part of the beach where the surfers are clustered, and the surfer who congregates where the surfboards are, are reacting individually to an environment that consists mainly of other individuals who are reacting likewise. The results can be unintended, even unnoticed. Nonsmokers may concentrate in the least smoky railroad car; as that car becomes crowded, smokers, choosing less crowded cars, find themselves among smokers, whether they notice it or not, and less dense, whether they appreciate it or not. . . .

The more crucial phenomena are, of course, residential decisions and others, like occupational choice, intercity migration, schools and churches, where the separating and mixing involve lasting associations that matter. The minor-league players who eat lunch at Dodgertown have no cafeteria line to scramble their home addresses; and even if they were located at random, they would usually not be casually integrated, because mixed residential areas are few and the choice, for a Black or for a White, is between living among Blacks or living among Whites—unless even that choice is constrained.

It is not easy to tell from the gross aggregate phenomenon just what the motives are behind the individual decisions, or how strong they are. The smoker on an airplane may not even know that the person in front of him is sensitive to tobacco smoke; the water skier might be willing to stay 400 yards off shore if doing so didn't just leave a preferred strip to other skiers. The clustered men and women at that cocktail party may be awfully bored and wish the hostess could shake things up, but without organization no one can do any good by himself. And people who are happy to belong to a club or to work where both English and French are spoken may find it uncomfortable if their own language falls to extreme minority status; and by withdrawing they will aggravate the situation that induced them to withdraw.

People who have to choose between polarized extremes—a White neighborhood or a Black, a French-speaking club or one where English alone is spoken, a school with few Whites or one with few Blacks—will often choose the way that reinforces the polarization. Doing so is no evidence that they prefer segregation, only that, if segregation exists and they have to choose between exclusive associations, people elect like rather than unlike environments. . . .

Arithmetic plays a role. . . . If Blacks are willing to be the minority but not smaller than one quarter, and Whites willing to mix equally but not in minority status, the limits are 3:1 and 1:1; and in a population 90 percent White, two-thirds of the Whites have to stay apart or they swamp the whole arrangement.

The dynamics are not always transparent to cursory analysis. There are chain reactions, exaggerated perceptions, lagged responses, speculation on the future, and organized efforts that may succeed or fail. Three people may break leases and move out of an apartment without being noticed, but if they do it the same week somebody notices and comments, alerting the residents to whether the Whites or the Blacks or the elderly, or the families with children or the families without, are moving away to avoid minority status and generating as they do the situation they thought they foresaw.

Some of the processes may be passive, systemic, unmotivated but nevertheless biased. If job vacancies are filled by word of mouth or apartments go to people who have acquaintances in the building, and if boys can marry only girls they know and can know only girls who speak their language, a biased communication system will preserve and enhance the prevailing homogeneities.

AN EXPERIMENT

Some vivid dynamics can be generated by any reader with a half-hour to spare, a roll of pennies and a roll of dimes, a tabletop, a large sheet of paper and a spirit of scientific inquiry or, lacking that spirit, a fondness for games.

Get a roll of pennies, a roll of dimes, a ruled sheet of paper divided into 1-inch squares, preferably at least the size of a checkerboard (64 squares in 8 rows and 8 columns), and find some device for selecting squares at random. We place dimes and pennies on some of the squares, and suppose them to represent the members of two homogeneous groups—men and women, Blacks and Whites, French-speaking and English-speaking, officers and enlisted men, students and faculty, surfers and swimmers, the well dressed and the poorly dressed, or any other dichotomy that is exhaustive and recognizable. We can spread them at random or put them in contrived patterns. We can use equal numbers of dimes and pennies or let one be a minority. And we stipulate various rules for individual decision.

For example, we could postulate that every dime wants at least half its neighbors to be dimes, every penny wants a third of its neighbors to be pennies, and any dime or penny whose immediate neighborhood does not meet these conditions gets up and moves. Then by inspection we locate the ones that are due to move, move them, keep moving them if necessary and, when everybody on the board has settled down, look to see what pattern has emerged. (If the situation never "settles down," we look to see what kind of endless turbulence or cyclical activity our hypotheses have generated.)

Define each individual's neighborhood . . .

to be the 8 surrounding squares; he is the center of a 3 x 3 neighborhood. . . . If he is discontent with the color of his own neighborhood, he moves to the nearest empty square that meets his minimum demands. . . .

Let us start with equal numbers of dimes and pennies and suppose that the demands of both are "moderate"—that each wants something more than one-third neighbors like himself. The number of neighbors that a coin can have will be anywhere from zero to eight. We make the following specification of demands. If a person has one neighbor, he must be the same color; of two neighbors, one must be his color; of three, four, or five neighbors, two must be his color; and of six, seven, or eight neighbors, he wants at least three.

It is possible to form a pattern that is regularly "integrated," and in which everybody is satisfied. A simple alternating pattern does it (Fig. 33.1), on condition that we take care of the corners.

Figure 33.1

No one can move, except to a corner because there are no other vacant cells; but no one wants to move. We now mix them up a little, and in the process empty some cells to make movement feasible.

There are 60 coins on the board. We remove 20, using a table of random digits; we then pick 5 empty squares at random and replace a dime or a penny with a 50/50 chance. The result is a board with 64 cells, 45 occupied and 19 blank. Forty individuals are just where they were before we removed 20 neighbors and added 5 new ones. The left side of Figure 33.2 shows one such result, generated by exactly this process. The #'s are

```
— # — # O # — O          — — — # — # — —
# # # O — O # O          — — — — — — — —
— # O — — # O #          — — — — — — — —
— O # O # O # O          — — # — # — # —
O O O # O O O —          — — — — — — — —
# — # # # — — O          # — — — — — — —
— # O # O # O —          — — O — O — O —
— O — O — — # —          — — — — — — — —
```

Figure 33.2

dimes and the O's are pennies; alternatively, the #'s speak French and the O's speak English, the #'s are Black and the O's are White, the #'s are boys and the O's are girls, or whatever you please.

The right side of Figure 33.2 identifies the individuals who are not content with their surrounding neighborhoods. Six #'s and three O's want to move; the rest are content as things stand. The pattern is still "integrated"; even the discontent are not without some neighbors like themselves, and few among the content are without neighbors of opposite color. The general pattern is not strongly segregated in appearance. One would be hard-put to block out #-neighborhoods or O-neighborhoods at this stage. (The upper left corner might be described as a #-neighborhood.) The problem is to satisfy a fraction (9 of 45) among the #'s and O's by letting them move somewhere among the 19 blank cells.

Anybody who moves leaves a blank cell that somebody can move into. Also, anybody who moves leaves behind a neighbor or two of his own color; and when he leaves a neighbor, his neighbor loses a neighbor and and may become discontent. Anyone who moves gains neighbors like himself, adding a neighbor like them to their neighborhood but also adding one of opposite color to the unlike neighbors he acquires. . . .

CHAIN REACTION

What is instructive is the "unraveling" process. Everybody who selects a new environment affects the environments of those he leaves and those he moves among. There

is a chain reaction. It may be quickly damped, with little motion, or it may go on and on and on with striking results. (The results of course are only suggestive, because few of us live in square cells on a checkerboard.)

One outcome for the situation depicted in Figure 33.2 is shown in Figure 33.3. It is "one outcome" because I have not explained exactly the order in which individuals moved. If the reader reproduces the experiment himself, he will get a slightly different configuration, but the general pattern will not be much different. Figure 33.4 is a replay from Figure 33.2, the only difference from Figure 33.3 being in the order of moves. It takes a few minutes to do the experiment again, and one quickly gets an impression of the kind of outcome to expect. Changing the neighborhood demands, or using twice as many dimes as pennies, will drastically affect the results; but for any given set of numbers and demands, the results are fairly stable.

All the people are content in Figures 33.3 and 33.4. And they are more segregated. This is more than just a visual impression; we can make a few comparisons. In Figure 33.2 the O's altogether had as many O's for

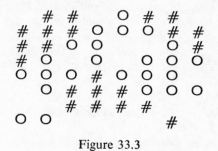

Figure 33.3

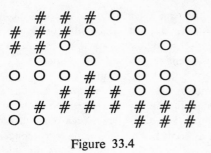

Figure 33.4

Figure 33.5

neighbors as they had #'s; some had more or less than the average, and 3 were discontent. For the #'s the ratio of #-neighbors to O-neighbors was 1:1, with a little colony of #'s in the upper left corner and 6 widely distributed discontents. After sorting themselves out in Figure 33.3, the average ratio of like to unlike neighbors for #'s and O's together was 2:3, more than double their original ratio and about triple the ratio that any individual demanded. Figure 33.4 is even more extreme. The ratio of like to unlike neighbors is 2:8, nearly triple the starting ratio and four times the minimum demanded.

Another comparison is the number who had no opposite neighbors in Figure 33.2. Three were in that condition before people started moving; in Figure 33.3 there are 8 without neighbors of opposite color, and in Figure 33.4 there are 14.

What can we conclude from an exercise like this? We may at least be able to disprove a few notions that are themselves based on reasoning no more complicated than the checkerboard. Propositions that begin, "It stands to reason that. . . ," can sometimes be discredited by exceedingly simple demonstrations that, though perhaps true, they do not exactly "stand to reason." We can at least persuade ourselves that certain mechanisms could work, and that observable aggregate phenomena could be compatible with types of "molecular movement" that do not closely resemble the aggregate outcomes that they determine. . . .

The reader might try guessing what set of individual preferences led from Figure 33.2 to the pattern in Figure 33.5.

The ratio of like to unlike neighbors for all the #'s and O's together is slightly more than 3 to 1; and 6 O's and 8 #'s have no neighbors of opposite color. The result is evidently segregation, but following a suggestion of my dictionary we might say that the process is one of *aggregation* because the rules of behavior ascribed both to #'s and to O's in Figure 33.5 were simply that each would move to acquire three neighbors of like color *irrespective of the presence or absence of neighbors of opposite color.* And correspondingly for O's. As an individual motivation this is quite different from the one that formed the patterns in Figures 33.3 and 33.4. But in the aggregate it may be hard to discern which motivation underlies the pattern and the process of segregated residence. And it may matter.

The first impact of a display like this on a reader may be—unless he finds it all "irrelevant"—discouragement. A moderate urge to avoid small-minority status may cause a nearly integrated pattern to unravel and highly segregated neighborhoods to form. . . . For those who deplore segregation, however, and especially for those who deplore more segregation than people were seeking when they collectively segregated themselves, there may be a note of hope. The underlying motivation can be far less extreme than the observable patterns of separation. What it takes to keep things from unraveling is to be learned from Figure 33.2; the later figures indicate only how hard it may be to restore such "integration" as would satisfy the individuals, once the process of separation has stabilized. In Figure 33.2 only 9 of the 45 individuals are motivated to move, and if we could persuade them to stay everybody else would be all right. Indeed, the reader might exercise his own ingenuity to discover how few individuals would need to be invited into Figure 33.2 from outside, or how few individuals would need to be relocated in Figure 33.2, to keep anybody from wanting to move. . . .

Biology and ecology are instructive. Biological evolution involves the responses of billions of individuals, each going about his own business, most of them—from the amoeba to the giraffe—without the slightest idea that they are engaged together in selective adaptation, separation of species, survival, and extinction. The results are statistical, collective, and aggregate; the process is molecular and individual. Minute shadings of advantage in survival and reproduction are statistically transformed into biological trends, as minute differences between the domestic and foreign price ratios of gold and silver could cause one metal or the other to disappear from circulation under bimetallism.

MICROMOTIVES AND MACROPHENOMENA

There is no specific alarmist point to all of this. The conclusion is not that cities will become ever more dense, races more separate, traffic more congested, food more contaminated, or whales extinct, or that typewriter keyboards will persist another century unchanged unless controls are ingeniously promulgated. The point is more general—that there is no universal teleology relating individual adaptations to collective results, neither a beneficent teleology nor a pernicious one.

Some adaptive processes work out fine and some do not. We expect competition in the prices of consumer goods to lead to some kind of market efficiency, but consumer competition in longer, heavier cars can be self-defeating. . . .

The fact that people voluntarily do something, or acquiesce in the consequences, does not mean that they like the results. Often the individual is not free to change the re-sult; he can change only his own position within it, and that does him no good. We might all be better off speaking Latin or using a different calendar, but nobody can do much about it by learning Latin or hanging a 13-month calendar on his wall. Nations may arm themselves with nuclear weapons while wishing the things had never been invented, just as someday citizens may carry concealed weapons in the belief that others do, wishing they had never been devised. The fact that I do not send a week's pay to the Department of the Treasury, requesting that it be used to subsidize development of external-combustion engines, does not mean that I want my congressman to vote against a program that, costing me a week's pay in taxes, may eventually make the sky bluer and the trees greener, and my eyes stop tearing long enough to enjoy both of them. . . .

We might also conclude that some severe problems result not from the evil of people but from their helplessness as individuals. This is not to say that there aren't callous, even malicious, noise and waste and vandalism, or that racial discrimination is not replete with behavior that is heartless, selfish, and illegal. But some is unwitting; some offers little choice; and some results from the magnification of small incentives into massive results. . . .

THE ROLES OF GOVERNMENT

Many of these inadequacies of the social decision process are expected to be remedied by government. The government is not only an ultimate authority, when compulsion or exclusiveness is required, it is also an instrument for initiative on a large or a monopolistic scale, and it is the address to which people send their complaints when they do not like the way their environment is shaping up. Sometimes the problem is solved without government, either through the market or through some nonmarket behavior or institutions, or at least the problem often seems solved. Commercially motivated contraceptives are helping to solve part of the population problem—the part over and above what remains when people individually have their way.

The range of techniques used by government is wide. It can simply signal, as with daylight saving or one-way street signs. It can regulate administratively, as with traffic police and safety inspectors. It can ration, as it does with fish and game, sometimes water and electricity or emergency rations. It can charge user fees, as with turnpikes and parking meters. It can facilitate legal arrangements, as with patents and copyrights and franchises for pay television. It can flatly prohibit, as with explosives in automobile tunnels, though sometimes the prohibition is enforced by a penalty that is more like a contingent fee on getting caught. A government can sometimes command, as with vaccination or, in some cities, the mandatory shoveling of sidewalks by the people who live along them. . . .

PRESCRIPTION, PROSCRIPTION, OR PRICES

One of the main divisions among governmental techniques—and one of the main controversies about government controls—is between making people pay for the things that they do that affect others, allowing them to go ahead and do it if the price is right, and simply stipulating what they should do and not do, with appropriate inspections and penalties for violations. We let people pay to use the scarce turnpike capacity; should we make them pay for the smoke they then emit? Should people be rewarded for recycling their refuse into harmless uses, or penalized for refusing to do so? . . .

Distributing scarce goods that have been constructed at public expense is commonly done by letting people pay for their use, if use can indeed be "sold" (as it usually cannot be with ordinary city streets). When we turn to the disposal of bads rather than the consumption of goods, it often seems a little anomalous to introduce the price system and to let people pay for the privilege of doing us harm. Especially if everyone prefers an absolute ban on the burning of trash to unrestricted burning, and we can get unanimous agreement on an ordinance, why backslide into "just a little burning" by those who can pay for it? And even if a few people would prefer unrestricted burning to an absolute prohibition, must a large majority of the rest of us defer to them and let them throw smoke into our atmosphere, legitimizing the whole arrangement by selling them permission?

The turnpike example can help a little in sorting out some of the issues. First, if the wind and the air have a certain capacity to dissipate smoke, or a river can digest a certain amount of sewage, up to some point at which further smoke or further sewage sharply worsens things, it may not make sense to let that capacity go unused. Letting those who have the most urgent needs sort themselves out by paying the price may not be a bad way of rationing this scarce capacity.

Second, if everybody has some urgent need but people have different urgencies, and if the object is to let everyone take care of his urgent needs but stop when the degree of urgency reaches some point, a price on the activity may not be a bad way of letting everybody decide for himself how urgent his need is. (Again, the system discriminates in favor of the rich only if it turns out that it's the rich who pay the price and if the proceeds are not used in an equitable way.) . . .

Prices convey *information* as well as *incentive*. Even the virtuous who want to do their part or to take only their rightful share need some signal, some measure, some way to gauge the seriousness of what they are doing to "them" out "there" when the problem is not just distinguishing right from wrong but knowing whose turn it is, or how much is one's share, or at what point the inconvenience of others outweighs one's own needs. Because the road to hell is alleged to be paved with good intentions—and this essay tries to give added reasons for believing that is so—road signs are critical. . . .

Allowing people to pay for the nuisances they create means compromise, of course.

Compromise means abandoning the goal of total victory in the war against poison, dirt, noise and unsightliness. . . . We have to pay a price for victory, and we usually have to pay it in the same currency in which we enjoy it. A good many bads are merely the reverse side of some goods, and the ratio of bad to good depends on the particular uses and beneficiaries and victims. DDT kills bedbugs and malarial mosquitoes and makes food cheaper, besides doing all those things that have recently been publicized; the most offending exhaust pipes are usually on the older cars and are owned by the poor; no-return bottles litter the countryside and fill the trash heaps, but returnable bottles contain remnants of stale beer and cola and draw flies while concentrating a lesser amount of "trash" where it matters more, in the store-fronts and on longer distance truck routes. . . .

Putting a price on pollution may be merely a complicated way of prohibiting it, or may be a way of legitimizing it. But it may also be a way of screening out the less essential or less worthwhile activities that harm the rest of us while permitting continuation of those that are comparatively beneficial. It may also be a way of collecting a kitty that, properly used, may be worth more to a good many among us than blue skies and water sports.

Prices, though, or fees or charges or property rights, are pertinent to only some of these problems, not nearly to all of them. We usually do not want to legitimize criminal activity by charging a "fee" rather than imposing a "fine." . . .

And some things are hard to price. Noise is one. Someday they may charge us for the liquids that leave our houses in pipes as well as the liquids that arrive in pipes. They may charge us for the special privilege of burning more gas than it takes to move our comparatively light bodies to and from work. We can quiet the factory whistles and prohibit billboards. But as people we can go on being as offensive as we please, forgetting to turn down our radios, being unsightly, spreading our germs, and throwing lighted cigarettes out car windows during a drought. Ships at sea may go on flushing their bowels in the ocean at night like undisciplined children at a municipal pond. And public unfriendliness may feed on itself in spite of ordinances against our expressions and gestures.

MORALITY AND THE COLLECTIVE GOOD

In the end, personal morality is a public asset; there is not much else to keep us from throwing bottles out our car windows, but we can wish that our nervous systems had been programmed through biological evolution to inhibit those actions that bring us mild individual gains at each other's expense. Virtue may be its own reward, but the reward is too often a collective good, shared only minutely by the virtuous individual.

Some animals have it, according to Konrad Lorenz. As animal life becomes complex, the young need to grow and are vulnerable. An incipient maternal instinct, however acquired, promotes the species in which it occurs. Something in a wolf cub causes him to roll onto his back when a hostile adult comes near, and something in the adult makes him incapable—his nervous system is just not programmed for it—of attacking the helpless cub that waves its feet in the air. The adult wolf is lucky to be so inhibited; he would never himself have survived as a cub were the inhibition not universal, or worse, his species would have been extinct long before it was his turn to be repelled by the sight and smell of a groveling cub.

But in many ways we poor humans have outgrown our biological heritage. Long before technology afforded us wealth, before refrigeration kept our food from spoiling, before we learned to protect herds of animals and to cultivate a year's supply of grain in a single season, there was no way to save but by putting fat under our skin. Along with others in the animal kingdom we developed that marvelous capacity to store surplus food in our very bodies, lugging it around wherever we went but keeping it fresh and alive in the process. And appetites evolved that were superfluous to the day's needs, so that without knowing it we added to our own bodies the flesh of fruits and animals. Those appetites can still give us pleasure, but that marvelous fatty stuff is about as useful as two tons of coal in the basement left over from the wartime shortages, and twice as disagreeable.

And so it is with our appetite for reproduction, not just the enjoyment of a partner but the delight in small children and even an inherited culture that values the immortality and the pride of creation that only children can give us.

God made the earth too small, it seems today. But in the blink of a cosmic eye an earth a hundred times as big would be too small too soon. The arithmetic is staggering. We can double more than twice every century, and in fewer years than have elapsed since Magna Charta we should all be able to inhabit dry land only on condition that no one try to sit down. Sooner or later it will be too much.

But when it becomes too much for us as individuals, we shall have gone too far. When sheer numbers make it no longer a joy to bring children into the world, our earth will have become that congested road through the wilderness that is just as attractive as no road at all. Up until that point it is always worth my while to add my car to the traffic.

The population problem is not unique. In the relation of molecular incentives to molar results, it is like dozens of familiar and tantalizing problems, of which this essay has been full of examples. It is uniquely important. And it may be uniquely difficult. As in the cars that passed that mattress on a holiday weekend, it is hard to reach a bargain with the generations that follow.

34. INEQUALITY, AFFLUENCE, AND ENVIRONMENTAL PROBLEMS

BARRY COMMONER

Reprinted from "The Social Issues," The Closing Circle: Nature, Man, and Technology (New York: Knopf, 1972). Copyright © 1971 by Barry Commoner. All rights reserved under International and Pan-American copyright conventions. Reprinted by permission of Alfred A. Knopf, Inc. Barry Commoner is Professor and Director of the Center for the Biology of Natural Systems at Washington University, St. Louis. He has been in the forefront of environmental discussion for two decades, first in connection with problems of nuclear fallout and later concerning the issues dealt with in this selection.

■ Along with the liberation and peace movements of the 1960s that urged a rethinking of America's role in the world, a third issue arose to vex the establishment and perplex everyone else. The environmental problem, the issue of "ecology," which earlier had been the interest of a few scientists (commonly considered crackpots, or at the very least persons given to fantastic exaggeration), became a broad-based issue of the quality of life, even of the continued existence of life.

The issue entered general public consciousness first through concern with air pollution. Los Angeles has long worried about its smog, but gradually people have learned that every major city has dangerously high levels of pollutants in the air. In some cities nylon hose disintegrates from pollutants ejected from nearby factories. Temperature inversions have produced smog so heavy that from time to time old people have died. Water pollution also has aroused public concern—Lake Erie is said to be biologically dead, Lake Michigan fast becoming so, and comedians joke about the difficult life of a fish in the Hudson River. Surely the environmental issue is a preeminent example of Schelling's model of individual choices and collective results.

Barry Commoner, a botanist, was an early leader among scientists in the environmental movement. In the 1950s he and fellow workers in a loose coalition of concerned scientists drew the nation's attention to nuclear fallout, the most lethal kind of pollution. After the nuclear test ban treaty they turned their attention to the broader issues of environmental degradation.

Clearly, the causes of the environmental crisis must be adequately understood to effect a cure, but the crisis has so rapidly become one of public concern and debate that the demand for knowledge now is beyond the ability of science to deliver. Thus Commoner observes that the environmental crisis is blamed on everything from rising population to affluence to "man's innate aggressiveness" to religion to technology to capitalism. The solutions range equally from abolishing capitalism to taxing those who pollute to riding bicycles and eating organic bread.

Commoner, however, finds the problem in a much more mundane location. While affluence and population growth certainly place a greater burden on the environment, he believes this burden would have been easily manageable were it not for technological developments in industry in the post-World War II period. The major causes lie in agricultural production, which is now dependent on nitrogen fertilizers and pesticides; in laundry which is now dependent on phosphates; in automobiles, which now produce great quantities of lead and nitrogen oxide; and in the proliferation of containers, from aerosol cans and beer bottles to nondegradable plastics.

Commoner's research indicates that when these factors are taken into account less than one-fourth of the increase in pollution since World War II can be attributed to population growth and increased affluence, and as much as three-fourths to the shift to what he calls "counter ecological" productive technologies. In what ways are patterns of inequality implicated in the environmental crisis, and in what ways will efforts toward solving that crisis affect issues of equity and be affected by such issues? Commoner's reference point for dealing with these problems is the social issues and economic meanings of a saner ecology.

Some of the crucial concerns about resources and distribution related to the environmental issue are dealt with in William Nordhaus and James Tobin, *Is Growth Obsolete?*, Cowles Discussion Paper no. 319, Yale University, 1971. An approach to an accounting of the impact of society on the environment is found in Alan V. Kneese, Robert U. Ayres, and Ralph C. D'Arge, *Economics and the Environment: A Materials Balance Approach* (Resources for the Future, Inc., 1970). A useful collection of social and physical science discussions of ecological issues *Environmental Quality and Social Responsibility*, ed. R. S. Kahre, J. W. Kolka, and C. A. Pollis (University of Wisconsin—Green Bay, 1972). ∎

IN MODERN INDUSTRIAL SOCIETIES the most important link between society and the ecosystem on which it depends is technology. There is considerable evidence that many of the new technologies which now dominate production in an advanced country such as the United States are in conflict with the ecosystem. They therefore degrade the environment. How can we account for this fault in modern technology? . . .

Reductionism [in science] has . . . tended to isolate scientific disciplines from the problems that affect the human condition. Such problems, environmental degradation for example, involve inherently complex systems. Life, as we live it, is not encompassed by a single academic discipline. Real problems that touch our lives and impinge on what we value rarely fit into the neat categories of the college catalog, such as physical chemistry, nuclear physics, or molecular biology.

For example, to encompass in our minds the terrifying deterioration of our cities, we need to know not only the principles of economics, architecture, and social planning, but also the physics and chemistry of the air, the biology of water systems, and the ecology of the domestic rat and the cockroach. In a word, we need to understand science and technology that is *relevant* to the human condition.

However, we in the scientific community have been brought up in a different tradition. We have a justified pride in our intellectual independence and know—for we often have to battle to maintain it—how essential this independence is to the search for truth. But scientists may sometimes tend to translate intellectual independence into a kind of mandatory avoidance of all problems that do not arise in their own minds—an approach that may cut them off from the real and urgent needs of society, and often from their students as well. As a result, science has become too isolated from the real problems of the world and a poor instrument for understanding the threats to its survival.

In sum, we can trace the origin of the environmental crisis through the following sequence. Environmental degradation largely results from the introduction of new industrial and agricultural production technologies. These technologies are ecologically faulty because they are designed to solve singular, separate problems and fail to take into account the inevitable "side effects" that arise because, in nature, no part is isolated from the whole ecological fabric. In turn, the fragmented design of technology reflects its scientific foundation, for science is divided into disciplines that are largely governed by the notion that complex systems can be understood only if they are first broken into their separate component parts. This reductionist bias has also tended to shield basic science from a concern for real-life problems, such as environmental degradation.

The isolation of science from such practical problems has another unfortunate consequence. Most people are less interested in the discipline of science than they are in its practical effects on their daily lives. And the separation between science and the problems that concern people has tended to limit what most people know about the scientific background of environmental issues. Yet such *public* knowledge is essential to the solution of every environmental problem. For these depend not only on scientific data, but ultimately on a public judgment which balances the benefits to be gained from a particular technology against the associated environmental hazards.

In effect, the citizen faces an important

question about modern technology: does it pay? Whether we ask this in the direct language of profit and loss or in the more abstract language of social welfare, the question is crucial. Sooner or later, every human endeavor—if it is to continue—must pass this simple test: is it worth what it costs?

It might appear that for most environmental issues this question has already been answered. After all, power companies seem eager to build plants for nuclear fuels rather than fossil ones and farmers rapidly adopt new insecticides and fertilizers. Apparently their cost accounting tells them that the new technologies yield the best available margin between income and costs. The environmental crisis tells us, however, that these calculations are not complete—that certain costs have not yet been taken into account.

For example, what are the true costs of operating a coal-fired power plant in an urban area? The obvious costs—capital outlay, maintenance, operating costs, taxes—are of course well known. But we have recently discovered that there are other costs and have even begun to put a dollar value upon them.

We now know that a coal-burning power plant produces not only electricity but also a number of less desirable things: smoke and soot, oxides of sulfur and nitrogen, carbon dioxide, a variety of organic compounds, and heat. Each of these is a nongood and costs someone something. Smoke and soot increase the householder's laundry and cleaning bills; oxides of sulfur increase the cost of building maintenance; for organic pollutants we pay the price—not only in dollars, but in human anguish—of some number of cases of lung cancer.

Some of these costs can be converted to dollar values. The United States Public Health Service estimates the overall cost of air pollution at about $60 per person per year. About one third of urban air pollution is due to power production from fossil fuels, representing about $20 per person per year. This means that we must add to the cost of power production, for each urban family of 4, about $80 per year—an appreciable sum relative to the annual bill for electricity.

The point of this calculation is obvious. The *hidden* costs of power production, such as air pollution, are *social* costs; they are met not by a single producer but by the *public*. To discover the true cost of the many benefits of modern technology, we need to look for, and evaluate, all the hidden social costs represented by environmental pollution.

Every environmental decision therefore involves a balance between benefits and hazards. . . . For any effort to reduce an environmental hazard will compete with the benefits available from the technological process that produces it. If radiation emission standards are made more rigorous, the health hazard from nuclear power operations could be reduced, but the added expense of achieving them would increase the cost of power and might render the nuclear industry incapable of competing with fossil-fuel power plants. This would severely curtail a major federally financed technological program and raise serious political issues. Similarly, it would be possible to reduce nitrate pollution from feedlots by returning the wastes to the land, where in nature they belong. But this would reduce the economy of the feedlot operation. Organic fertilizers could be reintroduced in place of inorganic nitrogen fertilizer in order to reduce the environmental hazard of excess nitrate in surface waters; but since inorganic fertilizers are cheaper to buy and to spread, crop production costs would rise. Urban pollution involves many cost/benefit decisions. For example, smog levels cannot be reduced without supplanting urban automotive traffic with electric-powered mass transit systems, or possibly by introducing new types of vehicles. The first of these actions would impose a massive economic burden on cities that are already unable to meet their social obligations; the second course would mean a serious disruption of one of the mainstays of our economy, the automobile industry. In the same way, the government's decision in 1970 to close the biological warfare arsenal at Pine Bluff, Arkansas, was protested by the local chamber of commerce, which expressed a readiness to accept the possible environmental hazard—and to enjoy the benefits of the 200 jobs associated with the arsenal—for the sake of "deterring" an enemy with the threat of bacterial attack.

We come then to a crucial question: who is to be the Solomon of modern technology and weigh in the balance all the good that comes of it against the ecological, social costs? Or, who will strike the balance between the concern of the prudent manager of a nuclear power plant for economy and the concern of a mother over the health of her child?

Confronted by decisions on nuclear power, radiation, nitrate levels, photochemical smog, bacterial warfare, and all the other technicalities of environmental problems, it is tempting to call in the scientific expert. Scientists can, of course, evaluate the relevant benefits: how many kilowatt hours of electricity a nuclear power plant can deliver and at what price, or the yield of corn to be expected from nitrogen fertilizer. They can also evaluate the related risks: the radiation dose to people in the vicinity of the power plant and the hazard to infants from nitrate levels exacerbated by fertilizers. These evaluations can be derived from appropriate scientific theories, principles, and data.

However, no scientific principle can guide the choice between some number of kilowatt hours of electric power and some number of cases of thyroid cancer, or between some number of bushels of corn and some number of cases of infant methemoglobinemia. These are *value* judgments; they are determined not by scientific principle but by the value that we place on economic advantage and on human life or by our belief in the wisdom of committing the nation to mass transportation or to biological warfare. These are matters of morality, of social and political judgment. In a democracy they belong not in the hands of "experts" but in the hands of the people and their elected representatives.

The environmental crisis is the legacy of our unwitting assault on the natural systems that support us. It represents hidden costs that are mounting toward catastrophe. If it is to be resolved, these costs must be made explicit and balanced against the benefits of technology in open, public debate. But this debate

will not come easily. For the public has little access to the necessary scientific data. Much of the needed information has been, and remains, wrapped in government and industrial secrecy. Unearthing the needed information and disseminating it to the public is, I believe, the unique responsibility of the scientific community. For to exercise its right of conscience, the public must have the relevant scientific facts in understandable terms. As the custodians of this knowledge, we in the scientific community owe it to our fellow citizens to help inform them about the crisis in the environment.

This partnership between scientist and citizen is, I believe, the clue to the remarkable upsurge of public action on environmental issues that we have witnessed in the United States in recent years. Here are some examples.

1. The Limited Nuclear Test Ban Treaty of 1963, a major reversal of United States foreign policy, is perhaps the first of the great ecological victories achieved by the partnership between the American public and the scientific community. For nearly a decade after Hiroshima, while the United States, the USSR, and Great Britain rapidly developed and tested nuclear weapons, the American public was kept in ignorance of the crucial environmental facts. No one knew that every explosion produced massive amounts of strontium 90 and other radioisotopes; that strontium 90 would be carried through the food chain and lodge in the developing bones of children; that *any* increase in radioactive exposure increases the risk of cancer and other radiation hazards. Rigid secrecy kept these facts from the public; the American people were paying the biological price of nuclear tests not even knowing that it had been asked of them.

However, beginning in about 1953, the independent scientific community began to agitate for the release of government-held data on fallout. By 1956 sufficient information had been released to provide scientists with an effective understanding of what was happening. At this point, led by Linus Pauling, scientists, first in the United States and later throughout the world, appealed through a petition for action to halt nuclear tests and the spread of fallout. This appeal brought no immediate action, but for the first time broad sections of the public began to understand the nuclear peril.

There then developed in the United States the scientists' information movement—the effort . . . of independent scientists organized in local committees under the aegis of the Scientists' Institute for Public Information to inform the public about the basic scientific facts on fallout. This campaign restored the missing element in the political process—the grist of data was supplied to the public conscience.

We have a fairly good historical record of the consequences. Previously unconcerned senators were moved to support the Nuclear Test Ban Treaty by a flood of passionate letters from parents who objected to raising their children on milk contaminated with strontium 90. The senators were not so much impressed that their constituents were irate (they are accustomed to that) but that they knew how to spell strontium 90! Presumably the prospect of facing not merely an irate voter but an informed one stirred them to action. Of course, there was also purely political pressure for the treaty; but that pressure succeeded, I am convinced, because it was armed—with the facts.

When the Test Ban Treaty was achieved, some observers expected scientists to lose interest in fallout. Instead, many of them saw that fallout was only part of a larger problem—the untoward environmental effects of modern technology—in which public education was also vital. It was at this point that the St. Louis Committee for Nuclear Information substituted "Environmental" for "Nuclear" in its name and converted its bulletin into the magazine now known as *Environment.*

2. A more recent example is the public victory over the Pentagon on the matter of disposal of nerve gas. For years a huge deadly supply of nerve gas was stored in tanks lying directly in the path of planes using the Denver airport. This menace went un-

noticed until scientists of the Colorado Committee for Environmental Information issued to the public a factual statement which pointed out that an unlucky plane crash might wipe out most of the Denver population. This, and other explanations by independent scientists in *Environment,* of how nerve gas had killed 6,000 sheep in Utah (a fact long denied by the Army) and the resultant public outcry, finally persuaded the government to remove the gas. On the advice of its experts, the army began to haul the gas by rail across the country in order to dump it in the Atlantic. At once scientists of the St. Louis Committee for Environmental Information pointed out the enormous risks involved in this procedure and showed that the material could be inactivated on the spot. Once more, the army's position was reversed. Curiously, the new decision to detoxify the material, like the earlier one to ship it, was also validated by the government's committees of experts. They corrected their initial mistake, and the government's policy was changed, but only after the relevant facts were unearthed by the scientific community—and brought to public attention.

3. For years the government spent billions of dollars and precious human resources on the development and production of biological weapons, only to abandon them not long ago when, despite the constraints of military secrecy, a few crucial facts about their uncontrollable dangers—if they were ever used—were brought home to the public by independent scientists: Matthew Meselson of Harvard, E. G. Pfeiffer of the University of Montana, Arthur Galston of Yale, and Victor Sidel of the Einstein Medical College, among others.

4. And what led to the recent government decision to halt the spread of DDT in the environment? Surely not the advice of industrial experts, who, along with many government advisers, for many years spoke only of the advantages of this insecticide. No, it was Rachel Carson who calmly and courageously unearthed the ecological facts and brought them eloquently to the public attention. Following her lead, other scientists spoke up. Armed with the facts, citizens sued for action.

Tragically late, action was taken. Nor is this task complete; as the U.S. markets for DDT are blocked, manufacturers increasingly ship the pesticide abroad.

5. The defeat of the SST over the massive, persistent opposition of the Nixon administration, the aircraft industry, and a number of labor unions is recognized as a crucial turning point in environmental politics. In 1969 Senator Gaylord Nelson of Wisconsin and his colleagues could muster only 19 votes against the SST in the Senate; in 1970 they defeated it by 52 votes. What happened in the intervening year is clear enough: the public became acquainted with the facts about the SST—its sonic boom, its possible effects on the ozone blanket that shields the earth from solar ultraviolet radiation, and its economic futility—and voiced their opposition. Their representatives listened. As one senator put it when asked to explain why he switched from support to opposition to the SST: "I read my mail."

6. And let us also pay tribute to Mr. Norvald Fimreite, a graduate student of zoology at the University of Western Ontario, for he holds the world record, I believe, for the fastest, one-man, large-scale ecological action. On March 19, 1970, he wrote to the Canadian Department of Fisheries and Forestry to report that he had found 7.09 ppm of mercury—a value 35 times greater than the allowable limit—in pickerel from waters that feed Lake Erie. The Canadian government responded at once. Within a month chloralkali plants were pinpointed as a source of the mercury; they have been forced to change their operations. Meanwhile the Canadian government has banned the taking of fish in the area; sport and commercial fishing have been halted and the polluters are threatened with legal action.

There are many other examples: the nuclear reactor planned for Bodega Bay, California, and abandoned when a local citizens' committee, aided by the St. Louis Committee for Environmental Information, helped publicize a report that showed that, since it sat on the great San Andreas fault, the reactor

might rupture in an earthquake; the Minnesota Committee for Environmental Information which made a study that led the state of Minnesota to adopt new reactor emission standards—much more stringent than AEC standards; the Northern California Committee for Environmental Information, which was instrumental in making Berkeley the first city to commit itself to natural, biological control of insects in its parks and streets; the scientists of the Rochester Committee for Environmental Information, who collected water samples that revealed the inadequacy of the city's sewage treatment—a new bond issue resulted; the New York Scientists' Committee for Public Information which unearthed an official report that showed that a new crosstown expressway, about to be adopted, would probably generate enough carbon monoxide to cause pedestrians to stagger in the streets—despite well-advanced plans, the project was dropped.

Add to all this the valiant efforts of Ralph Nader and the devoted students who have worked with him to uncover and make public the facts about air and water pollution and the inadequacies of protective regulations. And add, also, the legal actions taken by conservation organizations, by community groups, or simply by single, determined citizens to halt environmental hazards. All these efforts have been based not only on public morality but on facts—unearthed by scientists and brought into public view through the newspapers, radio, television.

There is one grim reason for all these successes: the country has been vastly ignorant of the extent and depth of the environmental crisis because crucial facts remained buried in inaccessible reports or shielded by official and industrial secrecy. When the facts were revealed, citizens were ready to weigh the benefits against the risks and make the moral judgment which is the spark to political action.

All this has taken some people by surprise. For there is a myth in some political circles that public policy is determined more by narrow self-interest than by concerns for values as nebulous as the integrity of the environment. They would argue as well that there is no way to establish the general public attitude toward the moral acceptability of a given balance between benefit and risk and that, realistically, this judgment can only be made by some appropriate governmental agency. The answer to this argument is that public opinion has, in fact, already established rather well-defined limits to the risks that are acceptable for the benefits to be derived from a wide range of activities.

The benefit/risk issue is associated with many aspects of personal life: driving a car, traveling in a train or an aircraft, skiing, working in an industrial plant or living near it, the use of X rays for medical diagnosis, watching a color television set, using a microwave oven or a synthetic insecticide. These are personal, voluntary acts. Other benefit/risk issues relate to large-scale social enterprises in which the risks are taken involuntarily. These include the widespread use of pesticides and fertilizers in agriculture, all forms of power production, air pollution due to urban traffic, and indeed all of the massive sources of environmental pollution.

Recently efforts have been made to evaluate, from the available statistics, the quantitative balance between the benefits and risks associated with such activities that has been accepted by the general public. For a number of such activities, Chauncey Starr has evaluated the risk (which he defines as "the statistical probability of fatalities per hour of exposure of the individual to the activity considered") and the benefit, calculated from the dollar equivalent value derived by the individual from the activity. The ratio of benefit to risk that is acceptable to the public can be seen from a plot of the risk against the benefit, calculated in these terms.

The results of such a plot are quite striking. When the value of the benefit is small, the acceptable risk is also relatively low; as the value increases, the acceptable risk also rises—but at a rate that is very large relative to the increase in value (the acceptable risk rises, approximately, in proportion to the cube of the benefit). Also, as the beneficial value of various activities increases, the ac-

ceptable risk reaches an upper limit. Since a wide variety of activities fit this general formula, we must conclude that there has been, deeply inherent in our society, some general standard of public judgment regarding the acceptable balance between benefit and risk. Moreover, the influence of a purely moral factor such as the distinction between an involuntary and voluntary activity is measurable in the results. Involuntary and voluntary activities fall on *separate* curves of the same general shape, but for the same benefit the acceptable level for involuntary risks is 10,000 times less than that acceptable for voluntary ones. These calculations show that the acceptable benefit/risk ratio is determined by a general public consensus; where regulatory agencies are involved, their actions appear to reflect rather than create the common public view. In effect, they place a numerical value on a matter of public morality—that, in Starr's words, "we are loath to let others do unto us what we happily do to ourselves."

Now, however, it has become apparent that we are in the midst of a revolution in public attitude toward the acceptability of levels of environmental deterioration which have for a long time been tolerated without general complaint. The explanation for this change is suggested by the clear 10,000-fold difference between the acceptable benefit/risk ratios of voluntary and involuntary activities. This reflects a more stringent public morality when actions of some members of society impose risks on others who are given no choice in the matter. The new assaults on the environment considerably intensify this moral factor. The public has now become aware, I believe, that the new environmental pollutants represent an assault by the present generation not merely on involuntary *living* victims—who have some recourse, however difficult—but on generations not yet born and therefore utterly defenseless. In response, the public is in the process of establishing a new set of acceptable benefit risk/ratios. For a given benefit, the new ratio will accept only a risk that is far below even that acceptable for involuntary risks imposed on the present population. This, then, is the moral response to the assaults on the integrity of the environment which threaten the well-being and even the survival of succeeding generations.

In politics, environmental protection is sometimes regarded as a "motherhood" issue; no one can really oppose it. In fact, it is often suggested that environmental issues are so innocuous that they serve to divert people from more serious, controversial issues—a kind of ecological copout from the problems of poverty, racial discrimination, and war. In practice, it hasn't quite turned out that way; as a political issue, environmental protection is neither innocuous nor unrelated to basic questions of social justice.

For example, in the ghetto, environmental protection is sometimes regarded as an irrelevant diversion from the plight of the Blacks. Some approaches to environmental action give substance to this view. This was dramatized during Earth Week 1970 at San Jose State College in California, where a student environmental program was climaxed by the burial of a brand new car, as a symbol of environmental rebellion. The event was picketed by Black students who believed that the $2,500 paid for the car could have been better spent in the ghetto. The San Jose burial reflects a kind of personalized approach to the environmental crisis which is sometimes adopted by ecological crusaders. They reason—erroneously, as we have seen —that pollution is caused by the excessive consumption of goods and resources by the United States population. Since the wastes generated by this intense consumption pollute our environment, the eco-activist is advised to "consume less." In the absence of the added statistic that in the United States the per capita consumption by Blacks is much less than that of the White population, such observations are not likely to make much sense to Blacks or to anyone who is concerned with social justice.

Disaffiliation of Blacks from the environmental movement would be particularly unfortunate, because in many ways Blacks are the special victims of pollution. A White suburbanite can escape from the city's dirt, smog, carbon monoxide, lead, and noise when he goes home; the ghetto dweller not only works in a polluted environment, he lives in it. And in the ghetto he confronts his own, added environmental problems: rats and other vermin, the danger of lead poisoning when children eat bits of ancient, peeling paint. And, through its history, the Black community can be a powerful ally in the fight against environmental degradation. The environmental crisis is a crisis of survival, an issue that is not familiar to middle class Americans. They have not yet learned how to face such a soul-shaking threat; witness our continued failure to appreciate that the existence of ready-armed nuclear weapons means that doomsday may be tomorrow. For Blacks, the issue of survival is several hundred years old. If they, too, have not yet mastered it, they have at least had a good deal of experience that may be enormously valuable to a society that, now as a whole, must face the threat of extinction. Blacks need the environmental movement, and the movement needs the Blacks.

There is also a close relationship between environmental issues and poverty. A classic illustration is provided by the recent events at Hilton Head, South Carolina. There, on a beautiful shoreline site, adjacent to large, well-kept estates, a chemical company proposed to build a large plant which, in the absence of unprecedented, expensive environmental controls, would certainly degrade the local environment. Opposed to the plant were the estate owners, conservationists, and shrimp fishermen who feared the aesthetic and ecological effects of the plant's effluents. In support of the plant were the chemical company and many of the poor people in the area, who saw the opportunity to relieve their long-standing unemployment. Where lies justice in this matter? It might be possible to compute the economic benefits of the plant and compare them with the economic cost of the effects of pollutants on shrimp fishing and on the local natural ambiance. Would it then be sufficient to compare the benefits with the costs and decide in favor of the more economical action? Clearly the matter cannot end there, for the environmental problem, even if "solved" in this way, raises other, more fundamental issues which are not solved by environmental action. For example, if the plant is blocked (which is, in fact, what happened), this action, in effect, says to the unemployed that their right to a job is less important than the integrity of the environment. The appropriate response may well be that a society that can find the means to save a marsh ought to be equally capable of finding the means to employ its citizens.

A similar situation arose in connection with the SST; unions strongly supported the project because its abandonment would throw some thousands of workers out of jobs. To a person thus unemployed, the immediate response may well be anger directed against the "eco-freaks" who opposed the SST. On further reflection, such a person might wonder about the rationality of an economic system that forces a person to fight for a job with the knowledge that the product would wake babies in the night and increase the incidence of ultraviolet-induced skin cancers.

There is an equally close link between environmental problems and the issues of war and peace. Like detergents and DDT, nuclear armament is a huge technological blunder. When in the 1950s the Pentagon generals and their scientific advisers decided to rely on nuclear weapons for the nation's defense, they were apparently unaware of what the scientific community, its voice strongly amplified by public response, has since told them: that it will not work, that no nation would survive a nuclear war.

In the same way, the Pentagon replied to an inquiry from the AAAS that it would not use herbicides in Vietnam if it believed that these agents would have "long-term ecological effects" on that tortured land. Now we know from the efforts of the AAAS and other independent scientists that the United States has indeed conducted ecological warfare in Vietnam. In response, the government has, at last, greatly restricted the military use of herbicides in Vietnam. There is equal force in the fact that the United States government has now abandoned the manufacture of biological warfare agents, after long defending them—against opposition from the scientific community—as effective and necessary for the nation's "defense."

It seems to me that these ecological insights raise very profound questions about the competence of our military to defend the nation, as they are charged to do. It adds force to the mounting evidence of purely military blunders in the United States war in Southeast Asia. It raises the momentous issue of at last freeing mankind from the threat of annihilation, from the intolerable burden of living, every day, within minutes of catastrophe.

The environmental crisis is hardly a "motherhood" issue. Nor is it a diversion from other social questions. For as we begin to act on the environmental crisis, deeper issues emerge which reach to the core of our system of social justice and challenge basic political goals.

The force of this challenge is revealed by the implications of two alternative routes of environmental action: action *of* the public and action *by* the public. Those who favor the first route march under Pogo's banner: "We have met the enemy and he is us." They are committed to personal acts that lessen environmental impact: they walk or bicycle rather than drive a car; they use returnable bottles and phosphate-free detergents; they produce no more than two children. These are the rudiments of a new, ecology-minded personal life-style. It is designed to minimize the two factors that intensify pollution that are under personal control: consumption and population size.

In contrast, action directed toward the third source of environmental impact—the counterecological design of production technology—is necessarily social rather than personal. As indicated earlier, this factor has a far more powerful effect on pollution levels than the other two. It will be recalled that, in the United States, population rise accounts for 12 to 20 percent of the increases in postwar environmental impact, while the technological factor accounts for 40 to 85 percent of these increases. If, to take a conservative illustration, the technological factor has had five times the effect of rising population, then there would have been the following alternative means by which we could have *prevented* the rise in pollution level since World War II. If we chose to allow population to grow, as it did, by about 43 percent, then *a 30 percent reduction* in environmental impact would have been required of productive technology. If, on the other hand, we chose to allow the environmental impact of technology to increase, as it did, by about 600 percent (in this example), then *an 86 percent reduction* in population size would have been required. . . . It seems rather clear that of the two factors, technology is by far the more effective one. On the other hand it is not subject to direct personal control.

Which route should we take? Should people be urged to consume less and produce fewer children in order to reduce pollution levels? Or should we, rather, concentrate on the ecological reform of technology? Or both?

Since powerful resistance is likely to delay technological reforms, and reduction in consumption is hardly sensible in the face of continued poverty and need, it is often proposed that the primary effort should be made to slow the growth of the United States population. Apart from the fact that a large *reduction* in population would be needed to achieve a noticeable effect on pollution levels, this is, of course, a perfectly logical argument. So long as we continue to use it, ecologically faulty production technology will certainly do less damage to the environment if fewer people demand its products. Clearly, there are logical grounds for supporting *both* ecological reform of production technology and the reduction of population growth as a basis of environmental improvement.

But there is more than logic and ecology at work here. For this same principle can be applied with equal logic to nearly every social problem. Indeed, under the impetus of recent environmental concern, it has been. Here are two examples.

A Secretary of Labor spends his years in office trying futilely to fight unemployment by creating more jobs; and only later, freed of the inhibitions of office and politics' restraints, faces the truth that there are too few jobs because there are too many people.

Considering the problems of air and water pollution, poverty, clogged highways, overcrowded schools, inadequate courts and jails, urban blight, and so on, it is clear that the United States has more people than it can adequately maintain.

This, it seems to me, sets the problem in its proper context: the nation's social system is grossly incapable of supporting the people who created it in their present and expected numbers; they are therefore suffering poverty, unemployment, environmental pollution, inadequate schooling, injustice, and the tyranny of war. Now, if the reason for this incompetence is that, even with maximum efficiency and complete social equity, the nation no longer has sufficient resources to support the expected population, we have no choice but to control its size. However, according to the United States Commission on Population Growth and the American Future:

There is little question that the United States has the resources, if it chooses to use them, to meet the demands of a population growing at the current rate as well as to correct various social and economic inequities.

This being the case, it seems to me that there is a clear dichotomy between the two routes toward social progress. We are engaged in a kind of political "zero-sum game": to the degree that population size is reduced, to that degree may we be able to tolerate some of the technological, economic, and social faults that plague us; to the degree that we repair these faults, to that degree can the nation successfully support a growing population.

How these considerations are to be balanced against one another depends on the collective sense of social justice inherent in the American people. Insofar as they are themselves willing to accept the personal burden of relieving the crisis in the environment, in unemployment, in education, in health, in urban decay, they will voluntarily reduce births. Insofar as the American people are unwilling to undertake this personal action, they will need to seek relief by altering the economic, social, and political priorities that govern the disposition of the nation's resources.

All this assumes voluntary public choice. However, some population-minded ecologists hold that "we must have population control at home, hopefully through a system of incentives and penalties, but by compulsion if voluntary methods fail." The outcome would be to constrain, by compulsion, the public choice between the two basic paths toward social progress. More simply stated, this is political repression.

Nor is it possible to disguise this ugly fact by notions such as "mutual coercion, mutually agreed upon." If a majority of the United States population voluntarily practiced birth control adequate to population stabilization, there would be no need for coercion. The corollary is that *coercion is necessary only if a majority of the population refuses voluntarily to practice adequate birth control.* This means that the majority would need to be coerced by the minority. This is, indeed, political repression.

In a way, it is fortunate that the environmental crisis has generated so much discussion of the population problem. The nation has for many years been tormented by the contrast between its unparalleled wealth and its inability to provide for its people an adequate environment, employment, schooling, health and social services, and a peaceful life. For a long time, this stark reality has been obscured by evasions, excuses, and a cloud of technical details. It seems to me that this screen has now, somehow, been penetrated by the environmental crisis. We can now see more clearly that the multiple national crisis of which it is a part, in MacLeish's words,

will not leave us until we believe in ourselves again, assume again the mastery of our lives, the management of our means.

35. THE CITY AS SANDBOX

GEORGE STERNLIEB

Reprinted from The Public Interest *No. 25, (Fall 1971), pp.14-21. Copyright © by National Affairs, Inc., 1971. George Sternlieb is Professor of Urban and Regional Planning at Rutgers University. He is a nationally known expert on housing, on suburban development, and on the inner city.*

■ A people concretize their patterns of social inequality in the physical world of the settlements they construct. The city historically has harbored the greatest inequalities, the largest numbers of those who have most and those who have least. Historically it also has been, perhaps for this reason, the place where equalitarian notions are born and nurtured. In the modern city, most particularly the modern North American city, the patterns of social classes, ethnic and religious groups, and inequality are spread out physically in the form of relatively homogeneous neighborhoods. In the smallest American towns "the other side of the tracks" describes the elemental division between a not-very-prosperous working and lower class and their better-off fellow citizens. In the large city even finer distinctions are possible.

The growth of suburbs outside the reach of central city governments has greatly complicated the consequences of the physical patterns of stratification. When Sternlieb speaks of "the city" he means the inner city and not the suburbs. To some extent he is talking about an artificial distinction forced by our peculiar habits of local government, which make different "cities" out of one metropolitan area that for all but political purposes everyone treats as a unit. Sternlieb points to a central fact in every metropolitan area in the country: the center is dying. Too few people want to live near the center of the city, and increasingly no one wants to establish his business or hold a job there if he has other options. The result of this interaction of social stratification, individual choice, rising affluence, and unchanging inequality is that the tremendous investment the central city represents—the physical, social, cultural, and political capital located there—is simply being abandoned.

The more people choose to leave, the more the center is left to the poorest and most disadvantaged sectors of the population, and the more dangerous the center becomes, and the more expensive for the few who choose to remain there. To the first wave of people who left the center to seek their dreams of a suburban existence, those pulled out of the city by the attractions of the countryside, are added those who are pushed out if they can possibly afford it because of the human and economic costs of remaining. In the end, then, the city becomes home only for the socially and economically weak, and they live there only because they have no other choice; they hate it and the system that confines them there. The result, Sternlieb suggests, is a sandbox, a place where society plays with its problems while the serious business goes on in the suburbs.

In suggesting further readings for selections on housing and on the melting pot that does not melt, we noted many references that are also central to this issue. In addition, the reader is referred to the *Urban Affairs Annual Reviews*, beginning with volume 1 (1967), published by Sage Publications, Inc. A very useful analysis of how stability in the midst of disorder is maintained in the inner city is Gerald D. Suttles, *The Social Order of the Slums: Ethnicity and Territory in the Inner City* (Chicago: University of Chicago Press, 1968). See also his *The Social Construction of Communities* (Chicago: University of Chicago Press, 1972). Anselm Strauss in *Images of the City* (New York: Free Press, 1961) analyzes the symbolism of the city in American systems of meaning. A useful collection of articles on the suburban phenomenon is John Kramer, ed., *North American Suburbs: Politics, Diversity and Change* (Berkeley: Glendessary Press, 1972); see also Jeffrey K. Hadden, Louis H. Massoti, and Calvin J. Larsen, eds., *Metropolis in Crisis: Social and Political Perspectives* (Itasca, Ill.: F. E. Peacock Publishers, 1967). A useful look at what cities were like in the heyday of their building is Stephan Thernstrom and Richard Sennett, *Nineteenth Century*

Cities, Essays in the New Urban History (New Haven, Conn.: Yale University Press, 1969). Interactions between city and the federal government in funding Sternlieb's sandbox are discussed by several authors in M. Fox, ed., *The New Urban Politics: Cities and the Federal Government* (Pacific Palisades, Calif.: Goodyear Publishers, Inc., 1972). ∎

HOW IS ONE TO WRITE about a Newark or a Youngstown? All the adjectives have been used up, as have all the warnings of disaster and dire happenings in the streets if "they" don't come across, all the stories of soaring syphilis rates, TB gone uncared for, children made vegetables by lead poisoning, rats running rampant, high infant mortality, increasing numbers of unwed mothers, schools and hospitals and garbage departments that don't work, or won't, etc. The cries of "wolf" have become so plentiful that we no longer listen and may even have begun to lose our fear of the beast itself. Yet there is something to be learned from a reshuffling of these dying embers of old rhetorical fires. For the Newarks of America are a foretaste of things to come, and if we want to understand the probable future that faces many of our older cities, then we will first have to get clear on what is happening—has already happened—in a place like Newark.

The bitterness of political conflict in such cities, and the intensity of their citizens' demand for an expansion of public services and public funding, provide a major clue. Of all the things people are prepared to fight over, their property interests are perhaps the most important, or at any rate the first; and of all a man's property interests, that in his job is usually the most important. Especially in cities like Newark, where the public sector has grown immensely while the private sector has decreased, the property interest which people possess—or seek—in their jobs gives local politics a peculiar importance. At one level, of course, such politics is precisely what it appears to be—an effort to promote the public interest. Thus, a housing program is an effort to provide housing for the poor; school reform aims at improving the achievement of pupils; a health program may be measured by its effect in raising the level of health and care. But beneath this there is another level of reality—that of who gets the action. Who will get (or keep) the job, the patronage? Who is going to build the new school? Who is going to make those sandwiches for the lunch program? Who is going to give out the contracts? As the size of the public sector grows, such questions become increasingly important and therefore increasingly divisive, for they engage the property interests of more and more people. Why should there be a fight for community control in Ocean Hill-Brownsville or Newark? There are many reasons, but one of the simplest and most important is that, for more and more people, new government programs are the only game in town; there is little else worth fighting for. Thus, for those who remain in the central city, fighting for such new programs is the only realistic response to the economic sterility of their environment.

EXPLOITED—OR MERELY DEFUNCT?

It is often said that our older central cities are essentially colonies—areas rich in resources which are systematically exploited by the suburban hinterlands. The residents of the latter drive into the city in the morning, use its services all day, and then creep out at night, taking with them much of the city's income and wealth. In one or another variant, this is the vision subscribed to by most city leaders, and they find it a satisfying one. For it implies that the Golden Return is at hand if only the city is given justice. The city's lack of such equity, which creates all its problems, is the result of a shortsighted plot by "outside" interests. Let there be a reallocation of wealth, and all will be well again.

The only problem with this notion is that it is untrue. The size of the constituency which lives outside the cities but still wants to preserve them at any cost grows smaller day by day. It is not exploitation that the core areas must fear; it is indifference and abandonment. The crisis of the cities is a crisis of function. *The major problem of the core areas of our cities is simply their lack of economic value.*

For a long time, the principal role of our inner cities was as a staging area for the floods of immigrants who came from Europe and elsewhere. Cities provided jobs, schools, and an infrastructure which helped earlier groups of immigrants move upward and outward. Although each of these groups left a residue of those who didn't make it, on the whole the city was an extremely successful processing center. Now that these great migrant flows have been reduced to a comparative trickle, the city has lost its raison d'etre. Formerly the focal point for cheap labor, uniquely amassable there in great volume, it now finds that competition from welfare payments keeps its labor far from cheap and that its traditional jobs have been taken over by Puerto Rico, Formosa, Hong Kong, Singapore, and the like. As its current group of immigrants begins to make it, they too are moving out; but because no new groups are moving in, the city emigrés leave behind a vacuum.

America's major cities are unique in that *they are losing population.* Everywhere else— in Moscow or Buenos Aires or Calcutta—the flow of the agrarian poor off the land to the big city is at its flood stage. We have already gone through that phase; we are now on uncharted territory. To be sure, the Puerto Rican migration may from time to time increase, depending on relative economic conditions, and small pockets of surplus population remain in the South. But for the most part, large-scale immigration to the city is a thing of the past, and much of the migration which does take place bypasses the older population centers for more promising areas.

The absence of replacements for the new emigrés from the city means that some of the first rungs in the nation's traditional ladder of upward mobility have been eliminated. The consequences of this development are already making themselves felt. One of the most common ways for earlier immigrant groups to accumulate capital was as slum landlords. They bought, as they could afford to buy, only the poorest and weakest of structures, which

they would rent, at whatever they could get, to their immigrant successors. By trading up the real estate ladder to bigger and better properties, these slumlords became prominent sources of capital for the business-oriented among their own ethnic group. But today, there is no new immigrant group to exploit. Slum tenement ownership has become a dead end, instead of an avenue to wealth—a fact symbolized by the abandoned slum dwelling.

Another way for earlier ethnic groups to move upward and outward was the exploitation of their own countrymen. Members of the immigrant group could rise as brokers between their ethnic labor pool and the external economy. If one wanted to build a sidewalk a generation or two ago, the cheapest labor available was Italian. Because the people who wanted sidewalks built rarely spoke Italian themselves, they dealt with bilingual Italian brokers, who would assemble and supervise the strong backs that were needed for the job. That was the stuff general contractors were made of. Or, to take another case, two generations ago the cheapest needle workers available were non-English-speaking Jews. Their labor was exploited by Jewish sweatshop owners, who served as go-betweens with the department stores of Grand Street. Of course the needle workers themselves had no chance to become rich; but the go-betweens did.

The need for strong backs and 15-hour-a-day sweated labor has been reduced to almost nothing by the transportation revolution, which has had the effect of homogenizing time and distance. Much of our labor-intensive work is now imported from abroad. Welfare legislation, minimum wages, maximum work hours, and the like have minimized the economic function of the conglomerations of poor-but-willing people in our cities. Similarly, the goad of hunger has been mitigated by the rising level of welfare payments. In Newark a woman with 3 children lives very badly on welfare payments, but these nevertheless average somewhere around $300 to $350 a month. To live at the same level, a man with a wife and 3 children would have to make about $5,500 a year. For unskilled labor, that sort of money just isn't available.

A NEW "FUNCTION"

Given that the older central cities have lost their capacity to serve as effective staging areas for newcomers, the question inevitably poses itself: What *is* the function of these cities? Permit me to suggest that it has become essentially that of a sandbox.

A sandbox is a place where adults park their children in order to converse, play, or work with a minimum of interference. The adults, having found a distraction for the children, can get on with the serious things of life. There is some reward for the children in all this. The sandbox is given to them as their own turf. Occasionally, fresh sand or toys are put in the sandbox, along with an implicit admonition that these things are furnished to minimize the level of noise and nuisance. If the children do become noisy and distract their parents, fresh toys may be brought. If the occupants of the sandbox choose up sides and start bashing each other over the head, the adults will come running, smack the juniors more or less indiscriminately, calm things down, and then, perhaps, in an act of semicontrition, bring fresh sand and fresh toys, pat the occupants of the sandbox on the head, and disappear once again into their adult involvements and pursuits.

That is what the city has become—a sandbox. Government programs in the core city have increasingly taken on this cast. A glance at Sar Levitan's *The Great Society's Poor Law,* or the Marris and Rein work, or for that matter Tom Wolfe's *Mau-Mauing the Flack Catchers* is enough to make clear the lack of effective flow of much poverty money to its ostensible targets. Instead, this money has been used to create a growing bureaucracy which is sustained by the plight of the poor, the threat of the poor, the misery of the poor, but which yields little in the way of loaves and fishes to the poor. This is the height of sandboxism. When old programs begin to lose their credibility or become un-

fashionable, they are given new names— therefore, they are new programs. The act of repackaging or relabeling is equated with creativity.

This is not to belittle the importance of government programs. They do have trickle-down effects; they are creating, if not efficiently then certainly in bulk, some measure of leadership, and this leadership is highly cynical about the nature of the faucet from whence all goodies flow and, possibly as a result, is increasingly effective. Perhaps most significantly, these programs have become forms of symbolic action. In their ritualistic aspects they are of particular value. They give psychic satisfaction to the patrons of the poor, convince outsiders—especially the media— that "something is being done," and indicate to the urban poor that someone up there really cares. In a word, these programs are placebos, and they often produce all the authentic, positive results which placebos can have in medical practice. One of the greatest shortcomings of the present administration in Washington is its failure to recognize the salutary placebo effects of social programs. The failure has been not so much in what it has done as in what it has called what it has done—not so much in the substance of its programs as in its rejection of the gamesmanship which does not merely accompany programs but is central to them.

The fact that so many programs are of only symbolic value is the result not of Machiavellian scheming but of simple incapacity. If the 1960s demonstrated anything, it was that the social sciences had not yet arrived at the point of being able to design programs that could be counted on actually to accomplish what they were supposed to accomplish. It is true that social scientists themselves were often quick to recognize the failure of a given program and would attempt to design a better one in light of that failure. But the new programs usually did not arise from any strong theory or experimentation; they were rather the complements of past failure. One simply took apparently salient parameters of the failed program and reversed them. The façade of intellectual rationalization was produced post hoc. Schools don't work because classes are too large and lack the personal touch? Make classes smaller. If smaller classes don't work, what is left? Ah! Skin color—the teacher's doesn't match that of the student; change the skin color. That doesn't seem to be working as well as one would have anticipated? It must be the supervisor's color—paint principal black. Principal black doesn't seem to provide the answer? Paint the board of education an appropriate hue. And when this entire mountain of strategems brings forth nothing but mice, bring the parents in. Parents don't want to come in? Pay them, we'll call them paraprofessionals. And so it has gone. The rationalizers of these programs dutifully turn out Ph.D. theses and proposals without end to justify the programs.

In this kind of "social science," anecdotal accounts began to pass as consequential theories and models for the design of new institutions. A typical specimen of the genus is the account of how I, a young draft dodger, full of beans and aware of the fact that I wasn't going to spend my career there, came into a class of young sullens; in six months they loved me. This sort of recital became dignified both as an indictment of the flywheels of our institutions and also possibly as a model for new educational institutions of the future. The former may well have validity, but the latter defies rationality. The wonder is not the existence of a number of these anecdotal descriptions but rather the childlike acceptance of them as a vision of a future that can be reproduced on a scale commensurate with the number of children and situations involved. The sordid fact that they enjoy such acceptance is but another indication of the extent to which we have begun to escape into fantasy.

THE FUTURE OF THE CENTRAL CITY

Jobs are leaving the central city. Except for insurance companies, banks, and other institutions which juridically find it difficult to leave, business institutions are virtually deserting the central cities. All major department store chains now do the bulk of their business in the suburbs; the efforts of urban renewal to retain major retail facilities in the core areas have died and are mourned by few. Smaller retailers in secondary urban shopping areas on the "trolley car streets" are also leaving or going out of business. The old mom-and-pop stores, candy stores, grocery stores on every block, fish stores, neighborhood bakeries, etc., are things of the far past. There has also been a flight of professionals. In the last 10 years, Newark has lost half its physicians, and many of those who remain have one foot in the suburbs and are just waiting for their practices to take hold before moving out. As for cultural activities, it is the first-run movie theaters rather than opera houses or symphony halls which have been of especially great economic importance to the vitality of the core city. In Newark, *there is not a single first-run theater left in the entire city of* 400,000, while in the suburbs one of the most desirable pieces of realty available is a site for a movie theater and shopping center. True, the museum and public library still exist downtown, but their wealthy patrons become fewer, galleries must be closed off for lack of money to pay guards, and book acquisition budgets and opening hours must be reduced as the city's budget crisis makes its impact felt.

Meanwhile, the suburbs have achieved critical mass, a scale of population and buying power which permits them to sustain amenities of a type and at a level which once only the central city was capable of sustaining. The shopping center which had at best a single department store branch now has three and soon will have four. The suburban music calendar is evolving from a marginal summer collection of odds and ends to a year-round independent activity. Small suburban hospitals have grown to thousand-bed monsters which can supply all the services and specialists available in the biggest central-city hospitals.

Who is left in the central city? Ride down the Central Avenues and Main Streets of our older cities and you will see that the new tenants are offshoots of the poverty program:

pseudotraining programs for the poor, enlarged offices of the welfare department, and the like. These are the focal points of the new central-city entrepreneurs, the people who, in the absence of a booming private economy, are trying to make it with government money. The predominance of these public-sector entrepreneurs is an index of the degree to which the central city—its inhabitants' training irrelevant to the needs of the larger society— has become a forgotten back alley in a nation whose principal business still is business.

This process of the "defunctioning" of the central city would have occurred even if there had not been a problem of race. It would have been considerably slower in that case, and the capacity of society to adjust to it would have been greater, for the pace of change in our central cities has unquestionably been speeded up by racial tensions and fears. But serious though that cost has been, perhaps the greatest cost of the race factor is that it has obscured the real nature of what is going on in the central city. Even if there were no racial difference in our society, there would probably still be as many people on welfare and as many under- or unemployed, and they would still be unwelcome among their more affluent fellow citizens.

What, then, of the future? The first point to be made is that there is no going back in time. The city as we have known it, and the forms of economic and social organization which characterized it, are simply irrecoverable. The folkways of our society have changed; they have also become homogeneous and monolithically dominant as no fashion has ever before been. The thin mist of eloquence emanating from upper middle class occupants of high-rise apartments cannot hide the fact that the dominant ethos today is a suburban one. It is as pervasive among minority groups as it is in the society as a whole. Thus, if we define the problems of the city as the gap between the reality of the cities as they exist today and a romanticized fantasy of cities as they used to be—as the economic center of the nation, as the font of civility and graciousness, as the source of everything that warms the hearts of social critics—then those problems are simply unsolvable and always will be unsolvable, at least for many of our older central cities.

Yet there is another way of defining the problems of the cities that does permit some real choice: Are they to become sandboxes entirely, or will we permit them to regain some useful economic function? Shall we optimize the machine, maximize capital investment and capital returns at the cost of human involvement, and then take the largesse so provided and redistribute it in the form of welfare or subsidized, irrelevant, unproductive make-work? Or should we reject the sandbox on the ground that useful, productive work is essential to human well-being, and design our policies to insure that everyone has an opportunity for such work, even if this involves cost to overall economic growth and wealth?

The plight of the inhabitants of our central cities, and the strategy we seem to be adopting to meet that plight, indicate that we are opting for the sandbox. What this will mean for our society in the future we do not fully know; but that the consequences are likely to be cruel and disagreeable has become only too clear.

36. METROPOLITAN DISPERSAL AND GROWTH

COMMISSION ON POPULATION GROWTH AND
THE AMERICAN FUTURE

Reprinted from "Population Distribution," The Report of the Commission on Population Growth and the American Future (Washington, D.C.: U. S. Government Printing Office, 1972, or New American Library edition, 1972).

■ Congress established the Commission on Population Growth and the American Future at the request of President Nixon to "formulate policy for the future" to deal with "the pervasive impact of population growth on every facet of American life." During the course of its two-year study the Commission enlisted many of the nation's leading scientists in more than 100 research projects. The Commission's report seeks to condense findings from the staff studies and the work of scientific consultants into a summary of facts about the growth and distribution of the American population, and to formulate policy implications and recommendations related to those facts. This section of the Commission's report deals with the distribution of population and, in particular with patterns of metropolitan growth and, migration, variations from one area of the country to another, and likely future developments in where Americans will live.

Given Sternlieb's analysis in the preceding selection, it is not surprising that Americans generally prefer to live in smaller communities; not only do they prefer the suburbs of large cities to the city itself, but most Americans say they prefer life in metropolitan areas that are not of great size. Yet the dynamics of economic development and of the initial population distribution have been such that the concentrations of population become larger and larger. But if, in fact people generally prefer smaller communities, why should not planning be consciously directed toward building new cities in relatively underpopulated parts of the country? Much of the enthusiasm for "new towns" is related to this kind of imagery, although in practice new towns have become simply another "in" phrase for large-scale suburbs still attached to a major city. The Commission's survey found that although at present only 45 percent of the population lives in open country or small towns and cities,

almost two-thirds of all residents say they would prefer to live in such surroundings. At the other extreme of population concentration, 27 percent live in a large city or suburb, but only 14 percent of the total regard that as the preferable place to be.

Additional analysis of population dispersion is contained in the research papers prepared for the Commission on Population Growth and the American Future, which are published separately by the Government Printing Office. ■

AMERICANS ARE a metropolitan people. Most families live in metropolitan areas; most births, deaths, and migration take place in them. But the traditions and nostalgia are farm and small town.

Our transition from rural to metropolitan has been rapid. At the beginning of this century, 60 percent of tht people lived on farms or in villages. When people now 50 years old were born, half the population was rural. In fact, it is only those below age 25 whose life experience is more attuned to a society that is two-thirds metropolitan and becoming more so. Perhaps we have been slow to cope with life in the metropolis because it is so new on the American scene. We struggle to solve the new problems of a metropolitan nation using old institutions suited to a simpler past. As one expert said to the Commission: "Small wonder we have an urban crisis; we are still trying to learn to live in this new demographic and technological world."

This country has experienced a demographic revolution in population distribution as well as in national population growth. Today, 69 percent of the American people live in metropolitan areas—cities of 50,000 or more, and the surrounding county or counties that are economically integrated with the city. Between 1960 and 1970, the population of the United States grew 13 percent, while the metropolitan population grew 23 percent. Nearly all metropolitan growth took place through the growth of suburbs and territorial expansion into previously rural areas. The United States has become mainly a nation of cities and their environs.

The surroundings in which metropolitan people live vary considerably, ranging from inner city to open country. And the metropolitan influence, through the highway and communications systems, affects people far beyond the central cities and adjacent counties. Distinctions between rural and urban people are diminishing. Some "urban" people reside in the countryside, and "rural" people can be found in the poverty areas of our cities.

Metropolitan population growth is a basic feature of the social and economic transformation of the United States—the transition from an agrarian, to an industrial, and now to a service-oriented economy. Metropolitan growth is the geographical dimension of these changes. Reflected in this process are increases in the productivity of agriculture, and the new dominance of commercial, professional, and industrial activities that thrive where people, equipment, money, and know-how are concentrated in space. It is a universal experience. As one of our consultants observed:

The concentration of national population within limited areas of national territory appears to be characteristic of practically all developed countries. It has little to do with overall population size or density . . . but rather is a reflection of the massive reorientation of population growth and life-styles associated with the industrial and technological revolutions of the last two centuries. Enormous changes in modes of population settlement, land use, and resource exploitation accompany these revolutions.

Metropolitan growth is the form that national and regional population growth have taken. The national population grew by 24 million in the 1960s. The metropolitan population grew by more than 26 million, while the nonmetropolitan population declined as migration continued, rural areas became suburban, and many smaller cities grew to metropolitan size. The states with rapid population growth—for example, California, Florida, and Arizona—have been states with rapid growth of metropolitan population. The regional shifts in population, from North to West and South, from the midcontinent to the coasts, have been focused in rapidly growing metropolitan areas.

The process has brought efficiency and confusion, affluence and degradation, individual advancement and alienation. The buildup of transport and communications has made possible increased contact and exchange, increased concentration and dispersal, and increased segregation of activities and people. While the metropolitan economy has reached new heights of productivity, the people who staff it, their families, and the businesses and roads that serve them, have settled miles and miles of formerly rural territory, creating a new enlarged community—a real city with common problems but no common government to manage it. Minority migrants have found better jobs and education, but in so doing have traded the isolation imposed by rural racism for the isolation of the inner city and the institutional racism of metropolitan America. And the growth and dispersion of the metropolitan population has brought wholly new problems of environmental management as well as social organization.

Population growth *is* metropolitan growth in the contemporary United States, and it means different things to different people.

To the man in Los Angeles, it means rapid growth throughout Southern California. The outcome is often unplanned and haphazard development that falls far short of realizing the full aesthetic potential of the climate and natural surroundings. Tract housing developments are marked off by smoggy and noisy expressways. It is the "good life" colliding with a fragile environment under palm trees.

To a housewife in Nebraska, it means the

loss of population in her small farming town —it reached its peak population in 1920. Family, friends, and neighbors, particularly the young and better trained, have moved away. Tax revenues are shrinking and essential public services are becoming more limited. She and her husband can remain where they are, but only at the cost of a difficult and uncertain livelihood.

To a Black person in Harlem, the process of metropolitan growth means discrimination that keeps him in a ghetto area with crumbling old apartments and abandoned houses. And it means that it is harder than ever to reach the jobs opening up in the suburbs as companies shift their operations outward.

Each of these problems relates to a different part of the country and a different set of circumstances. All are related to the evolution of a metropolitan America.

METROPOLITAN GROWTH

In its geographical dimension, population growth has been a dual process of concentration on a national scale and dispersion and expansion at the local level. More and more of our people live in metropolitan areas. At the same time, the greatest central cities have been losing population, and the territory of metropolitan settlement has expanded even faster than population. Consequently, average metropolitan densities have declined somewhat.

The older industrial areas of the North were the first to develop a high degree of metropolitan concentration. Two-thirds of the Northeast was urban in 1900; by 1970, this proportion was four-fifths, and more than one of every two Americans residing in a metropolitan area lived in the North. Recently, however, the North has lost much of its magnetism. Instead, the most rapid growth has been in the South and West where migration, supplementing growth from natural increase, has produced high metropolitan and regional growth rates.

In 1900, more than four-fifths of the South

was rural. By 1970, over half was metropolitan. The Atlanta area grew 37 percent during the 1960s. In Texas, the metropolitan population grew 24 percent from 1960 to 1970 and accounted for virtually all of the state's growth. At the end of the decade, three-fourths of the state population was metropolitan. In the west, the Arizona metropolitan population grew 42 percent from 1960 to 1970. Migration contributed as much to Arizona's growth as did natural increases—the balance of births over deaths. Over 80 percent of the growth was concentrated in the state's two metropolitan areas— Phoenix and Tucson—so that in 1970 three-fourths of the population was metropolitan. Migration accounted for half of California's growth in the 1960s; but, by the end of the decade there were signs that the annual net migration from other states was very low if not zero. Still, because past migrants included so many young adults at the beginning of their childbearing years, state growth remained high. The degree of metropolitan concentration in California was also high. In 1970, it was the highest in the nation at 93 percent.

The most rapid growth in the past decade occurred in metropolitan areas with populations of 1 to 2 million. As a class, these areas grew an average of 27 percent, twice the rate for the total population of the United States. In this size class 13 of the 21 areas are in the South and West, and all areas of this size that grew *more* than 27 percent are in the South and West. (See Table 36.1.)

The 12 areas having more than 2 million people grew at an average rate of 12 percent, slightly under the rate for the total population of the United States. As a class, they grew just enough to retain their natural increase. Because they are so large, their slow growth rate nonetheless resulted in the addition of 6 million people. These large areas are mainly the old urban centers of the North. Of the 12 areas in this class, only Los Angeles and San Francisco are in the West, and only Baltimore and Washington are in the South.

TABLE 36.1

Metropolitan Area Population, 1970	Number of Areas, 1970	Population in 1970 Boundaries (millions)	Population Increase, 1960 to 1970 (in 1970 boundaries)	
			Number (Millions)	Percent (Increase)
All Areas	243	139	20	14
2,000,000 or more	12	52	6	12
1,000,000 to 2,000,000	21	28	6	27
500,000 to 1,000,000	32	22	3	18
250,000 to 500,000	60	20	3	16
Under 250,000	118	17	2	14

SOURCE: U. S. Bureau of the Census, *Census of Population and Housing: 1970, General Demographic Trends for Metropolitan Areas, 1960 to 1970*, Final Report PHC(2), 1971. The figures shown in this table differ somewhat from those cited elsewhere in the text due to differences in areal definitions. If one compares the population of metropolitan areas as defined in 1960 to the corresponding population within areas as defined in 1970, there is an increase of 26 million people. But, if we look at growth occurring within fixed metropolitan boundaries as defined in 1970, as in this table, there is an increase of 20 million. The latter figure does not allow for territorial extension of existing areas or the growth of additional areas to metropolitan status between 1960 and 1970.

SOURCES OF METROPOLITAN GROWTH

The total metropolitan population grew by 26 million in the 1960s. About one-third of this growth was from territorial expansion of existing centers and the emergence of other communities into metropolitan status; two-thirds was the result of population growth within constant boundaries.

Within metropolitan boundaries as defined in 1960, 74 percent of growth was natural increase—the excess of births over deaths—and 26 percent was net migration, consisting of immigrants as well as migrants from nonmetropolitan areas of the United States. As the nonmetropolitan population becomes a smaller fraction of the nation's total, its relative importance as a source of migration declines. If current trends continue, other parts of the United States will contribute 4 million migrants to the metropolitan population between now and the year 2000, while immigrants will add about 10 million.

The dominance of natural increase and the smaller role of migration show how far metropolitan growth has advanced. When two-thirds of the people are metropolitan, their fertility has a greater effect on the growth of metropolitan population than does migration from nonmetropolitan areas. Natural increase is the dominant source of metropolitan growth because we have had so much migration to metropolitan areas in the past.

MIGRATION

We are a geographically mobile society. Expansion and movement have been central themes in a history in which metropolitan growth is but a recent chapter.

Migration is basically a process of adjustment. For the individual, it represents a personal adjustment to changing life circumstances and opportunities. For most of us, moving has led to better things. Whether across town or across the country, movement provides access to areas of greater opportunity. Immobility of people often reflects their isolation from opportunities available in the mainstream of society—social, economic, and political.

For the nation as a whole, migration helps achieve a balance between social and economic activities on the one hand and population numbers on the other. As we move about the country, our actions create broad social, economic, and political realignments, as well as adjustments in our personal lives. Balance is achieved through three broad types of movement: (1) the shift from economically depressed regions, often rural, to areas of expanding employment and higher wages, usually metropolitan; (2) the movement of the population within metropolitan areas—the flight from the central city to the suburbs —historically an adjustment to changing housing needs and a desire for more space; and (3) the system of migration flows among metropolitan areas by which migrants participate in a nationwide job market, moving to areas offering economic advancement and often personal environmental preferences.

Nearly 40 million Americans, or 1 in 5, change homes each year. Roughly 1 in 15— a total of 13 million people—migrates across a county line. These rates have remained virtually unchanged over the quarter century for which data are available. In part because of the relative decline in rural population, the majoriy of people moving to metropolitan areas, especially those moving long distances, are now coming from other urban areas.

Whether it is a short or a long haul, those who move are typically the better educated, more skilled young adults, seeking a better life. Nearly a third of all migrants are in their twenties, and they bring with them young children: a tenth of all migrants are between the ages of one and four.

Migration, then, represents more than the numbers suggest. Where 5 million young adults take their young children and reproductive potential each year affects where future population growth will take place, and where heavy demands for housing and health and educational services will be felt. It also determines where some of our most capable young people, with most of their productive lives ahead, will contribute to the nation's future.

Especially since World War II, metropolitan migrations have included large numbers of Blacks. Their transition from rural to metropolitan life has been faster, more recent, and more extensive than that of Whites; 74 percent of the Black population of the United States is now metropolitan, compared with 68 percent of Whites. Blacks, more than Whites, tend to live in the larger metropolitan areas, and four-fifths of them live in the central cities.

Recent streams of migration among regions also have varied substantially by race. In the 1960s, there was a net movement of Whites out of the North, to the West and South. Blacks moved from the South to the North and West. The net effect was an exchange of population between the North and South, with the West experiencing net in-migration of both Whites and Blacks. In the South, it was the nonmetropolitan areas that experienced the heaviest out-migration of Blacks. The main areas receiving White in-migrants were Florida, the Washington-Baltimore area, and large metropolitan areas in Texas.

LOCAL VARIATIONS

Differences in migration produce large differences in the rates at which individual metropolitan areas grow. The Washington, D.C. area, for example, grew 39 percent in the 1960s, but Pittsburgh's population declined. Although the total metropolitan population of Texas grew 24 percent, three-fifths of its metropolitan areas grew slowly or not at all.

Most migrants to an individual area come from other metropolitan areas. What is happening is that a small number of areas are attracting a disproportionate number of people moving from one metropolitan area to another. Between 1960 and 1965, some 60 metropolitan areas, accounting for 25 percent of all the metropolitan population, drew migrants at a rate at least twice that for the total system of metropolitan centers, and absorbed nearly half of all metropolitan growth. In this same period, 82 other metropolitan areas had more people leaving than arriving. The population size of the fastest growing areas ranged from small to very large, but the lion's share of metropolitan growth was taken by the larger of these fast-growing areas.

With the drying up of nonmetropolitan sources of migration and a general decline in the rate of natural increase, migration among metropolitan centers might result in some 60 to 80 metropolitan areas actually losing population by 1980. Many others would simply not grow. We indicate later in this report why we believe that the usual apprehensions over this prospect are ill-founded. But we also believe that far more research is needed to understand the potential consequences of such trends.

RURAL AREAS AND SMALL TOWNS

Over the decades, there has been an immense transfer of population and reproductive potential through migration from town and countryside to urban areas. The total rural population in 1900 was 46 million, or 60 percent of the population of the United States. Seventy years later, rural population had risen by only 8 million to a total of 54 million, while the total national population had nearly tripled. By 1970, the rural population was only 26 percent of the total.

High fertility rates in rural areas would have produced pressures for out-migration in any event. But the mechanization of agriculture made a small number of workers very productive, reduced the job market, and added to migration pressures. Since 1940, the farm population has dropped from 32 million to less than 10 million. Today, farmers, farm workers, and their families are only 5 percent of the nation's population.

Early in the century, those who moved were mainly White—the children of rural immigrants of the late 19th century, and people from Appalachia, the Ozarks, and other depressed rural areas. More recently, there was the great movement of rural Blacks from the South to the largest cities of the North and West.

Most migrants, regardless of race, bettered themselves economically, and in terms of their standard of living. In a recent government survey, most said their move was a success: They were better off financially, and were happier as a result of the move.

Here is Mrs. Mariah Gilmore, aged 60, who lived in the tiny hamlet of DeValls Bluff, 30 miles from Little Rock until her husband died in 1967.

I was without an income. After his death, I looked for work, but was unable to find anything other than ironing, which didn't pay enough money to maintain a house and buy groceries, too.
There were months that I might pick or chop cotton, but due to this being seasonal work, I couldn't make a living. . . . I had to come to Little Rock to see about finding a job because I didn't have nothing to live on.

Mrs. Gilmore found a job as a maid in a hotel for $35 a week. She also found her way into a federally funded work-training program operated by Pulaski County. She was eventually able to take a better position at the University of Arkansas Medical Center in Little Rock. Although she improved her economic status, Mrs. Gilmore confesses she would really prefer to live in DeValls Bluff, if she could have the same job. DeValls Bluff is still home to her.

The migraton from rural areas has been such that in the past decade nearly half of all counties lost population. These losses occurred in a belt from Canada to the Rio Grande between the Mississippi River and the Rockies, in the deep south, and in the Appalachian Mountains. For example, four-fifths of the counties in West Virginia declined in population in the 1960s, with virtually all counties losing population through net out-migration. West Virginia lost one-third of its people in their twenties by migration during the decade.

The territory involved in this rural exodus is immense; but, relative to the national population, the number of people leaving is small. The growth of the nation has been so great that even if all rural counties were repopulated to their historical maximum, they would absorb a population equivalent to no more than five years of national growth.

Nationally, decline in the farm population has been offset by growth in the nonfarm rural population, made possible by growth in nonfarm employment. These people now outnumber the farm population by five to one. If this employment trend should spread, rural population may begin to stabilize in some areas where depopulation has been the rule. Such signs are already apparent, as in the recent reversal of the trend in Arkansas.

Paralleling the decline in the rural percentage of population has been a decline in the proportion of the population located in towns and cities of less than 50,000. Population growth has pushed many of these places into the metropolitan category, but others have lost population. Such is the history of many small towns in Iowa and the Dakotas. In such towns population decline reflects a national system that increasingly requires critical minimum concentrations of economic activities in one location. Lacking adequate roads, power lines, sewers, proximity to large urban centers, and other advantages that would attract new kinds of economic activity and revive growth, they suffer from chronic high-level unemployment and a shrinking economic base. This triggers out-migration, mainly of the young and better educated, and leaves behind an older population that is disadvantaged in terms of education and training and less likely to depart, even in the face of economic hardship. In this case, migration removes surplus population, but it also tends to weaken further the town's competitive position. The future of these places and, more important, the future of the people who live in them, present problems that need continued government attention.

Yet this decline is far from universal. More than half of all nonmetropolitan municipalities grew during each of the last three decades. Between 1940 and 1970, the number of nonmetropolitan places increased from 12,800 to 13,800, and their total population grew from 23 to 33 million. An increasing percentage of this population is in places over 10,000. The places closest to metropolitan areas were more likely to grow than those situated in remote locations.

Nor is it clear that population growth is good for all small towns or cities any more than for all metropolitan areas. For some types of activities—recreation, for example—many rural areas may already have more people than desirable, even though density and population size are well below urban levels. The typical small college town, which has experienced rapid growth in the last decade, might well benefit from stabilization of its population as college enrollment levels off.

The continued growth of some small towns and cities, and the vitality of others whose populations are not growing, challenge the popular notion that small town life is disappearing. On the other hand, the association between growth and proximity to a metropolitan center indicates that many of the small towns are growing because they are part of an extensive metropolitan area whose influence goes beyond the census-defined boundaries. Although rural in physical setting, the life style is urban. Many of these areas have become part of the process of metropolitan growth and dispersal.

METROPOLITAN DISPERSAL

The territory of metropolitan America has expanded even faster than its population. Roads and communications extend the reach of today's metropolitan areas deep into their hinterland. Villages and towns become part of the city-system, grow, and the metropolis expands. At the same time, internal changes sharpen differences within areas. Major variations in ethnic diversity, environmental hazard, socioeconomic status, and income, as well as in fertility and mortality exist within rather than between metropolitan areas. Moreover, the most extensive depopulation in the contemporary United States is occurring in central crities of metropolitan areas.

Fifteen of the 21 central cities with a 1960 population of a half-million or more had lost population by 1970. In fact, declining central cities lost more people in the 1960s than were lost by declining rural counties. Over half the 1970 metropolitan population lived outside the central city, and suburban areas captured almost all the metropolitan growth during the decade. Continuing dispersal and expansion means that the density of the central cities and of the great metropolitan areas as a whole is falling slightly as the border gets pushed further and further outward.

The territorial expansion of metropolitan areas has resulted from the movement of business and the more affluent and White population out of the central city, and from a shift in the locus of new growth—residential, industrial, commercial—to the expanding periphery. These changes have been so pervasive that many suburban areas now provide all the basic services and facilities generally found in the city—shopping, jobs, and entertainment, as well as residences. The suburban resident has a decreasing need to come into the city. Many work at industries along the beltways circling many cities. Others, particularly white-collar workers, commute daily to the city, but otherwise live essentially a suburban life.

Simultaneous with this dispersal has been the concentration of the Black population in the central city, entrenching the already established pattern of racial separation. Even among relatively affluent Blacks, the proportion living in the suburbs is low compared to their White counterparts. In the 1960s, the Black population increased by a third. By 1970, 41 percent of metropolitan Whites and 78 percent of metropolitan Blacks lived in central cities. Suburbs continued to be almost totally White. Six central cities were over 50 percent Black, and this number is expected to increase over the next decade.

Outside the central city there is an extensive sorting-out process. Suburban communities typically are internally homogeneous, but differ from one another along social and economic lines, with the rich in some, the less affluent in others. Variations among suburbs are becoming as important as those between the central city and suburbs as a whole.

These processes—expansion and differentiation—pose critical problems for the contemporary United States. They do so in part because of the multiplicity of governmental jurisdictions encompassed and created by the expanding metropolis, and because of the ease with which the city line becomes the border between "them" and "us."

The first problem is racial and economic separation—Blacks and the poor in the inner city, Whites and the better-off in the suburbs. While job opportunities have been moving to suburban areas, the disadvantaged remain locked in declining areas of the central city. These areas have many of the same characteristics as the depopulating rural areas: a population with low skills and inadequate education, deteriorating and abandoned housing, poor public facilities. Conditions are aggravated by selective outmigration. Those who can, leave. Those unable to cope with the problems of social and economic isolation remain.

The demography of racial separation is grim. Blacks and other non-Whites, now 22 percent of central-city populations, are projected to comprise about 40 percent by the year 2000. Long before this average is reached by all cities, it will have been surpassed by many. At least in a geographical sense, the "two societies" envisioned by the Kerner Commission are emerging.

A second problem is the relationship of the "real city"—the functionally integrated metropolitan area—to the legal entities that are supposed to govern it. Since the turn of the century, the legal boundaries of the central city have remained relatively fixed, while the functional city has expanded to include many suburban jurisdictions as well. The Secretary of the Department of Housing and Urban Development recently referred to this problem, pointing to the need to deal with problems of transportation, housing, and location of jobs in relation to other daily activities at the metropolitan level. Instead, we are trying to cope with the problems arising from a new form of collective living—metropolitan—with a fragmented political structure suited to the needs of an earlier era. Disparities exist between the resources and responsibilities of different units of local government. Core cities with limited and sometimes shrinking tax bases are still responsible for needy elements of the population—the elderly, poor, unemployed, and non-White—left behind by the suburban exodus.

A third problem lies in the expanding periphery of metropolitan areas. During the rapid expansion of suburban areas since World War II, we failed to plan for anticipated growth; instead, we allowed it to spread at will. Whether or not we are past a population explosion, it is clear that the land-use explosion of "spread city" is currently in full bloom. In the 1970s and 1980s, the baby-boom generation will marry, have children, and set up house in the suburbs, creating a tremendous demand for the conversion of rural land to urban use. Without proper efforts to plan where and how future urban growth should occur, and without strong governmental leadership to implement the plans, the problems of sprawl, congestion, inadequate open space, and environmental deterioration will grow on an ever-increasing scale.

PUBLIC ATTITUDES

Partly because of the problems of urban living, partly as an expression of nostalgia for what is perceived as the "good old days," and perhaps partly in anguish over the condition of modern life—for whatever reasons—Americans express dissatisfaction with the city and think something should be done. When asked where they would prefer to live, they show pronounced preferences for small towns and rural areas. Following (Table 36.2) are some of the results from our survey of public information and attitudes.

Thus, 34 percent of people surveyed said they would prefer to live in open country, but only 12 percent of them were classified as actually living there now. These results correspond to the results of many similar national surveys. What do they mean?

A recent survey of Wisconsin residents asked the same questions, but added a question on preferred proximity to a large city. The results show a preference to live in smaller places *within commuting distance of a metropolitan central city*. In fact, if we take them at their word, 70 percent of the Wisconsin survey respondents would prefer to live near a metropolitan area, whereas only 54 percent now do.

We do not know if the results of the Wisconsin survey reflect national attitudes. If they do, it means people want the best of both worlds—the serene and clean environment of rural areas and the opportunity and excitement of the metropolis. Perhaps it is not accidental that much metropolitan growth in fact occurs in peripheral areas with a semi-rural environment. Ironically, people moving to such areas typically find that they soon lose their more desirable aspects—semirural areas rapidly become suburban.

Even if current trends should prove to reflect majority preferences, about one-fourth of the population in medium- and large-sized metropolitan areas think that the place where they live is too big. Over half of the population feel that the federal government should "discourage further growth of large metropolitan areas" or should "try to encourage people and industry to move to smaller cities and towns." One-third disagree, and the rest express no opinion. Americans are urban and becoming more so, but many people evidently dislike the trend.

WHERE DO THE TRENDS LEAD US?

In 1970, about 71 percent of our population was metropolitan; it is expected to be 85

TABLE 36.2

	Where do you live now? (Percent)	Where would you prefer to live? (Percent)
Open country	12	34
Small town or city	33	30
Medium-sized city or suburb	28	22
Larger city or suburb	27	14
Total	100	100

Source: National Public Opinion Survey conducted for the Commission by the Opinion Research Corporation, 1971.

percent by the year 2000. (The census figure for 1970 was 69 percent. Our projections were based on a modified definition of metropolitan areas; hence the difference.)

Natural increase is the primary factor affecting the growth of metropolitan population as a whole. To measure its effect, we asked the Census Bureau to project growth within fixed (1960) metropolitan population boundaries, supposing there were no additions to metropolitan population through territorial additions or migration from within the United States or from abroad. Even assuming growth at the 2-child rate, we found that the metropolitan population would grow by nearly 40 million people between 1970 and the year 2000, through natural increase alone. If to this we add migration, territorial expansion of existing areas, and the growth of other centers to metropolitan size, it is clear that a metropolitan future is assured.

If the national population should grow at the 2-child rate, projections based on recent trends indicate that there will be 225 million people living in metropolitan areas by the end of the century. This would represent the addition of 81 million people to the 144 million persons who comprised our metropolitan population in 1970. An average of 3 children per family would cause our metropolitan population to swell to a total of 273 million by the year 2000, an increase of 129 million over the 1970 figure. Thus, our metropolitan population at the end of the century will be nearly 50 million greater if American families average 3 rather than 2 children.

Where will these people live? In 1970, more than 4 out of every 10 Americans were living in a metropolitan area comprised of 1 million or more people. By the year 2000, the projections indicate that more than 6 of every 10 persons are likely to be living in these large areas. Not all of the additional people will be added to the 29 metropolitan areas of 1 million or more that existed in 1970. In the year 2000, there will be a total of 44 to 50 such places, depending on how fast the total population grows. If present trends continue, the locus of continued increases in our total population will be large metropolitan areas.

This is to be expected so long as the total number of people in metropolitan areas keeps on growing.

We tried to learn how much the growth of the large metropolitan areas might be reduced if the growth of smaller, less congested places were stimulated. Commission researchers picked 121 places ranging in size from 10,000 to 350,000 whose growth in the past decade indicated that they might be induced to grow more rapidly in the future. They listed all places of this size that had grown faster than the national average during the 1960s and were located more than 75 miles from any existing or projected metropolitan area of 2 million people or more.

Such places had a total population of 14 million in 1970. If they were to grow by 30 percent each decade, their population in the year 2000 would be about 31 million. If this were to happen, our calculations suggest that these places might absorb about 10 million of the growth which is otherwise expected to occur in areas of 1 million or more, assuming the 2-child national projection. However, these large areas would still increase by 70 million under the 2-child projection, and by 115 million under the 3-child projection. If the smaller areas were to grow faster than 30 percent, they would, of course, divert more growth from the large areas. But to obtain substantial effects, these smaller places, would have to grow 50 percent per decade. At that point, one must ask if the cure is any better than the disease.

Moreover, most of the smaller areas which are capable of attracting many people are in urban regions, or would be by the year 2000. Thus, stimulating their growth would have the useful effect of decongesting settlement in urban regions, but would do little to retard urban region growth.

URBAN REGIONS

The evolution of urban communities has proceeded from farm, to small town, to city, to large metropolitan area. It is now proceeding to the urban region—areas of 1 million people or more comprised of a continuous zone of metropolitan areas and intervening counties within which one is never far from a city. The reach of the urban economy has so increased that the most logical scale at which to grasp the trend is at the urban region level.

There have been tremendous changes in the geographic scale at which we live. Transportation technology, particularly our extensive highway system, permits us to move great distances within a short period. Some people commute daily between New York and Boston or Washington. Urban people in search of open space and recreation travel considerable distances to enjoy a weekend camping trip. A century ago, Central Park was the city park for New York. Now the "city" is the urban region along the Atlantic seaboard and its park is the Shenandoah National Park on Skyline Drive. It is perhaps a weekend park, not one visited daily; but, on a three-day weekend, the license plates on visiting cars will be from Pennsylvania, New York, D.C., and Virginia. The scale at which we live is expanding well beyond formal metropolitan boundaries. In the future, our daily experience may well reach out into the far corners of urban regions and beyond.

An urban region is not a single "supercity"; it is a regional constellation of urban centers and their hinterland. Although substantial portions are comprised of more or less continuous geographic settlement, the urban region offers—and continues to provide—a variety of residential settings within the functional sphere of a metropolitan economy. This mosiac of environments ranges from rural (southern New Hampshire or Indio, California) to cosmopolitan (Chicago or Los Angeles). Such environments coexist within a common functional framework without intruding spatially on each other. Even in the largest urban region, running along the Atlantic coast from Maine to Virginia, and westward past Chicago, it is estimated that only one-fifth of the area is currently in urban use.

These regions grow not only through the increase of population but by geographic expansion. In effect, they are a product of the automobile era and new communication technology which encouraged the outward movement of industries and residences from the city proper. Density within these regions has remained relatively constant and low, even though population size has increased.

Urban regions appear to be a prominent feature of the demographic future of this country. In 1920, there were 10 urban regions with over one-third of the total population. By 1970, about three-fourths of the population of the United States lived in the urban regions which already exist or are expected to develop by 2000.

The total land area encompassed by urban regions is estimated to double in the period 1960 to 1980, while the number of such areas is expected to increase from 16 to at least 23. By 2000, urban regions will occupy one-sixth of the continental United States land area and contain five-sixths of our nation's people. (See Figure 36.1).

If our national population distributes itself according to these projections, 54 percent of all Americans will be living in the two largest urban regions. The metropolitan belt stretching along the Atlantic seaboard and westward past Chicago would contain 41 percent of our total population. Another 13 percent would be in the California region lying between San Francisco and San Diego. . . .

Even if the broad trends have been projected accurately, the experiences of individual metropolitan areas may differ considerably from the estimates prepared for us. Within the general system of metropolitan centers, some will probably stabilize or decline; others, having a disproportionate number of young people, or attracting much migration, will continue to grow rapidly, even if national population stabilizes. Finally, there may well be new frontiers of growth that have not yet been established or discovered by social scientists. Our projections, then, should be taken as a description of a possible future —one that is essentially the outcome of trends now observable—but not as a prediction of

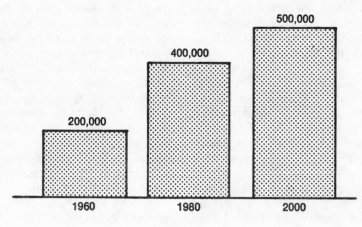

FIGURE 36.1

Expansion of Urban Regions
Square Miles

The territory of urban regions is doubling in the period 1960 to 1980. By the year 2000, urban regions will encompass one-sixth of the United States land area (excl. Alaska and Hawaii).
Source: Jerome P. Pickard, "U. S. Metropolitan Growth and Expansion, 1970-2000, With Population Projections" (prepared for the Commission, 1972).

what will happen or a prescription of what is desirable.

POPULATION STABILIZATION, MIGRATION, AND DISTRIBUTION

How would stabilization of the national population affect migration and local growth? First, shifts in population composition—chiefly age and family structure—would alter the tempo of migration. Second, changes in the balance between natural increase and migration would influence local growth. Because of the momentum of past growth and the time it will take to achieve a stabilized population in the United States, the full effects will be long range.

An older population with smaller families would be slightly less mobile. Long-distance moves would be relatively less numerous because of the decline in the proportion of the population aged 20 to 24, which is most apt to move. Smaller families would reduce the need of repeated residential moves, since such moves are often an adjustment to changing housing needs.

Perhaps the most significant effect of population stabilization on the distribution of population is the most obvious; Zero growth for the nation will mean an average of zero growth for local areas. It may be that the most effective long-term strategy for stabilizing local growth is through national stabilization, not redistribution.

Stabilization would slow the growth of the largest metropolitan centers, which are already growing only at the same rate as the nation, and it would shift somewhat more of the available growth to small- and intermediate-size centers. Replacement-level fertility would mean that migration in and out of a metropolitan area would be an extremely important component of local growth; and continued selective growth through migration would tend to accentuate uneven growth among different metropolitan areas. Natural increase would no longer balance out net outmigration, so a significant number of metropolitan areas could be expected to lose population.

However, even if the population of our country were to stop growing today, we would still have problems associated with rural depopulation and metropolitan growth. Our large metropolitan areas would still have problems of congestion, pollution, and severe racial separation.

According to the Commission's survey, 54 percent of Americans think that the distribution of population is a "serious problem"; half believe that over the next 30 years it will be at least as great a problem as population growth. This is in accordance with our belief that to reduce problems of population growth in no way absolves us of the responsibility to address the problems posed by the distribution of population.

INDEX

ABM. *See* Antiballistic missile system.
Abortion, 179, 188, 379, 384; research, 3; women's rights, 259
Abrams, Charles, 160
Abt Associates day care budgets, 276
ADC. *See* Aid to Families with Dependent Children.
Aerospace programs, 342; benefits contribution, 396; government expenditures, 394 human achievement, 401; systems *table*, 344
Africa, 369, 373
Agnew, Spiro, 146
Agriculture: environmental crisis, 420, 426; migration pressures, 442; Third World, 364, 367
Aid to Families with Dependent Children (ADC, AFDC) 89, 90-96, 100-02; failings, 105
Alger, Horatio, 268
Allison, Graham, 338
Ameliorative problems, 5
Andrzejewski, Stanislaw, 56
Anomie, 32, 38, 39; moral regulation, 36; systemic hypothesis, 222
Antiballistic missile system (ABM), 337, 346-47
Antonovsky, Anton, 170
Anxiety, 17; hospitalization, 186; working class lifestyle, 141
Apathy, lower class goals, 308, 309
Apollo program, 342, 345
Architectural Forum, The, 150
Architecture, 149; Pruitt-Igoe housing project 155
Aristotle, 42, 43
Assimilation model, 264, 266-07
Astor, John Jacob, III, 53
Atomic Energy Commission, 396

B.A. degree, FAA awards, 123
Balance of power: strategic theory, 337; Third World, 365
Barber, Bernard, 45, 50; status dysfunctions, 317
Beare v. *Smith*, 292, 293
Becker, Howard S.: model of social processes, 11; objective condition of problem, 2; sorting and defining problems, 10
Behavior, human: administration regulation, 314; aspects of, 2; control of, 403; deprivation, 74; deviant, 5, 6
    rewards and punishments, 46; status, 49
    government and social decision, 416; lower class organization, 179, 309; neighborhoods, 415; norms, 46, 47;

reproduction and child care, 380; role-taking, 315; rules of, 407; voting, 291, 293; welfare, 97, 98
Bell, Daniel, postindustrial society, 25
Berg, Ivar, 115; labor force, 118
Biological warfare, 424, 428
Birth control. *See* Family planning.
Black Muslims, 220
Black Panthers, 224
Black power, 157; radical decentralization, 303, 305
Blacks: achievement tests, 115; AFDC 94; assimilation model, 266; central city, 444; cultural democracy, 360; day care centers, 275; education, 124; environmental protection, 427; income, 80, 84, *tables* 226-28, 230-33, 235; integrated housing, 155; IQ variation, 127; job competition, 123; metropolitan migration, 441; Mexican Americans, 281 political strategy, 312; poverty, 113; professional status, 290; progress of 1960's, 225-40; Pruitt-Igoe housing project, 147; revolt, 19; taste culture, 357; unrest 216-224; voting, 289, 294; welfare, 95, 97; White attitudes toward integration, 241-50; women and civil rights, 263; working mothers, 270
Blake, Judith, 191
Blauner, Robert, 281, 286
BLS, *See* Bureau of Labor Statistics
Blue-collar workers, 90; educational achievements, 121; health, 182, 184; IQ, 132; problematic behavior, 135; voting participation, 289; working class, 138
Body esteem, 182
Boeing, 342, 345, 346, 347, 351; *table*, 344
Bokser, Ben Zion, 257
Bonuses, 87
Britain, 34, 36; national political culture, 39
Brown v. *Board of Education*, 290
Building and construction: costs, 159, homeownership and rental programs, 167; job market in 1960's, 239; Pruitt-Igoe housing project, 154; subsidy formulas, 163;
Building codes, 149
Bureaucratic theory, 337-38
Bureau of Labor Statistics (BLS), 193, 195, 196
Burke, Edmund, 57
Burnham, Walter Dean, 288, 293
Busing, 248; *tables*, 248, 249
Buying power. *See* Purchasing power.

California, 284-86
California, University of (UC), 117-18
Campbell, Arthur A., 190, 192, 197
Cantril, H., 218; Black status, 220
Capital gains tax, 206
Carmichael, Stokely, 281
Carson, Rachel, 8, 424
Cash transfers, 63, 64
Censorship, 354-55; taste culture, 360
Census Bureau:
    Current Population Survey, 234; metropolitan population boundaries, 446; mortality rates, 173, 175; population and income tax, 200; poverty, 160, 194; pregnancy, 198; racial differences, 225; subsidized family planning, 192
Central city, 435-36
Chain reactions, 414
Chauvinism, 400
Chicanos, 286
Child care. *See* Day care.
Children: AFDC, 91; credit income tax, 109-10; day care services, 268-79; education programs, 124; industrial societies, 385; parental character, 27; and physicians, 185; poverty, 105; Pruitt-Igoe housing project, 154; public housing, 151, 152, 153; working class lifestyle, 138
China: Third World, 363, 372, 373
Choice, freedom of 12, 65; economic efficiency, 64; family planning, 379; multifamily buildings, 166; public policy, 403
Cicero, 57
Cities: authority over public programs, 300; environmental crisis, 421; ethnic identity, 22; ethnic neighborhoods, 251; family planning, 381, 194; housing, 147, 149, 159, 160; inner cities, 431; metropolitan fragmentation, 304; Mexican Americans, 285; political strategy, 312; riots and violence, 223; socioeconomic system, 74; strategy of power, 310; urban design, 156; welfare 92, 98
Civil rights movement, 221; Black college students, 216; communication strategy, 311; radical decentralization, 301; strategy of power, support for, 241
Civil service, 120
Clark Kenneth B., 72, 311
Class, Social. *See* Stratification, social.
Cleaver, Eldridge, 281
Cloward, Richard, 66, 97, 98
Coercion, 8
Cohen, David K., 115, 124

Coleman report, 219
Collective interest, 405, 407-08; morality, 418-19
Collectivism, 23
Colleges and universities:
  Blacks, 216, 221, 229, 236; education subsidies, 116; enrollment and town population, 443; IQ, 128; organizational participation, 307; prointegration, 245; surplus of graduates, 119; working class anxiety, 142
Colonialism, 281-86; Third World, 366
Commission on Population Growth and the American Future, 429, 437
Commission on Pornography, U.S., 10
Commodities, primary, Third World, 368
Commoner, Barry, 393, 420
Communication strategy, 311-12
Communism, 29, 59
Communist Manifesto, 31
Community action, 299-306; programs, 155, 157
Community Work and Training (CW&T), 101
Competition:
  cities and welfare payments, 433; distribution, laws of, 55; employment economy, 86; nonelites, 59; Third World, 365
Conflict colonialism, 285
Conformism, 46
Congestion, 408-09
Conservation, 393
Conservative decentralization defined, 300
Conservatives:
  education, 123; government and consent, 61; humanitarianism, 63; manipulation of consensus, 58; merit standards, 128; population control, 385; radical decentralization, 302; taste culture, 357; welfare rolls, 98; working class, 137
Constitutionalism, 52; elite, 59, 61; power and privilege, 60
Contraception. See Family planning.
Corporate income taxes, 202
Costs:
  college and working class, 142; day care, 276, 277; environmental crisis, 422; family planning, 189, 386; housing, 152, 155, 159, 166, 257; negative income tax programs, 75; public assistance, 105; public colleges, 118; taxes and benefits, 106; radical decentralization, 302; wartime labor, 122; weapons systems, 351; see also Prices
Credentialism, 115
Credit income tax, 103, 107-09; redistribution, 112
Crime:
  Blacks, 254; Forest Hills public schools, 253; middle class and suburbs, 22; poverty, 21, 72; power and privilege, 60, 61; public housing, 147, 152; research, 3; social evaluations, 2
Cultural relativism, 359
Culture, 353-60; Third World, 364
Cutright, Phillips, 191, 195
CW&T (Community Work and Training), 101

Dahl, Robert, 337
Dahrendorf, Ralf, 41; manipulation of consensus, 58
Davis, Kingsley, 44, 50; population crisis, 375
Day care, 268-79; AFDC, 92; distribution of children tables, 274, 275; social services, 100
Daylight saving, 404
DDT, 418, 424
Death (biological). See Mortality rates.
Delinquency:
  mortality rates, 174; poverty, 72
Delta index,
  income distribution tables, 226, 227, 230, 233, 237
Democratic myth, 35
Democratic theory, 338
Demography, 437; AFDC, 92; future of urban regions, 447; racial separation, 444; Third World, 372
Demonstrations:
  Black protest, 221; Mexican Americans, 283
Deprivation and exclusion, 72; allegiant political culture, 36; Blacks, 216; minimum subsistence level, 74; structure of reference groups, 35
Desegregation:
  policy authority, 300; working class resistance, 135
Developing nations. See Third World
Disasters, natural, 5
Discrimination:
  income distribution, 81; women, 262; see also Blacks; Minority groups; Race relations; Racism
Distribution, laws of, 53-56
Division of Labour, The (Durkheim), 39
Divorce and separation:
  AFDC, 90; lower class, 73; poverty, 72; women and BLS level, 197
Doctrine of less eligibility, 99
DPV. See Dryfoos-Polgar-Varky formula.
Drift hypothesis, 178
Dropouts, 71; education subsidies, 118
Drugs:
  lower class, 181; working class, 142
Dryfoos, Joy G., 188
Dryfoos-Polgar-Varky formula (DPV), 191, 193
DuBois, W. E. B., 240
Durkheim, Emile, 38; Division of Labour, The, 39; moral community, 45
Dysfunctions, 50

Ecology. See Environmental crisis.
Economic colonialism, 281
Economics:
  Britain, 36; collective interest, 408; distribution, laws of, 55; priorities, 64; proportions, 29; Third World, 365; weapons system production, 351
Economic theory, 338
Edelman, Murray, 313
Education, 115-18; age, sex and color table, 237; birth rate, 387; Blacks, 218; class differentials, 34; discrimination and women, 262; distribution of income, 79, 85; elitism, 58, 397; hunger and learning, 27; job train-ing, 119-23; length of, 28; meritocracy, 49; migration patterns, 441; mortality rates, 177; prointegration tables, 245, 246; segregation, 290; tax support for, 211, 212; teaching standards, 303; and wealth, 31; working class, 142; working mothers, 272
Elections, 288; missile gap, 349; Vietnam war, 325 voter reregistration, 296
Elite, 59; colonialism, 282; community planning, 301; environment degradation, 389; evaluation of problems, 8; housing and neighborhoods, 149, 156; Mexican Americans, 285; radical decentralization, 301; revolution, 60; rule of might, 57-58; service workers, 135; social policy changes, 249; Third World, 366; urban renewal, 150; welfare, 98
Elitism, 397-98; achievements, 401
Ellsberg, Daniel, 322
Employment:
  metropolitan growth, 440; negative income tax, 103; payroll taxes, 203, 204; race and sex table, 235; rural population, 442; welfare recipients, 96
Employment Service, U.S., 119
Energy, 390; pollution, 422
Environment, 126; housing, 148; IQ differences, 125
Environmental crisis, 423; national ignorance, 425; origin, 421; population problem, 430; public morality, 426; social questions, 428; urban growth, 445
Establishment, the working class, 143
Estate and gift taxes, 203
Ethnic groups:
  neighborhoods and housing, 149; schooling, 133; see also Blacks; Minority groups
Evaluative differentiation, sanctions of behavior, 48
Excise taxes, 202, 206
Expressways, 404-05

FAA (Federal Aviation Agency), 123
Falk, Richard, 333
Fallout, 424
Family Assistance Plan (FAP), 100, 103
Family planning, 188-99, 384-88, tables, 192, 193, 199; availabiity of information, 196; population crisis, 375; struggle for survival, 60; Third World, 372
Farley, Reynolds, 225
FBI, 316
Federal Aviation Agency (FAA), 123
Federal Communications Commission (FCC), 316, 318
Federal Housing Authority (FHA), 155, 158; application for funds, 166
Federal Reserve Board, 82
Feminism, 259, 263; assimilation model, 266
Fertility, 188; control, 195, 377; metropolitan population, 440; replacement level, 448; rural areas, 442; surveys, 195
Fertilizers, 422
FHA. See Federal Housing Authority.
Fimreite, Norvald, 425

Food stamps, 64, 91, 96, 309
Ford Foundation, 283
Forest Hills housing project, 251-58
Foster, John, 337, 347
Foster care. *See* Day care.
Fourteenth Amendment, 291
France, Anatole, 58
France, 372, 373
Frazier, Franklin, 240
Freedman, Marcia, 120
Freedom, 31, 99
Fried, Edward R., 268
Frieden, Bernard J., 157
Friedman, Milton,
   negative income tax, 103, 110
Fuller, Richard C., 7; social prob-
   lems defined, 1; value conflict, 5
Functional theory, 44, 45

Galbraith, John Kenneth, 338
Game playing, 314
Gans, Herbert J., 148, 150; culture,
   353; egalitarianism, 18; lower class
   peer groups, 309
Gay liberation, 3
Gelb, Leslie, 331
General Dynamics, 342, 345, 346, 351,
   table, 344
General Grant-Morningside Gardens
   complex, 255-56
Genetics. *See* Heredity and genetics
Geographic mobility:
   income distribution, 81; violence,
   152; working class, 139
Ghettos:
   colonized groups, 281; cultural
   democracy, 360; education pro-
   grams, 115; housing, 149, 151, 155;
   institutionalized pathology, 72, 73;
   Mexican Americans, 286; program
   planning, 301; rioting, 223
G. I. Forum, 284, 285
Gini index,
   income distribution *tables,* 226, 227,
   230, 233, 237
Glazer, Nathan, 251; Black economic
   position, 65; welfare, 95
GNP. *See* Gross National Product.
Goals, 306, 324
Goldthorpe, John H., 32, 52
Goods and services, 78; distribution,
   laws of, 55; working class, 137
Government expenditures, 201; in-
   come transfer, 106; *see also* Grants;
   Subsidies; Welfare, social
Grants:
   community development programs,
   300; rehabilitation, 165; rent sup-
   plements, 158; social insurance, 90;
   war on poverty, 104
Great American Status Scramble, 130
Great Society, 124
Greeley, Andrew M., 241
Gross National Product (GNP):
   affluence, 24; defense spending, 336;
   medical care, 169; taxation, 203; unskilled workers, 75; working class,
   136
Gross reproduction rate (GRR), 377
Growth, Economic:
   Black community, 258; distribution
   of income, 78, 79; gap between
   Blacks and Whites, 225; incentives
   to work, 63; nation-state, 366; per
   capita income, 391; Third World,
   365, 389; welfare, 94; working class,
   144

GRR (Gross reproduction rate), 377
Guaranteed income, 75, 103; tax-ex-
   periment, 11; working class support,
   145
Guttman scale, 243, 247

Halberstam, David, 340
Halperin, Morton H., 323
Hansen, W. Lee, 115, 201; education,
   116
Hardin, Garrett, 409
Hausman, Leonard, 101
Headstart program, 124, 261
Health
   childrens services, 268; infant mor-
   tality, 34; rise in fertility, 382; *see
   also* Medicine
Health, Education and Welfare, U.S.
   Department of (HEW), 91, 103
Heredity and genetics:
   educational program, 115; IQ, 125,
   126; mortality rates, 178
Hermalin, Albert, 225
Herrnstein, Richard J., 125
Hiestand, Dale, 123
High school:
   IQ, 128; middle level jobs, 119;
   organizational participation, 307;
   racial differences and enrollment,
   236; working class view, 142
Hilsman, Robert, 329
Hobbes, Thomas, 57
Homeownership:
   aid and FHA, 158; low income,
   162; new construction market, 167;
   property taxes, 205; purchasing
   power, 136
Horowitz, Irving Louis, 362; interna-
   tional stratification, 16
Hoopes, Townsend, 333
Housing, 29, 64, 147-57; federal sub-
   sidies, 157-68, *table,* 158; high and
   low income apartments, 255; level
   of quality, 24; minority groups,
   254; racial desegregation, 251
Housing and Urban Development,
   U.S. Department of (HUD), 159,
   161; experimental housing allowances, 166; functional city, 444
Humanitarianism, 63
Human Sexual Response (Masters and
   Johnson), 265
Humphrey, Hubert, 223
Hybrid model, 264, 267

Illegitimacy:
   AFDC, 91, 94; poverty, 72
Illiteracy, 122
Immigration:
   inner cities, 433; Mexican Americans, 284 social disorganization, 4
Incivisme, 36
Income, 45; *tables,* 79-83; action organizations, 312; advanced societies,
   37; Blacks *tables,* 226-28, 230-33;
   BLS budget, 193; city workers, 432;
   day care, 274, 275; distribution of,
   19, 64, 77-88; education, 117, 134;
   evaluative differentiation, 48; family planning programs, 191, 192,
   198; Gini and delta indexes, 226;
   housing, 159, 162; hybrid model of
   equality, 267; incentive, 23; lower
   class, 72, 306; managerial structure,
   39; median, 21, 24; medical costs,

194; mortality rates, 177; national
   assistance level, 32; post WW II
   affluence, 21; quality of life, 65;
   restructuring, 87; subsidy formulas,
   163; taxation, 105, 200-14, 314,
   tables, 107-11; Third World, 366;
   War on Poverty, 74; welfare bene-
   fits, 96
Indians, American. *See* Minority
   groups.
Individualism,
   pursuit of liberty, 23
Industrialization, 367
Inflation, 88; working class, 141, 142
Integration, 241; attitudes *tables,* 242-
   49; experiments *figures,* 431-35; status of Blacks, 238
Intergenerational mobility, 82, 84
Intermarriage, 241
Internal colonialism, 286
Interstate Commerce Commission, 318
Intrauterine device. *See* IUD.
IQ (Intelligence quotient) 115, 125-
   34; day care benefits, 278
Isolation:
   hospitalization, 186; housing, 153;
   inner city, 438; middle class, 141;
   urban design, 150; women, 266;
   working class lifestyle, 139
IUD (Intrauterine device), 196, 376,
   379, 380, 383

Jacobs, Jane, 304
Jaffe, Frederick S., 188
Japan, 379
Jensen, Arthur, 125
Jews. *See* Minority groups.
Job Training, 118-24; bonuses, 87;
   culturally disadvantaged, 74; dis-
   tribution of income, 85; failure of
   programs, 147; income supplemen-
   tation, 113; next generation, 75;
   welfare, 102; WIN program, 101
Johnson, Lyndon:
   ABM gap, 346; family planning,
   376; Vietnam, 323, 325
Justice defined, 30

Kahn, Herman, 337
Kain, John F., 156
Kant, Immanuel, 51
Kelley, Stanley, Jr., 291
Kelso, Louis,
   individualistic model, 23
Kennedy, John F.,
   War on Poverty, 71
Kennedy, Robert F., 146
Kerner Commission report, 239, 444
Key, V. O., Jr., 295
Kinsey study, 197
Kinship:
   New Mexico, 282; working class
   views, 139
Kissinger, Henry, 337
Knowledge and power, 28
Kurth, James R., 336

Lampman, Robert, 112; income tax,
   200
Labor
   division of, 48;
      distribution, laws of, 53, 55;
      patient-physician relationship,
      185; working class, 139

force:
Blacks, 232, 239; job categories, 120; Mexican Americans, 285; skills, 86, 119; Third World, 367; women, 91, 386; working mothers *tables*, 270, 271
industrial, 53
market:
Blacks, 229; educational requirements, 122; employment opportunities, 104
shortages, 86, 87; supply and demand, 37; unions, 61
Landlords, 161; property taxes, 202; slum housing, 148; welfare families, 164
Laski, Harold, 26
Lasswell, Harold D., 41
Latin America, 364; family planning, 379; migration patterns, 372; parliamentary rule, 369; sovereignty, 366
Law:
absolute equals, 50; AFDC program, 92; new elite, 58; penalties, 47; taxation, 214
League of United Latin American Citizens (LULAC), 284
League of Women Voters, 262
Legislation, 24, 124; public colleges, 118; public housing, 163; taxation, 64, 205; welfare services, 100
Leisure, 60
Lenski, Gerhard, 52; functional theory of stratification, 45
Levitan, Sar, 434
Levy, Marion J., 45
Liberals:
crime, 254; merit standards, 128; population control, 385; radical decentralization, 302; social programs, 124; taxation, 201; welfare rolls, 98; working class, 137; worth of education, 123
Life expectancy. See Mortality rates.
Lipsky, Michael, 300
Lockheed, 342, 345, 346, 347, 351, *table*, 344
Lorenz, Konrad, 418
Lower class:
coping with reality, 73; defense and survival, 154; goals for community action, 306-12; health and medicine, 179-87; housing, 148, 151, 152; mortality rates, 178; poverty, 72; taste culture, 355; threat of violence, 153; urban design, 150; working class, 137, 138, 144
LULAC (League of United Latin American Citizens), 284
Lurie, Irene, 96

McDonnell, Douglas, 342, 345, 346, 347, 351; *table*, 344
McGovern, George, 103; comprehensive tax reform, 19
Machine (political), 304
MacLeish, Archibald, 430
McNamara, Robert S., 52; military buildup, 339
Malnutrition, 172
Man-in-the-house rule, 99
Man in the street, 9
Manipulation of concensus, 58
Markets:
distribution, laws of, 55; distribution of income, 78; efficiency of, 65

Marriage:
family planning, 385-87; lower class, 73; sex equality, 264; working class lifestyle, 139
Marx, Karl, 31, 50
Mass media, 58; companion-in-marriage, 259; culture, 354, 357; lower class housing, 152; working class, 137, 143, 146
Mead, George Herbert, 315
Medicaid, 90, 92, 169, 268
Medically indigent, 189, 190, 191; medical care, 194
Medicare, 64, 96, 169
Medicine:
careers for women, 268; family planning, 381; lower classes, 179; mortality rates, 178; paternalism, 397
Mercury, 425
Meritocracy, 49; defined, 115; intelligence, 128, 130, 134
Merton, Robert, 304; deviant behavior, 5; structural-functional approach, 12
Mexican Americans. See Minority groups.
Michanek, Ernst, 389
Middle class:
Blacks 222, 240; control of power and privilege, 60; dispensing of benefits, 398; force 56-61; fragmentation of central city, 304; health, 181, 184, 185; housing, 150, 151, 256; job opportunities, 80; law and order, 354; lifestyle, 136; material affluence, 72; medicine, 180, 187; political elite, 59; taste culture, 355; voting turnout, 296; women, 263
Middle East, 371
Migration:
AFDC, 105; Blacks, 222; metropolitan growth, 439; Mexican Americans, 283; population, 377, 439, 448
Military, 56;
expenditures, 400; independent organizations, 57; policy and weapons 336-39; remedial training, 122; security and paternalism, 396; Third World bases, 370
Military Air Command, 342
Military-industrial complex, 287, 336, 338
Military Organization and Society (Andrzejewski), 56
Mill, John Stuart, 398
Miller, S. M., 24, 179
Minimum subsistence level, 74
Minority groups:
AFDC, 90; assimilation model. 266, 268; central city, 436; distribution of income, 80, 84, 87; housing, 147; merit standards, 129; Mexican Americans, 280-86
organizational action, 310
political organization, 312; unemployment, 92; welfare eligibility, 99; see also Blacks
Minuteman (missile), 339, 340
MIRV. See Multiple independently targeted reentry vehicles.
Model cities, 149, 155
Models:
cash transfers, 64; designation of population, 303; educational institu-

tions, 435; individualism, 23; international balance sheet, 391; parental role, 263; quagmire machine, 328; regulatory agencies, 313; relative deprivation, 217, 221; social processes, 11; stratification, 264; symbolic participation, 312; welfare rise, 93
Monopolization defined, 368
Monopoly
distribution, laws of, 55
Montgomery, Roger, 149, 156
Montgomery, Ala.,
bus boycott, 18
Moore, Joan W., 280
Moore, Wilbert E., 44, 50, 55
Moral damage, 73
Morality, 5; collective good, 418; Durkheim, Emile, 45; environmental crisis, 426; norms, 48; policy innovations, 11
Mortality rates, 172-79; *tables*, 174, 179; class differentials, 169; infants, 34; population growth, 377; Third World, 372
Mortgages, 162, 163, 164
Mosea, Gaetano, 59
Moynihan, Daniel P.:
AFDC rates, 94; opportunity, 23
Multiple independently targeted reentry vehicles (MIRV), 337, 340-41, 352
Mumford, Lewis, 255
Mutual role-taking, 315; administrative agencies, 316
Myers, Richard R., 7; social problems defined, 1; value conflict, 5
Myrdal, Gunnar, 225, 239

NAACP, 252
Nader, Ralph, 425
Nagel, Thomas, 393, 394
NASA, 343, 344
National Academy of Sciences, 395
National Fertility Study (NFS), 195, 196
National Industrial Conference Board, 119
Nationalization
Third World, 365
National Opinion Research Center (NORC), 242, 244; integration scale, 249, 250
National Organization for Women, 264
Need, distributions, laws of, 53
Negative income tax (NIT), 75, 78, 103, 110-13; credit income tax, 108; guaranteed income, 11
Negroes. See Blacks.
Neighborhood organizations, 307
Nelson, Gaylord, 425
Nerve gas, 424
Net reproduction rate (NRR), 387
Neugarten, Bernice, 182
New Deal, 144, 313
New Left, 144
New Mexico, 282-83
New towns, 437
NFS. See National Fertility Study.
Nhu, Ngo Dinh, 329
Nisbet, Robert A.,
structural-functional approach, 13
NIT. See Negative income tax.
Nixon, Richard M., 103, 316; ABM

gap, 346; Blacks, 223; population growth, 437; Vietnam, 323
NORC. *See* National Opinion Research Center.
Norms:
conflict of weak and strong, 317; deviant behavior, 6; hidden social problems, 1; rewards for conformity, 49; sanctions, 46, 47
North American Rockwell, 342, 346, 347, 351; *table*, 344
NRR (Net reproduction rate), 387
Nuclear Test Ban Treaty, 423, 424

Obstetrics, 186
Occupational mobility,
distribution of income, 84
Occupational selection:
IQ, 132; sitting still, 133
Office of Economic Cooperation and Development (OECD), 391
Office of Economic Opportunity (OEO), 74, 103; day care centers staff, 276
Okner, Benjamin A., 205
Old age,
social insurance, 89
Oligopoly
distribution, laws of, 55
OPA, 314, 316, 318
Opinion, public:
force and the new elite, 58; polls, 136
Opportunity, 27; human capital, 104; public higher education, 117; training, 28; wages, 86, 88
Organization of Arab States, 366
Orwell, George, 50
Overqualification, 121

Parity payments, 320
Parks, Rosa, 18
Parsons, Talcott, 50, 183; stratification, 44, 45
Pascal, Blaise, 57
PASSO (Political Association of Spanish Speaking Organizations), 284
Paternalism, 396-97
Pathology, 3
Patriotism,
working class, 139, 144
Patron, 282
Patronage, 48, 359
Pauling, Linus, 423
Pearson Report, 391
Pechman, Joseph A., 200, 205
Penalties,
IQ, 128; norms and sanctions, 47; role-taking, 315
Pentagon papers, 322
Periodic registration. (Reregistration), 295
Personal registration, 293, 294; statutes, 289, 290
Pettigrew, Thomas F., 216
Physicians, 184
Picketing
communication strategy, 311
Pill, the 196, 380, 381, 383
Piven, Frances Fox, 66, 97, 98
Placebos, 434
Planned Parenthood, 193; clinics, 191
Planned Parenthood-World Population

(PPWP), 90; poverty income cutoffs, 192
Planning, social, 404
Planning, urban, 149, 157, 252
Pluralism:
taste cultures, 360; Third World, 364
Pluralist model, 264-65
Polaris (missile), 339, 340
Political Association of Spanish Speaking Organizations (PASSO), 284
Politics, Parties and Pressure Groups (Key), 295
Poll tax, 291
Pollution, environmental, 393, 409-10; individual prices, 417; population growth, 390; *see also* Environmental crisis
Population:
distribution of, 437, 449
metropolitan *table*, 440
preference *table*, 445
major cities, 433; migration and local growth, 448; population levels, 428; struggle for survival, 60; world crisis, 375-88
Poverty, 70-76, 113; Blacks and progress, 238; central city, 435; crime, 21; distribution of income, 84, 88; elimination as an ideal, 63; environmental crisis, 427; family planning services, 191, 194; housing projects, 157; IQ, 125, 127, 134; line, 70, 84 credit income, 108; family planning programs, 191; suburbs, 160 malnutrition, 172; national assistance level, 32; negative income tax, 11; strategy of power, 310; taxation, 105; welfare colonialism, 66; working class, 137
Power, 43, 45; administration regulation, 313-21; Blacks, 144; communication strategy, 311; culture, 353; defined, 33; distribution, laws of, 53, 54; institutionalized, 49; IQ. 125, 133; political and economic 31; possessions, 30; radical decentralization, 300; strategy of, 310; student behavior, 305; taste culture, 357; transformation of force, 56; urban neighborhoods, 19; utilization of knowledge, 28; working class, 143;
PPWP. *See* Planned Parenthood-World Population
Pregnancy, 190, 192, 197; family planning, 195; rhythm method, 196; social consequences, 198
Prestige, 43, 45; culture, 353; distribution, laws of, 54; evaluative differentiation, 48; gossip, 46; national, 399; occupations, 132
Prices:
cost of living, 71; day care, 270; lower class, 72; pollution, 417-18; taxation, 201, 208; Third World, 366; welfare, 93; *see also* Costs
Primitive society, 56
Privilege defined, 54
Production:
techniques of, 87; technological advance, 56
Productivity:
academic, 267; agricultural, 438; education, 120, 121; measure of society, 401; Third World, 368; wartime, 122; working class, 146

Professionals:
Blacks, 229; feminist-assimilation model, 266; middle class, 186; mortality rates, 173; voting participation, 289
Progressive income tax, 78; economics of war, 86
Progressive tax, 118; defined, 202
Propaganda, 58
Property tax, 205; neighborhood values, 201; value added tax, 211-14
Pruitt-Igoe housing project, 147, 148, 154
Public assistance, 89; day care, 269; inadequacies, 105; lower minimum budget level, 193; poverty gap, 111; *see also* Welfare, social
Public Health Service, U.S., 422
Public housing, 152; *see also* Housing
Purchasing power, 78; Blacks, 217; credit income tax, 108; Gross National Product, 136; new home construction, 167; racial differentiation, 228, 240; suburbs, 435

Quagmire machine, 328-34
Quantitative change
weapons systems, 350
Quota system,
distribution of income, 87

Race relations, 221, 237-38; central city 436; city and suburb separation, 444; prevention of riots, 224; sorting and scrambling, 411
Racism:
electoral processes, 289; Mexican Americans, 286; pressure groups, 8; welfare colonialism, 66
Racketeering, 6
Radical decentralization:
assessment of policies, 304; Black population, 301; defined, 300; national social welfare system, 303
Radicals, 58, 61
Rainwater, Lee:
lower class, 179, 306; poverty, 70; slum problems, 148; working class, 135
Rawls, John, 398
Redistribution:
preservation of inequalities, 65; public assistance, 78, 106; social policy definition, 64
Redistributive change,
defined, 349
Regressive tax,
defined, 202
Rein, Martin, 62, 89
Relative deprivation, 216, 218, 220, 221; Black position, 225; racial protests, 223
Religion:
family planning, 195; integration attitudes, 245; *table*, 247; new elite and force, 58; Third World, 370; zero population growth, 378
Rent supplements, 256, 257
Reproduction, 181
Research and development:
elitism, 397; family planning, 189; MIRV, 341; production techniques, 86, 87; public health, 169; sociological perspectives, 3; technical and organizational procedures, 347

Reston, James, 328
Retirement,
    working class views, 140
Revenue Act (1971), 205
Revolutionary movements, 221; elite 58, 60
Rewards:
    IQ, 128; positive sanctions, 47
Rhythm method, 379
Riots,
    relative deprivation theory, 223
Rivlin, Alice M., 268
Robinson, Joan, 65
Rolph, Earl, 107, 112
Roman Catholic church, 386
Roper Associates, 121
Rossi, Alice S., 260
Rousseau, J. J., 43, 50
Rowe, Mary P., 275
Rubington, Earl, 12; sociological perspectives, 3
Runciman, W. G., 34-36, 37; deprivation and Blacks, 220

Safeguard (ABM), 346
Safety:
    child care, 274; paternalism, 397
Salaries. See Wages and salaries.
Sales tax, 202, 206
Sanctions, 49; acceptability, 315; distributive status, 47; norms, 46, 47; regulatory agencies, 317; structures of power, 50
Sandboxism, 434, 436
San Jose burial, 427
Scattered site housing, 251, 254, 257; defined, 253
Schelling Thomas, 337, 403
Schlesinger, Arthur, Jr., 333, 339
Schools:
    culture, 353; inner city, 435; IQ, 128; interracial contact, 240; radical decentralization, 305; segregation, 249; Third World, 371
Schultze, Charles L., 268
Schwartz, Richard, 45
Security, national, 201
Segregation:
    lower class, 72; neighborhoods, 415; pluralist model, 264; schools, 388; sorting and scrambling, 411; urban housing, 220; white southerners, 221
Self-help strategy, 311
Sentinel (ABM), 346
Separation,
    ethnic groups, 240
Sheatsley, Paul B., 241
Shinn, Allen, 291
Short-term leasing, 165
Silent Majority, 136
Silent Spring (Carson), 8
Skills,
    mortality rates, 174
Slavery,
    defined, 30
Slums, 433; clearance, 147, 150, 301; goals of living, 306; institutionalized pathology, 72, 73; minority groups, 253
Snow, C. P., 371
Socialism, 31
Social security:
    distribution of income, 78; welfare mothers, 91
Social Security Act, 89, 100, 101
Social Security Administration (SSA),

190, 191; poverty and family planning, 193
Social services:
    defined, 100; see also Day care; Welfare, social
Sombart, Werner, 44
South, the:
    Black migration, 441; income level, 229; communication strategy, 311; moral community, 400; population growth, 439; racial integration, 242; strategy of power, 310
Sovereignty, political, 57
Spanish-speaking Americans. See Minority groups.
Spheres of influence, 366
Spread city, 445
SSA. See Social Security Administration.
SST. See Supersonic transport.
Standard of living, 70; Blacks, 217; Third World, 391; women, 266; working class, 137
Starr, Chauncey, 426
Status inconsistency, 219
Sterility, 191, 196
Sterilization, 188, 379, 384
Stern, Philip, 20
Sternlieb, George, 393, 431, 437
Strategic Air Command, 342
Strategic theory, 337
Stratification, social, 15, 43, 53; Blacks, 220; college determinant, 28; distribution, laws of, 48, 55; education, 116; functional theory, 44; hierarchy, 34; inner cities, 431; international issues, 361; manipulation of consensus, 58; meritocracy, 49; models, 264; mortality rates, 171, 172; non-competing groups, 37; norms, 47, 50; origin, 45; power, privilege and prestige, 52, 287; rank order, 46; reference groups, 36; stability of, 33; taste cultures, 356; voting turnout, 295; working class, 144
Strauss, Anselm, 156
Strikes, 143
Students for a Democratic Society, 299, 308
Studies in Family Planning, 379
Subsidies:
    day care, 269; education, 116; family planning services, 194; federal housing, 147, 157-68, table 158; home purchase, 256; mail rates, 321; rent, 24, 64; wage scales, 87; working mothers, 273
Suburbs:
    Black population, 444; central city, 435; housing and lower income, 159; stratification, 431
Suffrage, 50; Blacks, 98; women, 263; see also Voting
Supersonic transport (SST), 350, 351; noise pollution, 425; unemployment, 428

Supply and demand, 54
Supreme Court of the United States:
    AFDC, 92; censorship and culture, 354; educational segregation, 217, 290; one-man one-vote principal, 20; taxation for education, 211; welfare eligibility, 99
Surcharge, 214
Surplus:
    distribution, laws of, 54, 56; political sovereignty 57

Survival, 56
Suttles, Gerald, 148, 154
Systemic hypothesis, 222

Tactical Air Command, 342
Taiwan, 383
Taste cultures, 355-60
Taxation, 64, 200-14, tables 203, 206, 207, 209, 212, 213; childbearing, 386; day care services, 279; education, 117; income, 78, 106-14 innovation experiment, 11; progressive, 24; property ownership, 20; transfer policies, 88; unequal public economy, 19; see also various taxes
Tax base, 204, 205, 207; core cities, 444
Tax Reform Act (1969), 205
Teachers:
    child care certification, 276; quality requirements, 267; wages and salaries, 53, 119
Technocratic theory, 337
Technology:
    advance of, 395; contraception, 379; distribution, laws of, 55; environmental crisis, 421, 428; plastic Wasp 9-5 America, 267; Third World, 369; transportation, 447; upgrading of jobs, 119; welfare, 98; working class, 137; working mothers, 272
Teeters, Nancy H., 268
Test scores,
    IQ, 126, 129, 130
Texas, 383-84; voting turnout, 296
Texas Rangers, 283
Thant, U, 376
Third World:
    birth rates, 383-84; government planning, 389; stratification, international, 362-73
Thompson, Victor, 314
Thurow, Lester, 70; distribution of income, 77, 115
Tijerina, Reies, 283
Tobin, James, 64, 97; guaranteed income, 103
Tumin, Melvin M., 45
Twins, identical,
    IQ, 125

UC (California, University of), 117-18
Underdeveloped countries. See Third World.
Unemployment:
    AFDC, 92; dropouts, 71; education, 119; health, 183; reduction, 75; small towns, 443; social insurance, 89; working class lifestyle, 141
Unemployment compensation, 204
Uniform tax rate, 109, 112
United Nations, 366, 375; family planning, 378, 379; income level, 389; world resources, 392
United States Congress:
    Mexican Americans, 283; military-industrial complex, 338; price index, 320; representation of poor, 20; taxation, 204, 205; welfare, 92, 100; Vietnam, 326, 327
Urban renewal, 150, 155; income, 160; Negro removal, 254, 301
Utopia, 50, 51

Vacancies, 165
Value added tax (VAT), 204, 207-14
Values, 12; choice, 62; culture, 354; hybrid model, 267; policy analysis, 67; role-taking, 315; social pathology, 4; systems of society, 50; voting rights, 291
Varky, George, 188
VAT. *See* Value added tax.
Veterans' Pension Act, 90
Vietnam, 323-35
Violence:
Black community, 223; Mexican Americans, 283, 286; public housing, 152, 153
von Furstenberg, Aaron, 64
Voting, 288-98; participation *tables,* 294, 297, 298; presidential elections, 305

Wages and salaries:
AFDC, 96; day care workers, 276, 277; differentials, 86; distribution of income, 85; educational achievements, 120; guaranteed income, 19; individual output, 46; industrial democracy, 38; lower class perspective, 309, metropolitan growth, 440; reduction in compensation, 52; restructuring of jobs, 86; standard of living, 75; taxation, 202, 203; welfare benefits, 93; working class, 135, 140
Wallace, George, 146
Waller, Willard, 5
War and wartime:
employment trends, 122; escalation, 57; wage patterns, 86; working class, 143
War on poverty, 73, 74, 104, 171; family planning, 188; tax revenues, 114
Warsaw Pact,   L
Third World, 363
WASP. *See* White Anglo-Saxon Protestants.
Ways, Max, 390
Wealth, 43; basis of identity, 30; distribution of 48, 64, 82, *table* 83; income, 77; IQ, 125, 134; personal, 32
Weapons, advanced, 336-52
Weber, Max, 48; tripartite division, 15
Weikart, David, 276
Weinberg, Martin S., 12
Weisbrod, Burton A., 115, 201; education, 116
Welfare, Social, 30, 89-102; budgets, 71; day care centers, 269; housing, 156, 164; principles of allocation, 63; radical decentralization, 303; rights and freedoms, 65; standard of living, 433
Welfare Rights Organization, 98
Well-baby clinics, 268
Westinghouse Learning Corporation, 273, 275
White Anglo-Saxon Protestants (WASPs), 264; IQ, 127
White-collar jobs, 90; Blacks, 219, 221, 234; health, 182, 184; mortality rates, 173; taste culture, 355
Whyte, William F., 304
Will, 27
WIN (Work Incentive Programs), 101
Wolfe, Tom, 434

Women:
AFDC, 90; Blacks and income, 232, *table* 233; day care services, 268-79; deprivation, 228; distribution of income, 79; education and job performance, 120-21; family planning, 190, 194, 380; health and employment, 183; job opportunities, 80, 81, 88, 119; middle class lifestyle, 137, 139; mortality data, 173; norms, 46; pregnancy, 186, 197, 198; sex equality, 259-68; welfare and wages, 95; working class isolation, 141; working mothers, 276
Women's liberation, 259; college campus, 267; distribution of income, 84
Work Incentive Program (WIN), 101
Working class, 135-46; group goals, 307; housing, 151; law and order, 354; urban renewal, 150; voting turnout, 296; women and health, 184
World Bank, 392
Wrong, Dennis, 45

Xenophobia, 400

Young, Michael, 49

Zero population growth, 378, 387, 448
Zoning, 149, 159, 161

SOCIAL PROBLEMS AND PUBLIC POLICY
Inequality and Justice
edited by Lee Rainwater

Publisher: Alexander J. Morin
Manuscript Editor: Elizabeth Pearson
Production Editor: Janet E. Braeunig
Production Manager: Mitzi Carole Trout

Designed by David Miller
Composed by Production Type, Inc., Dallas, Texas
Printed and Bound by George Banta Company, Inc.,
    Menasha, Wisconsin